LABOR MANAGEMENT LAW

ANSWER BOOK

2019 Edition

PLI'S COMPLETE LIBRARY OF TREATISE TITLES

ART LAW

Art Law: The Guide for Collectors, Investors, Dealers & Artists

BANKING & COMMERCIAL LAW

Asset-Based Lending: A Practical Guide to Secured Financing
Consumer Financial Services Answer Book
Equipment Leasing–Leveraged Leasing
Financial Institutions Answer Book: Law, Governance, Compliance
Hillman on Commercial Loan Documentation
Hillman on Documenting Secured Transactions: Effective Drafting and Litigation
Maritime Law Answer Book

BANKRUPTCY LAW

Bankruptcy Deskbook
Personal Bankruptcy Answer Book

BUSINESS, CORPORATE & SECURITIES LAW

Accountants' Liability
Anti-Money Laundering: A Practical Guide to Law and Compliance
Antitrust Law Answer Book
Broker-Dealer Regulation
Conducting Due Diligence in a Securities Offering
Corporate Compliance Answer Book
Corporate Legal Departments: Practicing Law in a Corporation
Corporate Political Activities Deskbook
Corporate Whistleblowing in the Sarbanes-Oxley/Dodd-Frank Era
Covered Bonds Handbook
Cybersecurity: A Practical Guide to the Law of Cyber Risk
Derivatives Deskbook: Close-Out Netting, Risk Mitigation, Litigation
Deskbook on Internal Investigations, Corporate Compliance, and White Collar Issues
Directors' and Officers' Liability: Current Law, Recent Developments, Emerging Issues
Doing Business Under the Foreign Corrupt Practices Act
EPA Compliance and Enforcement Answer Book
Exempt and Hybrid Securities Offerings
Fashion Law and Business: Brands & Retailers
Financial Product Fundamentals: Law, Business, Compliance
Financial Services Mediation Answer Book
Financial Services Regulation Deskbook
Financially Distressed Companies Answer Book
Global Business Fraud and the Law: Preventing and Remedying Fraud and Corruption
Hedge Fund Regulation
Initial Public Offerings: A Practical Guide to Going Public
Insider Trading Law and Compliance Answer Book
Insurance and Investment Management M&A Deskbook
International Corporate Practice: A Practitioner's Guide to Global Success
Investment Adviser Regulation: A Step-by-Step Guide to Compliance and the Law
Legal Guide to the Business of Marijuana
Life at the Center: Reflections on Fifty Years of Securities Regulation
Mergers, Acquisitions and Tender Offers: Law and Strategies
Mutual Funds and Exchange Traded Funds Regulation
Outsourcing: A Practical Guide to Law and Business
Privacy Law Answer Book
Private Equity Funds: Formation and Operation
Proskauer on Privacy: A Guide to Privacy and Data Security Law in the Information Age
Public Company Deskbook: Complying with Federal Governance & Disclosure Requirements
SEC Compliance and Enforcement Answer Book
Securities Investigations: Internal, Civil and Criminal

Securities Law and Practice Deskbook
The Securities Law of Public Finance
Securities Litigation: A Practitioner's Guide
Social Media and the Law
Soderquist on Corporate Law and Practice
Sovereign Wealth Funds: A Legal, Tax and Economic Perspective
A Starter Guide to Doing Business in the United States
Technology Transactions: A Practical Guide to Drafting and Negotiating Commercial
  Agreements
Variable Annuities and Other Insurance Investment Products

COMMUNICATIONS LAW

Advertising and Commercial Speech: A First Amendment Guide
Sack on Defamation: Libel, Slander, and Related Problems
Telecommunications Law Answer Book

EMPLOYMENT LAW

Employment Law Yearbook
ERISA Benefits Litigation Answer Book
Labor Management Law Answer Book

ESTATE PLANNING AND ELDER LAW

Blattmachr on Income Taxation of Estates and Trusts
Estate Planning & Chapter 14: Understanding the Special Valuation Rules
International Tax & Estate Planning: A Practical Guide for Multinational Investors
Manning on Estate Planning
New York Elder Law
Stocker on Drawing Wills and Trusts

HEALTH LAW

FDA Deskbook: A Compliance and Enforcement Guide
Health Care Litigation and Risk Management Answer Book
Health Care Mergers and Acquisitions Answer Book
Medical Devices Law and Regulation Answer Book
Pharmaceutical Compliance and Enforcement Answer Book

IMMIGRATION LAW

Fragomen on Immigration Fundamentals: A Guide to Law and Practice

INSURANCE LAW

Business Liability Insurance Answer Book
Insurance Regulation Answer Book
Reinsurance Law

INTELLECTUAL PROPERTY LAW

Copyright Law: A Practitioner's Guide
Faber on Mechanics of Patent Claim Drafting
Federal Circuit Yearbook: Patent Law Developments in the Federal Circuit
How to Write a Patent Application
Intellectual Property Law Answer Book
Kane on Trademark Law: A Practitioner's Guide
Likelihood of Confusion in Trademark Law
Patent Claim Construction and *Markman* Hearings
Patent Law: A Practitioner's Guide
Patent Licensing and Selling: Strategy, Negotiation, Forms
Patent Litigation
Pharmaceutical and Biotech Patent Law
Post-Grant Proceedings Before the Patent Trial and Appeal Board
Substantial Similarity in Copyright Law
Trade Secrets: A Practitioner's Guide

LITIGATION

Arbitrating Commercial Disputes in the United States
Class Actions and Mass Torts Answer Book
Depositions Answer Book
Electronic Discovery Deskbook
Essential Trial Evidence: Brought to Life by Famous Trials, Films, and Fiction
Expert Witness Answer Book
Evidence in Negligence Cases
Federal Bail and Detention Handbook
How to Handle an Appeal
Medical Malpractice: Discovery and Trial
Product Liability Litigation: Current Law, Strategies and Best Practices
Sinclair on Federal Civil Practice
Trial Handbook

REAL ESTATE LAW

Commercial Ground Leases
Friedman on Contracts and Conveyances of Real Property
Friedman on Leases
Holtzschue on Real Estate Contracts and Closings: A Step-by-Step Guide to Buying and
    Selling Real Estate
Net Leases and Sale-Leasebacks

TAX LAW

The Circular 230 Deskbook: Related Penalties, Reportable Transactions, Working Forms
The Corporate Tax Practice Series: Strategies for Acquisitions, Dispositions, Spin-Offs,
    Joint Ventures, Financings, Reorganizations & Restructurings
Foreign Account Tax Compliance Act Answer Book
Internal Revenue Service Practice and Procedure Deskbook
International Tax & Estate Planning: A Practical Guide for Multinational Investors
International Tax Controversies: A Practical Guide
International Trade Law Answer Book: U.S. Customs Laws and Regulations
Langer on Practical International Tax Planning
The Partnership Tax Practice Series: Planning for Domestic and Foreign Partnerships,
    LLCs, Joint Ventures & Other Strategic Alliances
Private Clients Legal & Tax Planning Answer Book
Transfer Pricing Answer Book

GENERAL PRACTICE PAPERBACKS

Anatomy of a Mediation: A Dealmaker's Distinctive Approach to Resolving Dollar
    Disputes and Other Commercial Conflicts
Attorney-Client Privilege Answer Book
Drafting for Corporate Finance: Concepts, Deals, and Documents
Pro Bono Service by In-House Counsel: Strategies and Perspectives
Smart Negotiating: How to Make Good Deals in the Real World
Thinking Like a Writer: A Lawyer's Guide to Effective Writing & Editing
Working with Contracts: What Law School Doesn't Teach You

Order now at www.pli.edu
Or call (800) 260-4754 Mon.–Fri., 9 a.m.–6 p.m.

Practising Law Institute
1177 Avenue of the Americas
New York, NY 10036

When ordering, please use Priority Code NWS9-X.

LABOR MANAGEMENT LAW

ANSWER BOOK

2019 Edition

Jones Day

Brian West Easley
David S. Birnbaum
Joanne R. Bush
Editors in Chief

Practising Law Institute
New York City

#250390

This work is designed to provide practical and useful information on the subject matter covered. However, it is sold with the understanding that neither the publisher nor the author is engaged in rendering legal, accounting, or other professional services. If legal advice or other expert assistance is required, the services of a competent professional should be sought.

QUESTIONS ABOUT THIS BOOK?

If you have questions about billing or shipments, or would like information on our other products, please contact our **customer service department** at info@pli.edu or at (800) 260-4PLI.

For any other questions or suggestions about this book, contact PLI's **editorial department** at plipress@pli.edu.

For general information about Practising Law Institute, please visit **www.pli.edu**.

LCCN: 2012207503
ISBN: 978-1-4024-3321-4

About the Editors

BRIAN WEST EASLEY (Editor in Chief) represents employers in all aspects of labor and employment law, with a focus on labor-management relations. He has extensive experience representing employers throughout the United States in collective bargaining, union organizing and decertification proceedings, unfair labor practice proceedings, strikes and picketing disputes, corporate campaigns, neutrality and card check agreements, arbitration proceedings, and labor litigation. Brian frequently advises employers on labor and employment aspects of domestic and cross-border mergers and acquisitions and advises distressed employers with respect to labor and employment issues in bankruptcy proceedings. His traditional labor practice includes representation of employers in the manufacturing, oil and gas, energy, mining, automotive, aerospace, railroad, transportation, private equity, media, retail, telecommunications, technology, hospitality, health care, and construction industries.

Brian's practice also includes trial and appellate litigation of employment disputes, representing employers before federal and state courts throughout the United States. In addition, he represents employers in class action litigation pertaining to wage and hour compliance, employee benefits, employment discrimination, affirmative action, and other labor and employment issues.

In addition to his work on PLI's *Labor Management Law Answer Book*, Brian was a contributing author to the labor law treatise *The Developing Labor Law and How to Take a Case Before the NLRB*. He frequently lectures on such diverse topics as labor-management relations, international labor and employment law, union organizing and corporate campaigns, arbitration, strikes and picketing, decertification and deauthorization proceedings, Railway Labor Act issues, affirmative action, the FMLA, and federal recordkeeping requirements.

DAVID S. BIRNBAUM (Editor in Chief) represents employers in labor and employment matters, with a focus on collective bargaining, arbitration, litigation, strikes and picketing disputes, corporate campaigns, and representation proceedings arising under the National Labor Relations

Act (NLRA) and the Railway Labor Act (RLA). In 2017, The *Legal 500 US* named David as one of five "Next Generation Lawyers" in the United States for labor-management relations in recognition of his numerous successes on behalf of leading employers in complex and high-profile matters. His traditional labor practice spans employers in the automotive, construction, health care, hospitality, manufacturing, media, mining, oil and gas, private equity, railroad, retail, telecommunications, and transportation industries.

David has extensive experience representing clients in connection with labor and employment aspects of corporate and municipal restructurings and bankruptcies as well as mergers and acquisitions. He also has significant experience with single and multi-plaintiff employment litigation and regularly counsels employers in all areas of labor and employment law. Clients with whom David has worked include Continental Automotive, CSXT, HCA, Kraft Heinz Company, National Railway Labor Conference, Saputo, Sutter Health, Verizon, Wal-Mart, and Washington Metropolitan Area Transit Authority.

David is the regional co-chair of the American Bar Association Committee on Practice and Procedure Under the NLRA. In addition to co-authoring *Labor Management Law Answer Book*, he serves as an editor to the leading treatises *The Developing Labor Law*, *How to Take a Case Before the NLRB*, and *The Railway Labor Act*.

JOANNE R. BUSH (Editor in Chief) is a skilled trial lawyer, litigator, negotiator, and advisor with more than thirteen years of experience counseling and representing employers in all aspects of employment and traditional labor law. She has successfully represented companies in complex wage and hour class and collective actions as well as employment discrimination, harassment, retaliation, whistleblower, and contract claims and has won trials involving Federal Railroad Safety Act whistleblower claims. Joanne also has significant experience representing and advising clients in restrictive covenant and trade secret disputes. Working with clients to establish best practices, avoid litigation, and accomplish corporate goals, Joanne provides strategic advice and day-to-day counseling on a variety of employment compliance issues. She drafts personnel policies, employment agreements, and severance agreements. Joanne also conducts manager training, wage and hour audits, and internal investigations of employee complaints, including sexual harassment.

As a traditional labor lawyer, Joanne negotiates collective bargaining agreements and represents employers in labor arbitration, unfair labor practice proceedings, union election and decertification proceedings, and labor litigation and advises companies regarding corporate campaigns, strike and contingency planning, bargaining strategies, interpreting collective bargaining agreements, and obligations under the National Labor Relations Act. Joanne also regularly advises on and negotiates the labor and employment aspects of corporate transactions, with a particular focus on the energy industry.

Joanne leads the Labor & Employment Practice in the Houston Office. She is co-chair of the Houston Chapter of the Cornell ILR Alumni Association and is vice president of membership for the Cornell Alumni Association of Greater Houston.

Acknowledgments

The editors would like to thank the following Jones Day attorneys for their hard work, dedication, and tremendous contribution to this publication: Blake T. Pulliam (San Francisco), Jessica Kastin (New York), Michael Rossman (Chicago), George S. Howard Jr. (San Diego), Aaron Agenbroad (San Francisco), Jacqueline Holmes (Washington, D.C.), Michael Ferrell (Chicago), Thomas R. Chiavetta (Washington, D.C.), Elizabeth Dicus (Columbus), Joseph Brennan (Cleveland), Kayla M. Davis (Washington, D.C.), and Liat Yamini (Los Angeles).

Table of Chapters

Table of Contents

Chapter 2   Enforcement of the National Labor Relations Act

Chapter 3   Protected and Unprotected Activity

Chapter 4   Representation Cases

Chapter 5   Duty to Bargain

Chapter 6 Collective Bargaining Agreements

Chapter 8   Unfair Labor Practice Case Procedures

Table of Contents

Chapter 9   Railway Labor Act

Chapter 10 Federal Preemption of State Regulation

Chapter 11 Regulation of Internal Union Affairs: Rights and Obligations of Unions and Union Members

Chapter 12 Labor Relations of Federal Contractors

Table of Contents

Table of Abbreviations

Acronyms, initialisms, and abbreviations used in this book

AAA	American Arbitration Association
ADEA	Age Discrimination in Employment Act
ALJ	administrative law judge
ALRA	Agricultural Labor Relations Act
ARB	Administrative Review Board
CBA	collective bargaining agreement
CBU	collective bargaining unit
CSRA	Civil Service Reform Act
DFR	duty of fair representation
DOL	United States Department of Labor
DPPA	Driver's Privacy Protection Act of 1994
EAJA	Equal Access to Justice Act
ERISA	Employee Retirement Income Security Act
FAA	Federal Arbitration Act
FAR	Federal Acquisition Regulatory Counsel
FLRA	Federal Labor Relations Authority
FMCS	Federal Mediation and Conciliation Service
FMLA	Family Medical Leave Act
FSA	Foreign Services Act
ILB	Injunction Litigation Branch
IRS	Internal Revenue Service
LMRA	Labor Management Relations Act

Acronyms, initialisms, and abbreviations used in this book

LMRDA	Labor-Management Reporting and Disclosure Act (or Landrum-Griffin Act)
LOA	letter of agreement
MFN	most favored nation
NLRA	National Labor Relations Act
NLRB	National Labor Relations Board
NMB	National Mediation Board
NRAB	National Railroad Adjustment Board
OLMS	Office of Labor-Management Standards
OMB	Office of Management and Budget
PLA	Project Labor Agreement
PRA	Postal Reorganization Act
QCR	question concerning representation
RICO	Racketeer Influenced and Corrupt Organizations Act
RLA	Railway Labor Act
ULP	unfair labor practice
USERRA	Uniformed Services Employment and Reemployment Rights Act
WARN Act	Worker Adjustment and Retraining Notification Act of 1998

1

Overview of U.S. Labor Law

The protection of employees' rights in the workplace, including the right to organize and engage in collective bargaining, is governed by a body of law known as labor law.

In the United States, modern labor law began with the Norris-LaGuardia Act of 1932, which outlawed contracts that required employees to agree, as a condition of employment, not to join a labor union ("yellow dog" contracts), and which restrained the power of federal courts to issue injunctions in labor dispute cases. In 1935, Congress passed the National Labor Relations Act, which established a mechanism for unions to establish their bargaining authority, required employers to deal with unions duly authorized as employee representatives, and prohibited employers from discriminating against employees who engaged in concerted activity. Other labor law initiatives include the Labor Management Relations Act of 1947, which regulates certain activities by labor organizations, and the Labor-Management Reporting and Disclosure Act of 1959, which regulates labor activities and establishes a set of internal union democracy safeguards.

Although union membership among employees in the private sector has been in decline since 1956, the NLRA remains relevant and vital to the modern workplace and the national labor market. The NLRA continues to define and protect employee rights in the workplace and the processes of union organizing and collective bargaining.

The Basics

Q 1.1   What is "labor law"?

Labor law is the body of law that protects the rights of employees to organize and engage in collective bargaining and that regulates the relationship between employers, employees, and the labor organizations representing them. The primary labor law governing employment in private companies in the United States is the National Labor Relations Act (NLRA), 29 U.S.C. § 151 *et seq.*, which is also known as the Wagner Act. The NLRA applies to employers who meet the minimum jurisdictional standards established by the National Labor Relations Board (NLRB). Labor organizations (often called unions) are voluntary associations that represent employees in collective bargaining with their employers for employer-supplied dues or fees. Unions, on behalf of groups of employees, act as intermediaries between employees and their employers and negotiate collective bargaining agreements with respect to their terms and conditions of employment. Employers and employees are covered by certain provisions of the NLRA even if the employees are not represented by a union. Employees have the right to engage in certain group activities, more commonly referred to as "concerted activities," related to their employment whether or not there is a union on the scene. Labor law also intersects with a number of other federal and state laws, including free-speech laws, property and trespass laws, and antitrust laws.

Q 1.1.1 How does "labor law" differ from "employment law"?

Although the terms "labor law" and "employment law" are often used interchangeably, "labor law" normally refers to the collective aspects of the law of the employment relationship—that is, those aspects dealing with the relations between unions, employers, and employees.

The term "employment law" normally refers to individual aspects of the law of the employment relationship—that is, those aspects that protect, and in some cases restrict, employees whether or not they are represented by or are members of unions. The states through their contract, tort, and agency law and particular statutes are active in this area. In addition, Congress has passed a number of employment laws, including the Fair Labor Standards Act of 1938, which establishes minimum wages and requires payment of overtime for work in excess of a forty-hour workweek. Beginning in the 1960s, Congress enacted laws prohibiting discrimination on the basis of protected categories such as race, gender, religion, disability, age, and national origin; a statute protecting occupational health and safety; whistleblower protections in particular areas; and a measure regulating retirement and welfare benefit plans. This set of state and federal laws, focused primarily on the relationship between employers and individual employees, makes up the body of rules that is generally referred to as "employment law."

Legislative Framework

Federal Statutes

Q 1.2   What are the principal labor laws that govern employment in the private sector?

There are three main federal statutes that regulate employee collective bargaining rights, labor management relations, collective bargaining agreements, and labor organizations in the United States:

(1)   the NLRA (Wagner Act of 1935, 29 U.S.C. § 151 *et seq.*);

(2)   the LMRA (Taft-Hartley Act of 1947, 29 U.S.C. § 185 *et seq.*); and

(3)   the LMRDA (Landrum-Griffin Act of 1959, 29 U.S.C. § 401 *et seq.*).

These statutes substantially occupy the field of labor management relations and preempt state laws touching upon these issues.

Q 1.2.1   What does the NLRA provide?

The NLRA (or the Wagner Act) was enacted in 1935 to protect the rights of employees to organize and engage in collective bargaining with their employers. In passing the NLRA, Congress declared a public policy to protect employees' rights and encourage collective bargaining. It requires covered employers to bargain with unions that are recognized as the legitimate representatives of workers. These principles are underscored in the two most commonly invoked sections of the NLRA: section 7 and section 8(a).

Section 7 sets out the rights of employees:

- to organize;
- to form, join, or assist labor organizations;
- to bargain collectively through representatives; and
- to engage in other concerted activities.

Section 8(a) sets out prohibited employer labor practices. These include:

- interfering with employees' section 7 rights;
- dominating or interfering with the formation of a union;

- discriminating in regard to hire, tenure, or any other term and condition of employment to discourage the exercise of section 7 rights;

- retaliating against employees for filing unfair labor practice charges or testifying during certain hearings; and

- refusing to bargain collectively with employees' labor representatives.

The NLRA established the NLRB to oversee the development of federal labor law and resolve particular labor management disputes. The NLRB regulates unfair labor practices and the process of representative selection.

Q 1.2.2   What does the LMRA provide?

Pent-up demand for wage increases after World War II led to a wave of strikes and rising inflation. In an attempt to curb claimed abuses of union power, Congress passed the Labor Management Relations Act (LMRA or Taft-Harly Act) in 1947. The original Wagner Act saw the problem of interference with section 7 rights principally as a matter requiring protection from employer unfair labor practices. The LMRA amended the NLRA to prohibit unfair labor practices by unions (now found in section 8(b) of the NLRA).

Specifically, the LMRA outlawed secondary boycotts and "closed shops" (where only union members were eligible for hire). Congress sought to limit compulsory unionism in a number of respects. In addition to the prohibition of the closed shop, it amended section 7 to include the right "to refrain" from collective activity and allowed states to pass so-called right-to-work laws prohibiting union shops (where all of an employer's employees in a particular bargaining unit are required to join or contribute to a union once hired). The LMRA amendments also added section 8(c) to clarify that partisan employer speech would not be considered an unfair labor practice:

> The expressing of any views, argument, or opinion, or the dissemination thereof . . . shall not constitute or be evidence of an unfair labor practice . . . if such expression contains no threat of reprisal or force or promise of benefit.

The LMRA also included provisions on enforcing collective bargaining agreements (section 301), employer payments to union representatives (section 302), and remedies for union unfair labor practices (sections 10(*l*) and 303).

Q 1.2.3   What does the LMRDA provide?

Enacted in 1959, the Labor-Management Reporting and Disclosure Act (LMRDA or Landrum-Griffin Act), in addition to implementing internal union democracy safeguards dealing principally with the relationship between the union and its members, created two additional union unfair labor practices: (1) closing down the "hot cargo" loophole, which had permitted unions to compel neutral employers to agree in advance to boycott struck products; and (2) regulating recognitional and organizational picketing by labor organizations.

State Right-to-Work Laws

Q 1.2.4   What is a "right-to-work" law?

A right-to-work law is a state statute that prohibits employers and unions from requiring employees to join a union or pay the equivalent of union dues.

Before the LMRA, unions and employers subject to the NLRA could agree to a closed shop, meaning employees at unionized workplaces could be required to become union members as a condition of their employment. If, for whatever reason, the employee ceased to be a member of the union, his or her employment could be terminated. The LMRA outlawed closed shops, but permitted "union shops," which require new employees to join a union, or pay union dues, within a certain period of time after hire. In a union shop, the employer must terminate any employee expelled from the union for failure to pay dues, but need not terminate an employee expelled from the union for any other reason. The LMRA also permits the "agency shop," in which employees must pay the equivalent of union dues but are not required to formally join a union.

The LMRA authorizes individual states to outlaw union shops and agency shops for employees who work in that state. Unions can represent employees in right-to-work states, but such employees cannot be forced to join a union or to pay the equivalent of union dues; nor can their employment be terminated for joining or refusing to join a union.

NLRA Jurisdiction

Covered Employees

Q 1.3   What kinds of employees are covered by the NLRA?

Broadly speaking, an employee is an individual who works for an employer for payment and who performs his work under the employer's control. The statutory term "employee" under the NLRA specifically includes any individual whose work has ceased, either as a consequence of or in connection with any current labor dispute or because of any unfair labor practice, and who has not obtained any other regular and substantially equivalent employment.[1] The definition specifically excludes certain individuals, as elaborated below.

Q 1.3.1   Do you have to be a member of a union to be protected by the NLRA?

You do not need to be a member of a union to be protected by the NLRA. Even for unrepresented employees, the NLRA guarantees important workplace rights. Employees are guaranteed protection of the rights outlined in section 7 of the NLRA, regardless of whether they are represented by an outside labor representative. In addition to the right to organize or join a union, section 7 gives employees the right, among other things, to:

(1)   talk together about working conditions;

(2)   attend meetings about a union or workplace issues;

(3)   read or distribute pamphlets in non-work areas before and after work, or during breaks or lunch periods;

(4)   wear union insignia;

(5)   sign union authorization cards;

(6) sign a petition or file a grievance about work issues;

(7) talk to co-workers about wages;

(8) refuse to support a union; and

(9) solicit other employees to engage in the foregoing.

There may also be limits on the employer's ability to require, as a condition of employment, that employees give up their right to engage in concerted activity.

Excluded Employees

Q 1.4   Which workers are excluded from coverage under the NLRA?

The NLRA's definition of "employee"[2] specifically excludes:

(1) agricultural laborers;

(2) employees in domestic service;

(3) anyone employed by his/her parent or spouse;

(4) independent contractors;

(5) supervisors;

(6) anyone employed by an employer subject to the Railway Labor Act, as amended; and

(7) anyone who is employed by a person who does not meet the definition of "employer."

An "employer" is generally defined as an individual or business that engages employees to perform work in exchange for wages or salary.[3] The definition of "employer" is discussed more fully in Q 1.5 below.

Additionally, certain other types of employees not expressly excluded in the NLRA are not included in the definition of "employee," such as managerial employees and confidential employees.

Q 1.4.1   Who qualifies as an "agricultural laborer" excluded under the NLRA?

Employees who regularly perform nonagricultural work are not "agricultural laborers" and are covered under the NLRA.[4] The NLRB borrows the definition of "agriculture" from section 3(f) of the Fair Labor Standards Act. This definition of agriculture contains a primary meaning, including actual farming activities such as cultivation, tilling, growing, and harvesting, and a secondary meaning, including practices performed as incident to or in conjunction with farming operations.[5] Secondary agricultural functions, such as packing, sorting, grading, and storing, are incidental practices that do not change the employer's product or enhance its value, but are simply part of preparing the product for marketing.[6] Employees that perform such incidental practices will be covered under the NLRA if the employees regularly handle any amount of farm commodities produced by a farmer other than the employer.[7]

Some states have their own labor relations laws that govern agricultural employees excluded from the NLRA. For example, California has a state Agricultural Labor Relations Act, which regulates unfair labor practices, representation issues, and collective bargaining for farm workers. Idaho, Kansas, and Arizona have similar laws relating to the rights of farm workers. Moreover, other states, such as Hawaii and Wisconsin, regulate labor relations in the farm industry under more general labor relations statutes.

Q 1.4.2   Who qualifies as an employee in "domestic service" excluded under the NLRA?

The "domestic service" exemption under the NLRA applies to any domestic assistant directly employed in the service of a homeowner or resident at his home. The homeowner or resident must control the wages, hours, and terms and conditions of the domestic assistant's employment. The exemption does not apply to in-home workers employed by a for-profit corporation that provides housekeeping services for elderly, low-income, emotionally disturbed, or mentally or physically disabled individuals.[8]

Q 1.4.3   What does it mean under the NLRA for an individual to be "employed by a parent or spouse"?

The exclusion of individuals employed by a parent or spouse applies to the children and spouses of sole proprietors and of co-partners. The exclusion also extends to children and spouses of individuals who have substantial stock interests in closely held corporations. To determine the applicability of this exception, the NLRB looks beyond what may be a nominal employer to the actual employer, which is "the one who possesses actual authority and concomitant responsibility to determine labor policy and bargain collectively with the employees' representative."[9]

Q 1.4.4   What is the test to determine whether an individual is an "independent contractor" excluded under the NLRA?

The NLRB applies common law agency principles to determine whether an individual is an independent contractor. Independent contractor status is determined in light of all of the incidents of the relationship between the parties, "with no one factor being decisive."[10] The factors include:

(1) whether the work performed is an essential part of the company's regular business;

(2) whether the person is engaged in an occupation or business that is distinct from the company's regular business;

(3) the length of time for which the person is employed or contracted;

(4) the skill required in the particular occupation;

(5) whether the company provides the tools and instrumentalities necessary to perform the work;

(6) the method of payment, whether by the time worked or by the job;

(7) the extent to which the company controls the details of the work;

(8)   the kind of occupation, including whether, in the locality in question, the work is usually done under the employer's direction or by a specialist without supervision;

(9)   whether the parties believe they are creating an employment relationship;

(10) whether the employer performs the same type of work performed by the contracted individuals; and

(11) whether the person has significant entrepreneurial opportunity for gain or loss.[11]

Q 1.4.5   Who is a "supervisor" excluded under the NLRA?

Section 2(11) of the NLRA defines a supervisor as "any individual having authority, in the interest of the employer, to hire, transfer, suspend, lay off, recall, promote, discharge, assign, reward, or discipline other employees, or responsibly direct them, or to adjust their grievances, or effectively to recommend such action," as long as his or her authority is not merely routine or clerical but requires the use of independent judgment.[12] The test for determining supervisory status is:

(1)   whether the individual has the authority to engage in any of the twelve functions listed in section 2(11) of the NLRA;

(2)   whether the exercise of such authority requires the use of independent judgment; and

(3)   whether the employee holds the authority in the interest of the employer.[13]

An employee who holds the authority to engage in any of the twelve functions is a supervisor, even if he or she has not yet exercised the authority.[14]

Q 1.4.6   Who qualifies as an employee of an entity subject to the Railway Labor Act?

For a complete discussion of the Railway Labor Act and which employees it does and does not cover, see chapter 9. See also QQ 1.6.4 and 1.6.5 below.

Q 1.4.7   Who is a "managerial employee" excluded under the NLRA?

Although not expressly excluded from coverage under the NLRA, managerial employees generally are not included in the definition of "employee" under Supreme Court precedent.[15] Managerial employees are those who "formulate and effectuate management policies by expressing and making operative the decisions of their employer and those who have discretion in the performance of their jobs independent of their employer's established policy."[16] Thus, discretionary authority to make or implement policy for the employer is the linchpin. In evaluating whether an employee is managerial, the NLRB considers the individual's actual job duties, authority, and relationship to management, rather than his or her job title.

Some examples of positions that the NLRB has held to be "managerial" include: staff nurses who directed nursing assistants in providing care to patients because they exercised managerial judgment that they acquired through their professional training;[17] a university's faculty members who helped formulate fundamental university interests when recommending or implementing its policies;[18] and a purchasing/inventory controller who was able to commit her employer's credit.[19]

Q 1.4.8   Who is a "confidential employee" excluded under the NLRA?

Those who qualify as "confidential employees" because they assist and act in a confidential capacity to persons who exercise managerial functions regarding labor relations are excluded from the definition of "employee" under the NLRA.[20] Notably, an employee is not a confidential employee unless there is a nexus to labor relations functions.[21] Moreover, employees who simply have access to confidential non-labor materials, such as confidential financial or business information or personnel records, are not considered confidential employees and are not excluded.[22]

Some examples of employees who are considered labor-nexus "confidential employees" include: a personnel/payroll administrator; an executive secretary to the employer's general manager; and a human resources officer who investigates employee discipline issues.

Other Employees

Q 1.4.9   Does the definition of "employee" under the NLRA exclude contingent or temporary employees?

Generally, contingent or temporary employees are covered by the NLRA.[23] However, such workers may be excluded from particular bargaining units under NLRB decisions.[24]

Q 1.4.10   ... undocumented aliens?

Aliens with or without permission to work in the United States are covered by the NLRA.[25] An employer that violates the NLRA with respect to undocumented aliens may be subject to unfair labor practice charges and remedial NLRB action. However, there may be limits on the NLRB's authority to award reinstatement or backpay to those who do not have permission to work in the United States.[26]

Q 1.4.11   ... retired employees?

The NLRA's definition of "employee" does not include retired employees.[27] Thus, the employer's obligation to bargain collectively with representatives of its employees does not extend to current retirees. However, retirees can properly be represented by a union that represents active employees for certain purposes.

Q 1.4.12   ... "salts"?

Individuals who engage in salting, commonly referred to as "salts," are paid union organizers trying to gain employment in order to obtain direct access to employees for organizing purposes and to circumvent the restrictions employers may legally place on non-employee union organizers from entering the workplace. Historically, employers could deny employment to applicants discovered to be salts.[28] In a victory for unions, the U.S. Supreme Court ruled that salts applying for jobs are "employees" under the NLRA, and therefore an employer may not fire, refuse to hire, or otherwise discriminate against an individual solely because he or she works for a union.[29] Salting is further discussed at Q 3.26.1.

Covered Employers

Q 1.5   Who is an "employer" subject to the NLRA?

In general, an employer is an individual or business that engages employees to perform work in exchange for wages or salary. The NLRA defines "employer" as "any person acting as an agent of an employer, directly or indirectly," but excludes those entities discussed below (see Q 1.6).[30]

Because the NLRA's jurisdiction is based on the Commerce Clause of the U.S. Constitution, the NLRB exercises jurisdiction only over matters that substantially affect interstate commerce. The NLRB has established very modest financial thresholds to determine whether an employer substantially affects commerce; few employers fall below those thresholds. For a complete list of the NLRB's jurisdictional standards, consult the Basic Guide to the NLRA, which can be found on the NLRB's website.[31]

Q 1.5.1   Who is an "agent of an employer" under the NLRA?

The NLRA provides, "[i]n determining whether any person is acting as an 'agent' of another person so as to make such other person responsible for his acts, the question of whether the specific acts performed were actually authorized or subsequently ratified shall not be controlling."[32] In interpreting the NLRA, courts and the NLRB apply common law rules of agency. A person is an agent of the employer if, "under all the circumstances, employees would reasonably believe that the alleged agent was reflecting company policy and speaking and acting for management."[33] Thus, a supervisor acting under apparent authority may be treated as an agent of the employer, even if his or her actions run counter to instructions. In some circumstances, third parties who are independent contractors for the employer, such as accountants, consultants, employment agencies, and security guards, may be considered agents of the employer for certain purposes under the NLRA.[34]

Excluded Employers

Q 1.6   Which employers are not subject to the NLRA?

The federal government, Federal Reserve Banks, state governments and their political subdivisions, entities covered by the RLA, and labor organizations expressly are not subject to the NLRA. These express exclusions, as well as others, are addressed below.

Q 1.6.1   Are there any exceptions to the rule that the federal government is not subject to the NLRA?

The Postal Reorganization Act of 1970 (PRA) incorporated the NLRA's provisions, though it did not amend the NLRA itself. Thus, employees of the U.S. Postal Service, an independent establishment of the federal government with its own board of governors, have collective bargaining rights. Under the PRA, the NLRB has the authority to determine appropriate bargaining units, supervise elections, and investigate unfair labor practice allegations. However, the PRA maintains the ban on strikes by federal employees.[35] No other federal government employees are covered by the NLRA.

Q 1.6.2   Even though federal and state governments are not subject to the NLRA, do their employees have collective bargaining rights?

Federal employees are covered by the Federal Service Labor-Management Relations Act, 5 U.S.C. § 7101 *et seq.*, which is administered by the Federal Labor Relations Authority. Employees covered by the statute may organize and engage in limited collective bargaining (excluding wages). They may not, however, engage in strikes or slowdowns. Many state and local government employees have enacted labor relations laws allowing union organization and collective bargaining; the general rule is that government employees at any level do not have the right to strike.

Q 1.6.3   When is an entity a "political subdivision" of a state?

The NLRA excludes states and political subdivisions of states from its definition of "employer." The term "political subdivision" encompasses more than merely counties and municipalities. The U.S. Supreme Court has held that an entity is a political subdivision of a state if it: (1) is created directly by the state so as to constitute a department or an administrative arm of the government; or (2) is administered by individuals responsible to public officials or the general electorate.[36] The second criterion is met, for example, if a controlling majority of the entity's board of directors is appointed by public officials. An entity is responsible to the general electorate only if the composition of the group of electors eligible to vote for the entity's governing body is sufficiently comparable to the electorate for general political elections in the state. The NLRB, thus, may exercise jurisdiction over an entity even if it performs primarily public functions. For example, while the NLRB does not exercise jurisdiction over traditional public schools, it has exercised jurisdiction over two public charter schools because each school was operated by a non-profit corporation, and the school's board of directors was not subject to direction or dismissal from public officials or the general electorate.[37]

Q 1.6.4   Which employers are subject to the RLA and thus excluded from the NLRA?

The RLA applies to common carriers, such as railroads and airlines, engaged in interstate or foreign commerce. If an entity is subject to the RLA, it is excluded from the NLRA's definition of "employer."[38]

Q 1.6.5   How is the determination made as to whether an entity is subject to the RLA?

The NLRB will determine whether an entity is subject to the RLA when a petition is filed or a charge alleging unfair labor practices raises this jurisdictional issue. To determine whether an employer is subject to the RLA, a hearing is held at the regional office level of the NLRB, and the record is sent to the Executive Secretary. The NLRB may submit the record to the National Mediation Board (NMB), which has jurisdiction under the RLA, to determine whether the employer is subject to the RLA. Typically, the NLRB defers to the NMB's determination as to whether an employer is subject to the RLA.

If the NMB has rejected jurisdiction in the past, the burden is on the party asserting current NMB jurisdiction to establish jurisdictionally significant changes since the prior NMB decision.[39]

For further discussion of the RLA, see chapter 9.

Other Employers

Q 1.6.6   Are labor organizations subject to the NLRA in their capacity as employers?

Labor organizations are specifically excluded from the NLRA's definition of "employer," "other than when acting as an employer." In other words, when a union acts as an employer, it is subject to the NLRA, and its employees are entitled to the NLRA's protections. Typically, the NLRB must exercise its jurisdiction over unions when the unions are acting as employers, unless to do so, in a particular case, would not effectuate the NLRA's policies.[40]

Q 1.6.7   Are Native American–owned and –operated enterprises subject to the NLRA?

Enterprises owned and operated by Native American tribes are sometimes subject to the NLRA. Formerly, the NLRB held that tribes and their enterprises located on reservations were exempt from the NLRA's definition of "employer" as government entities. There were only two exceptions to this rule: (1) when the self-directed enterprise is located off the reservation grounds; or (2) where an enterprise located on the reservation is not wholly owned or controlled by the tribe.

In 2004, the NLRB abandoned the on/off reservation analysis.[41] Instead, the NLRB considers the function, rather than the ownership or location, of the enterprise. The NLRB will not assert jurisdiction when an enterprise serves a traditional or governmental function, but the NLRB will assert jurisdiction over purely commercial enterprises that substantially affect interstate or foreign commerce.

The NLRB's abandonment of the on/off reservation analysis has been challenged by Native American tribes, members of Congress, and the Department of the Interior. In July 2011, a federal district court in Oklahoma held that the NLRA did not give the NLRB jurisdiction over commercial enterprises run by Native American tribes on reservation lands. The court noted that the NLRA is silent as to whether the NLRB has jurisdiction over Native American tribes and that long-standing principles provide that ambiguities in a federal statute must be resolved in favor of Native American tribes. The court held that the NLRA's silence on the issue of the NLRB's jurisdiction did not establish congressional intent to strip Native American tribes of their inherent authority to govern their own territory. The district court enjoined the NLRB from exercising any such jurisdiction and the NLRB appealed to the Tenth Circuit.[42] The district court and Tenth Circuit allowed the Acting General Counsel to file an amended complaint directly with the NLRB.[43] The NLRB disagreed with the Oklahoma district court's holding and held that the Board could assert jurisdiction over Native American tribes unless:

(1)   the law "touche[d] exclusive rights of self-government in purely intramural matters";

(2)   the application of the law would abrogate treaty rights; or

(3)   the statutory language or legislative history of the law suggested that Congress did not intend the law to apply to Indian tribes.

If none of these three exceptions is present, the NLRB can assert jurisdiction unless policy considerations weigh against taking jurisdiction.[44] The NLRB found that none of the exceptions applied and no policy considerations weighed against exercising jurisdiction over the Chickasaw Nation's operation of the WinStar World Casino, which had primarily non-Indian employees and patrons and which advertised both in and outside the tribe's jurisdiction. The Chickasaw Nation appealed the NLRB's decision to the U.S. Court of Appeals for the Tenth Circuit.[45] U.S. Representative Kristi Noem (R-SD) and U.S. Senator Jerry Moran (R-KS), along with other members of Congress, introduced bills that would clarify that the NLRA does not give the NLRB jurisdiction over Native American tribes on reservation lands.[46] The Department of the Interior also wrote to the General Counsel of the NLRB expressing the department's position that the NLRB lacks such jurisdiction.[47]

Q 1.6.8   Are religious institutions subject to the NLRA?

Generally, the NLRB accords "employer" status under the NLRA to religiously affiliated institutions when their purpose is not to promote the religion or its values, but to achieve some other commercial or social end. As such, hospitals with religious affiliations typically are subject to the NLRA.[48]

Religious primary and secondary schools, on the other hand, are usually not "employers" under the NLRA. The NLRB and the federal courts use different standards to determine whether religiously affiliated colleges and universities are "employers" under the NLRA. The D.C. Circuit Court of Appeals has held:

> A school is exempt from NLRB jurisdiction if it: (1) holds itself out to students, faculty and the community as providing a religious educational environment; (2) is organized as a "nonprofit"; and (3) is affiliated with, or owned, operated, or controlled, directly or indirectly, by a recognized religious organization, or with an entity, membership of which is determined, at least in part, with reference to religion.[49]

The court later affirmed that this is not an intrusive inquiry; it ensures that schools claiming exemptions are "*bona fide* religious institutions," while avoiding NLRB inquiry into the substance and contours of their religious beliefs and missions.[50]

The NLRB asserts, however, that it must carefully examine the religious nature of the college environment to determine whether propagation of a religious faith is the primary purpose of the college or whether the college's purpose and function are primarily secular.[51] Opponents of the NLRB's "substantial religious character" test assert that such stringent review is unconstitutional under the religion clauses[52] of the U.S. Constitution because the review requires the NLRB to engage in improper inquiry into the school's religious doctrine and make unlawful judgments regarding the school's good-faith statements regarding its religious purposes.

Future decisions in this area may be influenced by the U.S. Supreme Court's 2012 ruling in *Hosanna-Tabor Evangelical Lutheran Church & School v. EEOC*.[53] In that case, the Supreme Court held that a religious organization's choice to hire or fire a teacher who had been ordained as a minister was protected from anti-discrimination laws because "the Free Exercise Clause . . . protects a religious group's right to shape its own faith and mission through its appointments . . . [and] the Establishment Clause . . . prohibits government involvement in such ecclesiastical decisions."[54] The opinion could be read to support a broad deference to religious organizations to shape their staff through religious appointments. However, the ruling could also be construed narrowly to support the NLRB's more stringent review into the secular or religious nature of an academic environment where professors are not ordained as ministers.

NLRB precedent is inconsistent as to whether non-teacher employees, such as custodians, are covered by the NLRA.[55]

Foreign Jurisdiction

Q 1.7   Does the NLRB have jurisdiction over labor disputes involving foreign countries?

The NLRB will not assert jurisdiction over disputes that arise in a foreign country, even if U.S. employees are involved. For example, the NLRB held that telephone equipment installers employed on projects in Iran or other foreign countries were not subject to the terms and conditions of a particular collective bargaining agreement.[56]

Notes to Chapter 1

1. 29 U.S.C. § 152(3).
2. *Id.*
3. *Id.* § 152(2).
4. *Id.* § 152(3).
5. Camsco Produce Co., 297 N.L.R.B. 905, 906 (1990).
6. *Id.* at 906.
7. *Id.* at 908.
8. *See* 2 JOHN E. HIGGINS, JR., THE DEVELOPING LABOR LAW 2425–26 (ABA 6th ed. 2012 & Supp. 2013) [hereinafter DEVELOPING LABOR LAW].
9. Foam Rubber City No. 2 of Fla., Inc., 167 N.L.R.B. 623, 624 (1967).
10. FedEx Home Delivery, 361 N.L.R.B. No. 55 (2014).
11. NLRB v. United Ins. Co., 390 U.S. 254 (1968); BKN, Inc., 333 N.L.R.B. 143 (2001); *see, e.g.*, FedEx Home Delivery, 361 N.L.R.B. No. 55 (2014) (finding drivers to be employees and not independent contractors under the NLRA because FedEx exercised control over the drivers' work; the drivers were not engaged in a distinct business; the work of the drivers was done under FedEx's direction; the drivers were not required to have special skills; FedEx established, regulated, and controlled the rate of the drivers' compensation; and the work of the drivers was part of the regular business of FedEx).
12. 29 U.S.C. § 152(11); *see also, e.g.*, Entergy Miss., Inc., 357 N.L.R.B. No. 178 (2011).
13. NLRB v. Health Care & Ret. Corp., 511 U.S. 571, 573–74 (1994); *see also* Modesto Radiology Imaging Inc., 361 N.L.R.B. No. 84 (2014) (holding that team leaders who reported to facility manager were not supervisors because they did not exercise independent judgment in setting employee schedules and there was no evidence of direct correlation between team leaders' evaluation scores of other employees and increased wages); GGNSC Springfield LLC v. NLRB, 721 F.3d 403 (6th Cir. 2013) (nurses were supervisors because they had discretion to choose whether to address misconduct by doing nothing, providing a verbal warning, or issuing a written memorandum that was a step in the company's progressive discipline program).
14. Fred Meyer Alaska, Inc., 334 N.L.R.B. 646, 649 n.8 (2001).
15. NLRB v. Bell Aerospace Co., 416 U.S. 267, 289 (1974).
16. Gen. Dynamics Corp., 213 N.L.R.B. 851, 857 (1974).
17. Schnurmacher Nursing Home v. NLRB, 214 F.3d 260, 268 (2d Cir. 2000).
18. NLRB v. Yeshiva Univ., 444 U.S. 672, 682 (1980).
19. Concepts & Designs, Inc., 318 N.L.R.B. 948, 957 (1995).
20. NLRB v. Hendricks Cty. Rural Elec. Membership Corp., 454 U.S. 170 (1981).

21.   Greyhound Lines, Inc., 257 N.L.R.B. 477, 480 (1981).

22.   *See* Brodart, Inc., 257 N.L.R.B. 380, 384 n.10 (1981); *see also* Fairfax Family Fund, Inc., 195 N.L.R.B. 306, 307 (1972).

23.   "Temporary" or "contingent" workers, also known as "on-call" or "casual" workers, are employees hired on a temporary basis to fill full-time or part-time jobs, with the understanding that their employment may be terminated at any time. The NLRB has found that temporary workers may not be deprived of NLRA rights. *See* Tamphon Trading Co., 88 N.L.R.B. 597 (1950) (ruling that "shipping stevedores" are casual employees who may not be deprived of rights under the NLRA); Yellow Freight Sys., Inc. v. NLRB, 37 F.3d 128 (3d Cir. 1994) (an employer violated section 8(a)(3) by refusing to hire as a regular employee a casual driver because of membership and association with the union); Mediplex of Conn., Inc., 319 N.L.R.B. 281, 295 (1995) (employer violated sections 8(a)(1) and 8(a)(3) when it discharged a temporary employee for union activity).

24.   The test for determining the eligibility of temporary or contingent employees to participate in a bargaining unit is whether or not they have an uncertain tenure. *See* Marian Med. Ctr., 339 N.L.R.B. 127 (2003). Temporary or contingent employees who are retained beyond their original term of employment and whose employment is thereafter for an indefinite period can be included in a bargaining unit. *See* MJM Studios of N.Y., 336 N.L.R.B. 1255 (2001). On the other hand, employees that are employed for one job only, or for a set duration, or that have no substantial expectancy of continued employment and are notified of this fact, must be excluded from the bargaining unit. *See* NLRB v. SRDC, Inc., 45 F.3d 328 (9th Cir. 1995); Kinney Drugs, Inc. v. NLRB, 74 F.3d 1419, 1427 (2d Cir. 1996); See's Candy Shops, Inc., 202 N.L.R.B. 538 (1973).

25.   Sure Tan, Inc. v. NLRB, 467 U.S. 883, 892 (1984).

26.   Hoffman Plastic Compounds, Inc. v. NLRB, 535 U.S. 137 (2002); Palma v. NLRB, 723 F.3d 176 (2d Cir. 2013) (refusing to award backpay to an undocumented alien even when the alien did not obtain job through fraudulent means).

27.   Allied Chem. & Alkali Workers Local 1 v. Pittsburgh Plate Glass Co., 404 U.S. 157, 167 (1971).

28.   NLRB v. Town & Country Elec., Inc., 516 U.S. 85 (1995).

29.   *Id.*

30.   29 U.S.C. § 152(2).

31.   *See* NLRB, Basic Guide to the National Labor Relations Act (1997), at 34. This pamphlet is available at www.nlrb.gov/sites/default/files/attachments/basic-page/node-3024/basicguide.pdf.

32.   29 U.S.C. § 152(13).

33.   Facchina Constr. Co., 343 N.L.R.B. 886, 893 (2004); *see also, e.g.*, Pratt (Corrugated Logistics), LLC, 360 N.L.R.B. No. 48 (2014) (finding labor relations consultant was agent of employer because managers instructed employees to meet with consultant on company time, and consultant listened to employee complaints and promised changes "real soon").

34. 2 DEVELOPING LABOR LAW, *supra* note 8, at 2570–71.
35. *Id.* at 2230.
36. NLRB v. Nat. Gas Util. Dist. of Hawkins Cty., Tenn., 402 U.S. 600 (1971).
37. Chi. Mathematics & Sci. Acad., 359 N.L.R.B. No. 41 (2012); Pilsen Wellness Ctr., 359 N.L.R.B. No. 72 (2013). The NLRB has not established a "bright-line rule" regarding charter schools. Whether the NLRB will exercise jurisdiction over a particular charter school will depend on the legal framework that governs the school's specific relationship with its state and local governments. Chi. Mathematics & Sci. Acad., 359 N.L.R.B. No. 41 (2012).
38. 29 U.S.C. § 152(2).
39. 2 DEVELOPING LABOR LAW, *supra* note 8, at 2357.
40. Office Emps. Int'l Union, Local No. 11, AFL-CIO v. NLRB, 353 U.S. 313, 318–20 (1957).
41. San Manuel Indian Bingo & Casino & Hotel Emps. & Rest. Emps. Int'l Union, 341 N.L.R.B. 1055 (2004), *aff'd*, 475 F.3d 1306 (D.C. Cir. 2007).
42. Chickasaw Nation v. NLRB, No. 11-cv-506, 2011 U.S. Dist. LEXIS 105675 (W.D. Okla. July 11, 2011).
43. Chickasaw Nation d/b/a WinStar World Casino, Case No. 17-CA-025031.
44. Chickasaw Nation, 359 N.L.R.B. No. 163 (2013) (internal citations omitted).
45. These decisions were remanded for consideration in light of NLRB v. Noel Canning, 134 S. Ct. 2550 (2014). *See, e.g.*, Order, NLRB v. Nat'l Cong. of Am. Indians, No. 17-CA-025031 (10th Cir. July 22, 2014).
46. Tribal Labor Sovereignty Act of 2013, H.R. 1226, S. 1477, 113th Cong. (2013).
47. Letter from Patrice H. Kunesh, Deputy Solicitor-Indian Affairs, Dep't of Interior, to Lafe Soloman, Acting Gen. Counsel, National Labor Relations Board (Dec. 7, 2011), http://turtletalk.files.wordpress.com/2011/12/nlrb-12-7-11.pdf.
48. 2 DEVELOPING LABOR LAW, *supra* note 8, at 2334–36. Note also that the NLRA was amended in 1974 to extend the NLRB's jurisdiction to employees of all "health care institutions." *Id.*
49. Carroll Coll., Inc. v. NLRB, 558 F.3d 568, 572 (D.C. Cir. 2009) (internal quotation marks and citations omitted).
50. *Id.*
51. Pac. Lutheran Univ., 361 N.L.R.B. No. 157 (2014) (holding Board will not decline to exercise jurisdiction over faculty members at a religious institution unless the institution demonstrates first that it holds itself out as providing a religious educational environment, and second that it holds out the petitioned-for faculty members as performing a religious function).
52. The "Establishment Clause" and the "Free Exercise Clause," U.S. CONST. amend. I.
53. Hosanna-Tabor Evangelical Lutheran Church & Sch. v. EEOC, 132 S. Ct. 694 (2012).
54. *Id.* at 706.

55.   *Compare* Hanna Boys Ctr., 284 N.L.R.B. 1080 (1987) (finding NLRB could exercise jurisdiction over non-teachers at residential facility run by Roman Catholic diocese), *with* St. Edmund's Roman Catholic Church, 337 N.L.R.B. 1260 (2002) (finding NLRB could not exercise jurisdiction over custodians who worked at a church or at the two schools operated by the church).

56.   GTE Automatic Elec., Inc., 226 N.L.R.B. 1222 (1976).

2

Enforcement of the National Labor Relations Act

The National Labor Relations Board is an independent agency of the U.S. government tasked with administering the National Labor Relations Act. Because the National Labor Relations Act is not a criminal statute, the NLRB cannot levy fines or penalties. Rather, the Board's remedial authority is limited to cease-and-desist orders and certain remedial actions including ordering backpay, offering reinstatement, issuing bargaining orders, and requiring the refund of illegally collected union dues. Board decisions are generally reviewable by federal courts, under a narrow scope of review: "substantial evidence" on findings of fact, and plenary review on conclusions of law.

The National Labor Relations Board

Overview

Q 2.1   What does the NLRB do?

The National Labor Relations Board (NLRB) is an independent agency of the U.S. government created to administer the National Labor Relations Act (NLRA). The NLRB has two main functions:

(1)   to conduct representation elections and certify the results; and

(2)   to prevent, investigate, and remedy unlawful acts, called unfair labor practices, by either employers or unions.

The NLRB also conducts de-authorization elections (which allow employees to determine whether they wish to continue operating under a union security agreement) and resolves jurisdictional disputes related to which employees are properly performing bargaining unit work. The NLRB does not act on its own volition in either function. It processes only those charges of unfair labor practices and petitions for employee elections that are filed with the NLRB in one of its regional offices. The NLRB has delegated some of its authority to the General Counsel and the Regional Directors under the General Counsel (see Q 2.2, below).

Organizational Structure/Basic Functions

Q 2.2   How is the NLRB structured?

When the NLRB was first established, it created an administrative scheme that, according to its critics, made it "prosecutor, judge, and jury."[1] In 1947, Congress remedied this appearance of a conflict of interest and established a single enforcement agency with divided authority. The NLRB now contains two independent units:

- the Board, and
- the General Counsel.

The NLRB has field offices in fifty-one locations in a number of states and Puerto Rico and is headquartered in Washington, D.C.[2] Each office is part of one of the NLRB's twenty-six regions, some of which contain subregions that were created as a part of a regional restructuring program in the early 2010s.

Staff in each region reports to a single regional director. As a result of the regional restructuring, the number of NLRB regional offices decreased from thirty-two to twenty-six, while the total number of field offices remained at fifty-one.[3]

In January 2018, the NLRB's General Counsel, Peter Robb, raised the possibility of restructuring the Board's field offices and the Regional Directors' role.[4] Among other things, Mr. Robb proposed: (1) replacing the Board's Regional Offices with "large Districts"; (2) demoting current Regional Directors from their Senior Executive Service (SES) positions to a lower-graded status; and (3) transferring Regional Directors' substantive decision-making responsibilities to managers who would work under the General Counsel's direction. It is unclear whether any of Mr. Robb's ideas will be implemented. Twenty-four Regional Directors have expressed "grave" concerns about the proposal.[5]

Q 2.3   What does the Office of the General Counsel do?

The Office of the General Counsel is independent from the Board and is charged with the investigatory and prosecutorial functions.

The General Counsel has final, unreviewable authority over the investigation of charges and issuance of unfair labor practice complaints. The General Counsel is appointed by the President, with consent of the Senate, for a four-year term. (The organization of the Office of the General Counsel is discussed below at Q 2.5.)

The General Counsel's office also oversees the regional directors, each of whom manages a regional office in one of the twenty-six regions throughout the United States. Each regional director oversees a staff of field examiners, a regional attorney, and field attorneys, as well as support staff. When employers are faced with unfair labor practice charges or petitions for representation, their first interaction is usually with a field examiner (also called a "Board Agent") or field attorney.

The General Counsel plays a critical role in determining which issues will appear before the NLRB for adjudication. The General Counsel's decision to dismiss a charge is not subject to further appeal and cannot be challenged in court. Accordingly, the General Counsel has nearly absolute discretion in determining whether to issue a complaint that would require the NLRB to overturn a precedent or otherwise make new agency law.

Q 2.4   What does the Board do?

The Board functions primarily as an appellate court and makes rulings based on a formal "trial" record. Administrative law judges appointed by the NLRB conduct the "trial" hearings and issue recommended decisions and orders that may be appealed to the Board.

The five members of the NLRB are appointed by the President of the United States, with consent of the Senate, for five-year terms. One of these members is selected by the President to serve as chairperson. While the full five-member Board occasionally sits together to hear a case, full Board participation is not required. When hearing cases, the Board's typical practice is to delegate its decision-making process to a three-member panel.

In addition to the five Board members, the NLRB comprises several subordinate offices and divisions that assist in enforcing the National Labor Relations Act. These include the following:

(1) Office of the Executive Secretary
(2) Office of the Solicitor
(3) Division of Judges
(4) Office of Representation Appeals
(5) Division of Information
(6) Inspector General

Q 2.4.1 What role is played by the Office of the Executive Secretary?

The Executive Secretary is the chief administrative and judicial management officer of the NLRB. The Executive Secretary assigns cases to the various Board members and tracks the processing of the cases. The Office of the Executive Secretary dockets all documents filed with the NLRB, serves NLRB decisions and orders upon the parties, and certifies copies of documents that are a part of the NLRB's files. The Executive Secretary also represents the NLRB in dealing with parties to cases and communicates on behalf of the NLRB with labor organizations, employers, employees, and the public.

Q 2.4.2 ... the Office of the Solicitor?

The Solicitor is the NLRB's chief legal officer and advises the NLRB on a number of issues, including:

(1) questions of law and policy;

(2) adoption, revision, or rescission of rules and regulations and statements of procedure;

(3) pending legislation amending or affecting the NLRA; and

(4) litigation affecting the NLRB.

The Office of the Solicitor also handles formal settlements forwarded for NLRB approval and drafts advisory opinions concerning whether the NLRB would assert jurisdiction in a particular case.

In addition, the Office of the Solicitor provides advice to the NLRB, the Office of the Executive Secretary, the Division of Information, and other offices on a variety of other matters, including issues arising under the NLRA, Administrative Procedure Act, Freedom of Information Act, Sunshine Act, and Privacy Act.

Q 2.4.3   ... Division of Judges?

The Division of Judges is a group of administrative law judges (ALJs) who conduct hearings once the General Counsel issues a complaint on an unfair labor practice charge. ALJs are employees of the agency, but operate largely independent of the General Counsel and the five-member Board. The ALJ acts much like a trial court judge in a bench proceeding. ALJs are barred by administrative law strictures from ex parte communications with any party on a matter in dispute. The ALJ hears the facts and arguments of each party and then renders an initial recommended decision with proposed findings of fact. That decision may be appealed to the Board. Offices of the ALJs are based in Washington, D.C., Atlanta, San Francisco, and New York City, but the ALJs will usually travel to the locality where the unfair labor practice occurred to hear the case.

Q 2.4.4   ... the Office of Representation Appeals?

The Office of Representation Appeals is attached to the Office of the Chairman of the NLRB and is responsible for processing appeals by parties from formal decisions issued by regional directors in representation cases, subject to review by the NLRB. The Office of Representation Appeals is also responsible for giving advice to regional directors on substantive and procedural questions, maintaining technical review and evaluation of the decisional activities of all regional directors, and recommending to the NLRB policy or legal changes in existing precedent governing representation cases.

Q 2.5   How is the General Counsel's Office organized?

The General Counsel's staff consists of four main departments:

(1)   Division of Operations Management
(2)   Division of Advice
(3)   Division of Enforcement Litigation
(4)   Division of Administration

Q 2.5.1   What role is played by the Division of Operations Management?

The Division of Operations Management assists the General Counsel with its administrative functions.

Q 2.5.2   ... the Division of Advice?

The Division of Advice provides legal advice to the General Counsel and to the regional offices and assists with injunction proceedings. The Division of Advice consists of three branches:

- Regional Advice,
- Injunction Litigation, and
- Legal Research & Policy Planning.

The Regional Advice branch provides guidance with respect to difficult legal issues arising in the processing of unfair labor practice charges and determines whether charges have merit. The Injunction Litigation branch implements the General Counsel's interim injunction program, which grants injunctive relief where necessary to preserve the effectiveness of an NLRB order. The Legal Research & Policy Planning branch provides agency employees with current summaries of NLRB and related court decisions.

The General Counsel requires cases involving certain novel or unsettled issues of labor law to be submitted to the Division of Advice for analysis and guidance. The General Counsel guidance regarding mandatory submissions to the Division of Advice was last updated on December 1, 2017,[6] and includes the following issues, among others:

- what level of obscene, vulgar, or other highly inappropriate conduct will still be considered concerted activity for mutual aid and protection;

- whether it is lawful under the NLRA for employers to prohibit the use of cameras or other recording equipment in the workplace;

- whether employees have a presumptive right to use their employers' email system to engage in section 7 activities;

- the breadth of permissible conduct by union representatives in *Weingarten* interviews; and

- whether the dues check-off obligation survives expiration of the collective-bargaining agreement.

Q 2.5.3   ... the Division of Enforcement Litigation?

The Division of Enforcement Litigation conducts the litigation wherein the NLRB is seeking enforcement of its orders. NLRB orders are enforced in the federal courts of appeals. The Division of Enforcement Litigation also conducts contempt proceedings, which may be brought when a party does not comply with a court-enforced NLRB order. This division also has an Office of Appeals that reviews regional directors' decisions not to issue a complaint on an unfair labor practice charge. Employers who have cases that go before an ALJ will often interact with the Division of Enforcement Litigation during the later (appellate) stages of the case.

Enforcement and Remedies

Penalties

Q 2.6   Can the NLRB impose fines or other monetary penalties?

The National Labor Relations Act is not a criminal statute, therefore, the NLRB does not levy fines or penalties. Instead, the NLRB effectuates the NLRA by crafting affirmative remedial actions such as ordering backpay, offering reinstatement, issuing bargaining orders, and requiring the refund of illegally collected union dues.

Q 2.7   How does the NLRB develop agency policy?

Like many federal agencies, the NLRB has two major ways of making policy determinations: (1) case-by-case adjudication, and (2) substantive rulemaking.

Rulemaking

Q 2.8   How does the NLRB use rulemaking?

The NLRB, like many federal agencies, has two major ways of making policy determinations: (1) case-by-case adjudication, and (2) substantive rulemaking. The adjudication process, described above, is similar to a court proceeding. Decisions rendered in adjudications bind only the parties, but are treated as precedential agency law.

Substantive rulemaking, by contrast, involves a kind of legislative function: The agency publishes a proposed rule in the *Federal Register*, allows an opportunity for public comments, and then considers those comments in deciding whether to promulgate the rule. The rule is prospective in operation and binding on all. Although the NLRB has the statutory authority, it has rarely used rulemaking. It has used rulemaking for certain procedural issues, such as agency procedures and guidelines. The U.S. Supreme Court has made clear that the NLRB has nearly absolute discretion regarding whether to use rulemaking or adjudication.[7] The scope of the NLRB's rulemaking authority, however, is limited by the NLRA and the U.S. Constitution.[8]

In 1990, the NLRB engaged in substantive rulemaking over the composition of appropriate bargaining units in the healthcare industry. This effort received a unanimous U.S. Supreme Court decision upholding the NLRB's authority and the rule.[9] During the Clinton administration, however, an attempt to promulgate a relatively inflexible rule declaring the single-location unit presumptively appropriate in representation cases turned out to be quite controversial, resulting in congressional resolutions to bar funding for any continuation of the rulemaking proceeding.[10]

The NLRB engaged in substantive rulemaking three times during the Obama administration. On August 30, 2011, the NLRB issued a final rule requiring private-sector employers to post notices advising employees of their rights under the NLRA.[11] The rule was challenged immediately and ultimately struck down by two circuit courts. The D.C. Circuit held that compulsory notice postings are in conflict with the NLRA's protection of non-coercive speech.[12] The Fourth Circuit held that the NLRA does not provide the Board with the authority to affirmatively act absent an unfair labor practice claim triggering the Board's jurisdiction.[13] The NLRB did not seek review of the decisions of the U.S. Supreme Court.

On December 21, 2011, the NLRB issued a final rule amending long-standing representation case procedures. The rule took effect April 30, 2012, but on May 14, 2012, the U.S. District Court for the District of Columbia held that the NLRB lacked the statutorily required quorum to promulgate the rules at the time the final rule was adopted.[14] Accordingly, the district court held that the rule was invalid. The NLRB appealed the district court decision to the D.C. Circuit, but ultimately agreed to a joint stipulation dismissing the case.[15]

On February 6, 2014, the NLRB issued a notice of proposed rulemaking that included many of the same amendments to the current representation case procedures that the NLRB unsuccessfully sought to implement in December 2011. Following the notice and comment period, the Board adopted the final rule with an effective date of April 14, 2015.[16]

On September 14, 2018, the NLRB Board published a Notice of Proposed Rulemaking regarding the joint-employer standard. If a company is found to be a joint-employer, it can be forced to bargain with the jointly employed workers. It can also be sued for unfair labor practices committed by the other employer. Under the Board's proposed rule, a company would only be a joint-employer if it possesses and exercises "substantial, direct and immediate control" over the essential terms and conditions of another employer's employees. Limited or routine control is not enough.

Adjudication

Q 2.9   How does the NLRB adjudication process work?

The adjudication process is described above (see QQ 2.3–2.5.3, discussing the roles of the various offices and divisions of the NLRB) and is similar to a court proceeding. Decisions rendered in adjudications bind only the parties, but are treated as precedential agency law.

Q 2.10   Can the NLRB overrule its precedent without being asked by any party?

The NLRB can decide cases on any ground in the record, even if that ground was not timely raised by any party. In *Dish Network Corporation*,[17] the NLRB questioned whether it could reconsider its precedent when the issue has not been timely raised by either the union or the Acting General Counsel under NLRB rules. The NLRB held those rules place limitations on parties, but do not limit the NLRB's authority. The NLRB can consider an argument and reverse precedent, even if it is not raised by any party, so long as the NLRB makes its decision based on the record.

Q 2.11   Does the NLRB have the authority to decide cases with only two members?

The NLRA authorizes the NLRB "to delegate to any group of three or more members any or all of the powers which [the NLRB] may itself exercise." A vacancy in the NLRB does not "impair the right of the remaining members to exercise all of the powers of the [NLRB]." "[T]hree members of the Board shall, at all times, constitute a quorum of the [NLRB], except that two members shall constitute a quorum of any group designated pursuant to the first sentence [above]."[18] In *New Process Steel, LP v. NLRB*,[19] the U.S. Supreme Court held these provisions to mean that the NLRB cannot act unless its powers are vested "at all times" in a group made up of at least three members. The Supreme Court, thus, invalidated a decision made by two members vested with the NLRB's powers because the third member's recess appointment expired before the decision was made. The Supreme Court noted the NLRB would have had a quorum if the third member of the delegated group had still been a member of the NLRB but merely had to recuse himself from the case.

In *Noel Canning v. NLRB*, the U.S. Supreme Court unanimously affirmed a D.C. Circuit decision holding that three of President Obama's recess appointments to the Board were unconstitutional.[20] The Recess Appointments Clause of the U.S. Constitution provides: "The President shall have Power to fill up all Vacancies that may happen during the Recess of the Senate, by granting Commissions which shall expire at the End of their next Session."[21] The Supreme Court held that the Recess Appointments Clause is broad, applying to both inter- and intra-session recesses. The Court further held that the clause applies to both vacancies that occur during a recess, and those that occur before and continue to exist through a recess. Finally, the Court held that pro forma sessions count as sessions, not recesses, consistent with the Constitution's delegation of authority to the Senate to determine how it conducts its own business.[22] President Obama appointed three NLRB members during the Senate's holding of "pro forma" sessions. The three appointees, thus, were not lawful members of the NLRB, the NLRB lacked a quorum, and a decision made that required those members to reach a quorum was unlawful.[23]

Because every NLRB decision may be appealed to the D.C. Circuit, the *Noel Canning* holding affected every NLRB decision issued from August 27, 2011, to August 12, 2013.[24] During that period, the NLRB relied on the since-invalidated recess appointments in an attempt to meet the NLRA's quorum requirement. On August 12, 2013, Congress confirmed the appointment of four new members to the NLRB.

Q 2.12   Can the NLRB reverse its prior decisions?

In theory, the NLRB subscribes to the doctrine of stare decisis, the legal principle by which judges and other adjudicators are obliged to follow the precedents established by prior decisions. In practice, however, the NLRB often reverses itself, especially when a new presidential administration is elected and appoints a new majority on the NLRB. The newly constituted NLRB typically is interested in reconsidering decisions of the previous majority in which a dissent was written.

Judicial Review

Q 2.13   Are NLRB decisions subject to judicial review?

The NLRB's decisions in unfair labor practice cases are normally subject to judicial review in U.S. federal courts, pursuant to section 10(e) and (f) of the NLRA.[25] In an unfair labor practice proceeding, the parties adjudicate their claims initially through an ALJ, with the

General Counsel acting as prosecutor. Once the ALJ issues a ruling, the parties may file exceptions. The ALJ is technically not the decision-maker; rather the five-member Board or a panel of the NLRB is the decision-maker. These exceptions are reviewed by the NLRB and result in an order. If a party does not file exceptions, the NLRB will simply issue an order accepting the judge's findings and recommendation. The order may be challenged by any party in a federal court of appeals. The NLRB's orders are not self-enforcing. An order issued by the NLRB does not have the force of law, and the NLRB has no authority to compel compliance. Therefore, to secure compliance, the NLRB will seek enforcement of its order in a U.S. court of appeals, or if a party files an appeal, the NLRB will file a cross-motion for enforcement.

In contrast, the NLRB's decisions in representation cases generally are not subject to judicial review. Only final orders of the NLRB are subject to review by federal courts, and representation decisions are not final orders under section 10(e) and (f). As more fully explained in chapters 8 and 9, questions concerning representation are typically decided by a Regional Director. The Regional Director's decision is then subject to discretionary review by the NLRB. Regardless of whether the NLRB refuses to review the decision or affirms the region's determination, the aggrieved party cannot bring the decision up on direct judicial review. Instead, a party dissatisfied with the NLRB's decision in a representation case must convert the case into an unfair labor practice proceeding, usually by refusing to bargain with the certified union.

Q 2.13.1   What is the scope of review when courts of appeals review NLRB decisions?

Courts will not disturb the NLRB's chosen remedy unless it is shown that the order is a "patent attempt to achieve ends other than those which can fairly be said to effectuate the policies of the [NLRA]."[26] In reviewing NLRB orders that turn on credibility determinations, federal courts give very substantial deference to the agency's findings of fact.[27] On questions of policy and sometimes questions of statutory interpretation, courts will defer to the NLRB's reasonable determinations unless the NLRA clearly provides an answer.[28]

Notes to Chapter 2

1.   *See* FREDRIC H. FISCHER, BRENT GARREN & JOHN C. TRUESDALE, HOW TO TAKE A CASE BEFORE THE NLRB 34 (ABA 7th ed. 1992).

2.   *See* NLRB, Basic Guide to the National Labor Relations Act (1997), at 33. This pamphlet is available at www.nlrb.gov/sites/default/files/attachments/basic-page/node-3024/basicguide.pdf.

3.   Restructuring of NLRB's Field Organization, 77 Fed. Reg. 72,886 (Dec. 6, 2012); Restructuring of NLRB's Field Organization, 78 Fed. Reg. 44,602 (July 24, 2013).

4.   Noam Scheiber, *Trump Appointee is Trying to Squelch Us, Labor Board Staff Says*, Jan. 25, 2018, https://www.nytimes.com/2018/01/25/business/economy/labor-board.html.

5.   Hassan Kanu, *Labor Board Officials Have 'Grave' Concerns About Restructuring*, Jan. 25, 2018, https://bnanews.bna.com/daily-labor-report/labor-board-officials-have-grave-concerns-about-restructuring.

6.   NLRB Gen. Couns. Mem. 18-02, Mandatory Submissions to Advice (Dec. 1, 2017), www.nlrb.gov/reports-guidance/general-counsel-memos.

7.   NLRB v. Bell Aerospace, 416 U.S. 267 (1974).

8.   *See* Nat'l Ass'n of Mfrs. v. NLRB, 717 F.3d 947 (D.C. Cir. 2013), *overruled on other grounds by* Am. Meat Inst. v. U.S. Dep't of Agric., 760 F.3d 18 (D.C. Cir. 2014).

9.   Am. Hosp. Ass'n v. NLRB, 499 U.S. 606 (1991).

10.   In 1995, during the Clinton administration, the NLRB proposed a rule to govern single-location units in all industries except public utilities, construction, and ocean-going maritime firms. Under the rule, absent "extraordinary circumstances," a single-location unit, if petitioned for by the union, would be deemed appropriate if (a) fifteen or more employees were employed at that location; (b) no other location of the employer was located within one mile; and (c) at least one supervisor was present at the location. The proposed single-location rule never became law. For three straight years following its proposal, the Republican majority in Congress attached "riders" to the NLRB's budget preventing the NLRB from spending any money on the single-facility proceeding. The NLRB ultimately withdrew the proposed rule, with Chairman Gould dissenting. 63 Fed. Reg. 8890 (1998).

11.   Notification of Employee Rights Under the National Labor Relations Act, 76 Fed. Reg. 54,006 (Aug. 30, 2011) (codified at 29 C.F.R. pt. 104).

12.   Nat'l Ass'n of Mfrs. v. NLRB, 717 F.3d 947, 955–56 (D.C. Cir. 2013), *overruled on other grounds by* Am. Meat Inst. v. U.S. Dep't of Agric., 760 F.3d 18 (D.C. Cir. 2014).

13. Chamber of Commerce v. NLRB, 721 F.3d 152, 154 (4th Cir. 2013).

14. Chamber of Commerce v. NLRB, 879 F. Supp. 2d 18 (D.D.C. 2012).

15. Chamber of Commerce v. NLRB, 2013 WL 6801164 (D.C. Cir. Dec. 9, 2013).

16. Representation Case Procedures, 79 Fed. Reg. 74,308 (Dec. 15, 2014).

17. Dish Network Corp., 359 N.L.R.B. No. 32 (2012); *see also* Tri-Cast, Inc., 274 N.L.R.B. 377 (1985). The NLRB ultimately declined to revisit *Tri-Cast* to avoid further delay in the resolution of the case. *In re* Dish Network Corp., 359 N.L.R.B. No. 32 (2012).

18. 29 U.S.C. § 153(b).

19. New Process Steel, LP v. NLRB, 130 S. Ct. 2635 (2010).

20. Noel Canning v. NLRB, 134 S. Ct. 2550 (2014).

21. U.S. CONST. art. II, § 2, cl. 3.

22. *Noel Canning*, 134 S. Ct. at 2550.

23. *Id.* at 2574.

24. *See* 29 U.S.C. § 160(f).

25. 29 U.S.C. § 160(e) provides: "The Board shall have power to petition any court of appeals of the United States . . . wherein the unfair labor practice in question occurred or wherein such person resides or transacts business, for the enforcement of such order and for appropriate temporary relief or restraining order. . . ." 29 U.S.C. § 160(f) provides: "Any person aggrieved by a final order of the Board granting or denying in whole or in part the relief sought may obtain a review of such order in any United States court of appeals in the circuit wherein the unfair labor practice in question was alleged to have been engaged in or wherein such person resides or transacts business, or in the United States Court of Appeals for the District of Columbia. . . ."

26. NLRB v. U.S. Postal Serv., 486 F.3d 683 (10th Cir. 2007).

27. 2 JOHN E. HIGGINS, JR., THE DEVELOPING LABOR LAW 3014–15 (6th ed. 2012 & Supp. 2014).

28. *See* Chevron U.S.A., Inc. v. Nat. Res. Def. Council, Inc., 467 U.S. 837 (1984); *see also* United States v. Mead Corp., 533 U.S. 218 (2001).

3

Protected and Unprotected Activity

The National Labor Relations Act (NLRA) protects the rights of employees and employers by defining those activities of employees that are protected and those labor practices of employers and unions that it deems unfair. This chapter examines the rights of employees, as well as the various actions and activities of employers and unions and the extent to which those activities are prohibited by the NLRA.

The Scope of NLRA Protection

Q 3.1   What types of employees are afforded protection by the NLRA?

The NLRA affords certain rights to most private-sector, non-supervisory employees.[1] Certain groups of persons are excluded from the definition of "employee" under the NLRA.[2] For details regarding the definition of "employee" under the NLRA, see QQ 1.3–1.4.12. For a discussion of whether "salts" are protected by the rights granted to employees under the NLRA, see Q 3.26.1.

Employees' Section 7 Rights

Generally

Q 3.2 What rights of employees are protected by the NLRA?

Section 7 of the NLRA provides employees with the following rights:[3]

- the right to self-organization

- the right to form, join, or assist labor organizations

- the right to bargain collectively through representatives of their own choosing

- the right to engage in other concerted activities for the purpose of collective bargaining or other mutual aid or protection

- the right to refrain from any or all of the above activities, except to the extent this right may be affected by an agreement requiring membership in a labor organization, or payment of union dues, as a condition of employment.

These "section 7 rights" apply in unionized and non-unionized workplaces; further, no union or organizing campaign is necessary.[4] Generally, for employee activity to be legally protected, it must:

(1) be concerted;

(2) be in furtherance of a protected objective regarding collective bargaining or other mutual aid or protection of employees; and

(3) involve the use of lawful, protected means.

Q 3.2.1 What is a "concerted activity"?

An employee's action is typically considered "concerted" if that employee acts with or for other employees, or is authorized to act on behalf of other employees.[5] Concertedness also exists when an individual employee's action is a "logical outgrowth" of previous group activity and when the employee is soliciting or responding to solicitations of co-worker group activity.[6] In contrast, a single individual, acting in his or her own self-interest only, is not engaged in concerted activity, and that individual activity is not protected by the NLRA.[7] Activities found *not* to be "concerted" include an employee's filing of a personal claim with a state or federal agency, and the solicitation of others to help with a personal issue.[8]

LABOR MANAGEMENT LAW FACT

It is well established that protected concerted activity under the NLRA may lose the veil of protection if it is carried out in an abusive, excessive, or otherwise indefensible manner, such as by using violence or illegal or unprotected means.[9] When employees, for example, engage in an in-plant strike or "slowdown," such activity has been held to involve the use of unprotected means and falls outside the protection of the NLRA.[10]

Q 3.2.2   What are activities "for the purpose of collective bargaining or other mutual aid or protection of employees"?

These may include employee efforts to improve working conditions and terms of employment (such as improved pay, hours, safety, or workload)[11] or to protest certain working conditions, such as overtime practices or workplace safety issues. Concerted complaints or grievances presented to employers and even informal discussions between employees about their working conditions can fall within the ambit of protected activity under the NLRA.[12]

The term "mutual aid or protection" broadens the scope of section 7 protected rights to include appeals to employees of the same employer or other employers outside of the bargaining unit. These issues typically arise in connection with the honoring of picket lines maintained by unions representing employees outside of the bargaining unit. The general rule is that employees honoring such a picket line are engaged in concerted activity "for mutual aid or protection" and lose protection only if they have agreed in their collective bargaining agreement not to honor picket lines during the contract term, or if the picketing is itself unlawful. That the activity is protected does not necessarily mean that the employer cannot hire replacements to ensure delivery commitments.[13]

The "mutual aid or protection" clause also broadens the scope of protected employee activity to include concerted activities to improve terms and conditions of employment. This clause protects employees who seek to improve working conditions by appealing to the courts, government agencies, or legislative bodies. The "mutual aid or protection" clause has been held to protect salespersons who expressed concerns regarding the hiring of a new cashier to a manager, and has also been construed to protect employees who sent a letter to management reflecting employees' discussions about possible mismanagement of the company, which the employees believed detrimentally affected their working conditions.[14] The clause has also been held to protect an employee who seeks to raise allegations of sexual harassment, even if the other employees involved did not agree or join the cause of the employee.[15]

Q 3.2.3   What is an employee's "right to refrain" from exercise of section 7 rights?

Section 7 was expanded by the Labor Management Relations Act in 1947 to guarantee employees the right "to refrain from any and all concerted activities."[16] This created tension between the two rights of employees protected by section 7: (1) the right to form, join, or assist labor organizations; and (2) the right to refrain from doing so.[17] An employer cannot discriminate against an employee who declines to become a member of the union or engage in concerted activity. However, under the "union shop" proviso to section 8(a)(3) of the NLRA, collective bargaining provisions requiring employees to pay the dues requirement assessed on union members are enforceable, to the extent of honoring the bargaining agent's demand to discharge an employee who refuses to pay the dues assessment.

Q 3.3   Are employers required to post notices of employees' section 7 rights?

Except government contractors, which must provide notice pursuant to Executive Order 13496, employers are not required to post notices of employees' section 7 rights. In 2011, the NLRB issued a rule that would have required private-sector employers to post notices advising employees of their section 7 rights under the NLRA.[18] The posting rule was enjoined by U.S. Courts of Appeal and never went into effect.[19] Accordingly, there currently is no requirement that non–government contractors post notices of employees' section 7 rights.

Protected Employee Activities

Strikes/Work Stoppages

Q 3.4   Are strikes and other work stoppages or slowdowns protected activity?

Inherent in section 7 is the right to strike, which is also expressly protected in section 13 of the NLRA.[20] A primary strike is considered "concerted" activity and it is generally protected, but it may be unprotected in particular circumstances:[21]

- if the strike violates a no-strike clause in the collective bargaining agreement;[22]

- if the strike disparages the employer's product or services without being connected to a labor dispute or that constitutes a "sharp, public, disparaging attack on the quality of the company's product and its business policies" in a manner "reasonably calculated to harm the company's reputation and reduce its income";[23]

- if the strike is in support of a secondary objective or uses secondary means that violate section 8(b)(4) of the NLRA;[24]

- if the strikers engage in serious misconduct such as damaging the employer's property, depriving the employer of its property, or threatening or causing violence;[25]

- if the strike or work stoppage is a "partial" strike (in which employees continue working on their own terms) or is an "intermittent" work stoppage;[26]

- if the strike's purpose is unlawful, such as a strike in support of an unfair labor practice.[27]

Political Rallies

Q 3.5   Does an employee engage in protected activity by attending a political rally?

Generally speaking, employees have no NLRA right to time off of work to attend political rallies. In 2008, the NLRB's General Counsel issued its "Guideline Memorandum Concerning Unfair Labor Practice Charges Involving Political Advocacy," which expressed the view that attendance at political rallies can constitute activity protected under section 7, with the caveat that the right can be lost depending on how it is exercised by employees.[28] The memorandum stated:

- Non-disruptive political advocacy related to an employment concern that takes place during the employees' own time and in non-work areas is protected.

- On-duty political advocacy is subject to restrictions imposed by lawful and neutrally applied work rules.

- Leaving or stopping work to engage in political advocacy may also be subject to restrictions imposed by lawful and neutrally applied work rules.[29]

Thus, an employee who chooses to engage in certain activities outside of the workplace (if otherwise concerted and for a protected objective) during a personal day may be protected by section 7. However, if an employee simply misses work without permission to attend a political rally or other employment-related event, he or she will likely not be protected.[30]

CASE STUDY: *A Day Without an Immigrant*

On May 1, 2006, across the United States, hundreds of thousands of immigrants, both legal and illegal, stayed home from work and school and avoided buying or selling anything, as part of the "Great American Boycott." The stated purpose of this one-day event, also referred to as "A Day Without an Immigrant," was to demonstrate the economic importance of illegal immigrants and to affirm their right to continue living and working here. The protestors opposed legislation that would impose greater requirements on immigrant employees and employers who would hire them and that would increase the penalties for violating those requirements.

In *Reliable Maintenance*,[31] the NLRB Office of the General Counsel, Division of Advice advised that employers lawfully terminated employees who missed work without permission to participate in or support "A Day Without an Immigrant" demonstrations. As the "Guideline Memorandum Concerning Unfair Labor Practice Charges Involving Political Advocacy" states, "As a matter of enforcement policy under the NLRA, we do not want to equate political disputes with labor disputes, or promote the use of strikes and similar activity for resolving what are essentially political questions." To be protected activity under section 7, then, there must be a direct nexus between concerns about employee working conditions and the specific issues that are the subject of the advocacy. The guideline found that there was such a nexus and that protests against the impediments to hiring immigrant employees fell within the scope of the "mutual aid or protection clause" of section 7 because even legal immigrant workers would be affected by the legislation. However, employees cannot skip work in order to participate in section 7 activity, paying no heed to the employer's nondiscriminatory attendance policy.

Representation During Investigations ("Weingarten *Rights*")

Q 3.6   Do employees have a section 7 right to be represented in investigatory interviews that might result in discipline?

The U.S. Supreme Court ruled in *NLRB v. J. Weingarten, Inc.* that union-represented employees have the right to have union representatives present during an investigatory interview that the employee reasonably believes might result in disciplinary action ("*Weingarten* rights").[32] Employees do not have *Weingarten* rights when a manager is only giving instructions or retraining an employee.[33] Determining when *Weingarten* applies requires a reasonable evaluation of all the circumstances. Even a conversation between a supervisor and an employee about the employee's misconduct may trigger *Weingarten* rights.[34] Employees also have a right, upon request, to have union representation for a "reasonable suspicion" drug or alcohol test required by an employer.[35]

The D.C. Circuit takes a narrower view than the NLRB regarding an employer's duties under *Weingarten*. In *Menorah Medical Center v. NLRB*, the D.C. Circuit concluded the employer did not unlawfully deny nurses' requests for union representation at nursing peer review committee hearings because, rather than a compulsory in-person interview, employees had the option of appearing, or, in lieu of appearing, filing a written response.[36] The court explained that Weingarten rights are infringed only when an employer *compels* an employee to appear at an interview that might put his or her job in jeopardy and denies him or her union representation.[37]

Q 3.6.1   Are employers required to offer employees union representation at investigatory interviews?

No. Employees must request a union representative to trigger their *Weingarten* rights. The request, however, "need only be sufficient to put the employer on notice of the employee's desire for union representation."[38] Statements or questions such as, "I would like someone there that could explain to me what was happening," "Should I have someone in here with me, someone from the union," and "Do

I need a witness" have been found sufficient to trigger *Weingarten* rights.[39]

If a union representative is unavailable, the employer "must give the employee time to obtain representation or, if it does not wish to accord the employee this right, proceed on the basis of information it could obtain through other means."[40] If no union representative is available, the employer must either discontinue the interview or offer the employee the choice between continuing the interview unaccompanied by a union representative or having no interview at all (in which case the employer is free to take disciplinary action based on information obtained from other sources).[41]

Q 3.6.2   What is a union representative's role during *Weingarten investigatory* interviews?

Employers may not limit a union representative's role in investigatory interviews to that of a silent observer.[42] Rather, union representatives must be permitted to "provide 'advice and active assistance'" to the employee.[43] For example, a union representative has the right to ask questions[44] and to object to questions posed by the employer reasonably perceived as harassing. A union representative may not, however, preclude the employer from using legitimate investigative techniques to obtain information.[45] Moreover, the union representative may not turn the meeting into an adversarial proceeding, may not prevent the employer from questioning the employee, and "may not interfere with legitimate employer prerogatives."[46]

Q 3.6.3   Do non-union employees have *Weingarten* rights?

Over the past two decades, the NLRB has changed its position regarding whether *Weingarten* rights extend to non-union employees. Currently, non-union employees are not entitled to have a co-worker present during investigatory interviews.[47]

Employee Communications: Solicitation and Distribution

Q 3.7 What forms of employee communications does the NLRA protect?

Employees have a section 7 right to engage in certain forms of "solicitation" and "distribution" on company property usually during non-working time. Employee rights are generally balanced against employers' property rights and rights to operate their businesses. An employee's right to communicate is not unlimited. The form of communication, to whom it is communicated, and when and where certain communication takes place all factor into whether the communication falls within the scope of protected section 7 rights.

For a discussion of solicitation/distribution by non-employee union organizers, see Q 3.10 below.

Q 3.8 What is "solicitation"?

The term "solicitation" refers to oral communications among employees concerning organization and terms and conditions of employment. "Solicitation" includes encouraging signatures on a petition (be it a union petition or otherwise), if it is for the purpose of discussing and improving the terms or conditions of employment. "Solicitation" also includes wearing union buttons and other insignia.

Q 3.8.1 Are employees permitted to solicit on company property?

Employers may prohibit employee solicitation during "working time," which is the time when an employee is being paid to actively work (and are not on a paid or unpaid break or meal period).[48] Rules prohibiting solicitation during "working time" are lawful because such rules imply that solicitation is permitted during nonworking time.[49] However, bans on solicitation during "company time," "business hours," or "working hours" are presumptively invalid because they include times during which employees are not working, such as breaks and meal periods.[50]

The nature of an employer's business may justify a solicitation ban in certain areas of the employer's premises.[51] For instance, a retail department store may prohibit employee solicitation on the selling floor even during non-working time.[52] On the other hand, a retail department store may not prohibit employees from soliciting in sections of the stores that are non-sale areas.[53] Similarly, a restaurant may prohibit solicitation even during employees' break and lunch periods in areas where customers are likely to be present.[54] A hospital can lawfully prohibit employee solicitation in immediate patient care areas.[55]

Q 3.9   Are employees permitted to distribute union literature on company property?

Employees generally have a section 7 right to distribute union or other literature regarding their collective concerns, but only during "non-working time" and in "non-working areas."[56] "Working areas" may include the shop floor, production areas, and other places where employees perform their jobs.[57]

While distribution can be prohibited in "working areas," a prohibition against distributing on "company property" is unlawful because "company property" includes non-work areas such as lunchrooms, locker rooms, and parking lots where employees *are* permitted to distribute written material.[58]

Employees may also be allowed to distribute union literature in certain "mixed-use areas," which are locations in which an employer permits both work and non-work activities to occur in the same space.[59] The Board recognizes two types of mixed-use areas: (1) "permanent mixed-use areas," which are areas that are perpetually used for both work and non-work activities; and (2) "converted mixed-use areas," which are work areas that periodically accommodate non-work (or a mix of work and non-work).[60] Employers may not prohibit distribution in permanent mixed-use areas; however, employers may prohibit distribution in converted mixed-use areas when the area is being used as a work area.[61]

Q 3.10   Do non-employee union organizers have a right to access company property to engage in solicitation and distribution?

Non-employee union organizers do not enjoy section 7 rights. An employer can lawfully prohibit non-employee union organizers from soliciting or distributing union literature on company property, such as in the company's parking lot or on a walkway reserved for the employees of the employer's manufacturing facility, if (1) the union organizers will be able to reach employees by making reasonable efforts through other available channels of communication and (2) the employer does not discriminate against the union by allowing solicitation or distribution of items by other non-employees.[62] The employer's property right, generally, will only have to yield where the location of the employer's facility or the living quarters of the employees place them beyond the reach of reasonable union efforts to communicate with them, such as where employees are working in remote locations such as lumber camps or are housed on employer property.[63]

While an employer has the general right to bar non-employee organizers from its own property, employers may not have a right to bar non-employees based on property rights of others. Therefore, to the extent an employer leases property from a third party, the employer may not have the right to prohibit non-employee organizing activity on a sidewalk in front of the employer that has not been conveyed in the lease.[64]

Employee Speech

Q 3.11   Is an employee's statement outside of work to third parties about an employer's business or products protected activity?

Employees' communications with third parties are generally protected by section 7 when they seek to improve the terms and conditions of their employment.[65] Thus, participating in a public protest over sanitation and safety issues,[66] complaining to an employer's clients about working conditions,[67] or making statements in an article[68] can all be protected activities.

Communications to third parties lose protection if they are unrelated to an ongoing dispute between the employees and the employer and are so "disloyal, reckless, or maliciously untrue as to lose the Act's protection."[69] An employee "exceeds the boundaries of protected activity when she falsely and publicly disparages her employer or its products and services. An employee may not appeal to the public by conveying information with 'reckless disregard of its truth or falsity.'"[70]

Employee communications that have been found to not be protected include:

- false statements by a nurse that accused her hospital employer of putting the safety of mothers and babies at risk by changing staffing practices in labor and delivery operating rooms;[71]

- an employee's allegations that a sandwich store would not permit its employees to call in sick, and as such, food was prepared by ill employees, where employees were never required to work when they were ill;[72] and

- an employee's statement to newspaper that following a layoff there were "gaping holes" in the employer's business, "leaving voids in the critical knowledge base for the highly technical business," as statements were "so disloyal" that they lost protection of the Act.[73]

 CASE STUDY: *Valley Hospital Medical Center*[74]

In *Valley Hospital Medical Center*, the hospital discharged an employee for comments she made that were reported in a local newspaper. The NLRB held that the comments made by the employee at a union rally, which were reported in a newspaper, were protected activity and not so disloyal as to lose NLRA protection. At the time the comments were made, the hospital and the union were in negotiations over staffing levels. At the union rally, the employee stated that, as a result of understaffing, "[y]ou don't get medications to patients on time. They could be lying in their own excrement. . . . You can't even do the basic things you want to do." These comments were deemed not to be disloyal, since they were not made at a critical time in the initiation of the hospital's business and, although critical of the hospital's product—patient care—they were not made in a manner reasonably calculated to harm the hospital's reputation and reduce its income. The NLRB found that the employee's intent was not to harm the hospital but rather to pressure the hospital into increasing staffing, which would improve nurses' working conditions.

Further, employer policies restricting communications with third parties may violate the NLRA unless there are significant countervailing employee interests.[75] For example, the NLRB has found it unlawful to maintain and enforce a policy prohibiting an employee from speaking to the media.[76]

Q 3.12 Are employees' social media posts considered protected activity?

Employees' social media posts may be protected activity when they relate to a broader discussion about work policies or terms of employment, such as job performance or compensation.[77] This is true even when the posts contain offensive language, insults, or sarcasm.[78] For example, employees may be engaged in protected concerted activity when they post on Facebook or Twitter about work policies or terms of employment.[79] In addition, clicking Facebook's "like" button can be considered protected concerted activity.[80]

An employee's social media posts may not be protected activity if the posts are complaints about individual co-workers or there is no evidence of concerted activity (for example, the employee never discussed the issue with other employees). For example, an employee's Facebook post containing unspecified criticisms where there was no evidence the post was intended for, or in response to, comments from co-workers was not considered protected concerted activity.[81] Further, an employee's social media postings can lose protection under the NLRA in the same manner as third-party communications.[82]

Non-Work Use of Employer's Equipment/Resources

Q 3.13 Do employees have a right to use an employer's equipment or resources to communicate about union issues?

Employees generally do not have a statutory right to use an employer's equipment or resources, such as an employer's fax machines, photocopiers, bulletin boards, or telephones, to communicate with other employees on union-related issues or on behalf of a union, as long as the restrictions are not discriminatory and are uniformly enforced.[83]

Q 3.13.1 Do employees have a right to use an employer's email system to engage in section 7 communications?

In *Purple Communications, Inc.*, the NLRB overruled previous Board precedent and held that employees who have access to an employer's email system in the course of their work have a presumptive right to use that email to engage in section 7 communications during non-working time unless the employer demonstrates that "special circumstances" make the ban necessary to maintain production or discipline.[84] The NLRB cautioned that "it will be the rare case where special circumstances justify a total ban on nonwork email use by employees" and that "ordinarily, an employer's interests will establish special circumstances only to the extent that those interests are not similarly affected by employee email use that the employer has authorized."[85] The NLRB specifically noted that its decision applies only to employees who have already been granted access to the employer's email system and does not require employers to provide such access.[86]

At the time of publication, the survival of *Purple Communications* is uncertain. In December 2017, the NLRB's General Counsel issued a Mandatory Submissions Memorandum that calls for mandatory submission to the Division of Advice all cases involving claims based on *Purple Communications'* holding that employees have a presumptive right to use their employer's email systems to engage in section 7 activities.[87] The Mandatory Submissions Memorandum also explains that the General Counsel is effectively overruling prior Advice Memoranda in which his predecessor noted the initiative "to extend *Purple Communications* to other [employer owned] electronic systems," such as the Internet, phones, and instant messaging systems that employees regularly use in the course of their work.[88]

In August 2018, the NLRB issued a public Notice and Invitation to File Briefs on whether the Board should adhere to, modify, or overrule *Purple Communications*.[89] The Board also invited comment on the standard it should apply to evaluate policies governing the use of employer-owned computer resources other than email.[90]

Wearing Union Insignia

Q 3.14   Can employees wear union insignia at work?

Wearing buttons, badges, and T-shirts that demonstrate union support or support for other workplace issues is considered a form of solicitation.[91] General provisions in employer handbooks or employment policies prohibiting employees from wearing union insignia while at work can be potential unfair labor practices subject to facial challenge even before they are enforced. The NLRB has ruled, with judicial approval, that an employer's policy that prohibits wearing or displaying tags, buttons, stickers, and other items "in support of any particular cause . . . while on duty" are unlawful, unless the employer can show that "special circumstances" justify the prohibition.

Q 3.14.1   What "special circumstances" may justify an employer policy that prohibits employees from wearing union insignia?

"Special circumstances" may involve maintaining production and discipline, ensuring safety,[92] preventing alienation of customers,[93] preventing adverse effects on patients in a healthcare facility,[94] or messages that are inflammatory and offensive.[95] An employer must put forth substantial, non-speculative evidence of the particular special circumstances that justify the restriction; the Board has found that generalizations or subjective beliefs do not suffice.[96] The Board reads the special circumstances exception narrowly and any rule based on special circumstances must be narrowly drawn to restrict wearing insignia only in areas or under circumstances that justify the rule.[97]

   CASE STUDY: *"W" San Diego*[98]

In this case, the NLRB held that a hotel's limitation on employees wearing buttons while in public areas was lawful because it fell under the "special circumstance" exception. The employer operated a 250-room hotel in San Diego. The employer marketed itself as providing an alternate hotel experience, referred to as "Wonderland," where guests could fulfill their "fantasies and desires" and get "whatever [they] want whenever [they] want it." In furtherance of the hotel's ambience, the employer required its public-contact employees to wear special uniforms to achieve a trendy, distinct, and chic look. Part of this uniform was a small "W" pin worn on the upper left chest. All other uniform adornments, including sweatbands, scarves worn as belts, and professional association pins, were prohibited.

One evening, an in-room delivery server who (the judge found) spent 30–40% of his work time in contact with the public put on a two-inch button, distributed by a union, that contained the wording: "JUSTICE NOW! JUSTICIA AHORA! H.E.R.E. LOCAL 30" in blue or red letters on a yellow background. The employer ordered the employee to remove the button.

The NLRB held that the employer had proved that special circumstances—interference with its public image—justified the no-button order while the employee was in public areas of the hotel where he would come in contact with guests. The employer failed, however, to show special circumstances that justified the employer's prohibition when the employee was in nonpublic areas of the hotel where he would not come in contact with guests. The NLRB rejected the employer's argument that it would be impractical for the employee to wear the union button in nonpublic areas while prohibiting the button in public areas because the employer did not introduce any actual evidence to support impracticality. The Board explained that simply removing a button—without any other alteration in employee uniform or appearance required—does not seem to present a barrier of impracticality, and Board precedent provides that the mere hypothetical impracticality of detaching a removable union insignia when moving between areas does not justify a blanket, property-wide prohibition.

Q 3.14.2   Can an employer prohibit union insignia based on special circumstances if it has allowed other insignia?

Disparate enforcement of a policy prohibiting insignia can undermine an employer's special circumstances defense.[99] Accordingly, an employer cannot prohibit union insignia if it has permitted other non-work insignia under similar circumstances.[100]

Q 3.14.3   What special rules regarding union insignia apply to healthcare facilities?

In the healthcare context, restrictions on wearing union insignia in "immediate patient care" areas are presumptively valid.[101] By contrast, restrictions on wearing union insignia in other areas of a hospital are presumptively invalid and violate the NLRA unless the employer shows "special circumstances" that justify the restriction.[102] In healthcare, special circumstances exist where the restriction is "necessary to avoid disruption of healthcare operations or disturbance of patients."[103]

In 2008, the Ninth Circuit overturned an NLRB decision that found a rule banning nurses from wearing buttons that said "RNs Demand Safe Staffing" in any area where they might be seen by patients or their families was lawful.[104] The court found that the NLRB had no evidence to support its conclusion that special circumstances justified the prohibition. The court focused on the lack of evidence in the record that the button actually disturbed patients. The presumption that restrictions on wearing insignia in immediate patient care areas are valid does not apply to a selective ban on only certain union insignia in immediate patient care areas.[105] In those circumstances, it remains the employer's burden to establish special circumstances justifying the restriction; specifically, that the prohibition was "necessary to avoid disruption of health-care operations or disturbance of patients."[106] Thus, if a hospital has in the past allowed employees to wear non-work-related buttons, signs, pins, or other insignia in immediate patient care areas, the hospital cannot prohibit union insignia in immediate patient care areas absent a showing that banning the union-related materials is necessary to avoid disrupting healthcare operations or disturbing patients.[107]

Unfair Labor Practices by Employers

Q 3.15 What types of employer conduct violate the NLRA?

Broadly speaking, an employer violates the NLRA when it commits an "unfair labor practice," defined by section 8(a) of the NLRA as:

(1) interfering with, restraining, or coercing employees in the exercise of their section 7 rights;

(2) dominating or interfering with the formation or administration of a labor organization;

(3) encouraging or discouraging membership in any labor organization by discrimination in regard to hire or tenure of employment or any term or condition of employment;

(4) discharging or discriminating against an employee for filing charges or giving testimony in NLRB proceedings;

(5) refusing to bargain collectively with the representatives of its employees.[108]

Employer Speech

Q 3.16 How does the NLRA govern employer speech?

The NLRA attempts to strike a balance between an employer's ability to express opinions concerning organizing efforts and an employee's rights to associate with a union and participate in organizing activity. An employer's free-speech right to communicate its views to employees is firmly established and cannot be infringed by a union or the NLRB. Section 8(c) of the NLRA provides that an employer's expression of any view, argument, or opinion will not be the basis of an unfair labor practice so long as the opinion "contains no threat of reprisal or force or promise of benefit."[109] At the same time, an employer may not interfere with, restrain, or coerce employees in the exercise of their rights to associate (or not to associate) with a union.[110] Each statement by an employer is assessed in the context of the labor relations dispute at issue, such that an otherwise permissible statement made in a context where other unlawful conduct occurs may itself be considered an unfair labor practice.[111]

Q 3.17 What types of employer speech violate section 8(a)(1) of the NLRA?

The following types of employer speech or expression, among others, have been found to violate section 8(a)(1) because they interfere with, restrain, or coerce employees in the exercise of their rights to associate with a union:

- communicating unsubstantiated predictions of plant closures in the event of unionization;

- threatening the loss of jobs or benefits for supporting a union;

- questioning an employee in a manner that tends to restrain, coerce, or interfere with the employee's rights under the NLRA;

- making statements that create an impression of surveillance;

- threatening that bargaining will start from "zero" or "scratch";[112]

- promising or granting benefits to employees for anti-union votes;

- soliciting grievances with the implied promise of improved conditions during the course of an organizing campaign;

- filing retaliatory state court lawsuits against employees and/ or unions, when such suits are preempted by the NLRA.

Q 3.17.1 When do an employer's predictions of plant closures or threats of lost jobs violate section 8(a)(1) of the NLRA?

An employer may communicate to employees "carefully phrased" predictions of the "demonstrably probable consequences" beyond the employer's control that it believes unionization will have on the employer.[113] These predictions must be based on objective facts.[114] For example, when based on objective fact, an employer may express a prediction of dire economic circumstances in response to a union's pledge to insist on application of an industry-wide agreement.[115] In addition, personal statements regarding plant closures or job losses by low-level employees not in a position to affect those changes may be lawful.[116]

An employer's prediction to close a plant or lay off workers in the event of unionization may violate section 8(a)(1) if the employer fails to cite any objective facts that would tend to show that unionization would prohibit the employer from competing, would result in lost jobs, or would cause the employer to close for reasons beyond its own control.[117] It is no defense that the employer phrases the prediction as a possibility rather than a certainty. Unlawful statements may include a statement conveying to employees that the union would "inevitably" make exorbitant demands, leading to plant closure.[118] Moreover, an employer's statement that it did not want employees "talking to anyone else" because the employer had "fired employees in the past for talking about their wages" was deemed to be unlawful.[119]

Q 3.17.2   When do an employer's statements create an "impression of surveillance" in violation of section 8(a)(1) of the NLRA?

An employer may observe employee union-related activity when employees conduct that activity openly and on or near the employer's premises.[120] However, an employer's actions beyond what is considered mere observation or that is "out of the ordinary" may constitute unlawful surveillance.[121] (See Q 3.22.)

An employer's statements create an unlawful impression of surveillance when the employer's statements or actions would lead employees to reasonably assume that their organizational activities have been placed under surveillance.[122] Thus, "members of management [cannot peer] over their shoulders, taking note of who is involved in union activities, and in what particular ways."[123] For example, an employer may create an unlawful impression of surveillance by stating that it knows how a representation election will turn out, including how many employees will vote for or against unionization.[124] An employer cannot tell employees to advise management if union supporters are "bugging" them or if they receive an unwanted union solicitation.[125] It is irrelevant whether the employer reached its conclusions through lawful means, rather than unlawful surveillance, because it is the impression conveyed to the employees that violates section 8(a)(1).[126]

Q 3.17.3   How may an employer describe the collective bargaining process to employees without violating section 8(a)(1) of the NLRA?

The NLRB has held that employer statements during an organizing campaign that collective bargaining will start from "zero" or from "scratch" may be unlawful. Statements regarding bargaining from scratch may be permissible when the statements merely describe the bargaining process; state what lawfully could happen during the give and take of bargaining; are tied to economic realities; or are in direct response to union promises.[127] Any statement concerning the possible adverse economic consequences of unionization must have an objective basis in fact to be lawful.[128]

Statements regarding bargaining from scratch violate section 8(a)(1) of the NLRA when, in context, they effectively threaten employees with the loss of existing benefits and leave employees with the impression that what the employees may ultimately receive depends on what the union can induce the employer to restore. Additionally, an otherwise permissible statement regarding bargaining from scratch may be found to be coercive when viewed in the context of other contemporaneous threats or unfair labor practices.[129]

Q 3.17.4   When does an employer's state court lawsuit against employees and unions violate section 8(a)(1) of the NLRA?

The NLRB may enjoin an employer's lawsuit as an unfair labor practice when the lawsuit is objectively baseless and filed with a retaliatory motive.[130] In addition, when an employer's state court lawsuit is preempted by the NLRA, the lawsuit may be enjoined as an unfair labor practice regardless of whether the lawsuit is baseless.[131]

See QQ 10.1, 10.2, and 10.3 for a discussion of what cases are preempted by the NLRA and LMRA.

Workplace Policies That Interfere with, Restrain, or Coerce Employees' Exercise of Section 7 Rights

Q 3.18   What types of company rules or handbook provisions unlawfully interfere with employees' section 7 rights?

The NLRB recently revised the standards used to determine whether facially neutral company rules or handbook provisions are unlawful under the NLRA. In 2017, the NLRB abandoned its previous "reasonably construe" standard[132] and adopted a new guide to evaluate whether a facially neutral rule—i.e., one that does not expressly restrict section 7 rights—violates the NLRA.[133] Now, "when evaluating a facially neutral policy, rule or handbook provision that, when reasonably interpreted, would potentially interfere with the exercise of NLRA rights, the Board will evaluate two things: (1) the nature and extent of the potential impact on NLRA rights, and (2) legitimate justifications associated with the rule."[134]

While the law under the Board's *Boeing* decision is still developing, the NLRB's General Counsel explained that it will categorize rules in three ways:[135]

- Category 1 rules are lawful, either because the rules do not prohibit or interfere with section 7 rights, or the impact on protected rights is outweighed by employer justification; examples are no-camera rules like those at issue in *Boeing*, rules seeking to enforce a harmonious workplace, and similar rules "requiring employees to abide by basic standards of civility."[136]

- Category 2 rules will require individualized scrutiny as to impact on protected activity and the employer's justifications for such rules.[137]

- Category 3 rules will be considered unlawful because they prohibit or limit protected conduct, and the employer's justifications do not outweigh the adverse impact on section 7 rights.[138] For example, a rule that prohibits employees from discussing wages or benefits would fall into Category 3 and be unlawful.[139]

The *Boeing* decision did not alter the standards the NLRB uses for certain types of rules—those where the agency has already struck a balance between employee rights and employer business interests—such as distribution and solicitation rules.[140] The decision also did not alter the Board's position that rules explicitly banning protected conduct are unlawful, nor did it change the Board's existing analysis that an employer may violate the NLRA by discriminatorily applying a facially neutral rule to restrict protected conduct.[141] (See Q 3.19 for a discussion regarding discriminatory enforcement of otherwise lawful rules.)

Following the *Boeing* decision, the NLRB's General Counsel issued a memorandum addressing its impact.[142] As to "Category 1" rules, the memorandum notes that "Regions should be cautious about dismissing allegations regarding rules that are not specifically listed here as Category 1 rules," and then lists the following as Category 1 rules: civility rules, no-photography and no-recording rules, rules against insubordination, disruptive behavior rules, confidentiality rules, rules against defamation and misrepresentation, rules barring the use of employer logos and intellectual property, rules requiring authorization to speak for the employer, and rules barring disloyalty.[143]

GC Memorandum 18-04 then discussed Category 2 rules, which "must be evaluated on a case-by-case basis to determine whether the rule would interfere with rights guaranteed by the NLRA, and, if so, whether any adverse impact on those rights is outweighed by legitimate justification."[144] Stressing the importance of evaluating the "context" of such rules, the memorandum states that they "should be viewed as they would by employees who interpret work rules as they apply to the everydayness of their job." The memorandum also notes that "other contextual factors" include the "placement of the rule among other rules, the kinds of examples provided," and "evidence that a rule has actually caused employees to refrain from Section 7 activity." The memorandum sets out a series of types of rules that it described as "possible" examples of Category 2 rules. Such rules include: broad conflict of interest rules that do not specifically target fraud and self-enrichment, confidentiality rules that broadly encompass "employer business" or "employee information," rules regarding disparagement or criticism of the employer, rules banning off-duty conduct that might harm the employer, and rules against making false or inaccurate statements.

Finally, the memorandum laid out the types of rules that fall into Category 3, which it described as "generally unlawful."[145] Such rules include confidentiality rules that specifically apply to wages, benefits, and other working conditions, and rules against joining outside organizations.

Q 3.19 What constitutes discriminatory application of a facially lawful policy?

An employer violates the NLRA when it enforces a facially neutral, otherwise lawful policy in a way that restricts section 7 rights.[146] As the Board explained, "unlawful discrimination consists of disparate treatment of activities or communications of a similar character because of their union or other Section 7-protected status."[147] For example, the Board recently found that an employer violated the NLRA when it allowed employees to use company-owned bulletin boards to solicit interest in an employee council, but refused to allow employees supporting a union to post pro-union materials.[148]

Q 3.20 Can an employer require its employees to waive any right to file joint, class, or collective claims regarding their employment?

Yes, if the waiver is part of a mandatory arbitration agreement that prohibits joint, class, or collective claims. In *Epic Systems Corp. v. Lewis*, the U.S. Supreme Court held that employers may lawfully enforce mandatory arbitration agreements that allow for only individual claims.[149] Reversing several NLRB and court decisions, the Supreme Court ruled that the Federal Arbitration Act (FAA) requires courts to enforce arbitration agreements as written and that the NLRA does not nullify the FAA with respect to arbitration agreements that prohibit joint, class, and collective claims because such group claims are not "concerted activities" protected by section 7 of the NLRA.

In reaching this decision, the Court rejected the argument that group claims are "other concerted activities for the purpose of . . . other mutual aid or protection,"[150] as provided in section 7.[151] The Court noted that section 7 focuses on the right to organize unions and bargain collectively, and found it unlikely that Congress intended section 7 to confer employees a right to class and collective actions since the procedure for such claims were hardly known when the NLRA was passed in 1935.[152] The Court also explained that, because the term "other concerted activities for the purpose of . . . other mutual aid or protection" appears at the end of a detailed list of activities speaking of "self-organization," "form[ing], join[ing], or assist[ing] labor organizations," and "bargain[ing] collectively," it must "embrace only objects similar in nature to those objects enumerated by the preceding specific words."[153] Thus, the Court concluded, the term "other concerted activities for the purpose of . . . other mutual aid or protection" like the activities that precede it, refers to "things employees 'just do' for themselves in the course of exercising their right to free association in the workplace, rather than the 'highly regulated, courtroom-bound "activities" of class and joint litigation.'"[154]

Outside of the arbitration context, courts differ on whether an employer can require employees to agree to waive any right to file joint, class, or collective claims where the waiver is not part of an arbitration agreement.[155]

Q 3.21   Can an employer require employees to waive their right to file unfair labor practice charges?

No, employers cannot require employees to waive their right to file an NLRB charge, but in the right circumstances, employees may effectively release their NLRB claims as part of a severance or separation package.[156] Recently, however, the Board has been critical of an employer's attempt to release claims under the NLRA, and has analyzed such releases and waivers under the same standard it uses to evaluate private settlements of pending NLRB charges.[157] In *A.S.V., Inc.*, the Board declined to enforce a release of claims because "the Union had not agreed to be bound by the severance agreements; that the General Counsel contested the validity of the agreements; that while the Respondent did not have a previous history of violating the Act, the severance agreements were executed in an atmosphere of serious, unremedied unfair labor practices; and that the agreements not only left many of the Respondent's unlawful actions unremedied, but also failed to provide for remedial notice to the plant's other employees and for reinstatement."[158]

Unlawful Surveillance

Q 3.22   When does an employer engage in unlawful surveillance of employee activity?

An employer generally can monitor employee behavior at work for legitimate and nondiscriminatory business reasons.[159] An employer may also observe public union activity without violating the NLRA so long as it does not "do something out of the ordinary."[160] Accordingly, an employer's mere observation of open and public union activity, such as picketing, on or near its property does not constitute unlawful surveillance.[161] Similarly, an employer's random or isolated viewing of a union gathering is not prohibited surveillance.[162]

An employer engages in unlawful surveillance when its observation of union activities can be reasonably construed as excessive or coercive surveillance, such that it unreasonably chills the exercise of the employees' section 7 rights.[163] Indicia of coerciveness include the duration of the observation, the employer's distance from its employees while observing them, and whether the employer engaged in other coercive behavior during its observation.[164] An employer may also violate section 8(a)(1) by creating the "impression of surveillance" among its employees.[165] The NLRB has found that taking photos or videos of employees' protected activities, without some legitimate justification, creates an unlawful impression of surveillance because such pictorial recordkeeping tends to create fear among employees of future reprisals.[166] Taking photographs with the mere belief that something might happen does not justify the employer's conduct when balanced against the tendency of that conduct to interfere with employees' right to engage in concerted activity.[167] The NLRB has found that photographing or videotaping peaceful section 7 activity is unlawful surveillance, even if the employees are unaware of it.[168]

In certain circumstances, the Board has found it lawful to photograph strikers as possible evidence for use in legal proceedings, especially where there is no showing that the employer also engaged in threats or actual reprisals.[169] The Board has also found it lawful to photograph picketers blocking employees from safely accessing a jobsite or union agents who stopped their trucks on a street, blocking traffic, while honking their horns in support of picketers.[170] In contrast, the NLRB has found that an employer's review, in response to employees' complaints, of archived video footage of employees distributing union literature in a breakroom was unlawful where the employees were engaged in lawful, protected activity.[171]

CASE STUDY: *Sprain Brook Manor Nursing Home*[172]

The NLRB held that the employer violated section 8(a)(1) of the NLRA by placing employees under surveillance while they engaged in protected concerted activity. During the course of the union's organizational campaign at the employer's facility, the employer's nursing home administrator stood at an exit door and observed employees meeting with union representatives in the parking lot area. The NLRB noted that, while an employer may observe open union activity on its property, it may not lawfully do something "out of the ordinary" to give employees the impression of surveillance.

In this case, the NLRB found that the nursing home administrator's actions were, in fact, "out of the ordinary." Specifically, the observation at issue occurred on the administrator's regularly scheduled day off. The administrator admitted that she was at the facility for the sole purpose of observing union activity. Accordingly, the NLRB determined that the administrator's conduct constituted unlawful surveillance.

The NLRB also found that the employer violated section 8(a)(1) by intimidating and coercing employees engaged in protected activity. After the union began its organizational campaign, the employer hired an additional (and armed) security guard who was deployed during shift changes. The NLRB noted that the employer provided no explanation for its decision to hire the additional guard and that the employer presented no evidence to establish that circumstances required additional security.

The NLRB applies the same standards to surveillance of employees' electronic activity as "surveillance in the bricks-and-mortar world"—that is, surveillance is lawful so long as it is not out of the ordinary.[173] While an employer may notify its employees that it monitors computer and email activity for legitimate business reasons and that employees have no expectation of privacy in their use of the company's email or computer systems, the Board noted that an employer would violate the NLRA if it were to increase monitoring of employees' emails during a union organizing campaign.[174] Social media adds a new area of concern regarding employer surveillance. Where a manager is connected to an employee as "friends" on Facebook, the manager may report to the employer information found on the employee's Facebook page if there is no evidence the manager was acting at the employer's direction or was on Facebook for the sole purpose of monitoring employee postings.[175] The NLRB recently found that a supervisor's review of suspected union sympathizers' personal Facebook profiles to find information about their union activity violated section 8(a)(1).[176] See Q 3.17.2 for a discussion of when an employer's statements create an unlawful impression of surveillance.

Unlawful Interrogation

Q 3.23 Can an employer question its employees about their union activities?

In determining whether an employer's questioning of an employee constitutes an unlawful interrogation, the NLRB considers the totality of the circumstances, including whether the employee is an open and active union supporter; whether there is a history of employer anti-union hostility or discrimination; the nature of the information sought (especially if it could result in action against individual employees); the position of the questioner in the company's hierarchy; the place and method of the interrogation; the timing of the interrogation; and whether other unfair labor practices were occurring or had occurred.[177] A statement need not be in the form of a question to constitute an unlawful interrogation.[178] However, an employer's statement of its own views that does not call for a response from the employee is not unlawful interrogation.[179]

Q 3.23.1   Can an employer instruct supervisors to poll subordinate employees regarding their feelings about unionization?

Generally speaking, employers cannot poll their employees to determine their union sentiments. Absent unusual circumstances, an employer violates section 8(a)(1) by polling employees unless the employer observes the following safeguards:

(1)   the purpose of the poll is to determine the truth of a union's claim of majority;

(2)   this purpose is communicated to the employees;

(3)   assurances against reprisal are given;

(4)   the employees are polled by secret ballot; and

(5)   the employer has not engaged in unfair labor practices or otherwise created a coercive atmosphere.[180]

In addition, the Board will permit polling only in limited situations. Because the purpose of the poll must be to test the truth of a union's claim of majority status,[181] a poll may only be conducted after the union has asserted majority status to the employer, such as by demanding recognition from the employer. At the same time, a poll taken while a petition for a Board representation election is pending is unlawful because, in the Board's view, it does not serve any legitimate interest of the employer that would not be better served by the forthcoming Board election.[182] As such, before a union is certified as the collective bargaining representative, an employer may conduct a poll during an initial organizing situation after the union has demanded recognition as a majority representative but has not yet filed a petition for a representation election with the NLRB. After a union is certified as the collective bargaining representative, an employer may poll its employees concerning their support for the incumbent union only if the employer first has a good faith doubt, based on objective considerations, of the union's majority status.[183] An employer must also provide an incumbent union with reasonable advanced notice of the time and place of the poll.[184]

Q 3.24 Can a non-union employer use employee committees to discuss working conditions with employees without violating section 8(a)(2) of the NLRA?

Section 8(a)(2) of the NLRA prohibits an employer from dominating or interfering with the formation or administration of a "labor organization" and from providing financial or other support to a "labor organization," regardless of whether a union is on the scene. In determining whether an employer violated section 8(a)(2), the Board conducts a two-step analysis.[185] First, the Board considers whether the group or entity involved is a "labor organization" as defined by section 2(5).[186] If the organization involved is a labor organization, then the Board considers whether the employer has engaged in any conduct proscribed by section 8(a)(2) (i.e., domination or interference with the organization's formation or administration, or unlawful support of the organization).[187] An employer does not violate section 8(a)(2) by dominating, interfering, or supporting a group that is not a "labor organization."

Q 3.24.1 What is a "labor organization" for purposes of section 8(a)(2)?

An organization, agency, or employee representation committee or plan is a "labor organization" if employees participate in it and it exists for the purpose, in whole or in part, of dealing with employers concerning grievances, labor disputes, wages, rates of pay, hours of employment, or conditions of work.[188] The NLRB has noted a distinction between "purpose" and "motive."[189] In particular, a group whose purpose is to deal with an employer concerning terms and conditions of employment is a "labor organization," regardless of whether the employer had a motive to avoid unionization.[190]

Any group may meet the statutory definition of "labor organization" even if it lacks a formal structure, has no elected officers, does not require the payment of initiation fees or dues, does not meet regularly, and does not have a formal framework for conducting meetings among the employees whose conditions of employment are the subject of committee dealings or for otherwise eliciting the employees' views.[191]

Moreover, it is not necessary that a group engage in formal collective bargaining to be a "labor organization" pursuant to section 2(5). The Board has explained that "dealing with" contemplates "a bilateral mechanism involving proposals from an employee committee concerning the subjects listed in Section 2(5), coupled with real or apparent consideration of those proposals by management."[192] A "bilateral mechanism" typically "entails a pattern or practice in which a group of employees, over time, makes proposals to management, [and] management responds to these proposals by acceptance or rejection by word or deed. . . ."[193] In *Electromation, Inc.*, the NLRB found that action committees were labor organizations because their purpose was to address employees' concerns about the terms and conditions of their employment by creating a bilateral resolution mechanism between the employees and their employer, and the employer expected committee members would obtain input from other employees who were not on the committee.[194] On the other hand, a group or employee committee is not a "labor organization" if it is not one through which employees participate or if its purpose is limited to performing an essentially managerial function, rather than to "deal with" the employer regarding terms and conditions of employment.[195] For example, the NLRB found that employee groups that were structured as self-managed work teams able to decide upon a range of operational issues, such as production, quality, training, attendance, safety, maintenance, discipline short of suspension or discharge, within set parameters were not "labor organizations" because their purpose was "to perform essentially managerial functions."[196]

Q 3.24.2   When does an employer unlawfully dominate, interfere, or support a "labor organization" in violation of section 8(a)(2)?

An employer unlawfully dominates a labor organization when it controls the form and structure of the labor organization such that the employees are deprived of complete freedom and independence of action guaranteed to them by section 7.[197] Thus, a labor organization that is the creation of management, whose structure and function are essentially determined by management, and whose continued existence depends on the fiat of management, is unlawfully dominated in violation of section 8(a)(2).[198] In *Electromation, Inc.*, for instance, the Board found the company unlawfully dominated the employee action committees where it unilaterally implemented the committees, articulated the goals of each committee, and decided on what committee each employee who volunteered would serve.[199]

While the determination of whether an employer has unlawfully dominated a labor organization is subjective, the Board has considered the following factors:

- the relationship between the employer and the labor organization;

- the nature of the negotiations between the employer and the labor organization;

- what control, if any, the employer has over the labor organization's membership;

- whether the labor organization has a constitution and bylaws;

- the nature and location of the labor organization's meetings;

- whether employees are compensated for time and attendance at such meetings; and

- whether supervisory personnel attend the labor organization's meetings and, if so, what role they play.[200]

An employer engages in unlawful interference when it participates in a labor organization's internal affairs. An employer's unlawful interference includes providing legal services to a union to assist it in its formation,[201] to defeat a representation petition filed by a rival union,[202] and to prepare contracts for negotiations.[203] The NLRB also found an employer engaged in unlawful interference when it permitted a supervisor to serve the union in a position that involved negotiations and grievance handling.[204]

The NLRB has found employers unlawfully supported a labor organization by recognizing a minority union as the exclusive bargaining representative of its employees,[205] paying a union a "kickback" for business referrals,[206] and soliciting employees to become members of the union and/or maintain their status as members of the union.[207]

An employer's mere cooperation with a labor organization, how-ever, is not unlawful.[208] The Seventh Circuit has explained that "[c]ooperation only assists the employees or their bargaining repre-sentatives in carrying out their independent intention."[209] In contrast, unlawful support, "even though innocent, can be identified because it constitutes at least some degree of control or influence over the labor organization."[210] For instance, an otherwise independent union's use of company time or property does not by itself constitute unlaw-ful employer support and assistance.[211]

While domination, interference, and support are all unlawful, the difference is relevant for purposes of the appropriate remedy.[212] The distinction between domination on one hand and interference or support on the other is one of degree.[213] The Supreme Court has explained that an unlawfully dominated labor organization deprives employees of their free choice to be represented by an agent acting as their true representative; a labor organization with which an employer has unlawfully interfered or supported is capable of acting as employees' true representative after the effects of the employer's unfair labor practices have dissipated.[214] Consequently, domination often may result in the disestablishment of the labor organization while mere interference or assistance results in a less severe remedy, such as withdrawal of recognition until recertification.[215]

Q 3.25 When does an employer unlawfully grant or promise a benefit or other improvement in terms of employment?

Section 8(c) generally allows an employer to express its views regarding a union and union representation provided the employer's "expression contains no threat of reprisal or force or promise of ben-efit."[216] Thus, the announcement, promise, or grant of benefits for the purpose of discouraging union support is unlawful.[217] The Supreme Court explained that "the danger inherent in well-timed increases in benefits is the suggestion of a fist inside the velvet glove. Employees are not likely to miss the inference that the source of benefits now conferred is also the source from which future benefits must flow and which may dry up if it is not obliged."[218]

The NLRB will presume improper motive and interference with employee rights when an employer announces, promises, or grants benefits to employees during a union organizing campaign.[219] An employer's actions will nonetheless be found lawful if it can show a legitimate business reason for the timing.[220] For example, an employer may lawfully announce, promise, or grant benefits in the midst of union organizing activity if such action is consistent with the employer's pre-existing policy or practice and the employer acts pursuant to such policy or practice and not with an unlawful motive.[221]

Discrimination in Employment

Q 3.26 When does discharge or other discipline of an employee constitute "discrimination" in violation of section 8(a)(3) of the NLRA?

Section 8(a)(3) prohibits an employer from encouraging or discouraging union membership by discriminating against applicants or employees with regard to employment.[222] An employer "discriminates" against an employee in violation of section 8(a)(3) when it takes adverse action against the employee because the employee engaged in protected concerted activities. This is a fact-intensive inquiry that often will turn on the following factors:

- Did the employer know of the employee's participation in concerted activity at the time of the discharge or other discipline?

- Did the employer previously tolerate the misconduct that the employer claims warranted the adverse action?

- Did the employer otherwise exhibit hostility to the union or other concerted activity?

The typical section 8(a)(3) case is a "pretext" case involving an employee claiming he was discharged for engaging in union or other concerted activity and the employer responding that the discharge or other discipline was for legitimate business reasons. It is the General Counsel's job to convince the administrative law judge, in the first instance, that the illegitimate reason motivated the discharge or other discipline.

There are circumstances, however, where an employer's decision to discipline an employee arises from both legitimate and illegitimate motives. In such "dual-motive" situations, if the NLRB General Counsel shows the employee's protected activity was a motiving factor in the discharge or other decision, the burden of persuasion shifts to the employer to prove the so-called *Wright Line* (or "same-decision") defense—that it would have made the same decision regardless of the employee's protected activity.[223] An employer does not violate section 8(a)(3) if it demonstrates that it would have taken the same adverse action absent the employee's protected activity.[224]

In *Starbucks Corp.*, an employer discharged an employee because, among other things, he used profanity in the presence of customers.[225] The employee got into a confrontation with an assistant manager after showing up off-duty with a group of other workers protesting a ban on wearing union pins. Even assuming the employee lost protection under the NLRA due to his outburst, the employer failed to show that it had in fact terminated him for the outburst. The NLRB noted that the discharge form completed by the store manager stated the employee was ineligible to be rehired in part because of strong union support, and the record therefore established that the discharge decision was motivated in part by the employee's protected pro-union activities.

Q 3.26.1   Can an employer lawfully refuse to hire "salts"?

"Salting" refers to a tactic where union organizers pose as job applicants and apply for employment with an employer to further union organizing goals.[226] Individuals who engage in salting, commonly referred to as "salts," are paid union organizers trying to gain employment so that they can obtain direct access to employees for organizing purposes and circumvent the restrictions employers may legally place on non-employee union organizers from entering the workplace.[227]

In 1995, the U.S. Supreme Court ruled that salts applying for jobs are "employees" under the NLRA, and therefore an employer may not terminate, refuse to hire, or otherwise discriminate against an individual because he or she works for a union.[228] More recently, however, the NLRB has held that a salt applicant must be genuinely interested in employment to receive the protections that the NLRA grants employees.[229]

CASE STUDY: *Allstate Power Vac, Inc.*[230]

In March 2007, Allstate Power Vac, Inc. ("Allstate") placed a classified newspaper ad seeking operators/drivers who had commercial driver's licenses (CDLs) and endorsements for hazardous materials handling (HAZMAT). On April 13, 2007, a union coordinator sent seven overt salts, two at a time, wearing union clothing and tape recorders, to apply for positions at Allstate and capture what was said during the application process. The salts asked the receptionist for employment applications and stated it was their intention to organize Allstate. She responded that Allstate was not interested in becoming a union shop but told them they could apply for one of the available driver positions. To apply for the positions, she explained, they would have to produce driver's licenses with CDLs and HAZMAT endorsements, which none of the salts had. When none could produce the licenses, she told them to come back and fill out applications when they had obtained their licenses. One of the overt salts asked whether he could apply to be a field technician, and the receptionist told him there were no openings but that, if he completed an application, she would keep it on file. He did not complete an application, nor did any of the salts make further efforts to apply.

The union filed unfair labor practice charges, and the Region issued a complaint. The administrative law judge dismissed the charge that Allstate unlawfully refused to hire or consider the union salts. The NLRB agreed, noting that the salts did not have the requisite qualifications for the driver positions, it was not established that Allstate was hiring or had concrete plans to hire field technicians, and none of the salts had actually applied to be field technicians.

Q 3.27   What employee activities are protected by section 8(a)(4)?

Section 8(a)(4) makes it unlawful for an employer to discharge or otherwise discriminate against an employee for filing charges or giving testimony under the NLRA.[231] The Supreme Court has explained that by adopting section 8(a)(4), "Congress has made it clear that it wishes all persons with information about such [unfair labor] practices to be completely free from coercion against reporting them to the Board."[232]

In addition to filing charges and testifying as part of the NLRB process, section 8(a)(4) has also been interpreted to protect employees who engage in the following activities:

- giving an affidavit or a sworn statement (but not live testimony) to an NLRB agent, even if no charges are filed;[233]

- appearing at a hearing in response to a subpoena, even if not called to testify;[234]

- speaking with coworkers about future testimony;[235]

- refusing to testify voluntarily on behalf of employers;[236] and

- testifying against former employers.[237]

Section 8(a)(4) similarly protects employees when their employer erroneously believes they have filed charges with or testified before the NLRB.[238]

Q 3.27.1   When does an employer violate section 8(a)(4) by discriminating against an employee who has filed charges with the NLRB or given testimony in an NLRB proceeding?

An employer violates section 8(a)(4) by taking adverse employment action against an employee as a result of his or decision to participate in activity protected by section 8(a)(4). Adverse action can range from termination to negative changes to the terms and conditions of employment. This includes refusing to grant a leave of absence,[239] deviating from usual disciplinary practices without a reason for the variance,[240] and making unfavorable schedule changes.[241] The following are also examples of adverse actions found to violate section 8(a)(4):

- conditioning rehiring an employee on the employee dropping unfair labor practice charges pending before the NLRB;[242]

- refusing to hire a job applicant;[243]

- refusing to rehire an employee who had filed an unfair labor practice charge, even where the original dismissal was for nondiscriminatory reasons;[244] and

- while previously injured employee's unfair labor practice charge was pending, refusing to consider reinstatement of the employee despite his doctor's note stating he was able to work.[245]

Unfair Labor Practices by Labor Organizations

Q 3.28 What types of conduct by labor organizations violates the NLRA?

Broadly speaking, a labor organization violates the NLRA when it commits an "unfair labor practice," defined by section 8(b) of the NLRA as:

(1) restraining or coercing employees in the exercise of their section 7 rights;

(2) causing or attempting to cause an employer to discriminate against an employee for the purpose of encouraging or discouraging union membership;

(3) refusing to bargain collectively with an employer;

(4) engaging in, inducing, or encouraging any employee to engage in a strike, boycott, or other coercive action for an illegal purpose;

(5) charging excessive or discriminatory membership fees;

(6) causing or attempting to cause an employer to pay or agree to pay for work that is not performed ("featherbedding");

(7) unless the labor organization is currently certified as the employees' collective bargaining representative, picketing or threatening to picket an employer to force it to recognize or bargain with the union or force the workers to accept the union as their representative if (a) another union already represents the workers, (b) a valid representation election was held in the past year, or (c) the union does not file a petition for an election with the NLRB within thirty days after the picketing starts.[246]

Restraint and Coercion

Q 3.29 When does a union unlawfully restrain or coerce employees?

Section 8(b)(1)(A) of the NLRA prohibits union tactics that involve violence, intimidation, reprisals, or threats that would reasonably "chill" employees' exercise of their rights to engage in organizing activity or their rights to refrain from doing so.[247] To be unlawful, a union's conduct must go beyond the general pressures implicit in economic strikes. Union actions that are reasonably calculated to lead to these effects are unlawful, regardless of whether the actions actually succeed in restraining or coercing the employees' exercise of their rights. The NLRB, however, does not require evidence of unlawful intent to support a finding of a violation of section 8(b)(1)(A).[248]

Certain union actions directed at non-employees may also unlawfully restrain or coerce employees in violation of section 8(b)(1)(A). Violent union conduct directed at non-employees unlawfully restrains or coerces employees when (1) it is substantially certain that employees will hear about the violent activity, or (2) the violence is committed in the presence of employees.[249]

A union may violate section 8(b)(1)(A) through the coercive conduct of its officers or agents, or by failing to repudiate coercive conduct by strikers, picketers, or employees conducted in the presence of union representatives.

Unlawful coercion may consist of physical acts specifically directed at an employee, such as physical assaults or threats of violence.[250]

Nonviolent physical force used to prevent employees from exercising their rights to engage in or refrain from union activities is also unlawful.[251]

Most cases involving section 8(b)(1)(A) violations, however, do not involve violence. The majority of cases concern threats of loss of employment, improper use of union discipline, discriminatory or other improper conduct by a union in violation of its duty of fair representation, or a union's practices that violate its obligations under hiring-hall or union-shop procedures.[252]

Unlawful coercion also includes other forms of pressure against employees, such as acts of a union while representing employees as their exclusive bargaining agent. A union violates section 8(b)(1)(A) if, while acting as the employees' statutory bargaining representative, it takes or withholds action in connection with employment because of the employee's concerted activities (or refusal to engage in such activities) or for any arbitrary reason such as an employee's race or gender.

The following are examples of acts of general restraint or coercion by a union or its agents that violate 8(b)(1)(A):[253]

- mass picketing in such numbers that non-striking employees are physically barred from entering the plant;

- acts of force or violence on the picket line, or in connection with a strike;

- threats of bodily injury to non-striking employees;

- threats that employees will lose their jobs unless they support the union's activities;

- statements to employees who oppose the union that the employees will lose their jobs if the union wins a majority in the plant;

- entering into an agreement with an employer that recognizes the union as the exclusive bargaining representative when it has not been chosen by a majority of the employees;

- refusing to process a grievance in retaliation for an employee's criticism of union officers;

- maintaining a seniority arrangement with an employer under which seniority is based on the employees' prior representation by the union;

- rejecting an application for referral to a job in a unit represented by the union based on the applicant's race or union activities.

Union Fines and Disciplinary Measures

Q 3.30   When does a union's fines assessed on its members violate the NLRA?

Section 8(b)(1)(A) recognizes a union's right to establish and enforce membership rules and to control its internal affairs.[254] A union may fine a member without violating section 8(b)(1)(A) so long as the fine does not impair an employee's rights under the NLRA.[255] Unions can enforce fines through suspension, expulsion, or the judicial process.

The following are examples of union fines that have been found to violate section 8(b)(1)(A):[256]

- fining an employee who crosses an unlawful picket line or a picket line that violates a no-strike agreement;

- fining an employee for crossing a picket line after the employee has resigned from the union;

- fining an employee for filing an unfair labor practice charge or for participating in an NLRB investigation; and

- fining an employee for filing a decertification petition (although the union may expel the member for doing so).

Q 3.30.1   Are there limits on the amount a union can fine its members?

Unions may only impose *reasonable* fines on its members.[257] However, there are no concrete standards against which to measure the reasonableness of a union's fine. A fine is lawful under the NLRA when it is imposed to enforce a properly adopted rule that reflects a legitimate union interest, does not contravene a policy of the NLRA, and is reasonably enforced against union members who are free to leave the union and escape the rule.[258] The NLRB lacks authority to evaluate the fairness or reasonableness of union fines where union discipline does not interfere with the employee-employer relationship or otherwise violate an NLRA policy.[259] In such cases, the determination of what constitutes a reasonable fine must be made by state courts based on "the law of contracts, voluntary associations, or such principles of law as may be applied" in their respective forums.[260]

Q 3.31   When is a union's discipline of its members unlawful?

Certain forms of union discipline are unlawful. Unlawful union discipline may include the following:[261]

- disciplining a member for refusing to engage in unlawful or unprotected activity;

- disciplinary measures that impact a member's employment relationship with his or her employer;

- discipline that impairs a member's access to the NLRB's processes, such as imposing discipline for filing an unfair labor practice charge;

- certain types of discipline against supervisor-members.

Q 3.31.1   What forms of union discipline are unlawful because they affect a member's employment relationship with his or her employer?

Where a union maintains a hiring hall, it cannot punish a member by refusing to refer that member for employment. A union is also prohibited from imposing discipline that has the effect of withholding a permit that a member needs for employment.[262] A union may not discipline a member by causing an employer to reduce that member's job seniority as punishment for the member's dispute with the union, by denying a member seniority he or she already earned, or by causing or attempting to cause the employer to discharge an employee because of an internal dispute between the member and the union.[263]

Indirect union actions that affect a member's relationship with his or her employer may also be unlawful under the NLRA. For example, a union's constitution or bylaws cannot require payments of fines or other internal union debts before the union will accept monthly dues.[264] Similarly, a union cannot seek the termination of an employee for failing to pay union dues, where the employee tendered the dues, but the union did not accept the dues because the employee failed to satisfy a separate union fine or debt.[265] Courts have taken a different view about whether a union may fine a member for reporting the misconduct of co-workers pursuant to an employer's policy.[266]

Q 3.31.2   What forms of union discipline impair a member's access to the NLRB's processes?

A union cannot impose a disciplinary measure, such as a fine or expulsion, that has the effect of impairing a member's access to NLRB's processes. Moreover, a union cannot discipline or threaten members for filing charges against the union or for testifying against other union members in arbitration proceedings. A union may, as a defensive measure, expel a member who files a decertification action, but the union cannot fine the member or seek his or her discharge from employment.[267]

Q 3.31.3   Are there limits on how a union can discipline supervisor-members?

Supervisors can lawfully become union members, although employers are not obligated to tolerate supervisor-members or to bargain with a union on their behalf.[268] In some industries where supervisors expect to return to the bargaining unit or participate in union benefit funds, employers may allow supervisors to retain their union membership. Under section 8(b)(1)(B) of the NLRA, unions cannot lawfully discipline supervisor-members who perform collective bargaining or grievance adjustment functions for their employer.[269] A union cannot discipline supervisor-members for working during a strike if the work deals with collective bargaining, grievance adjustment, or closely related activities such as contract interpretation because such discipline would constitute unlawful coercion of the employer's labor relations decisions.[270] The union can, however, discipline supervisor-members for any rank-and-file work they perform during a strike.[271]

Q 3.31.4   Can a union discipline members who have resigned?

The U.S. Supreme Court upheld the NLRB's view that, irrespective of limitations on the right to resign from union membership contained in a union's constitution, employees have a section 7 "right to refrain" from union activity and to resign union membership at any time, even in the midst of an ongoing strike.[272] A union thus violates the NLRA when it fines members who vote for a strike and then work during a strike after resigning from the union.[273]

The prohibition of fines after resignation also prohibits strike assistance programs that require participating members to reimburse benefits paid to them if they subsequently resign from the union and return to work for the struck employer.[274] Even though it is not called a "fine," such financial reimbursement requirement is a financial penalty imposed on members for resigning and thus violates members' right to resign.[275]

Discrimination by a Union

Q 3.32   When does a union cause an employer to discriminate against employees in violation of section 8(b)(2)?

Section 8(b)(2) makes it an unfair labor practice for a labor organization to cause an employer to discriminate against an employee in violation of section 8(a)(3) of the NLRA[276] (which prohibits an employer from discriminating against an employee in regard to wages, hours, and other conditions of employment for the purpose of encouraging or discouraging membership in a labor organization—see Q 3.28).

A union cannot cause an employer to discharge employees or otherwise affect their employment status for reasons other than failing to pay the financial costs of union representation.[277] Unions are also prohibited from causing an employer to discriminate against employees for resigning their membership in the union.[278] For example, where an employee engages in protected activity by announcing his or her intention to withdraw from the union, and the union subsequently threatens the employee with loss of overtime work and requests that the employer stop scheduling the employee for overtime work, the union violates the NLRA.[279]

Sections 8(b)(2) and 8(a)(3) both exclude from their prohibitions clauses in collective bargaining agreements that require payment of union dues (although not necessarily full-fledged membership) on or after the thirtieth day of employment.[280] The union can seek the discharge of employees who do not pay such dues without violating section 8(b)(2), and the employer does not violate section 8(a)(3) in discharging the employee for such non-payment.

In addition, unions and employers can negotiate seniority-based preferences. For example, it is lawful for an employer and a union to enter into an agreement whereby the employer agrees to hire new employees exclusively through the union hiring hall, so long as there is neither a provision in the agreement nor a practice in effect that discriminates against non-union members in favor of union members or otherwise discriminates on the basis of union membership.[281] Both the agreement and the actual operation of the hiring hall must be nondiscriminatory; referrals must be made without reference to union membership or arbitrary considerations such as race.[282] However, a union may, in setting referral standards, consider legitimate criteria such as giving priority to workers with greater experience in the industry.[283] It may also charge referral fees if the amount of the fee is reasonably related to the cost of operating the referral service.[284]

The following are examples of union violations of section 8(b)(2):[285]

- forcing or attempting to force an employer to enter into or to enforce an illegal union security agreement;

- demanding that an employer discriminate against employees because of their failure to make lawful dues payments to the union, when there is no valid union security agreement in effect;

- attempting to use otherwise lawful union security provisions of a contract to collect payments other than those that may be lawfully required;

- seeking the discharge of an employee under a union security agreement for failure to pay a fine levied by the union;

- agreements or informal arrangements with employers that unlawfully condition employment, job benefits, or preferential treatment on union membership, on the performance of union membership obligations, or on arbitrary grounds;

- causing an employer to discharge employees because they circulated a petition urging a change in the union's method of selecting shop stewards;

- causing an employer to discharge employees because they made speeches against a contract proposed by the union;

- making a contract that requires an employer to hire only members of the union or employees "satisfactory" to the union;

- causing an employer to reduce employees' seniority because they engaged in anti-union activities.

Notes to Chapter 3

1.   29 U.S.C. § 152(2) (excluding from the definition of "employer" federal, state, and municipal governments and unions); *id.* § 152(3) (excluding from the definition of "employee" "any individual employed as a supervisor").

2.   *Id.* § 152(3).

3.   *Id.* § 157.

4.   NLRB v. Phx. Mut. Life Ins. Co., 167 F.2d 983, 988 (7th Cir. 1948).

5.   *See, e.g.*, Air Contact Transp., 340 N.L.R.B. 688 (2003) (noting that questions raised by individual at a staff luncheon regarding relationship between employer's evaluation system and pay raises considered concerted activity); Compuware Corp. v. NLRB, 134 F.3d 1285, 1288 (6th Cir. 1998) (relevant question is whether employee acted with the purpose of furthering group goals); Int'l Transp. Serv., Inc. v. NLRB, 449 F.3d 160, 166 (D.C. Cir. 2006) (denying protection to an employee who picketed for a one-person bargaining unit); NLRB v. Hotel Emps. Int'l Union Local 26, 446 F.3d 200, 207 (1st Cir. 2006) ("To qualify as concerted activity, '[i]t is sufficient that the [complaining] employee intends or contemplates, as an end result, group activity which will also benefit some other employees.'") (quoting Koch Supplies, Inc. v. NLRB, 646 F.2d 1257, 1259 (8th Cir. 1981); *see also* William R. Corbett, *Waiting for the Labor Law of the Twenty-First Century*, 23 BERKELEY J. EMP. & LAB. L. 259, 292 (2002).

6.   *See, e.g.*, Every Woman's Place, Inc., 282 N.L.R.B. 413, 413 (1986) (finding employee's call to DOL was concerted because she and her co-workers had already brought their concern to management's attention at least four times).

7.   *See* World Color (USA) Corp., 360 N.L.R.B. 227 (2014) (finding a supervisor's statement to an employee about that employee's Facebook post did not violate the NLRA because the post consisted only of unspecified criticisms and did not include communications between or on behalf of co-workers), *enforcement denied on other grounds*, 776 F.3d 17 (D.C. Cir. 2015).

8.   *See* 29 U.S.C. § 157; *see also* Joanna Cotton Mills Co. v. NLRB, 176 F.2d 749, 752 (4th Cir. 1949) (noting that the words "concerted activities" in section 7 are "limited in meaning by the words with which they are associated"; protection of concerted activities under section 7 is "expressly limited" to activities pursued for the specific purposes stated therein).

9.   *See* Five Star Transp., Inc. v. NLRB, 522 F.3d 46 (1st Cir. 2008) (employees whose letters to local school district were found to be disparaging of the employer and primarily addressed nonemployment-related concerns were not engaged in protected activity); *see also* Elko Gen. Hosp., 347 N.L.R.B. 1425 (2006) (employer justified in terminating employee who, during a captive-audience pre-election meeting, stated that her husband had had a bad experience at the employer's

hospital facility and that she wished the employer was still run by the county, and tried to end the meeting by calling on her co-workers to leave the meeting and return to work); KHRG Emp'r LLC, 366 N.L.R.B. No. 22 (Feb. 28, 2018) (employer justified in terminating an employee who, while participating in protected activity, violated the employer's security protocol). *But see* Plaza Auto Ctr., Inc., 360 N.L.R.B. 972 (2014) (finding employee's statement that his manager was an "asshole" in a discussion about compensation policies was not so egregious as to lose protection under the NLRA).

   10.   Elk Lumber Co., 91 N.L.R.B. 333 (1950). *But see* Bridgeport Ambulance Serv., Inc., 302 N.L.R.B. 358, 363–64 (1991) (explaining that a wildcat strike was protected activity because "the employees' demands and statements during this period w[ere] not in derogation of the Union or contrary to, or inconsistent with, the Union's bargaining position"), *enforced*, 966 F.2d 725, 729 (2d Cir. 1992).

   11.   *See* Cynthia L. Estlund, *What Do Workers Want? Employee Interest, Public Interests, and Freedom of Expression Under the National Labor Relations Act*, 140 U. PA. L. REV. 921, 928 (1992).

   12.   *See, e.g.,* Rockwell Int'l v. NLRB, 814 F.2d 1530 (11th Cir. 1987) (an employee who objected at an employee meeting to the supervisor's lecture about the volume of radio headsets was engaged in protected activity); *see also* Citizens Inv. Servs. Corp., 342 N.L.R.B. 316, 317 (2004), *enforced*, 430 F.3d 1195 (D.C. Cir. 2005) (employee, acting both individually and as de facto spokesperson for other employees, engaged in protected activity when he wrote emails to management complaining about the employer's commission structure); Timekeeping Sys., 323 N.L.R.B. 244 (1997) (employee engaged in protected activity when he sent email message to fellow employees in response to employer's new vacation plan); NLRB v. Oakes Mach. Corp., 897 F.2d 84 (2d Cir. 1990) (employer who fired employees who mailed a letter to the employer's parent company complaining of working conditions and bonuses committed an unfair labor practice).

   13.   *See, e.g.,* Bus. Servs. by Manpower, Inc., 784 F.2d 442 (2d Cir. 1986); *see also* NLRB v. Browning-Ferris Indus., 700 F.2d 385 (7th Cir. 1983).

   14.   *See, e.g.,* Eastex, Inc. v. NLRB, 437 U.S. 556 (1978); *see also* Pontiac Osteopathic Hosp., 284 N.L.R.B. 442 (1987); Oakes Mach. Corp., 288 N.L.R.B. 456 (1988); Phx. Mut. Life Ins. Co., 73 N.L.R.B. 1463 (1947).

   15.   Fresh & Easy Neighborhood Mkt., Inc., 361 N.L.R.B. 151 (2014).

   16.   *See* 29 U.S.C. § 141 *et seq.*

   17.   NLRB v. Drivers Local Union, 362 U.S. 274 (1960).

   18.   Notification of Employee Rights Under the National Labor Relations Act, 76 Fed. Reg. 54,006 (Aug. 30, 2011) (codified at 29 C.F.R. pt. 104).

   19.   Ass'n of Mfrs. v. NLRB, 717 F.3d 947 (D.C. Cir. 2013); Chamber of Commerce v. NLRB, 721 F.3d 152 (4th Cir. 2013).

   20.   29 U.S.C. § 163: "Nothing in this [Act], except as specifically provided for herein, shall be construed so as either to interfere with or impede or diminish in any way the right to strike, or to affect the limitations or qualifications on that right."

21.	Recent guidance from the NLRB's General Counsel identified work stoppages on employer premises as an issue that must be submitted the Division of Advice. NLRB Gen. Couns. Mem. 18-02, Mandatory Submissions to Advice (Dec. 1, 2017). Accordingly, the Board's rules regarding work stoppages on employer premises may change.

22.	*See* The Right to Strike, NAT'L LABOR RELATIONS BD., www.nlrb.gov/strikes ("strike that violates a no-strike provision of a contract is not protected by the Act, and the striking employees can be discharged or otherwise disciplined, unless the strike is called to protest certain kinds of unfair labor practices committed by the employer").

23.	MikLin Enters. v. NLRB, 861 F.3d 812, 820, 824–25 (8th Cir. 2017) (citing NLRB v. Local Union No. 1229, 346 U.S. 464 (1953) ("Jefferson Standard").

24.	*See* Secondary Boycotts (section 8(b)(4)), NAT'L LABOR RELATIONS BD., https://www.nlrb.gov/rights-we-protect/whats-law/unions/secondary-boycotts-section-8b4.

25.	*See* The Right to Strike, NAT'L LABOR RELATIONS BD., www.nlrb.gov/strikes.

26.	Honolulu Rapid Transit Co., 110 N.L.R.B. 1806 (1954); EYM King of Mo., LLC, 365 N.L.R.B. No. 16 (Jan. 24, 2017) (non-unionized workers' one-day strike was protected activity and was not an unlawful intermittent strike); Consol. Commc'ns Holdings, Inc., 366 N.L.R.B. No. 172 (Aug. 27, 2018) (employer violated sections 8(a)(1) and (3) by disciplining employee for role in organizing and participating in a brief stand-and-stretch demonstration because demonstration did not constitute an unprotected work slowdown as employees did not refuse to perform duties or reduce the rate of work and the demonstration did not have a disruptive effect).

27.	*See* The Right to Strike, NAT'L LABOR RELATIONS BD., www.nlrb.gov/strikes.

28.	*See* NLRB, Office of the General Counsel, GC Mem. 08–10, Guideline Memorandum Concerning Unfair Labor Practice Charges Involving Political Advocacy (July 22, 2008), https://www.nlrb.gov/reports-guidance/general-counsel-memos.

29.	*Id.*

30.	*See, e.g.*, Quantum Elec., Inc., 341 N.L.R.B. 1270 (2004) ("Leaving work early is not protected activity even when the object of leaving is to engage in protected activity.").

31.	Reliable Maint., Case No. 18-CA-018119, NLRB Div. of Advice Mem. (Oct. 31, 2006).

32.	NLRB v. J. Weingarten, Inc., 420 U.S. 251 (1975).

33.	Success Vill. Apartments, Inc., 347 N.L.R.B. 1065 (2006).

34.	*See, e.g.*, PAE Aviation & Tech. Servs., 366 N.L.R.B. No. 95 (May 24, 2018) (employer violated section 8(a)(1) when it denied employee's request to have a union representative present during conversation about employee's alleged misconduct).

35.	Ralphs Grocery Co., 361 N.L.R.B. 80 (2014) (finding unlawful termination of employee for refusing to submit to drug and alcohol test after he requested union representation but management was unable to find a representative). Recent guidance from the NLRB's General Counsel identified *Weingarten* rights in the context of employer-mandated drug testing as an issue that must be submitted to the Division of Advice. NLRB Gen. Couns. Mem. 18-02, Mandatory Submissions to Advice (Dec. 1, 2017). Accordingly, the Board may change its application of *Weingarten* to circumstances involving employer-mandated drug testing.

36. Menorah Med. Cent. v. NLRB, 867 F.3d 1288 (D.C. Cir. 2017).

37. *Id.*

38. *See* Consol. Edison Co. of N.Y, Inc., 323 N.L.R.B. 910 (1997).

39. *See* Circus Circus Las Vegas, 366 N.L.R.B. No. 110 (June 15, 2018) (collecting cases).

40. Manhattan Beer Distribs. LLC, 362 N.L.R.B. No. 192 (Aug. 27, 2015), *enforced*, 670 F. App'x 33 (2d Cir. 2016); *see also* Circus Circus Las Vegas, 366 N.L.R.B. No. 110 (June 15, 2018) (finding the employer committed an unfair labor practice by not affirmatively ensuring that the employee had union representation at a meeting regarding the employee's suspension); *but see* Bellagio, LLC v. NLRB, 854 F.3d 703, 708–09 (D.C. Cir. 2017) (denying enforcement of Board's unfair labor practice finding where employer "worked diligently" to comply with the employee's request for union representation; after employee declined to contact a union agent himself, two supervisors attempted, to no avail, to locate a union representative, and before ending the interview, the employee was given the option to fill out a written statement, which he refused to do).

41. Ralphs Grocery Co., 361 N.L.R.B. 80, 86 (2014).

42. *See In re* Barnard Coll., 340 N.L.R.B. 934 (2003).

43. *See* Washoe Med. Ctr., Inc., 348 N.L.R.B. 361 (2006) (internal citations omitted).

44. *See* Greyhound Lines, 273 N.L.R.B. 1443 (1985).

45. *See* N.J. Bell Tel. Co., 308 N.L.R.B. 277 (1992).

46. NLRB v. J. Weingarten, Inc., 420 U.S. 251 (1975).

47. *See* IBM Corp., 341 N.L.R.B. 1288 (2004) (a non-union employer has a right to investigate an employee without the presence of a co-worker); *see also In re* Request for Rulemaking Regarding Reconsideration of IBM Corp., 341 N.L.R.B. 1288 (2004), Order (May 3, 2017) (declining petitioner's request to NLRB to use its discretionary rulemaking power to reverse its decision in *IBM Corp.* and extend *Weingarten* rights to non-unionized employees).

48. Valmont Indus. v. NLRB, 244 F.3d 454 (5th Cir. 2001).

49. Our Way, Inc., 268 N.L.R.B. 394 (1983).

50. Marriott Corp., 223 N.L.R.B. 978 (1976) ("rules which prohibit solicitation during 'working hours' . . . are generally presumptively invalid").

51. *Id.*

52. Meier & Frank Co., 89 N.L.R.B. 1016 (1950).

53. *See* McBride's of Naylor Rd., 229 N.L.R.B. 795 (1977).

54. *See id.*

55. Beth Isr. Hosp. v. NLRB, 437 U.S. 483 (1978).

56. Stoddard-Quirk, Mfg., 138 N.L.R.B. 615 (1962) (explaining that, unlike oral solicitation, an employer may prohibit distribution at all times in working areas because literature and other materials may create a hazard if discarded in a production area); Times Publ'g Co., 231 N.L.R.B. 207 (1977) ("The Board has consistently held that, pursuant to a valid rule, distribution may be prohibited from working areas because it can interfere with the employer's interest in order and discipline at employee work stations.").

57. *See* Stoddard-Quirk, Mfg., 138 N.L.R.B. 615 (1962) (identifying production area as a work area); Patio Foods v. NLRB, 415 F.2d 1001, 1003 (5th Cir. 1969) (holding that a loading area was a work area because loading trucks is a vital part of the production process even if it is performed outside the plant building); *see also* Brockton Hosp., 333 N.L.R.B. 1367 (2001) ("Board precedent has long held that merely because a work function or functions occur in a given space does not render that space a 'work area' within the meaning of the Board's rules regarding distribution. Rather, the Board has looked at the quality and quantity of work, which occurs in the area at issue, and examines whether the work is more than de minimis and whether it involves production.").

58. *See, e.g.*, Laidlaw Transit, Inc., 315 N.L.R.B. 79 (1994).

59. *See* Mercedes-Benz U.S. Int'l, Inc. v. Int'l Union, UAW, 838 F.3d 1128 (11th Cir. 2016) (reviewing Board and circuit court cases involving distribution in mixed-use areas).

60. *Id.* at 1140.

61. *Id.*

62. *See* NLRB v. Babcock & Wilcox Co., 351 U.S. 105, 112-13 (1956); *see also* Lechmere, Inc. v. NLRB, 502 U.S. 527, 540-41 (1992) (applying rule to a customer parking lot at a retail store); Albertsons, Inc., 351 N.L.R.B. 254 (2007) (employer's rule that prohibited non-employees from soliciting and distributing information on the employer's premises at all times was lawful because the employer's property was private and not equivalent to a public forum).

63. *See, e.g.*, Lake Superior Lumber Corp., 70 N.L.R.B. 178 (1946), *enforced*, 167 F.3d 147 (6th Cir. 1948).

64. *See* Polly Drummond Thriftway, Inc., 292 N.L.R.B. 331 (1989).

65. *See* Eastex, Inc. v. NLRB, 437 U.S. 556, 565 (1978); *see also* Allstate Ins. Co., 332 N.L.R.B. 759 (2000) (employer unlawfully disciplined employee for magazine interview critical of employer where several employees participated and interview was done in part to alert other employees of the complained-of conditions).

66. Goya Foods of Fla., 525 F.3d 1117 (11th Cir. 2008) (NLRB properly found that employer committed an unfair labor practice when it discharged three employees who had participated in a public protest over sanitation and safety issues related to rodent infestation at employer's warehouse).

67. Compuware Corp. v. NLRB, 134 F.3d 1285 (6th Cir. 1998), *cert. denied*, 523 U.S. 1123 (1998) (concluding that employer had unlawfully discharged employee for violating company work rule prohibiting employees from complaining to

company's third-party clients about working conditions where employee had acted on behalf of a group of employees and not simply on his own behalf).

68.   Valley Hosp. Med. Ctr., 351 N.L.R.B. 1250 (2007) (finding a nurse's statements during press conferences and in an article regarding her employer hospital's staffing ratios and how patient care could be affected were protected, even though the nurse criticized the hospital's main product—patient care—because the statements were not made in a manner reasonably calculated to harm the employer's reputation and reduce its income, and the statements were neither disloyal nor maliciously false), *enforced sub nom.* Nev. Serv. Emps. Union, Local 1107 v. NLRB, 358 F. App'x 783 (9th Cir. 2009).

69.   *In re* Am. Golf Corp. (Mountain Shadows), 330 N.L.R.B. 1238, 1240 (2000), *enforced sub nom.* Jensen v. NLRB, 86 F. App'x 305 (9th Cir. 2004); *see also* NLRB v. Elec. Workers Local 1229 (Jefferson Standard), 346 U.S. 464 (1953) (concluding that employees who made a "sharp, public, disparaging attack upon the quality of the company's product and its business policies" were not protected where the criticisms were unrelated to a labor controversy).

70.   St. Luke's Episcopal-Presbyterian Hosps., Inc. v. NLRB , 268 F.3d 575, 580 (8th Cir. 2001).

71.   *Id.*

72.   MikLin Enters., Inc. v. NLRB, 861 F.3d 812, 825 (8th Cir. 2017).

73.   Endicott Interconnect Techs., Inc. v. NLRB, 453 F.3d 532, 537 (D.C. Cir. 2006).

74.   Valley Hosp. Med. Ctr., 351 N.L.R.B. 1250 (2007).

75.   Veritas Health Servs., Inc., 366 N.L.R.B. No. 135 (July 24, 2018) (finding unlawful an employer's instruction to employees not to speak to third parties and/ or the media about their protected concerted activities and/or their terms and conditions of employment).

76.   *Id.*

77.   Triple Play Sports Bar, 361 N.L.R.B. 308 (2014) ("The employees engaged in protected concerted activity by taking part in a social media discussion among off-site, off-duty employees, as well as two non-employees."), *enforced sub nom.* Three D, LLC v. NLRB, 629 F. App'x 33 (2d Cir. 2015).

78.   *Id.*

79.   *Id.*

80.   *Id.*

81.   World Color (USA) Corp., 360 N.L.R.B. 227 (2014), *enforcement denied on other grounds*, 776 F.3d 717 (D.C. Cir. 2015).

82.   Richmond Dist. Neighborhood Ctr., 361 N.L.R.B. 833 (2014) (finding that a Facebook discussion between two workers who advocated specific insubordinate acts lost protection under the NLRA).

83.   Mid-Mountain Foods, 332 N.L.R.B. 229, 230 (2000) (no statutory right for employees to use the employer's television in breakroom to show a pro-union campaign video), *enforced*, 269 F.3d 1075 (D.C. Cir. 2001); Eaton Techs., 322 N.L.R.B. 848, 853 (1997) ("It is well established that there is no statutory right of

employees or a union to use an employer's bulletin board."); Champion Int'l Corp., 303 N.L.R.B. 102, 109 (1991) (stating that an employer has "a basic right to regulate and restrict employee use of company property" such as a copy machine); Churchill's Supermarkets, 285 N.L.R.B. 138, 155 (1987) ("[A]n employer ha[s] every right to restrict the use of company telephones to business-related conversations. . . ."), enforced, 857 F.2d 1474 (6th Cir. 1988), cert. denied, 490 U.S. 1046 (1989); Union Carbide Corp., 259 N.L.R.B. 974, 980 (1981) (employer "could unquestionably bar its telephones to any personal use by employees"), enforced in relevant part, 714 F.2d 657 (6th Cir. 1983).

84. Purple Commc'ns, Inc., 361 N.L.R.B. 1050 (2014) (overturning Register Guard, 351 N.L.R.B. 1110 (2007)).

85. Id. at 1063.

86. Id. at 1050.

87. NLRB Gen. Couns. Mem. 18-02, Mandatory Submissions to Advice (Dec. 1, 2017).

88. Id.

89. Notice and Invitation to File Briefs, Case No. 28-CA-060841 (Aug. 1, 2018); see also https://www.nlrb.gov/news-outreach/news-story/board-invites-briefs-regarding-employee-use-employer-email.

90. Id.

91. Republic Aviation Corp. v. NLRB, 324 U.S. 793 (1945).

92. Albis Plastics, 335 N.L.R.B. 923 (2001) (need to identify employees with safety training justifies prohibition of union stickers on caps); but see Ne. Indus. Serv. Co., 320 N.L.R.B. 977, 978, 980 (1996) (finding restriction on employees wearing stickers on hardhats not justified by special circumstance because, inter alia, stickers impaired employer's ability to inspect hardhats no more than employer-supplied helmet decals bearing employer's name).

93. Pathmark Stores, 342 N.L.R.B. 378, 378–79 (2004) (T-shirts with slogan "Don't Cheat About the Meat!" suggested employer was cheating customers and thus threatened genuine harm to customer relationship); but see In-N-Out Burger, Inc., 365 N.L.R.B. No. 39 (Mar. 21, 2017) (fast food employer could not ban "Fight for 15" buttons where it failed to show buttons would tarnish the restaurant's "sparkling clean image"), enforced, 894 F.3d 707 (5th Cir. 2018).

94. NLRB v. Baptist Hosp., 442 U.S. 773, 781 (1979).

95. Komatsu Am. Corp., 342 N.L.R.B. 649 (2004) (employer lawfully prohibited employees from wearing shirts that made "clear appeal to ethnic prejudices" by comparing employer's outsourcing and Japan's December 7, 1941 attack on United States); but see AT&T, 362 N.L.R.B. No. 105 (June 2, 2015) (employer could not prohibit employees from wearing a button stating "WTF Where's The Fairness" because the "WTF" acronym would be understood to mean "Where's The Fairness").

96. In-N-Out Burger, Inc. v. NLRB, 894 F.3d 707, 715 (5th Cir. 2018); Medco Health Sols. of Las Vegas, Inc., 364 N.L.R.B. No. 115, at *6 (Aug. 27, 2016).

97.   Leiser Constr., LLC, 349 N.L.R.B. 413, 414–15 & n.17 (2007) (finding lawful employer's ban on "unquestionably vulgar and obscene" sticker depicting someone or something urinating on a "non-union" rat, given narrowly tailored nature of ban and fact that employer did not prohibit any other union stickers), *enforced*, 281 F. App'x 781 (10th Cir. 2008).

98.   "W" San Diego, 348 N.L.R.B. 372, 372–76 (2006); *see also* NLRB v. Starbucks Corp., 679 F.3d 70 (2d Cir. 2012) (reversing the NLRB and finding lawful Starbucks' policy that allowed employees to wear only one piece of union insignia on their uniforms, finding Starbucks had a legitimate interest in having employees wear Starbucks-branded buttons, and allowing the employees to wear multiple union buttons in addition to Starbucks-branded buttons risked diluting the Starbucks brand).

99.   Stabilus, Inc., 355 N.L.R.B. 836, 838 (2010) (holding that, even if it justified its policy under the special circumstances test, the employer "nonetheless acted unlawfully by disparately enforcing the policy against statutorily protected activity while not enforcing it against other similar activity under similar circumstances").

100.   Nemacolin Country Club, 291 N.L.R.B. 456 (1988) (an employer's order to an employee to remove her union button, worn directly above her name tag, was unlawful; in the past, management's interest had not been evoked when waitresses had worn other types of pins and buttons on their uniforms); Titus Elec. Contracting, Inc., 355 N.L.R.B. 1357, 1357 (2010) (finding employer violated section 8(a)(1) when it sent an employee home to change out of a union shirt because employer did not send home employees who wore shirts with various nonunion, non-company logos).

101.   St. John's Health Ctr., 357 N.L.R.B. 2078 (2011).

102.   *See* Mesa Vista Hosp., 280 N.L.R.B. 298, 299 (1986) (Outside immediate patient care areas, and outside other areas where the hospital establishes an adverse effect on patient care, employees retain the right to wear union insignia while working. An employer may further restrict the right by demonstrating "special circumstances."); *see also* Mt. Clemens Gen. Hosp. v. NLRB, 328 F.3d 837, 846–48 (6th Cir. 2003) (restrictions on wearing union-related buttons are presumptively valid in patient-care areas, while restrictions on wearing union-related buttons in non-patient care areas are presumptively invalid in the absence of special circumstances).

103.   *See* Beth Isr. Hosp. v. NLRB, 437 U.S. 483, 507 (1978); *see also* NLRB v. L.A. New Hosp., 640 F.2d 1017, 1020 (9th Cir. 1981).

104.   Wash. State Nurses Ass'n v. NLRB, 526 F.3d 577 (9th Cir. 2008).

105.   Saint John's Health Ctr., 357 N.L.R.B. 2078, 2079 (2011) (finding hospital's prohibition against union ribbons stating "Saint John's RNs for Safe Patient Care" in immediate patient care areas unlawful where hospital distributed a button that said "Saint John's mission is patient safe care" and allowed nurses to wear it in immediate patient care areas).

106.   HealthBridge Mgmt., LLC, 360 N.L.R.B. 937, 938 (quoting Beth Isr. Hosp. v. NLRB, 437 U.S. 438, 507 (1978)), *enforced*, 798 F.3d 1059 (D.C. Cir. 2015).

107. Saint John's Health Ctr., 357 N.L.R.B. 2078, 2079 (2011).

108. 29 U.S.C. § 158(a).

109. *Id.* § 158(c).

110. *Id.* § 158(a)(1); *see also* 29 U.S.C. § 157.

111. *Id.* §§ 158(a)(1), (c); *see also* NLRB v. Gissel Packing Co., 395 U.S. 575 (1969).

112. Surprenant Mfg. Co. v. NLRB, 341 F.2d 756, 761 (6th Cir. 1965).

113. NLRB v. Gissel Packing Co., 395 U.S. 575 (1965).

114. *Id.*

115. *Id.*

116. *See* Daikichi Sushi Corp., 335 N.L.R.B. 622 (2001); *see also* Benjamin Coal Co., 294 N.L.R.B. 572 n.2 (1989); NLRB v. Gissel Packing Co., 395 U.S. 575 (1969); Dish Network Corp., 359 N.L.R.B. 311 (2012).

117. Gissel Packing Co., 395 U.S. at 618.

118. *See, e.g.*, Daikichi Sushi Corp., 335 N.L.R.B. 622 (2001); *see also* AP Auto. Sys., 333 N.L.R.B. 581 (2001).

119. Alternative Energy Applications, Inc., 361 N.L.R.B. 1203 (2014).

120. Partylite Worldwide, Inc., 344 N.L.R.B. 1342 (2005).

121. Arrow Auto. Indus., 258 N.L.R.B. 860, 860 (1981), *enforced*, 679 F.2d 875 (4th Cir. 1982).

122. Frontier Tel. of Rochester, Inc., 344 N.L.R.B. 1270, 1276 (2005).

123. Flexteel Indus., 311 N.L.R.B. 257 (1993).

124. Hopp Topp Mfg. Co., 250 N.L.R.B. 1232, 1244 (1980).

125. Shamrock Foods Co., 366 N.L.R.B. No. 117 (June 22, 2018).

126. *See, e.g.*, Metfab, Inc., 344 N.L.R.B. 215 (2005); *see also* Daikichi Sushi Corp., 335 N.L.R.B. 622 (2001).

127. BP Amoco Chem.-Chocolate Bayou & Paper, 351 N.L.R.B. 614, 617 (2007).

128. *Id.*

129. *See, e.g., id.* ("Such statements are unlawful and objectionable when, in context, they effectively threaten employees with the loss of existing benefits and leave them with the impression that what they may ultimately receive depends in large measure on what the Union can induce the employer to restore."); *see also* Fed. Logistics & Operations, 340 N.L.R.B. 255, 255 (2003) ("Although such statements are not per se unlawful, the Board will examine them, in context, to determine whether they effectively threaten employees with the loss of existing benefits and leave them with the impression that what they may ultimately receive depends in large measure upon what the Union can induce the employer to restore, or—conversely—whether they indicate that any reduction in wages or benefits will occur only as a result of the normal give and take of collective bargaining.") (internal quotations omitted).

130. Bill Johnson's Rests., Inc. v. NLRB, 461 U.S. 731 (1983); BE&K Constr. Co. v. NLRB, 536 U.S. 516 (2002).

131. Webco Indus., 337 N.L.R.B. 361 (2001) ("[I]f a suit is preempted, it violates Section 8(a)(1) if it tends to interfere with, restrain, or coerce employees in the exercise of their Section 7 rights.").

132. Under the previous standard, facially neutral work rules were found unlawful if employees could "reasonably construe" them to prohibit section 7 activity. *See* Lutheran Heritage Vill.-Livonia, 343 N.L.R.B. 646, 647 (2004).

133. Boeing Co., 365 N.L.R.B. No. 154 (Dec. 14, 2017).

134. *Id.*, slip. op. at 4.

135. *Id.*

136. *Id.*

137. *Id.*

138. *Id.*

139. *Id.; see also* ImageFIRST, 366 N.L.R.B. No. 182, n. 3 (Aug. 27, 2018) (concluding that rule that barred "discussion of payroll information" was unlawful).

140. *See* Boeing Co., 365 N.L.R.B. No. 154, slip. op. at 16.

141. *Id.*, slip. op. at n.15.

142. NLRB Gen. Couns. Mem. 18-04, Guidance on Handbook Rules Post-Boeing (June 6, 2018).

143. *Id.* at 2–15.

144. *Id.* at 15–17.

145. *Id.* at 17–20.

146. *See* Register Guard, 351 N.L.R.B. 1110, 1119 (2007), *enforced in relevant part*, 571 F.3d 53 (D.C. Cir. 2009).

147. *Id.* at 1119 (citing Fleming Cos. v. NLRB, 349 F.3d 968 (7th Cir. 2003); Guardian Indus. Corp. v. NLRB, 49 F.3d 317 (7th Cir. 1995)).

148. UPMC, 366 NLRB No. 185 (Aug. 27, 2018).

149. Epic Sys. Corp. v. Lewis, 138 S. Ct. 1612 (2018).

150. Section 7 provides employees a right to "self-organization, to form, join, or assist labor organizations, to bargain collectively through representatives of their own choosing, and to engage in other concerted activities for the purpose of collective bargaining or other mutual aid or protection," 29 U.S.C. § 157.

151. Epic Sys. Corp., 138 S. Ct. at 1624.

152. *Id.* (explaining that F.R.C.P. did not create the modern class action until 1966, that the Fair Labor Standards Act collective action provision post-dated the NLRA by years, and that section 7's failure to mention group actions reinforces that the statute does not address such procedures).

153. *Id.*

154. *Id.* at 1625.

155. *Compare* Killion v. KeHE Distribs., LLC, 761 F.3d 574, 590–91 (6th Cir. 2014) (concluding that right to a collective action could not be waived outside of an arbitration agreement) *with* Benedict v. Hewlett-Packard Co., 2016 BL 99857, at *6 (N.D. Cal. Mar. 29, 2016) (concluding that employees can waive their right to proceed in a class or collective action even where the waiver is not tied to an employment agreement.)

156. Hughes Christenson Co., 317 N.L.R.B. 633 (1995), *enforcement on other grounds*, 101 F.3d 28 (5th Cir. 1996); BP Amoco Chem.-Chocolate Bayou, 351 N.L.R.B. 614, 615 (2007).

157. A.S.V., Inc., 366 N.L.R.B. No. 162, slip op. at 50 (Aug. 21, 2018) ("the Board has also stated that, in exercising its discretion, it will refuse to be bound by any settlement that is at odds with the Act or the Board's policies.") (quoting Indep. Stave, 287 N.L.R.B. 740, 742 (1987).

158. A.S.V., Inc., 366 N.L.R.B. No. 162, slip op. at 2 (Aug. 21, 2018).

159. *See* Caterpillar, Inc., 322 N.L.R.B. 674, 683–84 (1996) (holding supervisor monitoring to ensure that employees are doing the work for which they are paid is not unlawful simply because employees choose to conduct union activity in the sight of the supervisor); Smithfield Foods, Inc., 347 N.L.R.B. 1225 (2006) (employer did not engage in unlawful surveillance by redirecting a security camera to the area where employee handbilling had taken place, where the employees engaged in handbilling had previously trespassed onto employer's property; employer's concern about further trespassing was reasonable).

160. Eddyleon Chocolate Co., 301 N.L.R.B. 887, 888 (1991) (quoting Metal Indus., 251 N.L.R.B. 1523 (1980)).

161. Intertape Polymer Corp. v. NLRB, 801 F.3d 224, 235 (4th Cir. 2015).

162. Aladdin Gaming, LLC, 345 N.L.R.B. 585 (2005), *enforced sub nom.* Local Joint Exec. Bd. of Las Vegas v. NLRB, 515 F.3d 942 (9th Cir. 2008).

163. NLRB v. S. Md. Hosp. Ctr., 916 F.2d 932, 938 (4th Cir. 1990).

164. Aladdin Gaming, LLC, 345 N.L.R.B. 585, 586 (2005), *enforced sub nom.* Local Joint Exec. Bd. of Las Vegas v. NLRB, 515 F.3d 942 (9th Cir. 2008); *see also* Sands Hotel & Casino, San Juan, 306 N.L.R.B. 172 (1992) (employer engaged in unlawful surveillance by posting a security guard near the employee entrance and another security guard with binoculars in an upstairs hotel room in order to observe employees and union agents soliciting union authorization card signatures across the street from the hotel), *enforced sub nom.* S.J.R.R., Inc. v. NLRB, 993 F.2d 913 (D.C. Cir. 1993).

165. *See* Classic Sofa, Inc., 346 N.L.R.B. 219 (2006); *see also* Rogers Elec., Inc., 346 N.L.R.B. 508 (2006).

166. Brasfield & Gorrie, LLC, 366 N.L.R.B. No. 82 (May 8, 2018).

167. F.W. Woolworth Co., 310 N.L.R.B. 1197 (1993).

168. *See* Kingsbridge Heights Rehab. Care Ctr., 352 N.L.R.B. 6 (2008); *see also* Cont'l Grp., Inc., 353 N.L.R.B. 348 (2008).

169. *See* Hilton Mobile Homes, 155 N.L.R.B., 873, 874 (1965); *see also* Town & Country Supermarkets, 340 N.L.R.B. 1410, 1415 (2004) (employer did not violate the NLRA when it photographed picketers who impeded access to store and intimidated customers for the purpose of obtaining evidence to support a court injunction to prevent future misconduct).

170. Brasfield & Gorrie, LLC, 366 N.L.R.B. No. 82 (May 8, 2018).

171. AdvancePierre Foods, Inc., 366 N.L.R.B. No. 133 (July 19, 2018).

172. Sprain Brook Manor Nursing Home, LLC, 351 N.L.R.B. 1190 (2007).

173. Purple Commc'ns, 361 N.L.R.B. 1050, 1064–65 (2014).

174. *Id.* at 1065.

175. Buel, Inc., Case No. 11-CA-22936, NLRB Div. of Advice Mem. (July 28, 2011) (there can be no unlawful surveillance if the employer's agent was invited to

observe), citing Donaldson Bros. Ready Mix, Inc., 341 N.L.R.B. 958, 960–61 (2004) (no unlawful surveillance where a supervisor attended a union meeting by invitation and subsequently reported to employer on what occurred there).

176. AdvancePierre Foods, Inc., 366 N.L.R.B. No. 133 (July 19, 2018).

177. Bozzuto's, Inc., 365 N.L.R.B. No. 145, slip op. at 1 (Dec. 12, 2017) (citing cases); *see also* EDP Med. Comput. Sys., 284 N.L.R.B. 1232, 1264–1265 (1987) (finding that two conversations, in and of themselves, might not be considered coercive, but when viewed in the context of the employer's section 8(a)(1) conduct, the questioning was coercive as it reasonably tended to color employees' perception of the character and reason for the inquiries).

178. *In re* SFO Good-Nite Inn, LLC, 352 N.L.R.B. 268, 268 n.3 (2008) (citing Children's Servs. Int'l & Serv. Emps. Int'l Union, Local 817, 347 N.L.R.B. 67, 79–80 (2006), *enforced*, 700 F.3d 1 (D.C. Cir. 2012).

179. *Id.* (manager did not unlawfully interrogate employees when he told employees that he did not know why they wanted the union and that the company would give the employees benefits because his statement did not call for an answer).

180. Struksnes Constr. Co., 165 N.L.R.B. 1062 (1967).

181. *See* Lackawanna Elec. Constr., Inc., 337 N.L.R.B. 458, 465 (2002), quoting Pub. Serv. Co. of Okla. (PSO), 334 N.L.R.B. 487, 504 n.10 ("an employer may not initiate a poll of employee sentiments in an attempt to create—as opposed to confirm—a good-faith doubt of the union's continuing majority support among employees").

182. Struksnes Constr. Co., 165 N.L.R.B. at 1063.

183. Allentown Mack Sales & Serv. v. NLRB, 522 U.S. 359 (1998).

184. Texas Petrochemicals Corp., 296 NLRB 1057, 1063 (1989), *enforced in relevant part*, 923 F.2d 398 (5th Cir. 1991).

185. Syracuse Univ., 350 N.L.R.B. 755 (2007).

186. Electromation, Inc., 309 N.L.R.B. 990 (1992), *enforced*, 35 F.3d 1148 (7th Cir. 1994).

187. *Id.* at 996.

188. 29 U.S.C. § 152(5).

189. Electromation, 309 N.L.R.B. at 996–97.

190. *Id.*

191. *Id.* at 994.

192. *Id.* at 995 n.21.

193. E. I. de Pont & Co., 311 N.L.R.B. 893, 894 (1993).

194. *Electromation*, 309 N.L.R.B. at 997; *see also* Keeler Brass Co., 317 N.L.R.B. 1110, 1114 (1995) (employee grievance committee existed for the purpose of "dealing with" employer where the committee and the company "went back and forth explaining themselves until an acceptable result was achieved" with respect to a discharge grievance and a company policy).

195. *Electromation*, 309 N.L.R.B. at 995; *see also* Crown Cork & Seal Co., 334 N.L.R.B. 699, 701 (2001).

196. *Crown Cork & Seal Co.*, 334 N.L.R.B. 699; *see also* Gen. Foods Corp., 231 N.L.R.B. 1232 (1977) (employee teams to which employer delegated authority to make job assignments to individual team members, assign job rotations, and schedule overtime were not "labor organizations"); John Ascuaga's Nugget, 230 N.L.R.B. 275, 276 (1977) (employee organization that resolved employees' grievances and did not interact with management was not a "labor organization").

197. Electromation, Inc. v. NLRB, 35 F.3d 1148, 1170 (7th Cir. 1994), citing Newport News Shipbuilding & Dry Dock Co., 308 U.S. 241, 249 (1939); NLRB v. Cabot Carbon, Co., 360 U.S. 203, 214 (1959).

198. *Electromation*, 309 NLRB at 995.

199. *Id.*

200. Spiegel Trucking Co., 225 N.L.R.B. 178, 179 (1976), *enforced*, 559 F.2d 188 (D.C. Cir. 1977).

201. G.L. Gibbons Trucking Serv., 199 N.L.R.B. 590, 592, 596 (1972).

202. Duquesne Univ., 198 N.L.R.B. 891, 892, 898 (employer's assistance to union in selecting a particular attorney to represent it in NLRB representation proceeding involving a rival union constituted section 8(a)(2) interference); Versatube Corp., 203 N.L.R.B. 456, 461 (1973) (employer's suggestion that it would pay the fees of an attorney to represent union in NLRB representation proceeding challenging union violated section 8(a)(2)), *enforced*, 492 F.2d 795 (6th Cir. 1974).

203. Sportspal, Inc., 214 N.L.R.B. 917, 926 (1974) (employer's promise to pay fees of union's lawyer incurred in preparing contracts during negotiations with employer violated section 8(a)(2)).

204. Power Piping Co., 291 N.L.R.B. 494, 497 (1988).

205. Allied Super Markets, Inc. (Retail Clerks, Local 1557), 169 N.L.R.B. 927 (1968).

206. Local 1814, Int'l Longshoremen's Ass'n, AFL-CIO v. NLRB, 735 F.2d 1384 (D.C. Cir. 1984).

207. Midtown Service Co., Inc., 171 N.L.R.B. 1306 (1968).

208. *See* Electromation, Inc. v. NLRB, 35 F.3d 1148 (7th Cir. 1994).

209. Chi. Rawhide Mfg. Co. v. NLRB, 221 F.2d 165, 167 (7th Cir. 1955).

210. *Id.*

211. Coamo Knitting Mills, Inc., 150 N.L.R.B. 579, 582 (1964); *see also* Modern Plastics Corp. v. NLRB, 379 F.2d 201 (6th Cir. 1967) (employer provided mere cooperation to a labor organization when it paid for food and drinks before its meetings and regular wages to employees who attended meetings).

212. NLRB v. Dist. 50, UMW, 355 U.S. 453 (1957).

213. *Id.*

214. *Id.* at 459.

215. *Id.* at 468.

216. 29 U.S.C. § 158(c); *cf.* Dentech Corp., 294 N.L.R.B. 924 (1989) (finding employer's threat to move business to Canada if the employees did not denounce the union was unlawful).

217. *See* NLRB v. Exch. Parts Co., 375 U.S. 405 (1964); *see also* Sun Mart Foods, 341 N.L.R.B. 161 (2004) (employer engaged in objectionable conduct by announcing to employees right before a union election that it would be remodeling its store where the employer had timed the announcement to influence the employees' choice in the election).

218. *Exchange Parts Co.*, 375 U.S. at 409.

219. Pac. FM, Inc., 332 N.L.R.B. 771, 773 (2000).

220. *Id.*

221. *See* Am. Sunroof Corp., 248 N.L.R.B. 748 (1980) (employer's grant of pay raise and institution of new pension plan within one day of union election were not unlawful because they were part of a previously established company policy); *see also* Towne Bus LLC, 350 N.L.R.B. 1253 (2007); Real Foods Co., 350 N.L.R.B. 309 (2007); Medline Indus., Inc., 218 N.L.R.B. 1404 (1975); Nalco Chem. Co., 163 N.L.R.B. 68 (1967); *cf.* Southgate Vill. Inc., 319 N.L.R.B. 916 (1995) (employer violated NLRA when it granted an across-the-board wage increase during a union campaign and did not have a prior practice of granting such increases).

222. 29 U.S.C § 158(a)(3).

223. Wright Line, 251 N.L.R.B. 1083 (1980), *enforced*, 662 F.2d 889 (1st Cir. 1981), *cert. denied*, 455 U.S. 989 (1982), *approved in* NLRB v. Transp. Mgmt. Corp., 462 U.S. 393 (1983).

224. *See id.; see also* Flamingo Las Vegas Operating Co., LLC, 360 N.L.R.B. 243 (2014) (applying *Wright Line* and holding that employer did not violate the NLRA by issuing a written warning to a security guard, despite the fact the security guard had previously testified against the employer in an unfair labor practice hearing, where the employer showed that it would have issued the warning even if the employee had not testified at the earlier hearing).

225. Starbucks Corp., 360 N.L.R.B. 1168 (2014).

226. The term "salting" originates from the concept of salting a mine, where metal or ore is introduced to the mine to create a false impression that the metal or ore is actually present in the mine. *See* James L. Fox, *"Salting" the Construction Industry*, 24 WM. MITCHELL L. REV. 681, 682 (1998).

227. *See* MICHAEL C. HARPER, SAMUEL ESTREICHER & JOAN FLYNN, LABOR LAW: CASES MATERIALS & PROBLEMS 191 (6th ed. 2007).

228. NLRB v. Town & Country Elec., Inc., 516 U.S. 85 (1995).

229. Toering Elec. Co., 351 N.L.R.B. 225, 228 (2007). Prior to *Toering*, the NLRB presumed that an individual who submitted an application for employment was an "employee" and thus entitled to protection against discriminatory hiring practices. *See, e.g.*, Progressive Elec., Inc. v. NLRB, 453 F.3d 538, 551-53 (D.C. Cir. 2006), *enforcing* 344 N.L.R.B. 426 (2005).

230. Allstate Power Vac, Inc., 354 N.L.R.B. 980 (2009).

231. 29 U.S.C. § 158(a)(4).

232. Nash v. Fla. Indus. Comm'n, 389 U.S. 235, 238 (1967); *see also* Briggs Mfg. Co., 75 N.L.R.B. 569, 571 (1947) (the purpose of section 8(a)(4) was "to assure an effective administration of the Act by providing immunity to those who initiate or

assist the Board in proceedings under the Act"); Gen. Servs., Inc., 229 N.L.R.B. 940, 941–43 (1977) (analyzing legislative history and Supreme Court and Board precedent regarding section 8(a)(4)).

233. NLRB v. Scrivener, 405 U.S. 117 (1972).

234. Williamhouse of Cal., 317 N.L.R.B. 699 (1995); *see also* Quality Millwork, 276 N.L.R.B. 591 (1985).

235. Weinreb Mgmt., 292 N.L.R.B. 428 (1989).

236. Retail Store Emps. Union, Local 876, 219 N.L.R.B. 1188, 1188–89 (1975) (employer violated section 8(a)(4) by terminating employee who refused, without malice, to voluntarily testify against co-worker where employee disclaimed first-hand knowledge of matters on which she was to be questioned), *enforced*, 570 F.2d 586 (6th Cir. 1978), *cert. denied*, 439 U.S. 819 (1978).

237. *See, e.g.*, Lamar Creamery Co., 115 N.L.R.B. 1113 (1956) (finding employer violated section 8(a)(4) when it refused to hire an applicant due to his participation in an NLRB proceeding against his former employer).

238. Maple City Stamping Co., 200 N.L.R.B. 743 (1972).

239. Hotel Holiday Inn de Isla Verde, 259 N.L.R.B. 496 (1981), *enforced*, 702 F.2d 268 (1st Cir. 1983).

240. *Id.*

241. *Id.* (after employee's unfavorable testimony in NLRB proceedings and his promotion to acting union president, employer changed the employee's schedule, hindering employee's ability to work his second job).

242. Everage Bros. Mkt., Inc., 206 N.L.R.B. 593 (1973).

243. Lamar Creamery Co., 115 N.L.R.B. 1113 (1956) (finding employer violated section 8(a)(4) when it refused to hire an applicant due to his participation in an NLRB proceeding against his former employer).

244. Motor City Elec. Co., 204 N.L.R.B. 460 (1973).

245. Globe Mfg. Co., 229 N.L.R.B. 1025 (1977).

246. 29 U.S.C. § 158(b).

247. 29 U.S.C. § 158(b)(1)(A).

248. *See, e.g.*, Painters Local 558 (Forman-Ford), 279 N.L.R.B. 150 (1986) (holding a message that conveyed potential unpleasant consequences for employee even if unintentionally communicated was coercive and violated section 8(b)(1)(A)).

249. *See, e.g.*, Retail, Wholesale & Dep't Store Union Dist. 65, 157 N.L.R.B. 615 (1966); *see also* Local 140 (Brooklyn Spring Corp.), 113 N.L.R.B. 815 (1955).

250. Teamsters Local Union No. 115, 344 N.L.R.B. 644 (2005).

251. *See, e.g.*, UNITE HERE! Local 5 (Aqua-Aston Hosp., LLC), 365 N.L.R.B. No. 169 (Dec. 16, 2017) (union unlawfully blocked or impeded employees from entering or exiting hotel's property during picketing).

252. *See, e.g.*, Armco, E. Steel Div., Ashland Works v. NLRB, 832 F.2d 357 (6th Cir. 1987); *see also* Elec. Workers (IBEW) Local 99 (Elec. Maint. & Control), 312 N.L.R.B. 613 (1993); Pattern Makers v. NLRB, 473 U.S. 95 (1985); Pattern Makers

(Mich. Model Mfrs. Ass'n), 310 N.L.R.B. 929 (1993); NLRB v. Carpenters Local 608 (Harte), 811 F.2d 149 (2d Cir. 1987); Theatrical Stage Emps. Local 7 (Universal City Studios), 254 N.L.R.B. 1139 (1981).

253. NLRB, Basic Guide to the National Labor Relations Act (1997), at 23, www.nlrb.gov/sites/default/files/attachments/basic-page/node-3024/basicguide.pdf.

254. 29 U.S.C. § 158(b)(1)(A) (section 8(b)(1)(A) "shall not impair the right of a labor organization to prescribe its own rules with respect to the acquisition or retention of membership therein").

255. Scofield v. NLRB, 394 U.S. 423, 432 (1969).

256. NLRB, Basic Guide to the National Labor Relations Act (1997), at 23, www.nlrb.gov/sites/default/files/attachments/basic-page/node-3024/basicguide.pdf.

257. *Scofield*, 394 U.S. at 430.

258. *Id.*

259. NLRB v. Boeing Co., 412 U.S. 67, 78 (1973).

260. *Id.* at 74.

261. *See* Coercion of Employees (Sect. 8(b)(1)(A)), NAT'L LABOR RELATIONS BD., https://www.nlrb.gov/rights-we-protect/whats-law/unions/coercion-employees-section-8b1a.

262. *See* Int'l Longshoremen's Ass'n, Local 1408, AFL-CIO v. NLRB, 705 F.2d 1549 (11th Cir. 1983).

263. *See* Int'l Union Auto. Workers (Pitt Processing Co.), 208 N.L.R.B. 736 (1974); Local 1104, Commc'ns Workers of Am., AFL-CIO v. NLRB, 520 F.2d 411 (2d Cir. 1975); *see also* 29 U.S.C. § 158(b)(2).

264. *See* Coercion of Employees (Sec. 8(b)(1)(A)), NAT'L LABOR RELATIONS BD., https://www.nlrb.gov/rights-we-protect/whats-law/unions/coercion-employees-section-8b1a.

265. Hershey Foods Corp., 207 N.L.R.B. 897 (1973), *enforced*, 513 F.2d 1083 (9th Cir. 1975).

266. *Compare* NLRB v. Gen. Teamsters Local No. 439, Int'l Bhd. of Teamsters, AFL-CIO, 175 F.3d 1173, 1174 (9th Cir. 1999) (finding union violated the NLRA by fining a member who reported co-workers' misconduct pursuant to employer's policy); *with* Int'l Union of Operating Eng'rs, Local 513, AFL-CIO v. NLRB, 635 F.3d 1233 (D.C. Cir. 2011) (finding the Ninth Circuit's *General Teamsters* decision unpersuasive and instead holding that the union did not violate the NLRA by fining a member for reporting another member's safety violation as required by the employer).

267. *See* Coercion of Employees (Sec. 8(b)(1)(A)), NAT'L LABOR RELATIONS BD., https://www.nlrb.gov/rights-we-protect/whats-law/unions/coercion-employees-section-8b1a.

268. Hanna Mining Co. v. Dist. 2, Marine Eng'rs Beneficial Ass'n, 382 U.S. 181, 188 (1965).

269. 29 U.S.C. § 158(b)(1)(B); Local 322, Laborers' Int'l Union, 229 N.L.R.B. 949, 950–51 (1977).

270. Toledo Lithographers Local 15-P & 272, 175 N.L.R.B. 1072 (1969), *enforced*, 437 F.2d 55 (6th Cir. 1971).

271. Fla. Power & Light Co. v. IBEW, Local 641, 417 U.S. 790 (1974).

272. NLRB v. Textile Workers Local 1029, Granite State Joint Bd., 409 U.S. 213, 216 (1972).

273. *Id.* at 217.

274. United Mine Workers (Canterbury Coal Co.), 305 N.L.R.B. 516, 518 (1991).

275. *Id.*

276. 29 U.S.C. § 158(b)(2).

277. NLRB v. Spector Freight Sys., Inc., 273 F.2d 272, 275 (8th Cir. 1960).

278. Postal Workers Long Island N.Y. Area Local, 350 N.L.R.B. 219, 221–22 (2007).

279. Nat'l Ass'n of Letter Carriers, Branch 86, 315 N.L.R.B. 1176 (1994).

280. NLRB, Basic Guide to the National Labor Relations Act (1997), at 1, www.nlrb.gov/sites/default/files/attachments/basic-page/node-3024/basicguide.pdf.

281. 29 U.S.C. § 158(f); *see also* Longshoremen's Local No. 13, 210 N.L.R.B. 952, 956 (1974) (union operating exclusive hiring hall unlawfully conditioned membership in class B upon sponsorship by class A, and eligibility to sponsor was conditioned on union membership), *enforced*, 549 F.2d 1346 (9th Cir.), *cert. denied*, 434 U.S. 922 (1977); Glass Bottle Blowers Local 149, 255 N.L.R.B. 715, 715–716 (1981) (unlawful seniority preference based on length of union membership).

282. Boilermakers Local 374 (Constr. Eng'g), 284 N.L.R.B. 1382, 1383 (1987) ("the referral rules themselves . . . cannot be discriminatory or arbitrary"), *enforced*, 852 F.2d 1353 (D.C. Cir. 1988); Laborers Local 1136 (S. Ill. Builders), 276 N.L.R.B. 1396 (1985); Rubber Workers (AFL-CIO) Local 12 (Bus. League of Gadsden), 150 N.L.R.B. 312, 314, 320 (1964), *enforced*, 368 F.2d 12 (5th Cir. 1966), *cert. denied*, 389 U.S. 837 (1967); *but see* Operating Eng'rs Local 302, Case 19-CB-6948, NLRB Div. of Advice Mem. (July 1, 1992) (union lawfully referred female and minority members out of order to contractors attempting to meet affirmative action goals that federal government contracts required).

283. 29 U.S.C. § 158(f)(4).

284. Pittsburgh Press Co. v. NLRB, 997 F.2d 652, 660 (D.C. Cir. 1992); *see also* Teamsters Local Union No. 667 (Spector Freight), 248 N.L.R.B. 260, 269 (1980) (referral fee cannot be "in excess of cost attributable to the services rendered").

285. NLRB, Basic Guide to the National Labor Relations Act (1997), at 26, www.nlrb.gov/sites/default/files/attachments/basic-page/node-3024/basicguide.pdf.

4

Representation Cases

The National Labor Relations Act (NLRA) encourages collective bargaining and the exercise by workers of full freedom of association, self-organization, and designation of representatives of their own choosing, for the purpose of negotiating the terms and conditions of their employment or other mutual aid or protection. This chapter examines the process by which employees decide whether, and by whom, to be represented, and how an appropriate collective bargaining unit is determined.

Question Concerning Representation

Q 4.1   What is a question concerning representation?

A question concerning representation (QCR) exists if a union desires to represent a group of employees and the employer does not voluntarily recognize the union as the employees' representative. In such case, the union, the employer, or the employees must petition the National Labor Relations Board (NLRB) for a representation election. A QCR also exists when a decertification petition challenges the representative status of a bargaining agent currently recognized by the employer. Section 9 of the NLRA empowers the NLRB to investigate petitions and conduct elections and provides a mechanism for resolving QCRs.

Resolving QCRs Without the NLRB Process

Voluntary Recognition of a Union

Q 4.2   Can an employer voluntarily recognize a union?

Yes. An employer can voluntarily recognize a union without an NLRB election where the employer and the union agree that (1) a majority of employees in a bargaining unit chooses the union as their representative, and (2) those employees constitute an appropriate collective bargaining unit. Unions often rely on card check and neutrality agreements to achieve recognition from employers.

Neutrality Agreement

Q 4.3   What is a neutrality agreement?

A neutrality agreement is an agreement between a union and an employer, sometimes negotiated as part of a collective bargaining agreement between an employer and a labor organization representing employees at one or more of the employer's facilities, in which the employer agrees not to oppose the union's efforts to organize unrepresented employees at the employer's facilities identified in the agreement.

Q 4.3.1   What do neutrality agreements typically provide?

Neutrality agreements typically provide that an employer will not engage in certain campaign tactics in opposition to a union organizing campaign, such as anti-union speech or conduct.[1] Captive-audience speeches, indirect threats to act against union supporters, and personal campaigning by supervisors are among the lawful or borderline-lawful techniques that employers have used to defeat unionization.[2] (Permissible and impermissible activities during a campaign are discussed at Q 4.51 *et seq.*) In some cases, the use of neutrality agreements can prevent unnecessary litigation before the NLRB regarding these issues and may facilitate the development of a harmonious relationship after recognition.[3]

Through a neutrality agreement, the parties agree to the rules governing permissible electioneering during an organizing drive. Neutrality agreements are a form of contract, so unions and employers may agree to a wide range of terms. Accordingly, neutrality agreements can take many forms, including, but not limited to the employer agreeing:

- to remain neutral in the event the union attempts to organize employees;

- to waive the right to an NLRB-conducted election;

- to follow certain procedures that govern the employer's conduct during a union organizing drive;

- to refrain from making disparaging comments about the union;

- to remain silent during an organizing drive.

The LMRA, however, prohibits an employer from paying, lending, or delivering any money or "thing of value" to a union that is seeking to organize the company's workers.[4] There is a circuit split among the federal courts of appeals as to whether an employer's agreement to provide organizational assistance to a union in a neutrality agreement violates the LMRA. In *Mulhall v. Unite Here Local 355*, the Eleventh Circuit found that an employer's agreement to: provide the union with information about and access to its employees; allow the union to organize through check cards rather than a secret ballot; and remain neutral to the union's organization efforts could be "things of value" in violation of the LMRA, particularly where the employer's agreement was in exchange for the union's agreement to provide $100,000 to support a state ballot initiative of the employer.[5] In contrast, the Third and Fourth Circuits found that an employer's organizational assistance does not provide any ascertainable value to the union and does not violate the LMRA.[6] The U.S. Supreme Court dismissed a petition to review the *Mulhall* decision, leaving this issue unsettled.[7]

Q 4.3.2   Are employers obligated to accept neutrality agreements?

Generally, neutrality agreements are not a mandatory subject of bargaining. Accordingly, employers are free to reject union demands for neutrality. However, the NLRB has held that a union can picket to pressure an employer to enter into a neutrality agreement because a union's mere request that an employer agree to a neutrality agreement does not constitute a "present" demand for recognition triggering section 8(b)(7) limits on recognitional picketing.[8] As such, picketing to obtain a neutrality agreement, unlike picketing to obtain a pre-hire agreement, may not violate the NLRA.

Q 4.3.3   How are neutrality agreements enforced?

Neutrality agreements are generally considered collective bargaining agreements subject to enforcement under section 301 of the Labor Management Relations Act. Accordingly, when a party seeks to enforce a neutrality agreement, it can (1) file suit in federal district court to enforce the agreement under section 301 of the LMRA[9] or (2) enforce the agreement through arbitration.[10] The NLRB has stated that "national labor policy favors the honoring of voluntary agreements reached between employers and labor organizations."[11] Thus, the question is really one of estoppel. A party, having chosen to proceed under an agreement and having derived benefits from it, should not be permitted to pick and choose which provisions it wishes to invoke and which it prefers to avoid.[12]

Card Check Agreement

Q 4.4   What is a card check agreement?

Under a card check agreement, an employer and labor union resolve a QCR by reviewing union authorization cards. The employer agrees that if a majority of the employees has signed such cards, it must recognize the union.[13]

Q 4.4.1   When are neutrality and card check agreements used by unions?

Unions often use neutrality and card check agreements with large employers with whom they already have an existing collective bargaining relationship. These agreements are very useful for unions in terms of organizing. Over 75% of organizing campaigns in which employers agree to both neutrality and card checks are successful. This is slightly higher than the unions' success rate in NLRB-supervised elections.

Q 4.4.2   Why do employers agree to neutrality and card check agreements?

Employers may choose to enter into neutrality and card check agreements for a variety of reasons, such as:

(1)   to obtain union concessions at another facility;

(2)   to avoid negative publicity or regulatory issues stemming from a union's "corporate campaign"; or

(3)   because they are facing political pressure.

Employers may also agree to neutrality in order to settle lawsuits, administrative charges, and other claims that unions often bring as pressure tactics.

Q 4.4.3 Are employers obligated to accept card check agreements?

An employer is under no obligation to accept a card count as proof of majority status, absent a clear agreement to do so. There must be a clear, express, and unequivocal statement by the employer that it intends to be bound by a card count.[14] Where the parties agree to such an agreement, the NLRB will hold them to it and will dismiss a petition filed by a union, even in circumstances where the union argues that the agreement will result in an arbitrator deciding unit placement and scope issues.[15] Absent such an agreement, an employer may refuse to recognize the union and demand an NLRB-conducted election without violating its duty to bargain.

 CASE STUDY: *In re Verizon Information Systems & Communications Workers of America*[16]

In Verizon Information Systems, the NLRB held that a union was bound by the terms of a neutrality and card check agreement that it had entered into. The union and employer executed a "Memorandum of Agreement Regarding Neutrality and Card Check Recognition," according to which the employer was required to provide substantial information about the employer's employees to the union. In addition, the agreement mandated that, in the event the parties were unable, after negotiating in good faith for a reasonable time, to agree upon the scope of an appropriate unit for bargaining, the issue of the scope of such unit should be submitted to final binding arbitration.

Pursuant to the terms of the agreement, the union received information about the employer's employees. The parties discussed the scope of appropriate bargaining units, but they were unable to

---

agree whether the employees should be organized into single-plant units. After the parties reached an impasse, the employer invoked the arbitration clause of the agreement, and the issue of the scope of the bargaining unit was scheduled for arbitration.

The union, however, informed the employer that it represented a majority of the employees and that, if the employees did not agree to recognition by card check, the union would file a representation petition with the NLRB. The union noted that, after the NLRB's determination of the appropriate bargaining units, the union could revert back to the card check or proceed with an election. The employer asked the NLRB to dismiss the petition or to hold it in abeyance so that the scope of the bargaining unit could be determined by the arbitrator, pursuant to the terms of the parties' agreement. The NLRB noted that national labor policy favored honoring voluntary agreements and that it would enforce such agreements, including agreements that explicitly addressed matters involving union representation between employers and labor organizations.[17]

The NLRB ruled that that the employer and union had reached complete agreement regarding a procedure for voluntary recognition outside of the NLRB's representation election processes. The NLRB observed that the union had obtained significant rights to information about employees, access to employees on the employer's premises, a pledge of employer neutrality, prompt recognition of the union by the employer upon a demonstration of majority support, and prompt commencement of good-faith bargaining. The union, having invoked the agreement, therefore, was held to its bargain, including arbitration over the scope of the bargaining unit. To do otherwise would permit the union to take advantage of the benefits accruing from its valid neutrality agreement while avoiding its commitment by petitioning to the NLRB for an election. The NLRB dismissed the union's representation petition.

Q 4.4.4   Can an employer and a union agree to substantive provisions to be included in a future CBA as part of their card check recognition agreement?

An employer and a union may agree to substantive issues that must be included in a future CBA as part of their card check agreement, so long as the employer does not recognize the minority union as the employees' exclusive bargaining representative.

In *Dana Corp.*, the Board found no violation of the NLRA where an employer and a minority union entered into a letter of agreement setting forth certain preliminary matters and a general framework for future bargaining in the event the union was able to obtain majority support. The letter of agreement also specified steps the parties would take if they were unable to reach a final agreement, including submission of outstanding issues to a joint committee and then to interest arbitration. The Board found that although the LOA created a framework for future collective bargaining, nothing in the LOA affected the employees' existing terms and conditions of employment and any potential impact on the employees would require substantial additional negotiations following recognition. As such, the Board determined that the LOA did not preclude the employees' free choice of representation and thus did not constitute an unfair labor practice.[18] The employer violates the NLRA, however, if it recognizes a minority union as the employees' bargaining representative and negotiates a complete CBA with that union to be signed when it obtains majority status.[19]

Polling

Q 4.5   Can an employer recognize a union's majority status through polling?

Polling employees regarding their support for the union is another informal way to recognize a union's majority status. The NLRB has held that, where an employer responds to a union's demand for recognition by seeking to determine majority status by, for example, polling employees, it may not lawfully deny the results.[20] The union's demand for recognition must precede the employer's polling to determine the union's majority status. Thus, polling that occurs before the demand for recognition will not waive the employer's right to a NLRB election.

The NLRB's decision in *Struksnes Construction Co.*[21] sets the standards for a lawful employer inquiry into a union's claim of majority support. Polling employees is a violation of section 8(a)(1) unless:

(1)   the purpose of the poll is to determine the truth of a union's claim of majority status;

(2)   this purpose is communicated to the employees;

(3)   assurances against reprisal are given;

(4)   the employees are polled by secret ballot; and

(5)   the employer has not engaged in unfair labor practices or otherwise created a coercive atmosphere.[22]

Challenging an Employer's Voluntary Recognition

Q 4.6   When may employees challenge an employer's voluntary recognition of a union as bargaining representative?

In 2011, the NLRB re-established its historical "recognition bar" doctrine in *Lamons Gasket*. Following an employer's voluntary recognition of a union, representation elections are barred for a reasonable period of time—no less than six months after the parties' first bargaining session and no more than one year. The NLRB's decision overruled its 2007 decision in *Dana Corporation*, which had given employees the right to challenge an employer's voluntary recognition of a union by filing a decertification petition within forty-five days' time after receiving notice of the employer's recognition of the union.

Under *Lamons Gasket*, to determine whether a reasonable period has elapsed, the NLRB applies the multifactor test set out in *Lee Lumber & Building Material Corp.*:

(1) whether the parties are bargaining for an initial contract;

(2) the complexity of the issues being negotiated and of the parties' bargaining processes;

(3) the amount of time elapsed since bargaining commenced and the number of bargaining sessions;

(4) the amount of progress made in negotiations and how near the parties are to concluding an agreement; and

(5) whether the parties are at impasse.[23]

The recognition bar is discussed further at Q 4.15.

Q 4.6.1   If a collective bargaining agreement is executed following an employer's voluntary recognition, is the contract binding?

A collective bargaining agreement executed on or after the date of voluntary recognition will be enforced, unless it can be demonstrated that the employer's voluntary recognition of the union was invalid.[24]

Agreement Not to Organize

Q 4.7   Can a union ever agree not to organize?

Yes. Employers and unions can enter into enforceable agreements providing that the union will not organize certain employees. The terms of these agreements vary, but they often contain provisions detailing specific locations where the union can seek to organize and specify a certain number of employees that the union can seek to organize. The NLRB will enforce an agreement not to organize as long as the agreement meets the following criteria:

(1) it contains an express promise;

(2) it is for a reasonable period of time; and

(3) it is the result of a bargain between the employer and the union.

In addition, a union can voluntarily relinquish its representative status. When a viable incumbent union disclaims and waives all interest in continuing to represent the employees covered by the collective bargaining agreement, the collective bargaining agreement ceases to act as a bar to future election.[25]

Withdrawal of Recognition

Q 4.8   Can an employer withdraw recognition of a union without an election?

Yes. An employer can withdraw recognition of, and refuse to bargain with, an incumbent union (subject to the contract, recognition, and election bars, discussed below), if the union, in fact, has lost majority support. An employer that believes the union lacks majority support may:

(1)   petition for an NLRB-supervised election contesting a union's majority status if the employer has a good-faith reasonable doubt as to the union's majority status;

(2)   withdraw recognition of, and refuse to bargain with, the union if the union, in fact, lacks majority status; or

(3)   conduct an internal poll of employee support for the union if the employer has a good-faith reasonable doubt as to the union's majority status.

The NLRB had a longstanding rule that, before an employer could take any one of the above steps, it needed "a good-faith reasonable doubt" as to whether a majority of its employees continued to support an incumbent union. The U.S. Supreme Court, in *Allentown Mack Sales & Service v. NLRB*, held that this reasonable good-faith doubt standard for polling, an employer's petition for election, and withdrawal of recognition was consistent with the NLRA.[26] However, in a later decision, the NLRB abandoned this approach. It developed a new standard for employer withdrawals of recognition, and now an employer who withdraws recognition from an incumbent union is required to prove that the union had, in fact, lost majority status at the time of the withdrawal.[27] The NLRB retained the good-faith reasonable doubt (that is, reasonable uncertainty as to the union's majority status) standard for employer election petitions and left open whether the standard for polling should be changed.

An employer's unilateral withdrawal of recognition is typically challenged by the union in ULP proceedings asserting a refusal to bargain. The NLRB, in *Levitz, Inc.*,[28] held that the employer must prove that the union had, in fact, lost majority support at the time the employer withdrew recognition.[29] Thus, an employer assumes the risk of a section 8(a)(5) complaint if it withdraws recognition on evidence other than the results of an election testing a union's majority status, even if the employer has a reasonable good-faith, but erroneous, belief that the union has lost its majority.[30]

   CASE STUDY: *Parkwood Development Center*[31]

An employer must be cautious when making an anticipatory announcement of withdrawal of recognition. In *Parkwood Development Center*, the employer declared on December 2, 2002, that it would be withdrawing recognition of the union as of the expiration of the collective bargaining agreement on March 8, 2003, because the employer had received a petition from a majority of the bargaining unit employees stating that they no longer wished to be represented by the union.

On March 8, 2003, the union presented a petition with employee signatures and authorization cards to the employer demonstrating conflicting evidence that the union continued to enjoy majority status. The NLRB ruled that the employer was not entitled to rely on its evidence existing on December 2, 2002, to support its withdrawal on March 8, 2003.

An employer can only follow through on an announcement of anticipatory withdrawal of recognition if the employer can prove actual loss of majority support on the date that recognition is subsequently withdrawn.

Q 4.8.1   What kind of evidence proves (or disproves) a union's loss of majority support?

"Actual loss" of majority status requires a showing of an actual numerical loss of the union's majority support. This can be established by direct evidence, such as employees' firsthand statements regarding their own personal opposition to the incumbent union. The employer may also present a petition that establishes that a numerical majority of unit employees no longer desire representation by the incumbent union. If, however, an employer's showing of "actual loss" is established solely or in part by hearsay evidence, such as employees' and supervisors' statements regarding other employees' union statements, the case will be subject to greater scrutiny by the NLRB.[32] An employer cannot rely solely on a decline in dues check-off authorizations; such a decrease is not determinative of a union's loss of majority status. The employer also cannot rely on a period of dormancy in negotiations with the union, particularly when the collective bargaining agreement, by its terms, renews itself.[33]

Any evidence presented by the employer in support of its withdrawal of recognition must also be untainted and valid. The NLRB, union, or employees, may present rebuttal evidence to show that the employer's evidence is unreliable. The NLRB General Counsel's office has identified the following examples of evidence that may taint an employer's evidence of "actual loss":[34]

- The employer had prior unremedied unfair labor practices.

- The employee petition used by the employer to demonstrate loss of majority support was sponsored by the employer.

- Employees were coerced into signing the petition used by the employer to demonstrate loss of majority support.

- Employees were misinformed as to the purpose of the petition used by the employer to demonstrate loss of majority support. This may occur where:

  (1) the employees were told the petition was for an election, as opposed to outright withdrawal of recognition;

(2)　the employees were told the petition was for an unrelated purpose; or

(3)　the petition did not contain any information or headings indicating its purpose was to demonstrate employee support for withdrawal of recognition.[35]

- Allegations of forged signatures. Faced with such evidence, the NLRB may authenticate the employees' signatures through affidavit testimony or questionnaires.

- Employee testimony or statements disavowing anti-union statements attributed to the employee. For example, if an employee joins the union after signing an anti-union petition, the employer is precluded from counting that employee among the opponents of the union in determining whether the union had lost majority support.[36]

Similarly, an employer cannot rely on signatures to an anti-union petition that were revoked prior to withdrawal, and the union is not obligated to warn the employer that it has collected such revocations.[37]

The NLRB, union, or employees may also present rebuttal evidence to show that the union enjoyed majority status at the time the employer withdrew recognition. This evidence includes pro-union petitions. The relevance of such rebuttal evidence depends, in part, on whether it existed before or after withdrawal.[38] The employer ultimately bears the burden of proving "actual loss" by a preponderance of the evidence.[39]

Q 4.9　Can an employer use a petition for election in an attempt to halt union organizing efforts?

When Congress enacted section 9(c)(1)(B) as part of the LMRA in 1947, it recognized the potential for abuse in giving employers expanded rights to petition for an election—that employers might file petitions for an election early in organizational campaigns in an effort to obtain a vote rejecting the union before the union had a reasonable opportunity to organize. So when it enacted section 9(c)(1)(B) as part of the LMRA in 1947, Congress included language limiting employer petitions to cases in which the union has presented a "claim to be recognized as the representative as defined in section 9(a)." The NLRB has consistently construed section 9(c)(1)(B) as requiring evidence of a union's "present demand" for recognition as the majority representative of an employer's employees before an employer may petition for a representation election. Absent such a claim for recognition, the employer is not entitled to an election. Employer petitions and what constitutes "present demand" are discussed further at QQ 4.11.6 and 4.12.

Petitions for an NLRB Representation Election

In General

Q 4.10 · What is the NLRB's 2015 rule on representation case procedures?

On December 15, 2014, the NLRB issued a final rule amending the longstanding regulations governing representation case procedures. The rule became effective on April 14, 2015, and has reduced the time between the filing of an election petition and the election itself by, among other things:

(1)   limiting the pre-election representation hearing to determining whether there is a question of representation and whether the unit is appropriate;

(2)   giving hearing officers the authority to limit the presentation of evidence during pre-election hearings to the party's contentions regarding the question concerning representation and the appropriate unit—hearing officers may defer issues concerning unit exclusions and individual eligibility until after the election is conducted to be considered only if those issues are outcome determinative;

(3)   giving hearing officers discretion regarding whether to permit parties to file post-hearing briefs, including the subjects to be addressed and the time for filing briefs, if the briefs are allowed;

(4) deferring all requests for NLRB review of the regional director's direction of election until after the election and consolidating any such request with election objections and post-election rulings—this also eliminates the recommended twenty-five-day period between the regional director's direction of election and the election itself, because parties no longer have a right to seek pre-election review from the NLRB;

(5) creating uniform procedures for resolving election objections and potentially outcome-determinative challenges in stipulated and directed election cases—the rule eliminates parties' ability to agree to mandatory NLRB review of election issues in a stipulated-election agreement;

(6) granting the NLRB discretion to deny review of regional directors' rulings absent "compelling reasons" justifying review; and

(7) eliminating what the Board deems to be other unnecessary and redundant representation case rules and regulations.[40]

This is not an exhaustive list of all the changes made by the 2015 rule. More details can be found in the final rule's "List of Amendments."[41]

Note that the provisions in this rule are substantially the same as those issued by the NLRB in 2011. The 2011 rule was invalidated by the U.S. District Court for the District of Columbia in 2012 because the Board lacked a quorum when the rule was issued.[42]

Filing the Petition

Q 4.11　How does a party commence representation proceedings before the NLRB?

The NLRB's election process is activated when one party petitions for an election in accordance with section 9(c) of the NLRA.[43] A petition may be filed by any person or labor organization acting on behalf of a substantial number of employees or by an employer after a labor organization has presented it with a claim to be recognized. The petition is filed with the regional director for the region in which the proposed or actual bargaining unit exists.[44]

The regional director then investigates the petition. If the regional director determines that a QCR exists, a secret ballot election will be directed. During the investigation into the petition, the regional director examines:

- whether the employer's business affects commerce within the meaning of the NLRA;

- the appropriateness of the bargaining unit; and

- whether there has been an adequate showing of interest by the employees in having the NLRB determine a QCR.[45]

LABOR MANAGEMENT LAW FACT

The NLRB requires that the filing of a petition seeking certification or decertification of a union be accompanied by a showing that 30% or more of the employees in the bargaining unit seek to be represented by the union or seek to decertify the currently recognized union.

Types of Petitions

Q 4.12   What are the different types of representation petitions the parties can file?

The NLRB has instituted different kinds of petitions depending upon the specific QCR and how the QCR is presented. The following are the different types of representation petitions that may be filed with the NLRB:

- RC petition (filed by employees or labor organizations);

- RD petition (filed by employees seeking decertification);

- UD petition (filed by employees seeking to de-authorize a union security provision);

- UC petition (filed by a labor organization or an employer seeking a unit clarification);

- AC petition (filed by a labor organization or an employer seeking an amendment of the union's certification); and

- RM petition (filed by an employer).

Q 4.12.1   What is the RC petition?

Certification of Representative. Under section 9(c)(1)(A)(i) of the NLRA, an RC petition may be filed by or on behalf of employees, alleging that a substantial number of employees wish to be represented for collective bargaining and that their employer declines to recognize their representative. The RC petition specifically asks whether any labor organization currently represents the petitioned-for group. Although RC petitions are commonly filed by a labor organization seeking to represent a group of employees that is currently unrepresented, an RC petition may be filed by a rival union seeking to unseat the employees' current collective bargaining representative. The petitioner must make a "showing of interest," meaning that it must present evidence demonstrating that at least 30% of the employees in the bargaining unit are interested in being represented by a particular labor organization. Where a representative has not previously been recognized or certified, such a 30% showing presents a QCR.

Q 4.12.2   ... the RD petition?

Decertification. An RD petition is typically filed by employees seeking to decertify their current collective bargaining representative. Under section 9(c)(1)(A)(ii), an RD petition may be filed by or on behalf of employees, alleging that a substantial number of employees assert that the certified or currently recognized bargaining representative is no longer their representative. The petitioner must make a showing of interest demonstrating that at least 30% of the employees in the bargaining unit favor an election. A petition for decertification presents a QCR, unless it was filed by a supervisor or was otherwise tainted by employer assistance, in which case the petition will be dismissed. (See QQ 4.23 and 4.23.1.)

Q 4.12.3   ... the UD petition?

Withdrawal of Union Security Authority. A UD petition ordinarily is filed by a group of employees interested in terminating their obligation to pay dues to their collective bargaining representative. Under section 9(e)(1), a UD petition may be filed by or on behalf of employees and must allege that 30% or more of the employees constituting an appropriate unit wish to rescind an existing union security agreement. (See Q 4.23.3.)

Q 4.12.4   ... the UC petition?

Unit Clarification. A labor organization or an employer may file a UC petition seeking clarification of an existing bargaining unit. A UC case is initiated by the filing of a petition alleging that a labor organization is currently recognized by the employer, but that the petitioner seeks clarification of the placement of certain employees or certain jobs in the unit under section 9(b) of the NLRA.

Generally, the NLRB will not clarify a bargaining unit during the term of a collective bargaining agreement when the agreement clearly defines the unit. The NLRB will consider a UC petition filed shortly after an agreement is executed when the parties dispute whether a certain classification should be part of the unit, unless there is an indication that the petitioner abandoned a request for clarification in exchange for some concession during the negotiations of the agreement.[46]

Q 4.12.5   ... the AC petition?

Amendment of Certification. A labor organization or employer may file an AC petition seeking amendment of an outstanding certification of bargaining representative. Amendments of certifications are most frequently sought when there is a change in the name or affiliation of the employer or the certified labor organization.

Q 4.12.6   ... the RM petition?

Employer Petition. Under section 9(c)(1)(B), an employer may file an RM petition, which alleges that a union has made a present demand for recognition as the exclusive bargaining representative or that the continued majority status of an incumbent union is in question.

Nothing in section 9(c)(1)(B) requires an employer to file a petition for an election; it merely gives the employer the option to petition the NLRB. An employer is not obligated to accept a union's proof of majority support, nor is the employer required to petition for an election if it refuses to voluntarily recognize the union. (See Q 4.23.2.) "Unless an employer has engaged in an unfair labor practice that impairs the electoral process, a union with authorization cards purporting to represent a majority of the employees, which is refused recognition, has the burden of taking the next step in invoking the [NLRB's] election procedure."[47]

Present Demand for Recognition

Q 4.13   What is a present demand for recognition?

The NLRA contemplates that a union that is not presently the majority representative may decide when or whether to test its strength in an election by the timing of its demand for recognition by the employer. The mere fact that the union is engaged in activities that it hopes will eventually lead to recognition by the employer is not evidence of a present demand for recognition such as would support the processing of an employer petition.[48] A union makes a "present demand for recognition" when, for example, it requests that the employer sign a collective bargaining agreement with the union.

Q 4.13.1   Does picketing constitute a present demand for recognition?

It depends. Informational picketing that truthfully advises the public that an employer does not employ members of, or have a contract with, a union does not, without more, establish that the union has made a "claim to be recognized" as required by section 9(c)(1)(B).[49] Further, area-standards picketing complaining of the employer's failure to pay area standard wages or benefits does not constitute a demand for recognition that would support an employer's recognition petition.[50] To establish that picketing is tantamount to the existence of a present demand, an employer must show that the picketing is done in conjunction with other union actions or statements establishing that the union's real objective is to obtain immediate recognition as the employees' representative. Other actions or statements indicating a "present demand" include a demand by the union for a contract or a statement by the union that picketing would cease as soon as the employer agreed to negotiate and sign an agreement.[51]

Once evidence of such action or intent exists, the employer may invoke the election process under the NLRB.

Dismissal of a Petition/Election Bars

Q 4.14   When will the NLRB dismiss a representation petition?

The NLRB will dismiss a representation petition when no QCR exists. Generally, there can be no QCR during a time period in which an incumbent union's majority status cannot be challenged. During these circumstances, the NLRB applies certain election "bars," including the contract bar, the recognition bar, the statutory one-year election bar, the certification bar, the blocking-charge rule, unlawful employer conduct, and the fluctuating work force rule.

Q 4.15   What is a contract bar?

A petition for an election may be brought any time when no existing agreement is in place. However, when a representation election petition is filed for a group of employees who are alleged to be covered by a collective bargaining agreement, the NLRB must decide whether the contract bars the petition by inquiring whether the contract in fact exists and whether it conforms to certain requirements. The basic requirements are:

(1) the agreement must be in writing and for a definite duration;

(2) the agreement must be signed by all parties;

(3) the agreement must contain substantial terms and conditions of employment deemed sufficient to stabilize the bargaining relationship;

(4) the agreement must clearly by its terms encompass the employees involved in the petition; and

(5) the agreement must cover an appropriate unit.

If the NLRB finds that a collective bargaining agreement exists and that all the requirements are met, the contract will be deemed to be a bar to an election.

The following agreements do *not* act as a bar to an election:

*   contracts not in writing or not signed;

*   contracts that do not specify a fixed term or are terminable at will;

*   contracts with an illegal union security clause;

*   contracts with an inappropriate bargaining unit;

*   contracts that on their face discriminate between employees on racial grounds;

*   contracts that cover union members only.

Q 4.15.1   When does a contract bar expire?

The contract bar reflects an agency policy in favor of contract stability and precludes the NLRB from directing elections among employees for the duration of a valid collective bargaining agreement for up to a three-year period. A collective bargaining agreement for a period of more than three years bars an election for only three years following the effective date of the agreement. In other words, the end of the contract bar is the expiration date of the collective bargaining agreement or, if the term of the collective bargaining agreement exceeds three years, the last day of the third year.

Balancing both the interest in contract stability and permitting the parties an opportunity to negotiate a renewal agreement free of the distraction of representational issues, the NLRB requires that a petition for an election must filed no earlier than ninety days from the expiration date of the agreement or the end of the three-year period and no later than sixty days from that date. Essentially, employees or rival unions have a thirty-day "open period" to file for an election. If the parties do not negotiate a renewal agreement before the expiration date or the end of the three-year period, representation petitions may be validly filed during the "hiatus" between agreements.

Q 4.15.2   What is the "open period" when a collective bargaining agreement does not act as a bar to election?

There is an open period during which a valid collective bargaining agreement ceases to operate as a bar to an election. Specifically, a petition for an election may be filed sixty to ninety days prior to the end of an existing collective bargaining agreement, or the three-year period, whichever is sooner. If the collective bargaining agreement involves a healthcare institution, the open period under which petitions can be filed runs from 120 days to ninety-one days before the end of the collective bargaining agreement. At the end of the open period (sixty to ninety days for non-healthcare employers), the NLRB will not accept any election petitions in order to allow the parties to the current collective bargaining agreement an opportunity to negotiate a new agreement without the threat of interruption.

Q 4.15.3   Does the contract bar continue if the parties extend the term of the agreement?

Modification of a collective bargaining agreement can extend the contract bar period. A contract will be considered extended if, during the term of an existing collective bargaining agreement, the parties agree to amend or execute a new collective bargaining agreement that contains a later terminal date than that of the existing collective bargaining agreement. An extension of the collective bargaining agreement generally does not act as a bar to an election petition that has been timely filed during the "open period."[52]

Q 4.16   What is the recognition bar?

The recognition bar, or voluntary recognition bar, is a kind of election bar that limits employees' right to a decertification or rival union petition after the employer voluntarily recognizes a union, regardless of whether a card check, neutrality agreement, or both preceded the recognition. Under *Lamons Gasket Co.*[53] (discussed further at Q 4.6, above), an election bar will be imposed for a reasonable period of time—no less than six months after the parties' first bargaining session and no more than one year. To determine whether a reasonable period has elapsed, the NLRB applies the multifactor test set forth in *Lee Lumber & Building Material Corp.*:

(1) whether the parties are bargaining for an initial contract;

(2) the complexity of the issues being negotiated and of the parties' bargaining processes;

(3) the amount of time elapsed since bargaining commenced and the number of bargaining sessions;

(4) the amount of progress made in negotiations and how near the parties are to concluding an agreement; and

(5) whether the parties are at impasse.[54]

The NLRB will not apply the recognition bar where, at the time of recognition, another union is seeking to organize the employer's employees.[55] Further, the NLRB will not dismiss a rival union's petition where the rival union can show it represented at least 30% of the unit at the time of recognition.[56]

Q 4.17 What is the statutory one-year election bar?

The statutory one-year election bar precludes the NLRB from holding a second representation election in the same unit within twelve months of a valid election.[57] Any election petition filed during this period will be dismissed. While a petition for an election can be filed up to sixty days prior to the end of the twelve-month period, the election may not be held until after the twelve-month period has expired. The twelve-month period begins running from the date of the election. Even if the NLRB holds a hearing with respect to challenges or objections, the election bar runs from the date of the representation election, not from the date that the NLRB resolves any post-election challenges or objections.

Importantly, the election bar only applies to the specific unit or subdivision in which the previous election was held. In other words, a new election may be held in a larger unit, such as a plant-wide unit, prior to the expiration of the twelve-month period.

The election bar does not apply to a prior voluntary recognition.

Q 4.18   What is the certification bar?

If a union receives the majority of votes in an election, the union will be certified by the NLRB as the exclusive bargaining representative of the employees. A certified union is entitled to an irrebuttable presumption of majority support for up to twelve months, and a petition filed during this twelve-month period will normally be barred.[58] This presumption of a union's continuing majority status is nearly conclusive. Absent "unusual circumstances," an employer must recognize a union for the entire certification year, even if it has evidence that the union has lost its majority status. Unusual circumstances include a schism within the certified union (serious organizational rift within the union), or radical fluctuation in the size of the bargaining unit within a short period of time.[59]

If the employer has committed unfair labor practices during the certification year, the NLRB will extend the certification bar to give the union the benefit of one full year of bargaining free of employer ULPs.[60]

Q 4.19   What is the blocking-charge rule?

The blocking-charge rule is an NLRB policy that authorizes the regional director to delay holding a representation or decertification election until pending ULP charges affecting the voting unit are resolved. The charging party must specifically request that the election petition be blocked, and must simultaneously file a written offer of proof in support of the charge. Ordinarily, if the offer of proof describes evidence adequate to prove the blocking charge, the petition will be held in abeyance.[61]

The NLRB may also choose to proceed while a charge is pending, depending on the following factors:

(1) the length of time the charge has been pending;

(2) the fact that employees in the unit have not had an election during that period;

(3) the fact that previous charges based on the same pattern of conduct as the pending charges were dismissed;

(4) the eleventh-hour filing of the charges;

(5)   the existence of a strike; or

(6)   the charging party's history of filing charges to delay representation proceedings.

See Q 4.61.5 for discussion of voter eligibility in elections that are held while a charge is pending.

The NLRB usually will not proceed to an election, absent the charging party's request to do so, until all pending ULPs are resolved. Absent a finding of a violation of the NLRA, or an admission by the employer of such a violation, there is no basis for dismissing a petition based on a settlement of alleged but unproven ULPs.[62]

Q 4.20   When are election petitions dismissed because of unlawful employer conduct?

The NLRB may dismiss an election petition where there is evidence that the employer unlawfully dominated or assisted the petitioning union. For instance, where supervisors assist in obtaining authorization cards, the regional director may dismiss the election petition. The NLRB will look at the totality of the circumstances to see if there was "a pattern of unlawful assistance sufficient to taint a proposed card majority."[63] If the authorization cards have been tainted due to supervisory participation, the showing of interest required for the election petition may be impaired, and the petition will be dismissed.[64] Dismissing a petition on these grounds will not affect a subsequent petition, provided a new showing of interest has been obtained without the assistance of supervisors.

Q 4.21   When will a fluctuating work force require dismissal of an election petition?

Generally, the NLRB will not hold an election where the employer is undergoing substantial changes or a representative employment complement has not yet been established. Such a dismissal will not bar a subsequent petition once the work force has stabilized. However, the NLRB will not dismiss the petition if the current number of employees constitutes a substantial percentage of the expected employee complement and covers nearly all of the anticipated job classifications.[65]

The treatment of seasonal employees is different from that of a fluctuating work force. The NLRB has consistently found a showing of interest among employees in a seasonal industry to be adequate, but usually requires the election to be held at the approximate seasonal peak since a truly representative vote in the off-season is not possible.[66] If the peak has already passed, the NLRB will generally fix the election date for the next seasonal peak.[67]

Withdrawal of a Petition

Q 4.22   Can a union withdraw a representation petition?

A union may request a voluntary withdrawal of a representation petition either orally or in writing, and a petition may be withdrawn only with the consent of the NLRB. NLRB policy favors a union's genuine voluntary request to terminate the proceeding, because the NLRA provides other parties with adequate alternate processes for seeking unionization when the union no longer desires to proceed on its petition.[68]

The NLRB will deny a request for withdrawal if:

- the withdrawal request is accompanied by inconsistent action by the union—for example, if the union engages in a strike or picketing for recognition at the time the withdrawal request is made, the request will be denied;[69]

- the withdrawal request is submitted while objections to the election are pending;

- a valid election has been conducted and the intent of the withdrawal is to circumvent the restrictions imposed on subsequent elections by section 9(c)(3).[70]

A union's statement that it will continue organizing in the future does not necessarily create a sufficient basis of inconsistent conduct on which to deny the union's request for withdrawal. The NLRB permits withdrawal regardless of whether the employer opposes the action. The NLRB's approval or rejection of the withdrawal request will not take into consideration the expenditure of resources, even when the request for withdrawal is made shortly before the election.[71]

Decertification

Q 4.23   Can employees remove a union as their bargaining representative?

Yes. Employees can remove a union as their bargaining representative through a procedure called decertification. Employees file a decertification (RD) petition (see Q 4.12.2) with the NLRB asserting that the currently certified or recognized union no longer represents the employees in the bargaining unit. This petition requires a 30% showing of interest and must be filed at a time the NLRB will consider a QCR—that is, there is no bar to an election.

Q 4.23.1   What are the requirements for filing a decertification petition?

Under section 9(c)(1)(A)(ii), an employee, group of employees, or individual must file a decertification petition requesting an election to determine whether a majority of the employees in the unit support the union. The petition must be supported by a showing of interest demonstrating that at least 30% of the employees in the current unit no longer desire to be represented by the incumbent union.

The petition must be filed in accordance with the contract, recognition, and election bars to elections. Generally, the NLRB will not order a decertification election within one year after a representation election. And a valid collective bargaining agreement will generally bar the filing of a decertification petition for up to three years, other than during the open period immediately before the contract expires. A decertification election, whatever its outcome, bars another NLRB election for a one-year period.

Q 4.23.2   Can employers "decertify" a union?

If the employer receives substantial evidence that the union no longer has the support of a majority of the bargaining unit, the employer can take the following action:

- petition for an NLRB-supervised RM election under section 9(c)(1)(B) contesting a union's majority status if the employer has a reasonable good-faith doubt of the union's continuing majority and it is during a time that a QCR will be entertained by the NLRB (see Q 4.12.6);

- unilaterally withdraw recognition from and refuse to bargain with the union if the union in fact lacks majority status; or

- conduct an internal poll of employee support for the union if the employer has a reasonable good-faith doubt as to the union's majority status (such a poll must satisfy certain procedural safeguards—see Q 4.5); poll results may be used to consider the other options set out above.[72]

Q 4.23.3   Can employees remove a union security clause from their collective bargaining agreement?

The objective of a de-authorization (UD) proceeding is to determine whether or not a majority of the eligible employees within a unit covered by a collective bargaining agreement desire to rescind the union security clause from the contract. A de-authorization case is initiated by the filing of a petition by employees whereby the employees indicate their desire to rescind the authority to maintain such a clause. The unit covered by the UD petition must have the same scope as the unit covered by the union security clause.[73] An employer may explain to employees their rights regarding the filing of a de-authorization petition, but the employer should be wary about encouraging such a filing so as to avoid tainting the petition or an unfair labor practice charge on account of employer coercion.

Q 4.23.4   Can a union use a blocking-charge strategy to interfere with a decertification election?

The NLRB has a general policy of suspending the processing of a decertification petition where a concurrent ULP is filed alleging conduct that, if proven, would interfere with employee free choice in a decertification election. This type of union-initiated charge is referred to as a "blocking" charge and is discussed above (see Q 4.19).

The regional director can, in his or her discretion, determine that the election should proceed despite the blocking charge, and will consider:

(1) the character, scope, and timing of the conduct alleged in the charge and the conduct's tendency to impair the employees' free choice;

(2) the size of the work force relative to the number of employees involved in the events or affected by the conduct alleged in the charge;

(3) whether the employees were bystanders to or the actual targets of the conduct alleged in the charge;

(4) the entitlement and interest of the employees in an expeditious election;

(5) the relationship of the charging parties to the labor organizations involved in the representation case;

(6) the showing of interest, if any, presented in the case by the charging party; and

(7) the timing of the charge.

Election Agreements

Q 4.24   What is a pre-election agreement?

Many NLRB elections are held pursuant to an agreement between the interested parties as opposed to an NLRB direction of election. After a petition is filed, the case is assigned to an NLRB agent for processing. If the region determines that the petition should be processed further, the agent will attempt to secure agreement of the parties. These agreements contain stipulations between the parties as to the appropriate unit, as well as the date, time, and location of the election.

There are several types of election agreements utilized by the NLRB's regional offices. These include:

- the stipulated-election agreement,

- the consent-election agreement, and

- the full-consent agreement.

Q 4.24.1   What is a stipulated-election agreement?

The stipulated-election agreement is an agreement between the parties (petitioners, intervenors, and employer) that establishes the appropriate unit, as well as the election details, but does not waive any post-election procedures with respect to the election. Under the NLRB's rules and regulations,[74] after a petition has been filed, and with the regional director's approval, the parties may enter into a stipulated-election agreement, which provides for a waiver of hearing, for an election. A stipulated-election agreement also must include a description of the bargaining unit, the time and location of the election, and the payroll period that will be used to determine eligibility to vote.

Q 4.24.2   What is a consent-election agreement?

The consent-election agreement is an election agreement where the parties agree to the appropriate unit and election details and agree to waive the parties' rights to request review of the election procedures from the NLRB. Under the NLRB's rules and regulations,[75] after a petition has been filed, the parties may, with the regional director's approval, enter into a consent-election agreement, which provides for the regional director to resolve any factual dispute arising from the consent election. The regional director's rulings and determinations of the election results will be final, as if issued by the NLRB. The agreement must include a description of the bargaining unit, the time and location of the election, and the payroll period that will be used to determine eligibility to vote.

Q 4.24.3   What is a full-consent agreement?

Under the NLRB's rules and regulations,[76] after a petition has been filed and with the regional director's approval, the parties may enter into an agreement whereby the regional director will settle any issue necessary to resolve the QCR. This agreement typically is referred to as a full-consent agreement. Under a full-consent agreement, the regional director's decision after any hearing will be final, as if issued by the NLRB, as will his or her rulings and determinations of the election results. Like a consent-election agreement and a stipulated-election agreement, a full-consent agreement must include a description of the bargaining unit, the time and location of the election, and the payroll period that will be used to determine eligibility to vote.

Representation Hearings

Q 4.25 What is an NLRB representation hearing and when is it held?

Pre-election representation hearings are part of the administrative process to determine whether a QCR exists. After the filing of a petition, if the parties cannot reach an agreement, a representation hearing will be conducted, during which all parties will have the opportunity to appear and present evidence about the issue in dispute. Unless a case presents unusually complex issues, the representation hearing is held eight days after the notice of hearing is served by the Region. The Region typically serves the notice of hearing on the same day that a petition is filed. After the hearing closes, a decision is issued in which an election will be ordered or the petition will be dismissed.

NLRB Hearing Officer

Q 4.25.1 Who presides over a representation hearing?

The hearing is conducted by an NLRB hearing officer, typically an employee from the regional office administering the petition. The hearing is essentially a fact-finding conference so that the regional director (acting as a delegatee of the NLRB) has the information he or she requires to make a determination regarding the appropriate unit. In theory, the hearing is investigative and non-adversarial; in practice, the employer and the union are adversarial parties. Accordingly, the hearing officer's role is non-adversarial. The hearing officer's job during the hearing is to guide, direct, and control the presentation of evidence at the hearing to ensure that a complete and accurate record is developed for the regional director. The hearing officer is charged with ensuring that the record is complete, while at the same time keeping the record as short as is commensurate with its being complete. The hearing officer does not make any recommendations. Decisions in the representation case are made, in the first instance, by the regional director (acting as a delegatee of the NLRB).

Q 4.25.2   What kinds of issues are adjudicated in NLRB representation hearings?

The NLRB's 2015 rule on representation case procedures includes several provisions governing the scope of issues litigated at representation hearings. First, the rule clarifies that the purpose of the hearing is to determine whether there is a question concerning representation. The regional director can therefore bar litigation of issues not necessary to resolving the question of representation. Second, the rule requires the non-petitioning party to submit a statement of position prior to the hearing, and any arguments not raised in that statement will be waived. Finally, the petitioning party is required to respond to this statement of position at the start of the hearing, and is bound by those responsive positions.[77]

The representation hearing will begin with a determination of jurisdiction. If the parties do not stipulate to the NLRB's jurisdiction, the hearing officer will take evidence on whether the NLRB may properly assert jurisdiction over the matter. The hearing officer will also assess the union's status as a labor organization and take evidence regarding same if necessary. Issues relating to contract bar, recognition bar, union merger, and accretion are also adjudicated at the representation hearing.

In most representation hearings, however, the bulk of the hearing is devoted to producing evidence pertaining to the scope and composition of the appropriate bargaining unit. The hearing officer will, therefore:

(1)   explore the parties' prior bargaining history, if any;

(2)   take evidence on the community of interest factors;

(3)   review the scope of the unit (for example, multi-facility or multi-employer);

(4)   address issues regarding residual units, healthcare units, craft and construction units, and department units, among others; and

(5) elicit the parties' positions on part-time employees, casual and on-call (or per-diem) employees, seasonal employees, and probationary employees.

The parties are generally not permitted to put on evidence regarding:

(1) the adequacy of the showing of interest;

(2) allegations that authorization cards were improperly procured;

(3) allegations regarding the commission of unfair labor practices, unless such ULPs are germane to the QCR;

(4) the eligibility of employees for union membership; and

(5) alleged union violations of federal law.[78]

Q 4.25.3 What is the statement of position and when is it due?

The statement of position is a form that solicits the employer's position on all issues that will be adjudicated at the representation hearing, including:

- whether the Board has jurisdiction over the petition;

- whether the proposed unit is appropriate (and if not, why);

- any job positions that should be added to or excluded from the unit to make it appropriate;

- any individuals whose voting eligibility the employer intends to contest;

- the existence of any election bars;

- the time, date, location, and format of the election; and

- any other issue the employer intends to raise.

Importantly, if an employer fails to raise an issue in a timely filed statement of position, it will be precluded from arguing that issue at the hearing or in later proceedings.

In addition to identifying issues that will be litigated, the statement of position must also include a list of all employees in the proposed unit. If the employer contends that the proposed unit is inappropriate, the employer must also include separate lists of the employees it contends should be added to or excluded from the unit.

The statement of position, including the preliminary voter list, must be filed with the Regional Director and served on all parties by noon on the business day before the hearing.[79]

Intervenors

Q 4.25.4   Which parties are permitted to participate in an NLRB representation hearing?

All parties have the right to participate in the hearing, as do any prospective intervenors (labor organizations who wish to intervene in the election). The representation hearings are open to the public unless otherwise ordered, and employees and other interested parties often attend.

Sometimes during representation hearings, an outside union will seek to participate in the election by making a motion to intervene. Such motions may be made orally or in writing. A request for intervention will only be granted where the intervenor can make a sufficient showing of interest. A single authorization card is sufficient to be deemed a participating intervenor. A participating intervenor can participate in the representation hearing and appear on the ballot, but cannot block a consent election. If an intervenor can present a showing of interest from 10% or more of the voting unit, the intervenor is deemed a full intervenor and can also block a consent election. An intervenor who can present a showing of interest from 30% or more of the voting unit has the additional ability to seek its own unit. For example, an intervenor with a 30% or more showing of interest from the maintenance employees in a plant-wide wall-to-wall unit can seek to sever the maintenance employee unit from the larger wall-to-wall unit.

Order of Proceedings

Q 4.25.5   What is the order of proceedings in NLRB representation hearings?

Under the NLRB's 2015 rule on representation case procedures, the hearing will be scheduled eight days after notice is served on the parties. At least one day prior to the hearing, the non-petitioning party must submit a statement of position on the issues as well as a preliminary list of all employees eligible to vote in a union election. At the start of the hearing, the petitioning party will be required to respond to this statement of position.[80]

Prior to a scheduled hearing, the hearing officer also will discuss the critical facts and issues with the parties and will make every effort to secure a stipulated-election agreement to avoid the delay and expense of a hearing. The hearing officer will prepare a written stipulation, for signature by the parties at the hearing, that covers all of the generally uncontested issues for hearings, as well as any other issues that are not in dispute.

There is no set order of presentation in a representation hearing. However, in most cases, the employer proceeds first. If the parties are unable to agree on the order of presentation, the hearing officer will direct the order of testimony. Witnesses at the hearing are sworn in by the hearing officer and are subject to cross-examination by the other parties. Documents and records, if relevant, are received into evidence as exhibits.

Q 4.25.6   Are parties permitted to file post-hearing briefs after a representation hearing?

Under the NLRB's 2015 rule on representation case procedures, post-hearing briefs are permitted only at the discretion the regional director. The timing and subject matter of the briefs are also set at the discretion of the regional director. Before the 2015 rule, post-hearing briefs generally were submitted as a matter of course.[81]

The Decision

Q 4.25.7   How and when is a decision in a representation hearing issued?

The hearing officer will prepare a report containing findings of fact and recommendations as to the disposition of each issue. The hearing officer will file his or her report with the regional director shortly after the close of the hearing. After reviewing the hearing officer's report, the regional director will issue a decision. The decision usually comes within a few days of either the close of the hearing or the submission of the parties' post-hearing briefs. The decision contains:

(1)   jurisdictional determinations;

(2)   a description of the appropriate bargaining unit (if necessary);

(3)   eligibility for voting of various part-time and temporary employees;

(4)   rulings on the union's status as a labor organization;

(5)   a determination on any potential recognition or contract bar issues; and

(6)   a determination on whether any outside labor organizations have properly intervened.

If the regional director's decision calls for an election, the decision will also contain a direction of election. This direction of election will ordinarily include the details of the election, such as its date, time, and place.

Q 4.25.8   Can the decision in a representation hearing be reviewed?

The parties may file a request for review of the regional director's decision with the NLRB. The NLRB will grant a request for review only if "compelling reasons" exist. Pursuant to the NLRB's rules and regulations,[82] compelling reasons include:

(1) a substantial question of law or policy is raised based on NLRB precedent;

(2) the regional director's decision contains a clearly erroneous prejudicial finding; and

(3) the conduct of the hearing or a ruling related to the hearing has resulted in prejudicial error.

The filing of a request for review does not stay the direction of election.

Appropriate Bargaining Unit

Overview

Q 4.26   What is a bargaining unit?

A bargaining unit is:

> a group of two or more employees who share a "community of interest" and may reasonably be grouped together for collective-bargaining purposes. . . . A unit is usually described by the type of work done or job classification of employees—for example, production and maintenance employees or truckdrivers. In some cases, the number of facilities to be included in a bargaining unit is at issue, and a unit may be described by the number of locations to be involved. . . . Generally, the appropriateness of a bargaining unit is determined on the basis of the community of interest of the employees involved. The NLRB may also consider factors such as any history of collective bargaining and the desires of the affected employees.[83]

Any election in a representation case must be conducted in an appropriate unit.

Q 4.27   Why is the issue of unit determination important?

Unit determination is of critical importance for at least three reasons: First, occupants of job classifications in the unit will be the electorate voting in the NLRB representation elections. Employers usually want broad units, while unions petition for narrow units because they are easier to organize and win over. Second, the unit defines the level of mandatory bargaining. The parties may agree to bargain on a broader basis, but if they cannot agree, the unit will be the basis for bargaining. Finally, the unit determines the area of concern for which the union owes a duty of fair representation and the impact of employer decisions on jobs in the unit will be a key subject matter for grievance arbitration between the parties.

Q 4.28   Who determines the scope and composition of the appropriate unit?

The NLRB has the ultimate authority to determine what constitutes an appropriate bargaining unit. Initially, the petitioner (a union, an employee, or the employer) defines the bargaining unit in filling out the petition. If one of the other parties objects to the scope of the bargaining unit, these differences can be resolved by an agreement between the parties. (See Q 4.24 *et seq.*) Typically, where the parties agree on an appropriate bargaining unit, the NLRB will honor the agreement.

If the parties do not agree, the regional director will hold a representation hearing to determine the appropriateness of the petitioner's proposed unit. (See Q 4.25 *et seq.*) If the employer opposes the petitioned-for unit, the employer generally will be required by the NLRB to state which unit or units it believes are "appropriate." The NLRB first examines the petitioned-for unit. If that unit is appropriate, the NLRB's inquiry ends. However, if the petitioned-for unit is not appropriate, the NLRB can examine alternative units suggested by the parties or select a different appropriate unit.

Q 4.29   How does the NLRB determine what is an appropriate bargaining unit?

The NLRB determines the appropriateness of a bargaining unit on the basis of whether employees in the petitioned-for unit share a sufficient community of interest to be organized as a discrete and cohesive group for collective bargaining purposes. There is no precise definition of "community of interest," and the NLRB makes determinations on a case-by-case basis. In general, the community-of-interest standard encompasses all aspects of the employment relationship, seeking to include in the unit only employees who have substantial shared interests as to wages, hours, and other terms and conditions of employment. These factors might include whether employees are covered by the same personnel policies, have the same supervisors, perform integrated work functions, or work in a location separate from others at a facility.

In addition to the community-of-interest test, the NLRB gives significant weight to the parties' history of bargaining, unless there are "compelling circumstances."[84] Other factors in a bargaining unit determination include:

(1) the extent and type of union organization involved (although this cannot be the controlling factor);

(2) the wishes of the employees; and

(3) the appropriateness of the proposed unit in relation to the organizational structure of the company.

Q 4.29.1 In the determination of the appropriate unit, how much weight is given to prior bargaining history?

Prior bargaining history will be given substantial weight when determining whether a particular unit is appropriate. For example, if a unit of employees had decertified one union and was being organized by another, the NLRB might examine the composition of the former unit. Also, in some instances the NLRB might look at the history, extent, and type of union organization in other plants of the same company or in the same industry.[85] Because it seeks to achieve stability in labor relations, the NLRB is unlikely to disturb a historical bargaining unit, whether established by certification or by agreement. Bargaining history is persuasive, but not dispositive; the party opposing a historical unit bears a heavy burden to demonstrate the unit is no longer appropriate.[86]

There are several notable exceptions in which substantial weight may not be given to prior bargaining history; these include instances where:

(1) bargaining history is associated with conduct contrary to NLRB policy or based on oral contract;[87]

(2) the duration of the bargaining history spans less than a year;[88]

(3) bargaining history is associated with separate and distinct units of employees;[89] and

(4) the workplace has undergone reorganization, decentralization, or some other substantial change.[90]

Note that bargaining history is different from "extent of organization." Extent of organization refers to employees or groups of employees the union has organized.

Q 4.29.2   ... "extent of organization"?

The NLRA allows the NLRB to consider the groups of employees on which the union has focused its organizing campaign, so long as it is only one factor used in making a unit determination.[91] Extent of organization may play a significant role in the NLRB's unit determination, but under section 9(c)(5) of the NLRA, it cannot be given controlling weight. Therefore, a unit based solely on the extent of organization will be inappropriate.

Q 4.29.3   ... the wishes of employees?

In cases where employees might appropriately be included in a number of units, employees sometimes are permitted to choose in a self-determination election which unit they want to join.[92]

Q 4.29.4   ... appropriateness of the organizational structure of the unit?

Employers usually want units to coincide with organizational structures, and the NLRB gives considerable weight to similarity of working conditions among employees, lines of supervision, and degree of functional integration in operations in making unit determinations.[93]

Q 4.29.5   May age, race, or gender be considered when determining the composition of a unit?

Age and race are never valid grounds for including or excluding certain employees in a bargaining unit.[94] Gender is also an improper consideration when composing a unit.[95]

Q 4.29.6   What other factors affect the composition and scope of an appropriate voting unit?

Under the express terms of the NLRA, the NLRB may not consider units appropriate that include both security guards and other employees, and professional employees may not be joined with non-professional employees without the former's consent. In addition, the NLRB provides substantial guidance on the composition of units in certain industries.

Q 4.30   Does the NLRB have to choose the most appropriate bargaining unit?

No. The NLRA does not require that a unit for bargaining be the only appropriate unit or even the most appropriate unit. Rather, the NLRA requires only that the petitioned-for unit be "appropriate."[96]

In some cases, employees might appropriately be included in any of several bargaining units. Due to the wide differences in employee organizations, Congress gave the NLRB broad authority to determine bargaining units. The NLRB will direct an election in a petitioned-for unit as long as it is deemed to be "appropriate" in light of the community-of-interest test. Because the petitioned-for unit need not be the most appropriate unit, a petitioning union may seek to include employee groups it believes will maximize its opportunity to win an election, as long as they constitute an appropriate unit.

Under NLRA section 9(c)(5), the NLRB cannot treat the extent of union organization as a controlling factor in determining the appropriate unit. In practice, however, the NLRB will tend to accept the unit the union has petitioned for if it is otherwise appropriate.

If an employer opposes a proposed unit on the grounds that it should be part of a larger, more inclusive unit of employees, the Board will consider whether the excluded employees have meaningfully distinct interests that outweigh their similarities with unit members. In making that determination, the Board will apply the traditional community-of-interest test, which generally considers whether the employees are organized into separate departments; have distinct skills and training; have distinct job functions and perform distinct work; are separately supervised; are functionally integrated with other employees; have frequent contact with other employees; interchange with other employees; and otherwise have distinct terms and conditions of employment. Notably, the Board no longer applies the *Specialty Healthcare* standard, which had placed the burden on employers to show that the excluded employees shared an "overwhelming community of interest" with the petitioned-for unit.[97]

Q 4.31 Can an NLRB determination of the appropriate unit be challenged?

Yes, but a party's ability to challenge the regional director's determination of an appropriate unit is extremely limited. Unit determination issues ordinarily are resolved by the regional director prior to holding an election. If the parties have agreed to unit composition, through a consent agreement or a stipulated election agreement, and the NLRB accepts the agreement, the parties cannot later seek review of the unit definition. Where the parties did not agree and, after a hearing, the regional director issued a decision and direction of election defining the unit, either party can file a request for review with the NLRB. However, the NLRB will grant discretionary review of the regional director's decision only in limited circumstances.

If review is granted, the NLRB's procedure for determining an appropriate unit under section 9(b) is to examine first the petitioned-for unit. If that unit is appropriate, then the inquiry into the appropriate unit ends. If the petitioned-for unit is not appropriate, the NLRB may examine the alternative units suggested by the parties, but it also has the discretion to select an appropriate unit that is different from the alternative proposals of the parties.[98] Once the NLRB has determined the unit, courts will not review the NLRB's decision except

possibly in the context of a later refusal-to-bargain unfair labor practice case against the employer. An employer that alters the scope
of the bargaining unit without the consent of the union or the NLRB
commits an unfair labor practice.[99]

Presumptively Appropriate Units

Q 4.32   What is a presumptively appropriate unit?

Certain proposed units are presumptively appropriate (subject to
rebuttal in a given case), including:

- a unit that includes all of the employer's employees, except
  for those employees excluded for statutory or policy reasons;

- a unit of all professional employees employed by the employer;

- a unit of all guards employed by the employer; and

- a single facility or plant where an employer operates multiple
  facilities or plants.

When the unit sought is presumptively appropriate, the burden
is on the party opposing the unit to show the unit is inappropriate.

Q 4.32.1   What kinds of employees cannot be included in a bargaining unit?

See Q 4.36.

Q 4.32.2   What kinds of employees are considered "professional" employees?

The Board may not certify a unit that comprises both professional
employees and non-professional employees without the former's
consent. Whether an employee can be classified as a professional
employee depends on the type of work performed by the employee,
not on the individual qualifications, experience, or educational background of the employee. Under section 9(b)(1) of the NLRA, a professional employee is any employee who is engaged in work that

(1) is predominantly intellectual and varied in character, as opposed to routine mental, manual, mechanical, or physical work;

(2) involves the consistent exercise of discretion and judgment in its performance;

(3) is of such character that the output produced or the result accomplished cannot be standardized in relation to a given period of time; and

(4) requires knowledge of an advanced type in a field of science or learning customarily acquired by prolonged course of specialized intellectual study in an institution of higher learning or a hospital.

The NLRB has applied the statutory definition to find the following groups of employees "professional":

- accountants;[100]
- architects;[101]
- graduate nurses;[102]
- industrial designers;[103]
- pharmacists and apprentice pharmacists;[104]
- newspaper journalists;[105] and
- full-time faculty members at a private, nonprofit university.[106]

See Q 4.42 for a discussion of "technical employees," who do not meet the requirements of "professional employees."

Q 4.32.3   Can professional employees be included in a unit with non-professional employees?

Professional employees are usually organized into separate units consisting only of professionals. Professional employees, however, can be included in a unit with non-professional employees if a majority of the professional employees votes for inclusion in such a unit.[107] Even where a majority of professional employees has voted to be included in a unit that also includes non-professional employees, those professional employees are not bound to that vote in future elections. Professional employees must be given a separate ballot in every representation election.

Q 4.32.4   What kinds of employees are classified as "guards" under the NLRA?

Under section 9(b)(3), the NLRB may not consider units appropriate that include both security guards and other employees. Guards are individuals employed to enforce rules to protect the employer's property or to protect the safety of people on the employer's premises against other employees and other persons.[108] Where an individual performs guard duties and non-guard duties, the NLRB will consider the individual a guard if the guard duties are an essential part of the job. Thus, part-time guards cannot be included in a unit with non-guards.

The NLRB has found "guards" to include individuals who protect the property of their employer's customers; firefighters; and unarmed production and maintenance employees who are regularly assigned as gate watchmen. On the other hand, the classification of "guard" does not extend to production and maintenance employees who only rarely and sporadically serve as watchmen; janitors who serve as night watchmen, checking exits, locks, and lights; employees who install and maintain alarm devices; or receptionists who control admission to offices but do not actually enforce plant security rules.

Q 4.32.5   When will the NLRB determine that a single-facility unit is appropriate?

Single-facility units are localized bargaining units such as a plant or store. Generally, a single-facility unit is presumptively appropriate, unless the employees of the single-facility unit have been merged into a more comprehensive unit or have been so integrated with the employees in another location as to lose their separate identity.[109] Where the presumption is present, it is the burden of the party seeking a multi-facility unit to rebut the presumption.

In determining whether a single-facility unit or a multi-facility unit is appropriate, the NLRB considers a number of factors, including:

(1)   bargaining history;

(2)   central control over labor relations;

(3) local autonomy;

(4) similarity of employees' skills, functions, and working conditions;

(5) supervision;

(6) degree of employee interchange;

(7) plant and product integration; and

(8) distance between locations.[110]

Q 4.32.6 When will the NLRB determine that a multi-facility unit is appropriate?

A multi-facility unit is a bargaining unit under which one bargaining agreement covers employees who work at different geographic sites. In certain industries, such as public utilities, construction, and ocean transportation, the NLRB has favored multi-facility bargaining units over single-facility units. The factors used to determine whether a multi-facility unit is appropriate are the same as those used to determine if a single-facility unit is appropriate.

Q 4.32.7 Is an employer-wide unit appropriate?

The NLRB previously presumed that employer-wide units can be appropriate.[111] In recent years, however, the NLRB has shown a general preference for finding single-facility units presumptively appropriate. In determining whether the single-facility presumption has been rebutted, the NLRB will analyze such factors as:

- centralized control over daily operations and labor relations and the extent of local autonomy;

- similarity of employee skills, functions, and working conditions;

- degree of employee interchange;

- distance between locations; and

- bargaining history.[112]

Q 4.32.8   Are multi-employer units ever appropriate?

A multi-employer situation exists when two or more employers band together for purposes of bargaining with a union. Multi-employer bargaining is common in industries such as construction, retail, hotel, and trucking. The NLRB will not hold an election on a multi-employer basis; rather, multi-employer bargaining is established only by mutual consent of the parties.[113] Employers can manifest their consent by expressly delegating bargaining authority to a multi-employer association or by past or current participation in the multi-employer bargaining process.[114] The formation of the unit must be voluntary, and the NLRB will not hold an election for a multi-employer unit if any of the parties object.

In determining appropriateness of a multi-employer unit, the NLRB will consider, among other factors, the following:

(1)   the history of collective bargaining;

(2)   the intent of the parties;

(3)   the nature and character of the joint bargaining;

(4)   the contract executed by the parties; and

(5)   whether effective withdrawal from multi-employer bargaining had occurred.[115]

Residual Units and Excluded Parties

Q 4.33   What if the proposed unit does not include all of the employer's employees?

When a proposed unit excludes a particular classification of employees, those excluded employees still are entitled to have an opportunity to be represented. As such, the regional director must consider the unit placement of all employees (as defined by the NLRA) of the employer. Groups of employees left out of established bargaining units may constitute an appropriate "residual" unit, provided they consist of all unrepresented but eligible employees.[116] For example, where a group of laboratory employees had been excluded from the production and maintenance unit and were therefore unrepresented, representation in a separate unit on a residual basis was held appropriate.[117]

It is NLRB policy not to create a residual unit where the employees could be included in the larger group[118] or where the unit sought is comprised of only a segment of all the unrepresented employees.[119] Where the record is insufficient to establish whether the requested residual unit includes all unrepresented employees, the NLRB will remand the matter to the regional director.[120] The regional director must ensure that the record includes a full description of all excluded classifications (other than classifications excluded from unit inclusion by statute or by NLRB policy) so as to allow the regional director and the NLRB to determine the excluded employees' unit placement.[121]

Q 4.34   Can parties enter into agreements that exclude certain groups of employees from a proposed unit?

Unions and employers may agree to stipulations that exclude certain groups or categories of employees from a unit. These stipulations must be entered into the record and supported by a statement of sufficient facts to justify approval by the regional director.[122] Once parties have stipulated to the exclusion of employees from a unit, they normally are bound by their agreement.[123] However, if the agreement clearly contradicts the NLRA or established policy, the NLRB can disregard the agreement and make its own determination. (See Q 4.29.5.)

Accretion to Existing Unit

Q 4.35   What happens to an existing bargaining unit when the employer starts a new operation?

When a company starts a new operation, the question arises as to whether the employees in the new operation are an "accretion" to the existing unit or a separate appropriate unit.

Q 4.35.1   What is the doctrine of accretion?

The NLRB defines an accretion as "the addition of a relatively small group of employees to an existing unit where these additional employees share a community of interest with the unit employees and have no separate identity."[124] The union representing the existing unit might insist that its collective bargaining agreement covers employees at the new facility (accretion), while the employer or a different union might claim the new employees are a separate appropriate unit.

Accretion issues arise in the following contexts:

(1)   deciding the scope of a contract bar;

(2)   petition for an election;

(3)   a unit clarification proceeding;

(4)   an unfair labor practice case where the general counsel alleges that an employer unlawfully added employees to a unit where there is no accretion and the union did not represent a majority of those added;[125] or

(5)   a dispute in front of a labor arbitrator, if there is a collective bargaining agreement between the parties, and the union maintains that the employer is failing to apply the collective agreement to a particular group of workers.

It is the policy of the NLRB to find accretions "only when the additional employees have little or no separate group identity . . . and when the additional employees share an overwhelming community of interest with the preexisting unit to which they are accreted."[126]

To resolve the issue, the NLRB will consider the following factors:

(1)   whether employees at the new and old facilities are separated physically or geographically;

(2)   whether they share the same supervision and have similar pay, hours, and working conditions;

(3)   the history of bargaining;

(4)   the type of work being done by the groups; and

(5)   the degree of employee interchange.

For example, the NLRB found that employees of a grocery store day care center were not an accretion to an existing unit of retail grocery store employees. The NLRB reasoned that the day care employees had little or no work contact or interchange with unit employees, performed completely dissimilar job functions, required specialized licensing and educational prerequisites for hiring, and had separate health insurance, savings, and pension benefits.[127]

Parties sometimes include an "after-acquired facilities" clause in their collective bargaining agreement. In this clause, the employer agrees to recognize a union as the representative of employees in facilities acquired after the execution of a collective bargaining agreement and to apply the contract to those employees upon proof of majority support for the union (for example, the union must show majority support through a card check). In such a situation, the NLRB will not order an election, and the employer will be required to honor the agreement.[128]

Bargaining Unit Eligibility of Specific Types of Employees

Q 4.36   Which employees may not be included in any bargaining unit?

The following groups of individuals are excluded from the definition of "employee" in section 2(3) of the NLRA and may not be a part of any bargaining unit:

- agricultural laborers;

- domestic servants of any family or person at his home;

- individuals employed by a parent or spouse;

- independent contractors;

- individuals employed by an employer subject to the Railway Labor Act; and

- individuals employed by a person who is not an "employer" as defined in the NLRA.

In addition, it is the NLRB's policy to exclude "labor nexus" confidential employees. For further discussion of excluded employees, see chapter 1.

Q 4.36.1   Who is considered an independent contractor?

Any individual having the status of an independent contractor cannot be part of a bargaining unit. The NLRB determines whether an individual is an independent contractor on a case-by-case basis by applying general principles of agency. The party asserting that an individual is an independent contractor bears the burden of proving that status.

In addition to the traditional test of whether the employer has the "right to control" the individual's work, the determination of whether an individual is an independent contractor may also consider, among other factors:

- whether the work performed is an essential part of the company's regular business;

- whether the individual is engaged in an occupation or business that is distinct from the company's regular business;

- the person's entrepreneurial opportunity for gain or loss;

- the length of time for which the person is employed or contracted;

- the skill required in the particular occupation;

- whether the company provides the tools and instrumentalities necessary to perform the work; and

- the method of payment of the individual.[129]

The NLRB has found, for example, that newspaper deliverers are independent contractors, where:

(1) the employer did not exercise control over the deliverers' work or discipline them;

(2) the deliverers provided their own mode of transportation; and

(3) the contracts with the employer indicated an intent to form an independent contractor relationship.[130]

Q 4.37   Can supervisors be included in a bargaining unit?

Although the NLRA (as amended by the LMRA) specifically excludes supervisors from the definition of employee,[131] the statute does not bar employers from allowing their supervisors to organize and bargain collectively. Under section 14(a) of the LMRA, supervisors may become union members, but employers may lawfully discharge such supervisors for involvement in union activities and can refuse to engage in collective bargaining with them or their unions.[132]

Q 4.37.1   Who are managerial employees?

Managerial employees are those who formulate and effectuate policies for the employer. Factors that indicate managerial status include:

(1) receipt of salary and participation in benefit programs in a manner equivalent to the corresponding payment by salary and a relatively flexible work schedule; and

(2) significant discretion in the formulation or implementation of policy for the employer, or the ability to make significant purchases or extend credit on behalf of the employer.

Q 4.37.2   Can managerial employees be included in a bargaining unit?

Managerial employees are considered representatives of management, and—as with supervisors—the employer can insist on their exclusion from any bargaining unit comprising non-supervisory and non-managerial employees even if the managers have no supervisory authority as such. Managerial employees also have no right to organize or bargain collectively.

Q 4.37.3   Can management trainees be included in a bargaining unit?

The placement of a management trainee within a unit requires a determination of the employee's supervisor and management status as well as the employee's community of interest with unit employees.[133] The determination will include the following considerations:

(1) whether the trainee's continued employment depends on entrance into management such that, if not accepted, the individual must leave the employ of the employer;

(2) whether the employer maintains a planned management training program; and

(3) whether management trainees and other employees have different working conditions or compensation structures.

For example, manager trainees whose training program, ranging from three to six years, was devoted to learning all store duties, but who had no authority to hire, discharge, adjust grievances, discipline employees, or make effective recommendations as to such actions, and who shared the same fringe benefits and working conditions with other employees lacked statutory indicia as supervisors and were thus included in the unit.[134]

Q 4.37.4   Are relatives of management, owners, or stockholders allowed to be part of a bargaining unit?

The NLRA specifically excludes any individual employed by his or her parent or spouse from the protections of the NLRA, and thus from inclusion in a bargaining unit. This exclusion from bargaining units includes the children and spouses of individuals who have substantial stock interests in closely held corporations. Employees who are children or spouses of sole or majority stockholders are excluded from bargaining units under this rule.

Q 4.38 Which employees are considered "confidential employees" not allowed to be part of a bargaining unit?

An individual is excluded from a bargaining unit as a "confidential employee" if that individual assists and acts in a confidential capacity with respect to a member of management who formulates, determines, and effectuates labor relations policies. Such an employee is called a "labor nexus" confidential employee and is treated as aligned with management, along with supervisory and managerial employees.

Access to, and use of, confidential labor relations information such as personnel files and discipline information are important factors in the determination of confidential-employee status. Also, access to information utilized in establishing wage and fringe benefit policies or formation of other employee policies may act to disqualify an employee as a confidential employee. Examples of confidential-employee status under the NLRA frequently include assistants to human resources directors and assistants to chief executive officers.

Q 4.39 Who qualifies as a "temporary worker" who may be excluded from a bargaining unit?

Outside of the construction industry, where employment tends to be on a project-only basis, those who are employed for only one project for a short duration or who do not have a substantial expectancy of continued employment are considered temporary workers and are generally excluded from the bargaining unit. For instance, workers who were hired for temporary positions not to exceed ninety days have been treated as not covered by the NLRA.[135]

Temporary workers, however, may be included in a bargaining unit if the employees have uncertain or indefinite tenure. Thus, employees who were given assurances of indefinite employment during job interviews or who were never informed that their employment was temporary have been held eligible to vote in a unit of warehouse employees.[136]

Often, temporary employees are formally employed by a temporary employment agency, (that is, a supplier employer), but are considered joint employees of the supplier employer and a host employer.

Over the past two decades, the Board has gone back and forth on whether employer consent is required for a unit that combines jointly employed temporary employees with the permanent employees of the host employer.[137] Under current Board law, such units are appropriate as long as the community-of-interest test is satisfied, and no employer consent is required.[138]

Q 4.39.1 Can seasonal workers be included in a bargaining unit?

Seasonal employees who have a reasonable expectation of re-employment to unit work in the foreseeable future may be included in a bargaining unit. Factors considered include:

(1) whether the employer draws from the same labor force each season;

(2) whether former employees are given preference in rehiring;

(3) whether the duties, working conditions, and supervision for seasonal employees are similar to those of permanent employees; and

(4) whether seasonal employees can become permanent employees.[139]

It is the NLRB's policy to direct elections involving seasonal employees at or near the peak of the season so that a maximum number of seasonal workers will have an opportunity to vote.[140] For instance, where the employer operates skiing facilities and hires seasonal workers during the ski season, the election must be held near the peak of the ski season.

Q 4.39.2 When is a probationary employee or trainee included in a bargaining unit?

Probationary employees are employees who will obtain permanent tenure upon satisfactory completion of an initial trial period. Probationary employees will be included in a unit along with permanent employees when the probationary employees (1) share the same duties and conditions of employment as permanent employees, and (2) have a reasonable expectation of continued employment upon completion of the probationary period.[141] Note that probationary employees must have actually started work prior to the election eligibility date in order to be included.

Q 4.40   Under what circumstances are strike replacement workers included in a bargaining unit?

An employer is not barred by the NLRA from hiring temporary or permanent replacements even for lawful economic strikers.[142] Generally, temporary replacements hired to perform work during a strike are not considered part of an appropriate unit and ordinarily are not eligible to vote in an NLRB election.[143] Temporary replacements are hired to fill jobs during a strike, with the understanding that their employment may be terminated after the strike has been settled.

In contrast, permanent replacement workers are normally considered bargaining unit employees and are eligible to vote in an NLRB election. Permanent replacements are hired to permanently replace economic strikers. The timing of the replacement worker's hire is the controlling factor in determining whether a permanent replacement will be eligible to vote as part of the unit. Permanent replacements hired prior to the election eligibility date are eligible to vote.

Notably, permanently replaced economic strikers may be eligible to vote under section 9(c)(3) of the NLRA if the election is held within twelve months of the strike's commencement. (See Q 4.61.5.) However, an economic striker loses eligibility to vote by abandoning his or her interest in returning to work, such as by accepting permanent employment with another employer. The NLRB presumes that economic strikers have not abandoned their interest in returning to work, and the party challenging the presumption bears the burden of proving that the strikers have abandoned their interest.[144] Additionally, an economic striker will not be eligible to vote if the employer has eliminated his or her job for non-strike economic reasons or if the employer has discharged or denied reinstatement because the striker engaged in misconduct warranting termination.[145] Where an employer claims that an unreplaced economic striker is ineligible to vote because his or her job was eliminated for non-strike-related reasons, the employer bears the burden of demonstrating that the jobs were in fact permanently eliminated and that its non-strike reasons for their elimination are legitimate.

Q 4.41   Are part-time employees included in a bargaining unit?

Regular part-time employees may be part of a unit that includes full-time employees if the part-time employees perform unit work on a regular basis for a sufficient period of time to demonstrate that they have a substantial and continuing community of interest with the remainder of the unit. Employees with varying hours of work, such as per-diem and on-call employees, may be included in a unit if they are regular part-time employees. The NLRB has established several tests to determine whether an individual is eligible to vote as a regular part-time employee.

The more common approach, known as the *Davison-Paxon* test,[146] holds that an employee is a regular part-time if he or she works an average of four or more hours a week in the quarter preceding the date set for determining eligibility for the unit.[147] Generally, the total number of hours worked in the calendar quarter should be divided by thirteen weeks to determine the average number of hours worked per week. Applying this test, the NLRB found that an employee hired to work in a theater company's box office during a four-week production was eligible to vote because he worked 172 hours during the quarter preceding the eligibility date.[148]

A second test, known as the *Marquette* test,[149] deems an employee as regular part-time if he or she works 120 hours in either of the two calendar quarters immediately preceding the voter eligibility date. This test was formulated for the healthcare industry to accommodate special circumstances in which on-call nursing department employees were required to sign six-month contracts agreeing to be available at specified times. Many of the on-call employees had worked a substantial number of hours over a three-month period, and the NLRB formulated a test that would permit inclusion of these employees but that would exclude the on-call employees who worked only twenty-three hours in a three-month period.

In the construction industry, a part-time employee is eligible to vote (1) if he or she has been employed for at least thirty working days within the twelve months preceding the eligibility date, or (2) if he or she has worked in the twelve months preceding the eligibility date and has been employed for at least forty-five working days in the twenty-four months preceding the eligibility date.[150] The construction industry formula excludes employees terminated for cause or who have voluntarily resigned prior to the completion of the last job on which they worked. It also does not apply to employers that clearly operate on a seasonal basis.

Irregular part-time employees are excluded from inclusion in any bargaining unit as casual employees.

Q 4.42 What employees are considered "technical employees," and in which bargaining unit do they belong?

Technical employees are employees who do not meet the strict requirements of the "professional employee" definition, but whose work is of a technical nature, involving the use of independent judgment and requiring the exercise of special training usually acquired in colleges, in technical schools, or through special courses.[151] Outside the acute-care hospital setting,[152] the placement of technical employees in a unit is based on all of the factors relevant to a community-of-interest inquiry, including:

(1) bargaining history;

(2) common supervision;

(3) similarity of skills and job functions;

(4) contracts or interchange with other employees;

(5) type of industry;

(6) location of employees within the plant;

(7) the desires of the parties; and

(8) whether any union seeks to represent the technical employees separately.[153]

Often, technical employees will not share a community of interest with a production and maintenance unit because their skills and job functions are so distinct. For instance, the NLRB has found that employees working as detailers do not share a community of interest with production and maintenance employees where

(1) their work is more similar to that performed by draftsmen than that performed by production workers;

(2) most of their time is spent performing specialized functions; and

(3) they work in a separate work area with different supervisors and different tools.[154]

On the other hand, a technical assistant in the engineering division of a nuclear power plant is properly included in a production and maintenance unit where his duties are functionally integrated with plant maintenance and he has extensive contact with unit maintenance employees.[155]

Q 4.43   What is a "craft unit"?

A craft unit is a unit consisting of a distinct and homogeneous group of skilled journeymen craftsmen, who, together with helpers or apprentices, are primarily engaged in the performance of tasks that are not performed by other employees and which require the use of substantial craft skills and specialized tools and equipment.[156]

Q 4.43.1   Do craft workers always have the right to be in their own unit?

When a separate craft unit is sought where no prior bargaining history exists, a representation petition seeking to establish the craft unit will generally be granted if the employees included have a separate identity of functions, skills, and supervision.[157] This includes consideration as to:

(1) whether the employees participate in a formal training or apprenticeship program;

(2) whether the employees' work is functionally integrated with the work of the excluded employees;

(3) whether the duties of the employees overlap with the duties of the excluded employees;

(4) whether the employer assigns work according to need rather than based on craft or jurisdictional issues; and

(5) whether the employees share common interests with other employees, including wages, benefits, and cross-training.[158]

For example, the NLRB has held that the following could each constitute a group of craft employees and be represented in a unit separate and apart from other employees: carpenters and upholsterers;[159] automobile mechanics;[160] tool-and-die makers and machinists;[161] and bakers.

If a representation petition seeking an inclusive unit comprising both craft and non-craft employees is sought, a determination election will be held. The self-determination election is used to determine the wishes of the craft employees—that is, whether the craft employees wish to be represented as a separate unit from other employees. In the meantime, the finding of an appropriate unit is put on hold. For example, where one union seeks a production and maintenance unit and another union seeks a craft unit of plumbing-pipefitting employees, including instrument repairmen and welders, elections were directed in three voting groups:

(1) production and maintenance employees,
(2) plumber-pipefitters and welders, and
(3) instrument repairmen.

The direction of election sets out the respective choices: the union seeking a separate unit or the union seeking the more comprehensive unit.[162] A majority of the crafts employees in a group must vote for the union seeking a separate craft unit, in which case the union seeking a craft unit is certified as the group's representative. If a majority does not vote for that union, those employees will be considered to have indicated their desire to remain in the comprehensive unit.[163] Their votes will be pooled with the votes of the employees from the first group. If a majority of the first group, including any pooled votes, votes for the union seeking the comprehensive unit, that union is certified as the representative in the comprehensive unit.

Q 4.43.2 Can a union seek to sever a craft unit from a broader existing unit including non-craft workers?

Section 9(b)(2) provides that the NLRB may not decide a craft unit is inappropriate because a broader unit had been established by prior NLRB determination, unless the craft workers in a self-determination election vote for the more inclusive representation. As a practical matter, the NLRB places considerable weight on the interest in preserving bargaining stability. Under certain circumstances, the craft severance bid will be recognized; a rival union can file a petition seeking recognition in a separate craft unit.

For example, where a petitioning union sought to sever a unit of powerhouse employees from an overall production and maintenance unit, severance was granted in view of all the circumstances, especially the short history of bargaining.[164] The NLRB noted that severance was not an attempt to carve out a craft group with a long history of collective bargaining shared with others, and considerations of stability did not require a denial of severance. Moreover, the powerhouse employees worked in a separate area, under separate supervision, with only occasional contact with the other employees. They were not involved in the production process, and they worked seven-day workweeks, as opposed to the other employees' five-day workweeks. Also, the powerhouse employees were in a special category for purposes of seniority and bumping rights.[165]

Q 4.44 Can maintenance employees obtain a unit separate from production employees?

Employees that make up a maintenance department do not constitute a homogeneous group of skilled craftsmen for whom craft severance is typically granted.[166] Rather, a maintenance group usually consists of a heterogeneous group of diversified workers who perform maintenance functions at locations all over the plant.[167] Although the NLRB has permitted separate representation of maintenance employees in the absence of a prior collective-bargaining history, the Board will not sever a group of maintenance employees from an existing production and maintenance unit where there has been a substantial collective bargaining history on a plant-wide basis.[168]

Q 4.45   Can warehouse employees be included in "wall-to-wall" units?

The general rule is that warehouse employees can be included in plant-wide ("wall-to-wall") units. Whether warehouse employees are included in units of other employees is determined considering the factors set out in the community-of-interest inquiry.[169] Of course, warehouse employees may petition for a separate unit, just as an employer can argue that a separate unit for warehouse employees is appropriate due to community-of-interest factors.

The retail store industry is an exception to the general rule that warehouse employees can be included in wall-to-wall units. In the retail store industry, there is a distinction between employees who perform warehouse duties and employees who perform other functions. The Board presumes that a separate unit of warehouse employees is appropriate where:

(1) the warehouse operation is geographically separated from the retail store operations;

(2) there is a separate supervision of employees engaged in the warehouse functions; and

(3) there is no substantial integration among the warehouse employees and those engaged in other functions.

Proposed warehouse units, however, have been rejected where the functions performed by the warehouse employees were integrated into the functions performed by employees in other areas, including production.[170]

Q 4.46   Can truck drivers be part of a unit that includes other employees?

Yes, truck drivers may be part of a separate unit or combined into a unit with other employees, but the complexity of modern industry generally prevents the application of fixed rules for the unit placement of truck drivers. There is a wide variation in employment conditions with respect to local and over-the-road drivers,[171] between the various industries, and from plant to plant in a given industry. For these reasons, substantial weight is given to the established course of dealings and agreements of parties. But when the parties disagree and there is no bargaining history and no union is seeking to represent the truck drivers separately, the pertinent facts must be considered "to determine wherein the predominant interests of truck drivers are vested."[172]

In making unit determinations involving truck drivers, the NLRB will consider the following community-of-interest factors: (1) whether the truck drivers and plant employees have similar duties, compensation structure, hours, supervision, and other conditions of employment; and (2) whether the truck drivers are engaged in the related production processes or operations, or whether the truck drivers spend a substantial portion of their time in such production or adjunct activities.[173] If the interests shared with other employees are sufficient to warrant their inclusion, truck drivers will be included in a broader unit. For example, in placing driver-salespersons within a unit, the NLRB found that truck drivers were so functionally integrated with plant employees as to preclude separate representation where:

(1)   the drivers spent a substantial amount of time performing the same function as other employees at the terminals, some of whom performed driving duties;

(2)   the drivers had the same supervision, pay scale, and benefits as other employees; and

(3)   the drivers' conditions of employment were substantially the same as that of the other employees.[174]

Q 4.47   Are clerical employees included in units with other kinds of employees?

Based on the type of work performed, clerical employees are usually divided into two distinct groups: (1) office clerical employees, and (2) plant clerical employees. Generally, plant clerical employees perform duties related to the production process, including maintaining inventory, ordering supplies, collecting time cards, and other tasks that assist production. In the course of their work, plant clericals usually have daily contact with production and maintenance employees, report to the same supervisors as unit members, and engage in work related to the production. Accordingly, plant clerical employees generally share a community of interest with the employees in the plant-wide unit.

Office clerical employees—those who perform duties related to general office operations, including tasks such as payroll, billing, and handling the company's phone and mail needs—are customarily excluded from production and maintenance units.[175] For example, the NLRB found appropriate a separate unit of office clericals, declining to include them in a unit of currently unrepresented production employees working in the stockyards, because the hours, working conditions, and educational backgrounds of the office clericals differed from the stockyard employees, with whom they had little work contact.[176] Indeed, office clerical employees generally do not share a community of interest with production and maintenance workers because the clerical employees perform routine office functions, usually have little contact with the production workers, do not engage in production work, and typically have different working conditions, such as hours, compensation, and benefits.

Q 4.48   Can college faculty be excluded from bargaining units?

In some cases, college faculty may be excluded from bargaining units. The U.S. Supreme Court has applied the managerial employee exemption to faculty members who enjoyed a substantial amount of discretionary authority in making and implementing academic policy for the institution.[177] Specifically, the Board has stated that it will primarily consider whether faculty has control over academic programs, enrollment, and finances. Control over academic policies and personnel decisions may be considered but given lesser weight. Moreover, the Board will look for actual control or ability to make effective recommendations, not mere "paper authority."[178] The party seeking to exclude faculty as managerial has the burden of establishing the exclusion.

College or school faculty may also be excluded pursuant to the supervisor exemption. For instance, department heads,[179] program directors,[180] and athletic directors[181] have all been found to be supervisors where they make hiring and firing decisions and determine work assignments. However, faculty members who do not make decisions regarding job status, or who participate in collective decision-making but represent their own interests and not the employer's, are not supervisors.[182] For discussion of the test for supervisors, see Q 1.4.5.

Q 4.48.1   Can part-time faculty be included in regular faculty units?

The NLRB has held that part-time faculty are so substantially different from full-time faculty that they cannot be included in the same unit.[183] In one such case, the NLRB found that part-time faculty members do not share a community of interest with full-time faculty because of the differences regarding compensation, participation in university government, eligibility for tenure, and working conditions.[184] Part-time faculty may organize as a separate unit from full-time faculty.[185]

Q 4.48.2   Can religious faculty at religious colleges be excluded from a unit?

Yes. The Board will assert jurisdiction over purely secular faculty at religious colleges and universities, but will not assert jurisdiction over faculty who are held out as performing a "specific role in creating or maintaining the school's religious educational environment."[186] For example, the Board has excluded faculty from the religious studies department at a catholic university while including faculty from other departments, such as those teaching calculus.[187]

Q 4.48.3   Can graduate students and undergraduate teaching assistants be included in regular faculty units?

Under current NLRB law, graduate students, research assistants, and undergraduate teaching assistants can be included in a unit with regular faculty if they perform work at the direction of the university and do so for compensation.[188] However, the Board has frequently reversed course on whether graduate students and undergraduate teaching assistants are statutory employees over whom it can assert jurisdiction, and it may do so again under the current Republican-majority Board.[189]

Q 4.49   What are the standard bargaining units for healthcare organizations?

Uniquely, in the healthcare industry, the NLRB has established specific units for acute-care hospitals (see below) through its rule-making process. In 1989, the NLRB issued new rules on collective bargaining units in the healthcare industry ("Healthcare Rule"), defining the eight standard units for union elections at acute-care hospitals. Except in extraordinary circumstances, the Healthcare Rule establishes that only the following units are appropriate units in an acute-care hospital setting:[190]

- all registered nurses (see Q 4.49.3);

- all physicians (including residents and interns) (see Q 4.49.4);

- all other professional employees (that is, all professional employees except for registered nurses and physicians—see Q 4.49.5);

- all technical employees (see Q 4.49.6);

- all skilled maintenance employees (see Q 4.49.7);

- all business office clerical employees (see Q 4.49.8);

- all guards (see Q 4.32.4); and

- all other non-professional employees (see Q 4.49.9).

In extraordinary circumstances, alternative units of healthcare employees may be found to be appropriate.[191] The party asserting these extraordinary circumstances exist must make an offer of proof of these circumstances on the record. Examples of extraordinary circumstances include:[192]

- where there is a bargaining history of nonconforming units;

- where units would include five or fewer people;

- consolidation of two or more of the units identified in the Healthcare Rule, absent some other statutory restriction (for example, combining professional with all non-professional employees);

- where the Healthcare Rule would result in residual units;

- where such unusual and unforeseen deviations in circumstances would make it unjust or an abuse of discretion to apply the rules to the facility involved.

The following are not considered to be extraordinary:[193]

- diversity of the industry, such as the sizes of the various institutions, the variety of services offered, including the range of outpatient services, and differing staffing patterns;

- increased functional integration of, and a higher degree of, contact between employees as a result of the advent of the multi-competent worker, increased use of "team" care, and the cross-training of employees;

- impact of nationwide hospital chains;

- recent changes within traditional employee groupings and professions—for example, the increase in specialization of registered nurses;

- effects of various governmental and private cost containment measures; and

- single institutions occupying more than one contiguous building.

Q 4.49.1   What is an "acute-care hospital"?

An acute-care hospital is (1) a short-term-care hospital in which the average length of stay is less than thirty days, or (2) a short-term-care hospital in which over 50% of all patients are admitted to units where the average length of stay is less than thirty days.[194] Many acute-care facilities have the goal of discharging the patient as soon as the patient is deemed healthy and stable. "Acute care" is generally associated with care rendered in an emergency department, ambulatory care clinic, or other short-term-stay facility. A hospital can be an acute-care facility even if it provides non-acute health services, such as long-term care, outpatient care, psychiatric care, or rehabilitative care.[195] But the NLRA specifically excludes facilities that are primarily nursing homes, psychiatric hospitals, or rehabilitation hospitals from the definition of "acute care" hospital in the Healthcare Rule.[196]

A hospital bears the burden to establish that it does not constitute an acute-care hospital.[197] In the case of *Park Manor Care Center*,[198] the NLRB stated: "[w]e hope . . . that after various units have been litigated in a number of individual facilities and after records have been developed and a number of cases decided from those records, certain recurring factual patterns will emerge and illustrate which units are typically appropriate."[199]

Q 4.49.2   How are units of healthcare employees determined outside the acute-care hospital setting?

The Board applies a modified version of the community-of-interest test, called the "empirical community of interest test," to healthcare workers outside the acute-care hospital setting. Under this test, which was established in *Park Manor*, the Board considers the standard community-of-interest factors, plus the factors and evidence considered relevant by the Board in the Healthcare Rule, plus prior cases involving either the type of unit sought or the type of health care facility in dispute.[200]

Q 4.49.3   What issues arise in the composition of a unit of registered nurses?

The Healthcare Rule establishes that units of registered nurses are appropriate. Licensing is an important factor in determining whether a particular employee or group of employees should be included in a registered nurse unit. In general, all registered nurses reporting to the director of nursing are included in this unit, unless properly excluded as supervisors, managers, or confidential employees. This includes graduate nurses, nurse permittees, non-nursing department nurses (for example, infection control nurses, diabetes nurses, home care coordinators, etc.), nurse anesthetists, nurse educators, and nurse practitioners. Whether a particular registered nurse belongs in this unit is determined on a case-by-case basis. Often, by agreement of the parties, one or more groups of employees are excluded. When deciding whether "admitting officers" and "utilization review coordinators" are included in a registered nurse unit, the NLRB will look to whether the employer requires a registered nurse license for the position. Other positions that do not require registered nurse licenses or are predominately administrative in nature are usually not included in registered nurse units.[201]

Note that a nurse will meet the statutory definition of supervisor where:

(1)   he or she has the authority to engage in one of the activities listed in the definition, such as hiring, firing, disciplining, or responsibly directing others;

(2)   exercising that authority requires the use of independent judgment; and

(3)   the nurse exercises the authority in the interest of the employer.[202]

A nurse who directs less skilled employees can be held to be a supervisor exercising authority in the interest of the employer even if he or she is exercising professional judgment for the purpose of patient care.[203]

Q 4.49.4   What issues arise in the composition of a unit of physicians?

A hospital's house staff physicians are considered employees under the NLRA and may constitute an appropriate bargaining unit. A house staff physician is an individual who has attended medical school, passed the medical board examinations, and is employed by a hospital, but who is receiving further training, such as in a medical or surgical specialty. These units of house staff physicians may include interns, residents, and fellows, where these students/apprentices receive compensation and benefits from the hospital and spend a high percentage of their time providing direct patient care. However, residents who rotate through hospitals as part of a joint program between the hospitals will not be included in a particular hospital's unit of physicians.

Many other physicians associated with an acute-care facility may be excluded from a unit because they are independent contractors. In addition, an open question remains as to whether research scientists with a Ph.D. or M.D. who are associated with a teaching and research facility should be included in a bargaining unit of physicians. Further, physicians may be excluded from bargaining units to the extent the physicians can be classified as supervisors or managerial employees.[204] For instance, at a health maintenance organization, the area chief, who is the senior physician on staff, may qualify as a supervisor within the meaning of the NLRA.[205]

Q 4.49.5   Which employees are typically included as "all other professional employees" under the Healthcare Rule?

The NLRB has found the following healthcare or hospital employees to be considered professionals under the NLRA:

(1)   audiologists;

(2)   physical and occupational therapists;

(3)   dieticians;

(4)   pharmacists;

(5)   psychologists;

(6)   recreational/play therapists (if related college degree is required);

(7)   medical technologists;

(8)   social workers; and

(9)   hospital business office employees whose college degree requirements and sophisticated work qualify them as professionals (for example, accountants, financial analysts, reimbursement specialists, and information technology specialists).[206]

Q 4.49.6   Which employees have been included in a healthcare unit of technical employees?

Technical employees are commonly distinguished from professionals by the fact that technical positions do not require a college degree (or at least a college degree in a specialized field) or that these positions do not require the completion of any educational or internship prerequisites to obtaining a license. In the healthcare context, technical employees must also be distinguished from the established unit of "all other non-professional employees." Unlike the "other non-professional employees," technical employees still have some degree of specialized training beyond high school, they use independent judgment and their training to perform their jobs, and their duties frequently provide direct support to diagnostic or patient-care services.

The NLRB has considered the following employees to be part of a unit of technical employees:

(1)   paramedics;
(2)   surgical technicians;
(3)   cerebrovascular laboratory technicians;
(4)   adolescent care workers and daycare coordinators; and
(5)   licensed practical nurses.[207]

The following employees have been found not to be part of a technical employee unit:

(1)   EKG technicians (because they have no special training or certification other than on-the-job training);

(2)   medical transcriptionists (because they share a community of interest with business office clericals);

(3)   radiology technologist assistants (because no license and no education beyond high school is required);

(4)   pharmacy technicians (because they exercise no independent judgment);

(5)   interpreters (because, while some higher education is required, their knowledge of medical, billing, and other hospital procedures is general, and anyone who speaks the required language can serve as a substitute);

(6) biomedical technicians (because they are involved in maintenance and repair of equipment, not in diagnostic work, and have skills similar to those of the more traditional skilled maintenance classifications);

(7) biomedical engineers (same);

(8) renal dialysis technicians (because they are only required to have a high school education, and no special training other than on-the-job training);

(9) physical therapy technicians (same); and

(10) health information/medical records technicians (because certification, while available, is not required, and the required education and skill level does not rise to the level of medical records employees found by the NLRB to be technical).[208]

Q 4.49.7 What are the qualifications for inclusion in the skilled maintenance unit under the Healthcare Rule?

A unit consisting of skilled maintenance employees includes employees who maintain, repair, and operate complex and sophisticated equipment and systems, such as a hospital's physical plant (HVAC, refrigeration, electrical, plumbing, and mechanical equipment and systems) or patient care equipment (diagnostic, therapeutic, monitoring, and life-support equipment). This unit also includes individuals who are trainees for these positions or who assist skilled maintenance employees in the performance of their duties.

Skilled maintenance positions usually require some trade or vocational schooling, an apprenticeship, or a college degree, in addition to requiring that the employee keep current on technological changes in building maintenance. Generally, these employees have separate supervision by the hospital's plant engineering or maintenance department, a higher wage rate reflecting their skills and training, and only incidental contact with employees outside of the maintenance department. Unskilled maintenance employees, including custodians and landscapers, are excluded from the skilled maintenance units.[209]

The NLRB has held the following groups of employees may be part of a skilled maintenance unit:

(1) telecommunications employees;

(2) plumbers;

(3) electricians;

(4) refrigeration mechanics;

(5) maintenance mechanics;

(6) painters;

(7) carpenters;

(8) computer engineers; and

(9) telecommunication, biomedical, electronic, and medical technicians.[210]

The rationale behind this is that skilled and unskilled maintenance employees do not share the same community of interest and thus are better placed in separate units.

Positions that have been excluded from the skilled maintenance unit include:

(1) computer operators;
(2) occupational therapy craftsman;
(3) yard maintenance;
(4) groundskeepers;
(5) non-electrical or mechanical equipment specialists;
(6) tool inventory employees;
(7) construction project coordinators;
(8) draftsmen; and
(9) printers.[211]

Q 4.49.8 Which employees are included in a healthcare business office clerical unit?

In promulgating the Healthcare Rule, the NLRB recognized a continuing distinction between business office clerical employees and other types of clerical employees. The NLRB noted that business office clerical employees perform distinct functions, such as handling finances and billing, and deal with reimbursement systems, such as Medicare and Medicaid. These employees are generally supervised separately in a business office and have little interaction with other non-professionals because the business office is often physically isolated.

The following employees have been included in the healthcare business office clerical unit:

(1) billing clerks working in the business office or whose billing work is in connection with the employer's main business office;

(2) collection clerks dealing with hospital insurers;

(3) purchasing clerks;

(4) payroll clerks;

(5) accounting clerks;

(6) admitting clerks working within the business office;

(7) data entry clerks; and

(8) data processing employees.[212]

The NLRB has held that certain other employees are not included in the business office clerical unit, including:

(1) receptionists located apart from the business office;

(2) nursing department secretaries;

(3) admitting clerks located outside of business office who have separate supervisors; and

(4) clerical employees who work on patient floors or are otherwise outside of the business office.[213]

Q 4.49.9 What are the typical groups of employees included in a healthcare "all other non-professional employees" unit?

The "all other non-professional employees" unit is the residual group of employees not included in the other seven presumptively appropriate healthcare units. Positions included in this group usually require a high school education or less and are unskilled or require less than six months of on-the-job training. Prior to the Healthcare Rule, these positions were often grouped in a service and maintenance unit.

Positions often made part of the "all other non-professional employees" unit include:

(1) patient transporters;

(2) nursing department clerks and other clerical employees who are not associated with the business office;

(3) medical transcriptionists;

(4) unskilled workers in diagnostic and treatment areas (EKG and EEG technicians, phlebotomists);

(5) nurse aides;

(6) patient consultants;

(7) receptionists;

(8) community relations coordinators; and

(9) service and maintenance employees who are not skilled maintenance employees.[214]

Union Organizing Campaign and Election

Q 4.50 What is the NLRB's role in the campaign and election process?

The NLRB's role in the campaign and election process is to ensure that employees can make a "free and untrammeled choice for or against a bargaining representative."[215] The NLRB has authority to monitor and police representation elections and campaigns and, under its *General Shoe* doctrine, seeks to ensure that neither party engages in conduct that impairs the "laboratory conditions" necessary for conducting a free and fair election. The test for conduct that interferes with laboratory conditions is more restrictive than the test for an unfair labor practice.

Employer Activity During a Campaign

Q 4.51   Are there restrictions on employer speech during a union organizing campaign?

Yes. In order to maintain a free and fair election, the NLRB prohibits several types of employer speech during a union campaign. (See also Q 3.16 *et seq.*) Employers may not make statements that contain threats of reprisal or promises of benefit to employees or deceptively use NLRB materials in a way that suggests the NLRB favors one choice in an election over another. Extensive appeals to racial or religious prejudice also impermissibly interfere with representation elections.

Where an employer has engaged in such conduct, the NLRB may invalidate the election, even if the conduct did not rise to the level of an unfair labor practice.[216] However, the NLRB will not set aside an election based on isolated or de minimis conduct.

Q 4.51.1   What is a "threat of reprisal"?

An employer threatens reprisal when an employee would perceive an actual or hidden threat in an employer's statement. The U.S. Supreme Court has distinguished unlawful threats of reprisal from lawful pre-election predictions. An employer "is free to communicate to his employees any of his general views about unionism or any of his specific views about a particular union, so long as the communications do not contain a 'threat of reprisal or force or promise of benefit.'"[217] An employer may even make pre-election predictions as to the effects it believes unionization will have on its company; however, the predictions must be "carefully phrased on the basis of objective fact."[218] For example, where an employer makes a prediction about the effects unionization will have on the company, any indication that the employer will take action against the employees not because of demonstrable economic realities, but because they voted favorably for union representation will likely result in a finding of a ULP or will void the results of a "no union" majority vote in an NLRB election.

The NLRB considers several factors to determine whether a statement is a threat of reprisal, including the timing of the statement, the definitiveness of the statement, the degree to which the statement was disseminated, the factual basis for the statement, and the level of authority possessed by the speaker.[219] Based on these factors, the NLRB has found a variety of statements to constitute threats of reprisal, including:

(1) predictions that union organization will cause loss of business and plant closure;

(2) predictions that organization inevitably will lead to loss of jobs;

(3) warnings that unionization will result in a decrease in wages or benefits; and

(4) predictions that, after unionization, the employer may enforce rules and policies more strictly.[220]

Q 4.51.2   Is conferral of benefits made during a campaign always prohibited?

No. An employer can confer benefits on employees during a union organizing campaign; however, the NLRB presumes that conferring new benefits is unlawful unless an employer can show that its actions were prompted by factors other than the pending election.[221]

Some employer actions, such as offering an employee money to vote in a particular way or bribing an employee to work against the union, are clearly unlawful and will be treated as an interference in the election.[222] However, other employer actions to improve benefits are not clearly unlawful. An employer may implement a planned benefit increase during a campaign, but changes during this critical period are made at the employer's peril. A critical inquiry is whether the employer's actions are consistent with its past practices or were made for the purpose of influencing the election outcome. The timing and manner of implementation are also important. The NLRB may find election interference if the implementation appears to be an attempt to influence the campaign.[223]

For example, the NLRB has found benefit improvements unlawful where they were:

(1)   given in the context of repeated references to the union;

(2)   made effective just before an election; and

(3)   given before an election when they could have reasonably been delayed until after the election.[224]

Employers may, however, reimburse the travel expenses incurred by an employee to vote in the NLRB election, as long as the payment is a good-faith reasonable estimate of the expenses.[225]

Promises of future benefits made by unions during campaigns receive more favorable treatment than promises made by employers. The rationale for this leniency is that a union is not in as strong a position to deliver on its promises as an employer. However, where a union promises benefits it "has the power to effectuate," the NLRB may find the promise interfered with the election. Similarly, a union may unlawfully interfere with an election if it actually confers significant benefits on employees during a union organizing campaign.[226]

Q 4.51.3   Can an employer withdraw, threaten to withdraw, or withhold employee benefits during a union organizing campaign?

No. An employer that discontinues existing benefits or other favorable conditions, such as breaks, during a union organizing campaign violates the NLRA.[227] In addition, threatening to change working conditions as a means of influencing a campaign constitutes unlawful interference.[228] An employer also may not suggest that election of a union representative would be futile or that economic hazards would be inevitable if employees elect a union representative.[229] Union threats of violence or unfavorable treatment are likewise prohibited.

Furthermore, under certain circumstances, a failure to implement a planned benefit increase may be considered improper interference in the election. The NLRB follows the general rule that an employer must proceed with granting benefits to employees if in the normal course of business it would have done so, absent a union organizing campaign.[230] Not giving an increase during a campaign after the employer had previously told employees of its decision to make the improvements will likely be seen as unlawful.[231]

Q 4.51.4   Are raffles permitted during union campaigns?

The NLRB has significantly limited employers' ability to conduct raffles to encourage employees to vote in representation elections. "Conducting a raffle" includes announcing a raffle, distributing raffle tickets, identifying raffle winners, and awarding raffle prizes.[232]

In certain circumstances, a raffle could be considered the same as a grant of increased benefits. An employer generally is banned from conducting raffles for its employees during a campaign if (1) eligibility to participate in the raffle or win prizes is in any way tied to voting in the election or being at the election site on election day, or (2) the raffle is conducted at any time during the period beginning twenty-four hours before the scheduled opening of the polls and ending with the closing of the polls.[233]

However, not all raffles are illegal. For example, a raffle was held lawful where the employer assured the employees that their participation was voluntary, the raffle was unrelated to their votes, the value of the prizes was not excessive, and the employer had conducted similar raffles in the past to encourage participation in charity fundraisers.[234]

Providing refreshments and holding parties prior to an election may also be permitted.[235]

Q 4.52   Can an employer deliver a speech to employees on its premises during the lead-up to a union election?

Employers may require employees to attend employee meetings or speeches during company time and on company premises. However, neither employers nor unions can deliver "mass assembly" speeches to groups of employees during the twenty-four hours preceding an election.[236] In a mail-ballot election, the prohibition on mass assembly speeches begins twenty-four hours before the ballots are mailed by the Regional Office.[237] Violation of this rule will result in the election being set aside. In addition, the NLRB prohibits prolonged discussions between employees and managers or union representatives in the polling area.[238]

The twenty-four-hour prohibition on captive-audience speeches does not apply to posters or other campaign literature; however, it does apply to statements included in paychecks.[239]

 CASE STUDY: *Kalin Construction Co.*[240]

On the day of an election, Kalin Construction Co. arranged for the polls to be set up in Office B, which, after the company blocked alternative routes, could only be accessed through Office A. As employees entered Office A, the company secretary handed them their pay envelopes, instructing them to "take time to look at it and understand it." It was the company's usual payday, and the checks were issued in the usual total amount. But it was not the usual practice for the secretary to distribute the paychecks.

When the employees opened their envelopes, the total pay amount was divided into two checks, the second of which was the amount the employer claimed represented the money employees would send to the union.[241] Enclosed with the checks were the following messages:

> Due to the current Organizing Drive the Operating Engineers Union is conducting, we feel obligated to inform you of the effects of joining such an Organization. Examine your Check carefully, for this is ALL you will receive each week UNDER UNION REPRESENTATION. Now open the other envelope. . . .

> This is the amount of your benefits that we pay you in cash each week as part of your pay. We have always thought that most Employees knew what to do with their OWN MONEY.

Under Union rules, we will send this Money to THEM, for which they will CHARGE YOU MORE MONEY TO HANDLE!
If you have any questions, please contact Cheryl or Jerry. Our doors are always open.

The union lost the election, and the unfair labor practice and election objection case came before the NLRB. The NLRB took the opportunity to adopt "a strict rule against changes in the paycheck process, for the purpose of influencing the employees' vote in the election, during a period beginning 24 hours before the scheduled opening of the polls and ending with the closing of the polls."[242] The "paycheck process" includes:

   (1)   the paycheck itself;
   (2)   the time of paycheck distribution;
   (3)   the location of paycheck distribution; and
   (4)   the method of paycheck distribution.[243]

Under the rule, any change in the paycheck process will result in the NLRB's setting aside the election, unless the employer can show that the change was motivated by a legitimate business reason unrelated to the election. As Kalin Construction Co. did not have a legitimate business reason for its changes, the election results were set aside.

Q 4.53   Can an employer lawfully ask employees whether they support or are affiliated with a union?

Generally, an employer violates section 8(a)(1) by making direct inquiries regarding whether employees support the union or have participated in union activities, unless they are open, known supporters of the union. Accordingly, an employer may not interview or interrogate employees as to whether they support the union or are affiliated with it during a union organizing campaign. The coerciveness of an interrogation is judged from the perspective of the employee in light of the surrounding circumstances, including the time, place, personnel involved, and known position of the employer.[244] The NLRB has stated that "any attempt by an employer to ascertain employee views and sympathies regarding unions generally tends to cause fear of reprisal in the minds of employees."[245]

In addition, absent unusual circumstances, polling employees as to their union sympathies will be unlawful unless the employer observes the following safeguards:

(1)   the purpose of the poll is to determine the truth of a union's claim of majority support;

(2)   the purpose is communicated to the employees;

(3)   assurances against reprisal are given;

(4)   the employees are polled by secret ballot; and

(5)   the employer has not engaged in unfair labor practices or created a coercive atmosphere.

Employers that attempt to discover employees' union sentiments indirectly, rather than by direct questioning or polling, can also violate the NLRA. For example, pre-election distribution of "Vote No" buttons to employees by a supervisor constituted illegal interrogation because the offer of the button by the supervisor and the acceptance or refusal by the employee required the employee to make an observable choice in the presence of the supervisor.[246]

Q 4.54   Can an employer limit access to its premises during a union election campaign?

An employer cannot lawfully bar off-duty employees from access to the exterior, non-working area of its property absent some legitimate business justification.[247] However, an employer may establish rules denying off-duty employees access to the interior of the employer's premises if such rules:

(1)   limit access solely to the interior of the facility and other working areas;

(2)   are disseminated to all employees; and

(3) are not applied discriminatorily against employees who support the union.[248]

Notably, a policy limiting off-duty access will not meet the third prong of this test if the employer permits access subject to a supervisor's prior approval. According to the Board, such a policy gives the employer too much discretion to decide when and why employees may access the facility, and is therefore facially unlawful.[249]

Employers may also restrict non-employee union representatives from soliciting support or distributing literature on employer property, unless employee living conditions "place the employees beyond the reach of reasonable union efforts to communicate with them."[250]

Q 4.55   Can an employer limit use of its email systems during a campaign?

No, but the Board is reconsidering the issue and is expected to modify its stance.[251] Under the Board's 2014 decision in *Purple Communications*, employees who already use an employer's email for business purposes have a presumptive right to use their work email to engage in union organizing and other section 7 activities during non-working time.[252] To rebut an employee's presumptive right to use an employer's email system, an employer must show that because of "special circumstances," the restriction is necessary to protect its legitimate interests. The Board has indicated that a total ban on non-business use of email will be justified only in rare circumstances. Even limited restrictions on access will be scrutinized to determine if there is an actual connection between the restriction and employer's asserted interest.

Q 4.56   Can an employer conduct surveillance of employees during a campaign?

Generally, surveillance of employees by an employer, whether conducted by supervisors, other employees, or third parties, is unlawful.[253] This is true whether or not the employees know they are being observed.[254] In addition, it is unlawful for an employer to create the impression among employees that it is engaged in surveillance.[255]

Photographing or videotaping employees engaged in union activities is considered unlawful surveillance, though the employer may show that the filming was justified because of safety or productivity concerns.

It is not surveillance for an employer to observe union activities openly conducted on its premises.[256] However, extended observation of such activities typically is considered surveillance because it could intimidate employees and restrict the free exercise of their rights to organize.[257]

Q 4.57   Can an employer discipline or discharge a supervisor for engaging in union activity?

Employers are unconstrained by the NLRA in insisting on the undivided loyalty of their supervisors and managers. Supervisors are excluded from the NLRA's definition of "employee" and are not protected under the NLRA; thus, supervisors can be disciplined or discharged for engaging in union activity.[258]

The NLRB has held that an employer's conduct in disciplining or discharging a supervisor out of a desire to assure the loyalty of its management personnel was lawful even though it had the incidental effect of causing other employees to fear that they would be disciplined or discharged for engaging in protected activity.[259] However, an employer cannot discipline or discharge a supervisor if the discipline or discharge interferes with employees' exercise of rights under the NLRA.[260] For example, an employer cannot discharge a supervisor for giving testimony adverse to an employer's interests or for refusing to commit unfair labor practices.[261] An employer also may not discharge a supervisor because of the union activities of a spouse, child, or other relative.[262]

Q 4.58   Can an election be set aside based on a supervisor's pro-union conduct?

Pro-union conduct by supervisors can constitute objectionable coercive conduct that may require setting aside the results of an election. An election can be set aside based on a supervisor's pro-union conduct if it (1) coerced or interfered with an employee's free choice in an election, and (2) materially affected the outcome of the election.[263]

The NLRB determines whether a supervisor's conduct coerced or interfered with an employee's rights by considering the nature and degree of the supervisor's authority over the employee and the nature, extent, and context of the conduct. The material-outcome determination is based on factors such as margin of victory, whether the conduct was widespread or isolated, the timing of the conduct, the extent to which the conduct became known, and the lingering effect of the conduct.

For example, the NLRB has held that pro-union supervisors engage in objectionable conduct when they solicit authorization cards from employees. In *Harborside Healthcare, Inc.*,[264] during a union campaign, a supervisor told other employees about the benefits of joining a union and asked them to sign cards authorizing the union as their representative in collective bargaining. The employer asked the NLRB to set aside the election, claiming that the employee was a supervisor and that her pro-union conduct during the organizing campaign coerced employees into voting for union representation. The NLRB overturned the election results, ruling that the pro-union position of one low-level supervisor was enough to taint the election.

Q 4.58.1 Can an election be overturned based on union interference during an organizing campaign?

Union misconduct during the critical period prior to the election can form the basis for setting aside the results of an election. Attempts by a labor organization to unduly influence the outcome of an election, such as electioneering near the polls, videotaping, threats of violence, or offering benefits or inducements, may amount to union interference. In addition, a union may interfere in an election by discriminating against employees based on how they vote or their willingness to sign authorization cards. For instance, a union was found to unlawfully interfere with an election when it offered to waive initiation fees only for employees who agreed to join the union prior to election, but did not offer the same waiver after the election.[265]

Q 4.58.2 Can an election be set aside based on third-party conduct?

An election can be set aside where the activities of third parties interfere with a free and fair election.[266] A third party can cause an election to be set aside even where it has no relationship to the employer or the union. The NLRB will set aside an election where there is an atmosphere of violence or a threat of violence that impairs employees' free choice.[267] However, an employer does not commit an unfair labor practice where the relevant third-party conduct is not attributable to the employer.

Q 4.58.3 Is an employer responsible for the conduct of third parties during a campaign?

An employer may be responsible for third-party conduct during a campaign if the third party is an agent of the employer.[268] Whether the third party had actual authority from the employer is not determinative of agency. Rather, the key factor is whether an employee could, under all the circumstances, reasonably believe that the third party was acting on behalf of the employer. For example, in a small community where the employer actively influenced community opinion against the union, the employer was held responsible for a third party's distribution of a leaflet containing a threat that unionization would result in plant closure.[269] In contrast, the NLRB determined that a co-owner's son who stated that pro-union employees would lose their jobs did not act as an agent of the employer and the threat was not attributed to management.

Administration of Elections—The NLRB Election Process

Timing of Elections

Q 4.59 When are elections held?

Under the NLRB's 2015 rules on representation case procedures, the regional director will schedule the election for the earliest date practicable. However, the employer must first provide the union with an "*Excelsior* list," identifying all employees eligible to vote (see Q 4.61). This list must be provided within two business days of the direction of election, and absent union consent, the election cannot be held any sooner than ten days after receiving this list. In practice, if the parties reach an election agreement, the election is typically held about twenty-two days after the petition is filed. If no agreement is reached and a representation hearing is held, the election is typically held about thirty-six days after the petition is filed.[270]

Notice of Election

Q 4.60   When and where does the Notice of Election have to be posted?

At the same time the regional director issues a direction of election, he or she will also send the employer a "Notice of Election."[271] The Notice of Election provides the voting unit with information regarding the logistics of the election. For example, the Notice of Election describes:

- the purpose of the election (namely, to determine the representative, if any, desired for the eligible employees for the purpose of collective bargaining with the employer);

- the process of the election (that it will be administered by the NLRB and employees will have the right to vote via secret ballot);

- the eligibility requirements (a description of the employees eligible to vote in the election);

- challenges (an explanation that challenged voters will be permitted to vote and the eligibility issues will be resolved later);

- the ballot (contains a "sample ballot" so that employees may review the ballot before actually participating in an election—see Q 4.66);

- observers (each of the interested parties may designate an equal number of observers to act as checkers at the voting place and during the counting of ballots, to assist in identifying voters, and to challenge voters); and

- a description of employees' NLRA section 7 rights, including the right:

  (1) to self-organize;

  (2) to refrain from organizing; and

  (3) to be free from threats or coercion during the election process.

Copies of the NLRB's official Notice of Election must be posted in conspicuous places in the workplace at least three full working days prior to 12:01 A.M. on the day of the election. In elections involving mail ballots, the election is deemed to have started the day the ballots are deposited by the regional office in the mail. In all cases, the notices are to remain posted until the end of the election. Posting places include, but are not limited to, bulletin boards and time card racks. Moreover, if an employer regularly communicates with employees electronically, the notice of election must be provided electronically, in addition to being physically posted.[272] The term "working day" means an entire twenty-four-hour period excluding Saturdays, Sundays, and holidays. Failure to post the election notices will be grounds for setting aside the election if timely objections are filed.[273] Notices may be posted in multiple languages if the employee population primarily speaks a language other than English.

Voter Eligibility

Q 4.61   What is the *Excelsior* or voter list?

During the election, NLRB agents and election observers identify eligible voters according to a list known as an *Excelsior* list.

The *Excelsior* list identifies all eligible employees by their full name, job classification, shift, and work location. The *Excelsior* list must also provide the home address, personal email address, and home and personal cell phone number of each eligible employee if such contact information is available to the employer. Employees who will be permitted to vote subject to challenge must be identified in a separate section of the list. The ranks of eligible employees should be based on the last payroll period ending before the approval of the election agreement or the NLRB's direction of election. The employer is required to provide the *Excelsior* list in electronic format to the regional director and the union within two business days after the direction of election is issued.[274]

Employers are responsible for compiling this list, and must file it with the Region and serve it on all other parties within two business days after the issuance of the direction of election. Employers must make a good faith effort to ensure that the list includes all available contact information and is free of errors and omissions. Personal contact information that is known to individual supervisors, particularly those who regularly text or call employees on their cell phones, may be considered available to the employer even if it is not listed in any HR files.[275] Employers are expected to make a good-faith effort to provide a list free of errors or omissions. If a list contains a significant number of omissions and the union loses the election by a narrow margin, the erroneous list may be determined prejudicial to the union and the election could be overturned. The NLRB has "consistently viewed the omission of names as more serious than inaccuracies in addressees"; whereas the vote margin may be relevant in cases of omissions, the NLRB has allowed greater latitude in cases of inaccuracies.[276]

The *Excelsior* rule is designed "to achieve important statutory goals by ensuring that all employees are fully informed about the arguments concerning representation and can freely and fully exercise their Section 7 rights."[277] The *Excelsior* rule helps achieve this goal of "an informed employee electorate" by giving unions the right of access to employees that employers already have, thus, enabling employees to hear from all parties on the unionization question.[278]

Q 4.61.1   Can the parties stipulate to a voter eligibility list?

The NLRB permits parties to a representation hearing to definitively resolve issues of voter eligibility prior to the election if they clearly evidence their intention to do so in writing. This is called a *Norris-Thermador* list, after the case that established the procedure.[279] Therefore, where parties enter into a written and signed agreement that expressly provides that issues of eligibility resolved therein shall be final and binding upon the parties, "such an agreement, and only such an agreement" is considered a final determination of the eligibility issues "unless it is, in part or in whole, contrary to the [NLRA] or established NLRB policy."[280] The written requirement is strictly applied, and the NLRB accepted an oral agreement only where both parties agree to its contents.[281]

The NLRB will not be bound by a stipulated voter eligibility list where the parties agree to allow a statutorily ineligible party to vote. For example, in *Inacomp America, Inc.*, an employee whose name was included on a stipulated election list resigned and left the employer before the election. The employee was not permitted to vote.[282]

Q 4.61.2   Can a voter's eligibility be challenged?

Yes. The challenge procedure provides a method whereby a voter's eligibility to vote may be called into question. Any observer has the right to challenge any voter for cause. The Board agent must challenge anyone whose name is not on the eligibility list or who has been permitted by the regional director or the NLRB to vote subject to challenge. Also, the NLRB agent must challenge a voter if he or she knows or has reason to believe that the voter is ineligible to vote (for example, the voter is in fact not employed in the proposed bargaining unit or is a supervisor), but only if none of the parties voices a challenge on that ground. A challenge should generally be made before the challenged voter receives a ballot.

When a voter is challenged, a small "c" is placed beside his or her name by the checking observer for the challenging party. After marking his or her ballot, the voter places the marked ballot in the challenged ballot envelope, seals the envelope, and drops the envelope in the box.

Typically voters are challenged because they:

(1)   do not appear on the *Excelsior* list;
(2)   are no longer employed;
(3)   are supervisors or managers;
(4)   are employed outside of the voting unit;
(5)   are temporary employees; or
(6)   are intermittent part-time employees.

Q 4.61.3   Are discharged employees allowed to vote in an NLRB election?

In general, to be eligible to vote, an employee must have been employed both on the eligibility date (usually the date the last payroll period ended prior to the approval of the election agreement or the issuance of the direction of election) and on the day of the election.[283] Therefore, a discharged employee is generally not an eligible voter. However, a discharged employee may vote subject to challenge where the discharged employee claims that he or she was discharged in violation of the protections of the NLRA. Discriminatory personnel actions cannot be used to make an employee eligible or ineligible to vote in an NLRB election. Where an employer's discharge of an employee is found to have violated section 8(a)(3) of the NLRA, it follows that the employee should properly be considered an employee at all relevant times. Therefore, discharged employees may vote, subject to challenge, and have their eligibility determined at a later time.

Q 4.61.4   Are employees on layoff allowed to vote in an NLRB election?

A laid-off employee is eligible to vote if, at the time of the election, the employee has a reasonable expectation of re-employment in the foreseeable future. Whether a worker has a reasonable expectation of recall is determined by looking to three factors:

(1) the employer's past experience;

(2) the employer's future plans; and

(3) the circumstances of the layoff, including what employees were told about the likelihood of recall.[284]

A reasonable expectation of recall is required to ensure that the voting employee is sufficiently concerned with the terms and conditions of employment in a unit to warrant his participation in the selection of a collective bargaining agent. There must be more than a mere possibility of recall to allow a laid-off worker to cast a vote.[285]

Q 4.61.5   Are strikers allowed to vote in an NLRB election?

As discussed above (see Q 4.40), employees engaged in an economic strike who have been permanently replaced are eligible to vote in an NLRB election where such election is conducted within twelve months of the strike. Employees who are both actively on strike and those on a rehire list are eligible to vote as long as the election is held within twelve months of the commencement of the strike. Unreplaced economic strikers and non-economic strikers are generally eligible to vote in NLRB elections.

Strikers may be rendered ineligible to vote in a union election for other reasons, including:

(1)   where a striker obtains permanent employment elsewhere;

(2)   misconduct that would render the striker unsuitable for employment; and

(3)   when an employer eliminates the striker's job for substantial non-strike-related reasons.

Replacement workers employed by an employer who locked out employees over bargaining issues are not eligible to vote in an NLRB election. In principle, replacement workers for employees out on a strike to protest employer unfair labor practices also cannot vote, although the NLRB's blocking-charge policy (see Q 4.19) first requires resolution of any pending charges. Strikers who strike in violation of the NLRA or a no-strike provision are usually ineligible to vote.

Q 4.61.6   Is an employee on a leave of absence allowed to vote?

Employees who are on sick leave, disability leave, or leaves of absence are presumed eligible to vote, absent an affirmative showing the employee has resigned or been discharged.[286] For example, in *Home Care Network, Inc.*,[287] the NLRB sustained the hearing officer's determination on three challenged ballots. The ballots belonged to three voters who worked as "home health aides," providing personal care and light housekeeping for clients in the clients' homes. Before the election, all three voters sustained injuries that prevented them from working. It was undisputed that they were not "absent without leave" and that they had been off work due to their medical conditions. It was also undisputed that the employer had not terminated any of the three voters or notified any of them that they were terminated. The employer also conceded that none of the three voters had resigned. Accordingly, all three voters were eligible to vote, and the challenges were overturned.

Q 4.61.7   Does the NLRB require voters to bring identification with them on election day?

The NLRB's *Casehandling Manual* (which can be found on the NLRB's website, www.nlrb.gov) provides that, in large or complex elections, the parties can agree, prior to the election, as to what identification will be required. If the parties cannot agree, the regional director determines what identifying information, beyond self-identification, should be required. In practice, however, the parties are typically unable to agree on identifying information beyond self-identification, and regional directors rarely require voters to bring driver's licenses or other identification.

Q 4.61.8   Can employees who have voluntarily resigned later vote in an NLRB election?

An individual who voluntarily resigns from the employer prior to an NLRB election is generally not eligible to vote in the election. The party challenging the individual's eligibility must show that the individual manifested a clear and unambiguous intent to resign before the election.[288]

Polling Place

Q 4.62   Where are NLRB elections held?

Generally speaking, NLRB elections are held on the employer's premises because this is a location that is accessible to most employees. The voting area should be located away from manager and supervisor offices and provide sufficient space for voting booths and employees to stand in line to be identified and vote. The NLRB has held elections at places outside of the employer's premises where (1) striking employees are eligible to vote and (2) there have been egregious unfair labor practices committed by the employer such that employees could not freely exercise their right to vote if required to do so on the employer's premises.[289]

Q 4.62.1   How long does it take to conduct an NLRB election?

The length of time for a union election depends on the size and geographic location of the voting unit. An election for a fairly small voting unit (less than 100 employees) can be held in one day, usually with two polling periods—one at the beginning of the shift and one near the end of the shift. Elections for voting units of more than 100 employees could be held in a single day but, depending on the shift times and when employees are scheduled to work, may last more than a single day. Where employees in the voting unit are located at multiple worksites, polling areas may be set up at each location to facilitate maximum opportunity to vote.

Q 4.62.2   Under what circumstances is it appropriate to reschedule an election?

NLRB elections are rarely rescheduled absent issues beyond the parties' control, such as inclement weather or the NLRB agent's failure to attend the election. Rather, if one or both parties object, it will proceed as scheduled and the parties' objections will be addressed at an objections hearing before results are certified. If an objection is found to have merit, the election is set aside and a new election is scheduled.

Q 4.63   How is the polling site controlled?

The NLRB agent and the interested parties inspect the polling place and review the procedures for the election during a pre-election conference. The NLRB agent and representatives of interested parties, including the election observers designated by the employer and union, generally assemble at the polling place anywhere from thirty to forty-five minutes prior to the opening of the polls. The Board agent examines the polling place with the parties and ensures that:

(1) there are no supervisor or manager offices in the immediate vicinity;

(2) there are no election-related postings in the immediate voting area;

(3) there is sufficient ingress and egress to the polling area; and

(4) all equipment is available and in place.

The Board agent also sets up the voting booth(s) and assembles the ballot box.

At the pre-election conference, the NLRB agent covers the following topics:

(1) prohibition of observers' electioneering and unnecessary conversation with voters;

(2) prohibition of observers' keeping lists of names of voters; and

(3) the procedure for checking voters' names and for challenging voters.

All observers at the pre-election conference will look into the ballot box while it is open and confirm that the box is empty. The Board agent will then close the ballot box and securely seal it.

Q 4.64   Who is present during the voting process?

During the voting process, the only persons who may be present are the NLRB agents administering the election, the observers, and the employees who are in the process of voting. Employer representatives (that is, supervisors and managers) and non-employee union officials may not be present in the voting area.

Q 4.64.1   Who are observers, and how are they selected?

Each party may be represented at the polling place by an equal, pre-designated number of observers. Some elections involve multiple polling places or multiple periods of voting. The observers represent their parties and monitor the election process. They also assist the NLRB agent in the conduct of the election. In extraordinarily large elections, three or more observers may be required; in all other elections, observers are usually limited to one or two per party.

In a small election, observers sit at the check-in table and identify voters by referring to the *Excelsior* list. Observers record which employees voted by checking off names on the *Excelsior* list. They also challenge voters who they believe are ineligible to vote. Observers are also responsible for ensuring that there is only one voter in the booth at any one time and for making sure that each voter deposits a ballot in the ballot box. In larger elections, observers will be placed near the ballot box for monitoring purposes and to assist in ushering employees through the voting lines, provide relief duties to other observers, and provide any other assistance necessary to ensure the election runs smoothly.

Parties designate their observers in advance of the election. The observers are usually employees of the employer. A supervisor is not permitted to serve as an observer, nor is a non-employee union official.

The Board agent provides observers with an official badge to wear during the election. Observers are generally discouraged from wearing any other insignia, but they are not prohibited from doing so.

Observers will attend the pre-hearing conference and receive instructions regarding their duties from the NLRB.

Q 4.65   What sort of electioneering is allowed during an election?

No electioneering is permitted at or near the polling place during the hours of voting. Agents of the parties are prohibited from conversing with voters in the polling area or in the line of employees waiting to vote. Agents of the parties (other than observers) are not allowed in the polling area during the election hours.

Election observers may not electioneer during their hours of observer duty, whether at or away from the polling place. Voters, on the other hand, do not need to remove insignia, such as buttons, even though it might constitute electioneering material.

Parties may distribute literature on the day of the election even though it takes place during the voting hours. However, electioneering materials visible from the polls are not permitted.

Ballots

Q 4.66   What does a ballot say?

Election ballots are provided by the NLRB, and the questions contained on those ballots depend on the type of election and the number of unions involved. In an election involving only a single union, the ballot inquiry is usually phrased as follows: "Do you wish to be represented for purposes of collective bargaining by: [name of the union]?" The employee is instructed to "mark an 'X' in the square of your choice." There is a square under the word "yes" and a square under the word "no". The employee is reminded not to sign the ballot. If the election involves more than one union, the employee is given the choice of marking "X" in the square designating "union A," "union B," or no union.

Employers and unions should refrain from reproducing sample ballots in campaign literature. Instead, employees should be instructed to review, prior to the election, the Notice of Election, which is provided by the NLRB and contains an accurate sample ballot.

Q 4.66.1   When are mail ballots used in elections?

Generally, the NLRB favors manual elections; the use of mail ballots for conducting elections is not common. The NLRB, however, occasionally uses mail ballots to conduct elections when circumstances make it difficult or impractical for employees to vote in a manual election.

The following situations normally warrant the use of mail ballots:

- where eligible voters are "scattered" and not present at a common location at common times (for example, work in different geographic areas, travel on the road, work different shifts, work combinations of full-time and part-time schedules);

- where there is a strike, a lockout, or picketing in progress.

In addition, the NLRB will consider:

- the desire of all the parties;
- the ability of voters to read and understand mail ballots;

- the availability of addresses for employees; and
- the efficient use of the NLRB's financial resources.

During elections, the NLRB may use mail ballots for absentee voting purposes, but the agency reserves discretion to deny a mail ballot to employees who are unable to attend the manual election. In the *Casehandling Manual*, the NLRB takes the following position:

> The Board does not provide absentee ballots. Specifically, ballots for voting by mail should not be provided to, inter alia, those who are in the Armed Forces, ill at home or in a hospital, on vacation, or on a leave of absence due to their own decision or condition.[290]

In a mixed manual-mail election, mail ballots should be sent only to those who cannot vote in person because of employer action (for example, assignment of employees to duties that make it impossible or impractical for them to come to a polling place). Pipeline employees, seamen, and traveling utility crews usually vote by mail. Like absentee ballots, mail ballots are not sent to those who are in the U.S. Armed Forces, are ill at home or in a hospital, are on vacation, or are on leave of absence due to their own decision or condition.

The NLRB does not use Internet or electronic voting procedures at this time.

Q 4.66.2   What is the procedure for counting the ballots?

The counting of the ballots takes place as soon after the close of voting as possible. The count takes place at any central location; in most elections, the ballot count occurs at the polling place. In a large election, if one of the polling places is large enough, the tally can take place there, otherwise it will be held in a nearby facility that can accommodate those who wish to view the count.

The actual participants in the count are the NLRB agents and official observers. Members of the press and other interested persons may also be present. However, the NLRB agent in charge of the election may limit the numbers of those present.

Prior to the count, the NLRB agent will announce the following to those present:

- A majority of the valid votes cast will decide the election. A tie vote will mean the union has not won, because it has not achieved a majority.

- Any ballot that clearly reflects the intention of the voter will be counted in accordance with the apparent intention, even though the marking is unorthodox (for example, where a voter places the word "yes" in the yes box, or the word "no" in the no box).

- A ballot the intent of which is not clear will be considered void.

- A ballot that contains a means of identifying the voter will be considered void.

- Only a board agent will touch any ballot, even if a ballot drops to the floor.

The board agent then counts the ballots by removing the ballots from the box, opening them one by one, calling out and displaying the preference expressed, and placing them face-up in piles according to the preference expressed. When the box is empty, the NLRB agent counts aloud the different piles, displaying each ballot to the witnesses as it is counted. The challenged ballots, unless voluntarily resolved by the parties, will not be counted during the vote count. The board agent then completes a "tally of the ballots" form, a copy of which is handed to each party.

Q 4.66.3 How are challenged ballots resolved?

As an initial matter, prior to the vote count, the parties often resolve some challenged ballots (that is, remove or sustain the challenge) by agreement. For example, where a voter was challenged because his or her name was not on the eligibility list and the parties can agree that the omission of the voter's name was inadvertent and the voter was eligible to vote, the challenge can be resolved. Challenged ballots that are not voluntarily resolved are not opened and counted during the vote count.

Some challenges are resolved because they are mooted by virtue of the fact that there were insufficient challenges to affect the results of the election. Specifically, challenges are not sufficient to affect the results of the election where, if added to the trailing choice, they would not change the outcome. For example, if 900 employees voted and 600 of them selected "yes" (that they wanted the union to be their representative for purposes of collective bargaining) and there are only ten challenged ballots, the challenged ballots would not be sufficient to affect the results and thus would require no "resolution."

For those challenges that are not voluntarily resolved or mooted, the challenges are usually resolved either through an administrative investigation or an administrative hearing.

In an administrative investigation, on each challenge the regional director ascertains from each party the following:

(1)   the position of the party;

(2)   the supporting arguments and law;

(3)   suggested witnesses; and

(4)   any other evidence the party may wish to bring in support of its position.

The regional director then informs the parties of his or her decision in either (1) a report, or (2) where elections objections have been filed, a supplemental decision on challenges. The report or supplemental decision sets forth the objective factors demonstrating that the challenges should be resolved in the manner described. Parties have the right to file exceptions or request review of the regional director's decision to the NLRB unless the report is made pursuant to a consent election. In the case of a consent election, the decision is final and there is no right of appeal.

Where the regional director has due-process concerns and feels that the challenge raises substantial and material factual issues, a hearing will be required. Substantial credibility issues concerning material facts are to be resolved at a hearing and not on the basis of an evaluation of the results of an administrative investigation. The

hearing will be scheduled as expeditiously as possible, and postpone-
ments will not be granted, absent good cause.

Post-Election Proceedings

Q 4.67   When do election results become final?

Following the election, the regional director issues a certification
at the end of the seven-day period for filing election objections. If a
party files election objections, the election results will not be certified
until the election objections have been resolved. In addition, voter
challenges sufficient in number to affect the election results must also
be resolved before an election can be certified.

Election Objections

Q 4.68   What are election objections?

Election objections are objections filed with respect to the conduct of the election or to the conduct affecting the results of the election. Election objections may only be raised by the employer, a union
whose name appeared on the ballot, or the petitioner. Objections must
be filed within seven days of the tally of the ballots. Objections to an
election are filed with the NLRB's regional director, and the burden
is on the objecting party to provide evidence that the election should
be set aside.[291]

Q 4.68.1   Can election objections be filed against a union?

Yes. Employers can file election objections against a union alleging
objectionable conduct such as:

- harassing and physically threatening employees who do not
support the union;

- threatening job loss or a decrease in wages and benefits if
the employees do not vote for the union; or

- making misrepresentations to the employees in order to obtain
union authorization cards.

Q 4.68.2   Can election objections be filed against the NLRB?

Yes. Parties may file election objections against the NLRB alleging objectionable conduct such as:

- that the NLRB agent failed to adequately guard the ballot box;
- that the NLRB agent fell asleep during the vote; or
- that the NLRB agent was late to the election.

Q 4.68.3   How are election objections adjudicated?

The party filing the objections must submit the objections to the regional director along with a short statement of the reasons each objection is being filed. The objecting party is also required to provide the regional director with evidence in support of the objections. Both the objections and the offer of proof must be submitted within seven days of tallying the ballots. However, upon a showing of good cause, the regional director may allow additional time to file the offer of proof.[292]

The evidence submitted should identify the nature of the misconduct on which the objections are based and should include a list of the witnesses and a brief description of the testimony of each witness. The objecting party should also submit any supporting documentation. If a party fails to submit sufficient evidence in a timely manner, the regional director will overrule the objections without any further processing.

The regional director then reviews the evidence submitted. If he or she finds that the objecting party failed to make a prima facie case, the objection can be overruled without an investigation. If a prima facie case is met, the regional director engages in an administrative investigation. During the investigation, if the regional director discovers additional conduct that might have undermined the election, he can consider this conduct as well. The parties, however, cannot amend their objections to include conduct not initially raised during the seven-day post-election period.

After the investigation is completed, the regional director either issues a report or proceeds to a hearing. Where initial efforts to resolve the issues are not successful and the parties' submissions of evidence appear on their face to raise substantial and material factual or legal issues requiring a hearing, the regional director usually does not conduct any further investigation and issues a notice of hearing setting the objections for hearing. The regional director must go to a hearing if the investigation reveals that there are substantial credibility issues related to material facts.

If the election objections require a hearing, the hearing is conducted by a hearing officer or an administrative law judge. The hearing must be scheduled within twenty-one days of the tally or as soon thereafter as possible. During the hearing, each party may present witness testimony through direct and cross-examination. Exhibits are also identified, authenticated, and offered into evidence. Parties may not file post-hearing briefs absent special permission from the hearing officer. If there are challenged ballots, any unresolved issues related to the ballot challenges are consolidated into the election objections hearing.

The hearing officer then prepares a report, which is reviewed by the regional director. The report includes credibility determinations made by the hearing officer. The regional director then issues a report on the election objections. The parties are permitted to file exceptions to the regional director's report with the NLRB.

If the regional director finds that the election objections were meritorious and affected the outcome of the election, the original election is set aside and a rerun election is scheduled.

Overturning an Election/Special Remedies

Q 4.69   What is the standard for determining whether objectionable conduct is sufficient to set aside an election?

Representation elections are not lightly set aside, and there is a strong presumption that ballots cast under the NLRB's procedural safeguards accurately reflect the voting unit's will. Accordingly, the burden of proof on parties seeking to have an NLRB-supervised election set aside is a heavy one. The objecting party must show that the conduct in question actually affected employees in the voting unit.[293]

The NLRB's usual policy, however, is to direct a new election whenever an unfair labor practice occurs during the critical period, because conduct violative of section 8(a)(1) is, almost always, conduct that interferes with the exercise of a free and untrammeled choice in an election.[294] An exception to this policy is "where the misconduct is de minimis: 'such that it is virtually impossible to conclude' that the election outcome has been affected."[295]

In determining whether misconduct could have affected the results of the election, the NLRB has considered the number of violations, their severity, the extent of dissemination, and the size of the unit. Other factors the NLRB considers include the closeness of the election, proximity of the conduct to the election date, and the number of unit employees affected.

Election issues that may provide a basis for invalidating an election include:

(1)   submission of an inaccurate, incomplete, or late voting list by the employer to the union;

(2)   campaign propaganda calculated to inflame racial prejudice of employees;

(3)   election speeches made on company time to mass assemblies of employees within twenty-four hours before the scheduled time for an election;

(4)   systemic employer visits to employees at their homes during the election campaign;

(5)   employer questioning, polling, or surveillance; and

(6)   threats of reprisal or promises of benefit.

Notably, the objectionable conduct must have occurred after the petition has been filed.[296] The NLRB will consider objectionable conduct occurring before the petition has been filed only "where it adds meaning and dimension to related postpetition conduct."[297]

For example, the NLRB has found that isolated instances of unlawful threats or interrogations, which were not disseminated to unit employees, did not rise to the level of conduct affecting the election.

In *Bon Appetit Management Co.*,[298] a low-level supervisor asked one employee how she was going to vote and threatened to cut her pay if she voted for the union. The NLRB held that the misconduct did not affect the election results because it was isolated and not disseminated, and election results were overwhelmingly in favor of the employer.

Q 4.70   What happens if an election is overturned?

When the original election is set aside based on objectionable conduct found either by the NLRB or the regional director, a rerun election is conducted. The voting unit or groups in a rerun election is the same as in the original election. The payroll period determining eligibility, however, will be the latest completed payroll period preceding the date of issuance of the notice of the rerun election. The preparation and pre-election check of the voting eligibility list should follow the rules applying to an original election.

The date, hours, place, and general conditions should be set in accordance with the terms of the original election. The voting procedures, the count, and the preparation and service of the tally of ballots are the same as in an original election, except that the form for the tally of ballots will indicate that the election is a rerun.

Q 4.71   Does the NLRB use any special remedies in election cases?

The NLRB occasionally has ordered special remedies for election misconduct where violations of the NLRA have made a free and fair election impossible. The NLRB uses restorative remedies for certain election issues, including access remedies and notice remedies. Access remedies provide employees with a way to communicate with unions without fear of retaliation from their employer.[299] Notice remedies inform employees of their rights and place limits on the employer's conduct to help ensure that further violations of the employees' rights will not occur.[300]

The foregoing special remedies are warranted where the NLRB finds that an employer's unfair labor practices were so numerous, pervasive, and outrageous that special notice and access remedies are necessary to dissipate fully the coercive effects of the unfair labor practices.[301] For example, in *Fieldcrest Cannon, Inc.*,[302] the NLRB held that special remedies were appropriate for four reasons:

(1) The employer responded to the organizing drive with extensive and serious unfair labor practices;

(2) The unlawful conduct pervaded the unit;

(3) Some of the unlawful conduct tended to have a long-term coercive impact on the unit; and

(4) Many of the violations were committed by high-level management officials.

The NLRB viewed the special remedies as necessary to dissipate the effects of the employer's unfair labor practices and to ensure that a future election could be held fairly.[303] Accordingly, the employer was required to publicly read a notice, provide employee lists to the union, allow the union reasonable access to the employer's facility in non-work areas and during employees' non-work time, and permit the union to deliver a thirty-minute speech to employees on working time prior to any future NLRB election.[304]

Another special remedy used by the NLRB when an employer commits an unfair labor practice that makes the holding of a fair election unlikely is a *Gissel* bargaining order (discussed in more detail in chapter 8).[305] When issuing a *Gissel* bargaining order, the NLRB considers the employer's unfair labor practices, the effects of the ULPs on elections, the likelihood of the employer committing ULPs in the future, and the need to ensure a fair election.[306]

Notes to Chapter 4

1.   *See* News Release No. R-2544, Nat'l Labor Relations Bd., NLRB General Counsel Arthur Rosenfeld Issues Report on Recent Case Developments (Nov. 17, 2004), www.nlrb.gov/news-outreach/news-releases; *see also* Verizon Info. Sys., 335 N.L.R.B. 558, 559 (2001); Adrienne E. Eaton & Jill Kriesky, *Union Organizing Under Neutrality and Card Check Agreements*, 55 INDUS. & LAB. REL. REV. 42, 47 (2001).

2.   James J. Brudney, *Neutrality Agreements and Card Check Recognition: Prospects for Changing Paradigms*, 90 IOWA L. REV. 819 (2005).

3.   Paul Weiler, *Promises to Keep: Securing Workers' Rights to Self Organization Under the NLRA*, 96 HARV. L. REV. 1769 (1983).

4.   29 U.S.C. § 186(a)(2).

5.   *See* Mulhall v. Unite Here Local 355, 667 F.3d 1211 (11th Cir. 2012).

6.   Adcock v. Freightliner LLC, 550 F.3d 369 (4th Cir. 2008); Hotel Emps. & Rest. Emps. Union, Local 57 v. Sage Hosp. Res., LLC, 390 F.3d 206 (3d Cir. 2004).

7.   Mulhall v. Unite Here Local 355, 667 F.3d 1211 (11th Cir. 2012), *cert. granted*, 133 S. Ct. 2849 (June 24, 2013), *cert. dismissed as improvidently granted*, 134 S. Ct. 594 (Dec. 10, 2013), *cert. denied*, 134 S. Ct. 822 (Dec. 16, 2013).

8.   New Otani Hotel & Garden, 331 N.L.R.B. 1078 (2001).

9.   29 U.S.C. § 185(a).

10.   Hotel & Rest. Emps. Union Local 217 v. J.P. Morgan Hotel, 996 F.2d 561 (2d Cir. 1993).

11.   Verizon Info. Sys. & Commc'ns Workers of Am., 335 N.L.R.B. 558, 559 (2001) (citing Pall Biomedical Prods. Corp., 331 N.L.R.B. 1674, 1677 (2000)); *see also* Retail Clerks v. Lion Dry Goods, Inc., 369 U.S. 17 (1962); Textile Workers v. Lincoln Mills of Ala., 353 U.S. 448 (1957).

12.   *Verizon*, 335 N.L.R.B. at 560–61 (citing Briggs Ind., 63 N.L.R.B. 1270 (1945)); *see also* Lexington House, 328 N.L.R.B. 894 (1999).

13.   Goodless Elec. Co., 332 N.L.R.B. 1035, 1038 (2000), *rev'd on other grounds sub nom.* NLRB v. Goodless Bros. Elec. Co., 285 F.3d 102 (1st Cir. 2002) (citing Snow & Sons, 134 N.L.R.B. 709 (1961), *enforced*, 308 F.2d 687 (9th Cir. 1962)).

14.   Jefferson Smurfit Corp., 331 N.L.R.B. 809 (2000) (relying on Nantucket Fish Co., 309 N.L.R.B. 794 (1992)).

15.   *Verizon*, 335 N.L.R.B. at 561.

16.   Verizon Info. Sys. & Commc'ns Workers of Am., 335 N.L.R.B. 558 (2001).

17.   *See id.* at 558; *see also* Pall Biomedical Prods. Corp., 331 N.L.R.B. 1674 (2000); Retail Clerks v. Lion Dry Goods, Inc., 369 U.S. 17 (1962); Textile Workers v. Lincoln Mills of Ala., 353 U.S. 448 (1957).

18.   Dana Corp., 356 N.L.R.B. 256, 257, 261–64 (2010).

19.   Majestic Weaving Co., 147 N.L.R.B. 859, 860–61 (1964).

20. Sullivan Elec. Co., 199 N.L.R.B. 809 (1972), *enforced*, 479 F.2d 1270 (6th Cir. 1973).

21. Struksnes Constr. Co., 165 N.L.R.B. 1062, 1063 (1967).

22. *Id.* at 1063.

23. Lamons Gasket Co., 357 N.L.R.B. 739, 748 (2011) (citing Lee Lumber & Bldg. Material Corp., 334 N.L.R.B. 399 (2001), *aff'd*, 310 F.2d 209 (D.C. Cir. 2002)).

24. *See* Lamons Gasket Co., 357 N.L.R.B. No. 72, at *14 (Aug. 30, 2011); Garner/Morrison, LLC, 356 N.L.R.B. No. 163 (May 27, 2011); Majestic Weaving Co., 147 N.L.R.B. 859, 860–61 (1964).

25. Am. Sunroof Corp., 243 N.L.R.B. 1128 (1979).

26. Allentown Mack Sales & Serv. v. NLRB, 522 U.S. 359 (1998).

27. Levitz Furniture Co., 333 N.L.R.B. 717 (2001). In *Levitz*, the employer received a petition containing signatures from what appeared to be a majority of unit employees stating that they no longer desired representation from the incumbent union, and informed the union that it intended to withdraw recognition at the end of the contract term. Within two weeks, the union informed the employer that it had objective evidence establishing that it retained majority support and was willing to show this evidence to the employer. The employer never examined the union's evidence and withdrew recognition from the union when the contract expired.

28. *Levitz*, 333 N.L.R.B. at 717.

29. *See* NLRB Gen. Couns. Mem. 02-01, Guideline Memorandum Concerning *Levitz* (Oct. 22, 2001), www.nlrb.gov/reports-guidance/general-counsel-memos.

30. *Id.; see also* Pac. Coast Supply, 360 N.L.R.B. 538 (2014).

31. Parkwood Dev. Ctr., 347 N.L.R.B. 974 (2006).

32. *Id. See also* Lily Transp. Corp., 363 NLRB No. 15 (Sept. 30, 2015) (employer could not prove actual loss of majority support based on unauthenticated petition signatures and hearsay testimony).

33. Port Printing Ad & Specialties, 344 N.L.R.B. 354 (2005).

34. Mem. GC 02-01, *supra* note 29.

35. Highlands Reg'l Med. Ctr., 347 N.L.R.B. 1404 (2006).

36. *Id.* at 1404.

37. Scomas of Sausalito, LLC v. NLRB, 849 F.3d 1147 (D.C. Cir. 2017).

38. NLRB Gen. Couns. Mem. 02-01, *supra* note 29.

39. *Id.*

40. Representation—Case Procedures, 79 Fed. Reg. 74,308 (Dec. 15, 2014) (to be codified at 29 C.F.R. § 102.60 *et seq.*).

41. *Id.*

42. Chamber of Commerce v. NLRB, 879 F. Supp. 2d 18 (D.D.C. 2012).

43. 29 U.S.C. § 159(c)(1).

44. 29 C.F.R. § 102.60.

45. 29 C.F.R. § 102.63–102.64.

46. Dixie Elec. Membership, 358 N.L.R.B. 1089 (2012) (NLRB refused to consider UC petition that was filed after the execution of the agreement and sought

to clarify the unit based on supervisory status, where no reasonable explanation was provided for the delay in filing and clarification would disrupt the collective bargaining relationship), *aff'd and incorporated by reference in* Dixie Elec. Membership Co. 361 N.L.R.B. 942 (2014), *aff'd*, 814 F.3d 752 (5th Cir. 2016).

47. Linden Lumber Div. v. NLRB, 419 U.S. 301 (1974).

48. *See* New Otani Hotel & Garden, 331 N.L.R.B. 1078 (2000); *see also* PSM Steel Constr., 309 N.L.R.B. 1302 (1992); Albuquerque Insulation Contractor, 256 N.L.R.B. 61 (1981).

49. Windee's Metal Indus. Inc., 309 N.L.R.B. 1074 (1992).

50. *See, e.g.*, Martino's Complete Home Furnishings, 145 N.L.R.B. 604 (1963); *see also* John's Valley Foods, 237 N.L.R.B. 425 (1978); Autohaus-Brugger, Inc., 173 N.L.R.B. 184 (1968); Old Angus Rest., 165 N.L.R.B. 675 (1967); Miratti's, Inc., 132 N.L.R.B. 699 (1961).

51. *See* New Otani Hotel & Garden, 331 N.L.R.B. 1078 (2000); *see also* Roberts Tires, 212 N.L.R.B. 405 (1974); Holiday Inn of Providence, 179 N.L.R.B. 337 (1969); Rochelle's Rest., 152 N.L.R.B. 1401 (1965); Capitol Mkt. No. 1, 145 N.L.R.B. 1430 (1964).

52. *See* Deluxe Metal Furniture Co., 121 N.L.R.B. 995 (1958); *see also* Shen-Valley Meat Packers, Inc., 261 N.L.R.B. 958 (1982).

53. Lamons Gasket Co., 357 N.L.R.B. 739, 748 (2011) (citing Lee Lumber & Bldg. Material Corp., 334 N.L.R.B. 399 (2001), *aff'd*, 310 F.2d 209 (D.C. Cir. 2002)).

54. *Lee Lumber*, 334 N.L.R.B. at 402.

55. Rollins Transp. Sys., 296 N.L.R.B. 793 (1989).

56. Custom Deliveries, Inc., 315 N.L.R.B. 1018 (1994).

57. 29 U.S.C. § 159.

58. Fall River Dyeing & Finishing Corp. v. NLRB, 482 U.S. 27, 37 (1987).

59. Children's Habilitation Ctrs., 289 N.L.R.B. No. 109 (1988), *enforced*, 887 F.2d 130 (7th Cir. 1989).

60. Mar-Jac Poultry, 136 N.L.R.B. 785 (1962); Fallbrook Hosp., 360 N.L.R.B. 644 (2014) (ordering a full year extension of the certification bar when employer had refused to bargain for most of the initial year).

61. 29 C.F.R. § 103.20.

62. *See* Truserv Corp., 349 N.L.R.B. 227 (2007); *see also* Passavant Health Ctr., 278 N.L.R.B. 483 (1986), *reinstated by* Truserv Corp., 349 N.L.R.B. 227 (2007).

63. Dairyland USA Corp., 347 N.L.R.B. 310 (2006).

64. Union Mfg. Co., 123 N.L.R.B. 1633 (1959).

65. Gen. Extrusion Co., 121 N.L.R.B. 1165 (1958).

66. *See* Cleveland Cliffs Iron Co., 117 N.L.R.B. 668 (1957); *see also* Bordo Prods. Co., 117 N.L.R.B. 313 (1957).

67. Dick Kelchner Excavating Co., 236 N.L.R.B. 1414 (1978).

68. *See* NLRB, CASEHANDLING MANUAL, PART TWO: REPRESENTATION PROCEEDINGS §§ 11110–11118 (Jan. 2017) [hereinafter CASEHANDLING MANUAL, PART TWO], https://www.nlrb.gov/reports-guidance/manuals.

69. Waumbec Dyeing & Finishing Co., 101 N.L.R.B. 1069 (1952).

70.　*See* Garden Manor Farms, Inc., 341 N.L.R.B. 192 (2004); *see also* Transp. Maint. Servs., LLC, 328 N.L.R.B. 691 (1999).

71.　Sears, Roebuck & Co., 107 N.L.R.B. 716 (1954).

72.　*Levitz*, 333 N.L.R.B. 717.

73.　Ill. Sch. Bus Co., 231 N.L.R.B. 1 (1977).

74.　NLRB Rules & Regs. § 102.62(b), www.nlrb.gov/reports-guidance/rules-regulations.

75.　*Id.* § 102.62(a).

76.　*Id.* § 102.62(c).

77.　29 C.F.R. §§ 102.63–102.66.

78.　BRENT GARREN, JOHN E. HIGGINS, JR. & DAVID A. KADELA, HOW TO TAKE A CASE BEFORE THE NLRB, ch. 7(II)(D) (BBNA 9th ed. 2016).

79.　29 C.F.R. §§ 102.63-102.66.

80.　29 C.F.R. §§ 102.63–102.66.

81.　29 C.F.R. §§ 102.66(h).

82.　NLRB Rules & Regs. § 102.67(c).

83.　NLRB, THE NATIONAL LABOR RELATIONS BOARD AND YOU: REPRESENTATION CASES, www.americanbar.org/content/dam/aba/administrative/labor_law/meetings/2010/annualconference/176.authcheckdam.pdf.

84.　Dodge of Naperville, Inc. & Burke Auto. Grp., Inc., 357 N.L.R.B. No. 183 (2012) ("compelling circumstances" may exist after merger if unit employees do not have an identifiable community of interest).

85.　A.H. Belo Corp. (Dall. Morning News), 285 N.L.R.B. 807 (1987).

86.　*See* Barron Heating & Air Conditioning, Inc., 343 N.L.R.B. No. 58 (2004); *see also* Canal Carting, Inc., 339 N.L.R.B. 969 (2003); NLRB, AN OUTLINE OF LAW AND PROCEDURE IN REPRESENTATION CASES § 12-220 (June 2017) [hereinafter NLRB LAW AND PROCEDURE], https://www.nlrb.gov/reports-guidance/manuals.

87.　*See* Crown Zellerbach Corp., 246 N.L.R.B. 202 (1980); *see also* Jos. Schlitz Brewing Co., 206 N.L.R.B. 928 (1973); Land Title Guar. & Tr. Co., 194 N.L.R.B. 148 (1972); NLRB LAW AND PROCEDURE, *supra* note 86, §§ 12-222, 12-224.

88.　*See Schlitz*, 206 N.L.R.B. at 928; *see also* Duke Power Co., 191 N.L.R.B. 308 (1971); NLRB LAW AND PROCEDURE, *supra* note 86, § 12-223.

89.　*See* Big Y Foods, 238 N.L.R.B. 855 (1978); *see also* N. Am. Rockwell Corp., 193 N.L.R.B. 985 (1971); NLRB LAW AND PROCEDURE, *supra* note 86, § 12-226.

90.　*See* Ready-Mix USA, Inc., 340 N.L.R.B. No. 107 (2003); *see also* Plymouth Shoe Co., 185 N.L.R.B. 732 (1970); Westinghouse Elec. Corp., 144 N.L.R.B. 455 (1963); NLRB LAW AND PROCEDURE, *supra* note 86, § 12-226.

91.　*See* NLRB v. Metro. Life Ins. Co., 380 U.S. 438 (1965); *see also* NLRB v. Lundy Packing Co., 68 F.3d 1577 (4th Cir. 1995).

92.　Globe Mach. & Stamping Co., 3 N.L.R.B. 294 (1937).

93.　Kaiser Aluminum & Chem. Corp., 177 N.L.R.B. 682 (1969).

94.　*See* Lindsay Newspapers, Inc., 192 N.L.R.B. 478 (1971); *see also* Holiday Inns of Am., 176 N.L.R.B. 939 (1969); New Deal Cab Co., 159 N.L.R.B. 1838 (1966); Metal Textile Corp., 99 N.L.R.B. 1326 (1950); NLRB LAW AND PROCEDURE, *supra* note 86, §§ 12-233, 12-235.

95. *See* Glass Bottle Blowers Local 106 (Owens-Ill.), 210 N.L.R.B. 943 (1974); *see also* Land Title Guar. & Tr. Co., 194 N.L.R.B. 148 (1972); Cuneo E. Press, 106 N.L.R.B. 343 (1953); NLRB LAW AND PROCEDURE, *supra* note 86, § 12-234.

96. Morand Bros. Beverage Co., 91 N.L.R.B. 409 (1950).

97. PCC Structurals, Inc., 365 N.L.R.B. No. 160 (Dec. 15, 2017) (overruling Specialty Healthcare & Rehabilitation Ctr. of Mobile, 357 N.L.R.B. 934 (2011)).

98. *See* Boeing Co., 337 N.L.R.B. 152, 153 (2001); *see also* Overnite Transp. Co., 331 N.L.R.B. 662, 663 (2000); NLRB v. Lake Cty. Ass'n for Retarded, 128 F.3d 1181, 1185 n.2 (7th Cir. 1997).

99. Dixie Elec. Membership, 358 N.L.R.B. No. 120 (2012), *aff'd and incorporated by reference in* Dixie Elec. Membership Co. 361 N.L.R.B. No. 107 (2014).

100. Armstrong Rubber Co., 144 N.L.R.B. 1115 (1963).

101. Wuster, Bernardi & Emmons, Inc., 192 N.L.R.B. 1049 (1971).

102. Reynolds Elec. & Eng'g Co., 133 N.L.R.B. 113 (1961). *But see* St. Francis Hosp., 271 N.L.R.B. 948 (1984).

103. Robbins & Meyers, Inc., 144 N.L.R.B. 295 (1963).

104. *See* Haag Drug Co. Inc., 146 N.L.R.B. 798 (1964); *see also* Longs Stores, Inc., 129 N.L.R.B. 1495 (1961); Skagg's PayLess Drug Stores, 134 N.L.R.B. 168 (1961).

105. *See* Express-News Corp., 223 N.L.R.B. 627 (1976); *see also* Jersey Publ'g Co., 76 N.L.R.B. 467 (1948).

106. Long Island Univ., 200 N.L.R.B. 408 (1971).

107. 29 U.S.C. § 159(b)(1).

108. Bellagio, LLC v. NLRB, 863 F.3d 839 (D.C. Cir. 2017) (concluding that casino surveillance technicians constituted guards).

109. *See* Dixie Belle Mills, Inc., 139 N.L.R.B. 629 (1962); *see also* Airco Inc., 273 N.L.R.B. 348 (1984).

110. Esco Corp., 298 N.L.R.B. 837 (1990).

111. W. Elec. Co. (Balt., Md.), 98 N.L.R.B. 1018 (1952).

112. *See* Hilander Foods, 348 N.L.R.B. 1200 (2006); *see also* Prince Telecom, 347 N.L.R.B. 789 (2006).

113. *See* Kroger Co., 148 N.L.R.B. 569 (1964); *see also* Greenhoot, Inc., 205 N.L.R.B. 250 (1973).

114. *See* Quality Limestone Prods., 143 N.L.R.B. 589 (1963); *see also* Milwaukee Indep. Meat Packers Ass'n, 223 N.L.R.B. 922 (1976).

115. *See* Cent. Transp., Inc., 328 N.L.R.B. 407 (1999); *see also* Chi. Metro. Home Builders Ass'n, 119 N.L.R.B. 1184 (1958); Cab Operating Corp., 153 N.L.R.B. 878, 879–880 (1965); Bennett Stone Co., 139 N.L.R.B. 1422, 1424 (1962); Sands Point Nursing Home, 319 N.L.R.B. 390 (1995); St. Luke's Hosp., 234 N.L.R.B. 130 (1978) (NLRB found that the history of multi-employer bargaining governed the scope of the unit).

116. *See* G.L. Milliken Plastering, 340 N.L.R.B. 1169 (2003); *see also* Carl Buddig & Co., 328 N.L.R.B. 929 (1999); Fleming Foods, 313 N.L.R.B. 948 (1994); Premier Plastering, Inc., 342 N.L.R.B. 1072 (2004).

117. S.D. Warren Co., 114 N.L.R.B. 410, 411 (1956). For other illustrations of groups found appropriate as "residual," see Cities Serv. Oil Co., 200 N.L.R.B. 470 (1972) (in a multiplant situation); Walter Kidde & Co., 191 N.L.R.B. 10 (1971) (plant clerical employees); Water Tower Inn, 139 N.L.R.B. 842, 848 (1962) (food service and kitchen employees); Hot Shoppes, Inc., 143 N.L.R.B. 578 (1963) (food preparation employees and related categories); Rostone Corp., 196 N.L.R.B. 467 (1972) (so-called hot mold employees).

118. Huckleberry Youth Programs, 326 N.L.R.B. 1272 (1998).

119. Armstrong Rubber Co., 144 N.L.R.B. 1115, 1119 n.11 (1963) (unit sought as "residual" did not contain all of the unrepresented employees).

120. *In re* G.L. Milliken Plastering, 340 N.L.R.B. 1169 (2003).

121. *See* NLRB, OFFICE OF GEN. COUNSEL, GUIDE FOR HEARING OFFICERS IN NLRB REPRESENTATION AND SECTION 10(K) PROCEEDINGS 81 (Sept. 2003) [hereinafter GUIDE FOR HEARING OFFICERS], www.nlrb.gov/sites/default/files/attachments/basic-page/node-1727/hearing_officers_guide.pdf.

122. *Id.* at 72.

123. *See* Allis-Chalmers Mfg. Co., 179 N.L.R.B. 1 (1969); *see also* Briggs Ind. Corp., 63 N.L.R.B. 1270 (1945).

124. *See* Safety Carrier, Inc., 306 N.L.R.B. 960, 969 (1992); *see also* Progressive Serv. Die Co., 323 N.L.R.B. 1182 (1997).

125. Ryder Integrated Logistics, Inc., 329 N.L.R.B. 1493 (1999).

126. Safeway Stores, Inc., 256 N.L.R.B. 918 (1981).

127. Giant Eagle Mkts. Co., 308 N.L.R.B. 206 (1992).

128. *See, e.g.,* Kroger Co., 219 N.L.R.B. 388 (1975); Shaw's Supermarkets, 343 N.L.R.B. 963 (2004).

129. *See* 29 U.S.C. § 152(3); *see also* NLRB v. United Ins. Co., 390 U.S. 254 (1968); Standard Oil Co., 230 N.L.R.B. 967 (1997); FedEx Home Delivery, 361 N.L.R.B. No. 55 (2014) (clarifying that entrepreneurial opportunity remained just one factor to consider and that analysis should focus on actual, not merely theoretical, opportunity), *enforcement denied*, 849 F.3d 1123 (D.C. Cir. 2017); NLRB LAW AND PROCEDURE, *supra* note 86, § 17-400.

130. Ariz. Republic, 349 N.L.R.B. 1040 (2007).

131. 29 U.S.C. § 152(3).

132. Rodriguez v. Conagra, Inc., 387 F. Supp. 951 (D.P.R. 1974), *aff'd*, 527 F.2d 540 (1st Cir. 1976).

133. *See* Nationsway Transp. Serv., 316 N.L.R.B. 4 (1995); *see also* Neisner Bros., Inc., 200 N.L.R.B. 935 (1972); NLRB LAW AND PROCEDURE § 17-506; GUIDE FOR HEARING OFFICERS, *supra* note 121, at 110.

134. Big "N," Dep't Store No. 307, 200 N.L.R.B. 935 (1972).

135. Davis Mem'l Goodwill Indus. v. NLRB, 108 F.3d 406 (D.C. Cir. 1997).

136. Kinney Drugs, Inc. v. NLRB, 74 F.3d 1419, 1435 (2d Cir. 1996).

137. M.B. Sturgis, Inc., 331 N.L.R.B. 1298 (2000) (combined unit need only satisfy the community-of-interest test), *overruled by* Oakwood Care Ctr., 343 N.L.R.B. 659 (2004) (requiring employer consent in addition to a community of

interest), *overruled by* Miller & Anderson, Inc., 364 N.L.R.B. No. 39 (July 11, 2016) (returning to the *M.B. Sturgis* standard).

138. Miller & Anderson, Inc., 364 N.L.R.B. No. 39 (July 11, 2016).

139. *See* L&B Cooling, 267 N.L.R.B. 1 (1983); *see also* Me. Apple Growers, Inc., 254 N.L.R.B. 501 (1981); NLRB LAW AND PROCEDURE, *supra* note 86, § 20-300; GUIDE FOR HEARING OFFICERS, *supra* note 121, at 113.

140. Bogus Basin Recreation Ass'n, 212 N.L.R.B. 833 (1974).

141. *See* Dynacorp/Dynair Serv., Inc., 320 N.L.R.B. 120 (1995); *see also* Johnson Auto Spring Serv., 221 N.L.R.B. 809 (1975); NLRB LAW AND PROCEDURE, *supra* note 86, § 20-610.

142. *See* Mackay Radio & Tel. Co., 305 U.S. 332, 345 (1938) (noting that it is not a ULP for the employer to "replace the striking employees with others in an effort to carry on the business"); *see also* Redwing Carriers, Inc., 137 N.L.R.B. 1545, 1548 (1962); Hot Shoppes, Inc., 146 N.L.R.B. 802, 804 (1964).

143. *See* O.E. Butterfield, Inc., 319 N.L.R.B. 1004 (1995); *see also* Macy's Mo.-Kan. Div., 173 N.L.R.B. 1500 (1969); Greenspan Engraving Corp., 137 N.L.R.B. 1308 (1962); Tampa Sand & Material Co., 129 N.L.R.B. 1273 (1961); NLRB LAW AND PROCEDURE, *supra* note 86, § 23-120.

144. Bio-Science Labs. v. NLRB, 542 F.2d 505 (9th Cir. 1976).

145. W. Wilton Wood, Inc., 127 N.L.R.B. 1675 (1960).

146. Davison-Paxon Co., 185 N.L.R.B. 21 (1970).

147. *See* N.Y. Display & Die Cutting Corp., 341 N.L.R.B. 930 (2004); *see also* Arlington Masonry Supply, Inc., 339 N.L.R.B. 817 (2003); NLRB LAW AND PROCEDURE, *supra* note 86, §§ 20-100 to 20-140.

148. Wadsworth Theatre Mgmt., 349 N.L.R.B. 122 (2007).

149. Marquette Gen. Hosp., Inc., 218 N.L.R.B. 713 (1975).

150. Steiny & Co., 308 N.L.R.B. 1323 (1992).

151. *See* Folger Coffee Co., 250 N.L.R.B. 1 (1980); *see also* Audiovox Commc'n Corp., 323 N.L.R.B. 647 (1997).

152. NLRB LAW AND PROCEDURE, *supra* note 86, § 19-510.

153. *See* Sheffield Corp., 134 N.L.R.B. 1101 (1962); *see also* Va. Mfg. Co., 311 N.L.R.B. 992, 993 (1993); Folger Coffee Co., 250 N.L.R.B. 1 (1980); NLRB LAW AND PROCEDURE, *supra* note 86, § 19-500.

154. S. Indus. Servs., Inc., 342 N.L.R.B. 215 (2004). Detailers take client blueprints and specifications for industrial steel and generate drawings on computer-aided design machines. The production employees then fabricate the items, and the erection crew assembles them in the field. "The detailers are not engineers, are not required to have an engineering and/or technical background . . . . Detailers work in a separate area from the production employees . . . . Detailers spend approximately 90 percent of their time in their own area performing specialized detailing functions, and approximately 5–15 percent of their time on the production floor communicating with 'production employees.'" *Id.* at 215.

155. Peco Energy Co., 322 N.L.R.B. 1074 (1997).

156. Burns & Roe Servs. Corp., 313 N.L.R.B. 1307, 1308 (1994).

157. *See* E.I. Du Pont de Nemours & Co., 162 N.L.R.B. 413 (1966); *see also* MGM Mirage, 338 N.L.R.B. 529 (2002); E.I. Du Pont de Nemours & Co., 192 N.L.R.B. 1019 (1971).

158. *See* Burns & Roe Servs. Corp., 313 N.L.R.B. 1307 (1994); *see also* E.I. Du Pont de Nemours & Co., 162 N.L.R.B. 413 (1966); NLRB LAW AND PROCEDURE, *supra* note 86, § 16-200.

159. *In re* MGM Mirage, 338 N.L.R.B. 529 (2002) (NLRB included upholsterers with carpenters in a unit, noting such a unit was an area practice; carpenters performed craft work, and together with the upholsterers, were separately supervised, and had limited interchange with other engineering department employees).

160. *See* Dodge City of Wauwatosa, 282 N.L.R.B. 459 (1986); *see also* Fletcher Jones Chevrolet, 300 N.L.R.B. 875 (1990).

161. Mason & Hanger-Silas Mason Co., 180 N.L.R.B. 467 (1970) (among the reasons given for granting them a self-determination election, in addition to noting that they constituted "a homogeneous, identifiable, traditional, departmental group with a nucleus of craft tool and die makers and machinists who are engaged in the skills of their trade," was the fact that they had retained their identity as a distinct group during their inclusion in the broader unit).

162. Union Carbide Corp., 156 N.L.R.B. 634 (1966).

163. *Id.*

164. *See* Towmotor Corp., 187 N.L.R.B. 1027, 1029 (1971); *cf.* Am. Bosch Arma Corp., 163 N.L.R.B. 650 (1967) (denying the petition, in a toolroom employee severance case, for a craft unit on the basis of the functional interrelationship of toolroom employees with other phases of the employer's production operation; frequent contact and common interest with production employees and with other skilled employees; a twelve-year bargaining history; and "the questionable qualifications of the Petitioner as a specialist in craft representation"); Paris Mfg. Co., 163 N.L.R.B. 964 (1967) (finding that a machinist group was not entitled to severance where, in the face of a long bargaining history, it was found that the employees in the group were primarily engaged in production work under the same supervision as the production employees, and there was no showing that "any of their alleged special interests have been prejudiced by their inclusion in the existing unit").

165. *See* F.N. Burt Co., 130 N.L.R.B. 1115 (1961); *see also* B.P. Alaska, Inc., 230 N.L.R.B. 986 (1977).

166. *See* Ore-Ida Foods, 313 N.L.R.B. 1016, 1019 (1994); *see also* Am. Cyanamid Co., 131 N.L.R.B. 909 (1961); Wah Chang Albany Corp., 171 N.L.R.B. 385 (1968); Gen. Foods Corp., 166 N.L.R.B. 1032 (1967); NLRB LAW AND PROCEDURE, *supra* note 86, §§ 16-130, 16-200.

167. Moloney Elec. Co., 169 N.L.R.B. 464 (1968).

168. Gen. Foods Corp., 166 N.L.R.B. 1032 (1967).

169. Esco Corp., 298 N.L.R.B. 837 (1990).

170. *See* A. Harris Co., 116 N.L.R.B. 1628 (1957); *see also* A. Russo & Sons, Inc., 329 N.L.R.B. 402 (1999); Esco Corp., 298 N.L.R.B. 837 (1990); Wickes Corp.,

201 N.L.R.B. 610 (1973), *rev'd on other grounds*, 231 N.L.R.B. 154 (1977); Frisch's Rests., 182 N.L.R.B. 544 (1970); NLRB LAW AND PROCEDURE, *supra* note 86, § 15-270.

171. It may also be appropriate to create different units that distinguish between local drivers and over-the-road drivers. This distinction is appropriate if the two groups are functionally distinct groups with interests that can be effectively represented separately for bargaining purposes. Ga. Highway Express, 150 N.L.R.B. 1649 (1965); *see also* NLRB LAW AND PROCEDURE, *supra* note 86, § 15-1333.

172. E.H. Koester Bakery Co., 136 N.L.R.B. 1006 (1962).

173. *Id.; see also* Overnite Transp., 322 N.L.R.B. 743 (1996); NLRB LAW AND PROCEDURE, *supra* note 86, §§ 15-131 to 15-136.

174. Tallahassee Coca-Cola Bottling Co., 168 N.L.R.B. 1037 (1968), *enforced*, NLRB v. Tallahassee Coca-Cola Bottling Co., 409 F.2d 201 (5th Cir. 1969).

175. *See* Hamilton Halter Co., 270 N.L.R.B. 331 (1994); *see also* Brown & Root, Inc., 314 N.L.R.B. 19, 23 (1994); Kroger Co., 204 N.L.R.B. 1055 (1973); Container Research Co., 188 N.L.R.B. 586, 587 (1971); NLRB LAW AND PROCEDURE, *supra* note 86, § 19-400 *et seq.*

176. Swift & Co., 166 N.L.R.B. 89 (1967).

177. NLRB v. Yeshiva Univ., 444 U.S. 672 (1980).

178. Pac. Lutheran Univ., 361 N.L.R.B. 1404 (2014).

179. Cardinal Timothy Manning, 223 N.L.R.B. 1218 (1976).

180. Fordham Univ., 214 N.L.R.B. 971 (1974).

181. Cardinal Timothy Manning, 223 N.L.R.B. 1218 (1976).

182. Ne. Univ., 218 N.L.R.B. 247 (1975).

183. N.Y. Univ., 205 N.L.R.B. 4 (1973).

184. *Id.* at 6–7.

185. *Id.*

186. Pac. Lutheran Univ., 361 N.L.R.B. 1404 (2014).

187. Saint Xavier Univ., 364 N.L.R.B. No. 85 (Aug. 23, 2016); *see also* Seattle Univ., 364 N.L.R.B. No. 84 (Aug. 23, 2016).

188. Columbia Univ., 364 N.L.R.B. No. 90 (2016).

189. *See* Leland Stanford Junior Univ., 214 N.L.R.B. 621 (1974) (holding that graduate students are "primarily students," not employees), *overruled by* N.Y. Univ., 332 N.L.R.B. 1205, 1206 (2000) (holding that graduate students are statutory employees), *overruled by* Brown Univ., 342 N.L.R.B. 483 (2004) (not employees), *overruled by* Columbia Univ., 364 N.L.R.B. No. 90 (2016) (statutory employees).

190. *See* 29 C.F.R. § 103.30(a); *see also* Am. Hosp. Ass'n v. NLRB, 499 U.S. 606 (1991); *see also* NLRB Gen. Couns. Mem. 91-3, Guidelines Concerning Application of Health Care Rule (May 9, 1991), www.nlrb.gov/reports-guidance/general-counsel-memos; NLRB Gen. Couns. Mem. 91-4, Health Care Unit Placement Issues (June 5, 1991), www.nlrb.gov/reports-guidance/general-counsel-memos.

191. *See* 29 C.F.R. § 103.30(b).

192. *See* 29 C.F.R. § 103.30(a); *see also* St. Margaret Mem'l Hosp. v. NLRB, 991 F.2d 1146 (3d Cir. 1993); St. Mary's Duluth Clinic Health Sys., 332 N.L.R.B. 1419 (2000); Kaiser Found. Health Plan, 333 N.L.R.B. 557 (2001); Dominican Santa Cruz Hosp., 307 N.L.R.B. 506 (1992); St. John's Hosp., 307 N.L.R.B. 767 (1992).

193. GUIDE FOR HEARING OFFICERS, *supra* note 121, at 83.

194. 29 C.F.R. § 103.30(f)(2).

195. *See id.; see also* A-1 Schmidlin Plumbing Co., 284 N.L.R.B. 1597 (1987); R.I. Hosp., 313 N.L.R.B. 343 (1993); Child's Hosp., 307 N.L.R.B. 90 (1992); NLRB Gen. Couns. Mem. 91-3, *supra* note 190.

196. 29 C.F.R. § 103.30(f)(2).

197. *See* CGE Caresystems, Inc., 328 N.L.R.B. 748 (1999); *see also* Park Manor Care Ctr., Inc., 305 N.L.R.B. 872 (1991).

198. *Park Manor*, 305 N.L.R.B. 872.

199. *Id.* at 875.

200. Park Manor, 328 N.L.R.B. 872 (1991), *overruled by* Specialty, 357 N.L.R.B. 934 (2011), *and reinstated by* PCC Structurals, Inc., 365 N.L.R.B. No. 160 (Dec. 15, 2017).

201. *See* Salem Hosp., 330 N.L.R.B. 560 (2001); *see also* Charter Hosp., 313 N.L.R.B. 951; Child's Hosp., Inc., 310 N.L.R.B. 560 (1993).

202. NLRB v. Ky. River Cmty. Care, Inc., 532 U.S. 706 (2001).

203. NLRB v. Health Care & Ret. Co. of Am., 511 U.S. 571 (1994).

204. FHP, Inc., 274 N.L.R.B. 1141 (1985).

205. *Id.*

206. *See* NLRB Gen. Couns. Mem. 91-4, *supra* note 190; *see also* Grp. Health Ass'n, 317 N.L.R.B. No. 37 (1995).

207. *See* Virtua Health, Inc., 344 N.L.R.B. 604 (2005) (paramedics); *see also* Lincoln Park Nursing & Convalescent Home, Inc., 318 N.L.R.B. 1160 (1995) (licensed practical nurses); R.I. Hosp., 313 N.L.R.B. 343 (1993) (surgical technicians and cerebrovascular laboratory technicians); Brattleboro Retreat, 310 N.L.R.B. 615 (1993) (adolescent care workers and day care coordinators); Meriter Hosp., 306 N.L.R.B. 598 (1992) (medical imaging quality control technicians).

208. *See* Marian Med. Ctr., 339 N.L.R.B. 127 (2003) (medical transcription-ists); *see also* R.I. Hosp., 313 N.L.R.B. 343 (1993) (radiology technician assistants, pharmacy technicians, and interpreters); Mercy Health Servs. N., 311 N.L.R.B. 1091 (1993) (biomedical engineers, renal dialysis technicians, physical therapy technicians, and health information/medical records technicians); San Juan Reg'l Med. Ctr., 307 N.L.R.B. 117 (1992) (biomedical technicians); Trinity Mem'l Hosp. of Cudhay, 219 N.L.R.B. 215 (1975) (EKG technicians).

209. *See* Ingalls Mem'l Hosp., 309 N.L.R.B. 393 (1992); *see also* Jewish Hosp. of St. Louis, 305 N.L.R.B. 955 (1991).

210. *See* St. Luke's Health Care Ass'n, 312 N.L.R.B. 139 (1993); *see also* Univ. of Pittsburgh Med. Ctr. v. NLRB, 88 F.3d 1300 (3d Cir. 1996) (telecommunications employees); Ingalls Mem'l Hosp., 309 N.L.R.B. 393 (1992) (biomedical technicians); Jewish Hosp. of St. Louis, 305 N.L.R.B. 955 (1991) (all others).

211. *See* Silver Cross Hosp., 350 N.L.R.B. 114 (2007) (computer operators); *see also* Ingalls Mem'l Hosp., 309 N.L.R.B. 393 (1992) (tool inventory employees, construction project coordinators, draftsmen, and printers); Jewish Hosp. of

St. Louis, 305 N.L.R.B. 955 (1991) (occupational therapy craftsmen, yard maintenance, grounds keepers, and equipment specialists).

212. *See* Charter Hosp. of St. Louis, 313 N.L.R.B. 951 (1994) (billing, collection, purchasing, payroll, accounting and admitting clerks); *see also* R.I. Hosp., 313 N.L.R.B. 343 (1993) (data entry and data processing employees).

213. *See* Lincoln Park Nursing & Convalescent Home, Inc., 318 N.L.R.B. 1160 (1995) (nursing department secretaries); *see also* Charter Hosp. of St. Louis, 313 N.L.R.B. 951 (1994) (receptionists); R.I. Hosp., 313 N.L.R.B. 343 (1993) (clerical employees who work on patient floors or otherwise outside the business office).

214. *See* Lincoln Park Nursing & Convalescent Home, Inc., 318 N.L.R.B. 1160 (1995) (nursing department clerks); *see also* Charter Hosp. of St. Louis, 313 N.L.R.B. 951 (1994) (receptionists); R.I. Hosp., 313 N.L.R.B. 343 (1993) (patient transporter, medical transcriptionists, EKG and EEG technicians, phlebotomists, patient consultants, and community relations coordinators); NLRB Gen. Couns. Mem. 91-4, *supra* note 190.

215. Gen. Shoe Corp., 77 N.L.R.B. 124 (1948).

216. *Id.*

217. NLRB v. Gissel Packing Co., 395 U.S. 575, 618 (1969).

218. *Id.; see also* Phillips 66, 360 N.L.R.B. No. 26 (2014) (predicted consequences of unionization cannot be considered objective economic realities if they are entirely within the employer's control).

219. Nat'l By-Product, Inc. v. NLRB, 931 F.2d 445 (7th Cir. 1991); *see also* Labrolia Baking Co., 361 N.L.R.B. No. 41 (2014) (mistranslated statement to non-English speaking employees that employer might have to hire a "legal workforce" if union election led to a strike constituted a threat of reprisal); Hendrickson USA, LLC, 366 N.L.R.B. No 7 (Jan. 25, 2018) (statements that workplace culture would "definitely" change constituted a threat of reprisal).

220. 1 JOHN E. HIGGINS, JR., THE DEVELOPING LABOR LAW 145–50 (ABA 7th ed. 2017) [hereinafter DEVELOPING LABOR LAW].

221. Guard Publ'g Co., 344 N.L.R.B. 1142 (2005).

222. Pembrook Mgmt., 296 N.L.R.B. 1226 (1989) (employer promised wage increases and bonuses if union was defeated and then granted such increases after election).

223. Crown Tar & Chem. Works, Inc. v. NLRB, 365 F.2d 588, 590 (10th Cir. 1966) (holding that employer's action in waiting to implement raises it had announced two months earlier was unlawful where it implemented the raises in the midst of an organizing campaign); Durham Sch. Servs., 360 N.L.R.B. No. 86 (2014) (same-day cash payments to correct for paycheck errors shortly before an election was an unlawful benefit when prior practice had been to correct for such errors in the next paycheck).

224. 1 DEVELOPING LABOR LAW, *supra* note 220, at 162–63.

225. Good Shepherd Home, Inc., 321 N.L.R.B. 426 (1996).

226. Gulf Caribe Mar. Inc., 330 N.L.R.B. 766 (2000).

227. Lake Mary Health Care & Rehab., 345 N.L.R.B. 544 (2005) (elimination of shift bonus during election period invalidates election); Lucky Cab Co., 360 N.L.R.B. No. 43 (2014) (employer unlawfully stated that the current leave of absence policy would be eliminated if union was elected).

228. NLRB v. Neuhoff Bros. Packers, 375 F.2d 372, 374–75 (5th Cir. 1967) (threats by supervisors to discontinue bonuses and to fire union adherents were unlawful).

229. Federated Logistics & Operations v. NLRB, 400 F.3d 920, 925 (D.C. Cir. 2005) (employer unlawfully stated that bargaining would start from "ground zero" and that it would move operations in the event of a strike).

230. Earthgrains Co., 336 N.L.R.B. 1119 (2001).

231. 1 DEVELOPING LABOR LAW, *supra* note 220, at 169–70.

232. *See* Atl. Limousine, Inc., 331 N.L.R.B. 1025 (2000); *see also* Comcast Cablevision-Taylor v. NLRB, 232 F.3d 490, 497 (6th Cir. 2000) (affirming *Atl. Limousine*).

233. *See Atl. Limousine*, 331 N.L.R.B. at 1025; *see also Comcast*, 232 F.3d at 497.

234. Sony Corp. of Am., 313 N.L.R.B. 420 (1993), *overruled in part by* Allegheny Ludlum Corp., 333 N.L.R.B. 734 (2001).

235. *Atl. Limousine*, 331 N.L.R.B. at 1029–30.

236. Peerless Plywood Co., 107 N.L.R.B. 427 (1953).

237. Guardsmark, LLC, 363 N.L.R.B. No. 103 (Jan. 29, 2016) (overruling Ore. Wash. Tel., 123 N.L.R.B. 339 (1959), which held that the prohibition begins when the ballots are mailed).

238. Milchem, Inc., 170 N.L.R.B. 362 (1968).

239. *See* Va. Concrete Corp., 338 N.L.R.B. 1182 (2003) ("vote no" text message sent to employees did not violate *Peerless Plywood* rule); *see also* Kalin Constr. Co., 321 N.L.R.B. 649 (1996) (prohibiting any changes to paycheck distribution process during twenty-four hours preceding election).

240. Kalin Constr. Co., 321 N.L.R.B. 649 (1996).

241. *Id.*

242. *Id.* at 650.

243. *Id.* at 652.

244. Blue Flash Express, Inc., 109 N.L.R.B. 591 (1954), *criticized in* Allegheny Ludlum Corp. v. NLRB, 104 F.3d 1354, 1359 (D.C. Cir. 1997) (criticizing the NLRB's general standard for non-polling inquiries in *Blue Flash* as abstract).

245. Struksnes Constr. Co., 165 N.L.R.B. 1062 (1967).

246. Kurz-Kasch, Inc., 239 N.L.R.B. 1044 (1978).

247. *See* Tri-Cty. Med. Ctr., Inc., 222 N.L.R.B. 1089 (1976); *see also* NLRB v. Pizza Crust Co. of Pa., Inc., 862 F.2d 49, 52–55 (3d Cir. 1988) (affirming standard set forth in *Tri-County*).

248. *Tri-County*, 222 N.L.R.B. at 1089.

249. Piedmont Gardens, 360 N.L.R.B. 813 (2014); Casino San Pablo, 361 N.L.R.B. 1350 (2014).

250. Lechmere, Inc. v. NLRB, 502 U.S. 527, 534 (1992).

251. *See* Caesars Entm't Corp. d/b/a Rio All-Suites Hotel & Casino, 28-CA-060841 (Board invited amici briefs on whether it should adhere to the current standard and if not, what standard should it adopt instead).

252. Purple Commc'ns, 361 N.L.R.B. 1050 (2014), *petition for review filed*, No. 17-70948 (9th Cir. 2017).

253. *See* Consol. Edison Co. v. NLRB, 305 U.S. 197, 217 (1938); *see also* NLRB v. Grower-Shipper Vegetable Ass'n, 122 F.2d 368, 376 (9th Cir. 1941).

254. *See Consol. Edison*, 305 U.S. at 217; *see also Grower-Shipper Vegetable*, 122 F.2d at 376.

255. *See* Arden Post Acute Rehab, 365 N.L.R.B. No. 109 (July 25, 2017) (employer created impression of surveillance by suggesting that surveillance cameras were used to monitor employee conversations); Promedica Health Sys., Inc., 343 N.L.R.B. 1351 (2004); *see also* Impact Indus., 285 N.L.R.B. 5 (1987) (creation of the impression of surveillance of union activities).

256. F.W. Woolworth Co., 310 N.L.R.B. 1197 (1993).

257. Timken Co., 331 N.L.R.B. 744 (2000).

258. *See* Stop & Go Foods, 246 N.L.R.B. 1076 (1979); *see also* NLRB v. Bell Aerospace, 416 U.S. 267 (1974).

259. Miller Elec. Co., 301 N.L.R.B. 294 (1991).

260. Parker-Robb Chevrolet, 262 N.L.R.B. 402 (1982).

261. *See* NLRB v. Oaks Mach. Corp., 897 F.2d 84, 92–93 (2d Cir. 1990) (employer unlawfully terminated supervisor for indicating willingness to testify); *see also* Phx. Newspapers, 294 N.L.R.B. 47 (1989).

262. Consol. Foods Corp., 165 N.L.R.B. 953 (1967), *enforced in part*, 403 F.2d 662 (6th Cir. 1968).

263. *See* Harborside Healthcare, Inc., 343 N.L.R.B. 906 (2004); *see also* Millard Refrigerated Servs., Inc., 345 N.L.R.B. 1143 (2005).

264. *Harborside*, 343 N.L.R.B. at 906.

265. NLRB v. Savair Mfg. Co., 414 U.S. 270 (1973); Manor Care of Kingston, 360 N.L.R.B. 719 (2014) (declining to set aside election results because isolated threats by pro-union employees to start punching people in the face did not create a general atmosphere of fear).

266. *See* Accubilt, Inc., 340 N.L.R.B. 1133 (2003); *see also* O'Brian Mem'l, 310 N.L.R.B. 943 (1993).

267. Al Long, Inc., 173 N.L.R.B. 447 (1968) (anonymous telephone calls threatening bodily harm, rifle shots by unknown persons, bomb threats, and massed and unruly picketing).

268. Dean Indus., 162 N.L.R.B. 1078 (1967) (by cooperating with the townspeople and accepting the benefits of their activities, the company was deemed responsible for their anti-union conduct).

269. *See* Star Kist Samoa, Inc., 237 N.L.R.B. 238 (1978); *see also* Albertson's, Inc., 344 N.L.R.B. 1172 (2005) (stating that the test to determine whether an employee is an agent of the employer is whether employees would reasonably

believe that the employee in question was reflecting company policy and speaking for management; holding that company's bookkeeper was an agent of the company when she told employees not to engage in protected activity).

270. NLRB Case Activity Report, Median Days from Petition to Election, https://www.nlrb.gov/news-outreach/graphs-data/petitions-and-elections/median-days-petition-election.

271. 29 C.F.R. § 102.67(k).

272. *Id.*

273. *Id.*

274. 29 C.F.R. § 102.67(l).

275. RHCG Safety Corp., 365 N.L.R.B. No. 88 (June 6, 2017).

276. Wash. Fruit & Produce Co., 343 N.L.R.B. 1215, 1222 (2004) (relying on and quoting Women in Crisis Counseling & Assistance, 312 N.L.R.B. 589 (1993)).

277. Mod Interiors, 324 N.L.R.B. 164 (1997) (citing N. Macon Health Care Facility, 315 N.L.R.B. 359, 360–61 (1994)).

278. Special Citizens Futures Unlimited, 331 N.L.R.B. 160 (2000) (citing Thiele Indus., 325 N.L.R.B. 1122 (1998)).

279. Norris-Thermador Corp., 119 N.L.R.B. 1301 (1958).

280. *Id.* at 1301.

281. *See* NLRB v. Westinghouse Broad. & Cable, 849 F.2d 15 (1st Cir. 1988); *cf.* Giummarra Elec., 291 N.L.R.B. 37 (1988).

282. Inacomp Am., Inc., 281 N.L.R.B. 271 (1986).

283. Plymouth Towing Co., 178 N.L.R.B. 651 (1969).

284. Apex Paper Box, 302 N.L.R.B. 67, 68 (1991).

285. Hughes Christensen Co. v. NLRB, 101 F.3d 28, 31 (5th Cir. 1996).

286. *See* Red Arrow Freight Lines, 278 N.L.R.B. 965 (1986); *see also* Pepsi-Cola Co., 315 N.L.R.B. 1322 (1995).

287. Home Care Network, Inc., 347 N.L.R.B. 859 (2006).

288. Orange Blossom Manor, 324 N.L.R.B. 846 (1997) (sustaining challenge because employee clearly and unambiguously expressed intent to resign)

289. *See* BRENT GARREN, JOHN E. HIGGINS, JR. & DAVID A. KADELA, HOW TO TAKE A CASE BEFORE THE NLRB, ch. 9(II)(C)(3) (BBNA 9th ed. 2016).

290. CASEHANDLING MANUAL, PART TWO, *supra* note 68, § 11302.4.

291. *See* Daylight Grocery Co. v. NLRB, 678 F.2d 905, 909 (11th Cir. 1982); *see also* Lamar Advert. of Janesville, 340 N.L.R.B. 979 (2003); Consumers Energy Co., 337 N.L.R.B. 752 (2002).

292. 29 C.F.R. § 102.69.

293. Wash. Fruit & Produce Co., 343 N.L.R.B. 1215 (2004).

294. Clark Equip. Co., 278 N.L.R.B. 498, 505 (1986); *overruled in part by* Nickles Bakery of Ind., 296 N.L.R.B. 927 (1989) (quoting Dal-Tex Optical Co., 137 N.L.R.B. 1782, 1786 (1962)).

295. Sea Breeze Health Care Ctr., 331 N.L.R.B. 1131 (2000) (quoting Super Thrift Markets, 233 N.L.R.B. 409 (1977)).

296. *See, e.g.*, Wash. Fruit & Produce Co., 343 N.L.R.B. 1215 (2004); *see also* Sewell Mfg. Co., 138 N.L.R.B. 66 (1962); YKK (USA), Inc., 269 N.L.R.B. 82 (1984); Peerless Plywood Co., 107 N.L.R.B. 427, 429 (1954).

297. Dresser Indus., 242 N.L.R.B. 74 (1979).

298. Bon Appetit Mgmt. Co., 334 N.L.R.B. 1042 (2001).

299. *See* Teamsters Local 115 v. NLRB, 640 F.2d 392 (D.C. Cir. 1981); *see also* Fieldcrest Cannon, Inc., 318 N.L.R.B. 470 (1995).

300. *Id.*

301. *See, e.g.*, Three Sisters Sportswear Co., 312 N.L.R.B. 853 (1993); *see also* Tex. Super Foods, 303 N.L.R.B. 209 (1991); Monfort of Colo., 298 N.L.R.B. 73 (1990), *enforced*, 965 F.2d 1538 (9th Cir. 1992).

302. Fieldcrest Cannon, Inc., 318 N.L.R.B. 470 (1995).

303. *Id.* at 472.

304. *Id.*

305. NLRB v. Gissel Packing Co., 395 U.S. 575 (1969).

306. *Id.*

5

Duty to Bargain

The National Labor Relations Act (NLRA) requires both employers and unions to bargain in good faith in an attempt to reach a collective bargaining agreement covering wages, hours, and working conditions for represented employees.[1]

Three provisions of the NLRA operate in concert to delineate the scope of the duty to bargain. Specifically, pursuant to section 8(a)(5) of the NLRA, an employer commits an unfair labor practice if the employer fails to bargain in good faith. A corresponding provision, section 8(b)(3), imposes on labor organizations a reciprocal obligation to bargain in good faith. A third provision, section 8(d), applies to both employers and unions and requires both parties to meet at reasonable times and to memorialize an agreement into a written document.

Scope of Bargaining Obligations

Onset and Duration of Duty to Bargain

Q 5.1   When does the duty to bargain initially arise?

Generally, an employer's duty to bargain arises when a union that properly represents a unit of employees (either through a National Labor Relations Board (NLRB) election or through lawful voluntary recognition) requests bargaining. It is the union's responsibility to start the bargaining process by making the initial request to bargain. The union's request must be clear and unmistakable.

A union obtains initial authority to bargain on behalf of unit employees only in the following circumstances:

- A union demonstrates to the employer that it represents a majority of the employees in an appropriate unit and the employer agrees to recognize the union. There is no obligation on the employer's part to recognize the union and commence bargaining provided it has not engaged in serious Unfair Labor Practices (ULPs) warranting a so-called *Gissel* bargaining order.[2]

- A majority of employees in an appropriate unit votes for representation by the union in an NLRB-supervised secret-ballot election resulting in Board certification of the union as bargaining agent.

- A union demonstrates majority support among employees in an appropriate unit but the employer's serious ULPs prevent a fair election from being held, resulting in the NLRB's issuance of a *Gissel* bargaining order.

Q 5.2 What does the duty to bargain require when a union is first certified or recognized?

Where a union is newly certified after an NLRB representation election, an employer is legally obligated to bargain for a minimum period of one year after the union is certified, plus any additional delay caused by the employer's unfair labor practices. During this one-year period, the union's majority status generally cannot be questioned by the employer. As a result, an employer is obligated to continue bargaining throughout the one-year period regardless of whether the employees who voted in the election remain employed, whether a majority of the employees still supports the union, or whether the employer entertains a good-faith doubt as to the union's continued majority status. In other words, there is an irrebuttable presumption that the union has majority status during the first year after certification. This same irrebuttable presumption of majority support applies up to the first three years of a collective bargaining agreement with a union.

A similar though more flexible rule applies when an employer voluntarily recognizes a majority union. The employer must bargain with the union for a "reasonable period of time" after recognition, which usually means a one-year period. In the case of a voluntarily recognized union, however, under current law employees can file a decertification petition during a forty-five-day period after recognition; in the case of a certified union, the NLRB will not entertain such a petition.

Q 5.2.1 Does the employer's obligation to recognize and bargain with the union end after the one-year period?

No. Furthermore, the presumption that the union has majority status continues. However, once the one-year period has ended, the presumption may be rebutted under certain circumstances. For example, employees or the employer may file a decertification petition requesting that the union be removed as the employees' representative. If a subsequent election results in the decertification of the union, then the employer is no longer obligated to bargain with the union.

Good-Faith Bargaining

Q 5.3   What does "good faith" mean?

Sections 8(a)(5) and 8(b)(3) of the NLRA require employers and unions to bargain in good faith with respect to wages, hours, and other terms and conditions of employment. In other words, it is not sufficient to simply confer regarding the terms and conditions of employment; it must be done in good faith. The NLRA does not define "good faith." Generally, however, it has been interpreted to require the parties to make a sincere and honest attempt to reach an agreement by offering proposals, considering the other side's proposals, and making counterproposals. The good-faith requirement imposes an obligation on both parties to make honest claims. Good faith does *not* require the parties to reach a settlement, to agree to any particular proposal, or to make a concession. However, it does require that, if an agreement is reached, a written contract incorporating those terms must be executed if either party requests it. The manner and extent of negotiations necessary to satisfy the good-faith requirement varies according to the situation. Protracted negotiations alone do not satisfy a party's obligation.

Q 5.3.1   What types of employer conduct can be considered evidence of bad faith in violation of section 8(a)(5) of the NLRA?

The NLRB and the courts have found that employers bargain in bad faith where the employer:

- sends to the bargaining table negotiators who do not have authority to make agreements on mandatory bargaining subjects;

- unreasonably delays negotiations;

- makes unilateral changes to terms and conditions of employment ("mandatory bargaining subjects");

- refuses to discuss proposals;

- shifts position during bargaining without explanation;

- withdraws concessions previously granted without explanation;

- refuses to provide relevant information;

- engages in merely "surface bargaining" (see Q 5.16 *et seq.*);

- prematurely declares an impasse and implements changes in mandatory bargaining subjects;

- conditions agreement on a mandatory subject to the union's concession on a permissive bargaining subject; or

- deals directly with employees over mandatory bargaining subjects.

Q 5.3.2   Are there any employer activities that, regardless of whether they were done in good or bad faith, are "per se violations" of the duty to bargain?

Yes; there are times where a single action, without more, indicates bad faith, resulting in a ULP. Specifically, these include:

- refusing to furnish when requested by the union certain information that is relevant and necessary for the union to perform its bargaining duty;

- refusing to discuss a mandatory subject of bargaining;

- refusing to execute a written contract incorporating an agreement that had already been reached;

- insisting on the inclusion in a contract of a permissive subject of bargaining; and

- refusing to meet at reasonable times.

Furthermore, employers who impose unilateral changes to existing terms or conditions of employment that are mandatory subjects of bargaining are generally found to have violated the duty, unless the subject has been bargained to impasse, a management rights clause gives the employer the right to make such changes, or the union has waived its right to bargain.

Q 5.3.3   When does a union refuse to bargain in good faith in violation of section 8(b)(3) of the NLRA?

A union may not refuse to bargain in good faith with an employer about wages, hours, and other conditions of employment if the union is the representative of that employer's employees. Section 8(b)(3) also requires a union to carry out its bargaining duty fairly with respect to the employees it represents. The union's duty to bargain in good faith is co-extensive with the duty imposed on employers under section 8(a)(5). As with the employer, there is no duty on the union, as bargaining representative, to agree to any specific proposal by the employer or to make any concessions to the employer. However, the union must bargain with an open mind in an attempt to reach an agreement. The union may not insist on specific terms without giving the employer an opportunity to bargain about those terms.

A union, or its designated representative, must be willing to meet at reasonable times with the employer or its designated representative. The union must confer in good faith on all mandatory subjects of bargaining or any other aspects of the agreement. Unions are further bound to sign a written agreement, upon request, if an agreement is reached.

Q 5.3.4   What are specific examples of violations of a union's duty to bargain in good faith?

A union violates its duty to bargain in good faith under section 8(b)(3) when it:

- insists on the inclusion of illegal provisions in a collective bargaining agreement, such as a closed shop or a discriminatory hiring hall;

- refuses to negotiate on a proposal for a written contract or to meet with employer's representative in bargaining;

- strikes against an employer in order to force a change in the scope of the bargaining unit;

- conditions the execution of an agreement on inclusion of a nonmandatory provision such as a performance bond or interest arbitration; or

- attempts to modify or terminate a labor contract by striking without serving the required statutory notice to the federal and state mediation agencies.

Obligation to Bargain over Discipline

Q 5.4   Are employers required to bargain with the union before taking disciplinary action if the union requests it?

Prior to the ratification of a first contract, a newly organized employer can unilaterally impose discipline on unit employees, if the employer follows the same disciplinary procedures it had established before the employees became unionized. This is true even if the discipline is, in part, discretionary, as long as the discipline is within the parameters of the progressive discipline procedure. Thus, where the employer has a clearly established disciplinary practice predating the union, it can unilaterally impose discipline as long as the imposition of discipline is based on objective standards and is applied consistently with past practice. An employer will be found to violate section 8(a)(5) of the NLRA if:

(1)   there existed a pre-election established past practice;

(2)   there was a post-election change to the practice; and

(3)   the change to the past practice constituted a material change in employees' terms and conditions of employment.

When a union has been certified but has not yet entered into a collective bargaining agreement, the employer must give notice and an opportunity to bargain before imposing certain types of serious, discretionary discipline—meaning forms of discretionary discipline that have "an inevitable and immediate impact on employees' tenure, status, or earnings," such as discharge, demotion, or suspension—unless the employer has a reasonable, good faith belief that an employee's continued presence on the job presents a serious, imminent danger to the employer's business or personnel.[3]

Once a contract is entered into, an individual disciplinary issue is usually not a "unilateral change" that requires bargaining. Typically, the terms of a collective bargaining agreement specify the circumstances under which disciplinary action can be taken and provide grievance procedures for obtaining review of the employer's disciplinary decisions. However, if the employer adjusts a work rule or disciplinary procedure of general application, the employer may be required to provide the union notice and an opportunity to bargain. To obviate such issues, many collective bargaining agreements contain specific provisions allowing the employer to implement or modify work rules during the term of the agreement.

LABOR MANAGEMENT LAW FACT

Under the NLRA, there generally are three different kinds of bargaining subjects:

(1)   mandatory subjects;
(2)   permissive subjects; and
(3)   illegal subjects.

Through case-by-case adjudication, the NLRB and the courts have defined which bargaining subjects fall into these three categories.[4]

Subjects of Bargaining

Mandatory Subjects of Bargaining

Q 5.5   What are "mandatory subjects" of bargaining, and what are the parties' duties with respect to them?

Mandatory subjects of bargaining are those generally referenced in section 9(a) of the NLRA as "rates of pay, wages, hours of employment, or other conditions of employment," and in section 8(d) of the NLRA as "wages, hours, and other terms and conditions of employment."[5] The NLRA compels collective bargaining with respect to mandatory subjects of bargaining. Unilateral modifications with respect to mandatory bargaining subjects in the absence of a bargaining waiver or bona fide impasse are generally unlawful.

With respect to mandatory subjects of bargaining:

- Both parties are required to bargain in good faith to impasse with respect to a mandatory subject.

- The "controlling" party, typically the employer, cannot make a unilateral change in a mandatory subject without first bargaining with the union to the point of impasse.

- The parties are under a duty to disclose information in their possession or control relevant to bargaining over a mandatory subject.

- Mandatory subjects can serve as "deal breakers," that is, lead to impasse and implementation by the controlling party if that party has otherwise engaged in good-faith bargaining.

- Unions can strike (assuming notice is given to mediation services) over disputes concerning mandatory subjects.

- Unilateral midterm modifications with respect to a mandatory subject "contained" in the collective bargaining agreement violate the duty to bargain, in addition to being possible violations of the agreement.

Q 5.5.1   What are considered "rates of pay" or "wages"?

The mandatory bargaining subject of wages has been given a broad construction by the NLRB and the courts to cover most of the common forms of compensation for labor performed, as well as the majority of agreements designed to protect standards of compensation.[6] The following are mandatory subjects of bargaining because they are considered "wages":

- basic hourly rates of pay;
- piece rates and incentive wage plans;
- overtime pay;
- shift differentials;
- paid holidays;

- paid vacations;
- commissions; and
- severance pay as compensation for services performed.

Q 5.5.2 Are bonuses considered "wages"?

Whether a bonus is considered to be a mandatory bargaining subject (that is, wages) depends on whether it is considered compensation for services rendered or a gift. If it is compensation, it is mandatory; if it is a gift, it is not.

The primary inquiry in making this determination is whether the payment of the bonus has occurred with sufficient regularity to become part of the compensation structure.[7] A bonus will be considered a gift and not mandatory where it is: (1) not tied to employment-related factors; and (2) not so fixed in nature that it becomes a part of the remuneration workers expect from their employment. Accordingly, irregular appreciation gifts made over a four-year period were held not to be wages, but a bonus system that consistently paid out $25 per month to employees based on job performance were wages and, thus, a mandatory bargaining subject.[8]

CASE STUDY: *NLRB v. Niles-Bement-Pond Co.*[9]

An employer must bargain over changes in a Christmas bonus. In NLRB v. Niles-Bement-Pond Co., the employer had, for years, paid employees Christmas bonuses equivalent to a percentage of the employees' earnings. When the employer implemented a retirement plan, it notified the employees that the new plan would cost more than the customary bonus and, consequently, the amount of the bonus would be changed. The employer refused to bargain with the union concerning the new amount of the bonus. The NLRB held that the bonus was part of "wages" and ordered bargaining.

Q 5.5.3   Which other employee benefits are considered "wages"?

Employee fringe benefits ordinarily are considered to be mandatory bargaining subjects. The word "wages" under the NLRA includes the direct and immediate economic benefits flowing from the employment relationship.[10] Thus, certain types of benefits are considered "wages" and are mandatory. For example, under certain circumstances, the following will be mandatory subjects of bargaining:

- pension benefits;
- group health insurance;[11]
- profit-sharing plans;
- stock purchase plans;[12]
- rental of company-owned housing;[13]
- company-provided meals and in-plant food prices;
- vacations, holidays, and sick leave;
- bereavement pay;
- jury duty pay; and
- change of payment from a weekly salary to an hourly rate.

Q 5.5.4   What kinds of employment terms fall within the scope of mandatory bargaining over "hours of employment"?

The NLRB has consistently held that hours, including work schedules, length of workday, overtime, and whether there should be Sunday work, are mandatory bargaining subjects.[14] For example, the NLRB has found violations of section 8(a)(5) in the following situations where an employer failed to bargain or give notice before:

- requiring employees who had previously worked only the morning or the afternoon shifts to instead work both shifts;

- changing employees' workweek schedules;

- implementing "swing shifts";

- changing from fixed shifts to rotating shifts;

- changing a contractually established five-day, forty-hour workweek to a four-day, forty-hour workweek.

Q 5.5.5   What kinds of employment terms fall within the scope of mandatory bargaining over "other terms and conditions of employment"?

The NLRB and the courts have adopted a relatively expansive view of the kinds of terms and conditions of employment that constitute mandatory bargaining subjects, and it is not possible to provide a comprehensive list. Common employment terms that fall within "other terms and conditions of employment" recognized as mandatory subjects of bargaining include the following:

- layoffs and recalls
- job transfers
- promotions
- seniority rights
- attendance policies
- work loads
- work duties
- subcontracting of unit work
- work rules
- leave policies
- employee on-site parking
- disciplinary process
- discretionary discipline
- grievance and arbitration process
- use of bulletin boards by unions
- dues check-off
- union security (where permitted by state law)
- definition of bargaining unit work
- employee physical examinations
- drug tests
- polygraph tests
- discounts on company products
- employee dress code[15]
- enrollment in E-Verify[16]

Q 5.6   Do mandatory subjects of bargaining include seniority, promotions, and transfers?

Yes; seniority, promotions, and transfers have long been recognized as mandatory subjects of bargaining.[17]

Seniority refers to the priority or status accorded an employee with regard to job retention, promotions, or other benefits, based on the employee's length of service. The length of an employee's service may be defined as the length of time an employee has been employed by the employer, or it may be defined by length of service in a plant, division, job title, or bargaining unit. The way an employer calculates seniority may be set out in a collective bargaining agreement or may be determined by the employer's past practices. Unilateral changes in seniority calculations or treatment of an employee's seniority status will generally violate an employer's obligation to bargain in good faith.

Promotion of employees within the bargaining unit is a mandatory subject of bargaining. Promotion of employees to positions outside the bargaining unit is not a mandatory subject, although treatment of supervisors returning to the unit is. Promotion of employees to supervisory positions outside the unit is generally not a mandatory subject unless the purpose or effect is to transfer bargaining unit work to non-unit employees.[18]

A transfer is a change in employee status and involves movement of an employee, such as to another job classification (that is, higher, lower, or lateral), to another plant, or to another shift. The procedures governing transfer of employees, as a general rule, are a mandatory subject of bargaining.[19]

Q 5.6.1   ... grievance procedures?

The types of grievances and the procedures used to adjust them generally are mandatory subjects for collective bargaining.[20] The collective bargaining agreement may limit the kinds of disputes that can be addressed through the grievance procedures. Even where the parties do not limit the issues that may be addressed through the grievance process, certain issues, such as representation issues and allegations of ULPs, are addressed through the NLRB processes rather than contract procedures. Importantly, an employer does not violate its duty to bargain where it disputes the right of the union to present an issue as a grievance and communicates the reasons for its position to the union.

Even after the expiration of the labor agreement, it is generally unlawful to unilaterally change the procedure for handling grievances, including refusing to meet with a designated union representative concerning grievances.[21] The promise to arbitrate itself does not generally carry over to this "hiatus" period between collective agreements, but the duty to process grievances does. Employers are also required to arbitrate pending grievances arising under a labor agreement with the union that was party to that agreement, even if that union has been superseded.[22]

Q 5.6.2 ... union security provisions, such as dues check-off and agency shop provisions?

Yes, union security provisions, such as a "dues check-off" provision in a collective bargaining agreement, fall within the area of mandatory bargaining.[23] A union security provision ensures that the union will continue to receive dues income. Dues check-off provisions allow an employer to withhold employees' union dues from their paychecks and, therefore, are a matter related to "wages, hours, and other terms and conditions of employment" within the meaning of the NLRA.[24] The NLRB held in 2012 and 2013 that an employer's obligation to check off union dues continues even after the expiration of a collective bargaining agreement.[25] However, those decisions were overturned by *Noel Canning.* Since the decisions were overturned, ALJs have been holding that an employer's failure to follow the dues check-off provision after expiration of a collective bargaining agreement does not violate the NLRA.[26]

Agency shop agreements also fall within the area of required bargaining. Under an agency shop agreement, an employee is not required to join the union, but is required to pay to the union an amount equivalent to union dues. An agency shop provision, therefore, differs from a union shop provision, which requires employees to join the union after hire and to maintain membership as a condition of employment (though an employee cannot be terminated where his loss of membership is for a reason other than failure to pay dues). The U.S. Supreme

Court has held that agency shop proposals impose no burdens in addition to those imposed by union shop proposals, which are lawful in states that permit them and are a mandatory subject of bargaining.[27] Although agency shop status is a mandatory subject of bargaining, the amount of agency fees assessed by the union is controlled by the union and is not subject to mandatory bargaining.[28]

LABOR MANAGEMENT LAW FACT

What is a hiring hall?

A hiring hall is an organization, operated or sponsored by a union, that refers workers to employers. An agreement between the employer and the union may be exclusive, meaning the employer only seeks new workers through the hiring hall, or nonexclusive, meaning the employer may use other sources, in addition to the hiring hall, to meet its hiring needs. An employer-union agreement to a hiring program that explicitly and directly discriminates based on union membership is unlawful. Thus, in referring workers, an exclusive hiring hall may not exclude nonmembers. Agreed-upon employment hiring preferences that are neither explicitly nor directly based on union membership may still violate the NLRA if they are so connected to union membership or affiliation that the foreseeable consequence is to coerce and/or encourage union membership. A contractual agreement to grant preferential rights to, say, employees with seniority in the industry, that appear to benefit some unionized employees is not per se unlawful or discriminatory where the agreed-upon criterion—here, seniority— is not so connected to union affiliation that it would foreseeably coerce or encourage union membership.

Q 5.6.3   ... hiring halls?

A nondiscriminatory referral or hiring hall to be operated by a union is a mandatory subject of bargaining. The NLRB has also held that, in the absence of some indication to the contrary, a hiring hall referral provision would not be presumed to expire with the contract.[29]

Q 5.6.4   ... employee surveillance or monitoring?

Yes, employers' installation and use of surveillance cameras in the workplace are mandatory subjects of bargaining.[30] The employer, thus, must notify the union of its proposal to use cameras and of the general reasons for the proposal. The unilateral installation and use of cameras by an employer in an area where employees regularly perform work or are permitted to take breaks may violate the NLRA if not bargained over with the union.

Q 5.6.5   ... "work rules"?

Generally, work rules, also known as plant rules, are considered subjects of mandatory bargaining, which means that an employer cannot unilaterally implement or change such rules.[31] Examples of work rules include rules related to attendance and tardiness, dress codes, parking regulations, rules about working overtime, and safety rules. The NLRB has carved out exceptions to the general rule that work rules are a mandatory subject of bargaining in cases where a change in a work rule had little or no impact on the employees as a group or on their working conditions. In addition, if a collective bargaining agreement contains a management rights clause giving the employer the broad right to make its own rules of conduct, the employer can unilaterally institute new rules without violating the NLRA. The management rights clause must clearly and unequivocally waive the right to bargain.[32]

Q 5.6.6   ... drug and alcohol testing for employees?

Ordinarily, drug and alcohol testing required for current employees is a mandatory subject of bargaining.[33] Drug or alcohol testing programs are considered to be a term or condition of employment and, therefore, are mandatory subjects of bargaining. However, drug or alcohol testing programs designed to screen job applicants generally are not mandatory subjects of bargaining. Because job applicants are not employees within the meaning of the NLRA, such testing is not deemed to vitally affect the terms and conditions of employment of bargaining unit employees.[34] Moreover, in most cases where the collective bargaining agreement contains a broad management rights clause, the right to bargain over drug and alcohol testing of current employees may be considered waived.

Q 5.6.7 ... discretionary discipline?

Discretionary discipline includes discharge, demotion, and other punishments that have an immediate impact on the tenure, status, or earnings of a bargaining unit employee. The imposition of a discretionary discipline policy is a mandatory subject of bargaining.

Permissive Subjects of Bargaining

Q 5.7 What are the permissive subjects of bargaining?

Permissive bargaining subjects are matters that do not fall within the scope of "wages, hours, and other terms and conditions of employment" and, thus, are not mandatory subjects of bargaining. However, permissive bargaining subjects are lawful matters that parties may, of their option, negotiate and include in collective bargaining agreements. Examples of permissive subjects of bargaining include provisions covering supervisors,[35] agricultural labor,[36] performance bonds,[37] some aspects of internal union affairs,[38] legal liability clauses,[39] and union recognition clauses.[40]

Unlike mandatory bargaining subjects, the noncontrolling party (typically, the union) cannot condition agreement or insist to impasse on the inclusion of permissive bargaining subjects in a collective bargaining agreement. Moreover, after the expiration of a collective bargaining agreement, parties do not violate their bargaining duty by unilaterally rescinding agreements on permissive bargaining subjects. For instance, where the collective bargaining agreement provides that the agreement on a permissive subject will not be modified "during the term of the agreement," a party is not prohibited from making a unilateral change after expiration with respect to the permissive subject. Likewise, where a party reserves the right to terminate or modify the agreement with respect to a permissive subject while the collective bargaining agreement remains in effect, the party may make the same unilateral change after the collective bargaining agreement's expiration.

Q 5.7.1   What are a party's rights and duties with respect to permissive subjects?

Either party may propose for inclusion in a collective bargaining agreement any clause addressing any permissive subject of bargaining. Neither party is required to bargain about permissive subjects. If the parties voluntarily bargain about a permissive subject, a party's refusal either to include the subject in the contract or to agree to a particular resolution of a voluntary subject is not unlawful. Conversely, a party's refusal to contract except upon the inclusion of a clause dealing with a permissive subject is per se a violation of the NLRA. When a permissive subject is included in a collective bargaining agreement, that subject is not transformed into a mandatory one even for the term of that agreement. It will be enforced by the usual contract enforcement mechanism, the parties' grievance and arbitration process. Once the contract has expired, there is no statutory requirement to continue to comply with the contract's treatment of a permissive subject.[41]

LABOR MANAGEMENT LAW FACT

Managerial decisions that lie at the "core of entrepreneurial control" are permissive, not mandatory subjects of bargaining. These decisions include actions fundamental to the basic direction of a corporate enterprise or that impinge only indirectly on terms and conditions of employment.[42] Bargaining over permissive subjects is lawful, but the employer has no duty to bargain over them and the union has no right to insist on its position with respect to them—that is, the union cannot treat disagreement over the subject as a deal breaker and strike over it. Moreover, the employer is under no duty to share relevant information it has with the union over such subjects. Nor will a midterm change in the treatment of such a subject, even if reflected in an extant collective bargaining agreement, constitute a violation of the duty to bargain.

Q 5.7.2   Which employer decisions lie at the "core of entrepreneurial control" and, thus, are not subject to mandatory bargaining?

Selling an enterprise and other situations that involve a significant investment or withdrawal of capital that will affect the scope and ultimate direction of an enterprise are matters essentially financial and managerial in nature. Decisions regarding these matters lie at the very core of entrepreneurial control and are not subject to mandatory bargaining. (See Q 5.7.) These managerial decisions often require secrecy, as well as the employer's freedom to act quickly and decisively.[43] An employer faced with the economic necessity of either moving or consolidating the operations of a failing business has no duty to bargain with the union respecting its decision to shut down.

Similarly, where a healthcare employer decides to no longer operate a pharmacy but instead rents space in its facility for a third party to operate the pharmacy, the healthcare employer generally does not have to bargain with the union about this decision. In such a case, the employer has made the entrepreneurial decision to leave the pharmacy business altogether; it is not subcontracting the employees' work. The effects of the decision on the unit employees, however, is a mandatory bargaining subject.

Other managerial decisions held to lie at the core of entrepreneurial control include:

- investing in labor-saving machinery;
- plant relocation for geographical, tax, public subsidy reasons versus labor costs;
- liquidation of assets;
- termination of a line of business;
- volume and type of advertising expenditures;
- showing all employees a videotape regarding newly instituted management principles;
- manner of financing and sales.

Q 5.7.3   When is an employer required to bargain over the effects of a permissive subject of bargaining?

Where an employer's decision has a direct impact on employment but involves a change in the scope and direction of the enterprise, such as a decision to exit a business segment or product line, the employer is not required to bargain over the decision, but is required to bargain over its effects. If a decision to change the scope or direction of a business is made for purely economic reasons other than labor costs, the decision itself is not "about" the terms and conditions of employment; such core entrepreneurial decisions are "akin to the decision whether to be in business at all," a unilateral decision that employers have an absolute right to make. However, these business decisions often directly affect the terms and conditions of employment and may result in employees' loss of employment. Accordingly, an employer that has made such a decision must give its employees' union notice and a reasonable opportunity to bargain over the effects of the decision, including such potential issues as job security, the order of layoffs, severance benefits, etc.

The U.S. Supreme Court has stated that, under section 8(a)(5), "bargaining over the effects of a decision must be conducted in a meaningful manner and at a meaningful time, and the NLRB may impose sanctions to insure its adequacy." Importantly, the Court did not state that the duty to engage in effects-bargaining must precede the employer's making the particular decision, but presumably would have to occur before its full implementation. The Court suggested, however, that the union lawfully "may secure in contract negotiations implementing rights to notice, information, and fair bargaining";[44] presumably such in-advance effects-bargaining clauses would be considered a mandatory subject of bargaining.

CASE STUDY: *Pan American Grain Co. v. NLRB*[45]

The First Circuit ruled that "an employer must bargain over a multiple-motive layoff based partially on labor costs." As a result of modernization work done in 1996, Pan American's staffing needs decreased, leading to a loss of one or two employees per year. During a 2002 strike, without bargaining, the company decided to lay off fifteen strikers and sent the employees a letter informing them that the layoffs were "due to economic reasons and as a result of a substantial decrease in production and sales." However, before the ALJ, the company claimed that the results of modernization were another factor causing the layoff. While recognizing that one factor leading to the layoff decision may have been an economic factor as a result of modernization, the NLRB held that the layoffs were at least partially motivated by labor costs and, thus, bargaining was required. The court found the NLRB's holding reasonably defensible and affirmed. In reviewing the remedy of reinstatement and full backpay, however, the court noted that Pan American should be allowed to present evidence at the compliance stage regarding the viability of rehiring individuals, given that no one had been hired since the 2002 layoff.

Q 5.8   Do permissive subjects of bargaining include subcontracting?

Employers may have an obligation to bargain over decisions to subcontract or otherwise remove work from the unit. In *Fibreboard Paper Products Corp. v. NLRB*,[46] the employer refused to bargain with a union regarding the employer's decision to subcontract maintenance work previously performed by unit employees in an attempt to reduce labor costs. The U.S. Supreme Court held that, where the employer simply replaced unit employees with a less costly subcontractor, the decision to subcontract the work is a mandatory subject of bargaining.

Even if the employer believes the labor cost negotiations will be futile, it is not relieved of an obligation to attempt to bargain over the decision with the union. The *Fibreboard* decision did not address whether other forms of "contracting out" or "subcontracting" were mandatory subjects of bargaining.

Since *Fibreboard*, an employer's decision to subcontract work previously performed by unit employees in an attempt to reduce labor costs has been held to be a subject of mandatory bargaining.[47] In addition, where subcontracting would result in a loss of significant amounts of overtime or lost jobs, the NLRB usually holds that the employer had a duty to bargain about the subcontracting.[48]

In some circumstances, an employer's decision to subcontract may be considered to fall into the category of core entrepreneurial decisions that are not subject to mandatory bargaining.[49] This may be the case if the subcontracting decision is:

(1)   the result of shutting down part of the employer's business;

(2)   a significant change in the employer's operations;

(3)   connected to the employer's decision to enter into a new line of business; or

(4)   related to employee matters that are not amenable to collective bargaining (for example, theft, outmoded facilities).

Even if the employer's decision to subcontract work is not a mandatory subject of bargaining, the employer may be obligated to bargain over the effects of such a decision. The employer may be under an obligation to notify the union of its intention to subcontract, so that the union may be given an opportunity to bargain over the rights of the employees whose employment status will be altered by the managerial decision. The employer may be obligated to bargain over such issues as severance pay, preferential rehiring, training assistance, seniority, and pensions.[50]

Q 5.8.1   ... relocation of unit work?

Relocation of bargaining unit work to a different part of an employer's business for the purpose of reducing labor costs is a mandatory subject of bargaining. Relocation means the transfer of work from a bargaining unit represented by a union to another facility operated by the same employer (regardless of whether employees at the other facility are represented by a union).

The NLRB has articulated a test to determine whether relocation of bargaining unit work is a mandatory subject of bargaining. First, the General Counsel must meet his burden to establish that the employer's decision to relocate unit work was not accompanied by a basic change in the employer's operation (establishing a prima facie case that the decision is a mandatory subject of bargaining). Second, the employer can rebut the prima facie case by showing that:

(1)   the work performed at the new location varies significantly from the work performed at the former location;

(2)   the work at the former location is to be discontinued and not moved to the new location; or

(3)   its decision involves a change in the scope and direction of the enterprise.

Alternatively, the employer can establish a defense by showing, by a preponderance of the evidence, either: (1) that direct or indirect labor costs were not a factor in the decision; or (2) if labor costs were a factor, that the union could not have offered concessions that would have changed the employer's decision to relocate.[51] Where bargaining is required, an employer is free to relocate work if it complies with its bargaining obligations and is not motivated by union animus.[52]

 CASE STUDY: *Komatsu America Corp.*[53]

The NLRB concluded, in a 2004 case, that an employer did not fail to bargain at a meaningful time and in a meaningful manner regarding its decision to move two assembly lines to Japan. The NLRB concluded that the employer satisfied its bargaining obligation by announcing the outsourcing initiative well in advance of its implementation and by bargaining at the union's request. The NLRB rejected the General Counsel's assertion that the company presented the union with a *fait accompli* by partially implementing its outsourcing decision when it imposed a reduction in force. Noting an increase in the employer's employee complement as business improved over time, the NLRB found no evidence of a causal nexus between the outsourcing initiative and the reduction in force.

Q 5.8.2   ... a "most-favored-nation" clause?

A "most-favored-nation" clause entitles the employer to any concessions the union grants other employers, such as more favorable wage and benefit levels negotiated with other employers. In most cases, the clause will provide that the more favorable terms are automatically incorporated into the collective bargaining agreement or that the employer is entitled to invoke the more favorable terms. Typically, MFN clauses are limited to the specific industry or to a specific geographic area. The NLRB has held that a most-favored-nation clause is a mandatory subject of bargaining.

Q 5.8.3   ... the scope of the unit?

The parties may agree to revise the scope of the bargaining unit to be covered by the contract they negotiate. Although the NLRB initially defines the unit for purposes of resolving questions concerning representation, the parties are free to agree on a somewhat different unit from the certified or recognized unit provided the unit is otherwise appropriate and the union retains majority support in the changed unit. The NLRB ordinarily accepts as lawful the bargaining units that the parties establish by consensual agreement.[54] The parties can also agree on altering the level of bargaining without changing the unit itself, such as when a union representing different locals of an employer agrees with the employer to conduct multi-local bargaining. Parties may also agree to provisions that potentially affect the scope of the unit, such as the elimination of outdated job positions and the addition of new job positions.

LABOR MANAGEMENT LAW FACT

What is interest arbitration?

Interest arbitration is when a third party is selected by the employer and the union to resolve any outstanding issues over the content of a new or renewal agreement. Parties resort to interest arbitration when they cannot agree about which proposals should be included in a new, renewed, or reopened contract. Rights arbitration, sometimes called "grievance arbitration," is when the parties are required to arbitrate claims arising under an existing labor agreement. While interest arbitration occurs during the course of negotiating a collective bargaining agreement, rights arbitration involves disputes over collective bargaining agreement interpretation.

Q 5.8.4   ... interest arbitration?

A clause providing for the settling of any of the terms of a future collective bargaining agreement by interest arbitration is a permissive subject of bargaining. Parties may voluntarily agree on an interest arbitration clause without violating the NLRA, but neither party may insist to impasse on its inclusion.[55] In limited circumstances, interest arbitration over wages has been held mandatory where employees could not work for other employers.[56]

Q 5.8.5   ... provisions that deal with employee-union affairs?

These are generally permissive subjects, and the union is the controlling party not obliged to bargain over joint determination with the employer. An employer may request bargaining about internal union matters, but may not insist on its position over such proposals—that is, it may not treat them as deal breakers or the cause of an impasse.[57]

Examples of permissive provisions dealing with union affairs include those:

- providing that non-union unit employees shall have a right to participate in and vote at union meetings;

- requiring a strike vote among employees before a strike occurs;

- requiring a contract be submitted for employee ratification before the execution of a collective bargaining agreement;

- providing that the contract would become void if the percentage of employees paying their dues by check-off dropped below 50%;

- requiring the union to provide withdrawal cards to any employee who might be transferred out of the unit; and

- requiring shop stewards be chosen jointly by the parties.

Q 5.8.6   ... retiree benefits?

Benefits for retired employees are normally considered to be a permissive subject of bargaining because retirees are no longer employees within the protection of the NLRA. However, although not a bargaining issue, employers should bear in mind that the union or retirees may have recourse under section 301 of the LMRA, the Employee Retirement Income Security Act, as well as section 1114 of the Bankruptcy Code, with respect to changes to previously agreed-to benefits. For example, under section 301, several courts have found that an expired labor contract can evince the intent of the parties to continue post-retirement benefits beyond the life of the agreement.[58] In addition, while a union may choose to bargain on behalf of retirees,[59] the union does not necessarily become the retirees' exclusive representative through which the retirees must then proceed.[60] Rather, a union must obtain consent from the retirees, actual or implied, before taking the retirees' benefits grievance to arbitration.[61] Notably, the NLRB has not decided whether a union owes retirees a duty of fair representation.[62]

Moreover, retirement benefits that will be received by employees who are currently in the bargaining unit and may retire in the future are a mandatory subject of bargaining.

Q 5.8.7 ... a "zipper" clause?

Yes. A "zipper" clause is a broad contract clause that states that the collective bargaining agreement is the complete agreement between the parties on all subjects. Such clauses typically involve a waiver of the union's right to request bargaining over new mandatory subjects not "contained in" the labor agreement.[63] (See also Q 5.22.3.)

Illegal Subjects of Bargaining

Q 5.9 Are there subjects about which employers and unions are not permitted to bargain?

Although the law permits, but does not compel, bargaining about permissive subjects, there is another category—*illegal* subjects—about which the parties may not include terms in the collective agreement. Among these subjects are closed shop provisions,[64] hiring hall provisions that give preference to union members,[65] "hot cargo" clauses that violate section 8(e),[66] contract provisions inconsistent with a union's duty of fair representation,[67] and contract clauses that discriminate among employees on unlawful bases, such as race, religion, sex, or national origin.[68]

Neither party may require the other to agree to contract provisions that are unlawful under the NLRA. Insistence upon an illegal provision violates the duty to bargain. More importantly, an illegal subject may never be properly included in a collective bargaining agreement.[69]

Q 5.9.1   What is a "closed shop" agreement?

A closed shop agreement is a form of union security agreement under which the employer agrees to only hire union members and employees must remain members of the union at all times in order to remain employed. Such agreements are prohibited by sections 8(a)(3) and 8(b)(2) of the NLRA. A closed shop agreement is distinguishable from a union shop agreement in that, under a union shop agreement, employers may hire nonmembers but require that they become members within a certain period (at least thirty days) after commencing employment.

Q 5.9.2   What is a "hot cargo" agreement?

A "hot cargo" agreement typically provides that employees will not be required by their employer to handle or work on goods or materials going to, or coming from, an employer designated by the union as unfair.

Q 5.9.3   Are hot cargo agreements permissible subjects of bargaining?

Hot cargo agreements are unlawful subjects of bargaining. Section 8(e) of the NLRA makes it an unfair labor practice for any labor organization and any employer to enter voluntarily into what is commonly called a "hot cargo" or "hot goods" agreement. Section 8(e) forbids employers and unions from making an agreement to stop doing business with any other employer and declares void and unenforceable any such agreement that is made. It should be noted that a strike, or any other union action including seeking grievance arbitration, to force an employer to agree to a hot cargo provision has been held by the NLRB to be a violation of section 8(b)(4). Where the employer acquiesces to the union's coercive action by ceasing to do business with the third party, however, it has not necessarily violated section 8(e) because its acquiescence does not constitute voluntary agreement.[70]

Exceptions to the hot cargo prohibition are allowed in the construction and garment industries. Moreover, a union in any industry can seek, and indeed insist upon, a "work preservation" agreement to keep within a bargaining unit work that is being done by the employees in the unit or to secure work that is "fairly claimable" in that unit.[71]

Q 5.9.4   Are there types of "super-seniority" clauses that are illegal subjects of bargaining?

A super-seniority system gives seniority to individual employees based on factors other than length of service. While contractual provisions granting super-seniority to union stewards with respect to layoff and recall are lawful,[72] more expansive clauses granting super-seniority to stewards for all purposes, including job bidding preference, are a violation of section 8(b)(2).[73] Super-seniority clauses are thus permitted only to the extent that they are necessary to ensure a steward's continued presence within the group of workers he or she represents. For example, a super-seniority clause giving a union the right to veto the discharge of a union steward would be presumptively illegal.[74]

In addition, giving super-seniority to replacements for striking employees will support a finding that the employer has violated section 8(a)(3) by discriminating against striking employees.[75]

Q 5.9.5   When are terminable-at-will clauses impermissible bargaining subjects?

The NLRB considers a clause making a collective bargaining agreement terminable at will an illegal bargaining subject.[76]

In *Chicago Typographical Union*,[77] the NLRB explained the difference between a failure to agree to a fixed term and an attempt to bargain for a contract terminable at will. The NLRB noted that a refusal to agree to particular fixed duration does not per se constitute a refusal to bargain in the same absolute sense that a refusal to agree to a contract in writing constitutes such refusal. But since a primary objective of a collective bargaining contract is to stabilize labor relations for periods of reasonable duration, insistence, in the absence of special circumstances, by an employer or a union upon a contract of indefinite duration terminable upon relatively short notice may evidence a bad-faith approach to the collective bargaining process.

Q 5.9.6   Can an employer or union bargain over a "hold-harmless" clause?

A hold-harmless clause is a clause that purports to alleviate liability for a party that commits a certain violation. The NLRB tends to consider such clauses a "roadblock" to collective bargaining. Hold-harmless clauses are, at best, permissive and in some circumstances may be illegal if they function to exculpate the parties from liability for wrongdoing.[78]

Unilateral Changes

Q 5.10   What is a unilateral change?

An employer in a collective bargaining relationship violates section 8(a)(1) and (5) of the NLRA if it unilaterally implements changes in its employees' terms and conditions of employment without first giving notice to the union of the change and providing the union with a reasonable opportunity to bargain over the same (either to agreement or impasse) before implementing the change.[79] The U.S. Supreme Court in *NLRB v. Katz*[80] explained that unilateral changes in terms and conditions of employment are inherently inconsistent with the duty to bargain and that an employer's unilateral change is as much a contravention of the objectives of the NLRA as is a flat refusal to bargain. However, an established past practice, regardless of whether it developed under a collective bargaining agreement, constitutes an existing term and condition of employment, such that an employer may implement actions, even those requiring some discretion, so long as it is consistent in kind and degree with what has been the customary practice in the past.[81]

Below are some examples of unilateral changes that have been considered unlawful because of the failure to bargain with the union to good-faith impasse:

- An employer's unilateral addition of cleaning duties to non-janitorial employees, particularly where the additional duties were more than a "mere continuation" of already assigned duties.

- An employer's unilateral decision to enforce a long-dormant policy that required employees who "called off" sick on the weekends to provide a doctor's excuse.

- An employer's unilateral posting of a particular job position at a lower pay grade than what the position had traditionally received.

- An employer's unilateral requirement that registered nurses become certified in advance cardiac life support when there was no evidence that the requirement reflected a regulatory mandate.

- An employer's unilateral decision to cease contributions to pension and annuity funds sponsored by the incumbent union after unit employees elected to change bargaining representatives. The NLRB required the employer to set the contributions aside for the benefit of the employees until the parties reached a new agreement or an impasse.[82]

Below are some examples of unilateral changes that were not considered material changes in a mandatory bargaining subject and, thus, could be made by the employer without prior bargaining:

- An employer's institution of a new parking policy that required employees to walk approximately 200 additional yards from their vehicles to the main building.

- An employer's implementation of a policy assigning employees a locker and issuing each employee a lock provided by the employer (held not material because employees were able to secure their lockers before and after the new policy, the only difference being that the employer now provided the lock).

- An employer's change in the dress code policy, prohibiting nurses from wearing acrylic or artificial nails, where the previous policy required that fingernails could not be longer than one-eighth of an inch past the tip of an employee's fingers and strongly discouraged the use of acrylic nails.

Q 5.10.1   Is an employer required to bargain with a union where a change to a non-unit employee's benefit affects a unit employee?

An employer does not need to bargain with a union over changes to the employee benefits of non-unit employees, even where those changes affect a unit employee. For example, an employer's unilateral implementation of a health plan in which non-unit employees lost the right to seek reimbursement of unpaid balances of their unit spouse's medical expenses was not unlawful because the employer changed the non-unit employee's plan and not the terms and conditions of employment for the unit employee. The fact that the change had an impact on the joint finances of the unit/non-unit couples was a result of marital status and not unit status. Unit employees retained the right to seek reimbursement of the unpaid balance of their non-unit spouses' medical expenses.[83]

Q 5.10.2 Can the employer make material changes to employees' terms and conditions of employment after the union is recognized, but before the first contract is ratified?

From the time a union petition is filed or the union is certified as the parties' bargaining representative until the ratification of the first contract, generally the employer must maintain the status quo with respect to the terms and conditions of employment.[84] Once a union has been recognized, an employer may not make a unilateral change to employees' terms and conditions of employment without bargaining with the union, regardless of whether or not the union has requested bargaining.[85]

Employer's Disclosure Obligations

Request for Information

Q 5.11 What are an employer's statutory bargaining obligations with respect to providing information to the union?

As part of an employer's statutory duty to bargain in good faith with the bargaining representative of its employees, section 8(a)(5) of the NLRA requires an employer to furnish certain types of information, upon request, to the employees' union representative. The purpose of this obligation is to enable the union to understand and intelligently discuss the issues raised in collective bargaining.

This obligation includes a duty to comply with legitimate requests in a timely manner. A significant, unjustified delay in providing requested information can constitute a violation of section 8(a)(5) of the NLRA. There is no rule for determining how long the employer can delay in providing information to the union before it violates the NLRA. The determination will be made on a case-by-case basis, in light of the surrounding circumstances.[86]

Relevance of Information

Q 5.12 What type of information must the employer provide to the union?

An employer must provide information that is relevant and necessary to allow the employees' representative to bargain intelligently and effectively with respect to wages, hours, and other terms and conditions of employment, as well as to properly administer and police a collective bargaining agreement. Thus, the question of whether particular information needs to be provided hinges on whether the information sought is probably or potentially relevant to the execution of the union's statutory duties. The standard for relevance is quite liberal. Generally, if information is even arguably related to the union's collective bargaining functions, it will be considered relevant and must be provided to the union.

Q 5.12.1 What types of information are considered presumptively relevant?

Certain types of information are so intrinsic to the employer-employee relationship that such information is considered presumptively relevant and must be provided by the employer to the union, absent compelling justification to the contrary, including:

- information pertaining to the identity and demographics of bargaining unit employees (names, addresses, phone numbers, hire dates, job titles, etc.);

- information pertaining to wages, hours, and other terms and conditions of employment, such as wage rates, shift premiums, hours worked, discipline history, and classifications of bargaining unit employees;

- information related to benefits or privileges received by bargaining unit employees, which can include, for example:

    (1) insurance policies;

    (2) amounts paid by the employer and employees for benefits;

    (3) the number of paid holidays;

    (4) pension plan information;

    (5) vacation requirements;

    (6) information regarding incentive plans;

    (7) information regarding the employer's annuity plan;

    (8) a list of laid-off employees; and

    (9) a list of employees receiving workers' compensation benefits;

- information pertaining to the health and safety (working conditions) of employees; and

- information relevant to anticipated or pending grievances.

Q 5.12.2   Does an employer have to provide to a union information that is not presumptively relevant?

An employer may be obligated to provide information that is not presumptively relevant, such as the employer's nonpublic financial information and wages and benefits paid to extra-unit personnel, but only if the union can demonstrate that the requested information is particularly relevant and necessary to one of the union's functions as a collective bargaining representative. For example, if the information does not pertain to employees in the bargaining unit, the union will be required to establish the relevance of the requested information. A union may be entitled to information about non-unit employees, for instance, if it has a reasonable belief that the non-unit employees are performing unit work, making such information potentially relevant to the union's right to monitor and enforce the collective bargaining agreement.[87] In such cases, an employer may insist on a reasonably tailored confidentiality agreement that limits the union's use of the information to the stated particular purpose to which the information bears relevance.

An employer also may be obligated to provide information that is not presumptively relevant if the union requests information pertaining to a suspected alter-ego relationship between the employer and a predecessor employer. The employer must turn over the requested information to the union so long as the union has an objective, factual basis for believing that the alter-ego relationship exists.[88] See Q 5.29.2 for a discussion of when an alter-ego relationship exists.

Refusal to Disclose Information

Q 5.13   What information can an employer refuse to provide a union?

An employer can refuse to provide information requested by the union where the information has no relevance to any legitimate union collective bargaining function.

Additionally, an employer can refuse to provide presumptively relevant information if it can show that:

(1)   the union requested the information in bad faith or for illegitimate purposes unrelated to the union's collective bargaining functions;

(2)   the employer has legitimate concerns for the safety of employees based upon incidents of violence or harassment (for example, information about employees who have crossed a picket line during a violent strike); or

(3)   the employer has legitimate confidentiality interests with respect to the information.[89]

Moreover, if retrieval or transmittal of presumptively relevant information is costly or overly burdensome the employer can refuse to provide such information or make alternative arrangements with the union. The NLRB will weigh the competing interests of the employer and the union and determine whether the information must be provided. The employer may, for example, require the union to pay for photocopying costs.[90] Similarly, the NLRB has also held that an employer did not violate the NLRA when it orally provided payroll information to the union despite the fact that the union requested the information in written form.[91]

In addition, where the information in question implicates legitimate privilege or confidentiality concerns, the parties will be directed to negotiate an alternative arrangement that does the least damage to those concerns.[92]

Financial or Confidential Information

Q 5.13.1 Does an employer have to provide its nonpublic financial information to a union?

An employer ordinarily does not have to provide financial information about its business to a union. In most cases, financial information is not presumptively relevant, and the employer is not required to disclose such information. Generally, only when the employer makes claims to the union related to such information—for example, claiming an "inability to pay" or pleading poverty in support of its bargaining position—is the employer required to provide financial information substantiating its claims. In these instances, it is the employer's statements to the union that has made the disclosure of the financial information relevant to the discussions with the union, and therefore subject to disclosure as the union has a right to test the veracity of the employer's statements in bargaining.[93]

Although unions are entitled to certain information regarding the subcontracting of work covered by a collective bargaining agreement and performed by bargaining unit members, employers are not necessarily obligated to disclose all financial information related to subcontracting. For example, the NLRB has held that while an employer was obligated to furnish the union with a list of jobs subcontracted and the terms of the contracts, it was not required to furnish information regarding amounts billed to the employer by the contractors.[94]

Further, where unions request information in the context of plant relocations, employers may be obligated to furnish financial information (such as sales contracts concerning the purchase and sale of a facility) where the information is necessary for the union to determine the rights of its members.

Q 5.13.2   Does an employer have to provide confidential employee information, such as medical information?

Where a union requests employee information that the employer claims is confidential, the NLRB will balance the union's interest in disclosure against the employee's privacy interests. For instance, an employer met its obligation to furnish information when it conditioned release of each individual employee's test scores on that employee's consent.[95]

An employer may be required to furnish aggregate medical data or individual medical records from which identifying information is redacted.[96] If necessary, the NLRB may also require limited disclosure of identifying information to healthcare providers in a confidential relationship with the patients.[97]

Union's Disclosure Obligations

Q 5.14   Is the union required to provide the employer with information as part of its statutory bargaining?

Yes, the union has a similar duty to provide relevant information in its possession or control.[98] The union's duty is not, however, triggered until an employer makes a request for the information. Decisions have found that unions have a duty to provide information regarding hiring-hall and staffing information, union pension and welfare plans, collective bargaining agreements with other employers, a list of employees on a union out-of-work list, and information that aids the arbitral process. A union does not have a duty to provide information from a fringe benefit fund, unless the union essentially controls the fund. If the union possesses the information and it is not readily available to the employer from another source, however, then the union may have an obligation to provide it.[99]

Bargaining Table Conduct

Hard Bargaining

Q 5.15   What is "hard bargaining"?

Hard bargaining describes a bargaining style whereby a party to the negotiations maintains a strong position from which it appears unwilling to yield.

Q 5.15.1   Is hard bargaining permissible?

Hard bargaining is permitted under the law and is not per se considered bad-faith bargaining in violation of section 8(a)(5) or 8(b)(3) of the NLRA.

In assessing an employer's conduct in negotiations, the NLRB considers the totality of the employer's conduct and the overall circumstances surrounding that conduct to determine whether the employer has bargained in good faith. Whether an employer has fulfilled its statutory duty to bargain in good faith depends on whether its conduct at the bargaining table demonstrates a bona fide effort to reach an agreement. Parties are not required, however, to make concessions or agree to any of the other parties' proposals.

Thus, an employer can take a resolute bargaining position without committing an unfair labor practice where the totality of the circumstances shows no dilatory tactics or an attempt to stall efforts to reach an agreement. For example, an employer's firm insistence on a contract extension will be considered lawful hard bargaining where the employer demonstrated good-faith bargaining by appearing at several negotiating sessions and continued to offer proposals and consider union proposals. Moreover, an employer is not required to agree to a concession and can lawfully refuse to yield on its various positions, so long as the totality of the circumstances indicates that the employer was engaged in good-faith bargaining. An employer could, for example, lawfully insist upon retaining its existing health benefits plan where it remained willing to discuss the issue and had reached agreement with the union on the vast majority of other bargaining issues.[100] If the insistence on a certain position does not detract from overall good-faith bargaining, it may be maintained indefinitely, even if it produces a stalemate.[101]

Surface Bargaining

Q 5.16   What is "surface bargaining"?

Surface bargaining is where a party goes through the motions of negotiating without making a bona fide effort to reach an agreement.

Q 5.16.1   Is surface bargaining permissible?

Surface bargaining violates the requirement that parties negotiate in good faith. The courts and the NLRB have held that an employer engaged in unlawful surface bargaining where the employer:

- maintains a "take-it-or-leave-it" attitude while going through the motions of bargaining;
- causes lengthy delays in scheduling bargaining sessions or arbitrarily schedules bargaining sessions;
- makes unreasonable bargaining demands, such as insisting on total control of the employment relationship;
- sends representatives who do not have the authority to negotiate;
- fails to offer proposals;
- fails or refuses to provide relevant information;
- threatens unilateral changes or impasse on multiple occasions.

Again, the NLRB will consider the totality of conduct in negotiations and the overall circumstances surrounding that conduct to determine whether a party has engaged in bad-faith surface bargaining.

Regressive Bargaining

Q 5.17   What is "regressive bargaining"?

Regressive bargaining is when a party either withdraws previously advanced proposals or adds additional provisions to delay or frustrate the bargaining process.

Q 5.17.1   Is regressive bargaining permissible?

An employer may make regressive bargaining proposals so long as the employer's proffered reasons are supported by good cause. Good cause will be presumed as long as the employer's reasons for its changed bargaining stance are not so illogical or unreasonable as to demonstrate an intent to frustrate the bargaining process and thereby preclude the reaching of any agreement. Accordingly, as long as the employer presents a reasonable basis for its changed negotiating stance, untainted by other bad-faith negotiating conduct, the employer's regressive bargaining will likely be upheld.

Bargaining and Employer Communications with Employees

Direct Dealing

Q 5.18   Can a unionized employer discuss bargaining issues directly with employees?

Generally speaking, an employer violates the NLRA when it bypasses the union and deals directly with employees with respect to mandatory bargaining subjects. However, the NLRB and courts have consistently upheld employers' rights to communicate directly to employees concerning the status of collective bargaining negotiations. Such communications are lawful if, viewed in the totality of the circumstances, the communications are accurate, are not coercive, do not evince an intent to bypass the union and deal directly with employees, and do not otherwise undermine the union's status as the employees' exclusive collective bargaining representative.

For example, the NLRB has found that an employer did not violate the NLRA when it communicated directly to its employees during ongoing contract negotiations through letters, bulletins, and formal and informal meetings. Through these means, the employer provided employees with information on the status of negotiations, explained company proposals that it had already presented to the union, refuted union allegations, and criticized the union's bargaining strategy and tactics, which the company said were the reasons for its inability to reach an agreement with the union. The NLRB found these communications to be lawful, emphasizing their non-coercive nature and the employer's overall good-faith bargaining conduct.

The NLRB has also found no violation of the NLRA where an employer:

- distributed leaflets describing the offer it made to the union during contract re-opener negotiations;

- mailed letters to its employees that further explained its proposal and urged them to vote;

- issued a press release and advertisements in local newspapers describing its final offer and urging employees to weigh the company's final offer against the alternative of a strike.

Impermissible Communications

Q 5.18.1 What are the limits of an employer's "free-speech rights" when it comes to employer-employee communications?

While an employer's free-speech right to communicate its views to employees is firmly established and cannot be infringed on by a union or the NLRB (see Q 3.16 *et seq.*), the scope of employer speech is not without limits:

- An employer may not attempt to influence employees' opinions by offering benefits or making threats.

- An employer may not present proposals to employees before they are presented to the union.

- An employer must be careful when engaging in speech that denigrates the union.

- An employer faces several restrictions (discussed below) when seeking employee input concerning the parties' bargaining proposals and positions.

Section 8(c) of the NLRA excludes from its protection communications that "contain[ ] [a] threat of reprisal or force or promise or benefit." (See Q 4.51 *et seq.*) Section 8(c) has been construed to prohibit an employer from making proposals directly to employees instead of to the union and to prohibit coercive communication campaigns. Examples of coercive conduct include extensive direct employee communications coupled with an inflexible bargaining stance; communication of employer offers to employees directly, outside the framework of formal negotiations; and letters to employees that portray the union's bargaining committee as individuals with no legitimate role to play other than to agree to the employer's proposals.

Q 5.18.2 When does an employer's communication to employees become a form of "direct dealing" in violation of the duty to bargain with the union?

Although employers are entitled to communicate with employees about the status of negotiations, the NLRB has consistently found that employers violate the NLRA when they communicate bargaining proposals directly to employees without first presenting those proposals to the union. However, just how much time must elapse between the time an employer presents its proposals to the union and the time it communicates its proposals directly to employees is unclear. The case law is inconsistent as to whether an employer's communication campaign, launched contemporaneously with union negotiations, violates the NLRA. In one case, a federal court of appeals refused to enforce an NLRB order holding that an employer violated the NLRA by sending proposals to the union at the same time the employer sent copies of the proposals to the employees. Likewise, an employer did not unlawfully deal directly with its employees, nor did it denigrate the union, when immediately after concluding negotiations with the union it held a meeting with employees to communicate its proposals and to explain that it had withdrawn from a multi-employer association.

Soliciting Employee Input

Q 5.18.3   Can employers directly seek employee input into bargaining proposals?

An employer can unlawfully undermine its employees' union by directly soliciting employee input concerning bargaining proposals. The NLRB has repeatedly held that efforts to directly solicit employee feedback concerning the relative merits of proposals that are the subject of ongoing negotiations violate the NLRA.[102] Generally, an employer may communicate to employees regarding the reasons for its actions and its bargaining objectives, but it may not seek to determine the degree of support bargaining unit employees have for either its proposal or the union's position on a subject of negotiations.[103]

Of note, the NLRB has found that an employer does not violate the NLRA merely by assembling a volunteer group of employees to provide input in shaping a proposal that will subsequently be bargained for with a union, where the employer told participating employees that it was seeking their input based on their professional expertise, emphasized that participation was voluntary, and expressly declared that their involvement in designing a plan did not entail bargaining or setting working conditions.[104]

Moreover, employers are entitled to seek employee input on issues unrelated to negotiations with the union or mandatory bargaining subjects. An employer did not violate the NLRA where it distributed a survey to all employees (not just those represented by the union) through non-specific, open-ended questions, seeking feedback on how to improve production efficiency.[105] The NLRB emphasized that the employer's bargaining proposals did not relate, except in a general way, to the survey responses; that the survey was consistent with, though more aggressive than, the employer's past practice of soliciting employees' input through a suggestion box; and that the survey was motivated by legitimate business concerns.

Bargaining Impasse

Q 5.19   What is a good-faith bargaining impasse?

The NLRA generally mandates that employers engage in good-faith collective bargaining over the terms and conditions of employment for bargaining unit employees. This statutory duty to bargain requires that employers meet with the union at reasonable times and make a good-faith effort to resolve their differences. Although the NLRA requires good-faith bargaining, the law does not require any party to agree to a concession, nor is a party required to engage in fruitless marathon discussions. "Impasse" is the term used to describe a deadlock in collective bargaining negotiations when neither side at that point in time will make further concessions. It is a situation in which one party is warranted in assuming that further negotiations will not resolve the parties' differences, or that further good-faith bargaining would be futile. "Impasse" is also the point in labor relations in which there is sufficient disagreement over a mandatory subject of bargaining to permit certain unilateral action on the subject by the controlling party (typically the employer).

Declaring an Impasse

Q 5.19.1   How do you know when parties have reached a good-faith bargaining impasse?

In determining whether negotiations have reached a good-faith bargaining impasse, the NLRB considers the totality of the circumstances, including:

(1)   the bargaining history;

(2)   the good faith of the parties in negotiations;

(3)   the length of the negotiations;

(4)   the importance of the issue or issues as to which there is disagreement; and

(5)   the contemporaneous understanding of the parties as to the state of negotiations.[106]

Bargaining history. If the parties have a longstanding collective bargaining relationship and have entered into a number of earlier contracts, a finding of impasse is more likely. A longstanding relationship, without any history of unfair ULPs, indicates that the parties can successfully negotiate where the differences are surmountable and supports the idea that the differences underlying the present deadlock are insurmountable. Conversely, it is more difficult to convince the NLRB that the parties have reached impasse in first-contract negotiations.

Good-faith bargaining. No bona fide impasse exists if either party has engaged in bad-faith bargaining. A finding that an employer has bargained in good faith is a necessary but not determinative factor in the NLRB's impasse analysis.

Length of negotiations. There is no rigid formula for determining how long parties must bargain before impasse occurs. The NLRB and the courts look at both the number of sessions where substantive negotiations occurred and the duration of each session.[107] In general, more time spent meeting translates into a higher likelihood of a finding of impasse, because it suggests that the parties made a reasonable effort to reach an agreement but have not been able to do so.

Importance of issues. A deadlock resulting in a bona fide impasse can occur over one or more issues that the parties recognize as important to their respective interests. Thus, the agreement or movement on minor items will not defeat a finding of impasse where there is deadlock on one or more items that one or both parties find critical to reaching an overall agreement.[108] Similarly, the fact that the parties have reached agreement on a few contract provisions of lesser importance and that their respective positions are in some respects closer does not negate the existence of a bona fide impasse. For instance, an impasse exists where the parties agree that wages are a critical issue, the union has agreed to an MFN clause with a multi-employer association that does not include the employer, but the employer will not agree to the wage rate in the multi-employer association's contract.

Contemporaneous understanding. This inquiry has been described as "a subjective attempt to discover what was going on in the minds of negotiators as they left the bargaining table." Words alone are not dispositive; rather, it is the entire course of dealing between the parties that must be considered when determining whether an impasse exists. Thus, a party's claim that it is still willing to negotiate over apparently deadlocked issues will not prevent a finding of impasse where the facts establish that an impasse exists. Moreover, a union's request for further bargaining will not break an impasse unless the union provides specific information that would allow the employer to reasonably conclude that it will not be entering into more fruitless discussions.

Q 5.20   What are the consequences of an employer declaring an impasse?

During bargaining, employers may formulate proposals to unions and insist upon the proposals so long as the employer bargains in good faith. Upon reaching an impasse, the duty to bargain is suspended and employers have several options available to them regarding seeking or implementing changes to the terms and conditions of employment.[109] For example, employers may resort to economic force, including lockouts, in support of their demands.

Once bargaining reaches an impasse, employers may also unilaterally implement changes to the terms and conditions of employment. Any new terms must be "reasonably comprehended" within the employer's pre-impasse proposals. This typically means implementing the last proposal put forth by the employer to the union regarding the term to be changed. Further, the collective bargaining process that resulted in an impasse must have been free from any ULP, such as the employer's failure to bargain in good faith.[110]

The employer need not implement all of its pre-impasse proposals, but the changes must be in line with, and not more favorable to the employees than, those offered prior to impasse. Conversely, an employer cannot implement a change that was not included in its pre-impasse proposals. If the employer's declaration of impasse is held to be premature or tainted by unremedied ULPs, any unilateral changes by the employer will have to be rescinded and may give rise to backpay liability.

Although an employer may normally implement employment terms after bargaining to impasse, an employer may not implement certain proposals that, even though they deal with mandatory subjects and thus can be "deal breakers," they envision ongoing unilateral employer determination of wages and benefits. For example, merit pay systems that allow employers to unilaterally determine wage rates and discretionary benefits–related proposals are ordinarily not subject to the implementation-after-impasse doctrine.

CASE STUDY: *McClatchy Newspapers v. NLRB*[111]

In *McClatchy Newspapers v. NLRB*, the U.S. Court of Appeals for the D.C. Circuit upheld the NLRB's finding of a narrow exception to the rule permitting an employer to unilaterally implement its final offer regarding a mandatory bargaining subject after contract expiration, where the parties have bargained in good faith to the point of impasse.

In *McClatchy*, an expired collective bargaining agreement set compensation through a combination of wage scales and discretionary merit increases. The employer proposed an entirely merit-based system, while the union sought to eliminate the merit component altogether. The parties reached an impasse over the wage terms, and the employer implemented its final offer, including its purely discretionary merit system. Thereafter, the employer granted merit increases without consulting the union.

The NLRB established an exception to the general implementation-after-impasse rule and held that the employer could not implement its merit-based system because the employer did not provide any "definable objective procedures and criteria" for assessing merit. Because the proposed merit system left wages entirely to the employer's discretion, the merit system did not really establish actual "terms and conditions of employment." Rather than encourage collective bargaining, implementation of a purely discretionary system effectively took the union out of the loop and undermined its ability to act as the employees' representative.

Absence of a Bona Fide Impasse

Q 5.20.1 Under what circumstances can a bona fide impasse be broken and the duty to bargain reawakened?

The fact that an impasse has been reached does not prevent the NLRB from finding a subsequent refusal to bargain. For example, the union's indication of a change in its bargaining position could reactivate the employer's bargaining duty as could the union's willingness to reopen negotiations unconditionally. The employer's failure to respond to the union's gesture could be considered a refusal to bargain in violation of section 8(a)(5) of the NLRA.

Further, any post-impasse unilateral changes an employer makes that exceed its pre-impasse offers to the union or that were never presented to the union may be interpreted as a refusal to bargain after impasse. Depending on the circumstances, a strike after impasse may also have the effect of breaking the impasse, obligating the parties to return to the bargaining table.

Q 5.20.2 Can employers make unilateral changes in the absence of a bona fide impasse?

In certain circumstances, an employer may make unilateral changes to the terms and conditions of employment without having first reached a bona fide impasse. These circumstances include situations where:

- the union clearly and unmistakably waived its right to bargain over the term or condition, either through contractual terms or inaction;[112]

- after the end of the certification year, the union no longer enjoys majority support;[113]

- purchasers of the assets of a business are setting the initial terms of employment and hiring;[114]

- the employer changes the terms and conditions for strike replacements after the termination of a collective bargaining agreement.[115]

Q 5.20.3   When will an employer's ULP preclude the finding of an impasse?

Unremedied ULPs committed by an employer may preclude finding that the parties reached a bona fide impasse. A common situation here would be an employer's failure to provide relevant information requested by the union. However, not all ULPs committed before or during negotiations preclude a bona fide impasse. Generally, "only serious unremedied ULPs that *affect* the negotiations will taint the asserted impasse."[116]

Midterm Bargaining and Waiver

Q 5.21   What does the duty to bargain require where a collective bargaining agreement already exists?

The execution of a collective bargaining agreement does not terminate an employer's duty to bargain collectively. There is, in principle, a continuous duty to bargain over wages and terms and conditions of employment unless the subject or term is, under section 8(d), "contained in" the collective agreement. A party's unilateral midterm modification of terms "contained in" the agreement is barred by the duty to bargain under sections 8(a)(5) and 8(b)(3), as defined in section 8(d). Thus, a union has the statutory right to require an employer to bargain before the employer makes a unilateral change with respect to a term or condition of employment treated in the collective bargaining agreement, unless the union waives its right to bargain over the subject. If the term the union requests bargaining over is a mandatory subject not contained in the agreement because the subject was never raised in bargaining and the parties have not agreed to a "zipper" clause (see QQ 5.8.7 and 5.22.3), an employer violates section 8(a)(5) of the NLRA if it refuses to bargain with the union to good-faith impasse over that subject.

Modifying the Collective Bargaining Agreement

Q 5.21.1   What can a party do if it wishes to change a provision in the collective bargaining agreement?

If a party wishes to change a provision in the collective bargaining agreement, it can request bargaining over the change. However, the other party to the collective bargaining agreement generally is not required to bargain during the term of the agreement over changes to the collective bargaining agreement unless the agreement specifically provides for either the reopening of the relevant provisions or the whole contract. Employers and unions must bargain, upon request, on mandatory subjects of bargaining that were neither covered in the agreement nor discussed in negotiations, unless the parties have negotiated a "zipper" clause or the union otherwise has specifically waived its right to bargain on such subjects.

Q 5.21.2   How does the NLRB determine whether an employer has modified a collective bargaining agreement in violation of sections 8(a)(5) and 8(d)?

Often, claims of midterm modification under sections 8(a)(5) and 8(d) overlap with claims of breach of contract. The NLRB generally will not find a midterm modification where the employer had a sound basis for its interpretation of the contract and was not motivated by union animus or bad faith.[117] In a modification case, the NLRB general counsel bears the burden to prove that the employer modified the collective bargaining agreement.[118] This burden is not met merely by showing that the general counsel's interpretation of the collective bargaining agreement is reasonable; the general counsel must show that the employer's interpretation is unreasonable.[119] In considering a section 8(d) modification complaint, the NLRB does not analyze which contract interpretation is better, leaving that determination to courts and arbitrators.[120]

Standards for Establishing Waiver of Bargaining Rights

Q 5.22   Can a union waive its right to bargain over an employer's midterm modification, and if so, how?

Either party can waive bargaining rights over a specific term or condition of employment or its right to bargain over any mandatory subject that otherwise might be open for midterm bargaining because it is not covered in the collective bargaining agreement. Because the employer is typically the controlling party, absent some limitation in the labor agreement or the NLRA, the issue of waiver of bargaining rights is typically an issue of whether the union has waived its right to insist on midterm bargaining or bar the employer's attempt at midterm modification. When the issue is whether the union can seek to require bargaining over a new term to the agreement, the zipper clause will be considered an effective waiver of any right to insist on such bargaining. Where the issue, however, is whether the employer can derogate from some significant practice beneficial to employees but not expressly treated in the collective bargaining agreement, the zipper clause, standing alone, does not constitute a waiver of the union's right to resist such changes without prior bargaining. Here, the NLRB requires that the union's waiver be "clear and unmistakable." Such waiver is difficult to establish, as the NLRB applies a high standard and typically construes any purported waiver narrowly. For example, the Board has required that "[t]he party asserting waiver must establish that the parties 'unequivocally and specifically expressed their mutual intention to permit unilateral employer action with respect to a particular employment term, notwithstanding the statutory duty to bargain that would otherwise apply.'"[121]

However, the U.S. Courts of Appeals for the D.C., First, and Seventh Circuits have declined to enforce the NLRB's clear and unmistakable test and have insisted on a "contract coverage" test that effectively treats the employer's midterm change as a contract violation rather than statutory violation.[122] Under the contract coverage test, if there is a contractual provision relevant to the dispute, then the dispute would be resolved by interpreting the contract language that the parties already have bargained and reached agreement on. Accordingly, where the collective bargaining agreement contains a relevant provision, the employer has not refused to bargain in violation of section 8(a)(5). For instance, where an employer revised its attendance and tardiness policy, the change was relevant to contract provisions regarding the employer's right to "make and enforce rules of conduct of employees," to "change reporting practices and procedures and/or to introduce new or improved ones," and to "discipline employees for breach of those rules."[123] Whether the employer violated the agreement in any manner would be a matter for the grievance and arbitration process.

Q 5.22.1   What constitutes "clear and unmistakable conduct" supporting a waiver of bargaining rights?

The NLRB's "clear and unmistakable" waiver standard requires that parties "unequivocally and specifically express their mutual intention to permit unilateral employer action with respect to a particular employment term." There are two ways this test can be met: (1) through express contractual language,[124] such as a zipper clause or a management rights clause; or (2) through conduct indicating the party has waived its right to bargain over an issue. Both forms of waiver are elaborated below.

Q 5.22.2   How does a "reopener" clause affect a party's duty to bargain during the term of a contract?

A reopener clause requires parties to bargain in good faith over any matters covered by a reopener provision, if the conditions for reopening are met. The most common form of reopener clause is a wage reopener clause that permits reconsideration of wages if, for example, the Consumer Price Index passes a specified point. In wage reopener negotiations, typically an employer may declare impasse and implement its final proposal, if all notice and good-faith bargaining requirements are met.[125]

Q 5.22.3   How may a "zipper" clause be used to establish waiver of bargaining rights?

A zipper clause is a provision that specifically states that the parties' contract covers all of the issues that were bargained over as well as those that could be bargained over between the parties. In that sense, it "zips up" the midterm duty to bargain. The NLRB has generally held, however, that a zipper clause can be used to maintain the status quo (by precluding union demands to add new terms), not to facilitate unilateral change by the employer.[126]

Q 5.22.4   What is a "management rights" clause, and how may it be used to establish waiver of bargaining rights?

A management rights clause specifically reserves certain rights to management that are not subject to bargaining. The clause may be general (for example, stating that all the normal prerogatives of management are retained by the company), or it can be very specific (for example, enumerating the specific powers to be exercised exclusively by management, such as the right to hire, promote, suspend, or discharge employees). A management rights clause ordinarily does not give an employer the right to make unilateral midterm changes to subjects treated in the collective bargaining agreement. Generally worded management rights clauses normally will not be construed as waivers of statutory bargaining rights and are, at best, guides for interpreting the labor contract in arbitration.

Keeping in mind that the waiver of bargaining question is fact-specific, some examples of where a management rights clause constituted waiver of a bargaining obligation are as follows:

- An employer did not make an unlawful unilateral change by a new disciplinary policy on attendance and tardiness where the management rights clause provided that the employer had the right to change or introduce new procedures and to make and enforce rules of conduct.[127]

- The employer did not make an unlawful unilateral change by changing its shift scheduling procedure where the management rights clause gave the employer the right "to determine and change starting times, quitting times and shifts," to "assign" employees, and to "change methods and means by which its operations are to be carried on."[128]

- An employer did not make an unlawful unilateral change when it required employees to complete a safety checklist before using equipment where the management rights clause provided that the employer "shall continue to make reasonable provisions for the safety and health of its employees."[129]

- A healthcare employer did not make an unlawful unilateral change by implementing a flu-prevention policy where the management rights clause gave the employer the right to "operate and manage the facility . . . require standards of performance . . . direct the nurses . . . determine the materials and equipment to be used . . . implement improved operational methods and procedures . . . and promulgate rules, regulations, and personnel policies."[130]

Some examples of where a management rights clause did *not* constitute waiver of a bargaining obligation are as follows:

- The employer made an unlawful unilateral change by attempting to relocate bargaining unit work and the management rights clause only gave management the right to determine what to produce.[131]

- The employer made an unlawful unilateral change by imposing drug and alcohol testing on bargaining unit employees where the management rights clause allowed management to issue "company rules" and did not make specific reference to drug and alcohol testing.[132]

- An employer made an unlawful unilateral change by eliminating an employee classification and terminating the employees in that classification even though the management rights clause gave the employer the right to classify, reassign, lay off, and discharge employees.[133]

Q 5.22.5 How does a party waive its right to bargain through conduct?

A party can waive its right to bargain through its actions or inactions during the course of the parties' bargaining history. The NLRB, however, has made clear that it will not lightly infer waiver in such situations. The NLRB will generally infer waiver only where the matter at issue has been "fully discussed and consciously explored" during negotiations and the union has consciously yielded or clearly and unmistakably waived its interest in the matter.[134] Courts and the NLRB will examine how often, and in what depth, the parties discussed the issues and what the parties' understanding was with respect to those issues. For example, the NLRB has found that a union bargained away language in an expiring contract that provided for a retroactive pay increase where the parties discussed the issue on several occasions and the union's members ultimately ratified an agreement with a different date for the pay increase.

Q 5.22.6 Can a union waive its right to bargain through inaction?

If an employer gives a union advance notice of its intent to make a change to a term or condition of employment, the union must request bargaining or it may waive any claims of unlawful unilateral change under the NLRA.[135] However, a union's acquiescence to certain prior changes to a matter subject to bargaining does not necessarily constitute a waiver of the right to bargain in the future regarding such a matter. In other words, the fact that an employer previously changed the terms of a particular program without bargaining does not necessarily preclude the union from demanding bargaining regarding an additional, subsequent change. Each time new rules are issued, the union has the option of requesting negotiations. An opportunity once rejected does not result in a permanent "close out."

In the context of decision and effects bargaining, a union may waive its right to bargain about an employer's decision to change its operations, and the decision's impact on employees, by failing to request bargaining after notification of the contemplated or impending decision.[136] Again, the union's waiver of the right to bargain must be "clear and unmistakable."

Post-Expiration Bargaining

Q 5.23 What types of changes can either party make in mandatory subjects after a union contract expires?

Even after a collective bargaining agreement expires and is no longer binding, the existing terms and conditions of employment must be kept in place simply by virtue of the duty to bargain found in section 8(a)(5). In general, the mandatory subjects treated in the collective bargaining agreement define the operational status quo during the "hiatus" period after the expiration of the contract and before a new contract has been agreed upon. If the employer wants to change any of those terms, the general rule is that the employer must bargain with the union to good-faith impasse on those terms. An employer, therefore, has a continuing duty to bargain with the union, and post-expiration the employer may not be able to rely on the management rights clause in an expired contract when making unilateral changes.

There are some exceptions to the rule that the mandatory subjects treated in the expired collective bargaining agreement define the operational status quo. With regard to the following cases, either party may decline to adhere to the provision of the expired agreement during the period between contracts:

- contract-dependent provisions where law requires an agreement, such as:

  - union security provision

  - dues check-off provision

- contract-dependent clauses where waivers of statutory rights are involved, such as:

  - no-strike clauses

  - rights arbitration clause versus duty to process grievances

Multi-Employer Bargaining

Participation and Withdrawal in Multi-Employer Association

Q 5.24   What is a multi-employer bargaining unit?

A multi-employer bargaining association is a group of employers who bargain collectively with a labor organization. This type of bargaining is found in the following industries:

(1) sports;
(2) trucking;
(3) mining;
(4) construction;
(5) some manufacturing; and
(6) maritime.

Regardless of whether an employer belongs to a multi-employer bargaining association, the employer can accept the provisions of a multi-employer collective bargaining agreement by signing a memorandum accepting the contract or by conduct indicating "me too" adherence. (See Q 5.24.3.)

A multi-employer bargaining unit requires the consent of all participating employers and the labor union(s) representing the affected employees. Generally, the employers form an association to bargain with the union. In principle, the unit is lawful only if the union is the majority bargaining agent for each constituent employer; in practice, the NLRB will give a good deal of weight to bargaining history before allowing a severance petition on a less inclusive basis than the overall multi-employer unit. The NLRB will not hold an election or certify election results in a multi-employer unit.

Q 5.24.1   How can an employer withdraw from multi-employer collective bargaining?

Although participation in multi-employer bargaining generally is voluntary, employers who elect to participate in multi-employer bargaining should be aware that the ability to withdraw from multi-employer bargaining is limited; it requires that written notice be sent within an appropriate window or as a result of specific circumstances. Absent timely withdrawal, an employer may find itself bound to the multi-employer collective bargaining agreement. In some situations, the Board may consider an employer bound to a multi-employer agreement, even after communicating a timely withdrawal, if the employer continues to actively participate in the association's labor relations activities (for example, bargaining or paying dues to the association).[137]

Under NLRB policy upheld by the U.S. Supreme Court, the timeliness requirement is met if the employer gives notice prior to the date on which negotiations are set to commence or before they actually commence. Accordingly, employers may only withdraw from multi-employer bargaining before the start of negotiations on a new contract. The employer must also consider the timing-of-notice requirements set out in a collective bargaining agreement.[138] However, an employer is entitled to actual notice of the scheduled commencement of contract negotiations. Absent such notice, the employer cannot be held to have untimely withdrawn from the multi-employer association.[139] For example, when an employer was given no prior notice that negotiations were beginning, its notice of withdrawal from the multi-employer association was timely when it was filed two weeks after the commencement of negotiations.[140]

Absent a showing of mutual consent or unusual circumstances, an employer will not be permitted to withdraw from a multi-employer association once bargaining begins. "Unusual circumstances" is narrowly defined. It does not include a bargaining impasse, the union's mounting of "whipsaw" strikes against particular employers, or the entering of "interim" agreements with particular employers. Untimely withdrawal is permitted by the NLRB, however, in situations where: (1) the employer otherwise is facing bankruptcy or similar financial problems; or (2) the multi-employer unit is effectively defunct.[141]

Q 5.24.2   Will an employer still be considered a member of a multi-employer association if its contract is different from other association members' contracts?

To establish a multi-employer association, each employer-member must have indicated from the outset an intention to be bound in collective bargaining by group rather than by individual action.[142] An employer-member may not assert that a multi-employer association does not exist or that a single unit is an appropriate bargaining unit where: (1) a union has collectively represented employees before the multi-employer association with regard to wages, hours, and other basic terms and conditions of employment; and (2) the individual contracts of each employer-member are identical, except for matters that are relevant only to the specific employer-members. Slight variations between individual contracts of employer-members do not support an assertion that a multi-employer association does not exist.[143]

The NLRB does not give controlling weight to the technicality of each employer-member having separate, signed agreements with the union when the NLRB determines whether or not a multi-employer unit exists. When employers consider themselves bound by the results of joint negotiations, it is immaterial that a master agreement is executed severally and not jointly. Such language indicates only the individual responsibility of each employer resulting from the multi-employer bargaining.[144]

For example, the individual collective bargaining agreement signed by each employer in a multi-employer association of supermarkets may contain minor differences based on the distinctions between the members. A collective bargaining agreement signed by one employer may need to account for additional store departments. Another collective bargaining agreement may need to account for bakery employees who are not employed by any of the other stores.[145]

"Me Too" Agreements

Q 5.24.3   When may an employer enter into a "me too" agreement with a union?

Once a union negotiates an agreement with a multi-employer association, the union customarily offers the same agreement to other employers in the area, including those that neither belong to a multi-employer association nor participated in the negotiations. These nonparticipating employers may bind themselves to the agreement negotiated by the union and the multi-employer association simply by executing what are known as "me too" agreements. Unless the employer affirmatively authorizes an acceptance of the agreement, the employer will not be considered to have a collective bargaining agreement with the union.[146]

A company's prior practice of becoming a "me too" signatory to an agreement reached by a union and another multi-employer association, therefore, does not create a presumption that the company will continue its participation in such agreements.[147]

It is perfectly legal and an established practice for an employer to timely withdraw from a multi-employer bargaining process and later adopt the collective bargaining agreement resulting from such a process. The union is not required to give the withdrawing employer the terms of the multi-employer collective bargaining agreement and may hold the employer to more stringent terms because the employer withdrew from the collective bargaining process. This practice is often used in the construction industry.[148]

Q 5.24.4 Where other groups of employees are already represented on a multi-employer or multi-plant basis, are new units of employees limited to that same type of representation?

The NLRB no longer requires a new unit of employees to organize on a multi-plant or multi-employer basis simply because other groups of employees have previously organized themselves on that basis. In *Joseph E. Seagram & Sons*,[149] the NLRB held that a unit of guards could seek single-plant recognition, notwithstanding an extensive history of collective bargaining for most of the employer's other employees on a multi-plant, employer-wide basis.

In *Seagram*, the NLRB noted that forcing employees who seek to organize for the first time to organize in a unit comprising employees spread across multiple plants or multiple employers would be, in practical effect, to deny those employees the right to collective bargaining and the fullest freedom in exercising the rights guaranteed by the NLRA. While the extent to which other employees have previously been organized is a factor when considering the appropriate scope of the new unit, this fact does not have controlling weight when considering whether to require a new unit of employees to bargain across multiple plants.[150]

The holding in *Seagram* has since been applied outside the multi-employer context. The NLRB will permit a new unit of employees to bargain on a single-employer or single-plant basis when those employees have characteristics and cohesiveness sufficient to permit them to bargain alone. For example, since *Seagram*, the NLRB has approved single-employer units of clerical employees and salespersons, despite the fact that the employer negotiated in a multi-employer association with respect to its other employees.[151]

Q 5.24.5   May an employer challenge the majority status of a union as a result of the employer's withdrawal from a multi-employer association?

When an employer withdraws from a multi-employer association, whether it may challenge the majority status of the union as representative of the now single-employer unit of employees depends on a number of factors. If the employers collectively and voluntarily recognized the union as representative of the employees as part of the multi-employer unit, absent additional evidence to the contrary, an employer may not challenge the majority status of the union based solely on its withdrawal from the multi-employer association. In this situation, because the union was voluntarily recognized, each employer implicitly declared that its employees favored the union. Majority status, thus, can be directly inferred from the employer's own conduct. The presumption of majority status originates with the constituent employer's implicit declaration of a majority in its single-employer unit.[152]

When the union was chosen by an election process involving employees across the employer-members of the multi-employer unit, however, some courts have held that the election result does not support a presumption of majority status when one of the employers withdraws from the association. For example, in *NLRB v. Richard W. Kaase Company*,[153] the union had been selected through an election involving the employees across all of the employers in the association. The court held that, despite the existence of a separate contract between the union and employer, there was no evidence showing that Kaase's employees themselves favored the union. Majority status in the Kaase single-employer unit had never been established. The court drew additional support for its holding from the following facts:

(1)   the union was not receptive to the employment needs of the workers;

(2)   the employer's workforce had recently been cut in half based on the company's sale to new owners; and

(3)   there were conflicting representation claims from a rival union.[154]

Another court denied a union the presumption of majority status upon the employer's withdrawal from a multi-employer association where the single employer's unit of employees comprised only a relatively small segment of the multi-employer unit that elected the union as its representative. In this case, however, a rival union's prior representation and a conflicting claim for representation also provided support for a finding of lack of majority status.[155]

Q 5.24.6   Can a multi-employer association and its members be liable for unfair labor practices during multi-employer bargaining?

Yes. One example involved a situation where a union requested information from the individual employers through the multi-employer association and the association unlawfully delayed in providing the information by waiting more than two months to convey the request to its members and by failing to communicate the request in a complete and accurate way.[156] Many of the individual employers also were found liable for failure to respond to the request, once received, in a timely manner. The association and the named members were ordered to timely provide the information and to post a notice of the violation on their premises.

Moreover, individual members may be held liable for the association's conduct if the conduct was within the association's apparent authority.

Successorship Issues

Q 5.25   What are the duties of a "successor employer," and when is an employer considered a "successor employer" for purposes of the NLRA?

A "successor employer" may have the following duties to the predecessor's employees and their union representative:

(1)   the duty to honor the predecessor's agreement (and past practices that inform and give meaning to the terms of the agreement);[157]

(2)   the duty to hire the predecessor's employees; or

(3)   the duty to redress unremedied ULPs committed under the predecessor's watch.

Generally, only the purchaser of the stock of the predecessor or the surviving entity of a merger with the predecessor gives rise to a full-fledged successorship embracing all three duties.

In a stock purchase agreement, the company acquiring the employer's stock typically will be bound to the existing collective bargaining agreement.[158] In such cases, the enterprise's ongoing operations typically are uninterrupted, without any substantial changes.

An assets purchase is handled differently. The U.S. Supreme Court has held that a purchaser of the assets of the predecessor is not obligated to honor the predecessor's labor agreement, but is required to redress unremedied ULPs committed by the seller. The purchaser is free to hire a completely new workforce as long as it does not discriminate against the predecessor's employees because of their union status or affiliation. However, the purchaser is obligated to recognize and bargain with a union representing the predecessor's employees when:

(1)   there is substantial continuity of operations,

(2)   the union makes a timely demand to bargain for an appropriate unit, and

(3) the employer has hired a "substantial and representative com-
     plement of employees, the majority of whom were represented
     by the union under the predecessor."[159]

Sale or Merger of a Company

Q 5.25.1   Is a purchaser bound by a "successorship clause" contained in the seller's unexpired collective bargaining agreement?

Some successorship clauses will purport to bind any successor
employer to the terms and conditions of the parties' collective bargaining agreement. Other successorship clauses will "require" the
employer/seller to condition the terms of any such transaction on the
purchaser's adoption of the terms of the collective bargaining agreement. These clauses may be enforceable against the seller but are not
enforceable against the assets purchaser under the NLRA or section
301 of the LMRA.[160] However, it is possible for unions to use these provisions to seek to block a sale as a means of enforcing its agreement
against the would-be seller.

Q 5.25.2   Is the seller bound by a successorship clause in the collective bargaining agreement?

A successorship clause in the collective bargaining agreement may
provide the union an avenue through which to seek an injunction if
the seller fails to ensure that the purchasing company adopts the collective bargaining agreement. When an injunction issues under such a
clause, the sale may be stayed until after the union and the seller have
arbitrated the issue pursuant to the terms in the collective bargaining
agreement.

Q 5.25.3   What steps can the purchaser take to avoid assuming or adopting a seller's labor contract?

A purchaser that assumes or adopts a seller's labor contract is bound
by it.[161] Courts recognize the adoption of a predecessor's collective
bargaining agreement where there is clear evidence of consent, either
actual or constructive, by the purchaser.[162] Some steps that might be
taken to avoid such a finding include:

- before commencing operations, expressly disavowing an intention to be bound by the contract by writing a letter to the union involved;[163]

- clearly stating that it will not be applying the seller's collective bargaining agreement (there are traps for the unwary in consulting with the seller's union on possible concessions that might be acceptable to the union);

- ensuring that the transaction documents do not inadvertently assume or adopt the collective bargaining agreement.[164]

Q 5.25.4   When will an assets purchaser be unable unilaterally to set the initial terms and conditions of employment?

In general, an assets purchaser may unilaterally set the initial terms of employment, subject to two recognized exceptions:

- where it is "perfectly clear" that the purchaser plans to hire all of the employees in the seller's unit without conditioning their hiring on the acceptance of changed terms and conditions of employment;[165]

- where the purchaser essentially forfeits the right to set initial terms of employment by discriminating against union employees (for example, refusing to hire union employees) or by making coercive anti-union statements (for example, informing employees that union representation will not be accepted or stating "we are not a union company" to employees during the hiring process).[166]

To avoid a finding that it is a "perfectly clear" successor, the assets purchaser should:

- refrain from announcing that it intends to hire the full complement of employees and preface any discussions with a union with a statement that no determination has been made regarding whether the predecessor's employees will be retained;[167]

- "clearly announce its intent to establish a new set of conditions prior to, or simultaneous with, its expression of intent to retain the predecessor's employees."[168]

Q 5.26 What are the purchasing employer's bargaining obligations with an incumbent union?

A successor employer must recognize an incumbent union for a "reasonable period of bargaining" without challenging the majority status of the union. If the successor employer expressly adopts the existing terms and conditions of employment as the starting point for bargaining, the "reasonable period of bargaining" is six months from the date of the first bargaining meeting.[169]

If the successor employer recognizes the union but unilaterally announces and establishes different initial terms and conditions of employment, the "reasonable period of bargaining" extends no less than six months from the date of the first bargaining meeting, but no more than one year. To determine whether this reasonable period has elapsed, the NLRB applies the multi-factor test set out in *Lee Lumber & Building Material Corp.*:

(1) whether the parties are bargaining for an initial contract;

(2) the complexity of the issues being negotiated and of the parties' bargaining processes;

(3) the amount of time elapsed since bargaining commenced and the number of bargaining sessions;

(4) the amount of progress made in negotiations and how near the parties are to concluding an agreement; and

(5) whether the parties are at impasse.[170]

Q 5.27 What are the selling employer's bargaining obligations with respect to selling or merging a company with union-represented employees?

The employer who is selling or merging a company has no duty to bargain over issues that are at the core of entrepreneurial control. Generally, the decision to sell or merge a company does not give rise to a duty to bargain for this reason. (See Q 5.7.2.) A selling employer is, however, required to bargain over the effects of the sale or merger before completing the transaction. To properly bargain over the "effects" the transaction may have on represented employees, the seller must provide: (1) meaningful notice to the union of the transaction; and (2) good-faith bargaining over mitigating measures concerning "effects" issues (for example, severance, outplacement and job counseling, transfer rights, payment for accrued vacation and holiday leave, seniority, and pension and benefits rights).

Transfer/Relocation of Employees

Q 5.28   When an employer transfers represented employees to a new division or location, what are the employer's responsibilities with respect to the union?

If a majority of the employees in the unit at the new facility are transferees from the original bargaining unit, there is a presumption that those employees continue to support the union. Where there is such a majority, the employer will be obligated to recognize and bargain with the union as the exclusive collective bargaining representative of the employees in the new unit. Absent a majority showing, the presumption does not arise and no bargaining obligation exists.[171]

The NLRB has also held that when a group of relocated employees is a separate appropriate unit, an existing collective bargaining agreement covering those employees in their original bargaining unit does not apply, absent explicit agreement by the employer and union that it should continue to apply. Instead, the parties are required to negotiate a new agreement.[172]

To the extent there are other represented employees at the employer's new facility, the NLRB will continue to treat the new unit as distinct from the old unit where:

(1) the two employee groups have always been separate and distinct;

(2) the existence of the pre-existing unit predated the arrival of the transferred employees; and

(3) after the arrival of the transferred employees the two groups remained separated, had no day-to-day contact, and retained separate supervision.[173]

Employers should always be aware, however, that transfers of business operations to avoid the obligations of the NLRA are a violation of the law.[174] The employer must present a legitimate economic justification for the change and the absence of union animus as the motivating factor for the change; otherwise the change in the employer's operation may be found to be discriminatory.[175]

Successor Liability

Q 5.29   Are there any defenses to purchaser liability for the seller's unremedied unfair labor practices?

To avoid liability for the seller's unremedied ULPs, the purchaser has the burden to prove its lack of knowledge at the time of purchase. It is no defense that the purchaser did not itself commit any ULP. The purpose of successor liability is focused not on the conduct of the successor, but instead on the need to prevent changes in business ownership from frustrating the NLRB's policy of remedying ULPs. Similarly, the NLRB has rejected arguments that the purchaser should not be liable because it believed in good faith that the seller remedied all ULPs prior to the transaction.

Q 5.29.1   When does an employer's sale constitute an "alter ego" transaction?

If two nominally distinct companies are considered "alter egos," the alter-ego employer may be bound by the other employer's labor contracts and may be held liable for the ULPs of the other employer. Generally, this applies when one employer has succeeded another, often through a change in corporate structure.

The alter-ego doctrine typically involves a single operation and two companies that are only nominally distinct. In particular, alter-ego cases typically involve a mere technical change in the structure or identity of the employing entity, frequently to avoid the effect of the labor laws, without any substantial change in its ownership, control, or management.[176]

Q 5.29.2   What factors will be considered when determining whether an employer's sale constitutes an alter-ego transaction?

When determining whether two nominally distinct entities are alter egos, the following factors are considered: substantially identical management, business purpose, operations, equipment, customers, supervision, and ownership.[177] While each of these factors is relevant, the NLRB does not require that they all be present for a company to be considered an "alter ego."[178]

In assessing these factors, courts have held the fact that two companies shared common services to be evidence of alter-ego status. This includes when the companies share common services for estimating, sales, accounting, data processing, check writing, invoice processing and payment, and computer services.[179]

In the absence of common ownership, the NLRB typically will not find an alter-ego relationship, unless the NLRB concludes that one company is controlling another and using it to evade its labor obligations.

Consolidation of Employees

Q 5.30   What is an "accretion," and what is an employer's duty to bargain after accretion?

The NLRB applies an "accretion" analysis in situations involving the consolidation of a represented group with an unrepresented group—for example, when an employer purchases another similar business and consolidates the purchased business's operations with its own.

In *Nott Co., Equipment Division*,[180] the NLRB explained that, where a unit of employees is simply moved from one location to another, there may be no reason to question the majority status of the union.[181] Similarly, where there is ordinary turnover of employees at a given location, there are policy reasons (for example, industrial stability) for not permitting that fact to give rise to a question concerning representation. But "where a new group of unrepresented employees is added wholesale to an extant unit . . . and that new group is equal to or outnumber[s] the extant group, there is a real basis for raising a question as to whether the union is the majority choice in the new unit."[182]

Thus, generally there is no accretion where the unrepresented group sought to be accreted is equal to or greater in number than the existing represented group.

Notes to Chapter 5

1.   For an in-depth discussion regarding which employers are and are not subject to the NLRA, see chapter 1. Unless specifically noted otherwise, this chapter relates only to an employer's obligations under the NLRA.

2.   NLRB v. Gissel Packing Co., 395 U.S. 575 (1969).

3.   Total Sec. Mmgt. Ill. 1, LLC, 364 N.L.R.B. No. 106 (2016).

4.   1 JOHN E. HIGGINS, JR., THE DEVELOPING LABOR LAW 1323 (ABA 6th ed. & Supp. 2014) [hereinafter DEVELOPING LABOR LAW].

5.   NLRB v. Borg-Warner Corp., Wooster Div., 356 U.S. 342 (1958).

6.   1 DEVELOPING LABOR LAW, *supra* note 4, at 1342.

7.   *Id.* at 1343; *see also* Advanced Life Sys., Inc., 364 N.L.R.B. No. 117 (2016) (finding that the employer had an established practice of granting annual Christmas bonuses and had unlawfully instituted a unilateral change, in violation of section 8(a)(5), by discontinuing this practice).

8.   *See also* Viejas Band of Kumeyaay Indians, 366 N.L.R.B. No. 113, slip op. at 1, 9–10 (2018) (finding that employer violated section 8(a)(5) by unilaterally changing past practice of giving bargaining unit and non-bargaining unit employees the same year-end bonuses without providing the union with notice and an opportunity to bargain).

9.   NLRB v. Niles-Bement-Pond Co., 199 F.2d 713 (2d Cir. 1952).

10.   W.W. Cross & Co. v. NLRB, 174 F.2d 875 (1st Cir. 1949).

11.   *See* W. Cab Co., 365 N.L.R.B. No. 78 (2017) (even when an employer is compelled to change the terms and conditions of employment to comply with applicable law (such as the Affordable Care Act), the employer must provide the union with notice and an opportunity to bargain over the discretionary aspects of such changes).

12.   Although stock purchase plans may be a mandatory subject of bargaining, not all such plans are. Pieper Elec., Inc., 339 N.L.R.B. 1232 (2003) (noting that a plan was a permissive subject of bargaining where: it did not operate as a retirement plan; shares acquired could not be bequeathed; and employees were required to sell back their stock to the employer if they quit, were discharged for cause, or were laid off for longer than a specific length of time).

13.   Employer-provided living accommodations fall within "wages" and "conditions of employment" where the accommodations are an integral part of the employment relations. Hart Cotton Mills, Inc., 91 N.L.R.B. 728 (1950), *enforcement denied*, 190 F.2d 964 (4th Cir. 1951).

14.   1 DEVELOPING LABOR LAW, *supra* note 4, at 1374.

15.   *Id.* at 1378–80.

16.   The Ruprecht Co., 366 N.L.R.B. No. 179, slip op. at 1 (2018) (finding employer's enrollment in E-Verify without satisfying its notice and bargaining obligations to the union was an unlawful unilateral change in a mandatory subject of bargaining, and ordering the employer to rescind its participation in the program at the union's request pending completion of the employer's pre-implementation bargaining obligations, even where after the charge was filed the parties had reached a collective bargaining agreement that included enrollment in E-Verify for new hires).

17.   *See id.* at 1381; *see also* U.S. Gypsum Co., 94 N.L.R.B. 112 (1951).

18.   1 DEVELOPING LABOR LAW, *supra* note 4, at 1381–82.

19.   Mission Foods, 350 N.L.R.B. 336 (2007) (employer engaged in unlawful unilateral action where it transferred an employee from sanitation department to another department where that employee performed different functions and worked fewer hours per week).

20.   1 DEVELOPING LABOR LAW, *supra* note 4, at 1398.

21.   Contract Carriers Corp., 339 N.L.R.B. 851 (2003).

22.   *See* Children's Hosp. & Research Ctr. of Oakland, 364 N.L.R.B. No. 114 (2016).

23.   NLRB v. Andrew Jergens Co., 175 F.2d 130 (9th Cir.), *cert. denied*, 338 U.S. 827 (1949).

24.   *See* Tribune Publ'g Co. v. NLRB, 564 F.3d 1330, 1333 (D.C. Cir. 2009) (citing Quality House of Graphics, Inc., 336 N.L.R.B. 497, 511 n.42 (2001)); *see also* Sw. Steel & Supply v. NLRB, 806 F.2d 1111, 1114 (D.C. Cir. 1986).

25.   Alamo Rent-A-Car, 359 N.L.R.B. No. 149 (2013), *set aside by* 2014 NLRB LEXIS 487 (NLRB June 27, 2014); WKYC-TV, Inc., 359 N.L.R.B. No. 30 (2012).

26.   *See, e.g.*, Lincoln Lutheran, 200 L.R.R.M. (BNA) 2033 (ALJ Aug. 11, 2014).

27.   Retail Clerks Local 1625 v. Schermerhorn, 373 U.S. 746, *on reargument*, 375 U.S. 96 (1963). The Supreme Court recently held that the extraction of agency fees from nonconsenting public sector employees, who are not covered by the NLRA, as a condition of their employment violates the First Amendment. Janus v. Am. Fed'n of State, Cty., & Mun. Emps., Council 31, 138 S. Ct. 2448, 585 U.S. ___ (2018), *overruling* Abood v. Detroit Bd. of Educ., 431 U.S. 209 (1977).

28.   Serv. Emps. Local 535 (N. Bay Dev. Disabilities Servs.), 287 N.L.R.B. 1223 (1988).

29.   1 DEVELOPING LABOR LAW, *supra* note 4, at 1387.

30.   Anheuser-Busch, Inc., 342 N.L.R.B. 560 (2004) (relying on Nat'l Steel Corp. v. NLRB, 324 F.3d 928 (7th Cir. 2003)).

31.   1 DEVELOPING LABOR LAW, *supra* note 4, at 1390–91.

32.   *Id.* at 1395–96.

33.   Johnson-Bateman Co., 295 N.L.R.B. 180 (1989) (drug and alcohol testing of employees who require treatment for injuries received while on the job).

34.   1 DEVELOPING LABOR LAW, *supra* note 4, at 1396–97.

35.   NLRB v. Retail Clerks (Safeway Co.), 203 F.2d 165 (9th Cir. 1953) (adjudging union in contempt for insisting on bargaining for supervisory employees in violation of consent decree), *enforcing* 96 N.L.R.B. 581 (1951), *cert. denied*, 348 U.S. 839 (1954).

36.   Mine Workers Dist. 50 (Cent. Soya Co.), 142 N.L.R.B. 930, 939 (1963).

37.   NLRB v. Reeves & Sons, 47 L.R.R.M. 2480 (10th Cir. 1961), *adjudicating contempt for violating* 273 F.2d 710 (10th Cir. 1959), *cert. denied*, 366 U.S. 914 (1961).

38.   NLRB v. Corsicana Cotton Mills, 178 F.2d 344 (5th Cir. 1949) (per curiam).

39.   Radiator Specialty Co., 143 N.L.R.B. 350 (1963), *enforced in part*, 336 F.2d 495 (4th Cir. 1964).

40.   NLRB v. Borg-Warner Corp., Wooster Div., 356 U.S. 342 (1958).

41.   1 DEVELOPING LABOR LAW, *supra* note 4, at 1448.

42.   *See* NLRB v. Royal Plating & Polishing Co., 350 F.2d 191 (3d Cir. 1965); *see also* Fibreboard Paper Prods. Corp. v. NLRB, 379 U.S. 203 (1964) (Stewart, J., concurring); Ford Motor Co. v. NLRB, 441 U.S. 488 (1979). *But see* Edgar P. Benjamin Healthcare Ctr., 322 N.L.R.B. 750 (1996) (refusing to extend the exemption from mandatory bargaining of decisions at the core of entrepreneurial control to include all decisions related to the employer's "core purpose").

43.   Gen. Motors Corp., 191 N.L.R.B. 951 (1971).

44.   First Nat'l Maint. Corp. v. NLRB, 452 U.S. 666 (1981).

45.   Pan Am. Grain Co. v. NLRB, 558 F.3d 22 (1st Cir. 2009).

46.   Fibreboard Paper Prods. Corp. v. NLRB, 379 U.S. 203 (1964).

47.   *See* Rock-Tenn. Co. v. NLRB, 101 F.3d 1441 (D.C. Cir. 1996); *see also* Torrington Indus., 307 N.L.R.B. 80 (1992).

48.   1 DEVELOPING LABOR LAW, *supra* note 4, at 1417.

49.   *See* Rock-Tenn. Co. v. NLRB, 101 F.3d 1441 (D.C. Cir. 1996); *see also* First Nat'l Maint. v. NLRB, 452 U.S. 666 (1981); Furniture Rentors of Am., Inc. v. NLRB, 36 F.3d 1240 (3d Cir. 1994).

50.   *See* NLRB v. Royal Plating & Polishing Co., 350 F.2d 191 (3d Cir. 1965); *see also* NLRB v. Rapid Bindery, Inc., 293 F.2d 170 (2d Cir. 1961); NLRB v. Lewis, 246 F.2d 886 (9th Cir. 1957); Inland Steel Co. v. NLRB, 170 F.2d 247 (7th Cir. 1948); NLRB v. Westinghouse Air Brake Co., 120 F.2d 1004 (3d Cir. 1941).

51.   Dubuque Packing Co., 303 N.L.R.B. 386, 391 (1991).

52.   1 DEVELOPING LABOR LAW, *supra* note 4, at 719.

53.   Komatsu Am. Corp., 342 N.L.R.B. 649 (2004).

54.   1 DEVELOPING LABOR LAW, *supra* note 4, at 1451.

55.   *Id.* at 1464.

56.   *See* Silverman v. Major League Player Relations Comm., Inc., 67 F.3d 1054, 1062 (2d Cir. 1995).

57.   1 DEVELOPING LABOR LAW, *supra* note 4, at 1468.

58.   *Id.* at 1350–51.

59.   Allied Chem. & Alkali Workers Local 1 v. Pittsburgh Plate Glass Co., 404 U.S. 157 (1971).

60. Anderson v. Alpha Portland Indus., 727 F.2d 177 (8th Cir. 1984).

61. *See* Cleveland Elec. Illuminating Co. v. Util. Workers Union, Local 270, 440 F.3d 809, 817 (6th Cir. 2006). *But see* Int'l Bhd. of Elec. Workers, AFL-CIO Local 1245 v. Citizens Telecomms. Co. of Cal., 549 F.3d 781, 786–88 (9th Cir. 2008) (holding that union is not required to obtain retirees' consent before arbitrating, in its capacity as representative of future retirees, disputes "relating to retiree benefits" that may affect current retirees' benefits, but finding that the arbitrator's decision should not be binding on current retirees).

62. Letter Carriers Branch 1227 (U.S. Postal Serv.), 347 N.L.R.B. 289 (2006).

63. 1 DEVELOPING LABOR LAW, *supra* note 4, at 1075–76.

64. Penello v. Mine Workers, 88 F. Supp. 935 (D.D.C. 1950).

65. NLRB v. Nat'l Mar. Union (Tex. Co.), 175 F.2d 686 (2d Cir. 1949), *cert. denied*, 338 U.S. 954 (1950).

66. Lithographers Local 17 (Graphic Arts Emp'rs Ass'n), 130 N.L.R.B. 985 (1961), *aff'd*, 309 F.2d 31 (9th Cir. 1962), *cert. denied*, 372 U.S. 943 (1963).

67. Longshoremen (ILA) Local 1367 (Galveston Mar. Ass'n), 148 N.L.R.B. 897 (1964), *enforced*, 368 F.2d 1010 (5th Cir. 1966), *cert. denied*, 389 U.S. 837 (1967).

68. *See, e.g.*, Metal Workers (Hughes Tool Co.), 147 N.L.R.B. 1573 (1964).

69. 1 DEVELOPING LABOR LAW, *supra* note 4, at 1479.

70. Local Freight Drivers Local No. 208, 224 N.L.R.B. 1116, 1124 (1976).

71. *See* NLRB, BASIC GUIDE TO THE NATIONAL LABOR RELATIONS ACT 25 (1997), www.nlrb.gov/sites/default/files/attachments/basic-page/node-3024/basicguide.pdf.

72. Dairylea Coop., 219 N.L.R.B. 656 (1975), *enforced sub nom.* NLRB v. Teamsters Local 338, 531 F.2d 1162 (2d Cir. 1976).

73. NLRB v. Joy Techs., 990 F.2d 104 (3d Cir. 1993).

74. Perma-Line Corp. v. Painters Local 230, 639 F.2d 890 (2d Cir. 1981).

75. Great Lakes Carbon Corp. v. NLRB, 360 F.2d 19 (4th Cir. 1966).

76. Massillon Cmty. Hosp., 282 N.L.R.B. 675 (1987).

77. Chi. Typographical Union, 86 N.L.R.B. 1041 (1949).

78. *See* Stamford Bd. of Educ. v. Stamford Educ. Ass'n, 697 F.2d 70 (2d Cir. 1982) (finding a hold-harmless clause of a labor contract invalid as "patently contrary to federal civil rights policy" because it fully indemnified a "commission of a civil wrong against a third person or persons").

79. *See, e.g.*, Comau, Inc., 364 N.L.R.B. No. 48 (2016) (finding that notice of a temporary closure and relocation was not timely where the employer informed the union of the closure the same day it became effective, with the transfer of employees occurring four days later).

80. NLRB v. Katz, 369 U.S. 736 (1962).

81. Raytheon Network Centric Sys., 365 N.L.R.B. No. 161 (2017), *overruling* E.I. de Pont de Nemours, 364 N.L.R.B. No. 113 (2016).

82. Cofire Paving Corp., 359 N.L.R.B. No. 10 (2012).

83. Torrington Co., 307 N.L.R.B. 485 (1992).

84. *See* NLRB v. Katz, 369 U.S. 736, 746 (1962) (generally, an employer may not unilaterally change a term or condition of employment during the collective bargaining process); *In re* Overnight Transp. Co., 335 N.L.R.B. 372 (2001) (stating that an employer is at risk of a violation if it unilaterally changes employees' terms and conditions of employment if the union is ultimately certified); Flambeau Airmold Corp., 334 N.L.R.B. 165 (2001) (an employer's unilateral change is unlawful if it is material, substantial, or significant).

85. Laney & Duke Storage Warehouse Co., 151 N.L.R.B. 248, 266–67 (1965).

86. Union Carbide Corp., Nuclear Div., 275 N.L.R.B. 197 (1985).

87. *See also* Diamond Trucking, Inc., 365 N.L.R.B. No. 64 (2017) (union had a "reasonable belief" that an alter-ego relationship existed, and it was therefore entitled to relevant information about that relationship).

88. Piggly Wiggly Midwest, LLC, 357 N.L.R.B. No. 191 (2012).

89. However, the employer must either timely assert a confidentiality interest or propose an accommodation to address the union's interest in obtaining relevant requested information. The Ruprecht Co., 366 N.L.R.B. No. 179, slip op. at 3–4 (2018); *see also* U.S. Postal Serv., 364 N.L.R.B. No. 27 (2016); Menorah Med. Ctr., 362 N.L.R.B. No. 193 (2015), *enforced in relevant part*, 867 F.3d 1288, 1300 (D.C. Cir. 2017).

90. United Aircraft Corp., 192 N.L.R.B. 382 (1971), *enforced in part and denied in part*, 534 F.2d 422 (2d Cir. 1975).

91. Cincinnati Steel Castings Co., 86 N.L.R.B. 592 (1949).

92. *See, e.g.*, NLRB v. New Eng. Newspapers, Inc., 856 F.2d 409 (1st Cir. 1988); *see also* Hercules, Inc. v. NLRB, 833 F.2d 426 (2d Cir. 1987).

93. *See, e.g.*, Wayron, LLC, 364 N.L.R.B. No. 60 (2016).

94. N.Y. Post Corp., 283 N.L.R.B. 430 (1987).

95. Detroit Edison Co. v. NLRB, 440 U.S. 301 (1979).

96. Oil, Chem. & Atomic Workers Local 6-418 v. NLRB, 711 F.2d 348 (D.C. Cir. 1983).

97. LaGuardia Hosp., 260 N.L.R.B. 1455 (1982).

98. Printing & Graphic Commc'ns Local 13 (Detroit) (Oakland Press Co.), 233 N.L.R.B. 994 (1977).

99. Am. Commercial Lines, 291 N.L.R.B. 1066 (1988); Food & Commercial Workers Local 1439 (Layman's Mkt.), 268 N.L.R.B. 780 (1984).

100. John S. Swift Co., 124 N.L.R.B. 394 (1959), *enforced in part and denied in part*, 277 F.2d 641 (7th Cir. 1960).

101. NLRB v. Herman Sausage Co., 275 F.2d 229, 231 (5th Cir. 1960).

102. NLRB v. Wallkill Valley Gen. Hosp., 866 F.2d 632 (3d Cir. 1989).

103. United Techs. Corp., Pratt & Whitney Aircraft Div., 274 N.L.R.B. 609, *enforced*, 789 F.2d 121 (2d Cir. 1986).

104. Permanente Med. Grp., Inc., 332 N.L.R.B. 1143 (2000).

105. Logemann Bros. Co., 298 N.L.R.B. 1018, 1019 (1990).

106. *See* Dish Network Corp., 366 N.L.R.B. No. 119, slip op. at 1 (2018) (citing Taft Broadcasting Co., 163 N.L.R.B. 475 (1967)).

107. Stein Indus., Inc., 365 N.L.R.B. No. 31 (2017) (employer violated the NLRA when it declared impasse after just four negotiating sessions. The parties failed to discuss all of the issues on the table, given the union's "willingness to bargain" and remain flexible to the employer's demands).

108. *But see* Southcoast Hosps. Grp., Inc., 365 N.L.R.B. No. 100 (2017) (although overall impasse may be declared based on a deadlock over a single issue, the impasse as to the single issue must have "led to a breakdown in overall negotiations," and in this case the union had continued to make substantial movement on a variety of issues, including significant moves made the same day the employer declared impasse).

109. NLRB v. Tex-Tan, Inc., 318 F.2d 472 (5th Cir. 1963).

110. *See* Brown v. Pro Football, Inc., 518 U.S. 231 (1996); *see also* First Nat'l Maint. Corp. v. NLRB, 452 U.S. 666 (1981); Fibreboard Paper Prods. Corp. v. NLRB, 379 U.S. 203 (1964); Nat'l Basketball Ass'n v. Williams, 45 F.3d 684 (2d Cir. 1995); Storer Commc'ns, Inc., 294 N.L.R.B. 1056 (1989); Akron Novelty Mfg. Co., 224 N.L.R.B. 998 (1976); Taft Broad. Co., 163 N.L.R.B. 475 (1967).

111. McClatchy Newspapers v. NLRB, 131 F.3d 1026 (D.C. Cir. 1997).

112. *See* Metro. Edison Co. v. NLRB, 460 U.S. 693 (1983); *see also* YHA, Inc. v. NLRB, 2 F.3d 168 (6th Cir. 1993); NLRB v. Spun-Jee Corp., 385 F.2d 379 (2d Cir. 1967); U.S. Lingerie Corp., 170 N.L.R.B. 750 (1968); Justesen's Food Stores, 160 N.L.R.B. 687 (1966); N.Y. Mirror, 151 N.L.R.B. 834 (1965); Motoresearch Co., 138 N.L.R.B. 1490 (1962).

113. *See* Levitz Furniture Co., 333 N.L.R.B. 717 (2001).

114. *See* Fall River Dyeing & Finishing Corp. v. NLRB, 482 U.S. 27 (1987); *see also* NLRB v. Burns Int'l Sec. Servs., Inc., 406 U.S. 272 (1972); Howard Johnson Co. v. Hotel Emps., 417 U.S. 249 (1974).

115. *See* Marbro Co., 284 N.L.R.B. 1303 (1987); *see also* Capitol-Husting Co., 252 N.L.R.B. 43 (1980); Imperial Outdoor Advert., 192 N.L.R.B. 1248 (1971).

116. *See* Dynatron/Bondo Corp., 333 N.L.R.B. 750, 752 (2001).

117. Bath Iron Works Corp., 345 N.L.R.B. 499, 502 (2005); *see also* Lenawee Stamping Corp., 365 N.L.R.B. No. 97 (2017).

118. *Id.* at 503.

119. *Id.*

120. *Id.*

121. Weyerhaeuser NR Co., 366 N.L.R.B. No. 169, slip op. at 3 (2018) (quoting Provena St. Joseph Med. Ctr., 350 N.L.R.B. 808, 811 (2007)).

122. *See* NLRB v. U.S. Postal Serv., 8 F.3d 832 (D.C. Cir. 1993); Bath Marine Draftsmen's Ass'n v. NLRB, 475 F.3d 14 (1st Cir. 2007); Chi. Tribune v. NLRB, 974 F.2d 933 (7th Cir. 1992); *see also* Weyerhaeuser NR Co., 366 N.L.R.B. No. 169, slip op. at 9 (2018) (Emanuel, dissenting) ("I write separately to note that multiple circuit courts have criticized the Board's continued use for the 'clear and unmistakable waiver' standard and have instead adopted a 'contract coverage' analysis to contractual defenses to refusal to bargain allegations.")

123. Provena Hosps., 350 N.L.R.B. 808, 818 (2007) (Battista, dissenting).

124. *See, e.g.*, Acad. of Magical Arts, Inc., 365 N.L.R.B. No. 101 (2017) (union clearly and unmistakably waived its right to bargain over the length and number of shifts because the contract authorized the employer "to schedule and change working hours, shifts and days off").

125. Speedrack, Inc., 293 N.L.R.B. 1054 (1989).

126. *See* IMI S., LLC, 364 N.L.R.B. No. 97 (2016).

127. Provena St. Joseph Med. Ctr., 350 N.L.R.B. 808 (2007).

128. Baptist Hosp. of E. Tenn., 351 N.L.R.B. 71 (2007).

129. Kennametal, Inc., 358 N.L.R.B. No. 68 (2012).

130. Va. Mason Hosp., 358 N.L.R.B. No. 64 (2012).

131. Dubuque Packing Co., 303 N.L.R.B. 386 (1991).

132. Johnson-Bateman Co., 295 N.L.R.B. 180, 184 (1969).

133. Embarq Corp., 358 N.L.R.B. No. 134 (2012).

134. Rockwell Int'l Corp., 260 N.L.R.B. 1346, 1347 n.6 (1982); *see also* Tramont Mfg., LLC, 365 N.L.R.B. No. 59 (2017) (employer violated the NLRA when it refused to bargain over the effects of its decision to lay off twelve employees. The fact that the union and employer had not entered into a collective bargaining agreement addressing layoffs was "crucial," and the union therefore had "not waived effects bargaining").

135. *See, e.g.*, Howard Indus., Inc., 365 N.L.R.B. No. 4 (2016) (because the union was on notice that the employer was seeking to change its gift policy under the procedures set forth in the collective bargaining agreement but failed to initiate negotiations with the employer within the ten-day notification period specified in the agreement, the union waived arbitration and other legal remedies concerning the creation or modification of the policy).

136. Golden Bay Freight Lines, 267 N.L.R.B. 1073 (1983).

137. *See, e.g.*, Artcraft Displays, 262 N.L.R.B. 1233 (1982); *see also* Kroger Co., 148 N.L.R.B. 569 (1964); NLRB v. Truck Drivers Local 449 (Buffalo Linen Supply Co.), 353 U.S. 87 (1957).

138. *See* Patterson Stevens, 316 N.L.R.B. 1278 (1995); *see also* Retail Assocs., 120 N.L.R.B. 388 (1958); LaCort v. Int'l Ladies Garment Workers Union, 315 N.L.R.B. 1036, 1051 (1994).

139. *See, e.g., Patterson Stevens*, 316 N.L.R.B. at 1286; *see also* Gary Jasper Enters., 287 N.L.R.B. 746 (1987); Acropolis Painting, 272 N.L.R.B. 150 (1984).

140. *Id.*

141. *See* LaCort v. Int'l Ladies Garment Workers Union, 315 N.L.R.B. 1036 (1994); *see also* Teamsters Union Local No. 378 v. Olympia Auto. Dealers Ass'n, 243 N.L.R.B. 1086 (1979).

142. *See* William T. Kirley Lumber Co., 189 N.L.R.B. 130 (1971); *see also* Kroger Co., 148 N.L.R.B. 569 (1964).

143. *Kirley*, 189 N.L.R.B. at 130.

144. *See, e.g., id.; see also* Johnson Sheet Metal, Inc., 179 N.L.R.B. 644 (1969); Wards Cove Packing Co., 160 N.L.R.B. 232 (1966); Korner Kafe, Inc., 156 N.L.R.B. 1157 (1966).

145. Winn-Dixie, Tex., Inc. (Foodway), 235 N.L.R.B. 1479 (1978).

146. NLRB v. Bos. Dist. Council of Carpenters, 80 F.3d 662 (1st Cir. 1996).

147. *See* NLRB v. Hayden Elec., Inc., 693 F.2d 1358 (11th Cir. 1982); *see also* Ruan Transp. Corp., 234 N.L.R.B. 241 (1978).

148. *Id.; see also* Phx. Air Conditioning, 231 N.L.R.B. 341 (1977).

149. Joseph E. Seagram & Sons, 101 N.L.R.B. 101 (1952).

150. *Id.* at 103.

151. *See, e.g.*, NLRB v. E-Z Davies Chevrolet, 395 F.2d 191 (9th Cir. 1968); *see also* Hyatt House Motel, 174 N.L.R.B. 1009; Joseph E. Seagram & Sons, 101 N.L.R.B. 101 (1952).

152. *See, e.g.*, NLRB v. Tahoe Nugget, Inc., 584 F.2d 293 (9th Cir. 1978); *see also* Sahara-Tahoe Corp. v. NLRB, 581 F.2d 767 (9th Cir. 1978).

153. NLRB v. Richard W. Kaase Co., 346 F.2d 24 (6th Cir. 1965).

154. *Id.* at 27, 30–31.

155. *See* NLRB v. Downtown Bakery Corp., 330 F.2d 921 (6th Cir. 1964); *see also* U.S. Molded Shapes, 141 N.L.R.B. 357 (1963).

156. United Elec. Contractors Ass'n, 347 N.L.R.B. 1 (2006).

157. *See* SMI/Div. of DCX-CHOL Enters., Inc., 365 N.L.R.B. No. 152 (2017) (when a successor employer adopts its predecessor's collective bargaining agreement, it also adopts its predecessor's past practices that inform and give meaning to the terms of the agreement).

158. Because a stock purchase is the continuation of the same legal entity under new ownership, absent terms in the collective bargaining agreement to the contrary, the stock purchaser would be bound by the collective bargaining agreement in effect prior to the purchase. Transmontaigne, Inc., 337 N.L.R.B. 262 (2001); Rockwood Energy & Mineral Corp., 299 N.L.R.B. 1136 (1990), *enforced*, 942 F.2d 169 (3d Cir. 1993).

159. Ride Right, LLC, 366 N.L.R.B. No. 16, slip op. at 2 (2018) (citing Fall River Dyeing & Finishing Corp. v. NLRB, 482 U.S. 27, 43, 47 (1987)). The parties stipulated to the substantial continuity of operations and the employer did not contest the timeliness of the union's bargaining demand or the appropriateness of the unit, leaving only the question of when the purchaser "employed a substantial and representative complement of employees and the makeup of the prospective unit at that time." 366 N.L.R.B. No. 16, slip op. at 2. The NLRB found that the purchaser "achieved a substantial and representative complement" when it assumed the predecessor's operations because "[a]t that point, it had substantially filled its job classifications, it was providing normal . . . service in the same manner as did [the predecessor], and it had no definite plan to expand." *Id.* at 3. Moreover, at that time, a majority of the employees the purchaser had hired to continue the predecessor's operations "had been represented by the [u]nion," thus obligating the purchaser to recognize and bargain with the union as the employees' representative. *Id.*

160. *See* Howard Johnson Co. v. Local Joint Exec. Bd., 417 U.S. 249, 264–65 (1974) (the purchaser of a business is not bound by the collective bargaining agreement of its predecessor, even though the predecessor's collective bargaining agreement contained a provision making the agreement binding upon any purchasers of the business); *see also* Int'l Oil, Chem. & Atomic Workers, Local 7-517, 170 F.3d 779, 783 (7th Cir. 1999) (successorship clauses in collective bargaining agreements "do not bind non-signatory successors"); New Eng. Mech., Inc. v. Laborers Local Union 294, 909 F.2d 1339, 1342 (9th Cir. 1990) ("The United States Supreme Court has continually indicated that a successor employer is only bound to bargain with a union which had a collective bargaining agreement with the predecessor."); Sheet Metal Workers Int'l Ass'n, Local No. 359, AFL-CIO v. Ariz. Mech. & Stainless, Inc., 863 F.2d 647, 651 (9th Cir. 1988) ("The United States Supreme Court has held that although a 'successor' employer may have a duty to bargain with the union recognized by its predecessor, it is not bound by the substantive terms of its predecessor's collective bargaining agreement unless it assumes or adopts those obligations.") (citing NLRB v. Burns Int'l Sec. Servs., Inc., 406 U.S. 272, 284 (1972)); *Howard Johnson Co.*, 417 U.S. at 264–65; Fall River Dyeing & Finishing Corp. v. NLRB, 482 U.S. 27 (1987); Johnson v. Pullman, Inc., 845 F.2d 911 (11th Cir. 1988) (in purchasing employer's plant, purchaser was not bound by "successorship" clause as would require it to adopt employer's collective bargaining agreement or to hire its past employees, since purchaser was not a party to the collective bargaining agreement); E. Bay Auto. v. Q&S Auto., LLC, 2005 WL 2171874, at *2 (N.D. Cal. Sept. 6, 2005) (unpublished) ("Successor employers, are not, however, ordinarily bound to the existing collective bargaining agreement between the union and its predecessor—even where the collective bargaining agreement expressly provides that it will be binding upon successor employers."); Chartier v. 3205 Grand Concourse Corp., 100 F. Supp. 2d 210, 213 (S.D.N.Y. 2000) ("[T]he existence . . . of a clause purporting to bind the employer's successors and assigns cannot itself bind the purchaser of the employer's assets absent assumption . . . by the purchaser.").

161. Atrium Plaza Health Care Ctr., 317 N.L.R.B. 606 (1995) (successor expressly agreed to be bound by predecessor's agreement).

162. NLRB v. World Evangelism, 656 F.2d 1349 (9th Cir. 1981) (successor was held to have assumed its predecessor's contract by actions that would lead a reasonable person to believe that agreement had been reached).

163. Banknote Corp. of Am., 315 N.L.R.B. 1041 (1994), *enforced*, 84 F.3d 637 (2d Cir. 1996) (no adoption where before commencing operations, successor sent unions letters expressly "disavowing the notion that . . . [it] had agreed to be bound the terms and conditions" of the predecessor's contracts).

164. United Food & Commercial Workers Union v. Morgan's Holiday Mkts., Inc., 202 F.3d 280 (9th Cir. 1999) (unpublished table decision) (requiring an employer to arbitrate pursuant to the predecessor's collective bargaining agreement where the merger agreement provided that [successor employer] "shall be responsible and liable for all liabilities and obligations of [predecessor employer]" because such language was viewed as an express assumption of the arbitration provisions of the collective bargaining agreement).

165. *See* NLRB v. Burns Int'l Sec. Servs., Inc., 406 U.S. 272, 284 (1972); Spruce Up Corp., 209 N.L.R.B. 194, 195 (1975), *enforced mem.*, 529 F.2d 516 (4th Cir. 1975) (finding the Supreme Court's "perfectly clear" successor exception announced in *Burns* "should be restricted to circumstances in which the new employer has either actively or, by tacit inference, misled employees into believing they would all be retained without change in their wages, hours, or conditions of employment, or at least to circumstances where the new employer ... has failed to clearly announce its intent to establish a new set of conditions prior to inviting former employees to accept employment"); *see also* Grenada Stamping & Assembly, Inc., 351 N.L.R.B. 1152 (2007) (employer was a "perfectly clear" successor that could not unilaterally change terms and conditions of employment where it invited all of predecessor's employees to accept employment and made no announcement that it intended to establish new terms and conditions of employment); Creative Vision Res., LLC, 364 N.L.R.B. No. 91 (2016); Adams & Assocs., Inc., 364 N.L.R.B. No. 193 (2016); Rosdev Hosp., 349 N.L.R.B. 202 (2007) (employer violated section 8(5) when it intended to hire all unit employees, failed to announce any potential changes in terms and conditions in employment, and changed the predecessor's practice with respect to leave accrual).

166. Downtown Hartford YMCA, 349 N.L.R.B. 960 (2007) (expressly affirming ALJ's finding that successor employer that discriminatorily refused to hire predecessor's employees lost its right to set initial terms and conditions of employment).

167. *See, e.g.,* Data Monitor Sys., Inc., 364 N.L.R.B. No. 4 (2016) (employer did not become a perfectly clear successor when it distributed job applications through the existing contractor and told employees to sign up for an interview if they were interested in employment); Paragon Sys., Inc., 364 N.L.R.B. No. 75 (2016) (employer did not become a perfectly clear successor when its job fair memo only communicated that the employer would be considering the incumbent officers as applicants and was not an invitation to accept employment).

168. Nexeo Sols., LLC 364 N.L.R.B. No. 44 (2016), slip op. at 5–6. *See* First Student Inc., 366 N.L.R.B. No. 13, slip op. at 3–4 (2018) (finding employer violated section 8(a)(5) where "[f]rom the very beginning of the transition process, well before the formal hiring process, the [employer] clearly and consistently communicated its intent to retain the [predecessor's] employees," and, while stating it would not adopt the predecessor's collective bargaining agreement, the successor failed to clearly announce its intent to condition offers of employment on employees' acceptance of changed terms); Cora Realty Co., 340 N.L.R.B. 366 (2003) (finding a purchaser violated the NLRA when it reduced employees' wages and discontinued their benefits but had told employees only that their schedules would change, implying that all other employment terms and conditions would remain the same).

169. UGL-UNICCO Serv. Co., 357 N.L.R.B. No. 76 (2011).

170. *Id.* (citing Lee Lumber & Bldg. Material Corp., 334 N.L.R.B. 399, 402 (2001), *aff'd*, 310 F.2d 209 (D.C. Cir. 2002)).

171. Gitano Distribution Ctr., 308 N.L.R.B. 1172 (1992).

172. *In re* United Steelworkers of Am., 338 N.L.R.B. 29 (2002).

173. *Id.*

174. Ladies' Garment Workers Local 57 v. NLRB, 374 F.2d 295 (D.C. Cir. 1967).

175. Dextra Indus., 273 N.L.R.B. 1660 (1985).

176. *See* Howard Johnson Co. v. Detroit Local Joint Exec. Bd., Hotel & Rest. Emps. & Bartenders Int'l Union, AFL-CIO, 417 U.S. 249 (1974); *see also* Reigel Elec., 341 N.L.R.B. 198 (2004).

177. *See, e.g.*, Island Architectural Woodwork, Inc., 364 N.L.R.B. No. 73 (2016).

178. Wilson v. Int'l Bhd. of Teamsters, 83 F.3d 747 (6th Cir. 1996).

179. Eichleay Corp. v. Int'l Ass'n of Bridge, Structural & Ornamental Iron Workers, 944 F.2d 1047, 1059 (3d Cir. 1991).

180. Nott Co., Equip. Div., 345 N.L.R.B. 396 (2005).

181. *Id.*

182. *Id.*

6

Collective Bargaining Agreements

Collective bargaining agreements document the general framework of an ongoing relationship between an employer and its employees by establishing terms and conditions of employment. Collective bargaining agreements, however, have characteristics that distinguish them from ordinary commercial contracts—a fact long recognized by courts. While a collective bargaining agreement generally outlines wages, hours, and working conditions, it cannot expressly define every term and condition of employment.

The U.S. Supreme Court has endorsed grievance arbitration as an alternative dispute resolution process to avoid excessive reliance on the courts or strike activity in collective bargaining relationships. Further, the grievance arbitration process allows the parties to develop a "common law of the shop" that captures the background understandings of the parties.

As expressed by the Court in *United Steelworkers v. Warrior & Gulf Navigation Co.*,[1] "the processing of disputes through the grievance machinery is actually a vehicle by which meaning and content are given to the collective bargaining agreement." A negotiated grievance arbitration process provides a means for the parties to reach a final resolution regarding the interpretation and application of collective bargaining terms. It is relatively informal, inexpensive, and expeditious compared to litigation.

Typical Components of a Collective Bargaining Agreement

Q 6.1 What are the typical components of a collective bargaining agreement?

A collective bargaining agreement typically includes:

- a recognition clause;
- a management rights clause;
- a no-strike/no-lockout clause;
- a union security clause; and
- an anti-discrimination clause.

Typical components of a collective bargaining agreement also include provisions addressing:

- employee compensation packages and benefits;
- seniority rights;
- layoff and recall procedures;
- hours of work;
- leave of absence;
- health and safety;
- transfers/promotions;
- union access;
- discipline and discharge;
- subcontracting to independent contractors; and
- the grievance procedure.

Q 6.2   What is a recognition clause?

A recognition clause is a standard provision in a collective bargaining agreement in which an employer formally recognizes a union (often after NLRB certification) as the exclusive representative of the employees in the bargaining unit and acknowledges the obligation of the employer to bargain only with the union over wages, hours, and working conditions of the bargaining unit employees. Most recognition clauses describe the employees or the job categories they occupy as being included in the bargaining unit and sometimes establish a procedure for incorporating new employees or jobs into the bargaining unit. A recognition clause may define the bargaining unit to encompass multiple sites or, alternatively, may be drafted to include only a subset of the employees at a particular facility covered by an applicable collective bargaining agreement. Additionally, a recognition clause may be interpreted by an arbitrator to restrict the employer's use of non-bargaining unit employees or subcontractors to perform bargaining unit work.

SAMPLE RECOGNITION CLAUSES

Unit Certified by NLRB

The Company recognizes the Union as the exclusive bargaining agency for those employees of the Company at its plant at _____, for whom the Union has heretofore been certified by the National Labor Relations Board in Case No. _____.

Office Clerical Employees

The Union is recognized as the sole and exclusive representative of all office clerical employees of the Company in the Office and Clerical Unit, as defined by the National Labor Relations Board in Case No. _____. This agreement shall apply only to those employees of the Company who are within the above-described bargaining unit.

Q 6.3   What is a management rights clause?

A management rights clause often contains a detailed list of those specific aspects of workplace control exclusively retained by management. Many management rights clauses reserve the employer's right to:

(1)   maintain company assets and property;

(2)   manage the business and direct employees who are subject to the agreement;

(3)   select and use items of equipment or methods of production;

(4)   open or close facilities;

(5)   exercise exclusive discretion to hire employees and direct the employer's work;

(6)   evaluate the performance of employees and suspend or discharge them for cause; and

(7)   lay employees off because of lack of work or for other lawful reasons.

A clause that clearly and specifically articulates management's rights empowers the employer to maintain authority in directing its workforce and its day-to-day operations and can serve as an effective defense against certain unfair labor practice charges and grievances. The more specifically a clause defines the rights retained by management, the more likely an employer will be found to have retained such authority in the event of an arbitration or NLRB case. Vague, ambiguous, or boilerplate management rights clauses are less likely to be helpful in the event of a dispute arising under its terms. Moreover, depending on the specific requirements of an employer's operations, a management rights clause may constitute a waiver of a union's bargaining rights with respect to specific issues and can, in certain situations, permit unilateral action by the employer during the term of the collective bargaining agreement.

Q 6.4 What are "no strike/no lockout" clauses?

Strikes and lockouts are "economic weapons" generally used by a union or an employer to gain leverage at the bargaining table. Many collective bargaining agreements contain provisions, often referred to as "no-strike/no-lockout" clauses, designed to prevent work stoppages during the term of the agreement. A no-strike clause is a provision whereby the union agrees that bargaining unit employees will not engage in strikes or slowdowns designed to halt operations during the life of the contract and that the union will not encourage bargaining-unit employees to engage in any such strike or work stoppage. Thus, although the NLRA grants employees the right to strike, if a collective bargaining agreement contains a no-strike clause, a strike during the life of the contract would not be protected and the strikers could be subject to disciplinary action, including termination from employment. In contrast, once the applicable collective bargaining agreement expires, absent an express commitment by the union, the bargaining unit will once again enjoy the legal right to strike.

Courts have reasoned that arbitration agreements in collective bargaining agreements constitute the parties' complete waiver of their rights to engage in a strike or lockout over arbitral issues that should be resolved by a neutral arbitrator. Indeed, the U.S. Supreme Court has held that a no-strike obligation is implied in the absence of an express no-strike clause where the issues driving the strike are subject to binding arbitration under the agreement.[2]

The importance of the no-strike clause is that it provides a predicate for disciplining employees who strike in violation of the no-strike promise and for seeking an injunction, notwithstanding the Norris-LaGuardia Act of 1932, if the strike is over an arbitral issue. (See Q 6.29 for further discussion of the Norris-LaGuardia Act and injunctions.) It is unlikely, however, that unions will face significant liability for breaching or inducing breach of the clause. While some arbitrators will award damages to a company stemming from a union's breach of a no-strike clause, other arbitrators have reasoned that there must be express contractual authority to award damages for such violations.

A collective bargaining agreement that contains a "no-strike" provision will often include "no-lockout" language prohibiting the employer from preventing the employees from entering the employer's premises or withholding work in order to gain concessions from the employees. Such complementary commitments are aimed at encouraging the parties to resolve collective bargaining disputes through the bargaining process, without the threat of economic loss to the employer or loss of work to its employees.

Q 6.5   What is a union security provision?

A union security clause requires employees, as a condition of employment, to maintain union membership or to pay union dues. While no employee is required to be a member of a union in order to maintain a job, in some states, private sector employees can be required to pay some amount of union dues and fees. That said, approximately half of the states have enacted right-to-work laws, which prohibit union security agreements and otherwise ban agreements requiring workers to join or financially support a union. Employees who live in right-to-work states cannot be required to pay union dues or become union members. And, the Supreme Court recently ruled that employees cannot be forced to pay fees to public-sector unions, abolishing union security provisions in public-sector agreements.[3]

Even in states where union security clauses are permitted, there are limits on how unions may spend funds collected pursuant to such provisions. For example, the Supreme Court held in *Communications Workers of America v. Beck*[4] that, while employers and unions can enter into union security agreements, the union cannot, over the objections of dues-paying non-member employees, expend funds collected pursuant to a union security clause on activities unrelated to collective bargaining, contract administration, or grievance adjustment. The Court further concluded that "such expenditures violate the union's duty of fair representation." For an employee to be protected by *Beck*, the employee must be a non-member and covered by a union security clause in a collective bargaining agreement. Under such circumstances, the union must provide notice to the non-member employees of their rights, including the right:

(1) to be or remain a non-member, subject only to the duty to pay initiation fees and dues;

(2) to object to paying for union activities not germane to the union's duties as bargaining agent and to obtain a reduction in fees for such activities;

(3) to be given sufficient information to enable the employee to intelligently decide whether to object; and

(4) to be apprised of any internal union procedures for filing objections.

In addition to providing notice, the union must also refrain from charging objectors for nonrepresentational expenses, provide objectors with a financial disclosure, and establish procedures for objectors to challenge the accuracy of the union's disclosure.

A maintenance-of-membership clause is a type of union security clause that does not require a worker to join the union, but does require any employee who voluntarily joins the union to remain a member of the union for the duration of the collective bargaining agreement. These clauses typically provide an escape period, either annually or at the end of the expiration of the contract, during which employees can withdraw from the union.

Q 6.6   What is an anti-discrimination clause?

Collective bargaining agreements commonly contain clauses prohibiting discrimination based on some or all of the following: race, color, creed, religion, gender, national origin, age, disability, marital status, and sexual orientation. Agreements may also include a statement that the employer will comply with any federal or state laws prohibiting discrimination. General anti-discrimination clauses are held to incorporate prohibitions against sexual harassment, but some parties choose to negotiate a separate, detailed sexual harassment policy, while other employers opt to unilaterally draft and implement a sexual harassment policy pursuant to the management rights clause.

Q 6.7   How does a collective bargaining agreement provide for the payment of wages?

The provisions outlining employees' compensation packages (which often include wage payments, bonuses, commissions, and incentive payments) are a critical component of any collective bargaining agreement. A collective bargaining agreement can calculate wages for bargaining unit employees in a number of different ways. Often, contracts provide wages based on job classification or seniority in the company or within a division or department of that company. Some contracts require employers utilizing multiple shifts to pay a shift differential on less desirable second or third shifts as a form of premium pay. These shift differentials can consist of a flat cents-per-hour bonus or a percentage of hourly earnings. Where shift differentials are used, collective bargaining agreements often specify whether the differentials are to be included in calculating other pay, such as a holiday, weekend pay, or pension credits.

Collective bargaining agreements often provide pay for certain specified holidays that typically include holidays recognized by state and federal governments. Holiday pay provisions typically protect employees against a loss of earnings when they do not work because the employer's operation is closed in acknowledgment of a holiday that falls during a work day. Some contracts additionally include pay for holidays that fall on days where the employees normally would not have been scheduled to work (for example, a weekend, or a Monday on which the employee typically would not work). Most contracts provide employees with holiday pay equal to their regular pay rate for holidays on which the employee does not work. Under the contract, however, holiday pay may be conditioned upon the employees' compliance with contractually stated work requirements, such as length-of-service requirements, and require employees to work their shifts immediately preceding and following a holiday in order to prevent holiday stretching. Finally, some contracts require employers to pay additional wages to those employees who are required to work on a holiday.

Collective bargaining agreements may also contain specific provisions pertaining to merit increases, including the objective standards for merit increases, and setting the regular review period or making such increases subject to review or negotiations. A wage provision may also generally provide for "across-the-board" wage increases for each year of the contract, longevity pay, and severance pay.

To address cost-of-living changes, many collective bargaining agreements either contain escalator clauses or provide for wage reopening during the term of the contract. Escalator clauses provide for automatic changes in wage rates in response to specified changes in the cost of living. Wage reopening clauses provide for the negotiation of new wage terms at specified intervals, when the cost of living changes by a specified percentage, or where there is a "substantial change."

Wage provisions also commonly contain information pertaining to payroll, including the frequency that an employee receives a paycheck and the process by which the employer will issue the checks (for example, paid at work, mail delivery, or electronic funds transfer). Generally, where the collective bargaining agreement contains contractual restrictions regarding those terms, arbitrators do not allow unilateral changes in the time or method of payment of wages.

Moreover, some collective bargaining agreements contain tiered wage systems that provide differing wage scales based upon seniority or other factors. Some state laws regarding wage-and-hour regulations are preempted by collectively bargained provisions.

Many collective bargaining agreements deal with the issue and allocation of overtime. For example, collective bargaining agreements can include provisions relating to a maximum amount of overtime an employee can work, the overtime rate, when overtime applies (for example, hours worked over eight per day and/or hours worked in excess of forty in any given work week), and when, if at all, double time is paid (for example, work in excess of twelve consecutive hours or on holidays or Sundays). Collective bargaining agreements may also include a provision providing for the equalization of overtime among the employees with a particular unit "as far as practicable" or "as equally as possible."

Q 6.7.1   How do employee benefits provisions work?

Because employee benefits are important in any collective bargaining relationship, collective bargaining agreements often specify employee benefits or incorporate ancillary agreements that set forth employee benefits. Health insurance and retirement benefits are typically high-cost benefit packages that form the primary focus of the benefits provisions in a collective bargaining agreement. Regarding health insurance benefits, issues covered in the collective bargaining agreement may include the availability of particular medical plans, the scope of employer and employee contributions to premium payments, and supplemental coverage including vision, dental care, and prescription drug coverage. If a collective bargaining agreement provides for a pension benefit, the agreement will typically explain the pension calculation, vesting rules, and any early retirement benefits. If such provisions are not set forth in the collective bargaining agreement, the agreement may incorporate plan documents that specify the benefits by reference.

Other types of employee benefits that may be negotiated for and set forth in a collective bargaining agreement include:

(1)   flexible spending accounts;
(2)   vacation plans;
(3)   life insurance;
(4)   short- and long-term disability insurance;
(5)   benefits for part-time, temporary, and seasonal workers;
(6)   benefits for domestic partners; and
(7)   tax-free savings plans.

An employer must generally bargain with a union before modifying retirement benefits for active employees, but no such obligation exists with respect to current retirees.[5]

Many collective bargaining agreements include provisions that permit the employer to make amendments to benefit plans under specific circumstances, but do not necessarily give employers discretion to choose between alternatives without union input. For example, in *Trojan Yacht*,[6] the collective bargaining agreement, effective June 7, 1989, authorized the employer to amend, prospectively or retroactively, the employees' pension plan to conform to ERISA or the Internal Revenue Code, or to any regulation promulgated under those statutes. Due to amendments to the Internal Revenue Code, the employer was required to adopt one of four model amendments proposed by the Internal Revenue Service by March 31, 1989, in order to retain the pension plan's tax-exempt status. However, when the parties negotiated the collective bargaining agreement after March 31, 1989, the employer did not mention the need to amend the plan. Instead, after the collective bargaining agreement became effective, the employer announced that it was retroactively freezing benefit accruals—that is, adopting IRS Model Amendment 3. The NLRB found that, while the employer may have had the contractual right to amend the pension plan to protect its tax-exempt status, it did not have the right to select and implement one of several possible amendments without giving the union notice and an opportunity to bargain about the subject.

In multi-employer bargaining relationships, where two or more separate employers negotiate together, often through a committee or trade association, the benefit plans tend to be administered separately from the collective bargaining agreements by joint union- and employer-appointed trustees (sometimes called "Taft-Hartley plans," because they are authorized by section 302(c)(5) of the Labor Management Relations Act). These plans provide mobile pension, healthcare, and other welfare benefits to employees who work on a project or other short-term basis for a particular employer while spending their career working for several employers in the industry. Funding deficiencies in multi-employer pension plans are the subject of the Multiemployer Pension Plan Amendments Act of 1980.

Q 6.8   How are seniority rights typically defined in a collective bargaining agreement?

A seniority system is an arrangement between an employer and its employees and/or union that requires an employer to take into account an employee's length of service when making particular decisions regarding job layoffs, promotions, or other employee benefits. Employees with greater seniority may receive additional compensation, benefits, or other competitive advantages over fellow employees in the workplace.

Seniority rights do not arise merely from the establishment of an employer-employee relationship or an even employer-union relationship. These rights only exist when provided by an individual employer-employee contract or a collective bargaining agreement. Seniority rights created by a collective bargaining agreement are subject to revision and renegotiation, even though the resulting changes may be retroactive or affect individual employees differently.[7] Collective bargaining agreement seniority provisions typically set out how employees will accrue seniority and what effect seniority or super-seniority may have on other employee rights and benefits under the collective bargaining agreement. The terms of a collective bargaining agreement may also create different classes of seniority, such as company-wide or in-classification seniority.[8] Seniority may be denied for probationary or part-time employees. Other provisions may state that a temporary worker, during his or her temporary status, can accumulate seniority that will apply when he or she is hired on a more permanent basis. A seniority plan will be upheld if it is reasonable and falls within the wide range of discretion given to the collective bargaining representative.[9]

There are two basic types of seniority provisions: (1) strict seniority clauses, whereby employees must give preference to the employee with the longest continuous service, without regard to any other consideration; and (2) modified seniority clauses, whereby seniority is considered along with other factors such as "fitness and ability," which includes skill, ability, aptitude, experience, and training. Contracts may also allow employers to disregard seniority upon a showing of a demonstrated need to do so.

Absent a collective bargaining agreement provision to the contrary, seniority rights do not vest in the employees. For example, a collective bargaining agreement may provide that an employee loses seniority due to:[10]

- termination of the collective bargaining agreement;

- relocation of the employer's facility upon purchase by or merger with another company;

- an internal transfer to another position or classification;

- absence from work; and

- discharge or resignation.

Q 6.8.1   Can seniority rights be transferred when, for example, a plant closes or is consolidated?

Issues regarding seniority often arise when plants are relocated or closed down, as employees may desire to transfer their seniority to another plant or to continue their seniority in the employment of the successor employer. Collective bargaining agreements can expressly provide for the transfer of seniority rights to other locations. Indeed, where collective bargaining agreements do not provide for company-wide seniority or integration of seniority lists and a plant-closing agreement states that such employees will be covered by the contract's new hire provisions, an employer may generally treat the employees from the closed plant as "new hires" upon transfer. When separate companies merge or plants are consolidated, seniority lists are often merged through one (or a combination) of several methods, including:

Endtail or *surviving-group principle*. The employees of the acquiring company receive preference over the employees of the acquired company. The employees of the acquired company are added, in seniority order, to the bottom of the acquiring company's seniority list.[11]

Dovetail or *length-of-service principle*. Employees from the acquired and acquiring companies are placed on a new list in order of their length of service. All employees are treated as if they had always been employed by the acquiring company.[12]

Follow-the-work principle. Acquired employees are given the opportunity to follow their work, if it can still be adequately identified, with seniority rights based on a separate seniority list. If the work merges into other work, the seniority lists may be integrated using the ratio-rank principle based on the amount of work brought into the consolidated group by each group of employees.

Ratio-rank principle. A ratio is derived from the number of employees on each company's seniority list. A new seniority list is formed by adding names from each company's respective seniority list according to the ratio. For example, if company *A*'s seniority list has 300 names and company *B*'s list has 100 names, three of company *A*'s employees will be added to the list for each employee added from company *B*. The first three employees on company *A*'s list will be the first three on the new merged list. Then the first employee on company *B*'s list will become the fourth employee on the new merged list.

Absolute-rank principle. Employees are placed on a new seniority list on the basis of the rank held on their respective prior seniority lists. For example, the two employees at the top of the prior lists take the first two places on the new merged list. The employee with the longer service gets the first place on the new list. This principle does not take into account the size of the two groups to be merged.

Q 6.8.2   What are super-seniority provisions?

Super-seniority provisions in a collective bargaining agreement provide particular employees with a right to benefits or other promotions over individuals with otherwise equal seniority. Super-seniority clauses that give seniority to union shop stewards or other officials over natural seniority must be scrutinized in light of sections 8(a)(2), 8(a)(3), 8(b)(1)(A), and 8(b)(2) of the NLRA. Any exercise of super-seniority raises potential problems under the NLRA because super-seniority clauses necessarily tie job rights and benefits to union activities, thereby encouraging union participation. Super-seniority clauses that are not on their face limited to layoff and recall are presumptively unlawful. Once the presumption attaches, the union and employer must demonstrate that a broader provision was required by legitimate and substantial business justifications. Absent such proof, the effects of the super-seniority clause will be limited to lawful recall and layoff rights.[13]

Q 6.9   What kind of provisions in a collective bargaining agreement govern layoff and recall procedures?

A collective bargaining agreement can contain provisions that govern layoff and recall procedures. A layoff provision may provide that layoffs will be conducted based on seniority, either within a department or plant-wide. Some contracts require that the employer give prior notice of layoffs to the union. Related provisions may provide that senior employees can "bump" into the jobs of employees with less seniority. Notably, once employees are on layoff, the contract will usually set forth procedures by which laid-off employees are brought back to work (that is, are recalled).

The federal Worker Adjustment and Retraining Notification (WARN) Act of 1988 and analogous state statutes require covered employers to provide certain notices in advance of plant closings and mass layoffs that are covered by the law. The employer must provide the notice to the employees or the union, as well as to state and local authorities. State law versions of the WARN Act may impose additional restraints on employers or expand the class of employers who are required to provide notice.

Q 6.10   How do collective bargaining agreements typically define hours of work?

Collective bargaining agreements may set forth the standard workday and workweek. Generally, an agreement may specify the number of hours an employee will work each day and the total number of hours the employee will work each week. This may include defining the beginning and end of the workday. These specifications often assist the employer and employee in determining when overtime will be owed to the employee.

Employers may also reserve the right in a collective bargaining agreement to determine employees' work schedules, and the collective bargaining agreement might provide the procedure used by an employer to schedule its employees. An agreement may include a provision stating that the employer will not guarantee employees a fixed number of hours per week. An agreement may also require the employer to provide notice or agree with the union prior to implementing changes in work schedules.

A collective bargaining agreement, as permitted by law, may also provide compensation or regulate the following nonproductive periods, among others:

- meals,
- rest periods,
- personal or production area clean-up,
- donning and doffing equipment,
- downtime due to lack of work or material necessary to complete a job,
- time spent on-call, and
- travel time.

Q 6.11   What types of leave provisions may be included in collective bargaining agreements?

Employees are not automatically entitled to a leave of absence from work. However, many types of leave-of-absence provisions can be found in collective bargaining agreements. As an initial matter, a contract may contain specific administrative procedures employees must follow when requesting a leave of absence. Moreover, provisions may set forth limits on the duration of leave from work, whether leave will be granted without loss of seniority, whether benefits will continue during leave, and who is eligible for certain types of leave. In some instances, the amount of leave available to a particular employee will differ based on how much seniority that employee has with the company.

Examples of leave that may be covered in a collective bargaining agreement include:

(1) leaves for union business;
(2) bereavement leave;
(3) jury duty leave;

(4)   military service leave;
(5)   education leave; and
(6)   family and medical leave.

For many types of leave, such as leave for military service and family and medical leave, the employer must comply with all applicable local, state and federal laws.

Q 6.11.1   What are typical provisions regarding family and medical leave?

Employers are required by the Family and Medical Leave Act of 1993 (FMLA) to provide unpaid family and medical leave if they employ at least fifty employees and other eligibility factors are met. As a result, employers must comply with the leave requirements of the FMLA as well as any more generous leave rights contained in state and local law and the collective bargaining agreement.

Q 6.11.2   What are the typical provisions regarding jury duty?

Many contracts include provisions entitling employees to jury duty and witness leave so they may serve on juries or appear as witnesses and attend legal proceedings. These provisions generally describe employee eligibility, notice, and return-to-work requirements. They also may include a discussion of how employees are to be compensated for such leave, including whether the leave is paid or unpaid and whether, for the purposes of calculating overtime and vacation eligibility, the leave is considered actual time worked. In the absence of an express provision, an employer is generally not required to pay jury duty benefits to employees. Many agreements, however, provide employees with their full salary less any jury fees received from the court. This is an area often governed by state or local law as well.

Q 6.11.3   What are the typical provisions regarding voting leave?

Many states require employers to grant paid voting leave during certain eligible elections. Provisions regarding voting leave may include requiring employees to fill out voting leave request forms designating specific hours in which employees can vote, requiring employees to prove voter eligibility and/or registration, and limiting the time an employer can take off to vote. Again, state and local laws may also impact voting leave.

Q 6.11.4 What are the typical provisions regarding military leave?

An employee's military leave is governed by the Uniformed Services Employment and Reemployment Rights Act of 1994, which delineates an employee's rights and obligations with respect to leave and reemployment, as well as any applicable state law. Therefore, contracts often include a provision stating simply that the employer will comply with the USERRA. Some contracts, however, expand the rights of the employees to include pay for time on military leave.

Q 6.11.5 What are the typical provisions regarding sick leave?

Sick leave may be negotiated as part of a collective bargaining agreement. Most collective bargaining agreements that provide sick leave grant employees one or more of the following:

(1) unpaid sick leave;

(2) employer-paid sick leave; or

(3) third-party paid sick leave (short-term disability insurance).

Unpaid sick leave provisions grant employees unpaid time off, while allowing them to retain seniority and other job protections during an absence from work. Contracts vary widely with respect to the availability and duration of unpaid sick leave; some only provide unpaid leave for illnesses or injuries, while others offer unpaid leave once an employee exhausts paid leave. Some contracts grant leave based on an employee's seniority while others grant it for the length of illness or injury. However, the availability and duration of the leave must meet federal and state requirements.

Employer-paid sick leave provisions may address the following issues:

(1) length-of-service requirement;

(2) any "wait periods";

(3) pay calculation;

(4) physician certification requirements;

(5) coverage of family illnesses;

(6) accumulation of unused sick leave; and

(7) whether accumulated but unused time will be paid at termination.

A number of states and local governments have recently enacted paid sick leave provisions, which set the minimum requirements that can be provided for employees in those locations.

With respect to third-party paid sick leave, terms of coverage (such as eligibility, duration, benefit formulas), if not mandated by state law, can be negotiated between the employer and the union. Third-party paid sick leave can also be left up to the employer and the insurance carrier, in which case the contract provision may state that short-term disability leave will be provided by the employer.

Q 6.11.6 What are the typical provisions regarding paid or personal time off (PTO)?

In recent years, many employers have moved away from separate sick and vacation provisions and instead combine all paid leave into a general "paid time off" or PTO provision, which gives employees flexibility and relieves employers from some administrative burden associated with sick leave policies. Collective bargaining agreements may provide for personal leave from work. PTO provisions may allocate time off of work based upon total service or attendance, and often otherwise mimic vacation policies.

Q 6.11.7 What are the typical provisions regarding union leave?

Employers and the union typically negotiate union leave to allow employees time off to conduct union business. These provisions vary greatly. A contract can expressly provide for union leave, or it can allow for such leave through personal leave provisions. Typically, union leave is unpaid.

Union leave provisions may address:

(1) the maximum length of the union leave;

(2) the number of employees who can be out on union leave at one time;

(3) whether life and health insurance coverage are continued during union leave;

(4) the definition of "union business"; and

(5) the administrative procedures to be followed when employees return from leave.

Union leave provisions also generally permit employers to obtain information regarding the nature of the union business and the likely duration of the absence in order to allow for an informed decision whether to grant or deny the leave sought.

Q 6.12   What type of safety and health provisions do collective bargaining agreements include?

Safety and health provisions are often included in collective bargaining agreements and can vary widely, from a statement that the employer is responsible for providing a safe workplace, to a more detailed safety policy, including regulations covering specific operations or the use of dangerous materials. The type of provisions the parties choose to include depends on several factors, including the amount of risk in the industry and the parties' bargaining relationship.

Parties should tailor the safety and health program to meet the needs of their particular workplace. Because safety and health are generally the employer's responsibility and a mandatory subject of bargaining, unions take different approaches. Some unions prefer to have the employer establish the safety and health rules and retain the right to file grievances regarding the effects of such rules. Other unions take an active role in promulgating the safety and health rules in the contract, including the establishment of a health and safety committee. An effective safety and health program can be beneficial to both the employees and the employer, often reducing workers' compensation costs and improving employee morale.

The employer is commonly responsible for issuing safety regulations and is required to post and distribute rules to employees. Some contracts require paid safety training for employees, address inspections, and investigations of on-the-job accidents, and allow for physical exams. Additionally, contracts frequently provide for the use of safety equipment and clothing, such as boots, gloves, and goggles. The contract may either list specific items the employer will furnish, or state that the employer will provide:

(1) necessary equipment;
(2) equipment as required by law; or
(3) equipment as established by prevailing industry practice.

The employer may agree to pay for all or a part of the costs for safety and health equipment.

At a minimum, a safety and health provision in a collective bargaining agreement should be drafted to ensure that the policies comply with all state and federal regulations, including the Occupational Safety and Health Act of 1970 and other laws applicable to particular industries.

Q 6.13   How are the issues of job transfers and promotions handled in collective bargaining agreements?

Promotions are defined as the transfer of an employee to a higher job classification. Although an employer's rights in selecting employees for promotion are generally unlimited, the collective bargaining agreement can dictate that promotions be determined by seniority alone or by seniority in conjunction with skill, ability, and experience.

Transfers may be defined as:

(1) the rotation of employees among jobs within their classification;

(2) moving employees between shifts;

(3) moving employees from one job to another in a different classification in the same job class;

(4) moving employees to a new machine; or

(5) moving employees to a new location for the same job.

Employers have the right to effect transfers, either temporary or permanent, unless otherwise restricted by agreement, law, or practice. Some collective bargaining agreements explicitly recognize management's right to transfer, while other agreements make the right to transfer subject to other terms of the collective bargaining agreement. Generally, arbitrators require that any restrictions on management's right to transfer be clearly stated in the agreement.

Q 6.14   How is the issue of union access addressed in collective bargaining agreements?

Generally, collective bargaining agreements address under what circumstances and to what degree the union will have access to the employer's facilities and its employees. A union access provision may provide:

(1) when and where the union can conduct its business and for what purposes the union can gain access to the facilities;

(2) the type of notice, if any, the union must give the employer of visits; and

(3) the extent to which a union's employee representative can use the employer's facilities, mail service, and business email for official union business.

The union access provision can also state that the union representative will not meet with employees during the employees' work hours, except in limited circumstances, and that union business shall not interfere with the employer's operations.

Q 6.15   How are the issues of discipline and discharge addressed in collective bargaining agreements?

An employer's ability to discharge employees covered by a collective bargaining agreement will depend on whether the agreement contains a "just-cause" provision. In the absence of a just-cause provision, some arbitrators imply such a limitation based on the reasoning that, without it, all the seniority and "work protection" clauses of the agreement would be meaningless. Under this view, parties must specify in their agreement that there is a no-just-cause requirement. Other arbitrators, however, believe that, where the collective bargaining agreement does not contain an express limitation on the right to discharge, the employer can discharge for any reason it chooses.

Many agreements, however, require cause for discharge and discipline. Examples of "cause" may include theft, repeated absences, or destruction of company property. If the listed offenses are not made exclusive, employers generally can also impose discipline for other conduct.

Q 6.16   What type of subcontracting language is found in collective bargaining agreements?

Many employers seek to use subcontractors to save labor costs in non-core work areas, such as janitorial and administrative work functions. Arbitrators generally hold that management has the right, absent an explicit restriction in the collective bargaining agreement, to subcontract work to independent contractors as long as the action is done in good faith, represents a reasonable business decision, does not violate the agreement, and does not seriously weaken the bargaining unit. Absent language in a collective bargaining agreement expressly allowing an employer to subcontract bargaining unit work, an employer may have to meet bargaining obligations before implementing its subcontracting strategy. Collective bargaining agreements may also require the employer to provide notice of its intent to subcontract. Bargaining over subcontracting is discussed in further detail in chapter 5.

Subcontracting clauses must be carefully drafted to avoid violating section 8(e) of the NLRA. For instance, "union-only" subcontracting clauses, which require employers to subcontract work only to certain unions or union employees, may constitute unlawful "hot cargo" provisions. (See Q 5.9 *et seq.*) However, "work preservation" clauses, aimed at prohibiting only subcontracting or transfers of bargaining unit work, have generally been held to be lawful. Agreements banning all subcontracting normally do not violate section 8(e). Before negotiating a subcontracting clause, an employer should carefully assess the needs of its business and determine areas where it can achieve labor cost savings by utilizing non-bargaining unit workers.

Q 6.17   How are grievance procedures addressed in collective bargaining agreements?

The scope of grievance procedures in collective bargaining agreements is ordinarily defined by the parties to the agreement. Some grievance procedures are broadly worded to permit virtually any employment dispute to be submitted to the contractual grievance machinery. Other grievance procedures narrowly define the scope of the disputes subject to resolution under the contractual process.

Grievances and the Arbitration Procedure

The Basics

Q 6.18   What is a "grievance"?

Given the variety of different approaches that prevail in collective bargaining agreements, there is no precise definition for the term "grievance." However, a grievance is commonly understood as a dispute related to the interpretation, application, or an alleged violation of a specific provision of the collective bargaining agreement. In contrast, disputes involving demands for changes to terms of a collective bargaining agreement (commonly referred to as "interest" disputes) and disputes regarding representation issues fall outside the generally accepted definition of a grievance under a collective bargaining agreement.

Q 6.19   How are grievances typically handled?

A typical contractual grievance procedure requires the parties to discuss the grievance at several junctures in an attempt to reach an amicable resolution and applies time limits for each stage. The objective of most grievance procedures is to resolve disputes during pre-arbitration stages rather than resorting to an arbitration hearing. An effective grievance procedure allows the parties to reach a compromise without the time and expense of a contentious arbitration hearing. Often, the first step in the grievance process is for the employee to take the grievance, with or without a union representative, to the first-line supervisor. If the grievance is not resolved, a formal, written grievance may be submitted and may be appealed through the successive stages of the process. Most arbitration clauses provide that, if the parties, upon exhaustion of the grievance procedure, fail to resolve the grievance, either party may invoke arbitration.

After all levels of the grievance procedure have been exhausted, the grievant and his or her union representative must decide whether to accept the employer's response to the grievance or to make an arbitration demand. The collective bargaining agreement typically provides that the party wishing to pursue arbitration must give notice of the intent to arbitrate within a specified period of time. The arbitration process is discussed in detail below at Q 6.22 *et seq.*

SAMPLE LANGUAGE:

Grievance and Arbitration Procedure

Step 1: The aggrieved employee is encouraged to present the grievance orally to his/her immediate supervisor, and the supervisor shall promptly attempt to resolve the complaint informally. If the grievance is not resolved in this manner, the Union representative shall reduce the grievance to writing, in duplicate, on a form provided by the Company, identifying the grievance, and setting forth the facts and any contract provisions giving rise to the grievance. Two (2) copies of the written grievance shall be presented by the Union representative to management within thirty (30) days (fifteen (15) for suspension and discharge) of the occurrence of the facts giving rise to the grievance. The management representative shall have seven (7) days, unless otherwise mutually agreed, in which to answer, adjust, or settle said grievance.

Step 2: If the grievance is not satisfactorily settled under Step 1 above, the representative of the Union may appeal and shall

---

present the written grievance to the Division Manager, or Department Head, within seven (7) days of the Company's answer under Step 1. The Division Manager, Department Head, or his/her designated representative, shall discuss the grievance and answer, adjust, or settle it with the appropriate Union area representative, or his/her authorized representative, within seven (7) days, unless otherwise mutually agreed, after the appealed grievance is presented.

Step 3: If the grievance is not satisfactorily settled under Step 2 above and is appealed to the third step, the grievance shall be presented to the Vice President of Human Resources, or his/her designated representative, by the Union's representative or local president. The Union representative will request a conference at the third step within thirty (30) days of the date of the appeal at the second level, and such meeting will be at a mutually agreeable location in the geographic location served by the bargaining unit. Following such conference, the written decision of the Company's representative at the third step shall be given to the Union within fifteen (15) days.

If the grievance cannot be settled by the above Grievance Procedure and is subject to the arbitration provisions of this Agreement, it may be referred to arbitration upon written request by the Union to the Company within sixty (60) days after a decision is rendered in Step 3 of this Grievance Procedure.

Resolving a Grievance Prior to Arbitration

Q 6.20   What are the steps in the pre-arbitration grievance process?

Pre-arbitration steps ordinarily reflect the interests of the parties, the structure of the employer, and the industry at issue. Although each collective bargaining agreement is unique, certain guidelines are helpful to ensure that the process functions smoothly and produces meaningful results. A provision defining the grievance arbitration process may establish the following:

- Who may file a grievance alleging that a party to the agreement has violated one of the collective bargaining agreement provisions.

- A grievance process comprising multiple steps providing for escalation of the dispute to higher levels of management and union representation in the event that the parties cannot reach agreement at the lower levels.

- The manner in which grievances are to be presented, including a requirement that the grievances be presented in writing in order to establish a record in the event that the dispute ultimately reaches arbitration.

- The method for appealing a grievance from one step to another in the grievance process.

- The time limits for initiating a grievance, appeals, responses from management, and demands for arbitration.

- The priority handling of certain grievances, such as grievances arising out of a discharge or an issue affecting the entire workforce.

Observing procedural requirements in the grievance arbitration process is important for employees, employers, and labor unions. An employer's flat refusal to process a grievance constitutes a violation of the NLRA.[14] Additionally, arbitrators may sustain or deny a grievance if a party fails to follow proper procedure, and may deny a hearing if a grievance is untimely. To preserve procedural defenses in the event a grievance proceeds to arbitration, deficiencies in the grievance process by another party should be documented as they occur.

Q 6.21 What is grievance mediation?

In certain situations, after the final step of an internal grievance procedure, unresolved grievances may be referred to mediation prior to arbitration as a last effort to amicably resolve the grievance.

Although not common, this step has been added to a growing number of collective bargaining agreements over the years.

In mediation, the neutral party does not have the authority to decide the case and has no binding power over the parties to the grievance. Rather, the mediator informally gathers the facts of the case and attempts to guide the two sides to a mutually acceptable agreement. Where mediation does not resolve the grievance, the mediator can deliver an advisory, non-binding, and confidential opinion regarding the grievance, which the parties can then use as a basis for further settlement discussion. Where mediation is used, the mediator should not act as the subsequent arbitrator, and the contents of the mediation proceedings are usually not admissible in the arbitration. For the mediation to be effective, the mediator should be selected from outside the company, and both parties must trust the mediator's competence and impartiality.

Submitting a Dispute to Arbitration

Q 6.22   What are the prerequisites for submitting a dispute to arbitration?

A threshold question in any arbitration proceeding is whether the parties' dispute is actually subject to arbitration. Arbitration is a matter of contract, and generally, parties cannot be required to arbitrate any disputes they have not specifically agreed shall be subject to arbitration.[15] Consequently, before agreeing to submit a particular dispute to arbitration, parties must resolve substantive arbitrability questions by first determining whether there is a valid agreement to arbitrate the particular dispute.

Substantive arbitrability determinations involve the question of whether the parties have a valid arbitration agreement that applies to the particular dispute at issue. As a rule, courts, rather than arbitrators, resolve disputes regarding substantive arbitrability.[16] The parties, however, may, by agreement, submit a question of substantive arbitrability to an arbitrator for resolution. Whether to submit a substantive arbitrability question to an arbitrator or a court is a strategic determination based upon the particular circumstances of the dispute. A court's role in resolving questions of substantive arbitrability under section 301 is extremely limited.

Assuming there is a valid arbitration agreement covering the dispute, the parties must also resolve procedural arbitrability questions by determining whether all procedural prerequisites to arbitration have been satisfied. However, once it is determined that the subject matter of a dispute is substantively arbitral, whether the parties have complied with procedural prerequisites set out in the labor contract is typically a matter left to the arbitrator.[17] According to the U.S. Supreme Court, the rationale for submitting such "procedural arbitrability" disputes to arbitrators is that procedural questions ordinarily cannot be answered without consideration of the merits of the matter. Procedural arbitrability questions typically involve disputes concerning whether the aggrieved party has followed all procedural prerequisites to arbitration under the parties' arbitration agreement. Examples of such questions include:

(1)   whether a proper grievance or arbitration demand was filed;

(2)   whether the grievance or arbitration demand is timely;

(3)   whether the parties have a justifiable controversy;

(4)   the res judicata effect of a prior arbitration award; and

(5)   whether any grievance procedures, such as meeting or notice requirements, have been satisfied.

The failure to comply with any such procedural prerequisites may or may not constitute grounds for refusal to arbitrate a particular grievance or dispute.

Q 6.23   How are arbitrators selected?

As an initial matter, the collective bargaining agreement may specify how the arbitrator(s) will be appointed. An arbitrator may be selected for a specific case or group of cases, or the contract may appoint a permanent arbitrator or a panel of permanent arbitrators to hear all arbitration cases pertaining to grievances that arise during the life of the contract. Many contracts provide the parties with the option of mutually selecting an arbitrator. Other contracts provide that the parties will select an arbitrator by striking or ranking names from a panel provided by a neutral agency.

Typically, the written grievance and the employer's response throughout the steps of the grievance procedure serve as the submission documents. These documents establish the issue(s) in dispute and delineate the arbitrator's authority. The parties are encouraged to stipulate the issue(s) to be decided by the arbitrator. If the parties cannot agree, the arbitrator will formulate the issue based upon the submissions of the parties. Issues should be framed with specific reference to the collective bargaining agreement because the arbitrator's authority to decide the issue is derived from the contract.

Q 6.23.1   Can arbitrators issue declaratory judgments?

As a general rule, arbitrators are reluctant to issue declaratory judgments or advisory opinions. Grievances involving "hypothetical" questions are generally premature as each case must be judged on its own facts. As one arbitrator has stated, "[t]he question of whether a rule is fair and reasonable cannot be confidently determined except in the context of a concrete case and upon consideration of the specific circumstances of a particular case in which the rule is invoked and applied."[18]

Arbitrators are more likely to issue an advisory opinion where the requesting party demonstrates that it is necessary to protect the party's interests under the contract or if both parties desire one. Parties can, for example, specifically provide in their contract for the use of advisory opinions.

Q 6.24   Who represents the parties?

Each party has the right to be represented in arbitration. Each party's choice of representative will vary depending on the case. In certain situations, the party's advocate during the internal grievance procedure will be chosen to present the arbitration case. In other circumstances, other union or company officials or their counsel will present the case. The parties may be represented by attorneys, but it is not unusual for union representatives or labor relations staff members to present the case. Moreover, in some industries or in expedited arbitrations, the parties may agree not to use attorneys. Generally, a union does not breach its duty of fair representation where it uses a union representative, rather than an attorney, to represent the grievant at the hearing.

Q 6.25   Who determines the rules governing the arbitration process?

Many collective bargaining agreements provide that the rules of a particular agency (for example, the American Arbitration Association, a private arbitration services organization, or the U.S. Federal Mediation and Conciliation Service) will govern the arbitration process. For example, the agency's rules may:

(1)   provide a framework for selecting arbitrators;

(2)   specify how the parties will determine the date, time, and place of hearing;

(3)   specify under what circumstances the arbitrator will grant a postponement;

(4)   specify whether a stenographic record of the hearing will be taken;

(5)   specify whether the parties will have an opportunity to submit post-hearing briefs;

(6)   specify the process by which evidence may be submitted;

(7)   specify the amount of time an arbitrator will have to issue an award; and

(8)   explain other administrative issues.

If the collective bargaining agreement does not adopt any agency's guidelines, arbitration procedures are dictated by legal requirements, the parties' agreement, and the preferences of the arbitrator hearing the dispute. If the dispute is determined to be arbitral, the procedural questions that are not governed by applicable laws and rules typically are left to the arbitrator.[19] It is the arbitrator's responsibility to ensure that the parties receive a full and fair opportunity to present their cases.

Q 6.26   Is an arbitration like a court trial?

An arbitration hearing is generally less formal than a trial in court and is not typically held in a courtroom, but instead in a meeting room or other private space. Many arbitrators do not strictly follow the Federal Rules of Evidence or other generally applicable rules of evidence. Based upon the terms of the collective bargaining agreement and the practice of the parties, a court reporter may or may not be present. Whether or not witnesses will be sequestered during the proceedings is also an issue typically dependent upon the specific contract, the history of the parties, or the discretion of the arbitrator.

Arbitration hearings generally begin with opening statements. The party that bears the burden of proof goes first; the other party goes second, with an opportunity to defer its opening statement until after the party bearing the burden of proof has rested its affirmative case. The union has the burden of proof in a contract interpretation case, as the union must show that a contract violation occurred in order to prevail. Therefore, in contract interpretation cases, the union typically presents its case first. In a discipline or discharge matter, the employer generally bears the burden of proof because it must usually establish the grievant was terminated with just cause. In such cases, the employer presents its case first.

Similar to a trial in a state or federal court, the parties present their cases through witnesses on direct examination, with opportunities for cross-examination and redirect. Generally speaking, evidentiary exhibits may be submitted to the arbitrator by agreement of the parties (joint exhibits), or through witness testimony during direct, cross-, or redirect examination. While some collective bargaining agreements provide for both closing arguments and post-hearing briefs, the prevailing practice is that the parties may either present a closing statement or submit a post-hearing brief. Moreover, some collective bargaining agreements provide for the submission of post-hearing briefs upon the completion of the hearing, while others provide some reasonable amount of time after the hearing during which the parties may submit post-hearing briefs for the arbitrator's consideration.

Q 6.26.1 What obligations do parties have with regard to discovery?

As a rule, traditional labor arbitration does not provide for formal pre-hearing discovery, such as depositions, interrogatories, requests for production, or requests for admission. Instead, access to pre-trial information is governed by the NLRA's statutory obligation to bargain in good faith. (See chapter 5 for additional information regarding a party's duty to bargain.) This duty requires an employer to provide relevant information to a union as is required for the union to properly perform its duties as the employees' bargaining representative. Likewise, the union is required to provide information it has that is needed by the employer to fulfill its responsibilities as a participant in the collective bargaining relationship.

Generally, parties are required to produce whatever documents a re relevant to the grievance. This includes witness statements, unless the statements are explicitly made confidential.[20] Even when statements are made confidentially, the employer likely must provide the names and job titles for the persons providing the confidential statements. The NLRB also held in *American Baptist Homes of the West* that an employer may be required to provide the confidential statements as well if the information requested by the union is relevant, unless the employer demonstrates a legitimate and substantial interest in confidentiality that outweighs the union's need for the requested information.[21] However, that decision was set aside as a result the Supreme Court's decision in *Noel Canning*.[22]

Although enforcement of the statutory duty to provide relevant information is subject to ULP proceedings filed with the NLRB, disputes regarding disclosure of relevant information are often submitted directly to the arbitrator for resolution. As a practical matter, given the time required to file and resolve a ULP charge with the NLRB, enforcement through NLRA processes of a request for information may be too late to affect the arbitration hearing.

In addition to the general duty to provide information, in some cases the parties' arbitration agreement itself may contain specific provisions regarding pre-hearing discovery. Such provisions may authorize the arbitrator to order parties to respond to discovery requests and to produce witnesses for depositions. Other contractual provisions may encourage the production of relevant information by restricting the use of documents or evidence that has not previously been given to the other party. Moreover, even in the absence of specific contractual provisions, arbitrators may consider the refusal to produce evidence when assigning weight and credibility to evidence that was not previously produced to an opposing party. As noted above, some arbitration agreements incorporate by reference arbitration rules and procedures of third-party arbitration administrators, such as the AAA and FMCS. The rules and procedures of these or other similar organizations may also contain provisions for prehearing discovery.

Additionally, arbitrators are generally deemed to have the authority to issue subpoenas to compel witness testimony and the production of documents or other information. An arbitrator's legal authority to issue subpoenas is derived from individual state arbitration acts, the Federal Arbitration Act, and/or section 301 of the LMRA. Subpoenas issued by an arbitrator are not self-enforcing. Accordingly, an action to enforce an arbitrator's subpoena must be brought in court. As a practical matter, this requires suspension of the arbitration hearing until the court rules on the issue of enforcement of the subpoena. If an action for enforcement in court is not practicable given the circumstances of the arbitration hearing, an alternative remedy is to seek an adverse inference from the arbitrator regarding the evidence that was subpoenaed. The procedure for requesting a subpoena is generally governed by the applicable arbitration agreement or arbitration rules.

Q 6.26.2   What is "expedited arbitration"?

Many collective bargaining agreements call for expedited arbitration of certain grievances. For instance, a collective bargaining agreement may specify that a grievance affecting all employees will be given priority and arbitrated on a shorter timeline than other grievances, even where other grievances were filed in advance of that grievance. Other collective bargaining agreements provide for expedited arbitration of discharge grievances. Moreover, the AAA has issued "Expedited Labor Arbitration Procedures," which were established "[i]n response to the concern of parties over rising costs and delays" in arbitration. The Expedited Labor Arbitration Procedures apply only where the parties have agreed to arbitrate under them and provide for the appointment of a neutral arbitrator who will promptly schedule the hearing and resolve the dispute within seven days of the hearing without reviewing post-hearing briefs.

Q 6.26.3   Can parties arbitrate multiple grievances in a single proceeding?

In the absence of an express clause in the collective bargaining agreement, the issue of whether multiple grievances may be heard by a single arbitrator is a procedural question for the arbitrator to decide. Generally, either party can seek simultaneous arbitration of all grievances that reach the arbitration stage at the same time, unless the collective bargaining agreement's arbitration clause clearly and unambiguously provides otherwise. Arbitrators generally reject the argument that an arbitration clause's use of the singular term "grievance" provides that multiple grievances cannot be compelled to the same arbitration. However, arbitrators have denied multiple-grievance arbitration where the parties' contract speaks to a singular "grievance" *and* there is an adequately established past practice of arbitrating only one grievance at a time.

Additionally, arbitrators have recognized other special circumstances that justify an exception to the general rule allowing multiple grievances, including:

(1)   the existence of individual grievances involving widely separated plants, brought under separate contracts, and where the witnesses are located in different places;

(2)   where there is an excessively high number of grievances;

(3)   the existence of specialized grievances requiring arbitrators with particularized experience; and

(4)   where multiple grievances would result in confusion, prejudice or substantial detriment to either party.

Once an arbitrator has been selected, a party generally needs to obtain both the arbitrator's and the opposing party's consent to add additional grievances.

Q 6.27   Do arbitration provisions in collective bargaining agreements preclude state and federal agencies from filing discrimination charges?

No. The Supreme Court has held that arbitration agreements do not preclude state and federal agencies from filing discrimination charges, even where those charges seek victim-specific relief. Government agencies are not bound by arbitration agreements where they are not party to those agreements.[23]

Enforcement of Arbitration

Q 6.28   How is the duty to arbitrate enforced?

Section 301 of the LMRA governs the enforcement of collective bargaining agreements negotiated pursuant to the provisions of the NLRA (as opposed to agreements negotiated pursuant to the Railway Labor Act). In 1947, Congress passed the LMRA, which amended the NLRA, in part, to encourage collective bargaining and to facilitate enforcement of collective bargaining agreements. Section 203 of the LMRA provides that a negotiated dispute resolution process is the preferred method to settle disagreements regarding the interpretation and application of collective bargaining agreements. This amendment to the NLRA specifically provides that the duty to bargain includes "the mutual obligation of the employer and the representative of the employees . . . to confer in good faith with respect to . . . the negotiation of an agreement, *or any question arising thereunder.*"[24]

Section 301 establishes a cause of action in federal courts to enforce collective bargaining agreements. Moreover, the U.S. Supreme Court has interpreted section 301 to authorize federal courts to develop a body of federal common law pertaining to collective bargaining agreements, a body of judge-made law that preempts state laws dealing with the enforcement or interpretation of labor agreements.[25] Consistently, federal courts have pointed to the NLRA and section 301 as evidence of clear legislative intent favoring the enforcement of arbitration provisions and have concluded that federal courts have the jurisdiction to enforce such provisions despite the Norris-LaGuardia Act,[26] which bars federal courts from issuing injunctions arising out of specified acts occurring in connection with labor disputes. The reason for enforcing arbitration provisions, addressed in *Textile Workers v. Lincoln Mills*, is that "the agreement to arbitrate grievance disputes is the *quid pro quo* for an agreement not to strike."[27]

Beginning with the *Steelworkers Trilogy* in 1960,[28] the U.S. Supreme Court developed a number of rules promoting the arbitration of disputes arising from a collective bargaining agreement as the preferred method of dispute resolution. First, a court's role in enforcing collective bargaining agreements is not to consider the merits of a grievance, but rather to "ascertain[ ] whether the party seeking arbitration is making a claim that on its face is governed by the contract."[29] Second, any doubts as to whether the grievance is covered by the arbitration clause should be resolved in favor of arbitration.[30] Third, as long as the arbitrator's award "draws its essence from the collective bargaining agreement," it must be enforced even if the arbitrator's interpretation of the contract is ambiguous or the court would have reached a different conclusion on the merits.[31]

Q 6.28.1   Can an individual be required to arbitrate an anti-discrimination claim pursuant to a collective bargaining agreement?

Generally, an individual employee cannot be compelled to submit an employment discrimination dispute based upon an alleged violation of federal civil rights laws to grievance and arbitration provisions under a collective bargaining agreement.

In the 1974 decision *Alexander v. Gardner-Denver Co.*,[32] the U.S. Supreme Court ruled that unions could not bargain away their members' individual rights to have their discrimination claims heard in court. The Court's stance regarding mandatory arbitration of statutory claims, however, appeared to shift in its subsequent decision in *Gilmer v. Interstate/Johnson Lane Corp.*[33] In *Gilmer*, the Court held that an individual employee could be required to arbitrate an Age Discrimination in Employment Act (ADEA) claim where he had waived his right to pursue the claim in a federal forum. *Gilmer*, however, did not explicitly overrule *Gardner-Denver*, and the *Gilmer* decision is distinguishable because it concerned a non-union setting in which the employee had signed an arbitration agreement in seeking to become a registered broker under the rules of the New York Stock Exchange.

In 2009, the Court recognized a narrow exception to the *Gardner-Denver* rule. In *14 Penn Plaza LLC v. Pyett*,[34] the Court held that arbitration provisions in collective bargaining agreements that clearly and unmistakably require arbitration of statutory employment claims, such as claims brought under the ADEA, are enforceable. In *14 Penn Plaza*, an anti-discrimination provision in the collective bargaining agreement specifically referred to the ADEA and other federal, state, and city laws banning employment discrimination. The clause further provided that all discrimination claims shall be subject to the grievance and arbitration procedures of the collective bargaining agreement as the sole and exclusive remedy for violations. In reaching its holding, the Court distinguished its earlier decision in *Gardner-Denver*, where the collective bargaining agreement contained an anti-discrimination clause, but did not mention Title VII or any other anti-discrimination statute, and did not empower the arbitrator to resolve disputes arising under statutory law. In *Gardner-Denver*, the arbitrator sat "as the proctor of the bargain" with authority to resolve contract claims; by contrast, in *Pyett*, the arbitrator was authorized also to resolve statutory discrimination claims as well as contract claims.

While most collective bargaining agreements contain non-discrimination provisions, *14 Penn Plaza* raises the question of whether it would be advantageous for the employer and unionized employees to negotiate a clause in the collective bargaining agreement that clearly provides for arbitration of statutory claims of discrimination. One unresolved question is whether employees are bound by the collective bargaining agreement's waiver of the judicial forum when the union does not take the case to arbitration.

Q 6.28.2   What is the extent of a court's authority in compelling arbitration?

In compelling arbitration, courts may consider only whether a valid agreement to arbitrate exists and whether the specific dispute falls within the substantive scope of the agreement. In deciding whether the parties have agreed to submit a particular grievance to arbitration, the court is not to rule on the potential merits of the underlying claims. Moreover, if the contract contains an arbitration clause, there is a presumption of arbitrability and "an order to arbitrate the grievance should not be denied unless it may be said with positive assurance that the arbitration clause is not susceptible of an interpretation that covers the asserted dispute."[35] Under this presumption, any doubts regarding whether a particular dispute is arbitral are resolved in favor of arbitration.

Q 6.28.3   Are arbitration awards subject to review?

Arbitration awards may be subject to review in federal district courts under section 301 of the LMRA. In determining whether to enforce an existing arbitration award, the court cannot rule on the merits of the grievance or refuse to enforce an award merely because its interpretation of the contract differs from the arbitrator's. Rather, a court can refuse to enforce an arbitrator's award if it fails to "draw[ ] its essence" from the agreement.[36] Arbitrators have no obligation to give the court reasons for their awards, and a mere ambiguity in an arbitrator's opinion from which an inference could be drawn that the arbitrator exceeded contractual authority is not grounds for refusing to enforce the award.

The general rule is that arbitrators are confined to interpreting and applying the parties' collective bargaining agreement and "may not ignore the plain language of the contract."[37] Where an arbitrator "ignore[s] the contract and dispense[s] his own brand of industrial justice," the rendered award fails to draw its essence from the parties' agreement and is unenforceable.[38] Thus, reviewing courts should be more open to vacating awards where the agreement expressly limits the arbitrator's authority and the arbitrator disregards that limitation. However, in practice, courts give tremendous deference to arbitrators, and arbitration awards are typically only overturned in cases of egregious misapplication of the terms of the collective bargaining agreement.

A court may also refuse to enforce an arbitration award where the remedial action ordered by the arbitrator violates strong and clearly defined public policy, ascertained by reference to laws and legal precedents rather than some general considerations of supposed public interests.[39] Parties can also seek to vacate an arbitrator's award on grounds of arbitrator corruption, misconduct, or partiality,[40] or where the award sustains or requires an illegal act.[41] Where a party challenges an award based on corruption, it need not show prejudice.

However, where it challenges an award based on arbitral misconduct or partiality, it is required to show prejudice.

Additionally, courts may penalize a party who brings a frivolous action to set aside an award or who, without justification, refuses to comply with an award and forces the other party to resort to court action for its enforcement. In such a situation, a court may require payment of the prevailing party's attorney fees and court costs.

Injunctions

Q 6.29   When may a court issue an injunction against a labor dispute?

The Norris-LaGuardia Act limits judicial interference in labor disputes by prohibiting federal courts from issuing injunctions that restrict or thwart actions taken in connection with a labor dispute, such as peaceful strike activity. The purpose of the LMRA is to promote peaceful resolution of labor disputes through voluntary arbitration. To this end, the LMRA grants federal courts jurisdiction over labor disputes involving collective bargaining agreements. The U.S. Supreme Court's decision in *Boys Markets v. Retail Clerks Union*[42] attempted to reconcile the seemingly conflicting commands of the Norris-LaGuardia Act and the LMRA.

In *Boys Markets*, the Court ruled that an employer could obtain an injunction against a strike if the collective bargaining agreement contained a no-strike clause, the strike involved a grievance subject to the arbitration process, and the injunction was warranted under "ordinary principles of equity."[43] The Court reasoned that the union's promise not to strike was the quid pro quo for the employer's promise to abide by binding arbitration and failing to restrain the union from striking over arbitral disputes would eliminate the employer's incentive to agree to arbitrate.[44] Thus, a *"Boys Markets* injunction" is a limited exception to the Norris-LaGuardia Act. Employers may obtain injunctions under section 301 against strikes pending the arbitration of a dispute. In addition to obtaining an injunction against strikes, an employer may seek a *Boys Markets* injunction for other employee activities that violate a no-strike clause, including a work slowdown,[45] a concerted refusal not to work overtime,[46] and other work stoppages based upon a concerted exercise of individual rights under the collective bargaining agreement.[47]

In a subsequent decision, *Buffalo Forge Co. v. United Steelworkers*,[48] the Court limited the availability of *Boys Markets* injunctions to strikes or other work stoppages over arbitral disputes. That case involves one union's honoring the picket line of another union, arguably in breach of the first union's no-strike pledge. The first union may have been liable for breach of contract, but an injunction could not issue under Norris-LaGuardia in the absence of the kind of undue pressure over the arbitration process inherent in a strike over an arbitral grievance.

Q 6.29.1   What is a "reverse *Boys Markets*" injunction?

A reverse *Boys Markets* injunction is an injunction to maintain the status quo pending arbitration and thereby preserve the remedial power of the arbitrator. While an injunction to maintain the status quo may be issued against either an employer or the union, reverse *Boys Markets* injunctions are most often sought against the employer to block the employer's plans to substantially change its operations in the face of union opposition. For example, such an injunction may issue where an employer's imminent plan to close a plant or a part of its operation or permanently lay off workers may render an arbitrator's award meaningless.

A reverse *Boys Markets* injunction will be issued where it is necessary to "prevent conduct by the party enjoined from rendering the arbitral process a hollow formality in those instances where . . . the arbitral award when rendered could not return the parties substantially to the status quo ante."[49] The arbitration process is rendered meaningless only if any arbitral award in favor of the union would substantially fail to undo the harm occasioned by the lack of a status quo injunction. Federal courts are to exercise great restraint in granting reverse *Boys Markets* injunctions, and traditional principles of equity apply to reverse *Boys Markets* injunctions. Thus, the union is required to show:

(1) it will suffer irreparable injury if the injunction is not issued;

(2) the potential harm to the employer from the injunction does not clearly outweigh the potential harm to the union without an injunction; and

(3) it has a reasonable likelihood of success on the merits.

Irreparable injury does not simply mean any injury resulting from a breach of contract that would not be fully redressed by an arbitral award; it means an injury so "irreparable that a decision in the Union's favor would be an empty victory."[50] A reverse *Boys Markets* injunction should issue only where an injunction is needed to preserve the remedial authority of the arbitrator should the arbitrator later find a violation. For example, it may be appropriate when a union challenges the employer's sale of the company because the "consummation of the sale before an arbitrator had an opportunity to rule on the Union's contention that the sale violated the labor agreement would have presented the arbitrator with a *fait accompli*."[51] On the other hand, there was no irreparable harm where a union challenged an employer's process of drug testing, because the arbitrator could provide other relief for any violation.[52]

Q 6.29.2   What are the requirements to obtain a *Boys Markets* injunction?

Courts will not automatically issue a *Boys Markets* injunction. At the outset, the collective bargaining agreement must contain a mandatory grievance and arbitration process, and the issue at the center of the employee activity must be covered by the provision. Additionally, the following prerequisites must be met:

(1) the strike or other conduct must be in breach of a contractual obligation not to strike (although an express no-strike provision is not required);

(2) the strike or other conduct must relate to a grievance that the parties are contractually required to arbitrate; and

(3) ordinary principles of equity require the court to issue an injunction.[53]

Ordinary principles of equity require the court to consider whether the alleged breaches "have caused or will cause irreparable injury to the employer; and whether the employer will suffer more from the denial of an injunction than will the union from its issuance."[54] The same presumption of arbitrability first declared in the *Steelworkers Trilogy* applies to the *Boys Markets* injunction analysis.[55]

Duty of Fair Representation

Q 6.30   What is the union's duty of fair representation?

A union acting as exclusive bargaining agency has a duty to represent fairly all of the employees in the bargaining unit. This includes a statutory obligation "to serve the interests of all members without hostility or discrimination toward any, to exercise its discretion with complete good faith and honesty, and to avoid arbitrary conduct."[56]

Most of the alleged violations of the union's duty of fair representation (DFR) occur in the grievance and arbitration context. Individual employees do not have an absolute right to have a grievance taken to arbitration. Union representatives generally have considerable discretion in the processing and presentation of grievances; negligence, poor judgment, or ineptitude are generally insufficient to establish a breach of the union's duty. However, the union may not arbitrarily ignore a meritorious grievance or process it in perfunctory fashion. Courts differ as to whether a union can be held liable for failure to call witnesses at the proceedings.

An employee can seek judicial enforcement of contractual rights if the union has the sole power under the agreement to invoke the higher stages of the grievance procedure and if the employee has been prevented from exhausting the contractual remedies by the union's wrongful refusal to process the grievance. However, a union's refusal is wrongful and, therefore, in breach of its duty of fair representation, only when the union's conduct is "arbitrary, discriminatory, or in bad faith." There is no definitive answer about what constitutes actionable arbitrariness on the part of the union. The majority of courts have ruled that, to be actionable, a union has to be more than negligent, but the courts differ regarding what level of culpability beyond simple negligence is required to state a claim for breach of the DFR.

DFR claims are actionable in federal court. Remedies include both injunctive relief and damages. The remedies imposed upon unions for breaches of its duty vary, but include:

(1) cease-and-desist orders;

(2) orders requiring unions to request the employer to reconsider the grievance;

(3) orders requiring unions to take the grievance to arbitration; and

(4) orders requiring unions to file a lawsuit in federal court to compel arbitration.

The NLRB may, in some circumstances, order a union to make an employee whole by awarding back pay and reimbursement of the employee's costs, including attorneys' fees.

The DFR also applies to contract negotiations but with much less vigor. Courts review the union's actions with respect to contract negotiations with a high level of deference. The union's conduct must be "so far outside a 'wide range of reasonableness,' . . . that it is wholly 'irrational' or 'arbitrary.'"[57] A union breaches its DFR if its bargaining position is motivated by hostility or illegal considerations.

Q 6.30.1   What is a "hybrid claim"?

Generally, an employee bringing suit against the union for an alleged breach of the DFR should also bring a section 301 action against the employer in the same suit, generally referred to as a hybrid claim. An employee cannot prevail on a hybrid section 301 claim against either the employer or the union if the employee can show only that the employer violated the labor contract or that the union breached its DFR. In other words, to prevail against either the employer or the union, the employee must be able to prove both elements.

Where an employee has successfully proven a section 301 hybrid claim, damages are apportioned between the employer and the union, according the fault of each. Generally, the employer is liable for those damages that occurred before the union's breach, and the union is liable for those damages that occurred after the union's breach.

While Congress did not enact a statute of limitations for section 301 actions, the U.S. Supreme Court has adopted the six-month statute of limitations applicable to claims brought under the NLRA as the limitations period for hybrid section 301 lawsuits.[58] The six-month period begins to run from the time "when an employee discovers, or should have discovered with exercise of due diligence, acts giving rise to the cause of action."[59]

Notes to Chapter 6

1.   United Steelworkers of Am. v. Warrior & Gulf Navigation Co., 363 U.S. 574 (1960).

2.   Teamsters Local 174 v. Lucas Flour Co., 369 U.S. 95 (1962).

3.   Janus v. State, Cty., Mun. Emps. Council 31, 138 S. Ct. 2448 (2018).

4.   Commc'ns Workers of Am. v. Beck, 487 U.S. 735 (1988).

5.   Chem. Workers v. Pittsburgh Plate Glass Co., 404 U.S. 157, 172 (1971).

6.   Trojan Yacht, 319 N.L.R.B. 741 (1995).

7.   *See, e.g.*, Hass v. Darigold Dairy Prods. Co., 751 F.2d 1096 (9th Cir. 1985); *see also* ILWU v. Kuntz, 334 F.2d 165 (9th Cir. 1964); Hardcastle v. W. Greyhound Lines, 303 F.2d 182 (9th Cir. 1953).

8.   *See, e.g.*, Ayala v. Union de Tronquistas de P.R., Local 901, 74 F.3d 344 (1st Cir. 1996); *see also* United Steelworkers v. Warrior & Gulf Navigation Co., 363 U.S. 574 (1960).

9.   *See* NLRB v. Dist. 23, United Mine Workers of Am., 921 F.2d 645 (6th Cir. 1990); *see also* Hass v. Darigold Dairy Prods. Co., 751 F.2d 1096 (9th Cir. 1985).

10.   Oddie v. Ross Gear & Tool Co., 305 F.2d 143 (6th Cir. 1962).

11.   Thomas v. Bakery, Confectionery, & Tobacco Workers Local 433, 982 F.2d 1215 (8th Cir. 1992).

12.   Rakestraw v. United Airlines, 981 F.2d 1524 (1992).

13.   *See* NLRB v. Joy Techs., Inc., 990 F.2d 104 (3d Cir. 1993); *see also* Teamsters Local 20 v. NLRB, 610 F.2d 991 (D.C. Cir. 1979); D'Amico v. NLRB, 582 F.2d 820 (3d Cir. 1978); Mechs. Educ. Soc'y of Am., Local 56, 287 N.L.R.B. 935 (1987); Gulton Electro Voice, 276 N.L.R.B. 1043 (1985); Dairylea Cooperative, Inc., 219 N.L.R.B. 656 (1975).

14.   29 U.S.C. §§ 151–69.

15.   *Warrior & Gulf*, 363 U.S. at 582.

16.   AT&T Tech. v. Commc'ns Workers of Am., 475 U.S. 643, 649 (1986).

17.   John Wiley & Sons, Inc. v. Livingston, 376 U.S. 543, 556–58 (1964).

18.   Trans World Air Lines, 47 Lab. Arb. Rep. (BNA) 1127, 1130 (1967).

19.   *John Wiley & Sons*, 376 U.S. at 558.

20.   Stephens Media, LLC, 359 N.L.R.B. No. 39 (2012).

21.   Am. Baptist Homes of W., 359 N.L.R.B. No. 46 (2012).

22.   Am. Baptist Homes of W., 199 L.R.R.M. (BNA) 2084 (NLRB June 27, 2014) ("In view of the Court's decision in *Noel Canning*, pursuant to Section 10(d) of the National Labor Relations Act, the Board hereby sets aside the above-referenced Decision and Order.").

23.   EEOC v. Waffle House, Inc., 534 U.S. 279 (2002).

24.   29 U.S.C. § 158(d) (1982) (emphasis added).

25. Textile Workers Union v. Lincoln Mills, 353 U.S. 448, 456–57 (1957).

26. 29 U.S.C. § 104.

27. *Lincoln Mills*, 353 U.S. at 455.

28. *See* Steelworkers v. Enter. Wheel & Car Corp., 363 U.S. 593 (1960); *see also* Steelworkers v. Warrior & Gulf Navigation Co., 363 U.S. 574 (1960); Steelworkers v. Am. Mfg. Co., 363 U.S. 564 (1960).

29. *Am. Mfg. Co.*, 363 U.S. at 568.

30. *Warrior & Gulf*, 363 U.S. at 583.

31. *Enterprise Wheel & Car*, 363 U.S. at 597.

32. Alexander v. Gardner-Denver Co., 415 U.S. 36 (1974).

33. Gilmer v. Interstate/Johnson Lane Corp., 500 U.S. 20 (1991).

34. 14 Penn Plaza LLC v. Pyett, 556 U.S. 247 (2009).

35. *Am. Mfg. Co.*, 363 U.S. at 568.

36. *Enterprise Wheel & Car*, 363 U.S. at 597.

37. *Misco*, 484 U.S. at 38.

38. Madison Hotel v. Hotel & Rest. Emps., Local 25, AFL-CIO, 144 F.3d 855, 858–59 (D.C. Cir. 1998) (quoting *Enterprise Wheel & Car*, 363 U.S. at 597).

39. *Misco*, 484 U.S. at 43.

40. *See* Longshoremen's Ass'n Local 1982 v. Midwest Terminals of Toledo Int'l, Inc., 560 F. App'x 529, 537, (6th Cir. 2014) (noting that appropriate question for review includes "Did the arbitrator commit fraud, have a conflict of interest or otherwise act dishonestly in issuing the award?" but noting that "judicial intervention should be resisted even though the arbitrator made 'serious,' 'improvident' or 'silly' errors in resolving the merits of the dispute.").

41. *Cf.* Air Line Pilots v. Trans States Airlines LLC, 638 F.3d 572 (8th Cir. 2011).

42. Boys Mkts. v. Retail Clerks Union, 398 U.S. 235 (1970).

43. *Id.* at 254.

44. Sinclair Ref. Co. v. Atkinson, 370 U.S. 195, 218 (1962) (Brennan, J., dissenting).

45. *See* Nat'l Elevator Indus. v. Elevator Constructors, 776 F.2d 374 (1st Cir. 1985); *see also* Otis Elevator Co. v. Elevator Constructors Local 1, 684 F. Supp. 80 (S.D.N.Y. 1988).

46. *National Elevator*, 776 F.2d at 378.

47. *See* Catalytic, Inc. v. Bldg. Trades Council, 829 F.2d 430 (3d Cir. 1987); *see also* Otis Elevator Co. v. Elevator Constructors Local 1, 684 F. Supp. 80, 83 (S.D.N.Y. 1988); Wireless Cable of N.Y. v. Elec. Workers (IBEW) Local 3, 1987 WL 17423, at *1 (S.D.N.Y. Sept. 17, 1987).

48. Buffalo Forge Co. v. United Steelworkers, 428 U.S. 397 (1976).

49. Lever Bros. Co. v. Chem. Workers Local 217, 554 F.2d 115, 123 (4th Cir. 1976).

50. Local Lodge No. 1266 v. Panoramic Corp., 668 F.2d 276 (7th Cir. 1981).

51. *Panoramic Corp.*, 668 F.2d at 276.

52. Local Union No. 733 of Int'l Bhd. of Elec. Workers v. Ingalls Shipbuilding Div., Litton Sys., Inc., 906 F.2d 149, 150–51 (5th Cir. 1990).

53. *Boys Markets*, 398 U.S. at 254.

54. *Id.*

55. Gateway Coal Co. v. Mine Workers Dist. 4, Local 6330, 414 U.S. 368 (1974).

56. Vaca v. Sipes, 386 U.S. 171 (1967).

57. Air Line Pilots v. O'Neill, 499 U.S. 65 (1991).

58. DelCostello v. Int'l Bhd. of Teamsters, 462 U.S. 151, 155, 169 (1983).

59. Wilson v. Int'l Bhd. of Teamsters, 83 F.3d 747, 757 (6th Cir. 1996).

7

Strikes, Picketing, Boycotts, and Lockouts

The National Labor Relations Act (NLRA) permits employers and unions to use a variety of tactics to achieve their goals. In addition to conducting strikes, unions may engage in picketing, distribute handbills, display banners, and even wage multifaceted "corporate campaigns." For their part, employers may conduct lockouts, permanently replace economic strikers, and discipline employees who engage in unprotected activity. This chapter explores the legal rules governing the use of these "weapons of economic warfare" by unions and employers.

Strikes

The Basics

Q 7.1   What is a strike?

A strike is the temporary or permanent withdrawal of labor by employees to put pressure on an employer. Strikes can take many forms, from a walkout with the complete refusal to perform work, to the refusal to perform only mandatory overtime work. As discussed below, only some types of strikes are protected by the NLRA. Just as employees have a protected right to engage in strike activities, employees also have a statutory right to cross picket lines and continue to work during a strike.[1]

Q 7.2   Do employees have an absolute right to strike?

Employees generally have the right under the law to strike subject to certain statutory limitations. However, the right to strike can be waived in a collective bargaining agreement (CBA). The great majority of CBAs contain "no strike/no lockout" provisions which restrict and often eliminate the right to strike or to lockout during the term of the CBA. An employee's right to engage in a strike or refuse to perform work derives from section 7 of the NLRA, which provides that employees have the right "to engage in concerted activities for the purpose of collective bargaining or other mutual aid and protection."[2] Not all employee strikes and work stoppages are legally protected by the NLRA.

The motivation for the strike or work stoppage and the tactics employed will generally determine the legality of the strike under the NLRA. Courts and the NLRB often are faced with balancing employees' right to engage in certain strike or work stoppage activities against property, contract, and other rights of employers. The applicable CBA between the employees' authorized labor representative and their employer often limits the right to engage in a strike and other forms of protected concerted activity.

Employer handbook provisions that might conflict with workers' right to strike may be unlawful. In *Ambassador Services, Inc.*,[3] the NLRB held that employees could reasonably construe a rule prohibiting "walking off the job and/or leaving the premises during working hours without permission" as chilling their right to strike. Rules that prohibited "willfully restricting production" and "walking off the job and/or leaving the premises during working hours without permission" were similarly unlawful.[4]

NLRA-Protected Strikes

Q 7.3   Which strikes are generally protected under the NLRA?

Generally, for a strike to fall within the legal protections of the NLRA, the strike must involve a "labor dispute." The term "labor dispute" is defined by the NLRA as follows:

> any controversy concerning terms, tenure or conditions of employment, or concerning the association or representation of persons in negotiating, fixing, maintaining, changing or seeking to arrange terms and conditions of employment, regardless of whether the disputants stand in the proximate relation of employer and employee.[5]

Protected strikes fall into two categories: economic strikes and ULP strikes. Employees who engage in protected strikes are generally protected from discipline or discharge, subject to exceptions.[6] Both types of strikes are discussed in detail below.

Strikes Not Protected by the NLRA

Q 7.4   Which kinds of strikes are not protected under the NLRA?

The NLRA provides protection only for lawfully conducted economic and ULP strikes. The NLRB and the courts have found various types of work stoppages to be illegal based on such things as improper tactics or improper motivations. Employees who engage in illegal strikes or other work stoppages are not protected under the NLRA and are subject to discipline or discharge.

Certain types of strikes or work stoppages, although not necessarily illegal, are unprotected under the NLRA. Examples of unprotected strikes or work stoppages include:

- sit-down strikes;
- intermittent strikes;
- partial strikes;

- production slowdowns;

- strikes over permissive or illegal subjects of bargaining;

- violations of a no-strike clause in a collective bargaining agreement; and

- wildcat strikes (that is, unauthorized strikes).

Q 7.4.1   What is a sit-down strike?

A sit-down strike generally occurs where employees refuse to work, take possession of the employer's premises, and attempt to exclude others from entering the employer's premises. The U.S. Supreme Court, in *NLRB v. Fansteel Metallurgical Corp.*,[7] held that sit-down strikes are unprotected due to the infringement of the employer's property rights. Thus, the employer did not commit a ULP when it discharged the employees who engaged in the unprotected sit-down strike.

Recent NLRB decisions suggest that employees engaged in a peaceful in-plant work stoppage may be protected in limited circumstances under the NLRA for a reasonable period of time. A peaceful work stoppage is one where employees have the sincere intent to address a work-related complaint, as opposed to interference with an employer's right to maintain ongoing control of the plant. For example, in *Benesight, Inc.*,[8] the NLRB held that the employees who engaged in an in-plant strike that was peaceful, focused on a specific work-related complaint, and "cause[d] little disruption of production by those employees who continue work" were engaged in protected activity.

Q 7.4.2   ... an intermittent strike?

Intermittent strikes are repeated work stoppages that are part of a planned strategy intended to harass the company, and/or to interfere with production or the provision of services. Intermittent strikes are viewed by the NLRB as "an arrogation of the [employer's] right to determine [employee] schedules and hours of work. . . . An employer is not required . . . to alter and adjust his operating schedules and hours to the changing whim which may suit the employees' or a union's purpose."[9]

Intermittent strikes are unprotected under the NLRA. To establish that a strike was part of an intermittent strike, the employer has to show a plan to engage in intermittent strikes, not merely separate strikes in reaction to different facts and circumstances. For example, the NLRB has found that recurring weekend strike activities that were part of a union's bargaining strategy to exert pressure on the employer were intermittent strikes, and thus, the employees' strike activity was unprotected conduct for which they could be disciplined.[10]

Intermittent strikes must be contrasted with single-walkout situations in response to different issues. A single short-term walkout in response to a discrete issue is presumptively protected, but if the walkout is part of a pattern or plan to usurp company time and harass the company, it is not protected by the NLRA. For example, when employees left work two to three separate times to attend union meetings on company time, the NLRB found that the employees were engaged in an unprotected intermittent strike.[11] Although employees are entitled to strike, they are not "entitled to walk out and return and to engage in this activity repeatedly."[12] The NLRB, adopting the administrative law judge's opinion, contrasted the two to three walkouts with a single short-term work stoppage to protest working conditions such as cold weather or a heavy workload, which would be a protected activity.

Q 7.4.3   ... a partial strike?

Partial strikes are unprotected work stoppages where employees refuse to perform certain, but not all, assigned tasks, while accepting pay and/or remaining on the employer's premises. The NLRB views such strikes as an attempt to usurp the employer's lawful right to assign work. As the NLRB explained:

> While employees may protest and ultimately seek to change any term or condition of their employment by striking or engaging in a work stoppage, the strike or stoppage must be complete, that is, the employees must withhold all their services from the employer. They cannot pick and choose the work they will do or when they will do it. Such conduct constitutes an attempt by the employees to set their own terms and conditions of employment in defiance of their employer's authority to determine those matters and is unprotected.[13]

For example, the NLRB found that an employee's conduct was not protected strike conduct when she solicited other employees to stop referring certain telephone calls to, interacting with, or referring service requests to the company's vendor after she found out that the vendor's employees might go on strike.[14] The employee's conduct amounted to a solicitation of a partial strike, and thus, the employer did not commit a ULP charge by terminating the employee for her conduct. Similarly, where nurse's aides refused to assist with a vacant section in a nursing home but continued to perform work in their own sections, the NLRB found that the nurse's aides engaged in an unprotected partial strike and the employer was justified in discharging the nurse's aides.[15]

Refusal to work mandatory overtime may constitute a partial strike when it is used as a bargaining tactic to put pressure on an employer.[16] However, concerted refusals to work non-mandatory overtime are protected activities and do not constitute an unprotected partial strike.[17]

Q 7.4.4   Are work slowdowns protected?

The NLRA protects only certain complete work stoppages. Work slowdowns, like partial strikes, are considered unprotected conduct. Slowdowns in production are also considered conduct for which employees can be disciplined or discharged. For example, in *Daimler Chrysler Corp.*,[18] the NLRB found that an employee engaged in unprotected activity when she solicited other employees to engage in a deliberate slowdown of production activities.

Another form of work slowdown is a "work-to-rule" campaign, where employees do only the minimum requirements of their job, or follow each work rule, including safety rules, to the letter. This tactic is designed to impede production by limiting efforts and frustrating management. The NLRB, in two separate decisions, has assumed, without affirmatively holding, that work-to-rule campaigns constitute unprotected partial strike activities.[19] In each case, the NLRB noted that work-to-rule situations raise "difficult issues."

Q 7.4.5   Are strikes over permissive or illegal subjects of bargaining protected?

The NLRA protects strikes over mandatory subjects of bargaining, such as wages, hours, and working conditions. While unions and employers may also lawfully negotiate over permissive subjects of bargaining, such as changes in the scope of the bargaining unit, it is illegal for a union to strike over a permissive subject of bargaining because there is no NLRA right on the part of the non-controlling party to use economic pressure to insist on its position over a permissive subject. It follows that unions are clearly prohibited from striking over an illegal subject of bargaining. Permissive and mandatory subjects of bargaining are covered in chapter 5; examples of permissive bargaining subjects that the union may not strike over include: a guaranty clause requiring the corporate parent to guarantee performance, an interest arbitration clause, an enlargement of the bargaining unit, and a decision to close down a product line.

Q 7.4.6   What remedies does an employer have when a union violates a no-strike agreement?

In a collective bargaining agreement, unions often waive employees' right to strike in certain circumstances. These no-strike clauses range from a broad prohibition of all strikes, work stoppages, and sympathy strikes, to clauses preserving the right to strike in response to certain actions, such as failure of an employer to participate in the grievance procedure. Thus, the scope of the no-strike clause will determine the extent of the prohibition on the employees' right to strike.[20] In addition to damage actions, employers faced with a strike in violation of a no-strike provision may seek a "Boys Market" injunction in federal court, if the relevant CBA also contains an arbitration provision covering the dispute.[21]

If a union strikes in violation of a no-strike clause, the employer may discipline or discharge the employees who strike. Further, the employer has the option of suing the union for damages for breaching a no-strike clause. The right to sue for breach of a no-strike clause stems from section 301 of the LMRA. Employers may seek monetary damages against a union, not against individual employees, and damages are appropriate in the amount of the actual losses sustained by the employer as a result of the breach of contract and that "may rea-sonably be supposed to have been in the contemplation of the parties as the probable result of such a breach at the time the agreement was made."[22]

No-strike clauses typically do not survive the expiration of a collec-tive bargaining agreement unless there is clear evidence that the par-ties intended the clause to survive the expiration of the agreement.[23]

Q 7.4.7   What is a "wildcat" strike?

When employees represented by a union engage in their own strikes or work stoppages without the union's authorization, such strikes are referred to as "wildcat" strikes.[24] Wildcat strikes may be unprotected if there is evidence that the strikers were attempting to deal with the employer without the union, or if the demands of the strikers are inconsistent with union demands and policies.[25] Employees who participate in unprotected wildcat strikes are sub-ject to discipline and discharge.[26] Wildcat strikes that do not meet such standards (that is, that are not attempts to deal without the union, or where the demands are consistent with the union's demands) may be protected, and an employer may not discharge or discipline employees for participating in protected wildcat strikes.[27]

Employees who participate in a wildcat strike in violation of a col-lective bargaining agreement's no-strike clause are engaged in unpro-tected activity and may be disciplined or discharged.

Strike Conduct

Q 7.5   Can employees engage in a sympathy strike or honor the picket line of another striking union?

An employee has a right to refuse to cross a lawful picket line maintained by the employee's union or another labor organization unless that employee's union has waived the employee's right in the collective bargaining agreement. The NLRB has held that a general no-strike clause does not necessarily waive the right of the represented employees to choose whether to honor another union's picket line.

The NLRB will look to the language of the no-strike clause to determine if the union's waiver of the right to engage in a sympathy strike covers both employees and the union and will also look to extrinsic evidence including the parties' discussions of the clause during bargaining. The NLRB does, however, employ a rebuttable presumption that a broad no-strike clause precludes unions from calling sympathy strikes.[28]

Although employees have a lawful right to refuse to cross a picket line, employers have a corresponding right to continue to run their business and may replace an employee who refuses to cross a picket line in limited situations. Employers may only exercise this right when they are acting "to preserve efficient operation" of their business.[29] Where employees' refusal to cross a picket line does not disrupt the employer's business in any significant way, replacement of those employees is not justified and will be held unlawful.[30]

Q 7.6   What constitutes strike misconduct?

While employees have the right to strike peacefully, employees who act violently or threateningly during a strike may lose their legal protections and be discharged. Discharging an employee for engaging in strike misconduct is not a ULP. In *Clear Pine Mouldings*, the NLRB held that serious misconduct or violence during a strike can lead to lawful discharge if, after considering all the circumstances, the conduct in question "would reasonably tend to coerce or intimidate employees in the exercise" of their rights, including the right to refrain from striking.[31] While some confrontation between strikers and non-strikers is inevitable, the NLRB has found various types of strike misconduct serious enough to justify discharge, including stone throwing at individuals not participating in a strike, cursing and insulting a healthcare employer's patients, and malicious destruction of private property.[32] On the other hand, the use of a water gun, even when pointed and squirted at a security guard, was not conduct that coerced or intimidated and, thus, was protected.[33] To establish a strike misconduct discharge defense, employers must show that they had an honest belief that the employee was guilty of strike misconduct of a serious nature.

Economic Strikes Versus Unfair Labor Practice Strikes

Q 7.7   What is the difference between an economic strike and a ULP strike?

Whether the employees are engaged in an economic strike or an unfair labor practice (ULP) strike is determined by the purpose of the strike. An economic strike is commonly defined as a dispute over terms and conditions of employment. Employees out on an economic strike are trying to persuade their employer to agree to certain bargaining demands. By contrast, a ULP strike occurs when employees are striking in whole or in part to protest ULPs committed by an employer. Examples of employer ULPs that can lead to a ULP strike include discrimination against union members, refusal to bargain in good faith, and unilateral changes in terms and conditions of employment.

The difference between an economic strike and a ULP strike has important practical consequences because, while employers lawfully can hire permanent replacements for economic strikers, they cannot lawfully hire permanent replacements for ULP strikers. Hence, whenever a ULP striker is ready to return to work, he or she can bump a replacement. In addition, the replacements for economic strikers are voting members of the bargaining unit, while the replacements for ULP strikers are not.

During either type of strike, state law will determine whether strikers are eligible for unemployment compensation benefits. In *New York Telephone Co. v. New York State Department of Labor*,[34] the U.S. Supreme Court ruled that states' laws on overtime compensation do not intrude into an area the Congress intended to reserve solely for federal labor law.

Finally, just as employees have a protected right to engage in strike activities, employees also have a statutory right to cross picket lines and continue to work.[35]

Q 7.7.1   Can a strike be both an economic strike and a ULP strike?

Yes, a strike can be motivated by both employee economic concerns and concerns about employer ULPs. The NLRB and the courts have required evidence that an employer's ULP was a contributing factor in a decision to strike for the strike to be deemed a ULP strike. For example, in *Citizens Publishing & Printing Co. v. NLRB*,[36] the U.S. Court of Appeals for the Third Circuit upheld the NLRB's decision that a strike was a ULP strike because there was evidence that the employees had decided to strike based on their concern that the employer was unlawfully subcontracting work from union employees. In that case, the union's disclosure to the employees that the NLRB would be issuing a ULP complaint about the alleged unlawful subcontracting "galvanized the bargaining unit members' belief that a ULP had been committed and served as the flashpoint for discussion about calling a strike."[37]

Furthermore, an economic strike can be converted into a ULP strike by the employer's commission of ULPs after the commencement of the economic strike. For example, in *Gloversville Embossing Corp.*,[38] the NLRB found that an employer's illegal statements to employees threatening them with termination after an economic strike commenced converted the economic strike into a ULP strike. To prove a conversion of an economic strike to a ULP, the NLRB and the courts have required evidence that the ULP actually prolonged the economic strike and that the strike was expanded to include a protest over the ULP.[39]

Employer's Response to a Strike

Q 7.8   How can an employer lawfully respond to an economic strike?

Employers have a number of options in response to an economic strike. Employers may temporarily subcontract union work during a strike,[40] but permanent subcontracting of union work during a strike may convert the strike to a ULP strike.[41] In addition, employers may lawfully stockpile inventories, readjust contract schedules, or transfer work from one plant to another, so long as there is no evidence of unlawful anti-union motivation.[42] Further, during an economic strike, an employer can hire temporary or permanent replacements for the strikers or use supervisory personnel to perform the work of the striking employees. Because temporary replacements cease working for the employer no later than when the strike ends, more questions arise regarding the hiring of permanent replacements.

Q 7.8.1   What are an employer's obligations when hiring permanent replacements?

When hiring replacements, employers have the burden to establish that the replacements hired are permanent by showing a mutual understanding between the employer and the replacements that the nature of the employment is permanent as opposed to temporary. An employer who promises replacement workers permanent positions but later discharges the replacements to make room for reinstated striking employees could face claims of breach-of-contract and other state law claims. The U.S. Supreme Court has held that such actions are not preempted by the NLRA. But employers generally may insulate themselves from suits by making any promise of permanent employment subject to the non-occurrence of a settlement with the union or an NLRB order on a ULP charge requiring reinstatement of replaced strikers.[43]

The NLRB held, in *Jones Plastic & Engineering Co.*,[44] that at-will employment of replacements is not necessarily inconsistent with permanent replacement status. Employment at-will generally means that either the employer or the employee can terminate the relationship without cause, and there is no defined term of employment. Despite the fact that the replacements were employed at-will, the NLRB evaluated the employer's offer letters and verbal statements to the permanent replacements and found sufficient evidence that there was a mutual understanding of job retention and that the individuals were in fact permanent replacements for the striking employees.

Q 7.8.2   Can replaced economic strikers ever get their jobs back?

A striking employee who has been permanently replaced still retains certain reinstatement rights even if he or she cannot displace the permanent replacement for the job. The rights of these employees were established by the NLRB's *Laidlaw Corp.* decision, wherein the NLRB defined the status and rights of economic strikers who had been permanently replaced:

[E]conomic strikers who unconditionally apply for reinstatement at a time when their positions are filled by permanent replacements: (1) remain employees; and (2) are entitled to full reinstatement upon the departure of replacements unless they have in the meantime acquired regular and substantially equivalent employment, or the employer can sustain his burden of proof that the failure to offer full reinstatement was for legitimate and substantial business reasons.[45]

Further, strikers who apply for reinstatement are entitled to their pre-strike preferential hiring rights from the parties' collective bargaining agreement.[46]

Q 7.8.3   How can an employer lawfully respond to a ULP strike?

During a ULP strike, an employer may hire temporary (but not permanent) replacements for the strikers or use supervisory personnel to carry on the business during the strike. Employees participating in a ULP strike must be immediately reinstated to their former jobs upon making an unconditional offer to return to work. The offer to return to work should be made by all employees seeking reinstatement; a letter listing some but not all employees seeking reinstatement will only be effectual for those listed employees. A union may, however, make a collective request covering all members. The offer need not be in writing; thus, an employee who presents himself and offers to return to work has made the appropriate unconditional offer. Further, the offer must be made without restrictions. An offer to return to work only if the employer recognized and bargained with the union was not an unconditional offer to return to work.[47]

Any replacements hired during the ULP strike must be dismissed, if necessary, to accomplish the reinstatement of the strikers.

Employees'/Union's Strike-Related Actions and Responsibilities

Q 7.9   Can employees walk out where they contend that the company is operating under abnormally dangerous conditions?

Even a broad no-strike clause in a collective bargaining agreement cannot prohibit strikes authorized by section 502 of the LMRA, which protects employees who stop working based on a good-faith belief of abnormally dangerous work conditions at the place of employment. Specifically, if an employee can establish such a good-faith belief, he or she is not required to continue to work in the unsafe conditions, and his or her conduct is not considered a strike.

The NLRB evaluates whether employees have met their burden to establish a good-faith belief of abnormally dangerous conditions on a case-by-case basis. In *TNS, Inc.*,[48] the NLRB articulated a multi-part test to establish protection under section 502:

(1)   the employee believed in good faith that work conditions were abnormally dangerous;

(2)   the employee's belief of abnormally dangerous working conditions was the cause of the work stoppage;

(3)   the employee's belief was supported by ascertainable, objective evidence; and

(4)   the perceived danger posed an immediate threat of harm to the employee's health or safety.

If the employee establishes protection under section 502, NLRB precedent provides that an employer is not allowed to hire permanent replacements for the employee.[49] At least one federal court of appeals has upheld the NLRB's multi-part test and its conclusion that permanent replacements are not allowed if employees establish section 502 protected activity.[50]

Q 7.10   When does an employee "abandon" his or her job during a strike?

Employees who participate in lawful economic or ULP strikes retain both their "employee" status for the duration of the strike and certain reinstatement rights, unless evidence exists that they have abandoned their jobs. To establish job abandonment, the NLRB and the courts will evaluate whether the employees have indicated, by their conduct or statements, an unequivocal intention to sever the employment relationship.[51] Even though section 2(3) of the NLRA seemingly requires loss of "employee" status where a striker has "obtained any other regular and substantially equivalent employment," the NLRB has held fairly regularly that a striker's resignation in order to accept another job or to obtain pension funds will not *in and of itself* be conclusive of job abandonment. The NLRB will examine other circumstances surrounding the striker's actions, including whether the striker resigned because it was the only way to obtain pension funds, whether the employee told the employer he had found other work, whether the employee abandoned the strike, and whether the employer had made an unconditional offer of reinstatement to an equivalent position which the striking employee rejected. An employer that demonstrates by "unequivocal evidence" that the striker intends to "permanently sever" the employment relationship is not required to offer reinstatement to that striker.[52]

Q 7.10.1   What if a striking employee accepts another job?

Employment status is lost if a striking worker accepts "regular and substantially equivalent" work elsewhere.[53] It is the employer's burden to show that a striker has obtained regular and substantially equivalent work, and the standard for regular and equivalent work can be high. The NLRB will closely compare the new job with the striker's current job to determine if it is a regular and equivalent job. Generally, the NLRB has found a new job to be regular and equivalent work if the employee generally works the same hours and has equivalent pay, working conditions, location, and seniority rights. The NLRB found that a position was not substantially equivalent when the job duties were different (for example, stocking groceries by hand at a retail level compared with stocking and pulling wholesale groceries using a fork-lift and other machinery), where the pay was several dollars less per hour, and where the employee maintained a "continuing interest in returning to his job."[54]

CASE STUDY: *KSM Industries, Inc.*[55]

In this case, employees resigned either during the strike or after the strike, but before they were recalled, after receiving instructions from management that resignation was the only way to receive benefits.

The NLRB affirmed an administrative law judge's finding that striking employees who were unlawfully denied recall or whose recall was delayed did not voluntarily abandon their jobs when they tendered resignations in order to receive payouts from retirement funds and for accrued vacation pay. The administrative law judge noted that "a striker's resignation in order to . . . obtain pension funds will not of itself be evidence of abandonment of the struck job. Rather, the NLRB will examine the relevant circumstances to determine whether the striker has expressed an unequivocal intention not to return to his former job."

On an additional issue, the NLRB affirmed the administrative law judge's ruling that strikers who responded "no" to a recall interest questionnaire sent by the employer did not abandon their job, because the interest questionnaire was not a valid offer of reinstatement. Even though the interest questionnaire clearly stated that "I understand that a 'NO' choice voluntarily terminates my employment with KSM Industries," the NLRB discounted the language because it could not say that an employee "would have responded the same way to an actual reinstatement offer."

Q 7.11   What notices are required before a strike can occur?

Section 8(d) of the LMRA requires that a party initiating termination or modification of a collective bargaining agreement give the other party to the contract written notice of its intent to terminate or modify the agreement sixty days prior to the collective bargaining agreement's expiration or the intended date of termination or modification.[56] The party that first "raises the possibility of industrial conflict by moving to open up the existing contractual arrangements"—in other words, the party that takes the initiative to change a contract—has the duty to notify the other party of its intent.[57] However, an employer who arguably claims authorization in the contract's management rights clause for a change opposed by the union under section 8(d) is likely not seeking to "modify such contract" within the meaning of that provision.[58] Additionally, both the union and the employer must notify the Federal Mediation and Conciliation Service and the relevant state agencies within thirty days after the notice of intent to modify or terminate the agreement has been provided to the other party. Once the federal and state agencies receive notification, they may contact the parties to the contract and offer mediation services in order to quickly and efficiently resolve negotiation disputes, if requested or necessary.

During this notification period, sometimes referred to as a "cooling-off" period, the collective bargaining agreement remains in effect and the NLRA generally prohibits the employees from striking and employers from locking employees out.[59] If the employees participate in a strike during the cooling-off period, they lose employee status under the NLRA and may be discharged or refused reinstatement. The restrictions on the right to strike during the cooling-off period apply only to economic strikes, not to ULP strikes.[60]

Q 7.11.1   Are there special notices required for strikes against healthcare institutions?

In the case of healthcare institutions, NLRA section 8(g) requires unions to provide longer notifications to the other party and the federal and state agencies. Specifically, there must be at least ninety days' notice to the other party of intent to terminate or modify the agreement, and at least sixty days' notice to the federal and state agencies. In addition to these longer notice periods, a union must give a healthcare institution ten days' notice of its intent to strike or picket, to ensure the safety of patients and continuity of care. The union's notice to the healthcare institution must specify the date and time of the commencement of the intended concerted work stoppage and cannot be unilaterally extended by the union.

If a union fails to provide the ten-day notice, employees who engage in the "concerted refusal to work" are not protected and may be subject to discipline by the employer, including the possibility of termination. For example, in *Beverly Health & Rehabilitation Services v. NLRB*,[61] the U.S. Court of Appeals for the D.C. Circuit held that the employer was not under any obligation to rehire workers who participated in a strike against the healthcare employer, because it was not a legally protected strike due to the union's failure to give the healthcare employer the required ten-day notice.

Employees engaged in an unauthorized walkout may retain their employee status on the theory section 8(g) applies only to action by a "labor organization."[62] However, if the union is involved in the strike or work stoppage, notice must be provided.

Q 7.11.2   Does the NLRB treat strikes differently from other concerted actions for purposes of section 8(g) notice?

The NLRB has held that section 8(g) notice is required for various types of "concerted work stoppages," including strikes, picketing, slowdowns, and even concerted refusals to work overtime.[63]

LABOR MANAGEMENT LAW FACT
Section 8(g) Notice Requirements for Healthcare Institutions
• Unions must give healthcare institutions a minimum of ten days' notice before engaging in a strike, picketing, or other concerted refusal to work.
• The notice must specify the date and time of the commencement of the strike or other concerted refusal to work.
• If the union fails to give notice, striking employees lose their status as NLRA employees and may be disciplined or discharged.

Picketing

The Basics

Q 7.12   What is labor picketing?

Picketing by a union in the course of a labor dispute may have varying objectives and may take different forms. Whether a union is engaged in "picketing," as opposed to other forms of worker protest activity, may have implications whether it has violated the union ULP provisions in sections 8(b)(4) and 8(b)(7) of the NLRA.

The term "picketing" is not defined by the NLRA, but includes one or more employees patrolling back and forth at an employer's business as part of publicizing a labor dispute. Patrolling is usually accompanied by signs or placards, although such are not necessary to constitute picketing. For example, the NLRB has found union representatives to be engaged in picketing where they placed signs in snow banks and waited in nearby cars to confront delivery drivers and answer questions.[64] Whether activity constitutes picketing focuses on the placement of individuals near the employer's place of business "to accomplish a purpose which advances the cause of the union, such as keeping employees away from work or keeping customers away from the employer's business."[65] A confrontational element is helpful but not a required component of picketing.[66]

 CASE STUDY: *Kentov v. Sheet Metal Workers' International Ass'n*[67]

In *Kentov*, the U.S. Court of Appeals for the Eleventh Circuit assessed whether the union's "street theater" demonstration constituted an unlawful secondary boycott. In protest of construction contractors' use of non-union labor for a hospital construction project, the union staged a mock funeral procession in front of a hospital for two hours, complete with representatives carrying an object resembling a coffin. The protesters walked back and forth in front of the hospital's entrance along with another union representative dressed in an oversized grim reaper costume carrying a large sickle. As funeral music blared from a flatbed trailer, other union representatives passed out handbills that accurately described allegations from state court lawsuits concerning four recent patient deaths at the hospital.

Although the street theater demonstration differed from traditional notions of unlawful secondary boycott activity, the court concluded that there was reasonable cause to believe that the union had violated the NLRA and affirmed an injunction against the union. The Court reasoned that, "[l]ike traditional secondary picketing, the Union's procession was a mixture of conduct and communication intended to provide the most persuasive deterrent to third persons about to enter the hospital."[68]

Q 7.13 Is picketing always lawful?

Some picketing is lawful, while other picketing may violate state law as well as the NLRA. Sections 8(b)(1)(A), 8(b)(4) and 8(b)(7) of the NLRA are most pertinent here. Legality does not turn on the number of persons involved in the picketing, but rather the purpose of the picketers and the means they employ.[69] There are several reasons that a labor union may picket an employer. Often, picketing is an attempt to dissuade others (for example, customers, employees, vendors) from entering the employer's business (crossing the picket line) and thereby to put pressure on an employer to meet the union's demands. Picketing can also be done to draw public attention to a dispute, or for another purpose. Among other objectives, picketing may be:

(1) for a recognitional or organizational objective;

(2) area standards–related;

(3) consumer-focused;

(4) informational;

(5) a secondary boycott; or

(6) in protest of an alleged ULP by the employer or alleged unlawful discharge.

The rules regulating picketing vary depending on which of these objectives is present.

In some cases, unions will claim that they are engaged in activities, such as bannering or handbilling, that communicate a union message without constituting picketing. The boundaries between these other activities and picketing are discussed in detail below.

Recognitional or Organizational Picketing

Q 7.14   What is recognitional or organizational picketing?

Recognitional picketing occurs when the union pickets an employer to cause the employer to recognize the union as the bargaining agent for its employees. Similarly, organizational picketing occurs when the union pickets an employer to cause the employees to support its bid for recognition. The NLRA regulates certain instances of recognitional and organizational picketing.

Q 7.14.1 How are recognitional and organizational picketing limited under the NLRA?

Pursuant to section 8(b)(4)(C) of the NLRA, a union is forbidden from picketing or using other pressures to compel an employer to recognize or bargain with a particular labor organization where the employer already has a duty to bargain with another union that has been certified by the NLRB as the representative of the employer's employees.[70] In other words, certified unions (with whom the employer is under a continuing duty to bargain) are protected from recognitional and organizational picketing by rival unions. Additionally, section 8(b)(7) of the NLRA restricts a union that is not certified as the representative of the employer's employees from picketing or threatening to picket:

(A) when the employer has lawfully recognized another union and no question concerning representation may appropriately be raised;

(B) when a valid NLRB election has been conducted among the employees the union seeks to represent within the prior twelve months (regardless of the outcome of the election); or

(C) for more than thirty days, unless a petition for recognition has been filed.

Informational/Publicity Picketing

Q 7.15 What is informational or publicity picketing?

Informational picketing, also known as publicity picketing, is aimed at informing the general public about matters of concern to the union, including:

(1) labor disputes;

(2) that the picketed employer does not employ members of the union; or

(3) that the employer does not have a contract with the union.

Q 7.15.1   When is informational/publicity picketing permitted?

To the extent this picketing is for a non-recognitional or non-organizational objective, it is not subject to section 8(b)(7).

If informational picketing has a recognitional or organizational objective and does not violate section 8(b)(7)(A) or (B), it may be permitted under the "publicity proviso" of section 8(b)(7)(C), and when not unlawful, informational picketing can continue for an indefinite time. At the same time, the publicity proviso also makes it clear that informational picketing with a recognitional or organizational object will not be protected by the proviso if the effect of the picketing is to induce employees of other employers (such as vendors and suppliers) to not pick up, deliver, or transport any goods, or to not perform services for the picketed employers.[71] Therefore, to fall within the proviso, the picketing must:

(1)   be an appeal to the public;

(2)   be truthful; and

(3)   not have the "labor effect" of inducing "any individual employed by any other person" to refuse to deliver, pick up, or transport goods or to refuse to perform any services.

Whether the picketing is addressed to the public or has a secondary aim can be difficult to determine. Picket signs that adhere closely to the language in the proviso and that are displayed only at public entrances to the employer likely come within the proviso. On the other hand, the NLRB and courts have found that "signal picketing," which discourages union members or other unions from performing work for the picketed employer, does not fall within the publicity proviso.

Another complication in assessing whether picketing is protected under the publicity proviso relates to whether it has had an impermissible labor "effect" on the employer. The NLRB has rejected a literal quantitative test and instead assesses whether the interruption "actually disrupted, interfered with, or curtailed the employer's business" in determining whether the picketing is unprotected.[72] Even so, decisions in this regard have been uneven. For example, the NLRB found three delivery stoppages, two work delays, and several delivery delays over the course of twelve weeks of picketing at eighteen retail stores insufficient to demonstrate the requisite "effect," causing the informational picketing to fall outside the publicity proviso.[73]

In a recent decision, the NLRB found picketing to violate section 8(b)(1)(A) (and therefore unprotected) where the picketers, although not on strike, blocked access on eight occasions to the employer's hotel, for two to four minutes on each occasion, causing on at least one occasion a disruption of traffic flow. Several of the drivers whose access was blocked were guests or valet drivers seeking to cross the picket line.[74]

Area Standards Picketing

Q 7.16   What is area standards picketing?

Area standards picketing is picketing for the purpose of informing the public that the picketed employer pays wages or benefits below the prevailing rate in the particular location. Area standards picketing is often used in the retail and construction industries. Most often, the picketing is an attempt to influence consumers not to patronize businesses identified as having substandard benefits and wages.

Q 7.16.1   How is area standards picketing limited under the NLRA?

Where the union's immediate objective in picketing is simply to protest the target's failure to adhere to area standards and the evidence is lacking that the union also has a recognitional or organizational object, the picketing is not regulated by section 8(b)(7). Accordingly, even if the picketing exceeds thirty days or induces people not to work or make deliveries, the picketing may not be illegal. However, if area standards picketing has an organizational or recognitional objective, it is subject to section 8(b)(7) and must conform with the rules for informational or publicity picketing to stay within the protection of the publicity proviso to section 8(b)(7)(C).

The NLRB's focus in these cases turns on evidence of the union's immediate purpose, rather than the union's "ultimate economic objective of recognition and organization" in "the long view." The NLRB maintains that a "union may legitimately be concerned that a particular employer is undermining area standards of employment by maintaining lower standards" and is, therefore, protesting.[75] Employers will sometimes challenge the union's assertion that it is only engaging in area standards picketing. The NLRB will then examine the circumstances and history between the union and employer to determine whether the asserted area standards object is genuine or a pretext for an unlawful recognitional or secondary picketing. To substantiate its claim of an area standards object, the union should have investigated whether the employer's practices are actually substandard.[76]

Secondary-Boycott Picketing

Q 7.17   What is a secondary boycott?

When a union engages in conduct, such as strikes and picketing, and thus exercises labor pressure against persons or employers that do business with the employer but that do not have a relationship to the labor dispute (the neutral or secondary employer), for the purpose of influencing the employer with whom the union has a dispute (the primary employer), the union's action constitutes an unlawful secondary boycott.

Q 7.17.1   Is a secondary boycott legal?

In 1947, Congress outlawed most but not all forms of the union secondary boycotts through sections 8(b)(4) and 8(e) of the NLRA. Unlawful secondary boycotts require both a proscribed object and proscribed means. The proscribed object is what is referred to as a "doing-business" objective—that is, the object of the union's conduct is to force or require an employer or person (the "neutral" employer) to cease doing business with another person or employer (the "primary" or "target" employer).

Section 8(b)(4)(B) prohibits union picketing or strikes against a neutral employer with whom the union does not have a primary labor dispute when a purpose of the picketing is to compel the neutral employer to stop doing business with the primary employer in an effort to force the primary employer to agree to the union's demands.[77]

The proscribed means is usually a strike or picketing directed at the neutral, secondary employer, which is a violation of section 8(b)(4)(i). Another form of proscribed means is pressure directed at management personnel of the target seeking to influence its exercise of managerial discretion. Here, the union pressure has to amount to a threat, coercion, or restraint to violate section 8(b)(4)(ii).

Q 7.17.2   When does a secondary boycott become an illegal threat of coercion?

To illustrate when union pressure is sufficiently coercive to violate section 8(b)(4)(ii), consider the following:

Labor picketing at the secondary situs. Where the union has a dispute with the primary employer (Employer A), the union may lawfully picket at Employer A's location. This primary picketing is lawful, even though it may have a secondary effect (for example, if a delivery truck refuses to cross the picket line). However, if the union were to picket the establishment of another employer (Employer B) that provides parts to Employer A with the purpose of encouraging Employer B's employees to stop deliveries to Employer A, the picketing is presumptively unlawful because it is directed at a secondary employer with the very object proscribed by section 8(b)(4)(ii)(B).[78]

Consumer picketing at the secondary situs. A twist on this analysis exists where the union pickets a particular product at the site of a neutral secondary employer. Such was the case in *NLRB v. Fruit & Vegetable Packers & Warehousemen, Local 760 (Tree Fruits).*[79] In *Tree Fruits*, the U.S. Supreme Court, clarifying that only consumer picketing aimed at the secondary employer was prohibited by section 8(b)(4)(ii)(B), made a distinction between consumer picketing to "shut off all trade with the secondary employer" and picketing that "only persuades his customers not to buy the struck product" and is "closely confined to the primary dispute."[80] In *Tree Fruits*, the union struck fruit packing companies that sold Washington State apples to Safeway supermarkets, placing pickets at a number of Safeway stores. The picketing was limited to the apples, did not interfere with the Safeway employees' ability to handle the apples or with deliveries generally, and occurred after the store opened and before it closed. On the other hand, if the neutral's principal business is selling or otherwise handling the struck product, the U.S. Supreme Court upheld the NLRB's view that the *Tree Fruits* struck-product consumer picketing exception does not apply, and that, even when the union limits itself to struck-product consumer rather than labor picketing, the picketing violates section 8(b)(4)(ii)(B).

Q 7.17.3   When is a secondary boycott not prohibited?

The "ally doctrine" provides an exception to the secondary-boycott prohibition. The doctrine is based on the premise that there cannot be a secondary boycott unless there are at least two employers. Therefore, a union may pressure the neutral employer in situations where the primary and neutral parties are considered a single employer. This includes situations where: (1) the neutral employer is actually an interested party or "alter ego" of the primary employer; or (2) the primary employer and the neutral employer are "struck-work allies."[81] In either case, once the general counsel has made out a prima facie violation, the union bears the burden of establishing that the employers are allies.[82]

Regarding corporate subsidiaries, the general rule is that separate subsidiaries of the same parent corporation with separate management, distinct bargaining units, and little interrelated business activities will likely be considered separate employers for purposes of the section 8(b)(4) prohibition. However, the analysis changes if the parent seeks to control aspects of the labor relations of the subsidiary, or the subsidiary and the parent are both commonly owned and their production or delivery systems are vertically integrated.

Even a wholly separate employer will lose the secondary-boycott protection if it ceases to be "neutral" in the labor dispute by agreeing to become a "struck-work ally" of the primary employer, for example, by performing the work disrupted by the labor dispute essentially as a subcontractor for the struck employer. The assessment of allied status is made on a case-by-case basis regarding the practical, day-to-day operations of the companies. Restoration of neutral status is possible if the ally informs the union that it has relinquished performance of the struck work.[83]

Q 7.17.4   What will make a third party a "single employer" or "alter ego" of the primary employer?

The NLRB and the courts have set forth the following criteria to determine whether two employers should be treated as a single entity:

(1) common ownership;
(2) common management;
(3) centralized control of labor relations; and
(4) interrelation of operations.[84]

Applying these criteria in *Boich Mining Co. v. NLRB*,[85] the court found two wholly owned subsidiaries of the holding company to be separate employers where each company maintained separate management and control over labor relations, despite the fact that the companies shared participation in a coal washing and blending process. The court placed little weight on evidence of the shared process because it did not involve a large amount of coal and was "a relatively minor arms-length business transaction for both companies."[86]

Q 7.17.5   When is a third-party employer considered a "struck-work ally" of the primary employer?

A third-party employer will be considered a struck-work ally of the primary employer if it performs the work that normally would be completed by the primary employer's employees if the employees were not on strike (that is, if it performs the struck work). In some circumstances, the NLRB and courts have explained, the picketing of a secondary employer who is performing the "farmed-out" work is not the kind of secondary activity that the NLRA was designed to prohibit. This is the case because, by doing the work, the secondary employer cannot say that it is completely uninvolved in the primary strike. Indeed the employer is securing a benefit for itself at the same time it is providing assistance to the primary employer.[87] Based upon this reasoning, if the work is being performed in a manner reducing the risk of lost future business to the primary, the secondary employer is not protected under section 8(b)(4)(ii)(B) where it "knowingly does work which would otherwise be done by the striking employees of the primary employer and where this work is paid for by the primary employer pursuant to an arrangement devised by the primary to enable him to meet its contractual obligations."[88]

Accordingly, the first issue relevant to the "struck-work" ally assessment is whether the secondary employer is actually performing the struck work. This is a question of whether the work performed is the same that had been performed by the striking employees. In some cases, the primary employer has had dealings with the secondary employer prior to the strike and there is evidence that the secondary employer is receiving additional work because of the strike. In other instances, the primary and secondary employers had no pre-strike dealings.

CASE STUDY: *NLRB v. Business Machine & Office Appliance Mechanics Conference Board (Royal Typewriter Co.)*[89]

Application of the ally doctrine is illustrated by the U.S. Court of Appeals for the Second Circuit's decision in *Royal Typewriter*. Royal serviced typewriters that had been sold and leased to its customers. When its technicians went on strike, the company advised its customers to select an independent repair company, and Royal agreed to reimburse payments. In most cases, Royal paid the independent repair companies directly. While the NLRB initially held the picketing of the independent repair companies to be unlawful secondary activity, the Second Circuit reasoned that the independent repair companies had notice of the strike based upon their receipt of the checks from Royal and that the arrangement was devised to enable Royal to meet its obligations to its customers. As a result, the independent repair companies were deemed allies of Royal that had lost the protection of the NLRA.

Employer's Response to Picketing

Q 7.18   If a union threatens to picket or begins recognitional or organizational picketing, how may an employer lawfully respond?

An employer may file a ULP charge with the regional office of the NLRB if a union unlawfully threatens to picket or begins recognitional or organizational picketing in violation of section 8(b)(7) of the NLRA. Under the NLRA, recognitional or organizational picketing cases are considered a priority, and the regional office should commence an investigation shortly after receiving the charge.[90] If, after an investigation, the regional director finds that there is probable cause to believe that a violation of the NLRA has occurred, the regional director is required to petition a district court for a section 10(*l*) injunction to stop the picketing.[91]

In addition, the employer can do any of the following in response to organizational picketing:

(1)   voluntarily agree to recognize the union, if the union can demonstrate that the majority of the employees support the union;

(2)   wait thirty days for the union to file a recognition petition or stop picketing; or

(3)   file its own petition (called an "RM petition") to force an NLRB election.

Q 7.18.1   What is a section 10(*l*) injunction?

Section 10(*l*) injunctions relate to union conduct, including picketing, that constitute a ULP under sections 8(b)(4), 8(b)(7), and 8(e).[92] Significantly, section 10(*l*) is a mandatory injunction provision that requires the NLRB's regional director to seek injunctive relief if there is "reasonable cause to believe" that one of the enumerated sections of the NLRA has been violated.[93] In the picketing context, the NLRB has sought section 10(*l*) injunctions in instances where the union has threatened or has engaged in picket-line violence, blocked ingress and egress to the employer's place of business,[94] or engaged in unlawful secondary picketing.[95]

Section 10(*l*) mandatory injunction proceedings are given priority over other NLRB cases.[96] Pursuant to section 10(*l*), district courts have the jurisdiction to grant injunctive relief and temporary restraining orders as deemed "just and proper."[97] Section 10(*l*) injunctions typically expire at the time the NLRB issues a decision as to the underlying ULP charge.

Q 7.18.2   What is an "expedited election" under section 8(b)(7)(C)?

Where a union has engaged in organizational or recognitional picketing that does not otherwise violate section 8(b)(7)(A) or (B) and does so for more than thirty days without filing a petition for election, the employer can file a section 8(b)(7)(C) charge (an RM petition), and thus secure the benefit of the "expedited election" proviso to 8(b)(7)(C). When the employer files an RM petition in such circumstances, the NLRB will hold an expedited election to determine whether the union has the requisite employee support for recognition. An RM election in these circumstances differs significantly from a typical representation election because it does not require a hearing to determine the scope of the bargaining unit, nor does the employer have to provide a list of eligible voters to the NLRB.

Q 7.19   Can an employer discipline an employee who engages in lawful recognitional or organizational picketing or a strike?

If an employee engages in unlawful recognitional or organizational picketing, the employee's participation is unprotected. If the picketing is lawful and otherwise peaceful, it is protected concerted activity under section 7 of the NLRA[98] and the employer is prohibited from interfering with or discriminating against employees who engage in such conduct.[99] An employer also violates the NLRA by engaging in the surveillance of employees (for example, by taking photographs of picketers),[100] or otherwise coercing employees engaged in protected section 7 activity (for example, by unnecessarily involving the police, interrogating employees or threatening them with adverse employment action). Such conduct may convert an economic dispute into a ULP strike. Any picketing for the immediate object of protesting the employer ULPs can continue indefinitely without violating section 8(b)(7)(C).[101]

Union's Picketing Rights and Limitations

Q 7.20   Where can a union picket?

Within certain limitations, the union may picket at the primary employer's site (the "primary situs"), a common site where multiple employers are present (the "common situs"), or a temporary site ("ambulatory site"). Additionally, as previously addressed, a union may picket a secondary employer who is deemed an ally. However, state law may impose limits on picketing that blocks access to or egress from the facility, creates an obstruction to traffic, or involves violence or creates a breach of the peace. Such state law is not preempted by the NLRA or barred by the Norris-LaGuardia Act's restrictions on federal injunctions in labor disputes. However, some states have enacted "little Norris-LaGuardia Acts" which limit the ability of state courts to issue injunctions in labor disputes.[102]

Q 7.20.1   Where can the union picket at the primary employer's site?

The union may picket in the outside areas of the primary employer's facilities, including before the primary employer's employees, suppliers, and customers who are working at those facilities. The union may also picket third-party employers performing work at the primary situs, even where the primary employer has established a "reserve gate" for use by the employees of the secondary employer. The union may picket at the reserve gate, but only where the third-party employers are performing work relating to the primary employer's normal business operations. At a multi-employer work site, the union may picket any access gate used by the primary employer, even if other companies also use that gate.

Q 7.20.2   How is common-situs picketing limited?

Common-situs picketing is when the union pickets a work site away from the primary employer's work site where both neutral and primary employees are working. The NLRA has developed guidelines for picketing a primary employer at a common situs—known as the "*Moore Dry Dock* standards"[103]—which state that:

(1)   picketing must occur at the site of the dispute;

(2)   the primary employer's employees must be present when picketing occurs;

(3)   picketing must be reasonably close to the location of the dispute; and

(4)   picket signs must clearly identify the primary employer.[104]

Common-situs picketing may be challenged if it violates the *Moore Dry Dock* standards and has the unlawful objective of disrupting the neutral employer so as to pressure it to cease doing business with the primary employer. Failure of the union to comply with one or more of the *Moore Dry Dock* standards does not, standing alone, constitute a per se violation of the NLRA; however, it creates "a strong but rebuttable presumption that the picketing had an unlawful secondary object."[105]

The NLRB recently held that common situs picketing was unlawful (and therefore unprotected) where employees of a janitorial services company picketed and leafleted at a building where both their janitorial company and other employers were present, and the picketers made direct appeals to a property manager, urging the property manager to pressure the janitorial company to improve their working conditions. Overruling an administrative law judge's decision, the NLRB held that the picketing did not comply with the Moore Dry Dock standards because leaflets distributed by the picketers referred to one of the neutral tenants at the common situs building. Additionally, the NLRB found clear evidence of a proscribed secondary intent in the picketers' direct appeals to a neutral employer (the building manager) to pressure the primary employer to change its practices.[106]

LABOR MANAGEMENT LAW FACT

Common-Situs Picketing and the "Reserve Gate" System

Construction sites offer a typical example raising common-situs picketing issues. Where the union contractors (primary employer(s) with whom the union has the ongoing labor dispute) and non-union contractors (neutral employers) are working at the same site to complete a project, the union may attempt to picket both in an attempt to slow down or shut down the job. The U.S. Supreme Court has rejected the argument that all employers working at a single site under a general contractor should be treated as one employer.[107] This is an important distinction because, although employees of a neutral contractor may be entitled to observe a lawful picket line (depending on the scope of the applicable no-strike clause), a union is prohibited from picketing the neutral contractors as a means of pressuring the primary employer to give in to its demands.

Outside the construction site context (where the site is usually not owned by any of the employers), a primary employer that owns the facility may seek to curtail the primary union's picketing of employees of the neutral employer working on the primary employer's premises by establishing a "reserve gate" system for the exclusive use of the neutral's employees. If the union continues picketing the neutral employer once a reserve gate system has been established, the union's conduct may be challenged as unlawful secondary-boycott activity. The rationale is that, under a valid reserve gate system, the union's picketing at a gate reserved for neutral employers demonstrates that it has not limited its picketing to places reasonably close to the situs of the dispute with the primary employer as required under the *Moore Dry Dock* principles. In essence, the reserve gate system allows the primary employer to establish a "common situs" situation on its own property.

> The establishment of a valid gate system is, therefore, of critical importance. Where such a system exists, the NLRB has rejected union claims that it was "confused" by the labeling of the gates and that the picketing at the gate reserved for neutral employers was "inadvertent and of short duration."[108]

Q 7.20.3   How does a "reserve gate" system limit where a union can picket at a common situs?

At a common situs, a union may picket common entrances used by both the primary and neutral employers and their employees and suppliers unless a reserve gate system is established. A reserve gate system is a means of physically separating primary and neutral employers, their employees, and suppliers at a common site.

If the reserve gate is properly established and marked, and the secondary employer(s) is not performing related work or work that would have required the shutdown of the primary employer, the union must confine its picketing to the gate reserved for the primary employer and its employees. To be effective, the reserve gates for the primary and neutral employers, and their respective employees and suppliers, must be clearly identified as such and located in separate locations. In addition, notice of the established reserve gates should be provided to the union, and the gates should be policed to ensure that the primary employer's employees, suppliers, and others doing business with the primary employer enter **only** the primary employer's reserve gate to prevent "mingled" or "tainted" use of the gate.

Q 7.20.4   What happens if a primary employer uses the gate reserved for the neutral employer, or vice versa?

The reserve gate system will be ineffective if a primary employer's employees or suppliers use the gate reserved for the neutral employer or vice versa. This results in the creation of a mixed-use gate, permitting the union to picket the gate. If the reserve gate system is destroyed due to mixed use, the employer should try to re-establish the gate system and notify the union and the affected contractors that the system has been rehabilitated.

Steps to Establishing a Reserve Gate System

1. The reserve gate must be distinct—that is, separate and apart from other entrances to the common site. The site should be assessed to determine the best way to isolate the reserve gate from the other entrances. The employer may use an existing gate or construct a new one.

2. Usage of the gate must be defined and clearly marked. Suggested signage language includes "THIS GATE RESERVED FOR SEPARATE AND EXCLUSIVE USE BY EMPLOYEES OF XYZ COMPANY, ITS SUPPLIERS AND VENDORS. ALL OTHER EMPLOYEES AND SUPPLIERS MUST USE THE ALTERNATIVE GATE THAT HAS BEEN ESTABLISHED FOR YOUR SEPARATE AND EXCLUSIVE USE."

3. Do not allow mixed use of the gate. Consider policing to avoid commingling, including the use of independent security to ensure usage rules are followed.

4. Notify the union that a reserve gate for the secondary employer's employees has been established and indicate that, going forward, any further picketing of the reserve gate will be construed as an illegal secondary boycott causing the employer to file a ULP charge with the NLRB against the union and possible lawsuit under section 303 of the NLRA. Clearly identify the location of the reserve gate and that of other gates on the site. Notification should be in writing. Notify all suppliers and vendors at the site as well.

5. If commingling occurs, promptly provide notice to the union and re-establish proper usage of the reserve gate.

Q 7.20.5   Can the primary employer establish a secondary or neutral situs at the primary situs?

Even where the employer owns the premises and conducts its normal operations there, the employer may establish a "reserve gate" for contractors who are not engaged in "related work" or work requiring the shutdown of the primary employer's operations (as in a strike). In such circumstances the union may not picket the reserve gate without violating section 8(b)(4)(B). The related-work doctrine is a significant exception to this principle; it allows union picketing where the contractor's work is related to the normal business operations of the primary employer.

In *Electrical Workers (IUE) Local 761 v. NLRB*,[109] the U.S. Supreme Court assessed whether the picketing of a gate reserved for employees of the independent contractors working at the primary employer's manufacturing plant violated section 8(b)(4). The NLRB found that the object of the union's picketing at the reserve gate was in violation of section 8(b)(4), because the union was trying to pressure the secondary contractors to cease doing business with General Electric. The Court, however, focused on the type of the work being performed by the contractors. Because the work performed by the contractors was "conventional maintenance work necessary to the normal operations of General Electric," their use of the reserve gate might have been a "mingled use" and if so, "would not bar picketing rights of the striking employees."

Notably, the NLRB has held that the related-work exception should not be applied in the construction industry as it would effectively privilege all labor picketing of the integrated tasks at a construction site in contravention of the Supreme Court's decision barring such picketing.[110] Instead, the legality of picketing in such circumstances is determined by the *Moore Dry Dock* standards outlined above.

Q 7.20.6   Is the union permitted to follow and picket a primary employer's employees from the primary situs to another site?

When the primary employer's employees are ambulatory (that is, moving from work site to work site), the union is permitted to engage in ambulatory picketing at the sites where the employer's employees perform work, within the limitations of the *Moore Dry Dock* rules.[111] The most common example of an ambulatory situs is each location where a delivery company's truck and employees are temporarily located for purposes of performing their delivery and/or pickup services.

Handbilling

Q 7.21   What is handbilling?

A handbill is any written or printed statement handed out to inform interested people of an event or dispute. Handbilling refers to a union's practice of distributing to the public handbills that contain information regarding a labor dispute urging the public to act or not to act in connection with that dispute.[112] This may include a request that the public cease patronizing a business because of its connection to a labor dispute.

Q 7.21.1   Does handbilling come within the secondary boycott prohibition of the NLRA?

Because it lacks the martial aspects of picketing and typically does not signal to labor unions and their supporters that employees should not cross the line, handbilling is considered a form of communication different from picketing. Picketing is a mixture of conduct and communication. The U.S. Supreme Court has stated that handbills can contain the same message as picketing, but generally do not have the same "signal" effect of triggering a nearly automatic response from members of other labor organizations to honor the union's boycott by withholding their services. The effectiveness of the handbills depends entirely on the persuasive force of the idea contained in the leaflet or the solidarity of consumers handbilled with the cause. Because handbilling lacks the conduct associated with picketing, handbilling is entitled to greater protection,[113] or, put differently, is subject to fewer restrictions in the NLRA.

CASE STUDY: *Edward J. DeBartolo Corp. v. Florida Gulf Coast Building & Construction Trades Council (DeBartolo II)*[114]

In *DeBartolo II*, the Court held that peaceful handbilling did not violate the NLRA. The Court reasoned that whether the handbilling was unlawful depended on whether the activity threatened, coerced, or restrained any person to cease doing business with another, within the meaning of section 8(b)(4)(ii)(B) of the NLRA. The Court noted that handbilling must involve some form of restraint or coercion— that is, more than mere persuasion—to prove a violation of section 8(b)(4)(ii)(B).

The union in *DeBartolo II* distributed handbills at entrances to a mall urging patrons not to shop at the mall because a contractor working at a department store at the mall paid non-union wages. The Court observed that the handbills truthfully revealed the existence of a wage dispute and urged potential customers of the mall to follow a wholly legal course of action, namely, not to patronize the retailers doing business in the mall. The union's handbilling was peaceful and did not involve any picketing, patrolling, or "labor effect." The handbills simply presented the benefits of unionism to the community and the dangers of inadequate wages to the economy and the standard of living of the populace.

The Court held that the evidence did not suggest that the leaflets had any coercive effect on customers of the mall. The Court rejected the general notion that handbilling a neutral employer as part of an ongoing dispute with a primary employer was unlawful simply because the handbilling has some economic impact on the neutral employer.

Q 7.21.2   When does handbilling violate the NLRA?

Where handbilling is accompanied by patrolling, the handbilling may be deemed to be picketing or coercive pressure and may be considered unlawful if engaged in for a "cease doing business" objective in violation of section 8(b)(4)(i)(B) of the NLRA.[115]

Q 7.21.3   Can a union handbill on private property?

In *Lechmere, Inc. v. NLRB*, the U.S. Supreme Court limited the ability of unions or union representatives to access private property. Where the employer has a facially nondiscriminatory no-solicitation rule and state law does not require access, non-employee union representatives may access employees or consumers on private property only where:[116]

(1)   the employees or consumers are otherwise inaccessible;

(2)   the private-property owner has permitted other similarly situated groups access, but denies a union that same access in a discriminatory manner; or

(3)   when permitted by a collective bargaining agreement or other contractual relationship.

The inaccessibility exception in *Lechmere* applies even when consumers are the intended audience of handbills. The private-property owner bears the initial burden of establishing it has a property interest entitling it to exclude persons. To prove consumers or employees are otherwise inaccessible for the purpose of handbilling, the union then bears the burden of showing that no other reasonable means of communicating its message to the employees or consumers exists. This includes showing that it would be unreasonable for the union to use mass media, including television and radio, to get its message across.[117]

A private-property owner discriminates against a union when it treats a union representative seeking to communicate on a subject protected by the NLRA less favorably than another person communicating on the same subject. The scope of discrimination that would permit access to otherwise protected private property is narrow. Impermissible discrimination may include favoring one union over another, or allowing employer-related information while barring similar union-related information. For example, a private shopping mall may not be able to permit a retail outlet to defend its labor practices while denying a union the opportunity to express its opinions on those practices.[118]

Historically, the NLRB has held that an employer's no-solicitation policy unlawfully discriminates against union activity if it allows charitable groups to solicit on company property. This *Sandusky Mall* doctrine has not fared well in some of the courts of appeals. The NLRB has also held that employer policies that broadly prohibit the distribution of literature on company premises "at all times" or require employees to obtain permission before distributing materials are unlawful.[119]

California state law provides that certain private shopping malls and shopping centers have the character of a public forum, resulting in the loss of protection given by *Lechmere* to private-property owners. For example, the Supreme Court of California held that a shopping mall violated a union's free speech rights under the California Constitution by refusing to allow the union to distribute leaflets inside the mall. Because the mall was a public forum, the property owner could not deny the union access; however, the mall was entitled to impose reasonable restrictions as to the time, place, and manner of the labor-related speech.[120]

Recently, the NLRB has announced a change in the way it will evaluate employer policies that potentially restrict employees' rights to engage in concerted activity under section 7 of the NLRA. In *The Boeing Company*,[121] the NLRB held that employer policies will be evaluated for "(1) the nature and extent of the potential impact on NLRA rights and (2) legitimate justifications associated with the rule." This new standard modifies the previous approach, under which the NLRB would evaluate whether employees could "reasonably construe" the policy to restrict section 7 rights (regardless whether there was any actual restriction.

Q 7.21.4   Can union members handbill on the property of a third party where they regularly perform work?

The NLRB has granted employees of a contractor the ability to engage in section 7 activity on the property of a third-party company where they regularly perform work. In *New York, New York Hotel & Casino*, the employees worked for a contractor that operated restaurants inside of the casino. The employees sought to improve their working conditions with the contractor by handbilling customers outside the restaurant on property owned by the casino. The NLRB held that while the employees were not employees of the casino, they had a greater right of access than non-employee union organizers. To determine the section 7 access rights of the contract employees, the NLRB engaged in a fact-intensive balancing of the employees' section 7 interests against the property rights of the casino, and ultimately concluded that the employees had a right to engage in section 7 activity in non-work areas of the casino property so long as the activity did not "significantly interfere" with use of the property."[122]

Bannering

Q 7.22   What is bannering?

Bannering is the union practice of displaying large signage (for example, an inflatable rat or a banner measuring fifteen feet by four feet) in front of businesses during ongoing labor disputes to discourage customers from patronizing those businesses. Bannering may be directed at primary or neutral employers. When unions place banners in front of neutral establishments, the union generally has a dispute with another company that does business with the neutral establishment.

Q 7.22.1   Does the NLRB consider bannering a protected activity under the NLRA?

Decisions from the NLRB during the Obama Administration held that stationary bannering activity is legally protected and not unlawful picketing, at least in cases where the bannering is not accompanied by martial patrolling or "coercive" conduct and does not induce a work stoppage. It is unclear whether the new NLRB majority, including members appointed by President Trump, will affirm these decisions. In *Southwest Regional Council of Carpenters*,[123] the NLRB upheld the tactic of bannering a neutral establishment, holding that it did not constitute an unlawful secondary boycott. The majority concluded that the tactic (1) did not amount to signal picketing (urging employees of the neutral employer to stop work) in violation of section 8(b)(4)(i)(B), and (2) was not a prohibited threat, restraint, or coercion of a neutral employer under section 8(b)(4)(ii)(B). The NLRB based its decision on *Carpenters & Joiners of America*,[124] which held that bannering did not constitute unlawful secondary picketing because, unlike unlawful secondary picketing, the practice was not confrontational. The NLRB has noted that it considers whether the display contains any elements of confrontation, including:

(1)   whether the banner is stationary;

(2)   whether it is located at a "sufficient distance" from vehicle and building entrances;

(3)   whether visitors are confronted by any actual or symbolic barrier as they arrive at or depart from a point of business; and

(4)   whether the banner is posted in such a manner that those entering the sites would perceive the individuals holding the banners as threatening.[125]

Bannering has also been held to be legally protected even when conducted outside a construction site not open to the general public, or outside a site where some employees already represented by the union are already working.[126]

 CASE STUDY: *Pacific Northwest Regional Council of Carpenters*[127]

Mauer Construction, a non-union general contractor, worked on remodeling projects at Macy's department stores. The union commenced a campaign to pressure Mauer to pay area standard wages and benefits. The campaign included bannering and handbilling outside a Macy's department store, though Mauer was not presently working or scheduled to work at the store.

Two union representatives stood next to a stationary ten-foot-by-five- foot banner located on a public sidewalk, close to the curb, near a store window at the main entrance to the Macy's. The banner stated "Macy's" in smaller print and "Low Wages = Poverty"

---

in larger print. The banner did not identify the union nor state the phrase "labor dispute" anywhere on the banner. Two groups of shoppers informed Macy's that they would not shop at the store because they perceived the banner implicated Macy's policies toward workers.

The handbills stated that Macy's had hired Mauer and that Mauer paid 20% below area standards. These leaflets urged customers to call Macy's and tell the managers to quit short-changing local labor. The leaflets also stated that the union was not promoting any work stoppages or refusal to deliver goods or services. The handbillers were not confrontational and did not block access to the Macy's store.

The case was referred to the Division of Advice, which considered whether the union's actions violated section 8(b)(4)(ii)(B). The Advice Memorandum stated that the banner was not misleading, in that it did not link Macy's to the labor dispute or refer to a labor dispute. The individuals standing alongside the banner did not identify themselves as union representatives. Because the Macy's was not presently undergoing any construction, the bannering would not create a misconception to the public that the union has a labor dispute with Macy's. Considering the totality of the circumstances, the Division of Advice stated that the bannering was not unlawful.

Union "Corporate Campaigns"

Q 7.23   What is a corporate campaign?

A corporate campaign is a coordinated effort by a union against a corporation that has opposed unionization, refused to agree to the union's bargaining demands, or in some way refused to yield on some issue of importance to the labor organization waging the campaign. The campaign is intended to force the employer to surrender to the union's demands, typically agreeing to a card check and/or neutrality agreement.

A union's corporate campaign may involve a variety of small or large economic, legal, political, and psychological tactics that, collectively, may pressure an employer to make concessions to a union. The union will seek to undermine the employer's business, including damaging the employer's relationships with shareholders, consumers, business partners, and governmental regulators, in order to advance the union's goals.[128]

A corporate campaign may involve:[129]

- visits by employees' union representatives to the offices of a company's parent and shareholders;

- enlisting politicians to hold hearings to investigate the company's treatment of its employees;

- public allegations, regulatory filings, and/or lawsuits asserting health and safety violations, environmental violations, civil rights abuses, wage/hour claims, and other perceived offenses by the company against employees or the larger community;

- seeking legislation and regulatory rulings contrary to company goals and interests;

- targeting and seeking to halt pending company projects that require regulatory approval;

- attempting to undermine employer attempts to obtain public financing; and

- strategic use of shareholder resolutions and proxy voting to pressure directors and senior management.

Q 7.24   How can employers lawfully challenge certain corporate campaigns?

Recently, employers have sought to challenge certain union corporate campaign tactics through lawsuits filed in federal and state courts. Employers have sought to both enjoin these tactics and also to obtain damages for harm caused by corporate campaigns.

In *BE&K Construction Co.*,[130] the NLRB held that filing and pursuing a reasonably based lawsuit does not violate the NLRA, regardless of the employer's motive for initiating the lawsuit or whether the lawsuit is ultimately successful. In *BE&K*, the union attempted to delay a contract won by a non-union company through picketing, handbilling, filing grievances, lobbying for new emissions standards, and filing a lawsuit alleging health and safety code violations. In response, the company filed a federal suit alleging violations of the LMRA, NLRA, and antitrust laws. The company's lawsuit was dismissed. The union asserted the company's federal suit constituted a ULP. The NLRB held the employer's lawsuit was reasonably based and, therefore, the employer's filing and maintenance of the lawsuit, however unsuccessful, did not violate the NLRA. The NLRB further held that the employer's motive in filing the lawsuit would not alter the lawfulness of an otherwise reasonably based claim.

The NLRB's holding in *BE&K Construction Co.* supports the use of reasonably based litigation to challenge union corporate campaign activity. The following claims have been filed against unions in an attempt to halt or recover damages for unlawful union activity:[131]

(1) federal Racketeer Influenced and Corrupt Organizations Act claims;

(2) state law defamation claims; and

(3) federal privacy law claims.

Q 7.24.1   How have employers pursued RICO claims against unions?

The federal RICO statute aims to eliminate organized crime and to combat corruption relating to enterprises, including corporations and unions.[132] The statute creates separate criminal liability for numerous offenses, including various state felonies, specified federal labor statutes, and specified federal criminal statutes (for example, extortion, mail and wire fraud, bankruptcy fraud, bribery). The RICO statute applies to union (as well as employer) activities[133] and has been used in civil litigation between labor unions and management in disputes relating to matters such as organizing, decertification, collective bargaining, and corporate campaigns.[134]

For example, RICO cases have been brought based on:

(1) direct threats to an employer's property or employees as part of organizing efforts;[135]

(2) extortion or sabotage by parties seeking an advantage in collective bargaining;[136]

(3) employers using bribes to subvert union organizing;[137] and

(4) abuses relating to employee health and welfare or pension plan assets.[138]

Section 1962(a) of RICO prohibits the use or investment of racketeering proceeds to acquire, establish, or operate an enterprise.[139] This section has been used in labor disputes involving allegations of:

(1) extortion to coerce collective bargaining agreements;[140]

(2) fraud or conversion with respect to pension plans;[141]

(3) bribery, extortion, and malicious prosecution to force employees from their jobs;[142]

(4) wrongful discharge;[143] and

(5) fraud with respect to wage and commission contracts.[144]

Section 1962(c) prohibits any person who is employed by, or associated with, an enterprise from participating in the conduct of its affairs through a pattern of racketeering activity.[145]

In the labor context, employers have asserted RICO claims in circumstances involving allegations:

- that a union tried to wrongfully force a prevailing wage contractor to become a union contractor by disseminating leaflets with false, harmful statements;[146]

- that a union tried to "run the company out of business" through mass picketing and leaflet distribution;[147]

- that striking unions engaged in extortion and violence against the company and non-striking employees;[148]

- that a union extorted it into signing a collective bargaining agreement.[149]

As of the time of publication, the degree of success of RICO litigation against unions remains unclear.

Q 7.24.2   When may an employer bring a defamation claim against a union?

If the union defames an employer, the employer can sue the union for defamation under state law, but not under the NLRA. Federal labor law partially preempts state libel law, requiring a plaintiff to prove "actual malice" in addition to the other defamation elements in order to recover. To show actual malice, a plaintiff must establish by clear and convincing evidence that the speaker made the statement with knowledge that it was false or with reckless disregard of whether it was false or not.[150] Accordingly, a defamation claim escapes labor law preemption only if there is a false statement of fact and the plaintiff proves actual malice by clear and convincing evidence.

Where either party to a labor dispute circulates false and defamatory statements during a union organizing campaign, the court has jurisdiction to apply state remedies if the complainant pleads and proves that the statements were made with malice and caused injury. However, even the most repulsive speech will enjoy immunity if it falls short of a deliberate or reckless untruth (actual malice). If no actual malice is found, then the state tort law is preempted by the NLRA and no recovery for defamation is allowed.

Q 7.24.3   How have employers pursued privacy claims against unions?

In *Pichler v. Union of Needletrades, Industrial & Textile Employees, AFL-CIO (UNITE)*,[151] a federal court of appeals held that a union unlawfully obtained and used confidential information for an impermissible purpose in violation of the federal Driver's Privacy Protection Act of 1994.[152] UNITE launched a union-organizing campaign targeting Cintas Corporation and its employees. UNITE believed that house calls were essential to the campaign's success, so it sought to determine the names and addresses of Cintas workers. As part of this effort, UNITE engaged in "tagging."

Tagging involves recording the license plate numbers on cars found in an employer's parking lots. Unions then use those license plate numbers to access information contained in the car owner's state motor vehicle records. UNITE accessed the motor vehicle records of approximately 2,000 cars located in the Cintas parking lot. This resulted in the union accessing not only employee information, but also the information of relatives or friends whose cars the employees had been driving. UNITE then visited the homes of many of these individuals.

The plaintiffs asserted that UNITE's actions violated their privacy rights under the DPPA. The DPPA lists only fourteen permissible purposes for obtaining or using personal information. Union organizing is not a permissible purpose under the DPPA. Because UNITE obtained and used confidential information for this impermissible purpose, UNITE violated the DPPA and was liable to the plaintiffs for violating their privacy rights.

Lockouts

Q 7.25   What is a lockout?

A lockout occurs when an employer withholds employment from its employees for the purpose of either resisting demands or gaining a concession. During a lockout an employer may or may not hire temporary or permanent replacement workers to fill in for the locked-out employees. An employer may lock employees out for the purpose of economically pressuring a union to support a legitimate bargaining position. An employer may also lawfully lock out its employees in the face of a strike.[153]

Q 7.25.1   When can an employer initiate a lockout?

An employer may impose an "offensive lockout" generally only when it reaches a bona fide impasse in bargaining with the union. The employer must engage in good-faith bargaining for an offensive lockout to be lawful under the NLRA and may not lock employees out in support of bad-faith bargaining positions or to avoid bargaining obligations. Prior to initiating a lockout, an employer should have presented a clear offer to the union, the acceptance of which would end the lockout. If a collective bargaining agreement contains a no-lockout clause, however, the terms of collective bargaining agreement control and the employer cannot initiate a lockout.[154]

A "defensive lockout" is a lockout that is called to prevent imminent and irreparable financial harm to the company or to protect a legal right, such as in the face of a whipsaw strike or a surprise or imminent walkout. In these circumstances, an impasse is not required.[155]

Employers often use lockouts in response to whipsaw strikes. (See Q 7.25.3.)

Q 7.25.2   When will a lockout violate the NLRA?

A lockout will be unlawful if it is declared for an unlawful purpose, such as to compel employee or union's acceptance of the employer's ULP. A bargaining lockout must be for the sole purpose of bringing economic pressure to bear in support of the employers or securing the premises in the event of an imminent strike.[156]

A lockout will be held to be unlawful where that lockout was declared:[157]

- for reasons motivated by anti-union animus;

- in response to a union or employee's organizing efforts;

- to discourage union membership;

- to discriminate against union members, whether through lay-offs or reinstatement;

- in support of unlawful surveillance or interrogation about union activities;

- to otherwise interfere with employees' exercise of rights under section 7 of the NLRA.

In addition, a partial lockout (of less than all of the bargaining unit employees) can violate the NLRA.[158]

Q 7.25.3   What is a whipsaw strike?

A union engages in a whipsaw strike when it strikes against some but not all members of a multi-employer association. A whipsaw strike attempts to obtain concessions or benefits from all of the employers in a multi-employer association by exerting pressure on one of the employers. The union attempts to divide the employers by striking only one employer to undermine its ability to remain united with the others. The whipsaw technique may be focused on causing a presumably stronger employer to yield to the union's demands, so that employer will carry the rest of the association with it.[159]

 CASE STUDY: *Dresser-Rand Co.*[160]

The union began an economic strike after the breakdown of negotiations for a successor collective bargaining agreement. The employer hired temporary and permanent replacement workers to maintain its operations. Thirteen union workers who were striking later crossed the picket line and returned to work. When the union announced that the remaining strikers were willing to return to work, the employer locked out all of the employees, including the thirteen workers who had previously crossed the picket line, but not any of the replacements. The employer later reinstated all of the workers. The union claimed that the employer committed several unfair labor practices before, during, and after the lockout, including providing preferential treatment to the thirteen crossovers at the conclusion of the lawsuit.

Whipsaw strikes are not per se unlawful. Like bargaining lockouts, they are a permissible bargaining tactic. In response to whipsaw strikes, the U.S. Supreme Court has held that employers may use multi-employer unit-wide lockouts and then use temporary replacements to maintain operations. Employers whose workers are not part of a whipsaw strike also have the right to lock out employees to exert counter-pressure on the union.[161]

CASE STUDY: *Buffalo Linen Supply Co.*[162]

An association of linen supply companies had bargained on a multi-employer basis with a union for thirteen years. While the association and the union had been parties to successive collective bargaining agreements covering the truck driver employees of the multi- employer unit, the most recent attempts to negotiate a new collective bargaining agreement were unsuccessful.

To put pressure on the employers, the truck drivers employed by one member of the association went on strike and picketed that employer's plant (a whipsaw strike). In response, the remaining employers in the association laid off their truck drivers after advising the union that the layoff was a result of the strike. The association informed the union that the employees would be recalled if the union withdrew its picket line and ended the strike at the initial employer. The parties' bargaining continued, and shortly thereafter, the parties executed a new collective bargaining agreement and terminated the strike and the lockout, and the truck drivers returned to work.

The union filed a ULP charge alleging that the association's layoffs were retaliatory and unlawful.

The NLRB held that the strike against the first employer carried an implicit threat of future strike action against any or all of the other employer-members of the association. The NLRB noted that the purpose of the union maintaining a strike against one employer and threatening to strike other employers in the group at future times was to cause successive and individual employer concessions to the union. Therefore, in the absence of independent evidence of anti-union motivation, the NLRB held that the association's action in locking out their truck drivers until termination of the strike against the first employer was defensive and privileged in nature, rather than retaliatory and unlawful.

Q 7.25.4   Can an employer use replacement workers during a lockout?

An employer may hire temporary replacement workers during a lawful lockout. Further, an employer lawfully may temporarily subcontract work during a lockout. At the end of the lockout, the employees must be returned to their jobs with their seniority intact.

If a lockout is unlawful, the hiring of temporary replacements will similarly be found to be unlawful.[163] Permanent replacements, however, may not be hired during a lockout.[164]

In addition, an employer may lawfully implement permanent subcontracting during a lockout, if the issue of permanent subcontracting work has been bargained to a bona fide impasse or the implementation of permanent subcontracting is not a subject of mandatory bargaining.[165]

Partial Lockouts

Q 7.26   Can an employer lock out some employees and not others?

When an employer can demonstrate a legitimate business reason for doing so, an employer may engage in a "partial lockout"—that is, locking out some but not all of its employees.[166] Partial lockouts are legal only when justified by operational needs.[167] The NLRB has held that an employer may engage in a partial lockout if it can "provide a reasonable basis for finding some employees necessary to continue operations and others unnecessary."[168] However, at least one federal circuit court has held that only extreme business exigencies will justify a partial lockout based upon operational needs.[169]

A partial lockout also must not be motivated by anti-union animus (for example, seeking to discourage union membership or discriminating among union members). An employer may not engage in a partial lockout that discriminates against employees merely because the employer anticipates those employees will honor a picket line or otherwise engage in protected activity. An employer's discriminatory partial lockout on the basis of a protected activity is unlawful even when it is supportive of an employer's bargaining position. An employer may not choose to lock out only union leaders or only employees it believes voted against a proposed contract. This type of discrimination is not a legitimate and substantial business justification for a partial lockout.[170]

An employer's partial lockout may be justified where the employer had a legitimate fear of repeated work stoppages; a partial lockout would thereby prevent a delay in production or a loss of customers. A partial lockout may also be unlawful where it was necessitated by the exigencies of the business operation, because operating on the basis of daily contract extensions was difficult, unproductive, and potentially dangerous to the public. The NLRB has also upheld a partial lockout where the employer's business required operating enormous kilns at extreme temperatures and other extraordinary time pressures in an effort to prevent explosions, injury, and other damage. A partial lockout may also be justified where the unit employees who remained at work have abandoned the bargaining demands being pursued by the union and the strikers.[171] An employer cannot justify a partial lockout when it successfully maintained operations without the use of crossover employees or non-strikers.[172]

Notes to Chapter 7

1.   29 U.S.C. § 157; *see also* NMC Finishing v. NLRB, 101 F.3d 528, 530–31 (8th Cir. 1996).

2.   29 U.S.C. § 157. The right to strike also derives additional support from section 13 of the NLRA. 29 U.S.C. § 163; Atl. Scaffolding Co., 356 N.L.R.B. No. 113 (2011) (holding that even unrepresented employees have a statutorily protected right to strike).

3.   Ambassador Servs. Inc., 358 N.L.R.B. No. 130 (2012).

4.   TT&W Farm Prods., Inc., 358 N.L.R.B. No. 125 (2012).

5.   29 U.S.C. § 152(9). A similar definition of "labor dispute" is found in section 13(c) of the Norris-LaGuardia Act of 1932. *See* 29 U.S.C. § 113(c).

6.   *See, e.g.*, Fortuna Enters., L.P., 360 N.L.R.B. No. 128 (2014) (holding that employees could lawfully engage in an on-site work stoppage to meet with senior-level managers and voice a grievance, even though the employer had an established procedure for resolving group grievances).

7.   NLRB v. Fansteel Metallurgical Corp., 306 U.S. 240, 253 (1939).

8.   Benesight, Inc., 337 N.L.R.B. 282 (2001).

9.   Honolulu Rapid Transit Co., 110 N.L.R.B. 1806, 1809 (1954).

10.   Care Ctr. of Kan. City, 350 N.L.R.B. 64 (2007).

11.   Embossing Printers, Inc., 268 N.L.R.B. 710 (1984).

12.   *Id.* at 710.

13.   Audubon Health Care Ctr., 268 N.L.R.B. 135, 137 (1983).

14.   Elec. Data Sys. Corp., 331 N.L.R.B. 343 (2000).

15.   *Audubon*, 268 N.L.R.B. at 137.

16.   Gaiu Local 13-B, Graphic Arts Int'l Union, 252 N.L.R.B. 936, 938 (1980).

17.   Hostar Marine Transp. Sys., Inc., 298 N.L.R.B. 188, 193 (1990); Inova Health Sys. & Nurses Ass'n for Patient Safety, 360 N.L.R.B. No. 135 (2014).

18.   Daimler Chrysler Corp., 344 N.L.R.B. No. 154 (2005).

19.   *See* Caterpillar, Inc., 324 N.L.R.B. 201, 202 n.4 (1997); *see also* Caterpillar, Inc., 322 N.L.R.B. 674, 675 n.6 (1996).

20.   *See, e.g.*, Engelhard Corp. v. NLRB, 437 F.3d 374 (3d Cir. 2006) (no-strike clause did not prohibit employees' picketing at a shareholder meeting because the clause only restricted picketing that resulted in the suspension of work).

21.   Boys Mkts., Inc. v. Retail Clerks Union, Local 770, 398 U.S. 235 (1970).

22.   Contempo Design, Inc. v. Chi. & Ne. Ill. Dist. Council of Carpenters, 226 F.3d 535, 552 (7th Cir. 2000).

23.   *See* CC-1 Ltd. P'ship, 358 N.L.R.B. No. 129 (2012); Ironton Publ'ns, 321 N.L.R.B. 1048, 1048 (1996).

24. *See, e.g.*, NLRB, Office of Gen. Counsel, Advice Mem., Case 28-CA-108504, ABC Union Cab (Nov. 4, 2013), http://mynlrb.nlrb.gov/link/document.aspx/09031d 45814b1fec (strike unprotected because it was in direct opposition to the union's position and strategy).

25. NLRB v. R.C. Can Co., 328 F.2d 974 (5th Cir. 1964).

26. NLRB v. Draper Corp., 145 F.2d 199, 205 (4th Cir. 1944).

27. E. Chi. Rehab. Ctr., Inc., 259 N.L.R.B. 996 (1982).

28. Children's Hosp. Med. Ctr. of N. Cal., 351 N.L.R.B. 569 (2007); *see also, e.g.*, Teamsters Local Union No. 688, 345 N.L.R.B. 1150 (2005) (holding that, absent any evidence to show that the parties intended otherwise, a no-strike clause that proscribed "any strikes [or] work stoppages" also barred sympathy strikes).

29. Redwing Carriers, Inc., 137 N.L.R.B. 1545, 1547 (1962).

30. Overnight Transp. Co., 154 N.L.R.B. 1271, 1275 (1965).

31. Clear Pine Mouldings, 268 N.L.R.B. 1044, 1046 (1984).

32. *See, e.g.*, Universal Truss, Inc., 348 N.L.R.B. 733 (2006) (employer did not violate NLRA when it discharged strikers who threw stones at non-striking employees and spray-painted and vandalized the employer's property); *see also* Avery Heights, 343 N.L.R.B. No. 128 (2004) (healthcare employer did not violate NLRA when it discharged striker for cursing and insulting patient and patient's family).

33. Detroit Newspaper Agency, 342 N.L.R.B. 233 (2004); *see also* Consol. Commc'ns, 360 N.L.R.B. No. 140 (2014) (finding that picketing employees' acts, which included making obscene gestures, following non-picketing employees, and harassing non-picketing employees while driving, were not sufficient to justify suspension or discharge, noting that "the instances in which the Board has found that strikers have forfeited the protection of the Act in almost all cases involve violent acts or threats of violent acts").

34. N.Y. Tel. Co. v. N.Y. State Dep't of Labor, 440 U.S. 519, 545–46 (1979).

35. 29 U.S.C. § 157; *see also* NMC Finishing v. NLRB, 101 F.3d 528, 530–31 (8th Cir. 1996).

36. Citizens Publ'g & Printing Co. v. NLRB, 263 F.3d 224, 235 (3d Cir. 2001).

37. *Id.* at 235.

38. Gloversville Embossing Corp., 297 N.L.R.B. 182 (1989).

39. Ryan Iron Works, Inc. v. NLRB, 257 F.3d 1, 13 (1st Cir. 2001).

40. Empire Terminal Warehouse Co., 151 N.L.R.B. 1359 (1965).

41. Am. Cyanamid Co. v. NLRB, 592 F.2d 356, 361 (7th Cir. 1979).

42. NLRB v. Brown, 380 U.S. 278, 283–84 (1965).

43. Belknap, Inc. v. Hale, 463 U.S. 491, 502 (1983).

44. Jones Plastic & Eng'g Co., 351 N.L.R.B. 948 (2008), *petition for review denied*, 544 F.3d 841 (7th Cir. 2009).

45. Laidlaw Corp., 171 N.L.R.B. 1366, 1368 (1968), *enforced*, 414 F.2d 99 (7th Cir. 1970); Tri-State Wholesale Bldg. Supplies, Inc., 2014 N.L.R.B. LEXIS 678 (Sept. 2, 2014).

46. *Laidlaw*, 171 N.L.R.B. at 1368.

47. Flambeau Plastics Corp., 172 N.L.R.B. 448, 449 (1968).

48.   TNS, Inc., 329 N.L.R.B. 602 (1999), *vacated in part*, 296 F.3d 384 (6th Cir. 2002) (court agreed that NLRB's test for section 502 coverage was permissible but found that the record lacked evidence to establish that the employees met the articulated coverage test).

49.   *Id.*

50.   *TNS*, 296 F.3d 384.

51.   LB&B Assocs., Inc., 346 N.L.R.B. 1025, 1029 (2006).

52.   NLRB v. Augusta Bakery Corp., 957 F.2d 1467 (7th Cir. 1992).

53.   29 U.S.C. § 152(3).

54.   Associated Grocers, 295 N.L.R.B. 806, 808 (1989).

55.   KSM Indus., Inc., 353 N.L.R.B. No. 117 (Mar. 26, 2009).

56.   29 U.S.C. § 158(d).

57.   United Furniture Workers of Am. v. NLRB, 336 F.2d 738, 741 (D.C. Cir. 1964).

58.   *Id.*

59.   29 U.S.C. § 158(d)(4).

60.   Mastro Plastics Corp. v. NLRB, 350 U.S. 270 (1956).

61.   Beverly Health & Rehab. Servs. v. NLRB, 317 F.3d 316, 321 (D.C. Cir. 2003).

62.   SEIU, United Healthcare Workers–W. v. NLRB, 574 F.3d 1213 (9th Cir. 2009).

63.   E. Chi. Rehab. Ctr., Inc. v. NLRB, 710 F.2d 397 (7th Cir. 1983); N.Y. State Nurses Ass'n, 334 N.L.R.B. 1094 (1999).

64.   Furniture Workers (Jamestown Sterling Corp.), 337 F.2d 936, 940 (2d Cir. 1964).

65.   Kentov v. Sheet Metal Workers' Int'l Ass'n, 418 F.3d 1259, 1265 (11th Cir. 2005) (citing Lumber & Sawmill Workers Local 9727 (Stolze Land & Lumber Co.), 156 N.L.R.B. 388 (1965)).

66.   Chi. Typographical Union No. 16 (Alden Press Inc.), 151 N.L.R.B. 1666, 1669 (1965).

67.   Kentov v. Sheet Metal Workers' Int'l Ass'n, 418 F.3d 1259 (11th Cir. 2005).

68.   *Id.* at 1265.

69.   *See, e.g.*, Laborers' E. Region Org. Fund, 346 N.L.R.B. 1251 (Apr. 28, 2006) (citing Serv. Emps. Union, Local 87, 312 N.L.R.B. 715 (1993)), *enforced*, 1996 U.S. App. LEXIS 30299 (9th Cir. Nov. 20, 1996); *see also* Sheet Metal Workers Int'l Ass'n, Local 15, 346 N.L.R.B. No. 22 (Jan. 9, 2006).

70.   29 U.S.C. § 158(b)(4)(C).

71.   *See id.* § 158(b)(4), (b)(7)(C).

72.   Retail Clerks Local 324 (Barker Bros.), 138 N.L.R.B. 478, 491 (1962).

73.   *Id.*

74.   UNITE HERE! Local 5, 365 N.L.R.B. No. 169 (2017).

75.   *See* Laborers Local 41 (Calumet Contractors Ass'n), 130 N.L.R.B. 78, 81–82 (1961); *see also* Laborers Local 840 (C.A. Blinne Contr. Co. II), 135 N.L.R.B. 1153 (1962).

76.   *See* Hoisting & Portable Local, Int'l Union of Operating Eng'rs (St. Louis Bridge Constr. Co.), 297 N.L.R.B. 485, 491 (1989); *see also* Local 88, Int'l Bhd. of

Teamsters, Chauffeurs, Warehousemen & Helpers (W. Coast Cycle Supply Co.), 208 N.L.R.B. 679, 680 (1974).

77.   29 U.S.C. § 158(b)(4)(B).

78.   520 S. Mich. Ave. Assocs. v. Unite Here Local 1, 760 F.3d 708 (7th Cir. 2014) (holding that a union may be liable for unlawfully coercing a secondary to cease doing business with an employer if the union's conduct amounts to harassment or involves repeated trespass; the court noted that although trespass and harassment differ from picketing because they do not create a symbolic barrier between a business and its customers, they significantly disrupt a business just as picketing does).

79.   NLRB v. Fruit & Vegetable Packers & Warehousemen, Local 760 (Tree Fruits), 377 U.S. 58 (1964).

80.   *Id.* at 72.

81.   Newspaper & Mail Deliverers Union of N.Y. (Gannet Co.), 271 N.L.R.B. 60, 67 (1984).

82.   *Id.*

83.   Laundry & Dry Cleaning Union Local 259 (Morrison's of San Diego), 164 N.L.R.B. 426 (1967).

84.   *Id.; see also* Massey Energy Co., 358 N.L.R.B. No. 159 (2012) (finding both parties liable for unfair labor practices of one party where court determined they were a single employer with common ownership, interrelated operations, limited common management, and centralized control of labor relations).

85.   Boich Mining Co. v. NLRB, 955 F.2d 431 (6th Cir. 1992).

86.   *Boich*, 955 F.2d at 435.

87.   NLRB v. Bus. Mach. & Office Appliance Mechs. Conference Bd., 228 F.2d 553, 558–59 (2d Cir. 1955).

88.   *Id.* at 559.

89.   *Id.*, 228 F.2d 553.

90.   29 U.S.C. § 160(*l*); *see also* 29 C.F.R. §§ 102.94–102.97.

91.   29 U.S.C. § 160(*l*).

92.   *Id.*

93.   *Id.*

94.   *See* Frye v. Dist. 1199, 996 F.2d 141 (6th Cir. 1993); *see also* Squillacote v. Meat Cutters Local 248 (Milwaukee Indep. Meat Packers Ass'n), 534 F.2d 735 (7th Cir. 1976).

95.   Kentov v. Sheet Metal Workers Local 15, 418 F.3d 1259 (11th Cir. 2005).

96.   29 U.S.C. § 160.

97.   *Id.*

98.   *Id.* § 157.

99.   *Id.* § 158(a)(1), (3).

100. Local Hotel, Motel, Rest. Emps. & Bartenders Union, AFL-CIO, 240 N.L.R.B. 240 (1979).

101. Int'l Hod Carriers Bldg. & Common Laborers, 135 N.L.R.B. 1153 (1962).

102. *See, e.g.*, CAL. CIVIL CODE § 527.3 and CAL. LABOR CODE § 1138.1.

103. Sailors' Union of Pac. (Moore Dry Dock Co.), 92 N.L.R.B. 547 (1950).

104. *Id.*

105. Local 7, Sheet Metals Workers' Int'l Ass'n, AFL-CIO (Andy J. Egan Co.), 345 N.L.R.B. 1322 (2005).

106. Preferred Bldg. Servs., Inc., 366 N.L.R.B. No. 159 (2018).

107. *See, e.g.*, NLRB Bldg. & Constr. Trades Council (Denver) (Gould & Preisner), 341 U.S. 675 (1951).

108. *Local 7*, 345 N.L.R.B. at 1325–26.

109. Elec. Workers (IUE) Local 761 v. NRLB, 366 U.S. 667 (1961).

110. NLRB v. Denver Bldg. & Constr. Trades Council, 341 U.S. 675 (1951); Bldg. & Constr. Trades Council (New Orleans & Vicinity) (Markwell & Hartz, Inc.), 155 N.L.R.B. 319 (1964), *enforced*, 387 F.2d 79 (5th Cir. 1967).

111. Teamsters, Local 776, 313 N.L.R.B. 1148 (1994).

112. Petrochem Insulation, Inc. v. NLRB, 240 F.3d 26 (D.C. Cir. 2001); *see also* BLACK'S LAW DICTIONARY 732 (8th ed. 2004).

113. *See* Edward J. DeBartolo Corp. v. Fla. Gulf Coast Bldg. & Constr. Trades Council (*DeBartolo II*), 485 U.S. 568 (1988); *see also* NLRB v. Retail Store Emps., 447 U.S. 607 (1980) (Stevens, J., concurring); Babbitt v. Farm Workers, 442 U.S. 289 (1979); Hughes v. Superior Court, 339 U.S. 460 (1950).

114. Edward J. DeBartolo Corp. v. Fla. Gulf Coast Bldg. & Constr. Trades Council (*DeBartolo II*), 485 U.S. 568 (1988).

115. 520 S. Mich. Ave. Assocs. v. Unite Here Local 1, 760 F.3d 708 (7th Cir. 2014) (holding that the union's practices of "barging into offices, bypassing security, following certain targets around stores, and shouting at employees" in addition to their persuasive acts of handbilling were unlawful coercive pressure).

116. *See* Lechmere, Inc. v. NLRB, 502 U.S. 527 (1992); *see also* NLRB v. Babcock & Wilcox Co., 351 U.S. 105 (1956).

117. *See Lechmere*, 502 U.S. 527; *see also* Indio Grocery Outlet, 187 F.3d 1080 (9th Cir. 1999); Oakland Mall (II), 316 N.L.R.B. 160 (1971); Food & Commercial Workers Local 880 v. NLRB, 64 F.3d 292 (D.C. Cir. 1996); NLRB v. Great Scot, 39 F.3d 678 (6th Cir. 1994).

118. *See* Hudgens v. NLRB, 424 U.S. 507 (1976); *see also* Salmon Run Shopping Ctr. LLC v. NLRB, 534 F.3d 108 (2d Cir. 2008); Sandusky Mall Co. v. NLRB, 242 F.3d 682 (6th Cir. 2001); Be-Lo Stores v. NLRB, 126 F.3d 268 (4th Cir. 1997); Davis Supermarkets v. NLRB, 2 F.3d 1162 (D.C. Cir. 1993).

119. *See, e.g.*, Target Corp., 359 N.L.R.B. No. 103 (2013); Shands Jacksonville Med. Ctr., Inc., 359 N.L.R.B. No. 104 (2013).

120. Fashion Valley Mall, LLC v. NLRB, 172 P.3d 742 (Cal. 2007).

121. The Boeing Co., 365 N.L.R.B. No. 154 (2017).

122. N.Y. N.Y. Hotel & Casino, 356 N.L.R.B. No. 119 (Mar. 25, 2011), *aff'd*, 676 F.3d 193 (D.C. Cir. 2012); *see also* Remington Lodging & Hosp., LLC, 359 N.L.R.B. No. 95 (2013) (security, maintenance, and valet parking, which typically occur at the entrance to a facility, do not transform the entrance into a "work area" where an employer can lawfully ban employee distributions).

123. Sw. Reg'l Council of Carpenters (New Star), 356 N.L.R.B. No. 88 (Feb. 3, 2011).

124. United Bhd. of Carpenters & Joiners of Am. (Eliason & Knuth), 355 N.L.R.B. No. 159 (2010).

125. Sheet Metal Workers Local 15, 356 N.L.R.B. No. 162 (May 26, 2011).

126. *New Star*, 356 N.L.R.B. No. 88 (2011).

127. *See* NLRB, Office of Gen. Counsel, Advice Mem., Case 19-CC-2042, Pac. Nw. Reg'l Council of Carpenters (June 19, 2008), http://apps.nlrb.gov/link/document.aspx/09031d458013e680.

128. *See* Ryan Ellis, *When Corporations Are Attacked: Look for the Union Label*, LABOR WATCH (Capital Research Ctr., Wash., D.C.), Apr. 2007; *see also* Jarol B. Manheim, *Corporate Campaigns: Labor's Tactic of the "Death of a Thousand Cuts,"* LABOR WATCH (Capital Research Ctr., Wash., D.C.), Jan. 2002.

129. Pennant Foods Co., 352 N.L.R.B. 451 (2008).

130. BE&K Constr. Co., 351 N.L.R.B. No. 29 (Sept. 29, 2007).

131. *Id*; Raineri Constr., LLC v. Taylor, 2014 U.S. Dist. LEXIS 151211 (E.D. Mo. Oct. 24, 2014).

132. *See* Organized Crime Control Act of 1970, § 901(a), tit. IX—Racketeer Influenced and Corrupt Organizations, Pub. L. No. 91-452, 84 Stat. 922, 941 (codified at 18 U.S.C. §§ 1961–68).

133. Longshoremen (ILA) Local 1814 v. N.Y. Shipping Ass'n, 965 F.2d 1224, 1235 (2d Cir.), *cert. denied*, 506 U.S. 953 (1992).

134. JOHN E. HIGGINS, JR., 2 THE DEVELOPING LABOR LAW 2500–01 (ABA 5th ed. 2006).

135. *See, e.g.*, Yellow Bus Lines v. Drivers Local 639, 883 F.2d 132 (D.C. Cir. 1989), *modified*, 913 F.2d 948 (1990) (en banc), *cert. denied*, 501 U.S. 1222 (1991); *see also* A. Terzi Prods. v. Theatrical Protective Union Local 1, 2 F. Supp. 2d 485 (S.D.N.Y. 1998).

136. *See, e.g.*, Landry v. Air Line Pilots, 901 F.2d 404, 426 (5th Cir.), *cert. denied*, 498 U.S. 895 (1990); *see also* Overnite Transp. Co. v. Truck Drivers Local 705, 704 F. Supp. 859 (N.D. Ill. 1989), *aff'd*, 904 F.2d 391 (7th Cir. 1990).

137. *See, e.g.*, Butchers Local 498 v. SDC Inv., 631 F. Supp. 1001 (E.D. Cal. 1986).

138. *See, e.g.*, United States v. Busacca, 936 F.2d 232 (6th Cir.), *cert. denied*, 502 U.S. 985 (1991) (use of funds to pay legal fees of union officer); *see also* Chi. Truck Drivers Pension Fund v. Bhd. Labor Leasing, 950 F. Supp. 1454, 1461–62 (E.D. Mo. 1996), *aff'd*, 141 F.3d 1167 (8th Cir. 1998) (alleging union filed inflated claims of withdrawal liability in bankruptcy court).

139. *See, e.g.*, Lightning Lube v. Witco Corp., 4 F.3d 1153, 1188 (3d Cir. 1993); *see also* Bldg. Indus. Fund v. Elec. Workers (IBEW) Local 3, 992 F. Supp. 162, 174 (E.D.N.Y. 1996), *aff'd*, 141 F.3d 1151 (2d Cir. 1998).

140. *IBEW*, 992 F. Supp. at 174–78.

141. *See* Saporito v. Combustion Eng'g, 843 F.2d 666 (3d Cir. 1988), *vacated*, 489 U.S. 1049 (1989); *see also* Hutchinson v. Wickes Cos., 726 F. Supp. 1315 (N.D. Ga. 1989).

142. Rose v. Bartle, 871 F.2d 331 (3d Cir. 1989).

143. In essence, these are whistleblower claims brought by former employees who were allegedly terminated for failure to participate in a RICO violation on behalf of their employer. *See* Bowman v. W. Auto Supply Co., 985 F.2d 383 (8th Cir.), *cert. denied*, 508 U.S. 957 (1993); *see also* Reddy v. Litton Indus., 912 F.2d 291 (9th Cir. 1990), *cert. denied*, 502 U.S. 921 (1991).

144. Busby v. Crown Supply, 896 F.2d 535 (5th Cir. 1986), *cert. denied*, 480 U.S. 949 (1987).

145. *See, e.g.*, Nat'l Org. for Women v. Scheidler, 510 U.S. 249, 259 (1994); *see also* Brannon v. Boatmen's First Nat'l Bank of Okla., 153 F.3d 1144, 1147 (10th Cir. 1998).

146. Paramount Enters. v. Laborers E. Region Org. Fund, 2014 U.S. Dist. LEXIS 23476 (D.N.J. Feb. 25, 2014) (granting union's motion to dismiss § 1962(c) RICO claim brought by employer, a prevailing wage contractor, claiming that union tried to wrongfully force the employer to become a union contractor by disseminating leaflets with false, harmful statements).

147. Mariah Boat v. Laborers, 19 F. Supp. 2d 893 (S.D. Ill. 1998).

148. Teamsters Local 372 v. Detroit Newspapers, 993 F. Supp. 1052 (E.D. Mich. 1998).

149. A. Terzi Prods. v. Theatrical Protective Union Local 1, 2 F. Supp. 2d 485 (S.D.N.Y. 1998).

150. N.Y. Times Co. v. Sullivan, 376 U.S. 254, 280, 285–86 (1964).

151. Pichler v. Union of Needletrades, Indus. & Textile Emps., AFL-CIO (UNITE), 542 F.3d 380 (3d Cir. 2008), *cert denied*, 129 S. Ct. 1662 (2009).

152. *See id.*

153. *See* Am. Ship Bldg. Co. v. NLRB, 380 U.S. 300 (1965); *see also* NLRB v. Greensburg Coca-Cola Bottling Co., 40 F.3d 669 (3d Cir. 1994); Local 825, Int'l Union of Operating Eng'rs v. NLRB, 829 F.2d 458 (3d Cir. 1987).

154. *See* 29 U.S.C. § 158(d); *see also* Brown v. Pro Football, Inc., 518 U.S. 231 (1996); Teamsters Local 369 v. NLRB, 942 F.2d 1078 (D.C. Cir. 1991); Royal Motor Sales, 329 N.L.R.B. 760 (1999).

155. Darling & Co., 171 N.L.R.B. 801 (1968).

156. Teamsters Local Union No. 455 v. NLRB, 765 F.3d 1198 (10th Cir. 2014) (holding that an otherwise lawful lockout does not materially affect negotiations and become unlawful when an employer threatens to permanently replace locked-out employees, but revokes the threat two days after lockout).

157. *See* Am. Ship Bldg. Co., 380 U.S. 300 (1965); *see also* Local 15, AFL-CIO v. NLRB, 429 F.3d 651 (7th Cir. 2005); NLRB v. Ancor Concepts, Inc., 166 F.3d 55 (2d Cir. 1999); Teamsters Local Union No. 639 v. NLRB, 924 F.2d 1078 (D.C. Cir. 1991); Am. Cyanamid Co. v. NLRB, 592 F.2d 356, 364 (7th Cir. 1979); Flora & Argus Constr. Co., 132 N.L.R.B. 776 (1961); N. Country Motors, 133 N.L.R.B. 1479 (1961); Ralph's Wonder, 127 N.L.R.B. 1280 (1960); Guard Servs., 134 N.L.R.B. 1753 (1961); Perry Coal, 125 N.L.R.B. 1246 (1959).

158. *See Local 15, AFL-CIO*, 429 F.3d at 656 (finding partial lockout is presumptively an unfair labor practice in absence of legitimate and substantial business justification).

159. *See* Don Lee Distrib., Inc. (Warren) v. NLRB, 145 F.3d 834 (6th Cir. 1998); *see also* McClatchy Newspapers, Inc. v. NLRB, 131 F.3d 1026 (D.C. Cir. 1997); Cal. *ex rel.* Lockyer v. Safeway, Inc., 355 F. Supp. 2d 1111 (C.D. Cal. 2005).

160. Dresser-Rand Co., 358 N.L.R.B. No. 97 (2012).

161. *See* Am. Ship Bldg. Co. v. NLRB, 380 U.S. 300 (1965); *see also* Brown v. Pro Football, 518 U.S. 231 (1996); NLRB v. Brown, 380 U.S. 278 (1965); NLRB v. Truck Drivers Local 449, 353 U.S. 87 (1957).

162. Buffalo Linen Supply Co., 109 N.L.R.B. 447 (1954).

163. *See* Boilermakers, Local 88 v. NLRB, 858 F.2d 756 (D.C. Cir. 1988); *see also* Harter Equip., Inc., 280 N.L.R.B. 597 (1986); Ass'n of D.C. Liquor Wholesalers, 292 N.L.R.B. 1237, 1258 (1989).

164. *But cf.* Int'l Paper Co. v. NLRB, 115 F.3d 1045, 1051 nn.4–5 (D.C. Cir. 1997) (leaving open the question); Johns-Manville Prods. Corp. v. NLRB, 557 F.2d 1126 (5th Cir. 1977) (employer's lockout and hiring of permanent replacements were justified by employees' in-plant sabotage).

165. *See Int'l Paper Co.*, 115 F.3d at 1046; *see also* Fibreboard Paper Prods. Corp., 379 U.S. 203 (1964); Rock-Tenn. Co. v. NLRB, 101 F.3d 1441 (D.C. Cir. 1996); Torrington Indus., 307 N.L.R.B. 809 (1992).

166. Bali Blinds Midwest, 292 N.L.R.B. 243 (1989).

167. *See* Midwest Generation, 343 N.L.R.B. No. 12 (2004); *see also* Bali Blinds Midwest, 292 N.L.R.B. 243 (1988); Laclede Gas Co., 187 N.L.R.B. 243 (1970).

168. Hercules Drawn Steel Corp., 352 N.L.R.B. 53 (Feb. 7, 2008).

169. Local 15, AFL-CIO v. NLRB, 429 F.2d 651 (7th Cir. 2005).

170. *See id.* at 651; *see also* Nat'l Fabricators v. NLRB, 903 F.2d 396 (5th Cir. 1990); Thrift Drug Co., 204 N.L.R.B. 41 (1973); McGwier Co. v. NLRB, 204 N.L.R.B. 492 (1973).

171. *See, e.g.*, Bali Blinds Midwest, 292 N.L.R.B. 243 (1988); Gen. Portland, Inc., 283 N.L.R.B. 826 (1987); Laclede Gas Co., 187 N.L.R.B. 243 (1970).

172. *Local 15, AFL-CIO*, 429 F.3d at 651.

8

Unfair Labor Practice Case Procedures

The NLRA defines certain actions by employers and unions as unfair labor practices. When a ULP is thought to have been committed, an unfair labor practice charge alleging a violation of one or more provisions of the NLRA may be filed against an employer or labor organization with a regional office of the NLRB. Upon the filing of a charge, the NLRB's jurisdiction is invoked, and it may investigate and remedy such ULPs.

Once a charge is received, it is investigated by an NLRB board agent, who, after gathering sufficient facts, makes a recommendation as to whether the charge has merit and whether a complaint should issue. A charge may be deferred for resolution through arbitration, and parties often seek private resolutions of their disputes through settlements. In cases that are not dismissed, arbitrated, or settled, the next step would be for the regional director on behalf of the general counsel to issue a complaint, after which the role of the NLRB switches from neutral investigator to prosecutor. Complaints may proceed to a hearing before an administrative law judge, who issues a recommended decision and, if a violation is found, an order to remedy ULPs.

The Basics

Q 8.1   What is an unfair labor practice?

An unfair labor practice is a violation of section 8 of the NLRA committed by an employer or a labor organization.

Sections 8(a) and 8(b) of the NLRA outline the different ULPs that can be committed by employers and labor unions. In practice, ULPs are often referred to by their subsection number.[1]

In addition, section (8)(e) of the NLRA prohibits employers and unions from agreeing to "hot cargo agreements," whereby a union and employer agree to refrain from dealing with or handling the goods of another employer or to refrain from doing business with another person. This provision is designed to outlaw certain secondary agreements, such as union-only subcontracting provisions. Section 8(e) provisos contain exceptions for the construction and garment industries. Hot cargo agreements are discussed in greater detail in chapter 5.

Finally, section 8(f) sets out exceptions to potential union violations for the construction industry related to pre-hire agreements.[2]

ULPs by Employer

Q 8.2   What kinds of employer actions are considered ULPs?

Sections 8(a)(1) through 8(a)(5) set forth ULPs that may be committed by employers.[3] Simply put, they are as follows:

(1)   interfering with employees' section 7 rights;

(2)   dominating or interfering with the formation or administration of a labor organization;

(3)   discriminating against employees for participating in, or refraining from, concerted or union activities;

(4)   retaliating against employees for filing charges or giving testimony;

(5)   refusing to bargain collectively.

Additional details regarding violations of section 8(a)(1)–(4) are provided in chapter 3; additional information regarding 8(a)(5) violations can be found in chapter 5.

Q 8.2.1   What employer actions violate NLRA section 8(a)(1)?

Employer conduct that interferes with employees' rights to organize or engage in collective bargaining may violate section 8(a)(1) of the NLRA. Section 8(a)(1) generally prohibits employer interference with, restraint of, or coercion of employees in the exercise of the rights guaranteed by section 7 of the NLRA. The rights guaranteed to employees under section 7 of the NLRA are discussed in greater detail in chapter 1 but, in general, include: the rights to self-organization; to form, join, or assist labor organizations; to bargain collectively through representatives of their own choosing; to engage in other concerted activities for the purpose of collective bargaining or other mutual aid or protection; and the right to refrain from each of these activities. Examples of section 8(a)(1) violations include:

• rules prohibiting solicitation, communications, or wearing of union insignia;

- threats and coercion directed against employees;

- promises of benefits or other inducements to discourage union activity;

- interrogation in the context of organizational campaigns;

- surveillance of union activities.

In practice, section 8(a)(1) also serves as a "catch-all" provision. Charges filed under other subsections of section 8(a) are often accompanied by a section 8(a)(1) allegation.[4]

Q 8.2.2   ... section 8(a)(2)?

Violations of section 8(a)(2) occur when employers dominate or interfere with the formation or administration of any union or contribute financial or other support to a "labor organization" as defined in section 2(5) of the NLRA. ULPs filed under section 8(a)(2) often involve so-called company unions, or the premature recognition of a union that does not have support of a majority of the employees in the relevant bargaining unit.[5] Examples of 8(a)(2) violations include:

- Where the employer allows one union access to the employer's premises, while denying access to another union.

- Where a supervisor assists a union by recruiting subordinates to sign authorization cards or threatens to terminate employees who do not join the union.

- Where the employer prematurely enters into a collective bargaining agreement with a minority union.

- Where the employer dominates or interferes with certain workplace employee committees that are considered to be labor organizations.

Q 8.2.3   ... section 8(a)(3)?

Generally, an employer cannot discipline or discharge employees because they belong to a union or engage in union activities. Section 8(a)(3) of the NLRA prohibits employers from discriminating with regard to hiring or tenure of employment, or as to any term or condition of employment, so as to encourage or discourage membership in any labor organization. This provision is interpreted broadly to prohibit discriminatory actions (such as discharge, refusal to hire, discipline, or refusal to reinstate) based on an employee's support for a union, membership in a union, or union activity, including serving as a union officer or participating in a lawful demonstration, or any protected concerted activity.[6]

Q 8.2.4   ... section 8(a)(4)?

Violations of section 8(a)(4) arise when an employer discharges or otherwise discriminates against an employee because he or she has filed charges or given testimony as part of the enforcement of the NLRA. This provision is often referred to as the anti-retaliation provision of the NLRA.[7]

Q 8.2.5   ... section 8(a)(5)?

An employer violates section 8(a)(5) when it refuses to bargain collectively with the representatives of his employees. This provision prohibits an employer's refusal to bargain in good faith with a duly recognized union as required by the NLRA.[8] Section 8(a)(5) has also been applied in a broad manner to prohibit other employer conduct, including:

- Refusal to recognize a union that has been duly certified.

- Making unilateral changes in the terms and conditions of employment before a good-faith bargaining impasse has been reached.

- Refusal to provide the union with certain requested information.

ULPs by Labor Organization

Q 8.3   What kinds of actions by a labor organization are considered ULPs?

Section 8(b) sets forth union activities that are considered union ULPs.[9] Simply put, they are as follows:

(1) restraining or coercing employees in their section 7 rights or an employer in the selection of its bargaining representative;

(2) causing or attempting to cause an employer to discriminate against an employee;

(3) refusing to bargain collectively;

(4) certain "secondary activity" designed to coerce a primary employer;

(5) charging excessive fees;

(6) "featherbedding";

(7) certain picketing aimed at gaining employer recognition.

Q 8.3.1 When does a union commit violations of section 8(b)(1)?

Section 8(b)(1)(A) makes it unlawful for a union to restrain or coerce employees in the exercise of their rights under the NLRA. As discussed in greater detail in chapter 3, these rights include the right to engage in (and the right to refrain from) self-organization, to form, join, or assist labor organizations, to bargain collectively through representatives of their own choosing, and to engage in other concerted activities for the purpose of collective bargaining or other mutual aid or protection.[10] Most cases involving section 8(b)(1)(A) violations concern threats of loss of employment, improper use of union discipline, or discriminatory or other improper conduct practiced by a union in violation of its duty of fair representation.[11]

Note that union "interference" with employee section 7 rights is not an express violation of section 8(b)(1)(A), whereas employer interference is a violation of section 8(a)(1). This reflects greater latitude in allowing unions to make promises in the course of election campaigns since they would need employer agreement to make good on those promises.

Violations of section 8(b)(1)(B) occur when unions restrain or coerce an employer in the selection of its representatives for the purposes of collective bargaining or the adjustment of grievances.[12] Permitting a union to use coercion in grievance or bargaining procedures would create a disincentive for employers to agree to take part in collective bargaining private grievance adjustment and would interfere with the exercise of their managerial judgment. See chapter 3 for a more detailed discussion and examples.

Q 8.3.2   ... section 8(b)(2)?

Unions violate section 8(b)(2) of the NLRA when they cause or attempt to cause an employer to discriminate against an employee in violation of section 8(a)(3). This includes union actions that assist an employer in discriminating against an employee for engaging in activity protected by the NLRA. Section 8(b)(2) violations are discussed in further detail in chapter 3.

Q 8.3.3   ... section 8(b)(3)?

Unions violate section 8(b)(3) when they refuse to bargain collectively with an employer. This section is the counterpart to employer section 8(a)(5) violations. Section 8(b)(3) violations are discussed in further detail in chapter 5.

Q 8.3.4   ... section 8(b)(4)?

A union commits an NLRA section 8(b)(4) violation when it engages in secondary activity, which includes strikes, picketing, boycotts, or other activity designed to pressure an employer with whom the union may have a dispute (the primary employer) by threatening or picketing a different employer with whom the primary employer has a business relationship (the secondary employer). This unlawful "secondary activity" is discussed in greater detail in chapter 7. In general, however, it is unlawful for a union to picket a secondary employer in an effort to coerce the primary employer to bargain with or make concessions to the union.

Q 8.3.5   ... section 8(b)(5)?

Violations of section 8(b)(5) occur when unions charge members excessive or discriminatory fees. There is no specific dollar amount that the NLRB will find per se discriminatory or excessive. Rather, the NLRB conducts a case-by-case analysis, focusing on the custom or practice of unions within the industry, the wages of the affected employees, and the union's intentions in setting the fees or dues. For instance, a union violates section 8(b)(5) where its purpose in setting a high initiation fee is to discourage entry into the industry.

Examples of excessive or discriminatory fees charged by unions in violation of section 8(b)(5) include imposing an initiation fee seven times an employees' weekly salary, and imposing non-uniform dues and fees, such as charging a higher fee to immigrants, without a reasonable justification for doing so. Section 8(b)(5) violations are discussed in further detail in chapter 11.

Q 8.3.6   ... section 8(b)(6)?

Section 8(b)(6) prohibits what is commonly referred to as "featherbedding," which occurs when a union requires the employer to pay in the nature of an exaction for services that are not performed or not to be performed, such as hiring or retaining employees in jobs where they do no actual work.[13]

Q 8.3.7   ... section 8(b)(7)?

Section 8(b)(7) prevents unions from picketing an employer for the purpose of organizing the employees or obtaining employer recognition, where: (1) the employer has lawfully recognized another union, or (2) the union does not represent the employees and fails to file a recognition petition within thirty days.

Filing a ULP Charge with the NLRB

Who Files

Q 8.4   Who may file a ULP charge?

Any person may file a charge, including employees, labor organizations, individuals who are not employees of the charged employer, an employer who is not a member of an employer association in a case where rights of that association's members are involved, and civil rights groups (on behalf of employees), to name a few.

The NLRB ordinarily does not investigate potential violations of the NLRA in the absence of a charge.

Q 8.5   Who is a charge filed with?

In most cases, charges are filed with a regional office of the NLRB in whose area the ULPs are alleged to have occurred. There are twenty-six regional offices and various resident offices (which are subdivisions of regional offices) that administer charges in the different geographical areas of the United States. It is also the charging party's responsibility under the NLRB's Rules and Regulations to serve a copy of the charge on each charged party.

Charge Forms

Q 8.6   What must a charge include?

The charge should include the names and addresses of the charging party and the charged party, as well as a clear and concise statement of the facts constituting the alleged violation of one or more provisions of the NLRA.[14] A charge must be sworn in front of a notary public, an NLRB agent, or someone authorized to administer oaths, or it must contain a declaration that its contents are true and correct to the best of the signer's knowledge.

Three types of charge forms are available in the Regional Offices of the NLRB and on the NLRB's website (www.nlrb.gov):[15]

(1) NLRB-501: Charge Against Employer

(2) NLRB-508: Charge Against Labor Organization or Its Agent

(3) NLRB-509: Charge Alleging Unfair Labor Practices Under Section 8(e) of the NLRA.

Unions generally can allege all of their charges on a single form. Employers, on the other hand, should be aware that not all types of allegations against unions can be included on a single charge form. For example, all charges involving jurisdictional disputes must be separated out on a single form. Likewise, all charges alleging recognitional picketing must be outlined on a separate form. A breakdown of the charges that may be grouped together on a single charge form are as follows:

- Secondary and other prohibited strikes and picketing may be grouped together on a single charge form.

- Recognitional picketing (section 8(b)(7)) violations may be combined on a single form.

- Violations of sections 8(b)(1), 8(b)(2), 8(b)(3), 8(b)(5), and 8(b)(6) can be included together on a single form.

The same form (NLRB-508) is used for all of the charges against the union, but because of the NLRB's case-numbering system, the charges must be broken out as described above.

Means of Delivery/Filing

Q 8.7   By what means may a charge be filed?

Most filings with the NLRB may be made in person, by mail (registered, certified, or regular), or by private delivery service. Certain documents may be electronically filed through the NLRB's website, which is now the NLRB's preferred method of filing for these documents. Charges, however, may not be filed electronically.[16] The charging party should include an original copy of the charge and a copy for each charged party, plus four additional copies. Service of papers to these other parties may be made in person, by mail (registered, certified, or regular), private delivery service, or email (if the document was electronically filed). Except for papers that were hand-filed with the NLRB, service should be made by the same means as was used for the filing with the NLRB.[17] Note that the NLRB Rules and Regulations do not permit facsimile service of a charge unless the opposing party has agreed to permit such service.

Timeliness of Charges; Deadlines

Q 8.8   When is a charge timely?

In most cases, a charge is timely if it is filed and served on the charged party or parties within six months of the alleged ULP, pursuant to section 10(b) of the NLRA. The time period is computed from the date of the alleged unlawful act rather than the date its consequences become effective.[18]

There are many ways in which a charge that appears untimely on its face may be revived. First, the section 10(b) statute of limitations period does not begin to run until the aggrieved party has clear and unequivocal notice, either actual or constructive, of the facts underlying the alleged violation. However, this notice rule cuts both ways, and a seemingly timely charge could be found untimely under certain circumstances. For example, an employee who received notice that he would be terminated but waited to file a charge until the termination became effective (more than six months from the date of the notice) was barred by section 10(b).[19] An employee's lack of knowledge of his rights under the NLRA is not a basis for tolling the limitations period.[20]

Second, an otherwise untimely charge can be revived under the theory of "continuing violations." For example, where there has been a series of contract breaches by an employer, the NLRB has held that each successive contract breach constitutes a separate ULP.[21]

Third, if a charge has already been filed by an aggrieved party, a new allegation can often be tacked on to the prior charge if the two allegations are "closely related." The NLRB uses a three-factor test in determining if two allegations are closely related:

(1) whether the untimely allegations involve the same legal theory as the timely charges;

(2) whether the untimely allegations arise from the same factual situation or sequence of events alleged in the timely charge; and

(3) whether similar defenses would be raised.[22]

Finally, an aggrieved party is relieved of the section 10(b) limitations period if the individual can show that he or she was serving in the armed forces during the six-month period.

Further, if the regional office decides to issue a complaint based on a particular charge, the complaint may assert allegations that are not specifically referenced in a charge if they are "closely related" to the allegations made in the charge. The NLRB applies the same three-prong closely related test detailed above to determine whether amendments to a complaint will be time-barred.

CASE STUDY: *Heartland Industrial Partners*[23]

The NLRB reaffirmed that allegations can be added to a complaint as long as they are closely related to a timely ULP charge. A side letter agreement between an employer and a union required that any subsequently acquired company of the employer would enter into an agreement with the union and include the same "subsequently acquired" provision in their agreement. The employer acquired two companies, and the first acquired company was required to execute an agreement with the union in January 2003. The second acquired company executed an agreement with the union in July 2003. An initial ULP charge was filed by the first acquired company in August 2003 alleging violation of section 8(e)'s "hot cargo" provision. An amended charge was filed in September 2004 asserting that the allegedly unlawful agreement between the employer and the union was reaffirmed each time a newly acquired company was required to execute a similar agreement. The NLRB determined that the complaint was not time-barred under section 10(b) because the original charge was timely with respect to the second company's agreement and the second company's agreement was sufficiently related to the first company's agreement. The NLRB reasoned that the original charge clearly gave notice to the employer and the union (the respondents) that the original agreement was being challenged under section 8(e), and the respondents would raise the same defenses to all agreements.

Q 8.9   How are filing deadlines calculated?

A filing must be received by the designated NLRB officer before the official closing time of the receiving office on the last day of the time limit. In computing any period of time, the day of the act or event after which the designated period of time begins to run is not included. The last day of the period is included, unless it is a Saturday, Sunday, or legal holiday, in which case the period runs until the official closing time of the receiving office on the next NLRB business day. When the period of time prescribed or allowed is less than seven days, intermediate Saturdays, Sundays, and holidays are excluded in the computation.

The NLRB will accept as timely filed any document that is hand-delivered to the NLRB on or before the official closing time of the receiving office on the due date or postmarked no later than the day before the due date. Documents postmarked on or after the due date are untimely. Postmarking also includes timely depositing the document with a delivery service that will provide a record showing that the document was tendered to the delivery service in sufficient time for delivery by the due date.

Q 8.9.1   Are deadlines the same for e-filing?

Filing rules are somewhat different when documents are filed electronically with the NLRB, Division of Judges, Office of Appeals, or Regional Offices.[24] A document is considered timely e-filed if the transmission of the entire document through the NLRB's website is accomplished before midnight (up to 11:59 P.M.) in the time zone of the receiving office on the due date.[25] More detailed instructions regarding the filing requirements for electronically submitted documents can be found on the NLRB's website at www.nlrb.gov.

Q 8.9.2   May a party request an extension of time for filing?

Yes. A request for extension of time to file a document must be filed no later than the official closing time of the receiving office on the date on which the document is due. If a request for extension of time is filed within three days of the due date, the request must be grounded upon "circumstances not reasonably foreseeable in advance."[26]

Q 8.9.3   What documents must be received by the NLRB on or before the last day for filing?

The NLRB specifies four types of documents that must be received by the NLRB on or before the official closing time of the receiving office on the last day for filing:[27]

- charges filed pursuant to section 10(b) of the NLRA;

- applications for awards, fees, and other expenses under the Equal Access to Justice Act (see Q 8.49.1 for more detailed discussion of EAJA);

- petitions to revoke subpoenas; and

- requests for extensions of time to file any documents for which an extension may be granted.

Q 8.9.4   How are service deadlines calculated?

The date of service is the day when the document is deposited in the U.S. mail or with a private delivery service that will provide a record showing the date the document was tendered to the delivery service. If the document is served in person, the date the document is delivered in person is the date of service. If service may be made by facsimile, the date of service is the date on which the transmission is received.[28]

Service rules are somewhat different for e-filed documents, and the NLRB's instructions with regard to e-filed documents may override its ordinary rules related to the service of hard copies.[29] Documents e-filed with the NLRB that require service on other parties must be served by email, if possible. If a party to be served does not have access to email service, notification by telephone regarding the substance of the e-filed document is required. Additionally, after telephoning the party, a copy of the document must be served on that party no later than the next day by either personal service, overnight delivery service, or facsimile (with the permission of the party receiving the document). Additional details regarding the rules for the timing of service of e-filed documents may be found on the NLRB's website, www.nlrb.gov.

NLRB Investigation of ULP Charges

Fact-Finding and Processing of a Charge

Q 8.10   How does the NLRB investigate a charge?

Once the NLRB regional office receives a charge, the regional director will assign an NLRB board agent or attorney to investigate the charge. At this stage of the investigation, the NLRB agent acts as a neutral fact-gatherer. The board agent's goal is to determine whether there is sufficient evidence to support the issuance of a ULP complaint.

The board agent will contact the charging party to gather details on the allegations underlying the charge. This may include talking to the charging party and third-party witnesses, obtaining affidavits, and requesting relevant documents. In certain circumstances, the NLRB may issue investigative subpoenas to compel witnesses to provide testimony needed for evaluating the merits of the charge.[30]

The *NLRB Casehandling Manual*, which can be found on the NLRB's website (www.nlrb.gov), provides detailed guidelines for charge investigations, including how the NLRB will handle attorney-represented witnesses.

Q 8.10.1   During the investigation, can the NLRB request to take witness affidavits?

Yes. Witness affidavits are a key part of ULP investigations. Affidavits provide a permanent record of a witness's testimony, which the NLRB agent can rely upon in making a decision regarding the case. Witness affidavits are confidential, and only pretrial statements given by a witness who actually testifies at the hearing will be subject to disclosure. The board agent will request to take a witness affidavit from the charging party and/or their witnesses in order to expedite processing the case in certain circumstances. Such circumstances include:

- The witness has traveled a substantial distance to the field office.

- The witness will be otherwise unavailable for a considerable period.

- The nature of the charge requires immediate investigation.

Q 8.10.2   Does the NLRB have authority to issue subpoenas to investigate charges?

Yes. Although "pretrial discovery" does not apply in NLRB proceedings, a limited "good-cause" exception exists to permit the taking of a deposition to preserve the testimony of a witness.[31] But special circumstances must be shown.[32] Subpoenas are used to require the attendance and testimony of witnesses at a deposition. Applications for investigative subpoenas should be filed with the regional director.

Q 8.11   What is the charged party's role in the investigation of a charge?

The board agent investigating the charge will often request that the charged party provide documents or make witnesses available for interviews and affidavits. The board agent will also invite the charged party to submit a written position statement setting forth its version of the facts and its legal arguments. Any information collected, however, may be used as evidence against the charged party in a later ULP proceeding. Therefore, the charged party may want to measure its level of cooperation at this stage of the investigation. While charged parties often refuse to present witnesses, generally it is advisable to cooperate to some extent with the NLRB agent because the regional office will rely on the facts gathered during the investigation to determine whether it should issue a ULP complaint.

Q 8.12   How long is the typical investigation?

The length of individual investigations will vary based on the complexity of the facts and legal issues involved. The NLRB has set internal targets to guide board agents in the processing of most charges. Depending on the type of charge, the NLRB sets a seven-, nine-, or twelve-week time target for the investigation of the charge.[33]

NLRB Formal Complaint

Division of Advice Memoranda

Q 8.13   How is the decision to issue a complaint made?

In addition to considering the law set out in the position statements of the parties, the NLRB agent may conduct his or her independent research into the applicable law.[34] Furthermore, where the legal issues involved are novel, complex, or controversial, the regional director may submit the charges to the Division of Advice for an opinion on whether a ULP complaint should issue. The Division of Advice, within the Office of the General Counsel in Washington, D.C., will review the submission and issue a public "Advice Memo" opining on whether the regional director should dismiss the charge or issue a complaint. The submission of a charge to the Division of Advice will generally delay the processing of the charge.

Additionally, the General Counsel periodically issues memoranda requiring the mandatory submission of certain types of charges to the Division of Advice.[35] For example, matters that have no governing precedent or matters in which the law is in flux as the result of NLRB or court decisions should be submitted to the Division of Advice. Submitting these cases to the Division of Advice helps to ensure that the NLRB develops a consistent nationwide response to these issues.

Issuing a Complaint

Q 8.14   How is a ULP complaint issued?

If, after gathering sufficient facts, the NLRB agent recommends to the regional director that the charge has merit and a ULP complaint should be issued, the NLRB agent typically notifies the parties of the determination and offers the parties a chance to settle prior to issuance of the complaint. If the parties do not agree to settle the charge, a complaint will be issued by the General Counsel, and the case will be scheduled for hearing.[36]

Amending a Complaint

Q 8.14.1   Can a ULP complaint be amended?

Amendments to ULP complaints are permitted as long as they are sufficiently related to existing allegations and no undue prejudice would be visited on the respondent. A complaint is not restricted to the precise allegations of the charge. As long as there is a timely charge, the complaint may allege any matter sufficiently related to or growing out of the charged conduct.[37] The test that applies for adding related allegations not included in the original charge is as follows:

(1)   whether the untimely allegation involves the same legal theory as the timely charge;

(2)   whether the untimely allegation arises from the same factual circumstances or sequence of events as the timely charge; and

(3)   whether the respondent would raise the same or similar defenses to both allegations.[38]

Amendments to complaints may be granted as follows:

- by the General Counsel;

- by the regional director issuing the complaint, prior to the hearing;

- by the ALJ assigned to the case, upon motion, at the hearing or until the case has been transferred to the NLRB;

- by the NLRB, upon motion, prior to the issuance of its order.

Dismissing a Charge

Q 8.15   What happens if the regional director determines a charge should be dismissed?

If the regional director determines that the charge should be dismissed, the regional office will typically afford the charging party an opportunity to withdraw the charge before issuing a formal dismissal.[39] Normally, this is done informally by a board agent contacting the charging party and soliciting a withdrawal. If the charging party agrees to withdraw the charge, the regional director will normally notify the parties of this fact and that the withdrawal request has been approved.[40] If the charging party refuses to withdraw the charge, the regional director will send a dismissal letter to the parties. The dismissal letter will be accompanied by an explanation of the regional director's reasons for refusing to issue a complaint and a description of the charging party's appeal rights.[41]

Appealing the Dismissal of a Charge

Q 8.16   Can a charging party appeal a dismissal of a charge?

The dismissal of a charge by the regional director may be appealed to the General Counsel's Office of Appeals. In most cases, the charging party must file an appeal within fourteen days of service of the dismissal. The General Counsel will review the case file and may hear oral arguments by all parties. Following such review, the General Counsel may sustain the regional director's dismissal or may direct the regional director to take further action. General Counsel decisions cannot be appealed, but parties may typically file a motion for reconsideration of the appeal decision within fourteen days of service of the appeal decision. Until the charge is finally dismissed by the Office of Appeals, it continues to exist during the appeals period and will not be time-barred if it is reinstated after the six-month statute of limitations.[42] The *NLRB Casehandling Manual* sets out, in detail, the procedures and standards used for these appeals, including motions for reconsideration of appeal decisions.[43]

Deferral and Deference to Arbitration

In General

Q 8.17   Can a charge be resolved where the parties are covered by a grievance and arbitration procedure?

Given that most collective bargaining agreements contain contractual grievance and arbitration procedures, the NLRB has adopted rules to coordinate these procedures with its case-handling process. Thus, it is possible for the General Counsel to "defer" a filed charge for resolution through arbitration. The NLRB may also defer in situations where the same matter is pending or has already been decided by an arbitrator.

Q 8.18   What standards apply to deferral to arbitral decisions?

The NLRB's deferral policy and the procedures implemented in furtherance of the deferral policy are complex.[44] Until recently, the Board applied longstanding pre-arbitration deferral standards articulated in *Collyer Insulated Wire*[45] and in *Dubo Manufacturing Corp.*,[46] and post-arbitration deferral standards articulated in *Spielberg Manufacturing Co.*[47] and expanded in *Olin Corp.*[48] However, on December 15, 2014, the Board upended longstanding precedent, announcing in *Babcock & Wilcox Construction* new standards for deferring to arbitral decisions in section 8(a)(1) and (3) cases.[49] (*Babcock* also addresses standards for grievance settlements, which are discussed in further detail below at Q 8.26.)

The new *Babcock* standards do not, however, automatically apply to every case filed on or after December 15, 2014. Rather, the Board stated in *Babcock* that, going forward, it would apply the new deferral standards in the following two types of cases: (1) cases where the collective bargaining agreement under which the grievance arose was executed after December 15, 2014; and (2) cases where the collective bargaining agreement under which the grievance arose was executed on or before December 15, 2014, the arbitration hearing occurred or the grievance settlement was executed after December 15, 2014, and the parties explicitly authorized the arbitrator to decide the statutory question or unfair labor practice issue either in the collective bargaining agreement itself or by agreement of the parties in a particular case.[50]

By contrast, the Board will apply the longstanding post-arbitration deferral standard articulated in *Spielberg Manufacturing Co.* and expanded in *Olin Corp.*, the pre-arbitration deferral standard articulated in *Collyer Insulated Wire* and in *Dubo Manufacturing Corp.*, and the grievance settlement deferral standard set forth in *Alpha Beta Co.*, to the following two types of cases: (1) cases where the arbitration hearing occurred or the settlement agreement was issued on or before December 15, 2014; and (2) cases where the collective bargaining agreement under which the grievance arose was executed on or before December 15, 2014, the arbitration hearing occurred or the settlement agreement was executed after December 15, 2014, and the parties did not explicitly authorize the arbitrator to decide the statutory question or unfair labor practice issue either in the collective bargaining agreement itself or by agreement of the parties in a particular case.[51]

The following questions address the deferral requirements under the "old standards" as they have been developed under the existing case law, followed by a look at how the deferral policies and procedures will be applied going forward under the brand-new Babcock standards.

Pre-Babcock: *Where Deferral Is Appropriate (The* Collyer *and* Dubo *Doctrines)*

Q 8.19   Before *Babcock,* how would the NLRB determine where deferral to arbitration is appropriate?

Under the doctrine articulated in *Collyer Insulated Wire,*[52] where a charge is filed by a party to, or an employee covered by, a collective bargaining agreement that contains a binding grievance arbitration procedure, the General Counsel may "defer" the charge for resolution through arbitration. Deferral is not automatic; it is a matter of the NLRB's discretion. The NLRB, in *Collyer,* observed that:

> where . . . [a] contract clearly provides for grievance and arbitration machinery, where the unilateral action taken is not designed to undermine the Union and is not patently erroneous but rather is based on a substantial claim of contractual privilege, and it appears that the arbitral interpretation of the contract will resolve both the unfair labor practice issue and the contract interpretation issue in a manner compatible with the purposes of the NLRA, then the NLRB should defer to the arbitration clause conceived by the parties.[53]

The NLRB has stated that a *Collyer* deferral to arbitration is appropriate where:

(1)   the parties have collectively bargained for binding arbitration procedures and the contract containing the arbitration procedures was in effect when the dispute arose;

(2)   the responding party is willing to submit to the grievance process for the allegations in the charge and will resort to arbitration if necessary;

(3)   the employer has agreed to waive any time limitations and other procedural defenses (other than the question of arbitrability); and

(4)   the allegations of the charge appear to be covered by, and are likely to be resolved through, the grievance/arbitration procedure.[54]

The NLRB generally finds that the fourth element (whether the allegations of the charge appear to be covered by, and are likely to be resolved through, the grievance procedure) is met when:

(1)   the issue "in its entirety" arose from the parties' collective bargaining agreement;

(2)   its resolution would be assisted by application of an arbitrator's "special skill and experience"; and

(3)   arbitration would provide a "fully effective remedy" in the event a violation was found to have occurred.

Even when it defers a charge pursuant to *Collyer*, the NLRB retains jurisdiction to ensure that the dispute is promptly settled or arbitrated. If arbitrated, following the issuance of an arbitration award, the regional office will determine whether the arbitration proceedings were fair and regular, the arbitrator adequately considered the charge issue, and the decision was not clearly repugnant to the purposes and policies of the NLRA. If the award does not meet these standards, the regional office will not defer to the award and will proceed to complete the investigation of the charge itself.

Under the *Dubo* deferral doctrine, the NLRB will defer processing a charge where a grievance involving the charge issue is already actively pending. Unlike the *Collyer* deferral policy, *Dubo* deferrals are not subject to appeal, as there is no obligation on the charging party's part to file or to continue processing a grievance. The NLRB postpones its determination while the parties voluntarily and actively pursue the dispute via the grievance/arbitration machinery in place. If the grievance is no longer pursued, the NLRB will resume its investigation of the charge. *Dubo* requires that the charging party choose either the NLRB or arbitration as the forum for the dispute.

Q 8.19.1   If the NLRB defers the charge under its *Collyer* deferral policy, does the charging party have any obligations?

Once a charge has been deferred, the charging party has an affirmative obligation to file a grievance under the parties' grievance procedure, if it has not already done so. If the charging party fails to promptly submit a grievance to the grievance/arbitration process, the NLRB will dismiss the charge. Moreover, the regional office will, on a quarterly basis, ascertain from the parties the status of the deferred proceedings. Once a response is received, the regional office will ensure that the deferred charge is processing properly.

Q 8.19.2   Are there any circumstances under which the NLRB will revoke its deferral and resume processing a charge?

If either the union or the employer fails to promptly process a grievance under the parties' grievance/arbitration procedure, the NLRB can revoke deferral. Additionally, if the charged party prevents or impedes resolution of the grievance, argues that the grievance is not timely filed, or refuses to arbitrate the grievance, the NLRB will revoke deferral.

Q 8.19.3   Can the charging party appeal the NLRB's deferral?

Under the NLRB's *Collyer* deferral policy, the charging party can appeal a deferral to the General Counsel. The NLRB provides an Appeal Form,[55] but the charging party is encouraged to submit a complete statement setting forth the facts and reasons why the charging party believes the decision to defer the charge was incorrect. The appeal is due fourteen days from the date of the deferral notification. The charging party must also provide notice to the other parties involved of its intent to file an appeal. The General Counsel will decide the appeal based on the arguments of all parties, and may sustain the regional director's deferral or may direct the regional director to take further action.

Pre-Babcock: *Where Deferral Is Not Appropriate*

Q 8.20   **What types of cases does the NLRB *not* defer to arbitration?**

Even where a particular dispute involves contractual relations between the parties and falls within the contract's arbitration clause, the NLRB may still decline to defer the matter to arbitration if the matter is one traditionally within the NLRB's expertise or outside the competence of the arbitrator. The NLRB commonly retains jurisdiction in situations involving the following:

- accretions or unit clarifications;
- a contract that conflicts with the NLRA (or that contains a provisions that is illegal);
- compliance with prior NLRB orders;
- statutory issues;
- arbitrator's inability to adequately remedy misconduct;
- charges related to a pending NLRB proceeding;
- failure to provide information.

Q 8.20.1   **Why does the NLRA not defer disputes involving accretions or unit clarifications?**

The NLRB will not defer disputes involving questions of representation, bargaining unit appropriateness, or accretion (whether employees may be added to an existing bargaining unit), because these issues are within the NLRB's special expertise. Additionally, since many unit clarification cases involve more than one union claiming representational rights under different contracts, resolution of such cases may lead to multiple conflicting arbitration awards. Thus, the NLRB has determined that unit clarification proceedings, not arbitrations, are the proper means of resolving such disputes.[56]

Q 8.20.2   What kinds of contract conflicts will cause the NLRB not to defer?

Where terms of the collective bargaining agreement directly conflict with provisions of the NLRA, or where it is unclear whether the employees' statutory rights are also covered by the contract, the NLRB will not defer. For example, in *U.S. Steel Corp.*,[57] the dispute between the union and the employer involved distribution of union literature on the employer's premises. The employer sought deferral to arbitration, citing various general contract provisions including one that mandated arbitration "of all complaints and grievances."[58] The NLRB, however, refused to defer because it was unclear whether the employees' section 7 rights to distribute union literature in some areas of the employer's premises were covered by the parties' collective bargaining agreement.

Q 8.20.3   What kinds of statutory issues will cause the NLRB not to defer?

The NLRB has established that legal questions concerning the NLRA itself are within the special competence of the NLRB rather than that of an arbitrator. For example, in *Native Textiles*,[59] the union claimed that the employer was refusing to recognize a designated representative for the purpose of processing grievances. The NLRB analyzed the issue and held that, because the right of employees to designate and be represented by representatives of their own choosing is a fundamental right guaranteed to employees by section 7 of the NLRA, the allegations at issue in this case were not simply a matter of contract interpretation, but rather an alleged interference with a basic statutory right of employees. Accordingly, the NLRB refused to defer the matter to arbitration, because the matter was one that required the NLRB to invoke its jurisdiction and exercise its expertise.

Q 8.20.4 In what kinds of situations would arbitration be an inadequate remedy?

The NLRB will not defer in situations involving, for example, a dispute among three parties in which there is no contractual dispute resolution method that binds all three parties.[60] In *Regional Import & Export Trucking Co.*,[61] the NLRB held it was inappropriate to defer issues currently being raised in a compliance proceeding to arbitration. In that case, both of the parties to the arbitration, the employer and the union, were jointly and severally liable under the terms of the NLRB's order for backpay due the charging party. In such circumstances, where both parties to the arbitration have interests adverse to the charging party (or grievant), deferral to arbitration is inappropriate.

Q 8.20.5 When does relatedness make deferral inappropriate?

The NLRB typically will not defer an allegation that is intertwined with another related allegation that is inappropriate for deferral. The NLRB has held that "[where it] must hear and resolve one issue, it makes no economic sense to refrain from deciding a closely related issue," and it would be inappropriate to require litigation of two closely related issues in more than one forum.[62]

Q 8.20.6 When does failure to provide information prevent a dispute from being deferred?

The NLRB generally will not defer the charge to arbitration where a charged party has failed to provide information in violation of section 8(a)(5) (addressing employer's refusal to bargain in good faith) or section 8(b)(3) (addressing union's refusal to bargain in good faith).

Q 8.20.7 Are there other circumstances in which deferral is not appropriate?

The General Counsel had urged the NLRB not to defer section 8(a)(1) and 8(a)(3) ULP charges to arbitration where it appeared that the arbitration process would take longer than a year.[63] But this direction has since been withdrawn.[64]

If resolution within a year is likely, then the regional office may defer. If resolution within that period is unlikely, the regional office should not defer in most circumstances; instead, the regional office must fully investigate the charge, and upon a finding of merit, submit the case to the Division of Advice for further analysis and guidance.[65]

Pre-Babcock: *Deferral to an Existing Arbitration Award (The Spielberg and Olin Standards)*

Q 8.21   Using pre-*Babcock* standards, when will the NLRB defer to an existing arbitration award?

The NLRB ordinarily will defer to an arbitration award that resolves a charge, unless the arbitration award is inconsistent with the purposes of the NLRA. Post-arbitration deferrals pre-*Babcock* are considered under the standards outlined in *Spielberg Manufacturing Co.*[66] In *Spielberg*, the NLRB dismissed a complaint alleging that the employer had violated sections 8(a)(1) and 8(a)(3) of the NLRA, and relied instead upon the earlier award of an arbitration panel. The NLRB explained: "In these circumstances we believe that the desirable objectives of encouraging the voluntary settlement of labor disputes will be best served by [recognizing] the arbitrators' award."

The NLRB has provided a four-pronged approach for determining when it should dismiss a subsequent charge and defer to the arbitration award:

(1)   the arbitration proceedings appeared to be fair and regular;

(2)   the parties to the arbitration agreed to be bound by arbitration;

(3)   the decision of the arbitration panel is not clearly repugnant to the purposes and policies of the NLRA; and

(4)   the ULP issue was presented to and considered by the arbitration tribunal.

For example, the NLRB would not defer to arbitration where all of the interested parties in the ULP could not participate in the arbitration, where evidence was deliberately withheld from the arbitrator, or where a grievant did not have sufficient time to prepare.

Q 8.21.1   When is an arbitrator's decision "clearly repugnant" to the NLRA?

A decision by the arbitrator is presumptively final. The NLRB will only overturn an arbitrator's decision in very limited circumstances. In these situations, the burden is on the party challenging deferral to an arbitrator's decision to show that the decision was "clearly repugnant" to the NLRA (in other words, not susceptible to any interpretation consistent with the NLRA).[67] "Clearly repugnant" is a fairly high standard for a party to meet. The NLRB does not require that the arbitrator's decision be entirely consistent with the NLRB's decisions. Additionally, it is not sufficient that the NLRB would have reached another decision. Rather, in order to be clearly repugnant, the arbitrator's award has to be palpably wrong; it must not be susceptible to an interpretation consistent with the NLRA. For example, an arbitration award that impairs employee right-of-access to the NLRB process would be repugnant to the NLRA. The NLRB has refused to defer where the arbitrator's award involved a waiver by the employee of his right to file a ULP.[68]

Q 8.21.2   When is a ULP "presented to and considered by the arbitration tribunal"?

A ULP issue must be presented to and considered by the arbitration tribunal. This requirement is met if the contractual issue that is the subject of the grievance procedure is factually parallel to the ULP issue before the NLRB, and the arbitrator was presented generally with the same facts relevant to resolving the ULP.

Deferral to Arbitration Under the New Babcock Standard

Q 8.22   Under *Babcock*, how does the NLRB determine where deferral to arbitration is appropriate?

In *Babcock*, the Board modified the criteria for administratively deferring a section 8(a)(1) or (a)(3) charge pending the outcome of the arbitral process. The Board will no longer defer cases to the arbitral process unless the arbitrator is "explicitly authorized" to decide the statutory issue (that is, either in the collective bargaining agreement or by agreement of the parties in a particular case). In modifying its longstanding *Collyer* standard, the Board reasoned that "[t]here is no apparent reason to defer to the arbitral process if it is plain at the outset that deferral to the arbitral decision would be improper."[69]

Deferral to Existing Arbitration Award Under the New Babcock Standard

Q 8.23   Under *Babcock,* when will the NLRB defer to an existing arbitration award?

In *Babcock*, the NLRB articulated a new standard under which it will defer to arbitration only if:

(1)   the arbitration procedures appear to have been fair and regular;

(2)   the parties agree to be bound by arbitration;

(3)   the party arguing for deferral shows:

    (a)   the arbitrator was *explicitly authorized* to decide the unfair labor practice issue;

    (b)   the arbitrator was *presented with and considered the statutory issue*, or was prevented from doing so by the party opposing deferral; and

    (c)   Board law *reasonably permits* the arbitral award.[70]

Significantly, the *Babcock* standard places the burden of proof on the party urging deferral.

Q 8.23.1   Under the *Babcock* standard, what is meant by "explicitly authorized"?

Under *Babcock*, "explicitly authorized" means that (1) the specific statutory right was incorporated into the collective bargaining agreement, or (2) the parties consented to authorize arbitration of an issue in a particular case.

Q 8.23.2   ... "presented with and considered the statutory issue"?

A party satisfies the requirement that the arbitrator was "presented with" the statutory issue by informing the arbitrator of the unfair labor practice allegation in a pending charge. Moreover, the arbitrator will have been found to have "considered the statutory issue" where he or she "identified that issue and at least generally explained why he or she finds that the facts presented either do or do not support the unfair labor practice allegation."[71]

Q 8.23.3   ... "reasonably permits"?

Board law "reasonably permits" the arbitral award where the award represents "reasonable application of the statutory principles that would govern the Board's decision" even if the arbitrator did not rule exactly as the Board would have ruled.[72] Under this new *Babcock* standard, arbitration awards are afforded more deference than they were under the "clearly repugnant" standard from *Spielberg* and *Olin*.

Settlements in NLRB Cases

Q 8.24   May the parties settle a charge without NLRB involvement?

Yes; parties often seek private resolutions of their disputes by settlements. If a complaint has not issued, the charging party can withdraw the charge without permission from the NLRB. Once a complaint has been issued, a charging party may withdraw a charge prior to the hearing only with the consent of the regional director who issued the complaint. After the hearing has begun, the charge may only be withdrawn upon motion, and then only with the consent of the ALJ. Following the hearing, after the case has been transferred to the NLRB, a charge can be withdrawn only upon motion and consent of the NLRB.[73] Thus, parties must obtain approval from the relevant NLRB authority when they wish to settle the charge.

Types of Settlements: Formal, Informal, and Unilateral

Q 8.25   What form does a settlement take?

Settlement of charges may be formal, informal, or unilateral. These settlements can take many different forms, involve different processes, and reach several different outcomes.[74]

Q 8.25.1   What is a formal settlement of a charge, and when is it appropriate?

If a complaint has been issued, the NLRB favors a formal settlement agreement by which the charged party agrees to the issuance of an NLRB order that directs the charged party to take action appropriate to the terms of the settlement. To ensure enforcement of the order, formal settlement agreements also require the charged party to consent to the NLRB's application for the entry of a court judgment. Posting of a notice to employees is an essential part of a formal settlement. The *NLRB Casehandling Manual* sets out, in detail, the procedures used for settlements.

Usually formal NLRB settlements are reserved for cases where investigation into the charge reveals egregious circumstances. For example, formal NLRB settlements are appropriate:

(1)   where the charged party is a recidivist;

(2)   where violence is involved;

(3)   where the amount of backpay involved is significant; and

(4)   where the charged party has a history of breaching informal settlements.

A formal settlement takes a significantly longer time to process, because it requires approval from the NLRB and a court judgment.

Q 8.25.2   What is an informal settlement of a charge, and when is it appropriate?

Most NLRB settlements are informal, as opposed to formal, and usually entail a standard form settlement agreement, which both the charged party and the NLRB sign, as well as printed notices of the settlement terms to the affected employees to be posted by the charged party. Normally, an informal settlement includes the consent of the charging party as well. Informal agreements provide for withdrawal of the complaint and are subject to the approval of the regional director. Generally, proof of compliance with the settlement is obtained by the regional director before the case is closed. Informal agreements are not subject to approval by the NLRB and do not need an NLRB order.

Although the informal NLRB settlement is not enforceable, if a party breaches the settlement, the regional office can revoke the settlement agreement, issue a ULP complaint, and go to a hearing before an ALJ. If the breaching party commits another charge, the NLRB may insist that the breaching party enter into a formal settlement.

Q 8.25.3   What is a unilateral settlement, and when is it appropriate?

Many NLRB settlements are unilateral in nature, because they are often signed only by the regional director and the charged party. Once the regional office and the charged party work out the terms of the settlement, the agreement is presented to the charging party. If the charging party does not agree with the regional office about the settlement, the charging party can appeal to the General Counsel.

If the regional office agrees to enter into a settlement before a hearing or before a complaint is issued, the charged party may file written objections to the settlement.

Q 8.26   What standards apply to deferral to settlement agreements?

Until recently, the Board applied settlement agreement deferral standards articulated in *Alpha Beta*.[75] However, on December 15, 2014, the Board announced in *Babcock & Wilcox Construction* new standards for deferring to grievance settlements in section 8(a)(1) and (a)(3) cases.[76]

The Alpha Beta Standard

Q 8.27   Under *Alpha Beta*, when will the NLRB defer to settlement agreements?

Under *Alpha Beta*, the Board allows for deferral to a settlement agreement if:

(1)   the proceedings appeared to be fair and regular;

(2)   all parties agreed to be bound by the settlement;

(3)   the agreement was not clearly repugnant to the NLRA; and

(4)   the parties considered the unfair labor practice issue.[77]

The New Babcock Standard

Q 8.28   Under *Babcock*, when will the NLRB defer to settlement agreements?

Under *Babcock*, the Board will only defer to grievance settlements if:

(1)   the parties intended to settle the unfair labor practice issue;

(2)   the parties addressed that issue in the settlement agreement; and

(3)   Board law reasonably permits the settlement agreement.[78]

The Board will examine the circumstances surrounding the settlement using the following factors that are applicable to other non-Board settlements:

(1)   whether all parties involved agreed to be bound by the non-Board settlement;

(2)   whether the proposed settlement is reasonable when compared to the alleged violation, the risks of litigation, and the stage of litigation;

(3)   whether there is any indication of fraud, coercion, or duress regarding the parties' settlement; and

(4)   whether the respondent has a previous record of violations or of breaching past settlement agreements resolving unfair labor practices.[79]

NLRB ULP Hearings

Service of Complaint/Notice of Hearing

Q 8.29   What happens if a case is not dismissed, arbitrated, or settled?

In cases that are not dismissed, arbitrated, or settled, the NLRB typically issues a complaint and notice of hearing, after which the role of the NLRB switches from neutral investigator to prosecutor. The regional director will assign an attorney or attorneys to prepare the ULP case for hearing and present the evidence to an ALJ. The charged party now becomes known as the respondent.

Q 8.30   How does a respondent answer a ULP complaint?

The respondent named in a ULP complaint must file an answer within fourteen days of service of the complaint, or the allegations in the complaint will be deemed admitted. The answer must admit, deny, explain, or disclaim knowledge of each of the facts alleged in the complaint and must include any affirmative defenses. The respondent or its representative should sign the answer. The answer may then be filed in hard-copy format or electronically and served on all parties.[80]

Q 8.30.1   Can a party ask for a postponement of the ULP hearing?

A party who wishes to postpone the start of a ULP hearing must present the request to either the regional director or the Division of Judges.

A request can be filed with the regional director under the following circumstances:

(1)   where all parties agree or no party objects;

(2)   where a new charge or charges have been filed that, if meritorious, might be appropriate for consolidation;

(3)   where settlement negotiations are in progress;

(4)   where issues related to the complaint are pending before the Division of Advice or Office of Appeals; and

(5)   where more than twenty-one days remain before the scheduled date of the hearing.

In all other circumstances, the NLRB requires that such motions be filed with the Division of Judges as set forth in the NLRB's Rules and Regulations at section 102.24. The motion should be filed in writing. Three copies should be served on the regional director or the Division of Judges, and copies must also be simultaneously filed with the other parties. The motion should explain in detail the reasons for the post-ponement request, the positions of the other parties with respect to the request, and the recommended dates for resetting the hearing.

Hearings may also be postponed at the last minute due to emergen-cies or unforeseen circumstances.

Q 8.30.2   When may parties file motions for summary judgment on a ULP complaint?

Parties may file motions for summary judgment with the NLRB no later than twenty-eight days prior to the scheduled hearing. This deadline changes to "promptly" if there are fewer than twenty-eight days between the filing of the answer and the scheduled hearing. The opposing party may file an opposition to the motion for summary judg-ment. In a motion for summary judgment, a party claims that some additional facts or circumstances not apparent from the face of the complaint should compel its dismissal.

Common grounds for summary judgment include:

• bar of the statute of limitations;

• relitigation bar (the alleged violations occurred prior to the trial of a previous ULP case involving the respondent and are related to the allegations in the prior case);

• deferral to arbitration.

A designated ALJ will issue a ruling on the motion. The ALJ may deny the motion or issue a notice to show cause why the motion should not be granted. The issuance of a notice to show cause will postpone the hearing.

Absent special permission from the NLRB, the ALJ's ruling is not directly appealable.[81]

Formal Trial Proceedings

Q 8.31   How is a ULP hearing conducted?

A ULP complaint will be litigated in a hearing before an ALJ. The NLRB's General Counsel prosecutes the charge, although the party that filed the charge may also appear, often through counsel. The charging party has the right to participate at trial by questioning witnesses and introducing evidence, but has no right to seek remedies that are inconsistent with the complaint or the General Counsel's theory of the case.

The ALJ has a great deal of discretion over how to conduct the hearing, but the typical order of proceedings is for the General Counsel, charging party, and respondent (in that order) to give their opening statements, followed by presentation of their cases-in-chief. Parties can file a brief or argue the case orally to the ALJ, but the majority of cases are briefed.

The ALJ will hear evidence, receive briefs, rule on motions and objections offered during the hearing, weigh the evidence, and issue a written decision containing factual findings and a recommended order.[82] Each party may then file exceptions to the ALJ's decision. A panel of Board members reviews the ALJ's decision and may ultimately adopt the ALJ's recommendations, in whole or in part. The Board members will then issue a final order. Either party may then petition for review of the NLRB's order in a federal court of appeals.

Q 8.31.1   How does a formal hearing compare to a federal court proceeding?

In practice, ULP proceedings are less formal than federal court proceedings. The ALJ serves much the same role, and has many of the same powers, as a judge presiding over a bench trial in federal or state court.

As much as practicable, ULP hearings are conducted in accordance with the Federal Rules of Evidence and Civil Procedure.[83]

The court reporter prepares the only official transcript of the hearing. The transcript is a public document, and anyone may request a copy at the cost of photocopying.

Q 8.31.2   What are the rights of the parties during the hearing?

Parties have much of the same rights at a ULP hearing as they would in a court proceeding. After a ULP complaint is issued, the General Counsel prosecutes the action. The General Counsel is usually represented by an NLRB attorney from the regional office. This attorney may be the NLRB agent who investigated the charge. The charging party is considered a party to the proceeding and may participate in the hearing, through counsel if so desired.

The General Counsel, all parties, and the ALJ have the power to call, examine, and cross-examine witnesses, and to introduce evidence into the record. They may also submit briefs, engage in oral argument, and submit proposed findings and conclusions to the ALJ.

In addition, NLRB rules permit "any person" to file a motion with the ALJ to intervene in the trial.[84] The issue of intervention is subject to the discretion of the judge and will not be disturbed absent abuse or prejudice.[85] For example, intervention has been permitted by ALJs when employees or groups of employees sought intervention to litigate the union's majority status or its solicitation of authorization cards.[86]

Q 8.31.3   Where and when is a ULP hearing held?

Typically, the ULP hearing is held in a hearing room at the regional office, but may be scheduled close to the situs of the dispute if the regional office is not geographically convenient. The hearing must be scheduled a minimum of fourteen days from the date of service of the complaint, but typically occurs a significant time later.[87]

Q 8.31.4   Does the NLRB issue subpoenas for ULP hearings?

Yes, the NLRB may issue a subpoena requiring the attendance and testimony of witnesses and production of documents at the hearing.[88]

Parties may file an application requesting subpoenas for their own witnesses with the regional director, who may then grant the request for the subpoenas. NLRB attorneys also may serve subpoenas. If the hearing has already begun, the application process goes to the ALJ presiding over the hearing.

Federal courts have the exclusive authority to enforce subpoenas. Only the NLRB may seek enforcement of the subpoenas in federal court. If a party requests that the General Counsel seek enforcement of a subpoena, however, the General Counsel must do so, unless the NLRB believes enforcement of the subpoena would be inconsistent with the NLRA or NLRB policies.[89]

Post-Hearing Briefs

Q 8.32   May a party file a brief after the close of the hearing?

Parties may request, but do not have an absolute right, to file a post-hearing brief. This request should be made before the close of the hearing. The ALJ may grant or deny the request, and may set a deadline for filing no later than thirty-five days after the close of the hearing.[90] In practice, post-hearing briefs are commonplace. In any case in which the ALJ believes that written briefs or proposed findings of fact and conclusions may not be necessary, the ALJ will notify the parties at the opening of the trial that he or she wants to hear oral argument in lieu of briefs.

The ALJ's Decision; The NLRB's Order

Q 8.33   What must be included in the ALJ's decision?

After the close of the hearing and, if applicable, the submission of post-hearing briefs, the ALJ will issue a decision. This decision must be in writing and ordinarily will contain specific findings of fact, conclusions, and the reasons or basis for those findings and conclusions, as well as a recommended decision and order.[91]

Q 8.33.1 What happens after the ALJ's decision is delivered?

After the ALJ issues the decision, the case is transferred to the NLRB. Once the time for filing exceptions and related briefs expires, the NLRB may issue its decision in the case. Typically, NLRB decisions are issued by a three-member panel.[92] The NLRB may permit oral argument before issuing its decision, but in practice this rarely occurs. The NLRB will decide whether to adopt, modify, or reject, in whole or in part, the ALJ's decision and recommended order. The NLRB may also impose remedies on any or all of the parties. If no party files exceptions to the ALJ's decision, the ALJ's recommendations automatically become the decision and order of the NLRB.[93]

Q 8.33.2 How do parties file an exception to the ALJ's decision?

Within twenty-eight days of the transfer, parties may file exceptions (or an appeal) to the ALJ's decision. After an exception has been filed, the party opposing an exception has fourteen days to file an answering brief in opposition to the exceptions. This response may also include the opposing party's own cross-exceptions to the ALJ's decision.[94]

With regard to the filing of exceptions, they must be filed with respect to each fact-finding and conclusion. If a party fails to except to a fact-finding or conclusion, that issue is waived. The NLRB's no-relitigation rule bars relitigation of a waived issue in a ULP proceeding that is related to the proceeding in which the waiver occurred.[95]

Q 8.33.3 Can a party file a motion for reconsideration, rehearing, or reopening of the record?

Yes; either party may file a motion for reconsideration, rehearing, or reopening the record within twenty-eight days of service of the NLRB's decision. These motions must be based on "extraordinary circumstances."[96] Requests for reconsideration are not necessary to preserve appeal. These motions are rarely successful, except under limited circumstances. For example, if the NLRB made a "housekeeping" mistake, such as issuing a remedy that is inconsistent with its decision, a party should file a motion for reconsideration so the NLRB can fix the error.

Q 8.34   How can a party challenge the NLRB's order?

Any person aggrieved by an NLRB order may obtain a review of the order in a federal court of appeals. This petition may be filed:

- in the circuit of the federal court of appeals in which the ULP was alleged to have occurred;

- in the circuit of the federal court of appeals where the aggrieved person resides or transacts business; or

- in the federal court of appeals for the D.C. Circuit.[97]

The federal courts of appeals apply a deferential standard when reviewing NLRB decisions. The reviewing court does not act as a fact-finder, but it does review whether the NLRB's findings of fact are supported by substantial evidence on the record considered as a whole. If the fact-finding is supported by substantial evidence it is deemed conclusive, even if the reviewing court might reach an opposite conclusion were it conducting an independent review. A decision of the NLRB will be overturned only if it is not supported by substantial evidence or if the NLRB incorrectly applied the law. The court may enforce, modify, or set aside the NLRB's order, in whole or in part.

Q 8.34.1   Are NLRB orders self-enforcing?

NLRB orders are not self-enforcing. This means that the order, standing alone, does not compel compliance. The NLRB must convert its orders into judicial decrees subject to the federal courts' contempt power in order to compel party action. Enforcement proceedings are initiated by the NLRB via procedures set forth in section 10(e) of the NLRA. The NLRB may seek enforcement in the federal courts of appeals in the circuit where the ULP occurred or where the respondent resides or transacts business. Generally, however, the NLRB petitions for enforcement only in the circuit where the ULP occurred. The NLRB can also cross-move for enforcement in the circuit where an aggrieved party first petitioned for review. In many cases, however, the parties voluntarily comply with the NLRB's orders without any petition for enforcement.

Q 8.34.2   What can the courts do with the NLRB's order?

Courts have the power to grant any temporary relief they deem proper and can enter a decree enforcing or modifying all, or part, of the NLRB's order. The courts also have the power to set aside in whole or in the part the NLRB's order.

Injunctions

Q 8.35   Is preliminary injunctive relief available to enjoin ULPs?

Preliminary injunctive relief is potentially available to remedy all types of ULPs. Section 10 of the NLRA empowers the NLRB to prevent employers, employees, unions, and other persons from engaging in any ULP. Upon the issuance of a ULP complaint, section 10(j) gives the NLRB the discretionary power to petition any federal district court for a temporary restraining order and/or preliminary injunction. Courts are given jurisdiction through section 10(j) of the NLRA to provide such injunctive relief upon the NLRB's petition and notice given to the party to be enjoined. Furthermore, injunctions are mandatory for certain types of "priority" ULPs set out in section 10(*l*).

Nothing in the NLRA gives the NLRB any authority to issue an injunction.

Mandatory Injunctions

Q 8.36   When are mandatory section 10(*l*) injunctions available to remedy ULPs?

Section 10(*l*) seeks to fill the time gap between the filing of a complaint and issuance of a final decision in cases in which considerable harm might occur in the interim. Section 10(*l*) embodies the determination by Congress that certain ULPs can cause such serious and unjustifiable interruptions to commerce as to require an immediate prohibition, pending trial by the NLRB, in order to avoid irreparable injury to the policies of the NLRA and the frustration of its statutory purpose. Mandatory injunctions are required for charges related to the following ULPs, once a regional director determines there is reasonable cause that the charge is true:

- secondary boycotts, section 8(b)(4)(A), (B), or (C) violations;
- unlawful picketing, section 8(b)(7) violations; and
- hot cargo agreements, section 8(e) violations.

Upon receiving a charge that could result in a 10(*l*) injunction, the regional director must begin an investigation. While the charging party may request that the regional director seek a 10(*l*) injunction, the charging party cannot pursue such injunctive relief on its own. Section 10(*l*) cases have priority over all of the regional office's non-section 10(*l*) cases. The investigation, submission of evidence, and determination of reasonable cause normally occur within seventy-two hours.[98]

Q 8.36.1 What is the procedure in court for seeking a 10(*l*) injunction?

Once the regional director finds "reasonable cause to believe the charge is true," the regional director must immediately petition a federal district court for injunctive relief. Only the regional director (as plaintiff), the charging party, and the charged party may appear in federal section 10(*l*) proceedings to present evidence, as permitted and/or required by the court. Courts have denied the intervention of other parties.

To obtain injunctive relief, the regional director must establish reasonable cause to believe that the alleged ULP was committed. The regional director does not have to prove the actual commission of the ULP. The regional director's burden of proof ranges from court to court: from showing that the allegations are substantial and non-frivolous, to a significant possibility that the NLRB will enter an enforceable order, to a traditional showing for equitable relief (that is, reasonable likelihood of success, no adequate remedy at law, and likelihood of irreparable harm).

The district court is limited to ruling on the existence of reasonable cause and may not invade in the province of the NLRB to make the determination of whether the ULP actually occurred. Once the court finds reasonable cause, it has jurisdiction to grant such injunctive relief or temporary restraining order as it deems just and proper. The judge has broad discretion to set the injunction for any length of time up to, but not longer than, the date the NLRB issues its decision. Temporary restraining orders may only be in place for five days.

The court's relief typically must focus on ending the violation and related conduct, preventing future violations, and ensuring the NLRB's order will have an opportunity to provide effective relief. The court's order (or dismissal of the petition) may be appealed to the federal court of appeals overseeing the district court.[99]

Discretionary Injunctions

Q 8.37 Under what circumstances will the NLRB seek a discretionary injunction under section 10(j) of the NLRA?

Unlike mandatory injunctions under section 10(*l*), the NLRB has discretion as to whether it chooses to seek injunctive relief under section 10(j). The NLRB may evaluate the ULP allegations and determine whether some or all of the violations alleged warrant injunctive relief.[100]

The purpose of a section 10(j) injunction is to maintain the status quo and prevent the charged party from accomplishing or continuing its unlawful acts, pending the NLRB's determination of the charges. In determining whether to exercise its discretion to request injunctive relief in federal court, the NLRB evaluates the strength of the alleged violation and whether its final relief would be effective to remedy the alleged ULP.

While discretionary injunctive relief is available for any ULP, in practice, the NLRB will typically exercise its discretion to seek injunctive relief only for the following categories of charges:

- interference with union organizational campaigns;
- subcontracting, relocations of work, or other changes to avoid bargaining obligations;
- withdrawal of recognition from the incumbent union;
- undermining of the bargaining representative;

- unlawful recognition of a union lacking majority support of the employees in the bargaining unit;

- successor employer refusal to recognize and bargain with an incumbent union;

- refusals to bargain in good faith that "pose a real danger of creating industrial unrest and/or of undermining employee support for the union";

- mass picketing, violence, threats, or damage to private property;

- failure to comply with section 8(d) or 8(g) notice requirements before striking or picketing (additional information regarding notice requirements under sections 8(d) and 8(g) can be found in chapter 7);

- refusal to permit employees to engage in activity protected by the NLRA in non-work areas of the employer's private property;

- union coercion to achieve unlawful object, section 8(b)(1)(B), 8(b)(2), and 8(b)(3) violations;

- retaliation for filing charges, giving testimony, or otherwise participating in or providing assistance to an NLRB investigation or hearing; and

- segregating assets, liquidating assets, or closing operations in a manner that creates a danger that there will be no remaining assets to satisfy a backpay order.

As a general matter, the NLRB will authorize section 10(j) injunctions in only a handful of cases each year. For example, out of 1,216 ULP complaints issued in Fiscal Year 2014, the Regional Offices submitted only 144 cases to the NLRB's Injunction Litigation Branch for consideration for section 10(j) injunctive relief. Of those 144 cases, the Board authorized only thirty-eight 10(j) petitions.

Nonetheless, the Office of General Counsel recently expressed its intention to aggressively seek 10(j) injunction in necessary circumstances. The office has pledged to place a particular focus on obtaining injunctive relief in successor refusal to bargain and successor refusal to hire cases.[101]

Q 8.37.1   When will the NLRB seek a discretionary injunction related to interference with union organizational campaigns?

The NLRB may seek a discretionary section 10(j) injunction in cases involving serious employer conduct intended to thwart the union's attempt to win recognition, such as threats, coercion, interrogations, surveillance, or unlawful discipline. These unlawful employer actions may occur prior to the filing of a petition for recognition, or in between the filing of the petition and the time of the election. The NLRB will typically seek injunctive relief that will enable the employees to exercise their lawful right to pursue majority status without the unlawful interference or coercion of their employer. Regional Offices have also been instructed to submit for section 10(j) consideration all cases seeking a *Gissel* bargaining order.[102] *Gissel* bargaining orders are discussed in greater detail below.[103]

Q 8.37.2   When will allegations that an employer is undermining a bargaining representative lead the NLRB to seek a discretionary section 10(j) injunction?

When charges involve egregious employer actions intended to undermine employee support for a union, the NLRB may exercise its discretion to seek a section 10(j) injunction. These employer actions include:

(1)   serious threats;

(2)   the discharge of key union officers or activists; or

(3)   implementing important changes in working conditions, either discriminatorily or without bargaining with the union.

Q 8.37.3   What will lead the NLRB to seek a section 10(j) injunction against a union?

The NLRB may exercise its discretion to seek injunctive relief against a union when a charge involves significant union restraint or coercion of employees. These cases typically involve union actions against those employees choosing to refrain from engaging in activities permitted under the NLRA, such as a strike. Actions that may lead to an injunction include:

(1)   mass picketing;
(2)   violence;
(3)   threats; or
(4)   damage to private property.

Q 8.38   May a charging party request section 10(j) injunctive relief?

A charging party may request NLRA section 10(j) relief along with, or after filing, its charge. The charging party, however, may not seek injunctive relief directly from the courts. Only the NLRB has the discretion to seek section 10(j) relief in a district court. The NLRB has final authority in deciding whether to seek such relief from the court.

Q 8.39   How does the NLRB determine if seeking section 10(j) relief is warranted?

The regional office will conduct an investigation into the propriety of seeking section 10(j) relief on its own initiative, or after receiving a request for section 10(j) relief from the charging party. Typically, a party opposing a request for section 10(j) relief is afforded an opportunity to submit a position statement to the regional office. After its investigation, the regional office will evaluate whether section 10(j) relief is appropriate.[104]

Q 8.39.1   If the regional office concludes that 10(j) relief is warranted, how does it pursue an injunction?

If it decides 10(j) relief is appropriate, the regional office will prepare a written memorandum to the General Counsel, through the Injunction Litigation Branch, making that recommendation.[105] The ILB will evaluate the recommendation, and if it agrees, it will draft a cover memorandum to be submitted to the General Counsel for authorization. Once the General Counsel signs off on the memorandum, it is forwarded to the NLRB for approval. The employer typically is not afforded an opportunity to oppose the section 10(j) request at this stage.

If the NLRB authorizes a section 10(j) petition, the regional office must then file a petition with the district court within forty-eight hours. Pursuant to the statute, a complaint must first be issued before the NLRB may petition for section 10(j) relief, so the regional office must issue a complaint before the actual petition may be filed in court.

Q 8.40   Who is authorized to file section 10(j) petitions for injunctive relief with the court?

As of December 28, 2007, the NLRB has temporarily delegated to the General Counsel the full and final authority on behalf of the NLRB to initiate and prosecute injunction proceedings under section 10(j). Thus, under the current practice, the General Counsel, and not the NLRB, will grant final approval for requests for section 10(j) relief. Once the General Counsel gives this approval, the regional office can file the section 10(j) petition with the district court.[106] Courts have upheld this and similar prior delegations under section 3(d) of the NLRA.[107]

Q 8.41   What factors will a court consider when evaluating a petition for injunctive relief under section 10(j)?

Federal courts are divided as to the appropriate standard for a section 10(j) injunction. The majority approach applies a two-step analysis: (1) the court determines whether there is reasonable cause to believe that the alleged unfair labor practice has occurred; and (2) if there is reasonable cause, the court then determines whether the grant of an injunction would be just and proper. The minority approach requires the movant to prove the traditional equitable criteria used in determining whether to grant a preliminary injunction, namely that:

(1)   the party is likely to succeed on the merits;
(2)   it is likely to suffer irreparable harm without preliminary relief;
(3)   the balance of equities tips in its favor; and
(4)   the injunction is in the public interest.

Still other courts apply a hybrid standard using the four-part equitable test as part of the "just and proper" standard but retaining a separate "reasonable cause" step.[108]

Most courts hold the NLRB to a relatively low standard on the "reasonable cause" analysis, finding that the standard requires the NLRB to show that its theory of the case is substantial and not frivolous. Other courts require a showing of a significant possibility that the NLRB will enter an enforceable order. Courts generally give the NLRB's position considerable deference in the "reasonable cause" analysis.

Courts are also split over the correct "just and proper" analysis. Some courts skip the analysis altogether, finding that an injunction must issue once the NLRB satisfies the reasonable cause standard; others courts look to the traditional equitable factors, and still others find that an injunction is just and proper when the relief is necessary to prevent frustration of the remedial purpose of the NLRA.

If the court denies the injunction, the NLRB has sixty days in which to decide whether to appeal the decision.[109]

Q 8.42   How long will a section 10(j) or section 10(*l*) injunction remain in effect?

A section 10(j) order remains in effect until the NLRB issues its final order in the underlying ULP case. At that time, the NLRB will either order the final relief requested or dismiss the complaint.[110] See the discussion that follows for standard NLRB remedies.

Section 10(*l*) injunctions issued without notice can last no longer than five days. Section 10(*l*) injunctions issued with notice run the same time period as section 10(j) injunctions.

Remedies

Q 8.43   What remedies are available for violations of the NLRA?

Pursuant to section 10 of the NLRA, the NLRB has the power to impose a variety of remedies to both cure past violations of the NLRA and prevent future commissions of ULPs. The NLRB also has broad discretion in determining the appropriate remedy, subject to limited judicial review. Courts generally will not disturb an order of the NLRB unless the order attempts to achieve ends other than those fairly said to effectuate the policies of the NLRA, including the promotion of industrial peace, the prevention of ULPs, and the protection of victimized employees. In effectuating the policies of the NLRA, the NLRB's proposed remedy must be tailored to the ULP it is intended to redress.

When the NLRB finds that a party committed a ULP, it generally issues a cease-and-desist order, but can also issue an "affirmative" order, requiring the violating party to take some specific action in the future. In other words, the NLRB often combines its available remedies. For example, a reinstatement order may be accompanied by an order to remit backpay, a cease-and-desist order, and a remedial notice posting order.

Cease-and-Desist Orders

Q 8.44   What is a cease-and-desist order?

When the NLRB determines that a party has committed an unlawful practice under the NLRA, the NLRB can impose a "cease-and-desist" order, ordering a violating party to refrain from continuing its unlawful actions.[111]

The scope of a cease-and-desist order depends on the circumstances of the particular violations at issue in the case. The NLRB prefers issuing narrow cease-and-desist orders prohibiting the specific conduct found to violate the NLRA and prohibiting the party from violating the NLRA in any similar fashion.

On the other hand, the NLRB can issue a broad cease-and-desist order, enjoining a violating party from all future violations of the NLRA or enjoining acts across the company's locations rather than just the location at issue. These broad cease-and-desist orders direct the violating party to stop interfering with, restraining, or coercing employees in any manner in the exercise of rights guaranteed by the NLRA. The NLRB does not favor these broad orders and generally issues them only where the violation is especially egregious or when the violating party has a long history of similar violations.

Notices to Be Posted

Q 8.45   When a party has committed a ULP, what notice must it post?

When the NLRB determines that a party has committed a ULP, the NLRB normally requires the party to post a notice informing employees of the NLRB's order and confirming the party's agreement not to engage in similar unlawful activity, in addition to any affirmative relief required by the order. When the NLRB orders a party to post a notice, the NLRB normally attaches the required notice to its opinion. The notice will state in plain language what the employer or union will and will not do, in compliance with the NLRB's order and the NLRA. The NLRB has held that the message to employees contained in the notice must be "expressed in simple and readily understandable language."[112] Depending on the workforce, the notices may need to be posted in several languages.

Q 8.45.1   Where and for how long does the notice need to be posted?

The NLRB normally requires the party to post notices in conspicuous locations where employees are likely to see them. The violating party must ensure that the notices are not covered, changed, damaged, or removed. The NLRB normally requires the party to post notices for sixty days. The NLRB does not require posting on company websites, but does sometimes require electronic posting within the company.

In some circumstances, the NLRB may find that physically posting the notice at the workplace is insufficient. For example, the NLRB may require the violating party to mail the notice to affected employees if a facility is closed when the notice should be posted.[113] Similarly, the NLRB can order the violating party to post notices at both the employer's headquarters and job sites and the union's offices and meeting places.[114] Where employees work primarily from home or in the field, the NLRB can require the violating party to post notices at various company locations and to mail the notice to each affected employee.[115]

Q 8.45.2   What does a notice look like?

Notices are usually printed on oversized paper and are in color. Here is an example of a notice that would be issued after the NLRB prevails at a ULP hearing:

FIGURE 8-1

Sample Notice to Employees

**NOTICE TO EMPLOYEES
POSTED BY ORDER OF
THE NATIONAL LABOR RELATIONS BOARD**

An Agency of the United States Government

The National Labor Relations Board has found that we violated federal law and has ordered us to post this notice and comply with its terms.

FEDERAL LAW GIVES YOU THE RIGHT

To form, join, or assist any union

To choose representatives to bargain with us on your behalf

To act together with other employees for your benefit and protection

To choose not to engage in any of these protected activities.

We will not do anything to interfere with these rights.

We will not maintain work rules containing overly broad prohibitions on the use and/or distribution of publications or literature.

We will not maintain work rules containing overly broad prohibitions on loitering.

WE WILL NOT interrogate our employees concerning their protected concerted activity.

We will not suspend employees because they invoke the right to be represented by a fellow employee during an interview that the employee reasonably believes could result in discipline.

We will make whole [Employee] for any losses [he/she] may have suffered as a result of our unlawful suspension of [him/her].

We will not in any like or related manner interfere with, restrain, or coerce employees in the exercise of the rights guaranteed them by section 7 of the NLRA.

Q 8.46   What are some of the other forms of relief the NLRB might order?

Other examples of affirmative remedial relief ordered by the NLRB include:

(1)   reinstatement orders for employees who were unlawfully discharged;

(2)   backpay orders for employees who lost wages as a result of a ULP; and

(3)   a bargaining order where an employer has failed to negotiate in good faith (or in some cases where an employer interfered with the fair and equitable election).

Job Placement; Reinstatement

Q 8.47   When does the NLRB order job placement or "instatement" as an affirmative remedy?

Job placement, or "instatement," is the typical remedy in an unlawful refusal-to-hire case. In order to find that an employer refused to hire a potential employee, the NLRB must find that:

(1)   there was a position available;

(2)   the applicant was qualified for the position; and

(3) the employer's animus toward the union was part of its deci-
     sion to not hire the applicant.

In those cases where there were more applicants than positions available, the NLRB uses compliance proceedings to determine who would
have been hired for the openings. Those applicants will be entitled to
job placement (and likely backpay).[116]

The applicants who would not have been selected are not entitled
to job placement, but instead are considered potential victims of an
unlawful refusal-to-consider practice. In a refusal-to-consider case, the
typical remedy includes an order to place the applicant in the position they would have been in, absent discrimination, for consideration
for future openings and an order to notify those applicants and the
regional director of future openings in "positions for which the dis-
criminatees applied or substantially equivalent positions."[117]

Importantly, some applicants, characterized as "salts," are union
organizers seeking to unionize from within the employer's business or
to establish the basis for a charge against the employer for failure to
hire. Salts are protected under the NLRA in some cases. This issue is
discussed in greater detail in chapter 3.

Q 8.47.1   When does the NLRB order reinstatement of a bargaining unit member?

Generally, the NLRB will order that an employee be reinstated where
the employee is discharged from employment due to the employer's
commission of a ULP. In determining whether reinstatement is appropriate, the NLRB considers the degree and type of unlawful conduct
by both the employer and the employee, the relationship between the
conduct, and the impact of selecting reinstatement as the appropriate remedy.[118] A reinstated employee is usually entitled to return to
the same position he or she held before the commission of the ULP or,
if the position is not available, to a substantially equivalent position.
The NLRB may even order that a reinstated employee displace the
employee hired to replace him or her.

Q 8.47.2   Are there instances where an employee will not be reinstated?

The NLRB may not order reinstatement of an employee who was discharged "for cause."[119] The NLRB has additionally refused reinstatement where the employer successfully argued that:

(1)   a reinstated employee is not qualified for the position;

(2)   the employee's misconduct makes him or her unsuitable for reinstatement; or

(3)   the reinstated employee would have been terminated notwithstanding the ULP.

The NLRB usually holds the employer to a high standard in making these arguments.

Backpay

Q 8.48   Can the NLRB order backpay?

Yes; the NLRB can and will award backpay to an employee who was denied employment or earnings due to the employer's violation of the NLRA. The goal of a backpay award is to restore the employee to the position he or she was in prior to the commission of the ULP. Backpay remedies can also be applied against unions for violations of sections 8(b)(1) and 8(b)(2) of the NLRA.

Q 8.48.1   How is backpay calculated?

Generally, in discharge cases, backpay is calculated from the initial unlawful action to a specific, unequivocal, and unconditional offer of reinstatement. Backpay usually continues to accrue until the respondent makes an offer of reinstatement. To determine when the satisfactory offer of reinstatement has been made, the NLRB examines whether the charged party went through the formalities of an offer, which did not result in actual reinstatement. The charged party, however, can establish facts negating its liability or mitigating the liability period. Further, the NLRB has broad discretionary power to tailor a backpay remedy to the facts of the case and can depart from its presumptive backpay period when the facts of the case demand.

Backpay is calculated by subtracting the employee's actual earnings from other employment that took place after the unlawful action, less the necessary expenses incurred by the employee in seeking and holding interim employment, from the earnings an employee would have had without the unlawful employment action. Under some circumstances, the amount the employee would have earned had he or she not quit, been discharged from, or refused interim employment are deducted from gross backpay. The difference is the net backpay award.

Backpay also includes other compensation lost as a result of the unlawful action, such as benefits, and any net backpay award should be adjusted to reflect such compensation.[120] Interest on backpay awards is compounded on a daily basis.[121]

Often in backpay cases, an agreement cannot be reached regarding the amount of backpay necessary to remedy the violations found in a ULP case. In these cases, the parties will go before an ALJ for a determination. Usually, these compliance proceedings begin with the regional director providing the charged party with a compliance specification that explains the methodology for the NLRB's determination of the backpay owed. The compliance specification is served on the responding party, and the responding party is provided access to the documents used by the NLRB in making the backpay determination. The respondent then has an opportunity to answer the compliance specification. At the hearing, the General Counsel has the burden of proof with respect to the appropriateness of the NLRB's backpay calculation.[122]

CASE STUDY: *Latino Express*[123]

Because backpay is generally awarded in a lump sum, the Internal Revenue Service considers backpay as having been earned in the year in which the award is made, even when the award reflects pay that should have been received over multiple years. A consequence of a lump-sum award is that it pushes some awardees into a higher tax bracket than they would have been in had they been paid at the regular intervals.

In *Latino Express*, the NLRB held this adverse tax consequence is contrary to backpay's purpose of making employees' whole. Thus, employers must compensate an employee for any heightened tax burden the employee faces as a result of a backpay award that covers multiple years. The General Counsel has the burden to prove that there will be an adverse tax consequence.

The employer must file a notice with the Social Security Administration designating how a backpay award should be allocated among prior quarters so that the employee does not face any future loss of Social Security benefits.

To assist parties in complying with *Latino Express*, the Acting General Counsel has created a Microsoft Excel spreadsheet that calculates the amount of federal and state income taxes the employee will be required to pay if she receives backpay in a lump sum and the amount of federal and state income taxes she would have paid had she received the backpay in the appropriate years. The employer must provide an additional amount to compensate for any increased taxes owed by the employee. The Acting General Counsel also has provided a notice that can be filed with the Social Security Administration.[124]

Recovery of Attorney Fees/Litigation Costs

Q 8.49   May the NLRB order a party to pay attorney fees and litigation costs?

Generally, the NLRB may grant attorney fees and litigation costs if the party's defenses to the charge are frivolous. If, instead, the defenses are "debatable," the NLRB will not order the party to reimburse costs and fees. The NLRB often classifies defenses turning on issues of credibility as debatable, because it reasons that parties should not be discouraged from seeking NLRB review where witness credibility issues are in doubt.[125] However, where a party relies on "transparently untruthful testimony" from a witness who "demonstrated unmistakably that he was not to be believed," the NLRB may award full litigation costs and expenses to the other party.[126] The NLRB may also hold a party liable for the bargaining expenses of the charging party where the party engaged in bad-faith bargaining.[127]

The filing and maintenance of reasonably based employer lawsuits against labor unions do not violate the NLRA, and the NLRB may not require an employer who brings such a suit to pay attorney fees to the union against which it filed the lawsuit.[128]

Q 8.49.1   Are there other ways a party can recover attorney fees?

If an employer or a labor organization prevails as a respondent in an adversary adjudication conducted by the NLRB, or prevails in a civil action, including proceedings for judicial review of agency action, brought by or against the NLRB, then the employer or labor organization can be awarded fees and other expenses as a prevailing party under the EAJA.[129] EAJA provides that a respondent who prevails in a ULP proceeding and who meets certain eligibility requirements (net worth, corporate organization, number of employees, etc.) is eligible to seek reimbursement for attorney fees, "unless the position of the general counsel over which the party has prevailed was substantially justified." The U.S. Supreme Court has defined the phrase "substantial justification" under EAJA as "justified to a degree that could satisfy a reasonable person" or having a "reasonable basis both in law and fact."[130] The NLRB has stated that substantial justification does not mean substantial probability of prevailing on the merits, and is not intended to deter the agency from bringing forward close questions or new theories of law.[131] The initial decision whether to award fees under EAJA is made by the adjudicative officer, but the NLRB makes the final administrative determination regarding fees.[132] On review, a court may modify the NLRB's failure to award fees only if the NLRB's decision was unsupported by substantial evidence.[133]

Bargaining Orders

Q 8.50   What is a bargaining order?

A bargaining order requires a party to negotiate in good faith with another party in an existing collective bargaining relationship. Bargaining orders can be issued against both employers and labor organizations. The NLRB generally requires bargaining orders in three situations:

(1)   where ULPs have precluded a fair election (*Gissel* bargaining order);

(2)   where the NLRB finds that one party has refused to bargain in good faith with the other party; or

(3)   where the NLRB finds that there was an unlawful withdrawal of recognition.

A bargaining order directs the parties to negotiate with one another for a specific period of time, and generally the union's majority status cannot be challenged during this period. The purpose of a bargaining order is to restore the parties to the position and bargaining opportunity they had prior to the commission of the ULP.

In addition, the NLRB has held that where a newly certified union is deprived of the opportunity to bargain for a substantial portion of the certification year through no fault of its own, the NLRB may extend the union's certification year insulation from representational challenges for an equivalent period of time.[134] When a refusal to bargain occurs during a certification year, that period will typically be one year, less the period of time (if any) during which the employer had bargained in good faith.

Q 8.50.1   What is a *Gissel* bargaining order?

A *Gissel* bargaining order requires the employer to bargain with a union that was never certified or determined through election, as long as the union had authorization cards from a majority of employees. A *Gissel* bargaining order may be imposed where a party committed egregious ULPs before a union election that so disturbed the election process it prevented a fair election; for this reason *Gissel* orders are generally considered extraordinary remedies. In 1969, the U.S. Supreme Court determined in *NLRB v. Gissel Packing Co.*[135] that a bargaining order was appropriate where the "employer has committed ULPs which have made the holding of a fair election unlikely or which have in fact undermined the union's majority and caused an election to be set aside."

Q 8.50.2   How does the NLRB determine that a *Gissel* bargaining order is appropriate?

When determining whether to grant a *Gissel* bargaining order, the NLRB examines "the seriousness of the violations and the pervasive nature of the conduct, considering such factors as the number of employees directly affected by the violations, the size of the unit, the extent of dissemination among employees, and the identity and position of the individuals committing the ULP."[136]

Gissel orders are entered in two categories of cases. The first, and rarer, category involves ULPs that are so outrageous or pervasive that more traditional remedies cannot fix the coercive effects.[137] For example, the NLRB has issued such category-one *Gissel* orders where an employer discharged an entire bargaining unit, or laid off nearly half of the unit's employees, and retaliated against employees testifying in support of the union.

The second category involves less pervasive practices that still undermine the strength of the union and undermine the election process.[138] The NLRB grants these orders only where because of employer ULPs a fair election cannot be held.[139] For example, the NLRB has issued a category-two *Gissel* bargaining order where the director of nursing at a hospital interrogated and placed surveillance on union

supporters, promised rewards for employees who spied on union supporters, threatened to discharge and fire supporters, fired three union
supporters without warning, and altered job duties to take employees
out of the bargaining unit.[140]

Whether the NLRB issues a category-one or a category-two *Gissel*
bargaining order is normally important mainly for purposes of the
NLRB's level of fact-finding and the level of deference granted by a
reviewing federal court. For example, in category-one cases, some
courts have stated that the NLRB need only make "minimal findings of
the lasting effect of ULPs" to support the order, and the NLRB's decision is entitled to greater deference in such a case.[141]

Q 8.50.3   What is the scope of a bargaining order?

A bargaining order specifies the acts that the charged party is
required to follow and a "reasonable period of time" for the bargaining
order to be in effect. Generally, the charged party must bargain collectively regarding rates of pay, wages, hours, and other conditions
of employment. To determine the period of time, the NLRB examines
several factors, including:

(1)   whether the parties are bargaining for their first contract;

(2)   whether the parties engaged in meaningful and good-faith
negotiations for any period of time and whether the parties
reached an impasse in negotiations;

(3)   the severity of the committed ULPs; and

(4)   the length of the interruption in bargaining caused by the
refusal to bargain.

Q 8.50.4   What happens if a party does not bargain
in good faith?

A party who believes another party is not meeting its obligation
to bargain in good faith can file a ULP practice charge with the NLRB.
The NLRB has authority under the NLRA to take the following actions:

(1)   issue a bargaining order to any party that is committing a ULP
by refusing to bargain;

(2) issue a cease-and-desist order to, for example, prohibit the enforcement of an illegal change in contract language;

(3) require an employer to post notices in the workplace stating the specific unfair labor practices it committed; and

(4) require the guilty party to take whatever affirmative steps might be necessary to remedy the effects of the violation.

Q 8.50.5   How do the NLRB and the courts determine whether a party is bargaining in good faith?

Whether a party's conduct satisfies the good-faith standard is resolved by the NLRB, subject to review by the federal courts. Generally, there is no bright-line standard used to determine whether a party is negotiating in good faith. Rather, the NLRB and the courts make the determination on a case-by-case basis, examining the totality of circumstances. In other words, the entire course of conduct during bargaining is examined, not simply an isolated incident of alleged misconduct. Matters considered in the good-faith determination include any unlawful conduct of the employer, the sequence of events, the time lapse between the refusal to bargain and the unlawful conduct, and the union's conduct. Conduct both at and away from the bargaining table is also considered. In addition to overt behavior, the NLRB also looks at the parties' underlying motivation. (See chapter 5.)

Preventing the Transfer or Opening of a Facility

Q 8.51   Can the NLRB prevent a company from transferring or opening a facility as a remedy for a ULP charge?

The NLRB asserted in *Boeing Co.*[142] that it has authority under the NLRA to block an employer from transferring a facility or establishing a new facility in a different location if the employer's action is in retaliation for union activity elsewhere.

On March 26, 2010, the International Association of Machinists and Aerospace Workers filed a charge with the NLRB alleging that Boeing had retaliated against union employees for past strikes in Washington

State by placing a new production line for the 787 Dreamliner airplane in a non-union facility in South Carolina. The NLRB issued a complaint, seeking to bar Boeing from opening the new facility. The complaint prompted heavy criticism from the business community and lawmakers, who asserted that the NLRB should not interfere with a company's decision on where to open a factory. The NLRB withdrew the complaint in December 2011, but only after Boeing and the union reached an agreement regarding the location of new facilities and the union recommended the dismissal of the complaint.

The controversial issue underlying the complaint remains unresolved. After dismissing the *Boeing* action, the NLRB stated that it might engage in the same complaint activity if faced with a similar problem.

Individual, Single-Employer, and Joint-Employer Liability

Q 8.52   Can an individual be held liable for interfering with protected activity?

In limited instances, an individual can be held responsible for a corporation's ULPs. The test for such individual liability (or piercing the corporate veil) in NLRA cases is: (1) whether the corporation and the individual have failed to maintain their separate identities; and (2) whether third parties may be damaged by the failure.[143] Where an individual plays no active role in the corporation's operations, he or she will not be held liable for the corporation's ULPs.[144]

Q 8.53   When can two employers both be liable for interfering with protected activity?

A non-acting joint employer can be liable for the ULP of an acting joint employer if the non-acting employer: (1) knew or should have known that the other employer was acting for unlawful reasons; and (2) acquiesced in the unlawful action by failing to protest it or to exercise any contractual right it might possess to resist it.[145] In addition, if two companies are operated as a single employer, they may be jointly liable for each other's violations.[146]

Q 8.54   When are two employers considered a "single employer"?

The determination of whether separate employers will be considered a single employer focuses upon how close the interrelationship is between the employers' integrated operations. A single-employer relationship exists where "two nominally separate employers are actually part of a single integrated enterprise so that, for all purposes, there is in fact only a 'single employer.'" The question is whether the two nominally independent employers, "in reality, constitute only one integrated enterprise."[147]

The NLRB and courts consider the following factors in determining whether two or more separate employers should be regarded as a "single employer":

(1)   functional integration of enterprises;

(2)   centralized control of labor relations;

(3)   common management; and

(4)   common ownership or financial control.[148]

None of the factors identified above is controlling, and not all need to be present. The NLRB, however, stresses the factors that show integrated functions, with particular emphasis upon centralized control of labor relations.[149]

Overall, single-employer status depends on all of the circumstances and has been characterized as an absence of the arm's-length relationship found among non-integrated companies. The fundamental inquiry is whether there exists overall control of critical matters at the policy level.[150]

Q 8.54.1   What evidence is considered as part of the "functional integration of enterprises" and "centralized control of labor relations" factors when determining if two employers are a single employer?

Evidence of functional integration of enterprises may consist of the sharing of employees and/or equipment or the sharing of bookkeeping/accounting functions. Functional integration may also be shown by evidence of operational integration, such as finishing products of the other, common purchasing and/or shared distribution facilities.

A party can demonstrate centralized control of labor relations by providing evidence that the employers have the same labor relations/human resources managers; human resources representatives perform hiring, firing, and discipline functions for both employers; or there is centralized control of wages and benefits for both employers, absent an arm's-length pricing mechanism. Centralized control is evidenced where supervisors or managers of one employer supervise and/or manage employees of other employer.[151]

Q 8.54.2   What evidence is considered as part of the "common management" and "common ownership" factors when determining if two employers are a "single employer"?

Evidence of common management includes the existence of similar officers and/or directors, and a common high-level management. Common ownership or financial control can be shown by separate employers owned by same parent company, or commingling of financial reports. In addition, common financial control can be shown when there are low or no-interest loans between the separate employers.[152]

Q 8.54.3   What are the potential concerns associated with being considered a "single employer"?

When two nominally distinct companies are considered to be a "single employer," each may be:

(1)   bound by the same labor contract;

(2)   held liable for the ULPs of the other employer; and/or

(3)   required to bargain with the union representatives of the other employer.

Further, certain otherwise unlawful union activity may be considered lawful (for example, picketing at one in support of a strike at the other).[153]

Q 8.55   When are two employers considered "joint employers"?

In contrast to the single-employer theory, the joint-employer concept does not depend upon the existence of a single integrated enterprise. Instead, the joint-employer concept assumes that the two employers are independent. When two separate employers are considered "joint employers," they may be liable for each other's ULPs and other unlawful employment practices.

The NLRB may find that two or more entities are joint employers of a single workforce if they are both employers within the meaning of the common law, and if they share or codetermine those matters governing the essential terms and conditions of employment.[154]

Prior to its decision in *Browning-Ferris Industries*,[155] the NLRB would not find joint employer status unless the control exercised by a putative joint employer over a single workforce was "direct and immediate."[156] Citing a changing economy, the NLRB switched course in *Browning-Ferris Industries* by holding that a purported joint employer need only possess the authority to control the terms and conditions of employment, either directly or indirectly, and regardless of whether or not that authority was ever exercised.[157]

In early February 2018, the NLRB reversed and vacated *Browning-Ferris Industries* in *Hy-Brand Industrial Contractors, Ltd.*[158] and returned to the pre-*Browning-Ferris Industries* standard requiring actual direct and immediate control in order to find joint employer status. The return to the old joint employer standard was, however, short-lived.

By order dated February 26, 2018, the NLRB vacated the *Hy-Brand* decision. It did so because of an apparent conflict of interest that arose because Member William Emanuel, who agreed with the majority to vacate *Browning-Ferris Industries*, had worked for a law firm that previously represented a party in *Hy-Brand*. By a 3-0 vote (in which Manuel did not participate), the Board ruled that Emanuel should have been disqualified from participating in the case, and, accordingly, vacated the ruling. As a result, *Browning-Ferris* was reinstated and, as of the date of publication, is the current joint employer standard.[159]

Q 8.55.1   When does an employer "possess the authority to control" terms and conditions of employment of employees with another employer?

Under the current *Browning-Ferris* standard, to justify treating two employers as joint employers, the NLRB will consider whether one employer has the authority to control the terms and conditions of the other employer's employees. This includes the ability to:

- effectively recommend which employees will be hired or discharged;

- directly administer disciplinary procedures;

- handle payroll;

- provide insurance;

- maintain personnel records;

- schedule employees' hours of work;

- supervise employees' day-to-day activities; and

- participate in the collective bargaining process.

Under the current standard, the NLRB acknowledges that a putative joint employer's control over any of these particular areas may be "too remote" to justify joint employer status but has failed to provide any examples, opting instead for the exceptions to be flushed out in future cases.[160]

Q 8.56   Can a successor company be held liable for its predecessor's unfair labor or employment practices?

Yes, a successor may be held liable for the predecessor's unremedied or outstanding ULPs and other unlawful employment practices. If the successor or its representatives are put on notice of outstanding charges against the prior employer or other unlawful conduct (for example, discrimination), the successor becomes jointly and severally liable for any monetary penalty. Notice of potential charges can come from the prior employer, the union, or employees.

There need not be actual consent or even actual knowledge of the existence of the ULP or unlawful employment practice for courts to impose successorship liability. It may be sufficient that a prospective purchaser have notice of the facts on which a later finding of a ULP or discriminatory conduct is based.[161]

Q 8.56.1   What remedies affect successor employers?

Purchasers who have knowledge of a predecessor's ULPs may be required to comply with NLRB orders and remedy ULPs of the predecessor.[162] Such successors are often titled "*Golden State* successors," after the U.S. Supreme Court's 1973 decision of the same name. Additional information regarding successor employers can be found in chapter 5.

Notes to Chapter 8

1. 29 U.S.C. § 158.
2. *Id.* § 158(f).
3. *Id.* § 158(a).
4. *Id.* § 158(a)(1).
5. *Id.* § 158(a)(2).
6. *Id.* § 158(a)(3).
7. *Id.* § 158(a)(4).
8. *Id.* § 158(a)(5), (d).
9. *Id.* § 158(b).
10. *Id.* § 158(b)(1)(A).
11. *See, e.g.,* Armco, E. Steel Div., Ashland Works v. NLRB, 832 F.2d 357 (6th Cir. 1987); *see also* Coca Cola P.R. Bottlers, 358 N.L.R.B. 1233 (2012); Carpenters Local 1507 (Perry Olsen Drywall), 358 N.L.R.B. 1 (2012); Elec. Workers (IBEW) Local 88 (Elec. Maint. & Control), 312 N.L.R.B. 613 (1993); Pattern Makers v. NLRB, 473 U.S. 95 (1985); Pattern Makers (Mich. Model Mfrs. Ass'n), 310 N.L.R.B. 929 (1993); NLRB v. Carpenters Local 608 (Harte), 811 F.2d 149 (2d Cir. 1987); Theatrical Stage Emps. Local 7 (Universal City Studios), 254 N.L.R.B. 1139 (1981).
12. 29 U.S.C. § 158(b)(1)(B).
13. *See* Am. Newspaper Publishers Ass'n v. NLRB, 345 U.S. 100 (1953); NLRB v. Gamble Enters., Inc., 345 U.S. 117 (1953).
14. NLRB, CASEHANDLING MANUAL (PART ONE), UNFAIR LABOR PRACTICE PROCEEDINGS §§ 10020–10020.4 (Sept. 2018) [hereinafter CASEHANDLING MANUAL], https://www.nlrb.gov/sites/default/files/attachments/basic-page/node-1727/ulpmanual-september2018.pdf.
15. Form NLRB-501: Charge Against Employer, www.nlrb.gov/sites/default/files/attachments/basic-page/node-3040/nlrbform501.pdf; Form NLRB-508: Charge Against Labor Organization or Its Agent, www.nlrb.gov/sites/default/files/attachments/basic-page/node-3040/nlrbform508.pdf; Form NLRB-509: Charge Alleging Unfair Labor Practices Under Section 8(e) of the NLRA, www.nlrb.gov/sites/default/files/attachments/basic-page/node-3040/nlrbform509.pdf.
16. *See* 29 C.F.R. § 102.114; *see also* CASEHANDLING MANUAL, *supra* note 14, § 11841.2.
17. 29 C.F.R. § 102.114.
18. Postal Serv. Marina Ctr., 271 N.L.R.B. 397, 397–400 (1984).
19. *Id.*
20. *See* Nat'l Ass'n of Mfrs. v. NLRB, 717 F.3d 947 (D.C. Cir. 2013). The D.C. Circuit held that the limitations period in section 10(b) is subject to only those equitable tolling doctrines that existed at the time the provision was enacted in 1947.

21.   A&L Underground, 302 N.L.R.B. 467, 469 (1991).

22.   *See, e.g.*, Redd-I, Inc., 290 N.L.R.B. 1115, 1116 (1988); *see also* WGE Fed. Credit Union, 346 N.L.R.B. 982 (2006).

23.   Heartland Indus. Partners, 348 N.L.R.B. 1081 (2006).

24.   CASEHANDLING MANUAL, *supra* note 14, §§ 11840, 11841.3–11841.5.

25.   *See* NLRB Operations-Management Mem. OM 09-34, Changes to Electronic Filing of Documents Requirements (Feb. 13, 2009), www.nlrb.gov/publications/operations-management-memos.

26.   29 C.F.R. § 102.111.

27.   *Id.*

28.   *Id.* § 102.112.

29.   CASEHANDLING MANUAL, *supra* note 14, §§ 11840, 11841.3–11841.5.

30.   *Id.* § 11770.

31.   Kenrich Petrochemicals, Inc. v. NLRB, 893 F.2d 1468, 1483 (3d Cir.), *cert. denied*, 498 U.S. 981 (1990).

32.   David R. Webb Co., 311 N.L.R.B. 1135 (1993); Dec. 12, Inc., 282 N.L.R.B. 475 n.1 (1986).

33.   *See* NLRB Gen. Couns. Mem. 02-02, Impact Analysis Program Modifications (Dec. 6, 2001). N.B.: All NLRB General Counsel Memos are available at www.nlrb.gov/publications/general-counsel-memos.

34.   CASEHANDLING MANUAL, *supra* note 14, § 10068.2.

35.   *See, e.g.*, NLRB Gen. Couns. Mem. 08-09, Submission of First Contract Bargaining Cases to the Division of Advice (July 1, 2008); *see generally* NLRB Gen. Couns. Mem. 07-11, Mandatory Submissions to Advice (Sept. 25, 2007).

36.   CASEHANDLING MANUAL, *supra* note 14, § 10068.3.

37.   *See* Payless Drug Stores, 313 N.L.R.B. 1220, 1220–21 (1994); *see also* Pincus Elevator & Elec. Co., 308 N.L.R.B. 684, 684–85 (1992), *enforced*, 998 F.2d 1004 (3d Cir. 1993).

38.   *See* Redd-I, Inc., 290 N.L.R.B. 1115, 1115–16 (1988) (citing NLRB v. Dinion Coil, 201 F.2d 484, 491 (2d Cir. 1952)); *see also* Old Dominion Freight Line, 331 N.L.R.B. No. 3, slip op. at 1–2 (2000).

39.   CASEHANDLING MANUAL, *supra* note 14, § 10122.

40.   *Id.* § 10068.3.

41.   *Id.* § 10122.1.

42.   Children's Nat'l Med. Ctr., 322 N.L.R.B. 205, 205 (1996).

43.   29 C.F.R. § 102.19; *see also* CASEHANDLING MANUAL, *supra* note 14, § 10122.

44.   *See, e.g.*, NLRB Gen. Couns. Mem. 73-31, Arbitration Deferral Policy Under *Collyer*—Revised Guidelines (May 10, 1973).

45.   Collyer Insulated Wire, 192 N.L.R.B. 837 (1971).

46.   Dubo Mfg. Corp., 142 N.L.R.B. 431 (1963).

47.   Spielberg Mfg. Co., 112 N.L.R.B. 1080 (1995).

48.   Olin Corp., 268 N.L.R.B. 573 (1984).

49.   Babcock & Wilcox Constr. Co., 361 N.L.R.B No. 132 (2014).

50. NLRB Gen. Couns. Mem. 15-02, Guidelines Memorandum Concerning Deferral to Arbitral Awards and the Arbitral Process, and Grievance Settlements in Section 8(a)(1) and (3) Cases (Feb. 10, 2015).

51. *Id.*

52. *Collyer*, 192 N.L.R.B. 837.

53. *Id.* at 841–42.

54. *Id.*

55. NLRB Form 4767, Notice of Appeal, www.nlrb.gov/sites/default/files/ attachments/basic-page/node-3040/nlrbform4767.pdf.

56. Boeing Co., 349 N.L.R.B. 957 (2007).

57. U.S. Steel Corp., 223 N.L.R.B. 1246, 1247 (1976), *enforced,* 547 F.2d 1166 (3d Cir. 1977).

58. *Id.* at 1247.

59. Native Textiles, 246 N.L.R.B. 228 (1979).

60. Laborer's Local 731 (Tully Constr. Co.), 352 N.L.R.B. 107 (2008).

61. Reg'l Imp. & Exp. Trucking Co., 306 N.L.R.B. 740 (1992).

62. Clarkson Indus., Inc., 312 N.L.R.B. 349 (1993).

63. NLRB Gen. Counsel Mem. 12-01, Guideline Memorandum Concerning Collyer Deferral (Jan. 20, 2012).

64. NLRB Gen. Counsel Mem. 18-02, Mandatory Submission to Advice (Dec. 1, 2017).

65. NLRB Gen. Couns. Mem. 12-01, Guideline Memorandum Concerning *Collyer* Deferral Where Grievance-Resolution Process Is Subject to Serious Delay (Jan. 20, 2012).

66. Spielberg Mfg. Co., 112 N.L.R.B. 1080 (1955).

67. *See* Olin Corp., 268 N.L.R.B. 573 (1984); *see also* Spielberg Mfg. Corp., 112 N.L.R.B. 1080 (1955).

68. Douglas Aircraft Co., 234 N.L.R.B. 578 (1978), *enforcement denied,* 609 F.2d 352 (9th Cir. 1979).

69. *Babcock*, 361 N.L.R.B., slip op. at 17.

70. *Id.* at 3.

71. *Id.* at 10.

72. *Id.* at 11.

73. 29 C.F.R. § 102.9.

74. CASEHANDLING MANUAL, *supra* note 14, §§ 10124–70.

75. Alpha Beta Co., 273 N.L.R.B. 1546 (1985).

76. Babcock & Wilcox Constr. Co., 361 N.L.R.B. No. 132 (2014).

77. *Id.*

78. *Babcock*, 361 N.L.R.B., slip op. at 18.

79. Indep. Stave Co., 287 N.L.R.B. 740 (1987).

80. 29 C.F.R. §§ 102.20–102.21; *see also* CASEHANDLING MANUAL, *supra* note 14, §§ 10280, 11840, 11846.5 (service requirements of answers filed by paper) 11841,

11846.4 (service requirements of answers filed by e-filing); *see also* NLRB Operations-Management Mem. OM 09-34, Changes to Electronic Filing of Documents Requirements (Feb. 13, 2009), www.nlrb.gov/reports-guidance/operations-management-memos.

81.   29 C.F.R. §§ 102.24–102.26; *see also* CASEHANDLING MANUAL, *supra* note 14, § 10283.

82.   29 C.F.R. § 102.35 (providing a description of the general powers and duties of ALJs).

83.   *Id.* § 102.39; *see also* NLRB, DIVISION OF JUDGES BENCH BOOK: AN NLRB TRIAL MANUAL (Aug. 2010), www.nlrb.gov/sites/default/files/attachments/basic-page/node-1532/nlrb_bench_book.pdf.

84.   29 C.F.R. § 102.29.

85.   *See, e.g.,* Auto Workers v. NLRB, 392 F.2d 801, 809 (D.C. Cir. 1967), *cert. denied,* 392 U.S. 906 (1968); *see also* Biles-Coleman Lumber Co., 4 N.L.R.B. 679, 682 (1937).

86.   *See, e.g.,* Taylor Bros., Inc., 230 N.L.R.B. 861, 861 n.1 (1977); *see also* J.P. Stevens & Co., 179 N.L.R.B. 254, 255 (1969), *enforced,* 441 F.2d 514 (5th Cir. 1971), *cert. denied,* 404 U.S. 830 (1971); Spruce Pine Mfg., 153 N.L.R.B. 309, 309 n.1 (1965), *enforced in part,* 365 F.2d 898 (D.C. Cir. 1966).

87.   29 C.F.R. § 102.15.

88.   *Id.* § 102.38.

89.   *Id.* § 102.31; CASEHANDLING MANUAL, *supra* note 14, §§ 11770–11808 (detailing NLRB procedures related to applying for, issuing, and enforcing subpoenas).

90.   29 C.F.R. § 102.42.

91.   *Id.* § 102.45.

92.   Between December 31, 2007, and March 27, 2010, the Board operated with only a two-member panel because the president had not filled three vacant positions on the Board. In Noel Canning v. NLRB, 134 S. Ct. 2550 (2014), the Supreme Court unanimously affirmed a D.C. Circuit decision holding that three of President Obama's recess appointments to the Board made during an "intra-session" recess between the Senate's holding of "pro forma" sessions were unconstitutional, a holding that affected every NLRB decision issued from August 27, 2011, to August 12, 2013. On August 12, 2013, Congress confirmed the appointment of four new members to the NLRB. The NLRB now has a fully constituted five-member Board for the first time since August 21, 2003. *See* Q 2.11, *supra,* for more details.

93.   29 C.F.R. § 102.48.

94.   *Id.* § 102.46.

95.   *Id.* § 102.67(f); *see also* Westwood One Broad. Servs., Inc., 323 N.L.R.B. 1002 (1997); Thomas-Davis Med. Ctrs. v. NLRB, 157 F.3d 909 (D.C. Cir. 1998) (remand required for NLRB to provide reasoned explanation for applying no-relitigation rule to proceedings involving different bargaining unit).

96.   29 C.F.R. § 102.48.

97.   *Id.* § 160(f).

98.   *Id.* § 160(l); *see also* NLRB Gen. Couns. Mem. GC 77-77; NLRB Gen. Couns. Mem. GC 77-9.

99. 29 U.S.C. § 160(l); *see also* Pye v. Teamsters Local 122, 61 F.3d 1013 (1995); Walsh v. I.L.A., 630 F.2d 864 (1st Cir. 1980); Sears, Roebuck & Co. v. Carpet, Linoleum, Soft Tile & Resilient Floor Covering Layers Local 419, 397 U.S. 655 (1970); Hendrix v. Operating Eng'rs Local 571, 592 F.2d 437 (8th Cir. 1979); Humprey v. Longshoremen, 548 F.2d 494 (4th Cir. 1977); Hirsch v. Bldg. & Constr. Trades Council, 530 F.2d 298 (3d Cir. 1976); Squillacote v. Graphic Arts Int'l Union, 540 F.2d 853 (7th Cir. 1976).

100. *See* NLRB, SECTION 10(j) MANUAL USER'S GUIDE 12 (Sept. 2002) (redacted electronic version) [hereinafter SECTION 10(j) MANUAL], www.nlrb.gov/sites/default/files/attachments/basic-page/node-1727/redacted_10j_manual_5.0_reduced.pdf.

101. NLRB Gen. Couns. Mem. 14-03, Affirmation of 10(j) Program (Apr. 30, 2014).

102. *See* NLRB Gen. Couns. Mem. GC 99-08, Guideline Memorandum Concerning *Gissel* (Nov. 10, 1999).

103. SECTION 10(j) MANUAL, *supra* note 100, § 2.1. *See, e.g.*, Pye v. Excel Case Ready, 238 F.3d 69 (1st Cir. 2001); *see also* NLRB v. Electro-Voice, Inc., 83 F.3d 1559 (7th Cir. 1996).

104. *See generally* SECTION 10(j) MANUAL, *supra* note 100.

105. *See generally id.*

106. *See* Press Release R-2653, NLRB, Labor Board Temporarily Delegates Litigation Authority to General Counsel; Will Issue Decisions with Two Members After Members Kirsanow and Walsh Depart (Dec. 28, 2007), www.nlrb.gov/news-media.

107. *See* Muffley *ex rel.* NLRB v. Spartan Mining Co., 570 F.3d 534 (4th Cir. 2009) (upholding the December 28, 2007, delegation to the General Counsel of 10(j) powers); *see also* Glasser v. Heartland—Univ. of Livonia, MI, LLC, 632 F. Supp. 2d 659 (E.D. Mich. 2009) (same); Kentov v. Point Blank Body Armor, Inc., 258 F. Supp. 2d 1325 (S.D. Fla. 2002) (upholding a similar delegation of 10(j) powers to the General Counsel in 2001).

108. For a discussion of the circuit split on this issue, see Muffley *ex rel.* NLRB v. Spartan Mining Co., 570 F.3d 534, 541 (4th Cir. 2009).

109. SECTION 10(j) MANUAL, *supra* note 100; *see also id.* at App. D.

110. SECTION 10(j) MANUAL, *supra* note 100, at 27.

111. *See generally* CASEHANDLING MANUAL, *supra* note 14.

112. Ishikawa Gasket Am., Inc., 337 N.L.R.B. 175 (2001).

113. *See* Excel Containers, Inc., 325 N.L.R.B. 17 (1997); *see also* Indian Hills Care Ctr., 321 N.L.R.B. 144, 144 n.3 (1996).

114. Best Roofing Co., 298 N.L.R.B. 754, 758 (1990).

115. Tech. Serv. Sols., 334 N.L.R.B. 116, 117 (2001).

116. *See* FES, 331 N.L.R.B. 9 (2000); *see also* Parkside Grp., 354 N.L.R.B. No. 90 (Sept. 30, 2009).

117. Tradesmen Int'l, Inc., 351 N.L.R.B. 399, 401 (2007).

118. Golden Day Schs., Inc. v. NLRB, 644 F.2d 834, 840 (9th Cir. 1981).

119. 29 U.S.C. § 160(c).

120. CASEHANDLING MANUAL, *supra* note 14, § 105365.1.

121. Ky. River Med. Ctr., 356 N.L.R.B. No. 8 (Oct. 22, 2010).

122. *See generally* CASEHANDLING MANUAL, *supra* note 14.

123. Latino Express, 359 N.L.R.B. No. 44 (2013).

124. NLRB Gen. Couns. Mem. 13-03 (CH), Reimbursement of Excess Income Taxes Paid and Reporting of Backpay Allocation to the Social Security Administration (Feb. 15, 2013).

125. Unbelievable, Inc., 318 N.L.R.B. 857, 860 (1995), *enforced in part*, 118 F.3d 795 (D.C. Cir. 1997).

126. *Unbelievable*, 318 N.L.R.B. at 861.

127. Dish Network Serv. Corp., 347 N.L.R.B. No. 69 (July 31, 2006).

128. BE&K Constr. v. NLRB, 536 U.S. 516 (2002).

129. 28 U.S.C. § 2412(d).

130. Pierce v. Underwood, 487 U.S. 552 (1988).

131. Galloway Sch. Lines, Inc., 315 N.L.R.B. 473 (1994).

132. Lion Uniform, Inc., Janesville Apparel Div. v. NLRB, 905 F.2d 120 (6th Cir. 1990).

133. Hovey Elec., Inc. v. NLRB, 22 F. App'x 509 (6th Cir. 2001).

134. Mar-Jac Poultry Co., 136 N.L.R.B. 785 (1962).

135. NLRB v. Gissel Packing Co., 395 U.S. 575 (1969).

136. Abromson LLC, 345 N.L.R.B. 171, 176 (2005).

137. Power, Inc. v. NLRB, 40 F.3d 409, 422 (D.C. Cir. 1994).

138. *Gissel*, 395 U.S. at 614.

139. *Power, Inc.*, 40 F.3d at 422.

140. Regal Health & Rehab. Ctr., 354 N.L.R.B. 466 (2009).

141. *Power, Inc.*, 40 F.3d at 422.

142. The Boeing Co., Case No. 19-CA-32431, Complaint (Apr. 20, 2011).

143. White Oak Coal Co., 318 N.L.R.B. 732 (1995).

144. SRC Painting LLC, 346 N.L.R.B. 707 (2006).

145. *See* Capitol EMI Music, 311 N.L.R.B. No. 103 (1993), *enforced*, 23 F.3d 399 (4th Cir. 1994); *see also* Tradesmen Int'l, Inc., 351 N.L.R.B. No. 27 (2007) (employer was jointly liable for its acquiescence in the unlawful refusal of its customer to permit a union member to work at the customer's jobsite in violation of section 8(a)(3)).

146. Sabee Co., LLC, 351 N.L.R.B. 1350 (2007) (evidence demonstrated that two companies were owned, in whole or in part, by the same individuals, shared office space and office staff, and manufactured the same products with shared machinery; same individual served as the chief executive of both companies and was responsible for all decisions regarding relations among and between the two companies, as well as all labor-related decisions for both companies; chief executive was also responsible for the financial decisions of both companies and testified that the companies' finances were commingled).

147. NLRB v. Browning-Ferris Indus., Inc., 691 F.2d 1117, 1122 (3d Cir. 1982).

148. *Id.*

149. *Id.*

150. *Id.*

151. *Id.*

152. *Id.*

153. *Id.; see also* Capitol-EMI Music, 311 N.L.R.B. 997 (1993).

154. NLRB v. Browning-Ferris Indus., Inc., 691 F.2d 1117, 1122 (3d Cir. 1982).

155. Browning-Ferris Indus. of Cal., Inc., 263 N.L.R.B. No. 186 (2015).

156. Airborne Express, 338 N.L.R.B. 597 (2002) ("The essential element in the [joint-employer] analysis is whether a putative joint employer's control over employment matters is direct and immediate.").

157. *Browning-Ferris Indus.*, 263 N.L.R.B. No. 186, slip op. at 15–16.

158. Hy-Brand Indus. Contractors, Ltd., 365 N.L.R.B. No. 156 (2017).

159. The NLRB, on September 14, 2018, published a Notice of Proposed Rulemaking seeking public comment regarding its joint employer standard for use in drafting a proposed rule concerning the appropriate standard for assessing joint employer status. *See* https://www.federalregister.gov/documents/2018/09/14/2018-19930/the-standard-for-determining-joint-employer-status. In so doing, the NLRB is potentially seeking to revert back to its *Hy-Brand* decision through regulation rather than adjudication.

160. *Browning-Ferris Indus.*, 263 N.L.R.B. No. 186, slip op. at 16.

161. *See, e.g.*, Golden State Bottling Co. v. NLRB, 414 U.S. 158 (1973); U.S. Pipe & Foundry Co. v. NLRB, 398 F.2d 544 (5th Cir. 1968).

162. *Golden State*, 414 U.S. at 180.

9

Railway Labor Act

Following several failed attempts to regulate labor relations in the railroad industry, Congress enacted the Railway Labor Act in 1926 with support from both railroad labor and management. The RLA was designed to serve several policy purposes. First, it established a framework for union representation, bargaining, and dispute resolution. Second, it affirmed the right of railroad employees to self-organize for the purpose of bargaining with management. Finally, it served the vital national policy of avoiding disruptions to interstate commerce. This final policy was driven by congressional recognition that railroads uniquely contribute to the flow of essential goods and services in the United States. To achieve this overriding purpose, the RLA contains provisions designed to avoid, limit, or delay the use of self-help remedies by unions and management when disputes arise in order to protect the public and private interests of third parties reliant on the orderly operation of commerce.

Provisions and Administration of the RLA

Entities Covered by the RLA

Q 9.1   Which employers does the RLA cover?

The RLA applies to "carriers" in interstate commerce—generally defined to include railroads[1] and airlines[2]—and derivative carriers,[3] that is, any company that is directly or indirectly controlled by, or under common control with, a railroad or airline and that performs a service in connection with transportation.

Q 9.1.1   Are all railroads and airlines considered "carriers" subject to the RLA?

Railroad carriers subject to the RLA include express companies and any railroad subject to the jurisdiction of the Surface Transportation Board (formerly the Interstate Commerce Commission). The Surface Transportation Board determines whether an entity is a railroad carrier based on an examination of the facts and circumstances of the entity's operations. A company does not need to operate rail engines or rail cars to fall within the RLA, so long as it falls within the Surface Transportation Board's definition of a railroad.

Airline carriers subject to the RLA include carriers of passengers or goods in interstate or foreign commerce or any airline that transports mail for the U.S. government. Typically, certifications issued by the U.S. government, along with the company's operations, establish whether the employer is subject to the RLA.

Q 9.1.2   When does a company qualify as a derivative carrier?

Whether subsidiaries or affiliates of railroads and airlines qualify as derivative carriers subject to the RLA is determined using a two-part test: (1) whether there is common ownership or control between the subsidiary or affiliate and the RLA carrier; and (2) whether the employees of the subsidiary or affiliate perform work traditionally performed by the employees of an airline or railroad.[4]

Q 9.2   Which employees are covered by the RLA?

The RLA defines "employee" to include every person "in the service of a carrier" subject to the carrier's direction and supervision. Employees are covered by the RLA regardless of whether they are part of a union.[5] Coverage under the RLA also extends to "subordinate official[s]"; thus, lower-level managers who would be excluded under the National Labor Relations Act may qualify as employees under the RLA. In fact, under the RLA, supervisory employees sometimes make up an entire bargaining unit. The RLA also covers part-time employees, probationary employees, employees on temporary leave, temporary employees with a reasonable expectation of continued employment, and furloughed employees. Employees based in the United States who perform work for a foreign-based carrier are covered by the RLA. Additionally, the RLA has been held to apply to foreign-based employees who work on international flights into and out of the United States.

With respect to independent contractors, the NMB has looked to NLRB precedent and follows a "right-to-control" analysis. Under this analysis, if the carrier controls the means of accomplishing the result, the worker is deemed an employee; if the carrier specifies only the result, the worker is deemed an independent contractor. The NMB has identified several additional factors relevant to determining whether an independent contractor qualifies as an employee under the RLA, including ownership of equipment used to perform the work, freedom to accept other work, entrepreneurial risk, pay and fringe benefits, tax status, and supervision.[6]

Entities Excluded from the RLA

Q 9.3   Which employers and employees does the RLA exclude from coverage?

The RLA specifically excludes trucking companies from its coverage.[7] However, the NMB has taken the position that a trucking company organized for the purpose of servicing a rail carrier is subject to the RLA.[8] The RLA also specifically excludes companies engaged in coal operations and feeder lines from its coverage. Private carriers, as opposed to public carriers, are not subject to the RLA. Private carriers are those that do not serve the public and do not hold themselves out as doing so.[9]

The RLA does not apply to management officials. The NMB looks to the authority of a manager to discharge, hire, discipline, supervise, establish assignments, create policy, and commit funds to determine whether an individual is an excluded management official or a subordinate official covered under the RLA. Employees stationed outside the United States and its territories who perform work completely outside the United States are also excluded. Job applicants and trainees are excluded from coverage under the RLA because they are not yet "in the service of" the carrier.

In recent years, Congress has considered several proposals that would delete "express company" from the definition of "carrier" under the RLA. The major impact of this amendment would be to remove truck drivers working for Federal Express from coverage under the RLA. Efforts to amend the RLA in this regard have not been successful.

Q 9.3.1   Who decides whether a particular entity is subject to the RLA?

Such issues are frequently decided by the National Mediation Board, the government agency responsible for handling representational disputes under the RLA. Because the jurisdiction of the National

Labor Relations Board does not extend to carriers subject to the RLA, the NLRB refers disputes involving the application of the RLA to the NMB for a jurisdictional determination. Determinations regarding application of the RLA to specific entities are subject to judicial review.

National Mediation Board

Q 9.4   Who administers the RLA?

The RLA is primarily administered by the National Mediation Board,[10] an executive agency consisting of three individuals appointed by the President with the advice and consent of the Senate. NMB members serve for a period of three years, but no more than two members of the NMB may be from the same political party. NMB members have authority to delegate functions to agency employees.

Q 9.4.1   How does the NMB administer the RLA?

The NMB performs several functions related to the RLA. First, the NMB has exclusive jurisdiction to investigate disputes related to the selection, election, and identity of an employee representative. This includes the responsibility to determine employee eligibility for coverage, the scope of the bargaining unit, and whether a carrier consisting of multiple entities will be treated as a single carrier under the RLA. The NMB also monitors representation elections to ensure that the process occurs without coercion or interference.

Second, the NMB mediates disputes between labor and management regarding changes to the bargaining agreement in the railroad and airline industries and actively promotes settlement of these disputes. Additionally, the NMB makes recommendations to the President regarding the potential likelihood and degree of disruption to interstate commerce when labor disputes may lead to work stoppages.

Third, the NMB performs administrative duties related to the RLA, such as exercising its rule-making authority to publish regulations[11] and publishing the *NMB Representation Manual*, which provides guidance on proceedings before the NMB.[12] The NMB also publishes notices, forms, and other materials to facilitate the execution of the RLA's provisions.

With the passage of the FAA Modernization and Reform Act of 2012,[13] the NMB is subject to increased oversight and transparency. For the first time, the NMB must follow the rulemaking requirements of the Administrative Procedures Act. Additionally, the U.S. Comptroller General must evaluate and audit the NMB's programs and expenditures at least every two years. The Comptroller General must also undertake an immediate review of the "processes applied by the [NMB] to certify or decertify" labor union representatives and must make recommendations to ensure that the processes are fair and reasonable to all parties.[14]

Q 9.4.2   Does the NMB have enforcement powers?

While federal courts are highly deferential to NMB decisions made within the scope of NMB jurisdiction, the NMB does not have enforcement powers. Thus, if a party does not comply with an NMB order, the party seeking compliance must obtain an enforcement order in federal district court.

Representation Elections

Q 9.5   How do representation elections work under the RLA?

The RLA expressly grants employees the right to organize and bargain collectively through representatives of their own choosing.[15] The RLA vests authority in the NMB to protect the right of representation and to investigate and control all aspects of representation disputes.[16] As part of this authority, the NMB administers representation elections, establishes election procedures, determines the scope of the bargaining unit, and certifies the union as the employee's representative. The NMB functions as a "referee" in representation elections under the RLA.

Q 9.5.1   How is a bargaining unit determined under the RLA?

The NMB is responsible for determining the identity of the appropriate bargaining unit under the RLA. The NMB has consistently interpreted the RLA to require employee representation on a system-wide basis according to employee craft or class. Thus, under the RLA, a union will only receive certification if it seeks to represent all employees performing a particular job function, regardless of work location. This contrasts sharply with location-based bargaining units under the NLRA. The rationale underlying the system-wide rule is that a strike or other disruption at one location may interfere with or halt a carrier's operations across its entire system. Thus, the system-wide representation requirement applies even where a carrier has employees performing similar work in functionally unrelated operations.

The NMB determines what constitutes a craft or class for purposes of representation based on "many factors, including the composition and relative permanency of employee groupings along craft or class lines; the functions, duties, and responsibilities of the employees; the general nature of their work; and the extent of community of interest existing between job classifications."[17] This inquiry is highly fact-specific, and an employee's job title or the manner in which a carrier groups employees for payroll or other purposes is not necessarily relevant to a class or craft determination. If necessary, the NMB can exercise its discretion to convene a craft or class hearing to determine the proper scope of a craft or class. In the railway industry, craft or class determinations are largely based on historical patterns of representation. The NMB has been slow to recognize new crafts or classes or to combine existing ones. Requests to combine crafts or classes based on economic necessity and cross-utilization have been mostly unsuccessful. Even though airlines are less consistent than railroads in how they utilize employees, craft or class groupings are only slightly less rigid in the airline industry.

Q 9.5.2   What are the procedures related to initiating and conducting representation elections under the RLA?

The NMB's involvement in representation elections occurs pursuant to its dispute investigation power. Thus, to initiate a representation election, an applicant must submit to the NMB a request to investigate the dispute (Form NMB-1). Under the FAA Modernization and Reform Act of 2012, an applicant must additionally file a "showing of interest" consisting of valid authorization cards from 50% of the workforce involved in the dispute.[18] Previously, NMB rules required a "showing of interest" threshold of only 35%. Valid authorization cards must indicate that an employee is interested in being represented by the applicant and must be signed and dated in the employee's handwriting. The date must be no more than one year prior to the date of the application for investigation of the dispute. If more than one applicant is seeking to represent the employees, the second applicant may intervene and become a party to the dispute. It is unclear under the FAA Modernization and Reform Act whether the second applicant must provide authorization cards from 35% or 50% of the workforce. Nevertheless, the National Mediation Board has interpreted the law to require all applicants—including any intervenors—to provide authorization cards from 50% of the workforce.[19]

After the NMB receives the application and showing of interest, a mediator is appointed to investigate the dispute. The mediator obtains a list of all employees eligible to vote in an election and uses the list to determine whether a sufficient showing of interest exists to hold an election. Once the NMB determines a representation election is warranted, the NMB generally conducts a secret-ballot election to determine whether a majority of employees supports representation by the union. RLA elections are generally conducted by mail, telephone, or Internet ballot, because bargaining units are designated on a system-wide basis with workers widely dispersed geographically. The NMB has discretion in determining when to hold an election, but NMB procedures state the time period should be no shorter than twenty-eight days.

For more than seventy-five years, the NMB's representation election procedures required a majority of eligible voters in the craft or class to cast a vote in order to elect a representative. The only way to vote against representation was to not vote at all: If less than a majority cast a ballot, no representative would be certified. In 2010, the NMB changed those procedures to a "majority of votes cast" approach. Elections under the RLA are now more similar to the approach under the NLRA: A representative will be certified if named on a majority of the ballots cast, regardless of how many eligible voters participate. However, in cases involving multiple union candidates, the NMB will conduct a run-off election if no option receives a majority of votes. The run-off election shall be between the options receiving the largest and second-largest number of votes in the initial election. The FAA Modernization and Reform Act of 2012 provides that the "no representative" option shall be included in the run-off election if it received the largest or second-largest number of votes.[20]

After resolving all challenges and objections to eligibility, the NMB counts the ballots and prepares a final report certifying the union or dismissing the petition. The NMB is not required to explain the reasons for its decisions, and challenges to NMB representation decisions are generally not subject to court review.[21] An NMB decision related to an election will only be overturned where the NMB utterly fails to fulfill its statutory duty to conduct an investigation.

Certification of a union representative raises a two-year "certification bar," during which the NMB will not accept an application for investigation of a representation dispute involving the same craft or class of employees. However, unlike the NLRA, no "contract bar" doctrine exists under the RLA. Thus, a competing union can seek election as a representative regardless of the existence or duration of a labor contract. If a new union is certified by the NMB following an election, it simply takes over administration of the prior union's contract.

Q 9.5.3   Can an employer voluntarily recognize an employee representative under the RLA?

Under the RLA, an employer may voluntarily recognize an employee representative. Voluntary recognition is valid even if the recognition is not on a system-wide basis. However, voluntary recognition of a union as the employee representative does not preclude the NMB from acting on a subsequent application for investigation of a representation dispute.

Q 9.5.4   How can a union be "decertified" under the RLA?

The RLA does not contain a provision directly authorizing union decertification, but the RLA implicitly guarantees the freedom of employee groups to choose not to be represented. Decertification can be accomplished by means of a "straw man" election, in which an employee group successfully petitions the NMB for an election involving a nominal representative. If the straw man is elected, it can disclaim its status. Unlike the NLRA, the RLA does not provide a method for an employer to challenge a union it believes has lost majority support.

Q 9.5.5   What limits does the RLA impose on carriers during a representation election?

The RLA prohibits carriers or unions from interfering with, influencing, or coercing employees in their choice of representative.[22] The NMB has the duty to ensure that no interference with the right to self-organize occurs. The NMB's test for whether interference exists is whether carrier or union conduct has "tainted laboratory conditions."[23] Carrier activities forbidden under the RLA include:

(1)   interfering with NMB voting procedures by providing misleading or inaccurate information to employees;

(2)   firing, demoting, or otherwise retaliating against union supporters;

(3)   favoring one representative over another;

(4)   granting or withholding employment benefits;

(5)   threatening negative consequences if a union is elected;

(6)   polling employees regarding union support; and

(7)   discriminating against pro-union literature.

A carrier or any agent of that carrier that willfully violates the interference provisions of the RLA can be subject to criminal penalties for violations,[24] although criminal charges are rarely brought in practice. If the NMB finds unlawful interference, it can order that the election be re-run.

Q 9.5.6   What rights does a carrier have to oppose the election of a union under the RLA?

The First Amendment to the U.S. Constitution protects a carrier's right to communicate its opinion regarding employee representation to its employees. The NMB balances the carrier's free-speech rights against the right of employees to be free from election interference in determining whether a carrier has interfered with employee rights under the RLA. The NMB evaluates carrier speech by examining the "totality of the circumstances." Standards of carrier speech under the RLA are more restrictive than speech permitted under the NLRA, especially in regard to "pervasive" campaign activity.[25]

Labor Relations Disputes

Q 9.6 How are labor relations disputes resolved under the RLA?

The RLA strongly encourages employers and employees to settle disputes in order to avoid disruptions to interstate commerce. The RLA expressly requires employers and employees to "exert every reasonable effort to make and maintain agreements concerning rates of pay, rules, and working conditions and to settle all disputes . . . in order to avoid any interruption to commerce." The manner in which a dispute is resolved under the NMB depends on how the dispute is classified.

Q 9.6.1 How are disputes classified under the RLA?

Under the RLA, disputes are classified into two categories: "minor disputes" and "major disputes." The classification of a dispute as minor or major determines the resolution procedures applied to the dispute and the remedies available. The classification does not relate to the value or importance of the dispute, but only to the subject matter of the dispute and the procedures and remedies applied to it. In practice, the major/minor dispute distinction can be difficult to apply. Federal district courts have jurisdiction to determine whether a particular dispute is minor or major, and the issue is frequently litigated.

Minor Disputes

Q 9.7 What are "minor disputes"?

Under the RLA, disputes "arising out of grievances or out of the interpretation or application of agreements" are classified as "minor disputes." These disputes typically arise when an employer attempts to implement a change to employment conditions that is opposed by the union. Because the RLA favors resolution of disputes through arbitration, a dispute will be characterized as minor so long as the carrier's proposed "action is arguably justified by the terms of the parties' collective bargaining agreement."[26] If a dispute is classified as minor, the employer has no duty to bargain regarding the change and may implement the proposed change while the dispute is pending.

Q 9.7.1   How are minor disputes resolved under the RLA?

Once a minor dispute arises, the parties have a duty to meet and confer in good faith to settle the dispute in the "usual manner up to and including the chief operating officer of the carrier designated to handle such disputes."[27] The parties must also adhere to statutory notice and scheduling procedures related to the duty to confer.[28] If the parties are unable to settle the dispute during internal dispute resolution procedures, either party can demand arbitration by filing a notice indicating the party's intent to submit the dispute to arbitration within thirty days.

Arbitration procedures differ for the railroad and airline industries. For the railroad industry, the RLA created the National Railroad Adjustment Board to act as a federally funded arbitration body charged with resolving minor disputes under the RLA. Review of NRAB decisions is available in federal court, but the standard of review is among the "narrowest known to law."[29]

As an alternative to the NRAB, the RLA allows parties to form and submit disputes to a private arbitration board, called a "Special Board of Adjustment," created in advance by the parties to resolve grievances. A third alternative allows either party to request the formation of a "Public Law Board," a private arbitration board funded by the NMB, to resolve the dispute. For Public Law Boards, the NMB designates two members, one representing the interests of each party, to arbitrate the agreement. If the two members are unable to resolve the dispute, the NMB then appoints a neutral third member to resolve the dispute. Decisions of such boards are also subject to review in federal court under the same narrow standard of review.

The airline industry does not have a counterpart to the NRAB because Congress did not create one when it amended the RLA to apply to airlines. Air carriers and unions instead created private arbitration procedures and boards known as "Systems Boards of Adjustment." Typically, these boards are evenly divided between management and labor initially, and later steps in the resolution process involve appointment of a neutral arbitrator to resolve the dispute. As with railroad arbitration, airline arbitration awards are judicially enforceable, and challenges to awards are rarely successful.

The RLA completely prohibits resort to self-help remedies, including strikes, in response to minor disputes. Rather, the sole remedy for resolving a dispute is arbitration. If one party resorts to self-help measures in response to a minor dispute, the other party can obtain an injunction in federal court. The RLA also makes arbitration mandatory and thereby prevents the parties from obtaining a court resolution to the dispute.

Major Disputes

Q 9.8   What are "major disputes"?

Major disputes under the RLA are those disputes involving the creation of new rights or destruction of existing rights under a collective agreement—that is, disputes related to the formation of collective agreements or a party's intent to change the terms of an agreement "affecting rates of pay, rules, or working conditions." Before making an intended change to an agreement, the party seeking the change must give at least thirty days' written notice of the intended changes. This is called a section 6 notice and must state the intended changes to the agreement sufficiently to put the other side on notice regarding the changes. In this way, the section 6 notice defines the subject matter and scope of the subsequent bargaining. Within ten days following the section 6 notice, the parties must arrange to confer and directly bargain regarding the intended changes.[30] This bargaining period continues indefinitely until either side determines it is no longer productive.

Q 9.8.1   How are major disputes resolved under the RLA?

If employees are represented by a union, the RLA prohibits either side from altering the status quo once a section 6 notice has been served. Thus, once the notice is served, neither side can change the agreement (including implied agreements based on past practice) until all of the bargaining and mediation procedures required under the RLA are exhausted, regardless of whether the agreement has expired. However, the RLA does not prevent carriers from implementing changes to the status quo when employees are not represented, subject to the prohibition against interfering with its employees' right of self-organization.

During the bargaining period, either side may invoke the mediation services of the NMB.[31] This usually occurs when the parties reach impasse on the most difficult outstanding issues. The NMB also has authority to initiate involvement in a labor dispute of its own accord.[32] After becoming involved in a dispute, the NMB appoints a mediator to assist the parties in resolving any remaining areas of disagreement. The parties then continue bargaining with the mediator acting in the role of facilitator.

Strikes Under the RLA

Q 9.9   Can employees covered under the RLA strike?

Employees covered under the RLA may strike, but only after exhausting the meditation process and only with respect to major disputes—that is, disputes relating to the formation of collective agreements or a party's intent to change the terms of an agreement "affecting rates of pay, rules, or working conditions."

Q 9.9.1   What if a strike or other work stoppage threatens to substantially disrupt interstate commerce?

If the NMB determines that the dispute threatens to substantially disrupt interstate commerce, the NMB may recommend that the President create an "Emergency Board." An Emergency Board consists of three or five neutral members appointed by the President. Following creation, an Emergency Board has thirty days to investigate the dispute and issue a report. The parties remain subject to the status quo requirement and may not engage in self-help activity during the Emergency Board investigation and for thirty days thereafter. In the past, Congress has intervened to prevent strikes by appointing a commission to further study the dispute or by passing a law adopting the recommendations of the Emergency Board, thereby legislatively imposing a contract on the parties. If employees strike in response to minor disputes, a carrier may obtain an injunction against the strikers.

Bargaining Agreements Under the RLA

Q 9.10 How long do bargaining agreements under the RLA remain in effect?

The length of time that RLA-governed bargaining agreements remain in effect varies between the airline and railroad industries. In the airline industry, bargaining agreements usually include a termination provision stating that the agreement will terminate a certain number of years in the future. At that point, the parties reconvene to engage in bargaining over a new agreement. This is similar to the practice of many industries under the NLRA. However, the RLA requires that the status quo remain in effect during the new round of bargaining.

Agreements in the railroad industry usually do not include a termination provision and therefore remain in effect indefinitely. Instead, new rounds of bargaining are initiated by means of a section 6 notice, which engages the bargaining and mediation procedures of the RLA. Even if the parties are unable to reach agreement through the entire RLA process and the parties reach the point of striking, the agreement remains in place until and to the extent changed by a subsequent agreement, although carriers may be permitted to unilaterally implement proposed changes to the extent necessary to operate in the face of employee self-help.

Q 9.11 Is there a duty to bargain under the RLA?

The RLA imposes on carriers the obligation to bargain or negotiate with a certified representative.[33] In addition, the RLA requires both carriers and unions to "exert every reasonable effort to make and maintain agreements" about "rates of pay, rules, and working conditions."[34] These provisions impose on both parties the substantive duty to bargain in good faith. The duty to bargain continues regardless of whether a carrier has a good-faith belief that a representative is no longer supported by a majority of the employees in the craft or class. The duty to bargain is enforceable in federal court, but the U.S. Supreme Court has admonished courts to use "great circumspection" before finding a party in violation of the duty to bargain.[35]

Q 9.11.1　Which subjects are mandatory subjects of bargaining?

Mandatory subjects of bargaining include "rates of pay, rules, and working conditions" which have been held to include almost all subjects that affect the interests of an employee. However, the U.S. Supreme Court has recognized that some decisions, specifically the decision to leave the railroad business entirely, are matters of management prerogative not subject to the duty to bargain. Courts have split on whether the duty to bargain under the RLA includes a duty to furnish information similar to the NLRA.

Q 9.11.2　Is multi-employer bargaining allowed under the RLA?

National, multi-employer bargaining is permitted under the RLA and is common in the railroad industry, where it is known as "national handling." However, carriers are not required to engage in new rounds of national handling even after participating in earlier rounds. A carrier that decides not to engage in national handling is not required to give a section 6 notice or bargain over the decision.

Q 9.12　Are union shop agreements permitted under the RLA?

The RLA was amended in 1951 to expressly authorize union shop agreements between unions and carriers. These agreements require employees, as a condition of employment, to pay union dues and other fees starting sixty days after beginning employment.[36] Failure to pay dues as required under a union shop agreement is a valid ground for termination of employment. Where financial conditions for union membership are uniform, membership must be available to all employees on the same terms and conditions. The RLA also authorizes dues check-off agreements that allow carriers to automatically deduct union dues and other fees directly from employee paychecks, provided the employee authorizes the deductions in writing.[37]

Notes to Chapter 9

1. 45 U.S.C. § 151, First.
2. *Id.* § 181.
3. *Id.* § 151, First.
4. ABM Onsite Servs.–W., Inc. v. NLRB, 849 F.3d 1137, 1140 (D.C. Cir. 2017).
5. Aircraft Serv. Int'l, Inc. v. Int'l Bhd. of Teamsters AFL CIO Local 117, 2012 WL 5194163 (W.D. Wash. Oct. 18, 2012), *rev'd on other grounds*, 779 F.3d 1069 (9th Cir. 2015) (en banc).
6. E. Air Lines, 9 N.M.B. 285, 296 (1982).
7. 45 U.S.C. § 151, First.
8. O/O Truck Sales, 21 N.M.B. 258, 272 (1994).
9. *See* Application of Transp. Workers of Am. (S. Air Transp.), 8 N.M.B. 31, 34 (1980).
10. 45 U.S.C. §§ 154–55.
11. 29 C.F.R. § 1201.1 *et seq.*
12. *See generally* NMB REPRESENTATION MANUAL, https://storage.googleapis.com/dakota-dev-content/Representation-Manual.pdf.
13. Pub. L. No. 112-95, 126 Stat. 11 (2012).
14. *Id.* §§ 1001, 1004.
15. 45 U.S.C. § 152, Fourth.
16. *Id.* § 152, Ninth.
17. NMB REPRESENTATION MANUAL § 9.1.
18. Pub. L. No. 112-95, § 1003.
19. 29 C.F.R. § 1206.2(b).
20. Pub. L. No. 112-95, § 1002.
21. Switchmen's Union v. NMB, 320 U.S. 297 (1943).
22. 45 U.S.C. § 152, Ninth; *see also* 45 U.S.C. § 152, Third & Fourth.
23. USAir, Inc., 18 N.M.B. 290, 323 (1991) (test is similar to the parallel test under the NLRA).
24. 45 U.S.C. § 152, Tenth.
25. USAir, Inc., 17 N.M.B. 377 (1990).
26. Consol. Rail Corp. v. Ry. Labor Execs.' Ass'n, 491 U.S. 299, 307 (1989).
27. 45 U.S.C. § 153, First (i).
28. *Id.* § 152, Sixth.
29. Gunther v. San Diego & A.E. Ry., 382 U.S. 257, 261 (1965).
30. 45 U.S.C. § 156.
31. *Id.* § 155, First.
32. *Id.*
33. 45 U.S.C. § 152, Ninth.

34. *Id.* § 152, First.
35. Chi. & N.W. Ry. v. United Transp. Union, 402 U.S. 570, 579 n.11 (1971).
36. 45 U.S.C. § 152, Eleventh (a).
37. *Id.* § 152, Eleventh (b).

10

Federal Preemption of State Regulation

Before the National Labor Relations Act, labor law consisted of a patchwork of state statutes and common-law torts. Although the NLRA contains no express preemption provision, the U.S. Supreme Court has recognized that one of the overarching goals of the NLRA was to consolidate the administration of the nation's labor policy into a single federal system. As such, "in passing the NLRA, Congress largely displaced state regulation of industrial relations."[1] Although ordinary preemption principles, such as frustration of federal purpose or field preemption, apply to the NLRA, the U.S. Supreme Court also has articulated three specific federal labor law preemption principles: *Garmon* preemption, *Machinists* preemption, and preemption under section 301 of the Labor Management Relations Act (LMRA), 29 U.S.C. § 186.

Garmon Preemption

Q 10.1   What is *Garmon* preemption?

Garmon preemption applies to actions implicating the primary jurisdiction of the NLRB. Under *Garmon* preemption, if the NLRA either arguably or actually protects or prohibits an activity, state regulation of that activity is generally forbidden.[2] *Garmon* preemption is designed to prevent conflict between local regulation and Congress's choice of the NLRB as the appropriate body to implement and enforce the substantive provisions of the NLRA.

In *San Diego Building Trades Council v. Garmon*,[3] the unions asked the employers to agree to terminate all employees who were not already union members and who did not apply for union membership within thirty days. The employers refused to do so, stating that their employees had not expressed a desire to join a union and that the employers could not enter into such an agreement with a union until the employees designated the union as its collective bargaining agent. Peacefully, the unions began to picket and to encourage others to boycott the employers in an effort to pressure the employers to enter into the agreement. In California state court, the employers sought and received damages and an injunction prohibiting the unions' picketing and exerting other pressures until one of the unions was designated the employees' collective bargaining agent. The employers also initiated a representation proceeding before the NLRB, which declined jurisdiction.

On appeal, the California Supreme Court sustained the lower court's award of damages and injunctive relief, holding that, because the NLRB had declined jurisdiction, the state courts had authority over the dispute. The California Supreme Court further found that the unions had engaged in unfair labor practices in violation of the NLRA, "and hence [were] not privileged under California law."[4]

When the case first came before the U.S. Supreme Court, the Court held the NLRB's refusal to exercise jurisdiction did not give states "power over activities they otherwise would be preempted from regulating."[5] On remand, the state court set aside the injunction, but upheld the damages award, finding that the unions' actions violated state labor law and tort law. The case came before the U.S. Supreme Court a second time, and the Court held that, in order to protect the primary jurisdiction of the NLRB over conduct regulated by the NLRA, the state has no jurisdiction to address activities actually or arguably protected or prohibited by the NLRA.[6] Accordingly, the California state courts did not have jurisdiction to award the employers damages for the unions' activities, which were arguably prohibited by the NLRA.

Q 10.1.1   What is the difference between "actually protected or prohibited" activity and "arguably protected or prohibited" activity?

The "actually protected or prohibited" prong of *Garmon* is essentially a manifestation of conflict preemption. The U.S. Supreme Court specifically stated that, where it is clear that the activities a state purports to regulate are protected by section 7 of the NLRA or constitute an unfair labor practice under section 8, the state's jurisdiction must yield to avoid a conflict of power, between the NLRB and a state court.

The "arguably protected or prohibited" prong of *Garmon* applies when it is unclear whether a particular activity is protected under section 7 or prohibited under section 8. Because the NLRB has primary jurisdiction to resolve labor management disputes, the courts have held that the determination of what is actually protected or prohibited by the NLRA belongs to the NLRB. Therefore, if something is even arguably protected or prohibited by the NLRA, the NLRB must resolve that question in the first instance. If the NLRB decides that the activity is regulated or prohibited by a section of the NLRA, the states are "ousted out of all jurisdiction."[7] Congress's interest in uniformly administered national labor laws animates this grant of primary juris-diction to the NLRB.

Notably, *Garmon* preemption is broad. Under the *Garmon* doctrine, both the state and federal courts are deprived of any jurisdiction to resolve the merits of claims involving activities either actually or argu-ably protected or prohibited by the NLRA.

 CASE STUDY: *J.A. Croson Co.*[8]

A non-union employer filed a lawsuit in state court alleging that a union employer violated the Ohio prevailing wage law by taking deductions from employees' wages on a public project to fund a union job targeting program. The union program sought to expand job opportunities for represented employees by subsidizing costs for union employers. The NLRB noted that job targeting programs and associated deductions from wages have long been considered protected activity under section 7, even when deductions are made in connection with public projects. Because the lawsuit challenged protected activity, it was preempted under *Garmon*. (See Q 10.1 for a discussion of *Garmon* preemption.) The NLRB held that "the filing and maintenance of [a preempted] lawsuit is an unfair labor practice without regard to whether it is objectively baseless,"so the employer's preempted lawsuit violated section 8(a)(1).[9]

Q 10.1.2   Are there any exceptions to the preemption of activities that are "arguably protected or prohibited" by the NLRA?

Exceptions to *Garmon* preemption arise, and a state may regulate conduct where:

(1)   a compelling state or local interest is involved;
(2)   the issue is of peripheral concern to the NLRA; or
(3)   the state is acting as a "market participant."

Q 10.1.3   What is the "compelling state or local interest" exception?

Typically, a compelling state or local interest provides a basis for permitting state regulation despite a claim of NLRA preemption. This compelling state interest is one for conduct like violence, concern over which is "deeply rooted in local feeling and responsibility."[10] The exception is usually applied to state laws that protect the health, safety, and welfare of citizens, such as state laws to prevent violence and imminent threats to the public order. The exception has also been applied to state personal tort laws, such as intentional infliction of emotional distress and malicious libel. However, both exceptions have been construed very narrowly.

Q 10.1.4   ... the "peripheral concern" exception?

A peripheral concern to the NLRA is conduct that does not threaten significant interference with the NLRB's jurisdiction. In *Sears, Roebuck & Co. v. Carpenter's Dist. Council (San Diego)*,[11] a union picketed the parking lot of a retail store to protest the hiring of employees who had not been dispatched from the union hiring hall. When the picketers refused to leave the employer's property, the employer sued for trespass. The U.S. Supreme Court held that the NLRA did not preempt an employer's state law trespass claims against union picketing because trespass implicated a "peripheral concern" of federal labor law, even if it was arguably protected by the NLRA. In the final analysis, the U.S. Supreme Court concluded that the state court jurisdiction was not preempted because the picketing likely violated state trespass laws and was arguably unprotected.

Q 10.1.5   ... the "market participant" exception?

Where the state is not acting in a regulatory capacity, but rather acting in a proprietary capacity like any other market participant, and where the state's actions are specifically tailored to its proprietary interest, there is no preemption.[12] For example, when the city of Pittsburgh conditioned a grant of tax increment financing to a hotel developer on the developer's acceptance of a labor neutrality agreement for projects receiving the funds, the NLRA did not preempt the condition.[13] Because the city was a constituent of the agency that issued the bonds to the developer and had a financial interest in the development, and because the condition was limited to projects receiving the funds, the city was not acting in a regulatory capacity, but rather in a proprietary capacity.

This exception is very narrow, and a state's regulatory use of its spending power for regulatory objectives is subject to an ordinary preemption analysis.[14]

Machinists Preemption

Q 10.2   When does *Machinists* preemption apply?

Under *Machinists* preemption, if an activity is not one that is protected or prohibited by the NLRA, but is one that Congress intended to leave completely unregulated (either by the NLRB or by the states), then state regulation of that activity is preempted.[15] Using *Machinists* preemption, the U.S. Supreme Court has repeatedly preempted state laws that affect the economic leverage of employers and unions in connection with organizing or collective bargaining, such as strikes, boycotts, and lockouts.

In *Machinists*, the Court held that the Wisconsin employment commission could not regulate a union's refusal to work overtime because Congress did not intend to permit regulation of such economic self-help, even if it were assumed that such activity was not protected by the NLRA. By prohibiting state and municipal regulation of areas that have been left to be controlled by the free play of economic forces, *Machinists* preemption "preserves Congress' intentional balance between the uncontrolled power of management and labor to further their respective interests."

Q 10.2.1   What are some examples of cases involving *Machinists* preemption?

- The City of Los Angeles' refusal to renew a taxicab franchise unless the taxicab company resolved a labor contract dispute was preempted under *Machinists* because the condition deprived the taxicab company of an essential economic weapon: the ability to wait out a strike.[16]

- A Massachusetts law mandating minimum healthcare benefits for insurance contracts that are the subject of collective bargaining was not preempted under *Machinists* because the NLRA "is concerned primarily with establishing an equitable process for determining the terms and conditions of employment, and not with the particular substantive terms of the bargain that is struck when the parties are negotiating from relatively equal positions."[17]

- A Pennsylvania law restricting union peaceful recognitional picketing was preempted because Congress intended this type of activity to go unregulated.

- A presidential executive order prohibiting the federal government from contracting with an employer using permanent replacement workers during a strike was precluded by the NLRA because an employer's use of replacement workers is an economic weapon that Congress intended to leave unregulated by the federal or state governments.[18]

- A city ordinance providing collective bargaining rights for independent contractor transportation providers was not preempted because the individuals covered by the city ordinance were independent contractors rather than NLRA-covered employees.[19]

Q 10.3 Are there any exceptions to *Machinists* preemption?

Circumstances where the *Machinists* preemption doctrine does not apply include the following:

(1) state regulations to establish minimum labor standards;

(2) cases involving compelling state or local interests of peripheral concern to the NLRA; and

(3) state actions as a market participant.

Q 10.3.1   What is the "minimum labor standard" exception?

State or local regulations that create generally applicable labor standards that do not substantially interfere with the collective bargaining process may not be preempted under the *Machinists* doctrine.[20] For example, a Massachusetts law mandating minimum health-care benefits for insurance contracts that are the subject of collective bargaining was not preempted under the *Machinists* doctrine because the NLRA "is concerned primarily with establishing an equitable process for determining terms and conditions of employment, and not with particular substantive terms of the bargain that is struck when the parties are negotiating from relatively equal positions."[21]

Q 10.3.2   What is the "state or local interest of peripheral concern" exception?

Regulation of conduct that touches issues "deeply rooted in local feeling and responsibility" that does not significantly impact the right to use economic weapons Congress intentionally left unregulated generally is not preempted under the *Machinists* doctrine.[22] In cases where an employer or union is alleged to have breached a contract or engaged in a tort, the party may not be able to avoid liability through a preemption argument. In rejecting an employer's argument that replacement workers' breach of contract and tort claims were preempted under the *Machinists* doctrine, the Supreme Court held, "[i]t is one thing to hold that the federal law intended to leave the employer and the union free to use their economic weapons against one another, but is quite another to hold that either the employer or the union is also free to injure innocent third parties without regard to the normal rules of law governing those relationships."[23] This exception has also been applied to trespass and nuisance claims.[24]

Q 10.3.3   What is the "market participant" exception?

States and local entities are not preempted from acting in a manner that has some effect on parties' use of economic weapons where the governmental entity is acting as a private actor, and not in its regulatory capacity.[25]

Section 301 Preemption

Q 10.4   What is section 301 preemption?

Section 301 of the LMRA confers federal court jurisdiction over "[s]uits for violation of contracts between an employer and a labor organization representing employees in an industry affecting commerce." The U.S. Supreme Court, however, has interpreted this phrase expansively, and today section 301 preempts a state law claim when a court, in reviewing an essential element of the claim, would be required to interpret the collective bargaining agreement.[26] "In practice, this test boils down to whether the asserted state law claim plausibly can be said to depend upon the meaning of one or more provisions within the collective bargaining agreement."[27]

Q 10.4.1   When does a state law claim "depend on the meaning" of a collective bargaining agreement?

State law claims will "depend on the meaning" of collective bargaining agreement provisions under two scenarios. First, a claim depends on the meaning of a collective bargaining agreement if it alleges conduct that arguably constitutes a breach of a duty that is created by or based on a collective bargaining agreement. For example, "a state-law tort action against an employer may be preempted by [section] 301 if the duty to the employee of which the tort is a violation is created by a collective-bargaining agreement and without existence independent of the agreement."[28] Second, where a claim's resolution necessarily requires an interpretation of the collective bargaining agreement, it will be preempted by section 301.[29]

The U.S. Supreme Court and the federal courts of appeal have relied on these principles to dismiss a wide range of state law claims because those claims are completely preempted by section 301. Such claims in particular circumstances include, among others, alleged bad-faith handling of an insurance claim, invasion-of-privacy claims, and malicious prosecution. Generally speaking, if a state rule purports to define the meaning or scope of a term in a collective bargaining agreement, it will be preempted by section 301. However, when a claim is based on a state rule that proscribes conduct or establishes rights and obligations that are independent of a labor contract, the claim will not necessarily be preempted.

Some examples of claims held not to be preempted by section 301 include in particular circumstances tortious interference with third-party contract claims, discrimination and retaliation claims, and claims involving individual employment contracts.

CASE STUDY: *Kofoed v. Shiprack*[30]

In Kofoed v. Shiprack, the Ninth Circuit affirmed the district court's holding that a union member's slander claim against a union representative was preempted under section 301. The union member claimed that the union representative made defamatory remarks about him to an employer so that the employer would not hire him. The Ninth Circuit held that the trial court would be required to interpret the collective bargaining agreement to determine whether the union representative's statements were privileged. Since the state law claim required an interpretation of the collective bargaining agreement, it was preempted by section 301.

Q 10.4.2   Will a state law claim always be preempted where a collective bargaining agreement is consulted in the course of litigation?

No. Courts have held that section 301 preemption is not required simply because resolution of the claim requires reference to the collective bargaining agreement. For example, the fact that a court must refer to a wage rate in a collective bargaining agreement to calculate damages does not make a claim preempted under section 301.[31] In addition, the mere fact that a party refers to a collective bargaining agreement in articulating its defense does not necessarily establish section 301 preemption. For example, where a union employee (truck driver) claimed that he was discharged in violation of public policy because he refused to drive in unsafe conditions that violated federal and state safety regulations, his claim was not preempted by section

301 simply because the federal safety regulations were also incorporated into the collective bargaining agreement. The court did not need to interpret the collective bargaining agreement in order to adjudicate the claim.[32] On the other hand, section 301 did preempt an employee's claim that his employer engaged in extreme and outrageous conduct when discharging the employee for allegedly defending himself during a fight with a co-worker. The issue of whether the employer's conduct meets the elements of an intentional infliction of emotional distress claim rests on whether the employer was legally entitled to discharge the employee, and this could only be determined by reviewing the terms of the collective bargaining agreement's "just cause" provision.[33]

Applicable Preemption Doctrine

Q 10.5 How does one determine which preemption doctrine applies in a particular case?

The following analytical steps can assist in deciding whether a claim is preempted:

1. If the claim alleges an unfair labor practice or activity arguably protected or prohibited by the NLRA, the claim likely falls within the primary jurisdiction of the NLRB and is preempted by *Garmon*.

2. Even if the claim is not preempted by *Garmon*, consider whether the claim is preempted under *Machinists* because it is based on the kind of activity that Congress intended to leave completely unregulated. If the claim involves regulation of employers' or unions' peaceful use of economic pressures in connection with organizing or collective bargaining, *Machinists* preemption will apply absent one of the exceptions discussed above.

3. Determine whether, regardless of how it is pled, the claim is a breach of a collective bargaining agreement within the scope of section 301; if so, it is likely preempted. Likewise, if a claim is not grounded in the collective bargaining agreement, but its resolution requires interpretation of a disputed term of the collective bargaining agreement, section 301 likely preempts the claim.

Notes to Chapter 10

1. Wis. Dep't of Indus., Labor & Human Relations v. Gould, Inc., 475 U.S. 282, 289–90 (1986).
2. *Id.* at 286.
3. San Diego Bldg. Trades Council v. Garmon, 359 U.S. 236 (1959).
4. *Id.* at 238.
5. *Id.*
6. *Id.* at 246.
7. *Id.* at 245.
8. J.A. Croson Co., 359 N.L.R.B. No. 2 (2012).
9. *See also* Fed. Sec., Inc., 359 N.L.R.B. No. 1 (2012) (filing and maintaining a suit preempted by the NLRA violated section 8(a)(1)).
10. *Garmon*, 359 U.S. at 244.
11. Sears, Roebuck & Co. v. Carpenter's Dist. Council (San Diego), 436 U.S. 180 (1978).
12. *See, e.g.*, Mich. Bldg. & Constr. Trades Council v. Snyder, 729 F.3d 572 (6th Cir. 2013) (Michigan law prohibiting government units from entering into Project Labor Agreements was not preempted by the NLRA because the state was acting as a market participant).
13. Hotel Emps. & Rest. Emps. Union, Local 57 v. Sage Hospitality Res., LLC, 390 F.3d 206 (3d Cir. 2004).
14. *See* Chamber of Commerce v. Brown, 554 U.S. 60 (2008).
15. Lodge 76, Int'l Ass'n of Machinists & Aerospace Workers v. Wis. Emp't Relations Comm'n, 427 U.S. 132 (1976).
16. Golden State Transit Corp. v. Los Angeles, 475 U.S. 608 (1986).
17. Metro. Life Ins. Co. v. Massachusetts, 471 U.S. 724 753 (1985).
18. Chamber of Commerce v. Reich, 74 F.3d 1322 (D.C. Cir. 1996).
19. Chamber of Commerce of the U.S. v. City of Seattle, 890 F.3d 769 (9th Cir. 2018).
20. Fort Halifax Packing Co. v. Coyne, 482 U.S. 1 (1987) (concluding that the *Machinists* doctrine did not apply because the Maine law requiring employers to pay severance to employees in the event of a plant closing did "not directly regulate[ ] any economic activity of either of the parties . . . [or] force[ ] a party to forgo the use of one of its economic weapons"); Livadas v. Bradshaw, 512 U.S. 107 (1994) (regulations claiming to be minimum labor standards are reviewed to determine their effect on the collective bargaining process).
21. Metro. Life Ins. Co. v. Massachusetts, 471 U.S. 724, 753 (1985); *see also* Am. Lodging & Hotel Ass'n v. City of Los Angeles, 834 F.3d 958 (9th Cir. 2016) (Los Angeles minimum wage ordinance for hotel workers not preempted).

22. *See Machinists*, 427 U.S. at 136 ("Policing of actual or threatened violence to persons or destruction of property has been held most clearly a matter for the States.").

23. Belknap, Inc. v. Hale, 463 U.S. 491, 500 (1983).

24. Retail Prop. Tr. v. United Bhd. of Carpenters & Joiners of Am., 768 F.3d 938 (9th Cir. 2014) (mall owner's state law claims against the union for the latter's disruptive protests were not preempted where the owner only sought to enforce reasonable restrictions against the union, not to preclude protests altogether); Helmsley-Spear, Inc. v. Fishman, 900 N.E.2d 934 (N.Y. 2008) (nuisance claim not preempted because "[l]oud drumming [during picketing] is not an integral part of the legislative scheme of the NLRA") (internal quotation marks omitted).

25. Building & Constr. Trades Council v. Associated Builders, 507 U.S. 218 (1993) (finding that neither *Garmon* nor *Machinists* preemption doctrines prevented government actors from freely participating in the marketplace in the same manner as private market participants where the state's interest is proprietary and not regulatory); *see also* Alameda Newspapers v. City of Oakland, 95 F.3d 1406 (9th Cir. 1996).

26. *See* Lingle v. Norge Div. of Magic Chef, Inc., 486 U.S. 399, 405–06 (1988); *see also* Livadas v. Bradshaw, 512 U.S. 107, 123 (1994).

27. Flibotte v. Pa. Truck Lines, Inc., 131 F.3d 21, 26 (1st Cir. 1997) (emphasis added).

28. United Steelworkers v. Rawson, 495 U.S. 362, 369 (1990).

29. Allis-Chalmers Corp. v. Lueck, 471 U.S. 202, 220 (1985) (finding section 301 preemption "when resolution of a state-law claim is substantially dependent upon analysis of the term of an agreement made between the parties in a labor contract").

30. Kofoed v. Shiprack, 180 L.R.R.M. 2612 (9th Cir. 2006) (unpublished).

31. Livadas v. Bradshaw, 512 U.S. 107 (1994).

32. Mowry v. United Parcel Serv., 415 F.3d 1149 (10th Cir. 2005).

33. Foy v. Giant Food, Inc., 298 F.3d 284 (4th Cir. 2002).

11

Regulation of Internal Union Affairs:
Rights and Obligations of Unions and Union Members

The Labor Management Reporting and Disclosure Act (also known as the Landrum-Griffin Act of 1959) is—along with the NLRA and the Taft-Hartley Act of 1947—one of the three main federal statutes constituting federal labor law. This chapter focuses on the internal union democracy safeguards dealing with the relationship between the union and its members established under the LMRDA, including the rights of union members, the administration of internal affairs such as union elections and union dues, and the reporting requirements of unions and employers. Additionally, this chapter discusses the rights of members of a collective bargaining unit who have renounced full membership in the union yet who still pay union dues.

Labor Management Reporting and Disclosure Act

Purpose and Scope

Q 11.1 What is the purpose and scope of the LMRDA?

Title I of the Labor Management Reporting and Disclosure Act creates a "Bill of Rights" for union members. These provisions provide union members with the right to nominate candidates for union office, vote in union elections, express opinions, and participate in union meetings. This section also imposes limits on how unions may impose dues and assessments. Elections and union dues are each discussed separately below.

Title II of the LMRDA creates reporting obligations for unions, union officers and employees, employers, labor relations consultants, and surety companies. Unions must file information reports, constitutions and bylaws, and annual financial reports with the Office of Labor-Management Standards of the U.S. Department of Labor. Unions must make reports available to members. Certain union officers and employees, employers, and labor relations consultants must file annual reports regarding particular transactions, agreements, or deals relating to unions. Surety companies that issue bonds required by the LMRDA must also report certain data, such as premiums received, total claims paid, and amounts recovered. Any individual or party that is required to file a report with OLMS must retain the records that verify those reports for at least five years after the reports are filed. The Secretary of Labor (Secretary) enforces the reporting requirements of the LMRDA.[1] The reports and other documents filed with OLMS are publicly available. Any person may examine and obtain copies of those records by visiting OLMS offices. The reports and documents are also available on the Internet at www.unionreports.gov. Reporting obligations are discussed more fully below beginning at Q 11.9.

Title III of the LMRDA restricts a union's ability to place a subordinate body under trusteeship. A union (the "parent union") may only establish and administer a trusteeship over another union (the "subordinate union") in accordance with the constitution and bylaws of the parent unions and only for the purpose of:

(1) correcting corruption or financial malpractice in the subordinate union, assuring the performance of collective bargaining agreements or other duties of the subordinate bargaining representative;

(2) restoring democratic procedures; or

(3) otherwise carrying out the legitimate objects of the subordinate union.

The most common example of a trusteeship is an international or national parent union imposing a trusteeship over a local subordinate labor organization. The LMRDA prohibits the parent union from engaging in certain acts involving the funds and delegate votes from the subordinate union. The parent union must also file initial, semiannual, and terminal trusteeship reports. The LMRDA gives the Secretary the authority to investigate alleged violations of Title III. Union members may also enforce the trusteeship provisions, except for the parent union's reporting requirements.[2]

Title IV of the LMRDA addresses the elections of union officers. Elections are discussed more fully below beginning at Q 11.3.

Title V of the LMRDA provides safeguards for unions. Union officers have a duty to manage the funds and property of the union solely for the benefit of the union in accordance with its constitution and bylaws. Officials who handle union funds or property must be bonded to provide protection against losses. Embezzlement or misappropriation of union funds or assets is a federal offense and precludes those persons from holding union office for up to thirteen years after conviction or the end of imprisonment.[3]

Title VI gives the Secretary the authority to investigate violations of the LMRDA. This includes the right to enter premises, examine records, and question persons in the course of the investigation. Unions are also prohibited from disciplining any member for exercising his or her rights under the LMRDA.[4]

"Bill of Rights"

Q 11.2 What are a union member's rights with regard to internal union affairs?

When enacting the Labor Management Reporting and Disclosure Act, Congress determined that union members should be guaranteed certain basic rights. Title I of the LMRDA creates a "Bill of Rights" for union members. If a union's constitution or bylaws are inconsistent with the Bill of Rights, those provisions are declared to be of no force or effect. The Bill of Rights provides union members with the following rights, some subject to reasonable rules and regulations in the union's constitution and bylaws:[5]

- to nominate candidates for union office;

- to vote in union elections and referendums;

- to attend and participate in membership meetings;

- to meet with other members to express any view, arguments, or opinions;

- to express at meetings the member's views on candidates for union office and business that is properly presented at the meetings;

- to have local union dues, initiation fees, and other assessments only increased by secret ballot after reasonable notice of the intention to vote on the question;

- to have dues, initiation fees, or assessments set only by:

  (1) secret ballot of all members;

  (2) majority vote of the delegates at a regular convention or, with proper notice, special convention; or

  (3) by a majority vote of the executive board pursuant to the express authority contained in the constitution and bylaws of the union (any such action will only have effect until the next regular convention of the union);

- to bring a lawsuit or administrative proceeding, regardless of whether against a union or its officers, or to appear as a witness;

- to communicate with legislators;

- to not be disciplined, fined, suspended, or expelled (except for nonpayment of dues), unless first served with a written list of the specific charges, given time to prepare a defense, and afforded a full and fair hearing;

- to have the right to request and receive a copy of a collective bargaining agreement if the member's rights are affected by the collective bargaining agreement.

Member rights with respect to elections and union dues are discussed in more detail in the corresponding sections in this chapter. (Rights of non-members are discussed below beginning at Q 11.16.)

Unions may adopt and enforce reasonable rules defining the responsibility of members to the union and restraining conduct by members that would interfere with the union in carrying out its contracts and other legal responsibilities.

Q 11.2.1   How can members enforce their Title I rights?

The vast majority of Title I rights are enforceable by a union member in a civil suit in federal district court. Union members may also seek injunctive relief. Members may be required to pursue, for up to four months, reasonable hearing procedures before bringing a suit or administrative proceeding against the union or any of its officers.[6] Union members and non-members affected by the agreement also have a right to inspect collective bargaining agreements.[7] Title I rights may be enforced by the union members and/or the Secretary.[8] Employers may not support or participate in union members' suits, proceedings, appearances, or communications, unless they do so openly as involved parties.

Union Elections

Member Rights

Q 11.3   What are a member's rights with regard to elections?

Any member in good standing has the right to:

(1)   nominate candidates;

(2)   be a candidate subject to reasonable, uniformly imposed qualifications; and

(3)   support the candidate of the member's choice.

All members in good standing must be given reasonable notice and opportunity to nominate candidates for election as union officers. The union must provide its members with notice of the positions to be filled and the process for submitting nominations. All members in good standing have the right to vote, subject to reasonable rules, uniformly imposed.

Title IV also gives union members rights and protections to enable them to reach other union members during officer election campaigns and to prohibit unions and employers from interfering in the campaigns. Union members may not be penalized, disciplined, or improperly interfered with in their exercise of their right to support the candidate of their choice generally, or the Secretary may sue in district court to set aside an invalid election.[9] (See Q 11.5.)

Election Requirements

Q 11.4 What requirements does the LMRDA impose on the election of union officers?

The LMRDA requires that all union officers be elected. Title IV of the LMRDA establishes minimum requirements to which all unions covered by LMRDA must adhere in the election of union officers. Beyond these minimal requirements, a union may conduct elections according to its constitution and bylaws, so long as those rules do not conflict with the provisions of the LMRDA.[10]

The LMRDA's election requirements apply to local unions, intermediate, national, and international unions, except for federations of these unions, such as the AFL-CIO. A local union not otherwise subject to the requirements of the LMRDA may still be required to elect delegates in the manner required by the LMRDA, if the delegates serve as part of an intermediate or parent union that is subject to the LMRDA.[11]

The LMRDA directs local unions to hold elections at least every three years, intermediate bodies at least every four years, and international unions at least every five years. Incumbent officers may be re-elected at the end of their terms of office.[12]

Officers of a local union must be elected directly by secret ballot from among the members in good standing. Officers of an intermediate, national, or international union may be elected by secret ballot from among the members in good standing or at a convention of delegates who were previously chosen by secret ballot. Each candidate may have observers at each of the polling and tallying places. All ballots, including used, unused, and challenged ballots, envelopes used to return marked ballots, tally sheets, and related election documents must be kept for one year.[13] A union may fill an unexpired term of office using a procedure set out in the union's constitution and bylaws.

Unions must permit candidates to distribute campaign literature at the candidate's expense. Any privilege the union extends to one candidate must be extended to all candidates. Neither unions nor employers may contribute to the campaign of any candidate.

Candidates

Q 11.4.1   Who are union officers that the LMRDA requires be elected?

Union officers include any constitutional officer, any person authorized to perform the functions of president, vice president, secretary, treasurer, or other executive functions of a labor organization, and any member of the union's executive board or similar governing body. Further, any union official with a policy-making authority or responsibility must be elected, even though that official does not fill an identified officer position. Shop stewards typically do not have to be elected, unless they exercise executive functions, are designated as officers in the union's constitution, or are members of the union's executive board. Business representatives of a union, whose duties include the responsibility for the control and management of the union's funds and fiscal operations, are considered officers under the LMRDA and must be elected. Any other individual, who is not already an elected officer, who votes for officers of an intermediate, national, or international union must be elected by secret ballot.[14]

Q 11.4.2   What limitations may be imposed on candidates for election as union officers?

Subject to restrictions based on prior criminal behavior, all members in good standing are eligible to be candidates and hold office in a union. Persons who have been convicted of embezzlement or certain other crimes specified by the LMRDA may not hold union office or employment for up to thirteen years after the conviction or after the end of imprisonment.[15]

Unions may also uniformly impose reasonable qualifications that their members must meet in order to serve as union officers. The following factors may be considered when determining whether a qualification on union office is reasonable:[16]

- the relationship of the qualification to the legitimate needs and interests of the union;

- the relationship of the qualification to the demands of the union office to which it is applied;

- the number of members who are disqualified by the application of the qualification;

- a comparison of the qualification with the requirements for holding office generally prescribed by other unions;

- the degree of difficulty union members have in meeting the qualification;

- whether members received adequate advance notice of the requirement;

- whether the qualification is part of the union's constitution, bylaws, or other enacted rules (a rule that is not set out in those provisions may not be the basis for denying a member from holding union office);

- whether the qualification requires positive action by union members—for example, meeting-attendance requirements (new qualification requirements may not be applied until members have had an adequate opportunity to comply with the obligations); and

- whether the qualification, though otherwise permissible, is being applied in a non-uniform or unreasonable manner.

For example, OLMS has stated that a union may require candidates to have been a member for a minimum period of time before the election, not to exceed two years in the case of a local union. Unions may also require that candidates attend a specified number of regular meetings during a period immediately preceding the election. However, such a rule will be unreasonable if it results in a significant number of members being declared ineligible.[17] A qualification for nomination based on geographic, craft, shift, or similar lines is normally considered reasonable for a position representing such a membership unit. A qualification may be unreasonable if it involves any requirement associated with race, color, religion, sex, or national origin or the payment of a filing fee.[18]

Enforcement; Protesting Elections

Q 11.5 How are the LMRDA's election requirements enforced?

A union member may file a complaint regarding a union officer election with the Secretary after exhausting or pursuing internal union remedies for three months. A challenged election is presumed valid pending a final decision. The member's complaint must be filed within four months of the action giving rise to the complaint. The complaint must list all of the violations known to the member. OLMS will then initiate an investigation of the election.

If an investigation discloses violations of the LMRDA that may have affected the outcome of the election, OLMS gives the union an opportunity to correct the violations through voluntary compliance, usually by re-running the challenged election under OLMS supervision. If warranted, OLMS may take legal action to set aside the challenged election and require a new election under OLMS supervision. If the union has not remedied the violation, the Secretary must bring a civil suit in federal district court. If the court also finds a violation, it may declare the election invalid and direct a new election supervised by the Secretary.[19] In general, Title IV's election provisions are enforced exclusively by the Secretary, with limited review of the Secretary's decision not to bring an action.

Union members also may not be penalized, disciplined, or improperly interfered with in their exercise of their right to support the candidate of their choice.

Union Dues

Q 11.6 What are union dues?

Union dues are regular, periodic payments of money by union members to financially support the goals of their organization. Dues are the cost of membership in a union. Many union members or other represented employees pay union dues out of their wages, although some unions collect dues separately from the employee's paycheck. The LMRDA allows both local and international unions to increase members' dues.[20]

Q 11.6.1   What are union dues used for?

Part of a member's dues may go to support the representational, research, legal, administrative, legislative, political, or other goals of the union's members on a national or international level. Another part may go to support the goals of the local union, including expenses incurred in handling grievances, arbitrations, bargaining, organizing activities, and rent. Union dues may also be used to pay the salaries and benefits of union employees. Dues may also go to pension, health, welfare, and safety funds or a union strike fund.

Q 11.6.2   Can employees who are not members of a union be required to pay union dues?

Yes, in the private sector. Non-members working under a private sector collective bargaining agreement containing a valid union security provision are typically required to pay union dues in the form of an "agency fee."[21] Dues obligations of non-members, as well as other rights and obligations of non-members, are discussed more fully beginning at Q 11.16. For public sector employees, however, the Supreme Court's 2018 decision in *Janus v. AFSCME* held that public employees cannot be required to pay agency or "fair share" dues as such fees may infringe upon employees' First Amendment rights and could be deemed a form of political advocacy.[22]

Q 11.6.3   Can an employer stop deducting dues from employees' paychecks after the collective bargaining agreement expires?

For more than fifty years, under the NLRB precedent set forth in *Bethlehem Steel*,[23] employers were under no obligation to continue deducting and remitting union dues pursuant to union security and dues check-off clauses contained within expired collective bargaining agreements. In *Lincoln Lutheran*, the Board reversed years of precedent, holding that an employer's obligation to deduct employees' dues from their paychecks will survive the collective bargaining agreement.[24] However, the tenure of *Lincoln Lutheran* remains in doubt as the Board's General Counsel has issued a memo to the regional offices requiring mandatory submission of this issue to the Board's Division of Advice, thereby signaling that the General Counsel is interested in having the Board revisit this issue.

Other Fees

Q 11.7   What other types of fees may be assessed by unions?

Unions may also charge:

(1)   initiation fees;
(2)   agency fees; and/or
(3)   assessments.

Q 11.7.1   What is an initiation fee?

A union may charge an initiation fee, which is imposed on all new members of a local union, so long as that fee is not excessive or discriminatory.

A union may waive initiation fees so long as the waiver is available to all eligible voters both before and after a union election and the waiver is not contingent on support for the union.[25] However, a union offer to waive initiation fees for only those employees who agree to sign authorization cards prior to a union election is an invalid waiver and may be held to undermine fair representation election conditions under the NLRA.[26]

Q 11.7.2   What are agency fees?

Dues-paying non-members subject to a union security agreement must pay agency fees equivalent to union members' dues, except that these "financial core" employees may object to paying certain amounts of the agency fees that will be used for political causes not germane to the organizing, bargaining, and contract administration efforts of the union (see Q 11.16.3 *et seq.*).

Q 11.7.3   What is an assessment?

An assessment is a charge levied on each member in the nature of a tax or some other burden for a special purpose, not having the character of being susceptible of anticipation as a regularly recurring obligation as in the case of "periodic dues."

While unions may impose assessments, a member may not be discharged from employment for failure to pay such an assessment. For example, a union may impose a one-time assessment to help defray the costs of helping other employees represented by the union strike another employer. A union may not refuse to accept tendered dues pending receipt of an assessment.

While the union may not enforce the payment of an assessment under pain of discharge, the union is still left with substantial internal powers to enforce the payment of an assessment. The union may take appropriate steps to enforce its assessment demand and rights of internal union membership so long as these steps remain matters confined to internal union administration and do not affect the right of a member to the acquisition or retention of a job.[27]

Excessive or Discriminatory Fees

Q 11.8   Are there limits on the amount of dues a union can collect?

Unions may not charge "excessive or discriminatory" fees as a condition of joining the labor organization.[28] While the National Labor Relations Act does not specify what constitutes excessive dues, the NLRB has the authority to determine whether a fee is "excessive or discriminatory" under section 8(b)(5) by considering the practices and customs of labor organizations in the industry and the wages of the affected employees.[29]

LMRDA Reporting Obligations

Q 11.9   What reporting obligations does the LMRDA impose on employers, unions, and labor relations consultants?

The LMRDA establishes financial reporting and disclosure requirements for employers, labor organizations, their officers and employees, and labor relations consultants related to certain activities, transactions, and agreements.[30] These reports provide workers with information critical to their effective participation in the workplace. This information helps workers make more informed choices regarding their collective bargaining rights and enables workers to increase their voice in the workplace.[31]

Q 11.9.1   What LMRDA reports are available publicly?

All reports and other documents filed with OLMS are publicly available. Any person may examine and obtain copies of those records by visiting OLMS offices, or by mail, telephone, and fax. The reports and documents are also available on the Internet at www.unionreports.gov. Anyone can view and print copies of union annual financial reports, employer and labor relations consultant reports, and union officer and employee reports for 2000 and later. Union annual financial reports are searchable by a variety of criteria, including union name, file number, affiliation, designation name and number, and location. The public can also view union constitutions, bylaws, and collective bargaining agreements. In addition, the public can find Form LM-10 Employer Reports, Form LM-20 and LM-21 Labor Relations Consultant Agreement and Activities Reports and Receipts and Disbursement Reports, and Form LM-30 Union Officer and Employee Reports.

Reporting Requirements for Employers

Q 11.10   What are an employer's financial disclosure and reporting requirements under the LMRDA?

The LMRDA requires employers to disclose publicly certain financial transactions and arrangements made with labor organizations, union officials, employees, and/or labor relations consultants. Subject to certain important conditions and exceptions set out in the statute, transactions and arrangements that must be disclosed include:[32]

- payments, directly or indirectly, to any labor organization, or employee or representative of such organization;

- payments to the employer's employees for the purpose of causing those employees to persuade other employees to exercise or not to exercise, or as to the manner of exercising, the right to organize and bargain collectively through representatives of their own choosing;

- expenditures made with a direct or indirect object of interfering with, restraining, or coercing employees in the exercise of the right to organize and bargain collectively through representatives of their own choosing, or to obtain information concerning the activities of employees or a labor organization in connection with a labor dispute involving the employer; and

- payments and agreements with labor relations consultants to perform the actions identified above.

A complete list of transactions and arrangements that must be reported can be found in the LMRDA.

All instances of reportable activity must be submitted to OLMS on a Form LM-10. A completed Form LM-10 and any additional pages must be mailed to the OLMS in Washington, D.C. within ninety days after the end of each fiscal year.[33] Employers are generally responsible for maintaining records that will provide, in sufficient detail, the information and data necessary to verify the accuracy and completeness of the report. These records must be kept for at least five years after the date the report is filed. These records may include vouchers, worksheets, receipts, and applicable resolutions.

Q 11.10.1   What exceptions or conditions are these disclosure requirements subject to?

Reporting requirements regarding the disclosure of an employer's use of attorneys or consultants to help persuade employees not to unionize includes a longstanding exemption that allows employers not to report having received such "advice" from lawyers and consultants on union organizing. The DOL has traditionally distinguished between "direct persuaders," who communicate directly with employees on behalf of employers, and advisors who have no direct contact with employees. Only those consultants engaging in direct persuasion have reporting requirements under the LMRDA. Reporting is not required with regard to payments to consultants to devise personnel

policies for the employer's use in discouraging employee organization, so long as the work product, whether written or oral, is submitted to the employer for his use and the employer is free to accept or
reject the submission. Where the attorney-consultant has direct contact with employees or he himself engages in the persuader activity,
the advice exemption does not apply.[34]

Reporting Requirements for Labor Relations Consultants

Q 11.11   What is a labor relations consultant?

A labor relations consultant is any person who, for compensation,
advises or represents an employer, employer association, or union
concerning employee organizing, concerted activities, or collective
bargaining.

Q 11.12   What are a labor relations consultant's financial disclosure and reporting requirements under the LMRDA?

Labor relations consultants have thirty days to mail a Form LM-20
and accompanying documents to OLMS in Washington, D.C. after
entering into an arrangement with an employer to undertake activities
(1) that will, directly or indirectly, persuade employees with respect
to exercising the employees' rights to organize collectively; or (2) that
are made in connection with a labor dispute involving the employer
and result in gathering information on employee or union activities.[35]
A consultant "undertakes" activities not only when it performs the
activity, but also when it agrees to perform the activity or to have them
performed. A Form LM-20 does not need to be filed if the information
gathered is solely for administrative, arbitral, or court proceedings.[36]
Any changes to the information reported in Form LM-20 must be filed
in a report clearly marked "Amended Report" within thirty days of the
change.

A labor relations consultant's reporting obligations include:

- the party or parties to the agreement or arrangement;

- the object and terms and conditions of the agreement or
  arrangement; and

- the activities performed or to be performed pursuant to the agreement or arrangement.

The reporting obligations for a consultant mirror those for the employer.

Any consultant required to file a Form LM-20 must also file a Form LM-21 Receipts and Disbursements Report. A Form LM-21 must be filed in each fiscal year in which the consultant received a payment pursuant to an agreement set out in a Form LM-20.[37]

Reporting Requirements for Unions

Q 11.13 What are a union's financial disclosure and reporting requirements under the LMRDA?

Unions subject to the LMRDA must file a financial report each year and maintain the underlying records for that report for at least five years after filing the report. A union's financial report must be electronically filed with OLMS on a Form LM-2, LM-3, or LM-4. These forms include the organization's assets, liabilities, receipts, salaries, loans, and other disbursements to officers and employees of more than $10,000. The particular form a union must use depends on the union's "total annual receipts." The term "total annual receipts" means all financial receipts of the union during its fiscal year, regardless of the source, including receipts of any special funds. A union should not include the receipts of a trust in which the union is interested, unless the trust is wholly owned, wholly controlled, and wholly financed by the union.[38]

Q 11.13.1 Who must file a Form LM-2?

Every union subject to the LMRDA, Civil Service Reform Act, or Foreign Service Act with total annual receipts of $250,000 or more must file a Form LM-2 for each fiscal year beginning on or after July 1, 2004. A Form LM-2 must be filed within ninety days after the end of the union's fiscal year based on a twelve-month reporting period. Unions may complete the form by typing financial information directly into the electronic form. OLMS also provides filing software that will permit unions that keep records electronically to transfer financial data from their accounting programs to the form.

A union imposing a trusteeship on a subordinate union must file an annual financial report on a Form LM-2 on behalf of the subordinate union. This is in addition to the initial and semiannual trusteeship reports the parent union must file based on the trusteeship. The Form LM-2 is due within ninety days after the end of the subordinate union's fiscal year and must report the financial activities of the entire fiscal year. If the trusteeship was imposed during the subordinate union's fiscal year, the initial Form LM-2 must cover the period prior to the imposition of the trusteeship and any reportable financial transactions occurring during the trusteeship. A terminal trusteeship financial report filed on a Form LM-2 is also required within ninety days after the termination of the trusteeship. Any Form LM-2 filed on behalf of a subordinate union must include the signatures of the trustees, in addition to the signatures of the president and treasurer, or equivalent union officers, of the union that established the trusteeship.

Q 11.13.2   ... Form LM-3?

A union subject to the LMRDA, CSRA, or FSA with total annual receipts of $10,000 or more, but less than $250,000, must electronically file a Form LM-3 with OLMS within ninety days after the end of the organization's fiscal year, based on the union's twelve-month reporting period. If the union is a subordinate union in a trusteeship with a parent union, the union must instead file a Form LM-2. Unions may complete the form by typing financial information directly into the electronic form. OLMS also provides filing software that will permit unions that keep records electronically to transfer financial data from their accounting programs to the form.

Q 11.13.3   ... Form LM-4?

A union subject to LMRDA, CSRA, or FSA with total annual receipts of less than $10,000 must electronically file a Form LM-4 within ninety days of the end of the labor organization's fiscal year, based on the union's twelve-month reporting period. If the union is a subordinate union in a trusteeship with a parent union, the union must instead file a Form LM-2. Unions may complete the form by typing financial information directly into the electronic form. OLMS also provides filing software that will permit unions that keep records electronically to transfer financial data from their accounting programs to the form.

Q 11.14   What are union officers' and employees' financial disclosure and reporting requirements under LMRDA?

The LMRDA requires labor organization officers and employees and their spouses and minor children to complete a Form LM-30 for certain financial transactions and financial interests for the purpose of publicly identifying an actual or potential conflict between the personal financial interests of the union officer or employee and his or her obligations to the union and its members. These disclosures discourage insider deals, favoritism, and selling out union members for personal gain and are intended to expose individuals who use their union positions for personal enrichment.

On October 26, 2011, the U.S. Department of Labor issued a final rule changing the Form LM-30 and who must complete the form. The rule took effect on November 25, 2011, for Form LM-30s covering fiscal years beginning on or after January 1, 2012.[39] Under the revised rule, union stewards or persons in similar positions, such as members of a safety or bargaining committee, will no longer have to file a Form LM-30. The rule also clarified the reporting requirements for union officials of national, international, and intermediate union officers and employees. These persons may need to report payments they receive from employers and businesses that are engaged in relationships with the lower levels of the union, in addition to transactions connected to the officer or employee's specific union level.

Union officers and employees have to report payments received only where such payments present a conflict of interest or reasonable potential for a conflict of interest. The new rule clarifies that union officers and employees no longer have to report "union leave" or "no docking" payments received from employers—payments to union officials who are also employees of the employer for work done for the union on employer time. In addition, bona fide financial transactions with credit institutions are no longer reportable if they are arm's-length transactions on the same terms received by other customers.

Q 11.15   What records does OLMS recommend unions retain in association with their reporting obligations under LMRDA?

A union must maintain financial records to assist in verifying any report filed with OLMS for five years after a report is filed. Unions must also retain any electronic documents, including record-keeping software, used to complete, read, and file the report. The union's president or treasurer, or the equivalent union officers, is required to maintain these records. OLMS recommends that unions retain the following records:[40]

- receipts and disbursement journals;
- canceled checks and check stubs;
- bank statements, dues collection receipts;
- employer check-off statements;
- per-capita tax reports;
- vendor invoices;
- payroll records;
- credit card statements and itemized receipts for each credit card charge;
- member ledger cards for former members;
- union copies of bank deposit slips;
- bank debit and credit memos;
- vouchers for union expenditures;
- internal union financial reports and statements;
- minutes of all membership and executive board meetings;
- accountants' working papers used to prepare financial statements and reports filed with OLMS; and
- fixed-assets inventory.

Q 11.15.1   When must a union disclose its constitution and bylaws to OLMS?

Every union covered by the LMRDA or the CSRA must adopt a constitution and bylaws and file two copies with OLMS, along with a Labor Organization Information Report, Form LM-1. The terms "constitution" and "bylaws" mean the basic written rules governing the organization. These documents must be submitted to OLMS within ninety days of becoming subject to the LMRDA or CSRA. The information provided includes the structure, practices, and procedures of the union.[41]

Any changes in procedures must be filed on an amended Form LM-1 submitted with the union's annual financial report. These include changes in practices and procedures which are not contained in the labor organization's constitution and bylaws.

Q 11.15.2   What obligation does a union have to provide its members with information that is reported to OLMS?

Every union must inform its members about the provisions of the LMRDA.[42] Unions must make a good-faith effort to explain to their current members the provisions of the LMRDA, including the LMRDA's reporting requirements, the rights of union members and the responsibilities of union officers. Because this obligation is ongoing, a one-time publication of the LMRDA to members is insufficient. Instead, effective notice requires, at a minimum, that each individual soon after obtaining membership be informed about the provisions of the LMRDA. Unions are not obligated, however, to advise or assist their members; the union's only duty is to provide members with notice of the provisions of the LMRDA.

There is little guidance on what methods of informing union members of their rights are sufficient, but the information must be delivered to each member. Posting a summary of the rights in the union office does not comply with the LMRDA.[43] Unions, however, do not have a duty to provide notice in a way preferred by members. For instance, a union may deny members' requests that the union publish a summary of the LMRDA rights on its website and include the rights in the union's constitution. Where a union published the LMRDA's provisions in three issues of the union's journal and in the union's welcome letter, such publications were held sufficient to satisfy the union's duty to provide notice.

In addition, every union required to submit a report under the LMRDA must make the information contained in such report available to all of its members. Union members may enforce this requirement by filing suit in state court or federal district court.

Q 11.15.3   Does every employee of the union have reporting requirements?

Officers and employees of labor organizations and their spouses and minor children may be required to publicly disclose certain financial transactions and financial interests in a Form LM-30. Union employees who provide exclusively clerical or custodial services are excluded from these disclosure requirements. Form LM-30s must be mailed to OLMS in Washington, D.C. within ninety days after the end of the union's fiscal year.

Officers and employees of labor organizations and their spouses and minor children must file a Form LM-30 disclosing the transactions identified in the LMRDA, which include:[44]

- legal and equitable interests in, transactions with, and economic benefits from an employer whose employees his/her union represents or seeks to represent;

- legal and equitable interests in, transactions with, and economic benefits from certain businesses that deal with the business of the employer whose employees the union represents or seeks to represent, or that deal with the union or a trust in which the labor organization is interested; and

- certain income and other economic benefits received from certain other employers or labor relations consultants.

Q 11.15.4   How are LMRDA reporting requirements enforced?

The Secretary may investigate violations and potential violations of the disclosure requirements of the LMRDA and may issue subpoenas to compel testimony or to obtain records and other materials when necessary to complete an investigation. The Secretary may also file a civil action in federal district court to bring about compliance with the LMRDA. Criminal fines and imprisonment may apply to certain reporting violations.[45]

Rights of Non-Members

Union Security Agreements

Q 11.16   What is a union security agreement?

A union security agreement is a contractual agreement between an organized labor association and an employer that establishes the extent to which union membership can be compelled, and whereby the employer agrees that, as a condition of employment, employees will be required to provide financial support to the union—that is, to pay union dues. (Union dues are discussed above at Q 11.6 *et seq.*)

Q 11.16.1   Can a union security agreement require union membership?

"Closed-shop" agreements, which require that employers hire only union employees, are forbidden by the NLRA. However, "union-shop" agreements, which require that employees join a union once employed, are valid under the NLRA.[46] Under a union-shop agreement, the requirement to join a union may not be imposed on employees until the later of either thirty days after the employee begins his or her employment, or thirty days after the union security agreement becomes effective.[47]

Moreover, despite any such union security agreement requiring union "membership" (that is, a union-shop agreement), employees subject to a valid union security agreement may renounce full membership in the union and thereby restrict their obligations to the "financial core."

Financial-Core Employees

Q 11.16.2   What are the limitations of financial-core employees' rights and obligations?

As dues-paying members of a collective bargaining unit who have renounced full membership in the union, financial-core members are, in essence, unit employees who cannot vote on union matters and who are not entitled to attend union meetings or otherwise have a voice in the internal affairs of the union. Further limitations on financial-core employees include the inability to nominate for office, hold office, or be a candidate for office in the union; to vote on dues increases or union contracts; or to attend any function of the union that is limited to union members.[48]

Notwithstanding these limitations, financial-core employees are still required to pay initiation fees and union dues.[49] They share in union expenditures for strike benefits, educational and retired-member benefits, and union publications and promotional activities. They keep their union jobs and all union benefits. However, since they are not constitutional members of the labor union, they are free from any union internal rules and regulations governing full constitutional members.

Courts have reasoned that the requirement that every employee pay dues, regardless of whether the employee joins the union, is not unreasonable where every employee should benefit from the union's efforts. For example, representational activities, such as collective bargaining, can lead to higher salaries and/or better working conditions for all employees working for that employer.[50]

Q 11.16.3   Are financial-core employees required to support union interests?

Section 8(a)(3) does not obligate financial-core employees to support union activities beyond those "germane" to collective bargaining, contract administration, and grievance adjustment. Employees who object to funding non-representational union activities pay reduced dues. These so-called *Beck* objectors (see Q 11.18) also have a right to challenge the union's calculation of the reduced dues. In response to such a challenge, the union bears the burden of justifying its calculation.[51]

Basic considerations of fairness and First Amendment rights require unions to give potential *Beck* objectors sufficient information to gauge the propriety of the union's fee. The union owes this duty to current *Beck* objectors, new employees, and other financial-core employees who have not chosen to be *Beck* objectors. Each of these employees must be told the percentage of union dues chargeable to them were they to become objectors.[52]

Q 11.17   What is the legal status of union security agreements?

Section 14(b) of the NLRA allows the states to enact laws that prohibit union security clauses.[53] These so-called right-to-work laws (see Q 1.2.4) thus enable employees to refrain from joining a union and decide not to financially support a union. These laws, however, do not prevent unions from being organized in the first place or bar unions from soliciting payment of union dues from its members and other represented employees.

Currently, twenty-seven states are right-to-work states: Alabama, Arizona, Arkansas, Idaho, Indiana, Iowa, Florida, Georgia, Kansas, Kentucky, Louisiana, Michigan, Mississippi, Nebraska, Nevada, North Carolina, North Dakota, Oklahoma, South Carolina, South Dakota, Tennessee, Texas, Utah, Virginia, West Virginia, Wisconsin, and Wyoming. In addition, national right-to-work legislation is currently under consideration. On February 1, 2017, the U.S. House of Representatives rolled out a right-to-work bill designed to prohibit unions from requiring non-members to pay fees for collective bargaining and other representational activities.[54] A similar bill (S. 545) was introduced in the Senate in March 2017 by Senator Rand Paul. Senator Paul asserted in July 2018 that there is presidential support for the bills should they hit President Trump's desk.

Q 11.17.1   Can employees vote to reject (de-authorize) a union security agreement?

The NLRA provides procedures for union security de-authorization petitions. Under the NLRA, an employee, group of employees, or others acting on behalf of the employee(s) may file a petition alleging that a substantial number of employees assert that their current union no longer represents them.[55]

Where 30% of the employees covered by the collective bargaining agreement file a petition stating they want the union's authorization rescinded, a de-authorization vote will be triggered.[56] A majority of eligible employees may then vote to rescind the authority of a union to enter into union security agreements with their employer. The vote, which is conducted by secret ballot, is known as a de-authorization election.[57]

 CASE STUDY: *Communications Workers of America v. Beck*[58]

In *Communications Workers of America v. Beck*, the union negotiated a union security agreement that required all represented employees, including those who do not wish to become union members (financial-core employees), to pay agency fees in amounts equal to the periodic dues paid by union members. Twenty financial- core employees initiated a suit challenging the union's use of their agency fees for purposes other than collective bargaining, contract, administration, or grievance adjustment. Specifically, the plaintiffs alleged that the union's expenditure of their fees on activities such as organizing the employees of other employers, lobbying for labor legislation, and participating in social, charitable, and political events violated the union's duty of fair representation, the NLRA, the First Amendment, and various common-law fiduciary duties.

The U.S. Supreme Court held that the agency dues obligation of financial-core employees does not include the obligation to support union activities beyond those germane to collective bargaining, contract administration, and grievance adjustment. The Court explained that section 8(a)(3), like its statutory equivalent in the RLA, authorizes the exaction of only those fees and dues necessary to "performing the duties of an exclusive representative of the employees in dealing with the employer on labor-management issues."[59]

Beck *Objections; Chargeable and Non-Chargeable Union Expenditures*

Q 11.18   What is a *Beck* objection?

After the Court's decision in *Beck*, financial-core employees and new employees are permitted to make a "*Beck* objection" to the use of their agency fees. This is an objection to the way unions expend the mandatory dues of those employees who choose not to participate in full union membership. *Beck* objectors essentially have the ability to place limitations on how their dues are spent, and to limit their contribution to payment of representational or "chargeable" expenses.[60] Accordingly, where an employee chooses not to join a union, but is still required to pay union dues under a union security agreement, the employee may assert his or her rights under *Beck*, thereby objecting to the use of his or her dues for nonrepresentational activities.

Q 11.18.1   What expenses qualify as unobjectionable "chargeable" expenses?

Beck objectors are required to pay only chargeable expenses and not expenses considered to be non-chargeable. Accordingly, it is important to determine what types of expenses fall into which of these categories.

Generally, chargeable expenses are those related to collective bargaining, contract administration, and grievance adjustment. The NLRB and courts have clarified that activities within an objector's bargaining unit are chargeable if they are "germane" to the union's representational role.[61] On the other hand, expenses for activities outside the objector's bargaining unit, such as for political and legislative activities and lobbying, are only chargeable if they are germane to the union's role and membership in the national organization benefits members of the local union.[62]

Beck imposes the same limitations on national union expenses as it does on local expenses; in other words, collection of local dues or fees for national expenses is valid only where the union uses the amounts to pay for germane or chargeable representational activities.[63] For example, the U.S. Supreme Court recently ruled that national litigation activities can be chargeable if related to chargeable matters, such as collective bargaining or contract administration.[64]

Q 11.18.2 What are some of the procedural issues involved in *Beck* objections?

Since the *Beck* decision, the NLRB and courts have identified several procedural issues with the practical implementation of *Beck* objections, some of which are discussed below.

Q 11.18.3 What obligations do unions have to notify employees of their *Beck* rights?

Initially, unions must notify employees of their rights to be a non-member (that is, a financial-core employee), subject to the obligation to pay certain fees and dues.[65] The union must also provide actual notice to employees of certain rights under *Beck* at or before the time a union seeks to require employees to pay union fees and dues under a union security clause.[66] For example, employees must be told of the following additional rights that are available to non-members:

(1) the right to object to paying for activities not germane to the union's bargaining activities;

(2) the right to obtain a reduction of fees for non-germane activities;

(3) the right to obtain information that enables them to decide whether to object to activities as not germane; and

(4) the right to be told the procedures for filing *Beck* objections.[67]

Unions must be able to show that they provided actual notice to employees; a good-faith effort is insufficient unless the employee had independent actual knowledge of his or her rights.[68] However, the notice requirement is not ongoing; in other words, the union is only required to give the employees notice once. Furthermore, the notice does not need to take a particular form; notice is valid as long as the union makes reasonable efforts to notify employees of their *Beck* rights.

After an employee objects under *Beck*, a union must disclose its financial expenditures to the objector and refrain from charging the objector for nonrepresentational expenses.[69] Unions must also provide objectors the opportunity, through established procedures, to challenge the union's disclosures.[70]

Q 11.18.4 What obligations do employers have to notify employees of their *Beck* rights?

Executive Order 13201, signed by former President George W. Bush, required federal contractors to post notice to employees of their *Beck* rights under federal law. This order was subsequently rescinded in Executive Order 13496, Notification of Employee Rights Under Federal Labor Laws, signed by President Barack Obama on January 30, 2009. For additional information on this topic, see chapter 12.

Under the NLRA, an employer must also provide notice of an employee's *Beck* rights when the employer discharges an employee where the employer knows that the union failed to inform the employee of his or her financial obligations.[71]

Q 11.18.5 Is there any limitation on when employees may file *Beck* objections?

Generally, the NLRB and courts have held that unions may create a limited window during which employees must file their *Beck* objections.[72] Courts have held that, as long as a union's actions "fall within a generous range of reasonableness," a union does not violate its duty of fair representation by imposing an annual window period (that is, where objections must be made, and can only be made, in a given month).[73]

However, a union may violate section 8(b)(1)(A) of the NLRA if it requires employees to renew their objections on an annual basis. The NLRB has stated that it will evaluate a union's reasons for maintaining renewal requirements on a case-by-case basis.[74]

Q 11.18.6   How are expenditures properly documented?

Unions do not need to provide an exhaustive and detailed list of all expenditures, but unions should disclose the major categories of expenses.[75] Accordingly, unions need not provide detailed supporting schedules of "chargeable" and "non-chargeable" expenditures, but must provide a summary of major categories of expenditure.[76]

In line with basic concerns of fairness, unions must provide "sufficient information to gauge the propriety of the union's fee" to non-member employees.[77] The information provided to non-members must also include verification by an independent auditor.[78] A letter from the union providing a breakdown of the major categories of expenditures and stating that an auditor has verified those expenditures is sufficient to assure an objector that the expenditures were made.[79] However, auditors are not required to determine the allocation of chargeable and non-chargeable expenditures,[80] though the auditor does need to verify that the union actually made the expenditures claimed.[81] There is currently a split among federal circuit courts about whether smaller unions must comply with the independent audit requirement.[82]

Q 11.18.7   Can *Beck* objectors challenge a union's expenditures?

Beck objectors are free to challenge a union's allocation of representational and nonrepresentational expenditures, and unions must provide objectors with reasonable procedures for them to file such a challenge.[83] In order to be "reasonable," the challenge procedure must not be arbitrary, unreasonably obstructive, or administered in bad faith.[84]

Beck objectors who have not otherwise agreed to the procedure are not required to exhaust internal union procedures, such as arbitration, before they challenge a union's agency fee calculation in federal court.[85] However, the NLRB has upheld expedient union hearings that cause only a minimal delay to the objector's ability to have his or her challenge heard by a neutral arbitrator.[86]

Notes to Chapter 11

1. 29 U.S.C. § 431 *et seq.*
2. *Id.* § 461 *et seq.*
3. *Id.* § 501 *et seq.*
4. *Id.* § 521 *et seq.*
5. *Id.* § 411 *et seq.*
6. *Id.* § 411(a)(4).
7. *Id.* § 414.
8. *Id.* §§ 412, 414.
9. *Id.* § 481 *et seq.*
10. In 2016, the Department of Labor issued guidance allowing for the option of remote electronic voting. *See* https://www.dol.gov/olms/regs/compliance/catips/2016/CompTip_RemoteElecVote.htm.
11. *Id.; see also Office of Labor-Management Standards (OLMS), Electing Union Officers,* U.S. DEP'T OF LABOR, www.dol.gov/olms/regs/compliance/ElecOfficer/elecofficer.htm (last updated June 30, 2017).
12. *Id.*
13. *Id.*
14. *Id.*
15. *Id.*
16. *Id.*
17. *See, e.g.*, Steelworkers, Local 3489 v. Usery, 429 U.S. 305 (1977).
18. *See* 29 U.S.C. § 481 *et seq.; see also Office of Labor-Management Standards (OLMS), Electing Union Officers,* U.S. DEP'T OF LABOR, www.dol.gov/olms/regs/compliance/ElecOfficer/elecofficer.htm (last updated June 30, 2017).
19. *See* Calhoon v. Harvey, 379 U.S. 134 (1964); Dunlop v. Bachowski, 421 U.S. 560 (1975) (required statement of reasons); Trbovich v. United Mine Workers, 404 U.S. 528 (1972) (right of affected members to intervene in Secretary's suit).
20. Corns v. Laborers Int'l Union of N. Am., 709 F.3d 901 (9th Cir. 2013) (the LMRDA allows an international union to increase members' dues if the members are represented at the international level by delegates).
21. Int'l Bhd. of Teamsters, Local Union 89 (United Parcel Serv., Inc.), 361 N.L.R.B. No. 5 (2014) (finding that where there is a union security agreement between the employer and the union, even employees that have been expelled from the union have an obligation to pay reduced dues as they continue to receive representational benefits).
22. *See* Janus v. AFSCME, 585 U.S. ___ (2018).
23. Bethlehem Steel, 136 N.L.R.B. 1500 (1962).

24.   *See* Lincoln Lutheran, 362 N.L.R.B. No. 188 (2015); *see also* Metalcraft of Mayville, Inc., 18-CA-178322, 2017 WL 956627 (2017) (recognizing the continuing validity of *Lincoln Lutheran* in holding that dues checkoffs have long been considered a matter related to working conditions and that the employer's "unilateral cessation of dues checkoff violated Section 8(a)(5).").

25.   Aero Indus., 314 N.L.R.B. 314 (1994).

26.   NLRB v. Savair Mfg. Co., 414 U.S. 270 (1973).

27.   *See* NLRB v. Food Fair Stores, Inc., 307 F.2d 3 (3d Cir. 1962); *see also* NLRB v. Int'l Ass'n of Machinists, Guided Missile Lodge 1254, 241 F.2d 695 (9th Cir. 1957); NLRB v. Die & Tool Makers Lodge No. 113, 231 F.2d 298 (7th Cir. 1956); NLRB v. Phila. Iron Works, 211 F.2d 937 (3d Cir. 1954); Anaconda Copper Mining Co., 110 N.L.R.B. 1925 (1954); Int'l Harvester Co., 95 N.L.R.B. 730 (1951); Elec. Auto-Lite Co., 92 N.L.R.B. 1073 (1950).

28.   29 U.S.C. § 158(b)(5).

29.   *Id.*

30.   *Id.* § 431 *et seq.*

31.   *Id.*

32.   *Id.* § 433.

33.   *See* 29 U.S.C. § 433(a); *see also* U.S. Dep't of Labor, Office of Labor-Mgmt. Standards, Form LM-10 Employer Report, www.dol.gov/olms/regs/compliance/GPEA_Forms/lm-10p.pdf.

34.   *See, e.g.*, Auto Workers v. Dole, 869 F.2d 616 (D.C. Cir. 1989).

35.   As with the reporting requirements for employers, the disclosures required of labor relations consultants are subject to certain statutory conditions and exceptions. *See* 29 U.S.C. § 433(b).

36.   *See* 29 U.S.C. § 433(b); *see also* U.S. Dep't of Labor, Office of Labor-Mgmt. Standards, Form LM-20 Agreement and Activities Report, www.dol.gov/olms/regs/compliance/GPEA_Forms/lm-20p.pdf.

37.   *See* 29 U.S.C. § 433(b); *see also* U.S. Dep't of Labor, Office of Labor-Mgmt. Standards, Form LM-21 Receipts and Disbursements Report, www.dol.gov/olms/regs/compliance/GPEA_Forms/lm-21p.pdf.

38.   29 U.S.C. § 431.

39.   Labor Organization Officer and Employee Reports, 76 Fed. Reg. 66,442 (Oct. 26, 2011).

40.   *See Office of Labor-Management Standards (OLMS), Fact Sheet: LMRDA Recordkeeping Requirements for Unions*, U.S. DEP'T OF LABOR, www.dol.gov/olms/regs/compliance/lmrdarecordkeeping.htm (last updated Feb. 25, 2010).

41.   *See* 29 U.S.C. § 431(a); *see also* U.S. Dep't of Labor, Office of Labor-Mgmt. Standards, Form LM-1 Labor Organization Information Report, www.dol.gov/olms/rcgs/compliancc/GPEA_Forms/lm-1p.pdf.

42.   29 U.S.C. § 415.

43.   Knight v. Int'l Longshoremen's Ass'n, 457 F.3d 331, 345 (3d Cir. 2006).

44. *See* 29 U.S.C. § 432; *see also* U.S. Dep't of Labor, Office of Labor-Mgmt. Standards, Form LM-30 Labor Organization Officer and Employee Report, www. dol.gov/olms/regs/compliance/GPEA_Forms/lm-30p.pdf.

45. *See* 29 U.S.C. §§ 439, 440; *see also Employment Law Guide: Other Workplace Standards: Union Officer Elections and Financial Controls*, U.S. DEP'T OF LABOR (Sept. 2009), www.dol.gov/elaws/elg/unions.htm.

46. 29 U.S.C. § 158.

47. *Id.*

48. *See* 29 U.S.C. § 158(a)(3); *see also* NLRB v. Gen. Motors Corp., 373 U.S. 734 (1963); Radio Officers v. NLRB, 347 U.S. 17 (1954); Marquez v. Screen Actors Guild, Inc., 525 U.S. 33 (1998).

49. Commc'ns Workers of Am. v. Beck, 487 U.S. 735 (1988).

50. United Food & Commercial Workers Locals 951, 7 & 1036 (Meijer, Inc.), 329 N.L.R.B. 730 (1999) (determining that "economists generally agree that there is a positive relationship between the extent of unionization of employees in an industry or locality and negotiated wage rates").

51. *See* Commc'ns Workers of Am. v. Beck, 487 U.S. 735 (1988); *see also* Cal. Saw & Knife Works, 320 N.L.R.B. 224 (1995).

52. *See* Penrod v. NLRB, 203 F.3d 41 (D.C. Cir. 2000); *see also* Chi. Teachers Union v. Hudson, 475 U.S. 292 (1986); Abrams v. Commc'ns Workers of Am., 59 F.3d 1373 (D.C. Cir. 1995).

53. 29 U.S.C. § 164(b).

54. NAT'L RIGHT TO WORK ACT, H.R. 785, 115th Cong. (2017).

55. *Id.* § 159.

56. *Id.*

57. *Id.*

58. Commc'ns Workers of Am. v. Beck, 487 U.S. 735 (1988).

59. *See Beck*, 487 U.S. 735; *see also* Chi. Teachers Union v. Hudson, 475 U.S. 292 (1986); Penrod v. NLRB, 203 F.3d 41 (D.C. Cir. 2000); Abrams v. Commc'ns Workers of Am., 59 F.3d 1373 (D.C. Cir. 1995).

60. *See Meijer, Inc.*, 329 N.L.R.B. at 69; *see also* Chi. Teachers Union v. Hudson, 475 U.S. 292 (1986); Penrod v. NLRB, 203 F.3d 41 (D.C. Cir. 2000); Abrams v. Commc'ns Workers of Am., 59 F.3d 1373 (D.C. Cir. 1995).

61. Lehnert v. Ferris Faculty Ass'n, 500 U.S. 507, 524 (1991).

62. Cal. Saw & Knife Works, 320 N.L.R.B. 224, 239 (1995).

63. *Lehnert*, 500 U.S. at 524.

64. Locke v. Karass, 555 U.S. 207 (2009).

65. *Cal. Saw*, 320 N.L.R.B. at 235 n.57.

66. *Id.* at 231–33.

67. *Id.* at 233.

68. Teamsters Local 162 (Platt Elec. Supply) v. NLRB, 568 F.2d 665 (9th Cir. 1978).

69.   United Food & Commercial Workers Int'l Union Local 700 (Kroger L.P.), 361 N.L.R.B. No. 39 (2014) (reaffirming *California Saw*, finding that a union does not violate the duty of fair representation where it does not inform employees of the specific amount of reduced dues and fees in its initial *Beck* notices).

70.   *California Saw*, 320 N.L.R.B. at 242.

71.   Hospital del Maestro, 323 N.L.R.B. 93, 94–95 (1997).

72.   *California Saw*, 320 N.L.R.B. at 235–36 (recognizing that "several courts have found permissible the use of a window period for filing objections").

73.   Nielsen v. Machinists Local Lodge 2569, 94 F.3d 1107 (7th Cir. 1996).

74.   *See* Machinists Local Lodge 2777, 355 N.L.R.B. No. 174 (2010) (annual renewal requirement violated the NLRA); *see also* United Auto Workers Local 376, 356 N.L.R.B. No. 164 (2011); Commc'ns Workers of Am., 359 N.L.R.B. No. 131 (2013) (union could not justify annual renewal requirement with assertion that it allowed the union to collect data on *Beck* objectors).

75.   Chi. Teachers Union Local 1 v. Hudson, 475 U.S. 292, 307 n.18 (1986).

76.   *California Saw*, 320 N.L.R.B. at 233.

77.   *Hudson*, 475 U.S. at 306.

78.   *Id.* at 307 n.18.

79.   United Nurses & Allied Prof'ls, 359 N.L.R.B. No. 42 (2012).

80.   *California Saw*, 320 N.L.R.B. at 241; *see also* Dashiell v. Montgomery County, 925 F.2d 750, 755 (4th Cir. 1991).

81.   Television Artists AFTRA (KGW Radio), 327 N.L.R.B. 474, 477 (1999).

82.   *See* Harik v. Cal. Teachers Ass'n, 326 F.3d 1042, 1047 (9th Cir. 2003) (local union with under $50,000 in revenue not required to obtain independent verification of expenditures). *But see* Otto v. Pa. State Educ. Ass'n, 330 F.3d 125, 134 (3d Cir. 2003) (requiring independent verification of expenditures despite small union).

83.   Carpenters Local 943 (Okla. Fixture Co.), 322 N.L.R.B. 825 (1997).

84.   *California Saw*, 320 N.L.R.B. at 242.

85.   Air Line Pilots Ass'n v. Miller, 523 U.S. 866, 878–79 (1998).

86.   *Meijer*, 329 N.L.R.B. at 730–31 n.4.

12

Labor Relations of Federal Contractors

This chapter looks at several executive orders whose provisions affect labor relations of federal contractors:

Exec. Order 13658   Establishing a Minimum Wage for Contractors

Exec. Order 13496   Notification of Employee Rights Under Federal Labor Laws

Exec. Order 13494   Economy in Government Contracting

Exec. Order 13495   Nondisplacement of Qualified Workers Under Service Contracts

Exec. Order 13502   Use of Project Labor Agreements for Federal Construction Projects

Exec. Order 11246   Equal Employment Opportunity

Exec. Order 13782   Revocation of Federal Contracting Executive Orders

Exec. Order 13812   Revocation of Executive Order Creating Labor-Management Forums

---

EXECUTIVE ORDER 13658

Establishing a Minimum Wage for Government Contractors

On February 12, 2014, President Barack Obama signed Executive Order 13658, raising the minimum wage paid by federal contractors to $10.10 per hour beginning January 1, 2015.[1] Executive Order 13658 states that raising the pay of low-wage workers increases their morale and the productivity and quality of their work, lowers turnover and its accompanying costs, and reduces supervisory costs. The order concludes that, as a result, there will be improved economy and efficiency in federal government procurement. On June 17, 2014, the DOL published a notice of proposed rulemaking seeking comments on its proposed regulations to implement the order.[2] The regulations became effective on December 8, 2014.[3]

Executive Order 13658

Minimum Wage for Federal Contractors

Q 12.1   What is the required minimum wage rate for federal contractors under Executive Order 13658?

Executive Order 13658 took effect January 1, 2015, increasing federal contractors' minimum rate of pay to $10.10 per hour for all "new contracts, contract-like instruments, and solicitations." The new minimum wage affects all new or renewed federal contracts after January 1, 2015. The order also "strongly encourage[d]" federal agencies to negotiate and attempt to include the $10.10 minimum wage rate in any contracts signed during 2014.[4]

The regulations implementing the Executive Order define "contract or contract-like instrument" as "an agreement between two or more parties creating obligations that are enforceable or otherwise recognizable at law." A "solicitation" is defined as "any request to submit offers, bids, or quotations to the federal government."[5]

Q 12.1.1   Will the minimum wage for government contractors increase again after January 1, 2015?

Under the DOL's regulations, the Secretary of Labor ("Secretary") is required to determine the minimum wage rate annually beginning on January 1, 2015, and to modify the minimum wage based upon changes in the Consumer Price Index for Urban Wage Earners and Clerical Workers.[6]

Q 12.2   Are all employees of a federal contractor eligible for the new minimum wage regardless of whether a contract is a federal contract?

The new minimum wage requirement applies to employees who are performing work "on or in connection" with federal contracts.[7] Employees are considered to be performing work "in connection" with federal contracts if they spend 20% or more of their work time performing duties necessary to the performance of the contract, even if they are not directly engaged in performing the specific work called for by the contract.[8] (See Q 12.2.2 for a discussion of the federal contractors that are exempt from the minimum wage requirement.)

Q 12.2.1   Does Executive Order 13658 affect prime contractors and subcontractors?

The Executive Order affects both federal prime contractors and subcontractors. As of January 1, 2015, all new contracts and "contract-like instruments" must include a provision that requires any subcontract to include, as a condition of payment, that the subcontractor pay the new minimum wage to its workers.[9]

Q 12.2.2   Are any federal contracts exempt from this requirement?

The regulations set forth six categories of contracts and contractors that are not subject to the order's minimum wage requirements:

(1)   Grants, within the meaning of the Federal Grant and Cooperative Agreement Act, as amended, 31 U.S.C. § 6301 *et seq.*;

(2) Contracts and agreements with and grants to Indian Tribes under the Indian Self-Determination and Education Assistance Act, as amended, 25 U.S.C. § 450 *et seq.*;

(3) Procurement contracts for construction that are excluded from coverage of the Davis-Bacon Act, 40 U.S.C. § 276a;

(4) Contracts for services that are exempted from coverage under the Service Contract Act, 25 U.S.C. § 6701 *et seq.*, unless expressly covered by the Executive Order and the regulations;

(5) Employees who are exempt from the minimum wage requirements of the Fair Labor Standards Act, 25 U.S.C. §§ 213(a) and 214(a)–(b); and

(6) FLSA-covered workers performing work in connection with covered contracts for less than 20% of their work hours in a given work week.[10]

In addition, on May 25, 2018, President Trump signed Executive Order 13838 (Exemption from Executive Order 13658 for Recreational Services on Federal Lands). Section 2 of the Order adds language lifting the $10.10 minimum wage and overtime requirements of Executive Order 13658 for certain federal contractor employees and permit holders. Specifically, the minimum wage and overtime requirements no longer extend to contracts for "seasonal recreational services" and equipment rental on federal lands.[11] River running, hunting, fishing, horseback riding, camping, mountaineering activities, recreational ski services and youth camps are among the services encompassed by Executive Order 13838.[12]

Q 12.2.3   Does the order affect tipped employees of government contractors?

Beginning January 1, 2015, federal contractors must pay tipped employees an hourly cash wage of at least $4.90 per hour. If the tipped employee does not receive the new minimum wage when the employee's tips are combined with the hourly cash wage, the employer must pay the employee an additional cash wage so that the employee receives the new minimum wage.[13]

Executive Order 13658 increases the hourly cash wage paid to tipped employees each subsequent year after 2015 until the hourly cash wage is 70% of the minimum wage. The amount of the annual increase is the lesser of: (a) $0.95; or (b) the amount necessary for the hourly cash wage to equal 70% of the minimum wage.

Enforcement

Q 12.3　How will the Department of Labor enforce the new minimum wage requirements?

The regulations allow any worker, contractor, labor organization, trade organization, contracting organization, or other person or entity to report suspected violations of the Executive Order by filing a complaint with the Wage and Hour Division of the Department of Labor.[14] The administrator may seek to resolve a complaint through conciliation, but can also institute an investigation either resulting from a complaint or on its own initiative.[15] The investigation may include interviews with the contractor and workers, as well as record inspection.[16]

If the Secretary issues a final order that a contractor has failed to pay the correct wages, the administrator may direct that any payments due under the contract be withheld to provide relief to the underpaid workers. The regulations also permit the Department of Labor to bring a civil action against the contractor if the withheld funds are insufficient or there are no more payments due under the contract. Any recovered funds will be directly reimbursed to the workers.[17] A contractor may request a hearing before an administrative law judge to dispute the administrator's findings.[18]

EXECUTIVE ORDER 13496

Notification of Employee Rights Under Federal Labor Laws

On January 30, 2009, President Barack Obama signed Executive Order 13496, revoking former President George W. Bush's Executive Order 13201, Notification of Employee Rights Concerning Payment of Unions Dues or Fees, which was signed February 17, 2001. Executive Order 13201 required notice to employees of their rights pursuant to *Communications Workers of America v. Beck.* Specifically, federal contractors previously had to post notice informing employees of their right not to join a union to retain their jobs and not to pay agency fees for non-representational union expenditures. (See chapter 11 for a greater discussion of when employees may have *Beck* rights and how they may exercise those rights.) The DOL published a final rule on March 30, 2009, rescinding all regulations and rules implementing Executive Order 13201.[19]

On August 3, 2009, the DOL published a notice of proposed rule-making seeking comments on its proposed regulations for implementing Executive Order 13496, which would require federal contractors to post notice of employee rights under the NLRA. The regulations became effective beginning June 21, 2010.[20]

Executive Order 13496

Notification of Employee Rights

Q 12.4 What notice are federal contractors required to post based on Executive Order 13496?

Executive Order 13496 requires all federal government departments and agencies to include a provision in all contracts, unless otherwise exempted, requiring federal contractors to post a notice informing employees of their rights under federal labor laws as defined by the Secretary in specified places throughout the workplace.

Q 12.4.1   What specific employee rights must be included in the notification?

The proposed regulations set out the following employees' rights for inclusion in the notice of employees' rights that must be posted by each covered contractor:[21]

- The right to organize a union to negotiate with an employer concerning wages, hours, and other terms and conditions of employment.

- The right to form, join, or assist a union.

- The right to bargain collectively for a contract through a duly selected union.

- The right to discuss the terms and conditions of employment with co-workers or the union.

- The right to join other workers in raising work-related complaints with the employer, government agencies, or members of the public.

- The right to seek and receive help from a union, subject to certain limitations.

- The right to take action with co-workers to improve working conditions.

- The right to strike and picket, unless prohibited by a no-strike clause or other limitations, taking into consideration that an employer may permanently replace strikers.

- The right to choose not to do any of those activities, including joining or remaining a member of a union.

The proposed notice also includes language setting out certain employer actions that are illegal under federal labor law, including:

(1) discriminating against employees or threatening to close a facility for engaging in union activity;

(2) prohibiting the wearing of union insignia, except under certain circumstances; and

(3)   conducting surveillance of peaceful union activities or gatherings.

The notice further provides the process for contacting the NLRB in the case of a suspected unfair labor practice.

Q 12.4.2   Are any federal contracts exempted from this requirement?

Contracts involving collective bargaining agreements or purchases under the simplified acquisition threshold are excluded from the requirements of this order. The Secretary may further exempt any department or agency from any or all requirements of the order if the Secretary finds that the application of the requirements would:

(1)   not serve the purposes of the order;

(2)   impair the ability of the government to procure goods or services economically or efficiently; or

(3)   not serve the national interest.[22]

General Enforcement; Compliance Review and Complaint Procedures

Q 12.5   How will the DOL determine compliance with the notice requirements?

The regulations give the Director of the Office of Federal Contract Compliance Programs (OFCCP) the authority to conduct a compliance evaluation of federal contractors. A compliance evaluation includes a review of the posted notice as well as whether the required provisions have been included in contractors' government contracts, subcontracts, and purchase orders. The results of the director's compliance evaluation will be recorded.[23]

An employee of a covered contractor may also file a complaint alleging that the contractor has failed to post the notice and/or has failed to include the notice in subcontracts or purchase orders.

Q 12.5.1   How does an employee of a covered contractor file a complaint alleging noncompliance?

Employee complaints may be filed with the Office of Labor-Management Standards or with the Office of Federal Contract Compliance Programs. Complaints must be in writing and include the employee's name, address, and telephone number; the name and address of the contractor; and a description of the alleged violation of Executive Order 13496 or the regulations. The OFCCP director will investigate the allegations and develop a case record.[24]

Q 12.5.2   What are the consequences of noncompliance?

If a complaint investigation or compliance evaluation indicates that the contractor has violated Executive Order 13496 or the regulations, the DOL must make reasonable efforts to secure compliance through conciliation. The contractor must correct the violation and commit, in writing, not to repeat the violation. If a violation is not resolved through conciliation, the matter will be referred to the Director of Labor-Management Programs and the Solicitor of Labor for the institution of administrative enforcement proceedings. Enforcement proceedings may also be brought for a contractor's refusal to cooperate with a compliance evaluation or a complaint investigation or for refusing to take action with respect to enforcing Executive Order 13496 with respect to a subcontractor.

Administrative enforcement proceedings will be before an administrative law judge. Exceptions to the ALJ's decision must be filed with the Administrative Review Board. After a final decision on the merits, the Administrative Review Board must determine the sanctions or punishment to impose. Sanctions and penalties will not be imposed if the head of the contracting agency objects to the imposition of penalties or if the contractor has not been afforded an opportunity for a hearing.

After giving the contractor an opportunity for a hearing, the Director of the Office of Labor-Management Standards (OLMS) may enforce a violation of Executive Order 13496 and the regulations by:[25]

- directing a contracting agency to cancel, terminate, or suspend any contract or portions thereof;

- issuing an order of debarment providing that one or more contracting agencies must refrain from entering into further contracts, or extensions or other modification of existing contracts, with any non-complying contractor;

- issuing an order of debarment providing that no contracting agency may enter into a contract with any non-complying subcontractor.

The contracting agency must report back to the Director of OLMS regarding its implementation of the sanctions and penalties. The director will periodically publish a list of the names of contractors and subcontractors that have been declared ineligible for future contractors or subcontracts due to violations of the executive order or its regulations.

A debarred contractor or subcontractor may be reinstated by sending a letter to the Director of OLMS. If the director finds that the contractor or subcontractor has come into compliance with the executive order and the regulations, and the contractor has shown that it will carry out the order and the regulations, the contractor or subcontractor may be reinstated.[26]

EXECUTIVE ORDER 13494

Executive Order 13494, signed on January 30, 2009, was later amended by Executive Order 13517 on October 28, 2009. This order, as amended, specifies certain costs that federal contracting departments and agencies are required to treat as unallowable.

Executive Order 13494 provides that the Federal Acquisition Regulatory Council, within 150 days, shall adopt such rules and regulations and issue such orders as are deemed necessary and appropriate to carry out the order. On April 14, 2010, the council issued its proposed rules.[27] The regulations became effective on December 2, 2011.[28]

Executive Order 13494

Allowable and Unallowable Costs

Q 12.6   What does it mean when costs in government contracts are unallowable?

Unallowable costs cannot be included in prices or cost reimbursements under contracts with the federal government. A company is not prohibited from incurring unallowable costs, but they cannot be recovered either directly or indirectly under federal government contracts. To manage unallowable costs, the contractor must establish separate accounts for these expenses and these costs must not be priced directly into federal government contracts during the proposal process. Such costs cannot be made a part of the expense pools that are applied to federal government contracts through an overhead, materials handling, or cost allocation at the accounting period close or during forward pricing rate planning. These unallowable costs must also be excluded from billing, claims, proposals, and disbursements from any applicable contract.

Q 12.7   What costs in government contracts have been made unallowable under Executive Order 13494?

Executive Order 13494, as amended, requires federal contracting departments and agencies to treat as unallowable the costs of any activities undertaken to persuade employees to exercise or not to exercise, the right to organize and bargain collectively.[29] The broad prohibition in the order excludes the cost of the following activities, when they are undertaken to persuade employees to exercise or not to exercise, or concern the manner of exercising, rights to organize and bargain collectively:

- preparing and distributing materials;
- hiring or consulting legal counsel or consultants;

- holding meetings (including paying the salaries of the attendees at meetings held for this purpose); and

- planning or conducting activities by managers, supervisors, or union representatives during work hours.

Executive Order 13494 requires that the rules adopted by the Federal Acquisition Regulatory Council to carry out the order may not interfere with the ability of contractors to engage in advocacy through activities for which they do not claim reimbursement.[30] Those proposed rules provide the following examples of activities that will be treated as unallowable costs under the order when these activities are undertaken to persuade employees to exercise or not to exercise, or concern the manner of exercising, rights to organize and bargain collectively:

- preparing and distributing materials;

- hiring or consulting legal counsel or consultants;

- holding meetings (including paying the salaries of the attendees of meetings);

- planning or conducting activities by managers, supervisors, or union representatives during work hours.

Q 12.7.1   What costs are allowable?

Allowable costs pursuant to Executive Order 13494, as amended, include costs directly related to the contractor's provision of goods and services, as well as those costs incurred while maintaining satisfactory relations between the contractor and its employees, including costs of labor-management committees, employee publications, and other related activities. Each of these costs is allowable so long as it does not involve the activities associated with unallowable costs, as noted above.[31]

The Federal Acquisition Regulatory Council's proposed rules provide that a contractor's costs incurred in maintaining satisfactory relations between the federal contractor and its employees will be treated as allowable costs, if these activities do not involve the prohibited persuasive purpose noted above. These allowable costs include the "costs of shop stewards, labor management committees, employee publications, and other related activities."[32]

Q 12.7.2   Does the NLRA preempt Executive Order 13494?

Critics question whether Executive Order 13494 is preempted by the NLRA because of the order's prohibitions on an employer's use of funds. The U.S. Supreme Court has held that NLRA preemption principles prohibited a California statute that barred employers from using state funds to speak to their employees about union-related matters. Also, a federal circuit court has also held invalid and inconsistent with the NLRA an order that would have barred federal agencies from contracting with employers that permanently replaced striking employees.[33]

EXECUTIVE ORDER 13495

**Nondisplacement of Qualified Workers
Under Service Contracts**

On January 30, 2009, President Barack Obama signed Executive Order 13495, stating the government's policy of nondisplacement of a predecessor employees where a service contract expires and a follow-on contract is awarded for the same service.

The order required the FAR to issue implementing regulations within 180 days. On March 19, 2009, the FAR issued proposed regulations to implement the order. The regulations became effective on January 18, 2013.[34]

Executive Order 13495

Nondisplacement of Qualified Workers

Q 12.8   When must a successor federal contractor hire its predecessor contractor's employees pursuant to Executive Order 13495?

Executive Order 13495 essentially requires a successful new bidder to an existing service contract to give all of the incumbent organization's employees working on the existing service contract first right of refusal of employment by the new awardee.

Q 12.8.1   What are the consequences for noncompliance?

Failure to comply with an order from the enforcing agency, the DOL, or a willful violation can result in debarment from further government contracts for three years.[35] (See also Q 12.11.3.)

Q 12.8.2   Are any contracts exempted from this requirement?

Executive Order 13495 does not apply to:

- contracts or subcontracts under the simplified acquisition threshold;

- contracts or subcontracts awarded pursuant to the Javits-Wagner-O'Day Act;

- guard, elevator operator, messenger, or custodial services provided to the federal government under contracts or subcontracts with sheltered workshops employing the severely handicapped;

- agreements for vending facilities entered into pursuant to the preference regulations issued under the Randolph-Sheppard Act; and

- employees who were hired to work under a federal service contract and one or more nonfederal service contracts as part of a single job, provided employees were not deployed in a manner to avoid the purposes of the Order.

Further, the head of a federal contracting department or agency may exempt his or her department or agency from the requirements of this order in certain specified circumstances.[36]

Predecessor Contractor's Responsibilities

Q 12.9 What are a predecessor contractor's responsibilities under the proposed regulations?

The predecessor contractor must provide the executive agency's contracting officer with a certified list of the names of all service employees working under the contract who may be covered, along with the anniversary dates of employment of each service employee. This must be provided no less than ten days before completion of the contractor's performance of services on the contract. This list will then be forwarded to the awardee contractor. If the predecessor fails to provide the list of names, the federal contracting officer may, upon request by the administrator of the DOL Wage and Hour Division, take such action as may be necessary to cause the suspension of the payment of the contract funds to the predecessor contractor until the list is provided to the contracting officer.

Awardee Contractor's Responsibilities

Q 12.10 What are the awardee contractor's responsibilities under the proposed regulations?

Absent an exception, the awardee contractor must, in writing or orally, make an express bona fide offer of employment to each service employee for a position for which the covered employee is qualified and shall state the time within which the employee must accept the offer. In no case shall the period in which the employee must accept the offer be less than ten days. The awardee's obligation to offer a right of first refusal exists even if the awardee's contractor has not been provided a list of the predecessor's employees or the list does not contain the names of all persons employed during the final month of contract performance.[37]

If the predecessor contractor's workforce comprises a significant number of workers who are not fluent in English, the offer shall be provided in both English and the languages with which the employees are familiar. Having a co-worker translate would satisfy this requirement. The contractor must maintain copies of any written offers of employment or a contemporaneous written record of any oral offers of employment, including the date, location, and attendance roster of any employee meetings at which the offers were extended, a summary of each meeting, a copy of any written notice that may have been distributed, and the names of the employees from the predecessor contract to whom an offer was made.

Q 12.10.1   Who is a qualified service employee?

The proposed regulations define "service employee" as any person engaged in the performance of a service contract, other than any person employed in a bona fide executive, administrative, or professional capacity. Questions of interpretation shall be referred to the nearest local office of the Wage and Hour Division. The awardee contractor bears the responsibility of proving that an employee does not qualify for the protections of the Executive Order and accompanying regulations.

Q 12.10.2   To which predecessor employees is an awardee contractor not required to make an offer?

A contractor is not required to offer employment to the following excepted employees of the predecessor contractor:[38]

- employees who will be retained by the predecessor contractor;

- employees who are not service employees as defined in the regulations;

- employees who the awardee contractor reasonably believes have failed to perform suitably on the job, based on past performance; the performance determination must be made on an individualized basis;

- employees who were hired by the predecessor to work under the predecessor's federal service contract and one or more nonfederal service contracts as part of a single job, unless the employees were deployed in a manner designed to avoid the purposes of the Executive Order.

The awardee contractor must presume that all employees do not qualify for the exceptions set out above. For an exception to apply, the employer must demonstrate a reasonable belief based on credible information provided by a knowledgeable source, such as the predecessor contractor, local supervisor, the employee, or the contracting agency. Information regarding the general business practices of the predecessor contractor or the industry is not a sufficient basis on which to claim an exception. Evidence of disciplinary actions taken for poor performance may demonstrate a reasonable belief that the employee failed to perform suitably. The contractor must maintain a copy of any evidence or record that forms the basis for any exception.

The awardee contractor may determine how many employees it will need to perform on the contract. For bona fide staffing or work assignment reasons, the awardee contractor may choose to employ fewer employees than the predecessor contractor. The awardee contractor, therefore, does not necessarily have to offer employment on the contract to all of the predecessor's service employees, only those necessary to meet the awardee's anticipating staffing needs. The contractor may determine which of the predecessor's employees will receive offers.[39]

If the awardee uses a smaller workforce, its obligation to offer employment shall continue for ninety days after the awardee's first date of performance on the contract. The contractor's obligation to offer a right of first refusal to the predecessor's service employees, thus, ends when all of the predecessor's contract employees have received a bona fide job offer or the ninety-day period has expired.

Q 12.10.3   Must an awardee's offer to a qualified predecessor employee be for the same position that employee previously held?

The awardee contractor is obligated to make an express bona fide offer of employment for a position for which the covered employee is qualified. An offer will be presumed to be a bona fide offer of employment even if it is for a position that is not similar to the one the employee previously held, but is one for which the employee is qualified. The offer may be under different employment terms and conditions, including changes to pay or benefits, if the reasons are not related to a desire that the employee refuse the offer or that other employees be hired for the offer. Questions as to the employee's qualifications must be decided based on credible information concerning the employee's education and employment history, with a particular emphasis on the employee's experience on the predecessor's contract.[40]

Compliance and Enforcement

Q 12.11   How can an employee enforce its right of first refusal against an awardee contractor under Executive Order 13495?

Any former employee who believes the awardee contractor has violated Executive Order 13495 or the regulations may file a complaint with the Branch of Government Contracts Enforcement of the Wage and Hour Division, U.S. Department of Labor[41] within 120 days of the alleged violation.

Q 12.11.1   How is a complaint of a violation investigated?

After receiving a complaint, the Wage and Hour Division may attempt conciliation and resolution of the issue consistent with the provisions of the order and regulations. The administrator of the Wage and Hour Division may initiate an investigation if conciliation is unsuccessful or the administrator otherwise decides to proceed on his or her own initiative. As part of the investigation, the administrator may inspect the records of the predecessor and successor contractors, question the contractors and employees, and require the production of documents.

The contractor must cooperate in any review or investigation of a complaint alleging noncompliance with the order or the regulations. Contractors may not interfere with the investigation or intimidate, blacklist, discharge, or in any other manner discriminate against any person for bringing, or cooperating with, an investigation or proceeding.[42]

Upon completion of an investigation, the administrator will issue to the parties a written determination as to whether a violation occurred. The determination must contain a statement of the findings of the investigation and the administrator's conclusions. The determination must also address appropriate relief and eligibility sanctions, where appropriate. If the administrator determines that lost wages or other monetary relief are due to an employee, the administrator may direct that a portion of any accrued payment owed to the contractor by the government be withheld. Upon final order of the Secretary that money is due, the administrator may direct that the withheld funds be transferred to the DOL for disbursement to the employee.[43]

Q 12.11.2 Can a contractor dispute the results of an investigation?

Yes. To contest the administrator's decision, a contractor must submit a request for a hearing to the Chief ALJ within twenty days of the date of the determination. The contractor must provide the Chief ALJ with a detailed statement of the reasons why the administrator's ruling was in error, including the facts in dispute. A copy of any request for a hearing must be sent to the other party, the administrator, and the associate solicitor, Division of Fair Labor Standards, DOL. The administrator may intervene as a party or as amicus curiae.

A petition for review of an ALJ's decision must be sent to the Administrative Review Board within twenty days, and also served on all parties. A petition for review shall refer to the specific findings of facts, conclusions of law, or order at issue. Copies must be served on the ALJ, the administrator, and associate solicitor. The ARB must issue a decision within ninety days of receipt of the petition for review and serve the decision on all parties. The ARB's decision shall be the final order of the Secretary.[44]

If the administrator, when issuing a determination, finds that there are no facts in dispute, the administrator shall send the decision within twenty days to the ARB. If a party disagrees with the administrator's determination that there are no disputed facts is in error, the aggrieved party may advise the administrator of disputed facts and request a hearing within twenty days of the determination. The administrator may deny the request, or refer the request for a hearing to the chief ALJ. If the administrator denies the party's request, the parties have twenty days to file exceptions with the ARB.

If a timely request for hearing or petition for review is filed, the determination of the administrator or ALJ shall be inoperative unless and until the ARB issues an order affirming the determination or decision, or the determination or decision otherwise becomes a final order of the Secretary. If a petition for review concerns only the imposition of ineligibility sanctions, the remainder of the decision shall be effective immediately. No judicial review shall be available unless a timely petition for review to the ARB is first filed.[45]

Q 12.11.3   What penalties may a successor contractor face for noncompliance?

After affording the contractor an opportunity for a hearing, if the Secretary finds that a contractor has failed to comply with any order or committed willful or aggravated violations of the order or regulations, the Secretary may order that the contractor and its responsible officers, and any firm in which the contractor has a substantial interest, be ineligible for any future contract or subcontract of the United States for a period of up to three years.

In addition to satisfying court costs, a contractor who violates this part must take appropriate action to abate the violation, which may include hiring each affected employee in a position on the contract for which the employee is qualified, together with compensation (including lost wages), terms, conditions, and privileges of that employment. The Equal Access to Justice Act does not apply to proceedings to enforce the Executive Order. Neither the ARB nor the ALJ have authority to award attorney fees or other litigation expenses.[46]

EXECUTIVE ORDER 13502

**Use of Project Labor Agreements
for Federal Construction Projects**

Executive Order 13502 was signed February 6, 2009. The order allows an executive agency to require the use of project labor agreements in connection with awarding any contract associated with a large-scale construction project with a total cost to the federal government of $25 million or more.[47]

On April 13, 2010, the FAR issued its final rule implementing Executive Order 13502.[48] The final rule encourages federal agencies to consider requiring the use of PLAs in connection with large-scale construction projects.

Executive Order 13502

Project Labor Agreements

Q 12.12   What is a project labor agreement?

Project labor agreements are agreements with contractors that establish the rules to be followed by firms that bid on construction projects. A PLA establishes the terms and conditions of employment for a specific project and binds all contractors and subcontractors on the project. A PLA typically requires a contractor to:

(1)   hire workers though union halls;

(2)   require non-union workers to pay dues during the construction project; and

(3)   force contractors to follow union rules on pensions, work conditions, and dispute resolution.

Q 12.12.1   When is an executive agency allowed to require a PLA?

The Executive Order provides that when PLAs would lead to economy and efficiency in federal procurement, labor management stability, and compliance with the law, the agency may require every contractor and subcontractor on the project to agree to negotiate or to become a party to a PLA with one or more appropriate labor organizations.[49] PLAs reached under the Executive Order must:

- bind all contractors and subcontractors on the construction project through the inclusion of appropriate specifications in all relevant solicitation provisions and contract documents;

- allow all contractors and subcontractors to compete for contracts and subcontracts without regard to whether they are otherwise parties to collective bargaining agreements;

- contain guarantees against strikes, lockouts, and similar job disruptions;

- set forth effective, prompt, and mutually binding procedures for resolving labor disputes arising during the project labor agreement;

- provide other mechanisms for labor management cooperation on matters of mutual interest and concern, including productivity, quality of work, safety, and health;

- fully conform to all statutes, regulations, and executive orders.[50]

The FAR's final rule implementing Executive Order 13502 also requires all PLAs to conform to these six provisions.

Q 12.12.2   What is considered a "construction" project?

The FAR's final rule broadly defines "construction" as "construction, rehabilitation, alteration, conversion, extension, repair, or improvement of buildings, highways, or other real property."

Construction Projects Requiring PLAs

Q 12.13 What factors should an agency consider when deciding whether to use a PLA for a particular construction project?

The FAR's final rule recommends that federal agencies making such an evaluation should consider:

- whether the project will require multiple construction contractors and/or subcontractors employing workers in multiple crafts or trades;

- whether there is a shortage of skilled labor in the region in which the construction project will be sited;

- whether completion of the project will require an extended period of time;

- whether PLAs have been used on comparable projects undertaken by federal, state, municipal, or private entities in the geographic area of the project;

- whether a PLA will promote the federal agency's long-term program interests, such as facilitating the training of a skilled workforce to meet the agency's future construction needs;

- any other factors that the federal agency decides are appropriate.

Q 12.13.1 How are the terms and conditions of the PLA determined?

The final rule permits a federal agency to specify the terms and conditions of the PLA to be used in the solicitation of a contract and then require the successful bidding contractor to become a party to a PLA containing those terms and conditions as a condition of being awarded the federal contract. The rules permit the federal agency to "seek the views of, confer with, and exchange information with prospective bidders and union representatives" in an effort to identify the appropriate terms and conditions of a PLA for a particular construction project. The federal agency may also facilitate agreement between prospective bidders and union representatives on those terms and conditions to be used in the solicitation.

The final rule also permits a federal agency to require a prospective bidder to submit a PLA as part of its offer, or to require the successful bidder to enter into a PLA once the contract has been awarded. The timing of a prospective or successful bidder's submission of a PLA depends on the notice language used by the federal agency in its solicitation of the contract.[51]

Q 12.14   What do critics say will be the effect of Executive Order 13502 on construction projects?

Critics of Executive Order 13502 assert that PLAs will significantly increase construction costs of federal projects, by discouraging open-shop firms from bidding. These critics assert that union-only PLAs virtually eliminate "merit-shop" contractors from competing for and winning construction projects, because union-only PLAs are typically awarded to unionized contractors. Further criticism against the use of PLAs includes requiring non-union companies with their own benefit plans to pay their workers' health and welfare benefits to union trust funds; requiring non-union companies to obtain apprentices exclusively from union apprenticeship programs, instead of federal and state-approved non-union apprenticeship programs; and requiring a non-union company to send its own employees to a union hiring hall.

EXECUTIVE ORDER 11246

Equal Employment Opportunity

Executive Order 11246, signed by President Lyndon B. Johnson on September 24, 1965, provides for employment nondiscrimination and equal opportunity in supply and service contracts. Executive Order 11246 was amended most recently on July 21, 2014, when President Barack Obama signed Executive Order 13672.[52] On December 3, 2014, the Department of Labor issued its final rule implementing Executive Order 13672, which took effect on April 8, 2015.[53]

Executive Order 11246

Q 12.15   What does Executive Order 11246 require?

All contractors, during the performance of a contract, are required to agree:[54]

- not to discriminate in employment on the basis of race, color, religion, sex, sexual orientation, gender identity, or national origin and indicate as such in all solicitations or advancements for employees;

- to take affirmative action to ensure applicants are considered, and that employees are treated during employment, without regard to race, color, religion, sex, sexual orientation, gender identity, or national origin;

- to send unions a notice of the contractor's commitments under the order; and

- to furnish information as required and provide access to books, records, and accounts by the contracting agency and Secretary to ascertain compliance.

Exemptions

Q 12.15.1   Are there any contracts that are exempted from these requirements?

The Secretary may exempt any contracting agency from the requirements of the order, if special circumstances in the national interest so require. The Secretary may also exempt certain classes of contracts whenever:

(1) work is to be performed outside the United States and no recruitment of workers within the limits of United States is involved;

(2) the contract is for standard commercial supplies or raw materials;

(3) contracts involve less than specified amounts of money or specified numbers of workers; or

(4) the contracts involve subcontractors below a specific tier.

The executive order also does not apply to a contractor that is a religious corporation with respect to the employment of individuals of a particular religion to perform work connected with the contractor. Further, the Secretary may exempt contractor facilities that are separate and distinct from the activities of the contractor related to the contract.[55]

Q 12.15.2   How does Executive Order 13782 impact Executive Order 11246?

As noted below, President Trump's Executive Order 13782 revoked Executive Order 13673. Executive Order 13673 encouraged compliance with Executive Order 11246 by requiring bidding employers to report violations of Executive Order 11246 as part of the bidding process so that federal contracting officers could determine to whom they should grant projects based on the bidders' compliance. Revocation of Executive Order 13673 thereby weakens the incentive to comply with 11246.

Compliance and Enforcement

Q 12.15.3   How is compliance with the order enforced?

Contractors must file compliance reports with the contracting agency or the DOL. These reports must contain information as to the practices, policies, programs, and employment policies, programs, and employment statistics of the contractor. Prospective contractors may be required to submit previous compliance reports from past contractors, if such reports exist.[56]

In the event of a contractor's noncompliance, the contract may be canceled, terminated, or suspended, in whole or in part, and the contractor may be declared ineligible for further government contracts, or other remedies invoked as provided.[57]

> ### EXECUTIVE ORDER 13812
>
> #### Revoking Executive Order Creating
> #### Labor-Management Forums
>
> On September 29, 2017, President Donald J. Trump signed Executive Order 13812, revoking Executive Order 13522 of December 9, 2009 (Creating Labor-Management Forums to Improve Delivery of Government Services), as extended by Executive Order 13708 of September 30, 2015 (Continuance or Reestablishment of Certain Federal Advisory Committees), which established the National Council on Federal Labor-Management Relations and related agency-level labor-management forums throughout the executive branch.

Executive Order 13812

Revocation of Executive Order Creating Labor-Management Forums

Q 12.16   What effect does Executive Order 13812 have on labor-management forums?

Executive Order 13812 directs the Director of the Office of Personnel Management and heads of executive departments and agencies to "promptly move to rescind any orders, rules, regulations, guidelines, programs, or policies implementing or enforcing Executive Order 13522."[58] Executive Order 13812 abolished the requirement that agencies form labor-management forums and participate in pre-decisional workplace matters with employees and union representatives.[59]

Q 12.16.1   What effect does Executive Order 13812 have on collective bargaining agreements?

Nothing in Executive Order 13812 abrogates provisions contained in any collective bargaining agreements in effect on September 23, 2017.[60] However, given the breadth of Executive Order 13812, some agencies may seek to renegotiate collective bargaining agreements that have embedded within them guidelines, rules, or policies associated with a labor-management forum. Furthermore, if a term or article of a collective bargaining agreement or memorandum of understanding is explicitly conditioned on creating a forum pursuant to Executive Order 13522, those provisions may be declared unenforceable under Executive Order 13812.

EXECUTIVE ORDER 13782

Revoking Federal Contracting Executive Orders

On March 27, 2017, President Donald J. Trump signed Executive Order 13782 to revoke Executive Order 13673, section 3 of Executive Order 13683, and Executive Order 13738.

Executive Order 13782

Revocation of Federal Contracting Executive Orders

Q 12.17   What did Executive Order 13673 do?[61]

Executive Order 13673 provided instructions for federal contracting officers to consider a contractor's compliance with certain federal and state labor laws before awarding a federal contract.[62] For projects with an estimated value greater than $500,000, bidding employers were required to report violations of fourteen federal labor laws as part of the bidding process in order to assist federal contracting officers determine to whom they should grant projects based on the bidders' compliance with labor laws.[63] The fourteen laws bidding employers were required to report violations of were:

- Fair Labor Standards Act
- Occupational Safety and Health Act (and state law equivalents)
- National Labor Relations Act
- Davis-Bacon Act

- Service Contract Act
- Executive Order 11246 (affirmative action)
- Executive Order 13658 (minimum wage)
- Section 503
- Vietnam Era Veterans' Readjustment Assistance Act
- Family Medical Leave Act
- Title VII
- Americans with Disabilities Act
- Age Discrimination in Employment Act
- Migrant and Seasonal Agricultural Worker Protection Act

Executive Order 13673 also prohibited the use of pre-dispute arbitration agreements with individual workers covering claims arising under Title VII or any tort related to or arising out of sexual assault or harassment for projects over $1 million.[64] Finally, Executive Order 13673 required certain disclosures on employee paystubs and a special notice of employment status to designated independent contractors.[65]

Q 12.17.1   What did section 3 of Executive Order 13683 do?

Section 3 of Executive Order 13683 added the Vietnam Veterans' Readjustment Assistance Act to the list of federal laws that bidding employers had to report violations of to be eligible to receive projects worth more than $500,000 under Executive Order 13673.[66]

Notes to Chapter 12

1. Exec. Order No. 13,658, Establishing a Minimum Wage for Contractors, 29 C.F.R. 10 (2014).
2. Establishing a Minimum Wage for Contractors, 79 Fed. Reg. 34,568 (June 17, 2014).
3. 29 C.F.R. § 10.1 *et seq.*
4. Exec. Order No. 13658, *supra* note 1.
5. 29 C.F.R. § 10.2.
6. *Id.* §§ 10.12, 10.5(b).
7. *Id.* § 10.1.
8. *Id.* § 10.4.
9. *Id.*
10. 29 C.F.R. §10.4.
11. 83 Fed. Reg. 25,341(2) (June 1, 2018).
12. *Id.*
13. Exec. Order No. 13658, *supra* note 1.
14. *Id.* § 10.41.
15. *Id.* §§ 10.42, 10.43.
16. *Id.* § 10.43.
17. *Id.* § 10.44.
18. *Id.* § 10.51.
19. *See* 74 Fed. Reg. 14,045; *see also* 74 Fed. Reg. 65,599.
20. 29 C.F.R. pt. 471.
21. *Id.* pt. 471, app. A.
22. Exec. Order No. 13496, Notification of Employee Rights Under Federal Labor Laws (Jan. 30, 2009), www.gpo.gov/fdsys/pkg/FR-2009-02-04/pdf/E9-2485.pdf; *see also* U.S. Dep't of Labor, Employee Rights Under the National Labor Relations Act, www.dol.gov/olms/regs/compliance/EmployeeRightsPoster11x17_Final.pdf.
23. 29 C.F.R. § 471.10.
24. *Id.* § 471.11.
25. *Id.* § 471.14.
26. *Id.* § 471.16.
27. *See* 75 Fed. Reg. 19,345, http://edocket.access.gpo.gov/2010/ 2010-8504.htm.
28. 48 C.F.R. § 31.000 *et seq.*
29. Exec. Order No. 13494, Economy in Government Contracting (Jan. 30, 2009), www.gpo.gov/fdsys/pkg/FR-2009-02-04/pdf/E9-2483.pdf.
30. *Id.*
31. *Id.*

32.　*See* 75 Fed. Reg. 19,345, http://edocket.access.gpo.gov/2010/ 2010-8504. htm.

33.　*See* Chamber of Commerce v. Brown, 128 S. Ct. 2408 (2008); *see also* Chamber of Commerce v. Reich, 74 F.3d 1332 (D.C. Cir. 1996).

34.　29 C.F.R. § 9.1 *et seq.*

35.　Exec. Order No. 13495, Nondisplacement of Qualified Workers Under Service Contracts (Jan. 30, 2009), www.gpo.gov/fdsys/pkg/FR-2009-02-04/pdf/E9-2484. pdf.

36.　*Id.*

37.　*Id.*

38.　*Id.*

39.　*Id.*

40.　*Id.*

41.　29 C.F.R. § 9.21.

42.　Exec. Order No. 13495, *supra* note 35.

43.　*Id.*

44.　*Id.*

45.　*Id.*

46.　*Id.*

47.　Exec. Order No. 13502, Use of Project Labor Agreements for Federal Construction Projects (Feb. 6, 2009), www.gpo.gov/fdsys/pkg/FR-2009-02-11/pdf/ E9-3113.pdf.

48.　48 C.F.R. § 22.501 *et seq.*

49.　*Id.*

50.　*Id.*

51.　75 Fed. Reg. 19,168.

52.　Exec. Order No. 13672, Further Amendments to Executive Order 11478, Equal Employment Opportunity in the Federal Government, and Executive Order 11246, Equal Employment Opportunity, 141 Fed. Reg. 42,971 (July 23, 2014), www. gpo.gov/fdsys/pkg/FR-2014-07-23/pdf/2014-17522.pdf.

53.　79 Fed. Reg. 72,985.

54.　Exec. Order No. 11246, Equal Employment Opportunity (as amended Dec. 16, 2002), www.dol.gov/ofccp/regs/statutes/eo11246.htm; *see also* U.S. Dep't of Labor, Office of Federal Contract Compliance Programs, Executive Order 11246, www.dol.gov/ofccp/regs/compliance/fs11246.htm.

55.　*Id.*

56.　*Id.*

57.　*Id.*

58.　Exec. Order No. 13812, Revocation of Executive Order Creating Labor-Management Forums, 82 Fed. Reg. 46,367 (Sept. 29, 2017), https://www.whitehouse. gov/presidential-actions/presidential-executive-order-revocation-executive-order-creating-labor-management-forums/.

59.　*Id.*

60.　*Id.*

61.   Executive Order 13673 was slightly amended by Executive Order 13738. *See* Exec. Order No. 13738, Amendment to Executive Order 13673, 81 Fed. Reg. 58, 807 (Aug. 23, 2016), https://www.gpo.gov/fdsys/pkg/FR-2016-08-26/pdf/2016-20713. pdf.

62.   Exec. Order No. 13673, Fair Pay and Safe Workplaces, 79 Fed. Reg. 45,309 (July 31, 2014), https://www.federalregister.gov/documents/2014/08/05/2014-18561/ fair-pay-and-safe-workplaces.

63.   *Id.*

64.   *Id.*

65.   *Id.*

66.   Exec. Order No. 13683, Amendments to Executive Orders 11030, 13653, and 13673, 79 Fed. Reg. 75,041 (Dec. 11, 2014), https://www.gpo.gov/fdsys/pkg/FR-2014-12-23/pdf/2014-30195.pdf.

Index

(References are to question numbers.)

A

Abnormally dangerous conditions
    walkouts based on good-faith belief of, 7.9
AC petitions, 4.12.5
Access remedies
    election misconduct, for, 4.71
Access to employer facilities and employees
    collective bargaining agreement provisions, 6.14
    limitation of access by employer, 4.53
    non-employee union organizers, right to access company
        property of, 3.10
Accretion
    consolidation of employees, applicability to, 5.29
    duty to bargain after, 5.29
    generally, 4.35, 4.35.1
Administrative law judges, 2.4.3
Agency fees, 11.7.2
Agency shops
    collective bargaining, agency shop agreements as mandatory
        subject of, 5.6.2
    generally, 1.2.4
Agents
    employer's agents, 1.5.1
Agreements not to organize, 4.7
Agricultural laborers
    exemption from NLRA, 1.4.1
Airline carriers, unionization of. *See* Railway Labor Act (RLA)
Alcohol testing programs
    collective bargaining, as mandatory subject of, 5.6.6

B

C

D

Financial-core employees
    Beck objectors. *See Beck* objections
    dues and fee requirements, 11.16.2
    generally, 11.16.2
    limitations on, 11.16.2
    union interests, requirements with respect to support of, 11.16.3
Fines or penalties
    Executive Order 13495, penalties for violations of, 12.11.3
    Executive Order 13496, sanctions or penalties for violations of
        notice requirements of, 12.5.2
    National Labor Relations Act (NLRA), lack of fines or penalties
        under, 2.6
    unfair labor practice, assessment of fines by union as
        generally, 3.30
        limits on fines, 3.30.1
Full-consent agreement, 4.24.3

G

Garmon preemption
    "actually protected or prohibited" activity, 10.1.1
    applicable preemption doctrine, determination of, 10.5
    "arguably protected or prohibited" activity, 10.1.1
    broad scope of, 10.1.1
    compelling state or local interest exception, 10.1.3
    exceptions
        compelling state or local interest exception, 10.1.3
        generally, 10.1.2
        market participant exception, 10.1.5
        peripheral concern exception, 10.1.4
    generally, 10.1
    J.A. Croson Co., 10.1.1
    market participant exception, 10.1.5
    peripheral concern exception, 10.1.4
    purpose of, 10.1
    Smart v. Local 702 Int'l Bhd. of Elec. Workers, 10.1.1
General Counsel's Office. *See* Office of General Counsel

H

I

J

L

M

N

O

Objections
    representation elections, objections to. *See* Election objections
Observers
    representation election, role and selection of observers for,
        4.64.1
Office of Executive Secretary, 2.4, 2.4.1
Office of General Counsel
    Division of Advice, 2.5, 2.5.2, 3.5, 3.13.1
    Division of Enforcement Litigation, 2.5, 2.5.3
    Division of Information, 2.4
    Division of Judges, 2.4, 2.4.3
    Division of Operations Management, 2.5, 2.5.1
    functions of, 2.3
    General Counsel, appointment and role of, 2.3
    generally, 2.3
    structure of
        Division of Advice, 2.5, 2.5.2
        Division of Enforcement Litigation, 2.5, 2.5.3
        Division of Operations Management, 2.5, 2.5.1
        generally, 2.5
Office of Representation Appeals, 2.4, 2.4.4
Office of Solicitor, 2.4, 2.4.2
Organizing campaign. *See* Union organizing campaign
Overtime, 6.7, 6.10

P

Part-time employees
    bargaining unit, inclusion in, 4.41
Partial lockouts, 7.26
Partial strikes, 7.4.3
Penalties. *See* Fines or penalties
Personal leave provisions, 6.11.6

S

T

U

Unfair labor practices; case procedures, joint liability *(cont'd)*
    single-employer theory of liability
        centralized control of labor relations factor, 8.54.1
        common management factor, 8.54.2
        common ownership factor, 8.54.2
        concerns associated with being considered single
            employer, 8.54.3
        determining whether two employers are considered
            single employer, 8.54, 8.54.1 *et seq.*
        functional integration of enterprises factor, 8.54.1
        generally, 8.53
    liability
        individual liability, 8.52
        joint liability. *See* subhead: joint liability
        successor liability
            generally, 8.56
            remedies affecting successor employer, 8.56.1
    notice, posting of
        contents of, 8.45
        duration of, 8.45.1
        generally, 8.45
        locations where notice should be posted, 8.45.1
        sample notice, 8.45.2
    orders of NLRB
        challenges to, 8.34
        court's power with respect to, 8.34.2
        enforcement of orders, 8.34.1
        generally, 8.33.1
        self-enforcing, orders are not, 8.34.1
    parties who may file charge, 8.4
    post-hearing briefs, 8.32
    postponement of hearing, request for, 8.30.1
    preventing transfer or opening of a facility as remedy, 8.51
    regional office of NLRB, filing of charge with, 8.5
    reinstatement as remedy
        circumstance where reinstatement will not be ordered,
            8.47.2
        generally, 8.47.1

V

W